EU ENVIRONMENTAL LAW AND THE INTERNAL MARKET

EU Environmental Law
and the
Internal Market

NICOLAS DE SADELEER

Professor of EU Law, Saint-Louis University
Jean Monnet Chair

OXFORD
UNIVERSITY PRESS

OXFORD
UNIVERSITY PRESS

Great Clarendon Street, Oxford, OX2 6DP,
United Kingdom

Oxford University Press is a department of the University of Oxford.
It furthers the University's objective of excellence in research, scholarship,
and education by publishing worldwide. Oxford is a registered trade mark of
Oxford University Press in the UK and in certain other countries

© N. de Sadeleer 2014

The moral rights of the author have been asserted

First Edition published in 2014

Impression: 1

Published in the United States of America by Oxford University Press
198 Madison Avenue, New York, NY 10016, United States of America

British Library Cataloguing in Publication Data
Data available

Library of Congress Control Number: 2013949376

ISBN 978-0-19-967543-2

Printed in Great Britain by
CPI Group (UK) Ltd, Croydon, CR0 4YY

Links to third party websites are provided by Oxford in good faith and
for information only. Oxford disclaims any responsibility for the materials
contained in any third party website referenced in this work.

Foreword

As is well known, the European Union (EU) started off as a markedly economic project, reflected in the names of the three integration organisations created in the 1950s, the European Coal and Steel Community, the European Economic Community (EEC) and the European Atomic Energy Community (Euratom). Mainly since the 1970s, things started to change and the integration agenda began to include values, objectives and principles which cannot be defined as purely economic or as promoting exclusively an internal economic market. Already in 1969, in *Stauder*, the European Court of Justice (ECJ) had held that the general principles of Community law include fundamental rights.

Among sectoral subjects and themes, environmental protection emerged early on as a frontrunner ("wallbreaker") for opening up the economic project to broader concerns. That declarations, programmes and directives started to see the daylight at the beginning of the 1970s can be seen against the background of the 1972 Stockholm Conference on the Human Environment, which demonstrated that environmental concerns also began to be seen as a universal challenge.

As before the Single European Act, the EEC Treaty did not contain any explicit legal basis for environmental protection, the European legislator resorted to an internal market legal basis and/or the then Article 235 EEC (now Article 352 of the Treaty on the Functioning of the European Union—TFEU) which enabled the Council to 'fill the gaps' if action of the Community was considered necessary to attain, in the course of the operation of the common market, one of the objectives of the Community. In both cases, unanimity was required.

In the same way as the ECJ already in 1969 had showed sensitivity with regard to human rights and fundamental rights concerns, it now showed a similar willingness to pay heed to the need to protect the environment by accepting, first (1980), that some environmental concerns could be addressed within the confines of the internal market legal basis and, then (1985) that environmental protection was one of the Community's 'essential objectives', despite the fact that Articles 2 and 3 EEC did not list the environment as one of its tasks or objectives. In 1978, the Court had accepted that restrictions on the free movement of goods could be grounded in 'mandatory requirements' which did not figure explicitly in the derogation clause provided for such restrictions in the Treaty (now Article 36 TFEU) and it did not take long before the Court acknowledged that such mandatory requirements could include environmental concerns, thus supplementing the explicit reference in the derogation clause to 'the protection of health and life of humans, animals or plants'.

After the legal basis had been revised (through the Single European Act (1987), and the Treaties of Maastricht (1992) and Amsterdam (1997)) to enable qualified majority voting in the Council and the full involvement of the European Parliament, EU environmental law has made great headway. This has taken place at the level of both primary (the TFEU) and secondary law, the latter mainly in the form of legislative acts adopted as regulations and directives. What is now Article 11 TFEU provides that environmental protection requirements be integrated into the definition and implementation of the Union's policies and activities while Article 191 TFEU instructs the Union to aim at a high level of environmental protection and lists the main principles of EU environmental law (such as the precautionary principle and the polluter-pays principle). EU environmental legislation is vast, detailed and stretches over a broad range of issues such as pollution and climate change, the management of waste and hazardous substances, the protection of nature and wildlife as well as assessment and participation procedures, the right to information and environmental liability.

It was thus inevitable that the ECJ, too, became heavily involved in environmental issues. At a time when the statistics established by the Court grouped together 'environment and consumers' as one subject-area, this subject-area was often at the top of the list on the number of cases decided. Whilst this is no longer the case after these two areas were split, it remains the case that the ECJ deals annually with a great number of environmental cases, reflecting broadly the topics regulated in EU legislation. At the time of writing, water protection, the protection of habitats and the right to information can be mentioned as examples of topics which seem to preoccupy the Court.

As will be illustrated and analysed in this book, environmental protection does not take place in a vacuum but is very much related to other subject-areas, such as the internal market, agriculture and fisheries, health protection, energy policy, and so on and so forth. Professor de Sadeleer's book pays a particular attention to the relationship between environmental protection and EU internal market law. There are, of course, many areas of tension and even conflict in this regard as it remains to be true, also after the entry into force of the Treaty of Lisbon (2007) at the end of 2009, that the internal market, according to Article 26 TFEU 'an area without internal frontiers in which the free movement goods, persons, services and capital is ensured', is an essential objective of the Union. That such tensions or conflicts should not be insolvable, however, is demonstrated by the fact that Article 3(3) of the Treaty on European Union (TEU) now not only provides for the establishment of an internal market but mentions also, inter alia, 'the sustainable development of Europe' and 'a high level of protection and improvement of the quality of the environment' among the objectives.

It falls upon both the Union legislator and the Union Courts, within the limits of their competences, to strike the right balance between these and other objectives and principles. This task is sometimes very challenging indeed. Professor de Sadeleer's book will no doubt be a very welcome contribution and I am convinced that it will prove its usefulness for both academics and practitioners, including EU judges at the Union and national courts.

Luxembourg 22 December 2013

Allan Rosas
Dr.Jur, Dr.Pol.Sc. h.c., Dr.Jur. h.c.
Judge at the European Court of Justice

Acknowledgements

In the late 1980s, when I was working in DG Environment of the European Commission on infringement proceedings lodged against Member States which had failed properly to implement environmental directives—including the Birds Directive—I could not have envisioned that, a quarter of a century later, I would embark upon a legal analysis encompassing subjects ranging from the use of watercrafts to the granting of State aids to renewable energy. Consequently, the thoughts expressed here are the fruit of countless discussions, consultations, seminars, conferences, lectures, student tutorials, and so on all across Europe. In the course of these activities, I have crossed paths with numerous brilliant lawyers and scholars who have in so many ways fostered my interest in EU environmental law and its awkward relationship with trade law that it would not be possible to thank them all.

That said, my first expression of gratitude goes to Thomas Roberts—without whom this book would not have seen the light of day—who translated many of the chapters into an enjoyable English text. My warmest thanks also go to Peter Craddock, who several years ago translated an earlier version of the chapter on free movement of goods, which has since been subject to a number of amendments. I am also particularly indebted to two former students, Laure-Anne Nyssen and Clio Liégeois, who carried out a tremendous amount of editorial work over the past few years. Needless to say, any remaining mistakes are entirely my own.

I discussed a variety of legal points regarding competition law with my PhD student Christophe Verdure, who helped me to decipher the intricacies of that branch of law and to whom my thanks are due. My special thanks also go to Virgilio Pereira for his suggestions about my comments on abuse of dominant position.

Generations of students who took my EU law classes in Brussels, Louvain, Paris, Lille, Bilbao, Fribourg, and Oslo have helped to hone my ideas regarding the conflict between trade and environment and, during my time as a guest professor, the Law Faculty of Lund University proved to be an excellent setting for writing the chapters on environmental rights and State aids. In addition, I am very grateful to my colleague Annika Nilson. Thanks also to my Marie Curie chair at Oslo University, and subsequently my Jean Monnet Chair at Saint Louis University, where I had the opportunity to organize a number of seminars and conferences across Europe on the topics discussed in this book and found new areas for research in an ever-developing field. My hope is that this book will be the most evident outcome of my Jean Monnet chair.

I would also like to thank the staff of OUP, particularly Alex Flach, for the care they have taken in producing this book.

My deepest thoughts, at the end of this journey, go to my father, whose European ideals never dimmed, as well as my wife, Åse, and my children, Irmeline and Christopher, for our endless discussions on the dilemma that is our society's short-term thinking about the consumption of natural resources in a vulnerable environment.

Last, given that the symbolic limit of 400 ppm of CO_2 was surpassed for the first time in May 2013 and that such levels have not been recorded in the nearly three million years since the Pliocene and, to make matters worse, that the years 2001–12 were all among the warmest since records began, I hope that this work will underscore the necessity for embarking upon more ambitious policies at EU level.

Contents

Table of Cases

EUROPEAN COURT OF JUSTICE

COURT OF FIRST INSTANCE/GENERAL COURT

INTERNATIONAL COURT OF JUSTICE

EUROPEAN COURT OF HUMAN RIGHTS

EFTA

WTO

ARBITRATION

BELGIUM

FRANCE

Table of Cases

NETHERLANDS

UNITED KINGDOM

USA

Table of Legislation

INTERNATIONAL NON-BINDING INSTRUMENTS

EU PRIMARY LAW

EU SECONDARY LAW BINDING ACTS

Decision

DIRECTIVES

REGULATIONS

EU SOFT LAW ACTS

Notices

List of Tables

List of Abbreviations

AJDA	*L'actualité juridique—droit administratif*
ALARA	as low as reasonably achievable
Amén-Env	*Aménagement-Environnement*
APT	*Adminstration publique trimestriel*
BAT	best available techniques
CAP	Common Agricultural Policy
CBA	Cost–benefit analysis
CBD	Convention on Biological Diversity
CCP	Common Commercial Policy
CDE	*Cahiers de droit européen*
CDM	Clean Development Mechanisms
CEE	charges having equivalent effect
CFP	Common Fisheries Policy
CLJ	*Cambridge Law Journal*
CLP	*Classification, labelling and packaging of substances and mixtures*
CML Rev	*Common Market Law Review*
CMLR	Common Market Law Reports
CPN	*Cours de perfectionnement du notariat*
CYELS	*Cambridge Yearbook of European Legal Studies*
EAEC	European Atomic Energy Community
EC	European Community
ECHA	European Chemicals Agency
ECHR	European Convention on Human Rights
ECLR	*European Competition Law Review*
ECR	European Court Reports
ECtHR	European Court of Human Rights
ECJ	European Court of Justice
EEA	European Environment Agency
EEC	European Economic Community
EEELR	*European Energy and Environmental Law Review*
EELR	*European Environmental Law Review*
EEZ	exclusive economic zone
EFFLR	*European Food and Feed Law Review*
EFSA	European Food Safety Agency
EFTA	European Free Trade Area
EIA	environmental impact assessment
EJCL	*European Journal of Consumer Law*
EJIL	*European Journal of International Law*
EJRR	*European Journal of Risk Regulation*
EL Rev	*European Law Review*
ELD	Environmental Liability Directive (2004/35/EC)
ELJ	*European Law Journal*
ELV	emission limit values
EMA	environmental multilateral agreement
Env L Rev	*Environmental Law Review*
EPL	*European Public Law*
EQS	environmental quality standards
ESDP	European Spatial Development Perspective

ETR	environmental tax reform
ETS	emissions trading scheme
EUCFR	European Charter of Fundamental Rights
EuR	*Europarecht*
FAO	Food and Agriculture Organization
GBER	General Block Exemption Regulation (800/2008)
GFL	General Food Law
GHG	greenhouse gases
GMO	genetically modified organism
ICJ	International Court of Justice
IE	Industrial Emissions
IMO	International Maritime Organization
IOPCF	International Oil Pollution Compensation Funds
IPP	integrated product policy
IPPC	Integrated Pollution Prevention and Control
JDE	*Journal de droit européen*
JEEPL	*Journal for European Environmental and Planning Law*
JEL	*Journal of Environmental Law*
JT	*Journal des tribunaux*
JTDE	*Journal des tribunaux droit européen*
JWT	*Journal of World Trade*
LIEI	*Legal Issues of Economic Integration*
MEE	measures having equivalent effect
MJ	*Maastricht Journal of European and Comparative Law*
NCA	national competition authority
NELJ	*Nordic Environmental Law Journal*
NGO	non-governmental organization
NJB	*Nederlands Juristenblad*
NJIL	*Nordic Journal of International Law*
ODA	Overseas Development Administration
OECD	Organisation for Economic Cooperation and Development
OLP	ordinary legislation procedure
POP	persistent organic pollutant
QMV	qualified majority voting
RAE-LEA	*Revue des affaires européenness*
RDCE	*Revista de Derecho Ambiental*
RdE	*Recht der Energiewirtschaft*
RDUE	*Revue de droit de l'Union européenne*
REACH	registration, evaluation, authorisation and restriction of chemicals
REDC	*Revue européenne de droit de la consommation*
RMC	*Revue du marché commun*
RMUE	*Revue du marché unique européen*
RPS	regulatory procedure with scrutiny
RTDE	*Revue trimestrielle de droit européen*
SEA	Single European Act
	Strategic Environmental Assessment
SEW	*Sociaal-Economische Wetgeving: Tijdschrift voor Europees en economisch recht*
SGEI	services of general economic interest
SLP	special legislative procedure
SME	small and medium-sized enterprises
SPS	Sanitary and Phytosanitary

TBT	Technical Barriers to Trade
TEU	Treaty establishing the European Union
TFEU	Treaty on the Functioning of the European Union
TMR	*Tijdschrift voor Milieurecht*
UNECE	United Nations Economic Commission for Europe
WCED	World Commission on Environment and Development
WFD	Waste Framework Directive (2008/98/EU)
WTO	World Trade Organization
YbEEL	*Yearbook of European Environmental Law*
YbEL	*Yearbook of Environmental Law*
YEL	*Yearbook of European Law*

General Introduction

Whilst environmental protection is not a recent concern, over recent years it has taken on a renewed intensity, characterized by the urgent need to find universal solutions to global warming, the erosion of biodiversity, as well as the depletion of natural resources. The interest pursued undoubtedly springs from the fact that the situation has, in many respects, become alarming and risks worsening if no ambitious action is taken.

Driven by fear of a disintegration of the internal market, concerns over portraying a less mercantile image of the EU, as well as the intention of safeguarding ecosystems and species under threat, a European environmental policy has thus gradually emerged. Although not mentioned in the 1957 Treaty of Rome, environmental concerns have, through various Treaty reforms, gradually been able to establish themselves as one of the primary values enshrined in the Treaties. Henceforth, environmental protection is not only a core objective of the Union but has also been placed on an equal footing with economic growth and the internal market. As far as secondary law is concerned, environmental issues also made headway. At first an obscure field in the 1970s, and having long remained the preserve of engineers and biologists, this policy and the law to which it gave rise have ended up asserting themselves both on public and private actors. Starting with a range of action programmes, EU environmental law has progressively grown from a sparse set of directives to a vast body of regulatory measures aiming both to regulate the main forms of pollution as well as to protect the main ecosystems along with some of their composite elements. Today it is possible to count more than 300 regulatory measures; that is, around 8 per cent of EU law.[1] Several EU agencies, 28 Member States, three European Free Trade Area (EFTA) States, hundreds of regions and Länder, and thousands of municipalities now implement EU secondary environmental law through a complex web of regulation that affects virtually every aspect of our lives.

Thanks to EU environmental law, much has been achieved over the last 30 years: bans on lead in petroleum products, the phasing-out of ozone-depleting substances, a reduction in nitrogen oxide emissions from road transport, improvements in waste-water treatment and water quality, a reduction in acidification, and improvements to some aspects of air quality.[2] This significant progress demonstrates that environmental policy and law do work. Even though recent years have seen a decline in legally binding instruments in favour of 'voluntary' agreements and the abandonment of a sectoral

---

[1] Given that the scope of environmental policy is dogged with controversy, the precise number cannot be precisely determined. According to the Directory of EU legislation in force, on 1 September 2010 there were 113 regulatory acts directly regulating chemicals, 365 acts addressing the wider area of pollution and nuisance, and a total of 1,321 covering the broader environmental realm. See also L. Krämer, '30 Years of EC Environmental Law: Perspectives and Prospectives' (2002) 2 YbEEL 160.

[2] European Environment Agency (EEA), *The European Environment. State and Outlook* (Copenhagen: EEA, 2005) 19.

approach in favour of a more global dimension, EU environmental law should continue to play a significant role over the course of this century.

However, despite the earlier progress that was made, the results of this policy have at
the very least been muted.[3] EU environmental and national policies are still facing a
daunting agenda of unfinished business[4] as well as a swathe of new challenges. By way
of illustration, air pollution still reduces life expectancy significantly,[5] major rivers are
still heavily polluted, the 2010 biodiversity conservation targets have not been met,[6]
and the amount of waste is increasing.[7] As regards new challenges, the most pressing is
that of climate change, the impact of which is becoming ever more frequent. Indeed,
the overarching target to limit climate change to temperature increases of less than 2°C
globally during this century[8] is unlikely to be met, in part because of greenhouse gas
emissions from other parts of the world.[9] A closer look at greenhouse gas emissions
within the EU reveals mixed trends: whereas emissions from large point sources have
been reduced, emissions from some mobile and diffuse sources, especially those which
are transport-related, have increased substantially.[10] To make matters worse, every step
forward—such as reductions in industrial pollution—appears to be cancelled out by the
appearance of new phenomena—mass consumption, more diffuse sources of pollution
proving more difficult to control—or unforeseen risks—biotechnology, nanotechnology, endocrine disruptors, etc. The deteriorating situation thus requires lawmakers
constantly to return to the drawing board for solutions.

In view of the cultural, social, and economic impact of environmental policy, the
relations between Treaty law and secondary environmental law have been subject to
intense debate in the academic literature for over a decade, fuelled by a swathe of
specialist law journals and various associations of lawyers.[11]

---

[3] EEA, *Europe's Environment. The Dobris Assessment* (Copenhagen: EEA, 1995) 599–611; EEA, *The
European Environment. State and Outlook* (Copenhagen: EEA, 2005) 18, 20, and 30; EEA, *Europe's
Environment. The Fourth Assessment* (Copenhagen: EEA, 2007) 22; European Commission, Environment
Policy Review 2008, COM(2009) 304; EEA, *Progress Towards the European 2010 Biodiversity Target*
(Copenhagen: EEA, 2009) 17–21; EEA, *The European Environment 2010. State and Outlook* (Copenhagen:
EEA, 2010) 15; OECD, *Environmental Outlook to 2050* (Paris: OECD, 2012).
[4] Within a single sector, the trends can be mixed: some pollutants might be declining whilst others are
increasing. The stabilization of the total amount of mineral nitrogen fertilizer consumption is a good case in
point in that respect. See the Report of the Commission on implementation of Council Directive 91/676/
EEC concerning the protection of waters against pollution caused by nitrates from agricultural sources
based on Member State reports for the period 2004–2007, COM(2010) 4 final.
[5] EEA, *Europe's Environment. The Fourth Assessment* (Copenhagen: EEA, 2007) 73.
[6] The Commission as well as the EEA have repeatedly acknowledged that the EU was unable to achieve
its global target of significantly reducing biodiversity loss by 2010. Eg European Commission, A mid-term
assessment of implementing the EC Biodiversity Action Plan, COM(2008) 864 final; European Commission, Communication on options for an EU vision and target for biodiversity beyond 2010, COM(2010) 4
final; EEA, *Progress Towards the European 2010 Biodiversity Target* (Copenhagen: EEA, 2009); EEA, *The
European Environment 2010* (n 3), 49–50.
[7] EEA, The *European Environment 2010* (n 3), 71–5.
[8] Communication from the Commission, 20 20 by 2020, Europe's climate change opportunity, COM
(2008) 30 final.
[9] EEA, *The European Environment 2010* (n 3), 27.
[10] EEA, *The European Environment 2010* (n 3), 34.
[11] Eg the *International Yearbook of Environmental Law*, the *Yearbook of European Environmental Law*,
the *Yearbook of International Environmental Law*, the *European Environmental Law Journal*...

However, despite the attention devoted to them,[12] these rules still come across as a regulatory jungle. Both their mutual intertwining as well as their technical or scientific nature give even the most rash of lawyers reason to pause. One of the main difficulties environmental law has been facing in the EU is related to the fact that the legal order of the EU was originally conceptualized in terms of economic integration, and had no regard for the precarious state of natural resources and *res comunes*, for which we are accountable to future generations.

At the core of economic integration lies the internal market that is based on the free movement provisions promoting access to the different national markets and on the absence of distortion of competition. The relationship between that form of economic integration and environmental protection has always been fraught with controversy. It has been argued that trade liberalization and free competition increase the wealth of trading nations so they are able to afford to implement environmental policies. On the other hand, economic growth at all costs may result in greater pressures on ecosystems. Moreover, the internal market and environmental policy have traditionally focused on apposite, albeit entangled, objectives: deregulation of national measures hindering free trade, in the case of internal market, and protection of vulnerable resources through regulation, in the case of environmental policy. In other words, whereas the internal market is concerned with liberalizing trade flows, environmental policy encourages the adoption of regulatory measures that are likely to impact on free trade. In addition, the internal market favours economic integration through total harmonization whilst environmental law allows for differentiation. To make matters more complicated, the relationship between the internal market and the environment has always been asymmetrical.

Given that environmental issues encompass a broad range of measures ranging from green energy, regulation of fisheries, cross-compliance in agriculture, product policy, waste management, or wildlife conservancy, the tensions with trading interests are likely to vary considerably depending on the regulation at issue. That said, the tensions between the two policies have been smoothed out through a mix of complementary means. On the one hand, an innovative interpretation of Treaty provisions enshrining economic freedoms has offered some leeway to national environmental agencies ('negative harmonization'). On the other hand, the two policies can also support

---

[12] P. Davies, *EU Environmental Law* (Farnham: Ashgate, 2006); N. de Sadeleer and C.-H. Born, *Droit international et communautaire de la biodiversité* (Paris: Dalloz, 2004); N. de Sadeleer, *Commentaire Mégret. Environnement et marché intérieur* (Brussels: ULB, 2010); A. Garcia Ureta, *Derecho Europeo de la Biodiversidad* (Madrid: Gomez-Acebo & Pombo, 2010); C. Hilson, *Regulating Pollution: A UK and EC Perspective* (Oxford: Hart, 2000); J. H. Jans and H. Vedder, *European Environmental Law*, 4th edn (Groeningen: Europa Law, 2012); L. Krämer, *EC Environmental Law*, 6th edn (London: Sweet & Maxwell, 2007); M. Lee, *EU Environmental Law. Challenges, Change and Decision Making* (Oxford: Hart Publishing, 2005); E. Louka, *Conflicting Integration. The Environmental Law of the EU* (Antwerp: Intersentia, 2004); P. Pagh, *EU MiljøRet* (Copenhagen: C. Ejler, 1996); V. Plaza Martin, *Derecho ambiental de la Unión europea* (Valencia: Tirant Lo Blanch, 2006); A. M. Moreno Molina, *Derecho comunitario del medio ambiente* (Madrid/Barcelona: Marcial Pons, 2006); J. Scott, *European EU Environmental Law* (London: Longman, 2001); J. Scott (ed.), *Environmental Protection. European Law and Governance* (Oxford: OUP, 2009); P. Thieffry, *Droit de l'environnement de l'UE* (Brussels: Bruylant, 2011). With respect to EU case law, see W. Douma (ed.), *European Environmental Case Law* (The Hague: Asser Instituut, 2002); L. Krämer, *Casebook on EU Environmental Law* (Oxford: Hart Publishing, 2002).

each other through the adoption of harmonized EU standards integrating the environmental dimension ('positive harmonization'). Needless to say, lawmakers and courts are always likely to face the need to reconcile the irreconcilable.

The confrontation between ecological imperatives and economic integration justifies a detailed examination of the compatibility of environmental protection regimes with the internal market. Informed by the desire to clarify and systematize, this book will attempt to set out in a concise manner the environmental protection rules contained in the Treaties and in key secondary legislation and the ways in which they interact with the internal market and competition law. Accordingly, the book will place particular emphasis on the compatibility of EU and national environmental protection measures with the provisions of the TFEU on the free movement of goods and services, the freedom of establishment, as well as freedom of competition. In particular, it sheds light on the ways in which EU Courts are trying to reconcile internal market obligations with environmental concerns.

The discussion will be structured as follows.

With the entry into force of the Treaty of Lisbon on 1 December 2009, environmental issues are not only cutting across traditional boundaries of 'official' disciplines, but are also entangled with other non-tradable interests, such as consumers and health concerns, which have been gathering momentum in EU Treaty law. Part I of the book will thus consider the place occupied by a broad range of objectives and obligations—sustainable development, high-level protection, integration clauses, policy principles, and fundamental rights—that are enshrined in the Treaty on European Union (TEU), the Treaty on the Functioning of the European Union (TFEU), the Charter of Fundamental Rights, and the European Convention on Human Rights (ECHR). It is suggested in Chapters 1 and 2 that this flurry of Treaty obligations contributes to an equilibrium between the economic core of EU integration and environmental concerns. In addition, environmental policy must be considered in its own rights. In order to define the objectives, principles, and decision-making procedures characteristic of EU environmental policy, the TFEU includes a title specifically dedicated to environmental policy. Chapter 3 is dedicated to the Treaty provisions that empower EU institutions to adopt harmonized rules with a view to protecting the environment. As will be seen, these measures can be related either to internal market policy (Art. 114 TFEU) or to the environmental policy (Art. 192 TFEU). Chapter 4 will set out in a concise manner the main environmental protection measures in key secondary legislation.

Part II will place particular emphasis on the compatibility of environmental protection measures with a number of key TFEU provisions on the free movement of goods and services, as well as freedom of establishment. The focus of this part is on the case law regarding consistency of environmental measures with Articles 28–30, 34–36, 49, 56, and 110 TFEU. Account must also be taken of the fact that several Treaty provisions require the EU institutions to take into account environmental requirements while establishing the internal market. Consequently, Part II will also consider the place occupied by environmental issues within the internal market. It will focus, in particular, on the scope of Articles 26 and 113–114 TFEU.

Part III will provide an in-depth analysis of the compatibility of environmental protection agreements with the TFEU provisions on the freedom of competition and State aids under Articles 101–108 TFEU.

Some clarification of a methodological nature is in order. A broad understanding has been adopted of the concepts of the environment and the internal market. From the perspective of sustainable development, the concept of the environment has, in addition to its core elements, an economic dimension as well as a social dimension. Our perspective is therefore broader than that adopted by most commentators who have discussed this issue.

Furthermore, with a view to bringing a fresh and original perspective to the study of environmental law, the book attempts to tackle the issue from a new angle: that of the spillover effect of environmental issues on a number of general obligations of EU Treaty law. Indeed, the original feature of environmental policy lies in the fact that by asserting its cross-cutting nature, it overturns the boundaries separating the different legal disciplines. Thanks to this spillover effect, the environmental concepts and principles quickly become disseminated throughout EU law. Conversely, environmental Treaty obligations are likely to gain support from concepts or principles proper to other policies such as health and consumers.

Finally, although this book has been designed in a practitioner-friendly way, it is also intended to be accessible for students. To keep the book manageable, not all the controversies related to the various Treaty provisions on the internal market and competition have been explored in depth; instead, it is assumed that readers are already acquainted with EU economic law. Furthermore, theoretical developments are illustrated throughout, along with the relevant case law. The manner in which the case law is exposed should help to put the legal concepts—measures having equivalent effect, discriminatory taxations, State aids, abuse of dominant position, etc—in a more practical context. For the sake of clarity, ample use is made of tables. All relevant sources and authorities are quoted fully, with special emphasis placed on case law in order to enable readers easily to seek further information. In so doing, it is hoped to give both practitioners and students the theoretical background they need to help them answer their own questions: do Treaty law and secondary law permit the national authorities to maintain such-and-such a regime of authorizations, to adopt a positive list of hazardous substances, to prohibit the placing on the market or the use of a hazardous product, to limit the importation of animals or plants, to levy environmental taxes that do not amount to State aids, or to conclude an agreement with private undertakings that does not impede competition?

Further developments regarding these issues may be followed on the author's website at <http://www.tradevenvironment.eu>.

PART I

INTRODUCTION TO EU ENVIRONMENTAL LAW

Part I Introduction

In Part I, we shall analyse the place occupied by environmental requirements in the Treaty on European Union (TEU), the Treaty on the Functioning of the European Union (TFEU), the Charter of Fundamental Rights (EUCFR), and the European Convention on Human Rights (ECHR).

Chapter 1 addresses the environmental requirements set out in both the TEU and TFEU. In particular, a great deal of attention is paid to different EU and TFEU provisions enshrining cross-cutting concepts that are likely to enhance environmental values. Specifically, there will be a discussion of the concept of sustainable development, the various integration clauses, as well as the obligation to achieve a high level of protection with respect to a number of non-tradable interests. As will be seen, these obligations are to a great extent intertwined. In so doing, we shall address the curious relations between environment policy and other policies likely to oppose the internal market.

Environmental issues cannot be restricted merely to technical standards: they prompt important questions of human rights. As will be discussed in Chapter 2, although fundamental rights and environmental interests have developed in parallel, these subjects intersect with increasing frequency.

Chapter 3 addresses the nature of environmental competence as well as the external relations of the EU in the environmental field. It deals with procedurals issues related to the enactment of legislative measures under Article 192 TFEU. Whilst the expansion of EU regulatory action aimed at environmental protection dates back to the start of the 1970s, it has, however, suffered, following the entry into force of the Single European Act, from differences in interpretation regarding the legal basis on which legislation adopted in this area is grounded. Given that environmental issues are entangled with the internal market, health, consumer, industrial, and agricultural issues, a number of legal bases are likely to be considered for adopting environmental measures. However, this debate is not neutral since the choice of legal basis is not simply a question of form but, instead, a question of substance, given that it has a considerable impact on the degree of harmonization which can be achieved; as a result, residual competences are deeply affected. Accordingly, the different legal bases which make it possible to ground regulatory intervention are also discussed.

Finally, Chapter 4 provides non-expert readers with a brief presentation of EU secondary law. Its goal is not to catalogue directives, regulations, and decisions, which are easily found on the internet, but to set out the principle sectors and instruments.

1

Environmental Objectives, Principles, and Criteria of the Environmental Policy in the TEU and TFEU

1. Introduction

The discussion in the first chapter will be structured as follows.

Before commenting on each of the TEU and TFEU provisions referring to the environment, it is necessary to consider, in Section 2, what exactly the elusive concept of environment covers.[1]

---

[1] Although they are widely used in secondary law, the concepts of pollution, ecosystems, biodiversity, precaution, risk, dangerous substances, and waste are not mentioned in Treaty law.

Section 3 then offers a brief historical perspective of environmental policy in relation to the internal market policy.

In view of Article 3(3) TEU, sustainable development, and hence the objective of environmental protection, cannot be dissociated from the internal market. Paragraph 3 of this provision places these objectives on an equal footing. Consequently, they must be analysed more in terms of reconciliation than of opposition. Moreover, environmental concerns are not isolated; they overlap with other policies that were originally regarded as ancillary to or liable to counter the goals of economic integration. In particular, consumer, health, and environmental policies share a range of common features, up to the point that one can speak of cross-fertilization between them.[2] Sections 4 to 5 offer the opportunity to consider the extent of cross-fertilization between different areas of EU law and, in so doing, they place special emphasis on the bonds uniting environment, consumer, and health policies.

Entirely devoted to the environment, Title XX of the TFEU does not limit itself to confirming the EU's competence in environmental matters: it sets out goals, states principles, and establishes criteria. Accordingly, that title calls for EU action to grow in strength and coherence. It is thus the aim of Sections 6 to 8 to examine in depth the series of goals, principles, and criteria guiding this policy encapsulated in Article 191 TFEU 'which the EU legislature must respect in implementing environmental policy'.[3]

2. Concept of Environment

What exactly is the environment? What is meant by this open concept is, indeed, ripe for discussion. Dating back to the start of the 1970s, the concept of environment is the implicit result of a compromise between two approaches which do not sit comfortably together. Taking things to extremes, one might say that there is, on the one hand, an objective dimension based on scientific criteria (state of species conservation, pollution thresholds, ecosystem approach, sustainable yields, total allowable catches, etc), which seeks to protect the biosphere per se. Thresholds have been established pursuant to scientific analysis classifying ecological risk. Clearly, nature protection law as well as most of water law aim at protecting ecosystems as such. This scientific approach stands in opposition to a subjective vision of relations between mankind and his surroundings (including economic, aesthetic, cultural, and recreational aspects), which focuses more on the quality-of-life dimension than the conditions favourable for life. Consequently, a species may be protected not by virtue of the role it plays within an ecosystem, but on account of its appeal to a broader public or its economic value. As a result, the protection of the biosphere is justified as a function of the interests of mankind.

In this respect, it should be pointed out that measures aiming to reduce noise, odours, air pollutants, as well as radiation, aim chiefly at improving the quality of

---

[2] As will be shown later, an understanding of the key role played by the precautionary principle in the area of environmental protection calls for a digression into public health. Conversely, the principle would not have been established as a guiding principle in the area of public health had it not originally been established in relation to environmental matters. By the same token, sustainable development appeals to consumer law.

[3] Case C-341/95 *Bettati v Safety Hi-Tech* [1988] ECR I-4355, para. 34.

human life. It is also to be noted that the case law of the European Court of Human Rights (ECtHR) signs up to an anthropocentric vision of the environment, as the rights enshrined under the ECHR are first generation rights. By the same token, in recognizing that 'the environment is not an abstraction but represents the living space, the quality of life and the very health of human beings, including generations unborn', the International Court of Justice (ICJ) has also endorsed an anthropocentric approach.[4]

Leaving aside this latent tension between two opposing viewpoints, one could well ask what is still natural about a heavily 'artificialized' world. How can we distinguish the environment from nature, from ecology, or from biology? Anxious to consume natural products, the uninitiated will fall into the depths of confusion on reading some of the judgments handed down by the Court of Justice in that regard.

For instance, the use in most Member States of the term 'bio' for goods not produced from organic agriculture will not mislead Spanish consumers, since goods produced from this type of agriculture are in general referred to using the term '*ecológico*'.[5] Similarly, notwithstanding the presence of traces of lead, cadmium, and pesticides, the term 'naturally pure' used on jars of jam will not be misleading for Austrian consumers.[6] In addition, the accidental presence of material derived from certain genetically modified organisms (GMOs) not exceeding a particular level in baby food is not subject to specific labelling requirements.[7] Finally, although it adversely affects the integrity of a Natura 2000 site, the conversion of a natural fluvial ecosystem into a largely man-made structure in Northern Greece can be justified on the ground that it 'may, in some circumstances, have beneficial consequences of primary importance for the environment'.[8] Given the severity of the impact of irrigation projects on the natural environment, the position of the Court on this question is controversial.[9]

As far as Treaty law is concerned, the concept of environment appears in several provisions of Treaty law—Articles 3(3) and 21(2)(d)–(f) TEU, Articles 11, 114(3), (4), and (5), 191–193, and 194(1) TFEU—without, however, being defined, no doubt out of fear of circumscribing its scope to overly specific areas. Likewise, EU secondary law pays little attention to defining what is meant by the term 'environment'. Attempts to define the boundaries of the concept often involve its enumeration through examples.[10]

---

[4] *Legality of the Threat or Use of Nuclear Weapons*, Advisory Opinion [1996] ICJ Rep. 29.

[5] Case C-135/03 *Commission v Spain* [2005] ECR I-6906, paras 36–41.

[6] Case C-465/98 *Adolf Darbo* [2000] ECR I-2321, para. 33.

[7] Case C-132/03 *Cadocons* [2005] ECR I-4167.

[8] Case C-43/10 *Nomarchiaki Aftodioikisi Aitoloakarnanias e.a.* [2012] OJ C355/2, para. 125.

[9] Indeed, 'irrigation and drainage projects invariably result in many far-reaching ecological changes', some of which 'cover the entire range of environmental components, such as soil, water, air, energy, and the socio-economic system'. See the Food and Agriculture Organization (FAO) and Overseas Development Administration (ODA), *FA O Irrigation and Drainage Paper 53* (Rome: FAO, 1995) 1.

[10] But a few EU secondary law acts determine what the concept of environment should encompass. See Directive 2011/29/EU on the assessment of the effects of certain public and private projects on the environment [2012] OJ L26/1, Art. 3; Commission Regulation (EC) No. 800/2008 declaring certain categories of aid compatible with the common market in application of Articles 87 and 88 of the Treaty (General block exemption Regulation) [2008] OJ L214/3, Art. 17; European Parliament and Council Regulation (EC) No. 1107/2009 concerning the placing of plant production products on the market [2009] OJ L309/1, Art. 3(13). See also the Aarhus Convention on Access to Information, Public Participation in Decision-making and Access to Justice in Environmental Matters (Aarhus, 25 June 1998), Art. 2(3).

Its protean nature means that it is difficult to define its boundaries exactly. Although everyone may be agreed on the core of what is meant by the concept of environment, disputes arise about the boundaries surrounding the core content. If there is a catch-all concept, then this is it. Immune to all efforts at legal classification, this chameleon-like concept may be limited under a narrow reading to NIMBY (not in my back yard) factors, whilst read more broadly it may be coterminous with the biosphere. Furthermore, it continuously overlaps with other concepts, such as ecology, nature, biodiversity, public health, worker protection, land use, living surroundings, or sustainable development, which nevertheless have not succeeded in taking its place. Despite this, EU institutions as well as Member State authorities continue to rely on the concept of environment.

From a legal perspective, the concept may not be ideal but it is the best we can do under the circumstances. First, the fact that the boundaries of this policy are not marked out with even a basic degree of precision enables EU lawmakers to extend their initiatives to a broad array of areas, reaching from nature conservation to the fight against global warming. However, such a broad scope is likely to give rise to conflicts with other EU policies.[11] Second, the use of a flexible notion has turned out to be indispensable because an excess of detail would render it quickly obsolete. In effect, this relative notion is strongly dependent on its context and its historical setting. Indeed, as understood in the twenty-first century, the concept of environment is much more substantial than that of the twentieth century. The issue now covers questions that were ignored until a short time ago, such as global warming, GMOs, product life-cycle analysis, or electromagnetic radiation. Last, but not least, given that natural habitats are shrinking, sea levels are rising, glaciers are melting, fish stocks are fished to the limits of their reproductive capacity, and rare natural resources are depleted, new issues are likely to gather momentum in the near future.

3. Stages of Integration of Environmental Requirements in Treaty Law

The relatively complex legal framework in which EU action in environmental matters is carried out requires a brief discussion of the principal stages of the integration of environmental concerns into the Treaty establishing the European Economic Community (EEC Treaty) and later into the European Community Treaty (EC Treaty) and the TFEU, taking into account the amendments which have been made to primary law since the late 1980s (the Single European Act (SEA), Maastricht, Amsterdam, Nice, and Lisbon).[12]

---

[11] See the discussion in Ch. 3, Section 4 below.

[12] See J. Holder and M. Lee, *Environmental Protection Law and Policy*, 2nd edn (Cambridge: CUP, 2009) 155–71; J. Jans and H. Vedder, *European Environmental Law*, 4th edn (Groeningen: Europa Publishing, 2012) 3–13.

3.1 From the Treaty of Rome to the Single European Act: the shaping of the environmental policy

The original Treaty of Rome was drafted at a time when environmental questions did not arise as such. Whereas the original objectives of the Treaty emphasized an essentially economic project,[13] it contained no general reference to consumer, health, or environmental protection. The absence of such provisions reflected the unimportance of these issues at the time the Treaty was drafted.

Given that many contemporary environmental problems—acid rain, transboundary watercourse management, eutrophication, conservation of migratory species, ozone depletion—are transboundary in nature, it came as no surprise that in the 1970s the EEC became the most relevant regional organization to address these issues.[14] The absence of provisions establishing specific Community competence over the fight against pollution did not prevent the Heads of State and Government from agreeing on the necessity to take action to save the environment when that issue became salient. The Declaration of the Council of the European Communities and of the representatives of the Governments of the Members States of 22 November 1973 stressed that the promotion of 'a harmonious development of economic activities and a continuous and balanced expansion' cannot be imagined 'in the absence of an effective campaign to combat pollution and nuisance' or 'the improvement in the quality of life and the protection of the environment'.[15] As a result, economic expansion, expressly mentioned as a goal of the Community under former Article 2 EEC, had to go hand in hand with environmental protection. Hence, economic growth was not to be assessed exclusively in quantitative terms but also qualitatively.

The 1973 Declaration marked the beginning of EU environmental policy. Against that background, the Commission enacted the first environmental action programme[16] and the Council adopted, at the beginning of the 1970s, the first directives which paved the way for the expansion of Community environmental policy. In the absence of specific legal bases, and prior to the entry into force of the SEA, the Council was obliged at times to base its intervention on Article 100 EEC (Art. 94 EC, Art. 113 TFEU),[17] and at other times on Article 235 EEC (Art. 308 EC, Art. 352

---

[13] Pursuant to Art. 2 EEC, the European Economic Communities were aiming at 'an harmonious development of economic activities, a continuous and balanced expansion... an accelerated raising of the standards of living'.

[14] It should be recalled that other international organizations have played a key role in Europe as regards environmental protection. Eg the 1979 Geneva Convention on Long-Range Transboundary Pollution has been adopted under the auspices of the UN Economic Commission for Europe and the 1979 Berne Convention on the Conservation of European Wildlife and Natural Habitats has been adopted under the auspices of the Council of Europe.

[15] Bulletin EC 1972, No 10.

[16] Five additional programmes have been enacted, setting out roadmaps for EU environmental policy. By virtue of Art. 192(3) TFEU, the environmental programme has to be adopted pursuant to the ordinary legislative procedure. With the exception of research and trans-European networks (Arts 172 and 182 TFEU), no other EU policy programmes are subject to the ordinary legislative procedure.

[17] Several directives were enacted under Art. 100 EEC, see Council Directive 73/404/EEC relating to the approximation of the laws of the Member States relating to the detergents [1973] OJ L347/51 and Council Directive 76/769/EEC on dangerous substances [1976] OJ L262/201.

TFEU),[18] and sometimes even on both provisions. Given that Article 100 EEC related to the functioning of the common market, that legal basis was chosen by the Council in order to adopt a number of environmental directives laying down technical standards for the placing on the market of hazardous products. Clearly, environmental issues have been intricately related to the functioning of the common market since the early 1970s.

However, both Articles 100 and 235 EEC also represented a significant obstacle to the expansion of a policy area which became mired in disputes; the requirement of unanimity within the Council placing a considerable brake on the implementation of an ambitious EU policy.[19] This explains why Community law was first of all the result of compromises between, on the one hand, Member States supporting a reinforced environmental policy and, on the other, States in favour of a less integrated policy. Furthermore, the adoption of environmental directives on the basis of these provisions was criticized on the ground that the EEC did not enjoy any genuine competence to deal with such matters, since it was not listed under the tasks conferred on the EEC pursuant to former Article 3 EEC and, at most, its competence was limited to regulating questions directly associated with the elimination of restrictions on intra-Community exchanges.[20] The European Court of Justice (ECJ) rapidly put an end to the doubts that hung over the legality of this competence. In a landmark judgment, the Court held that 'it [was] by no means ruled out that provisions on the environment may be based upon Article [115 TFEU]' (ex Art. 100 EC).[21] In any event, the intervention of the Community was justified by the fact that 'provisions which are made necessary by considerations relating to the environment and health may be a burden upon the undertakings to which they apply and if there is no harmonization of national provisions on the matter, competition may be appreciably distorted'.[22] Later, the Court of Justice had to solve the question whether environmental considerations could override one of the fundamental principles of the EEC, the free movement of goods. The Court expressed the view that a directive on the disposal of waste oils had to be 'seen in the perspective of environmental protection, which is one of the Community's essential objectives'[23] and, thus, justified that restrictions were imposed on the 'fundamental principles of Community law',[24] which consist of the 'principles of free

---

[18] This allowed the Council to adopt, on the basis of ex Art. 234 EEC, measures less directly bound to the common market, such as those relating to the protection of flora and fauna. See, eg, Council Directive 79/409/EEC on the conservation of wild birds [1979] OJ L103/1.

[19] The rule of unanimity required by Arts 100 and 235 EEC allowed each Member State to block or delay the adoption of any Commission proposal, or even to negotiate its adherence by obtaining important concessions. However, Member States opposing harmonization were more keen on gaining concessions rather than vetoing the Commission's proposal. See D. Chalmers, 'Inhabitants in the Field of EC Environmental Law' in P. Craig and Gráinne de Búrca (eds), *The Evolution of EU Law* (Oxford: OUP, 1999) 658.

[20] E. Grabitz and C. Sasse, *Umweltkompetenz der Europäischen Gemeinschaften* (Berlin: E. Schmidt, 1977) 93; G. Close, 'Harmonization of Laws. Use or Abuse of Power under the EEC Treaty' (1978) 3 *EL Rev* 461.

[21] Cases C-91 & 92/79 *Commission v Italy* [1980] ECR I-1099 and 1115.

[22] *Commission v Italy* (n 21).

[23] Case C-240/83 *Association de Défense de Brûleurs d'Huiles Usagées (ADBHU)* [1985] ECR I-531, para. 13.

[24] *ADBHU* (n 23), para. 15.

trade, free movement of goods and freedom of competition'.[25] The significance of this judgment lies in the fact that the Court had for the first time recognized environmental protection as an 'essential objective'. Later, as with the areas of health and consumers, the case law of the ECJ listed environmental issues as one of the mandatory requirements authorizing restrictions to be placed on the free movement of goods enshrined in ex Articles 30–36 EEC (Arts 34–36 TFEU).[26] These societal values were thus recognized at the expense of market integration.

3.2 The Single European Act: the recognition of a new Community competence

Although there was already, in the course of the 1980s, extensive secondary legislation covering water and air, noise, chemicals, waste, and nature protection, there were no specific environmental competences in the Treaty. With a view to filling this gap, the SEA baptized in 1987 EEC environmental policy as a new Community competence under three heads:

- pursuant to ex Article 3 EEC, as autonomous EEC action, the protection of the environment was now recognized as a fully fledged EEC objective;
- pursuant to ex Article 130r EEC (Art. 191 TFEU), as a compulsory element of other policies pursued by the EEC;
- and, finally, pursuant to ex Article 100a(3) EEC (Art. 114(3) TFEU), as a specific element in the completion of the internal market.

For the first time, environmental obligations were encapsulated in the Treaty. The SEA clarified to some extent the choice of the legal basis: environmental measures not related to the common market no longer needed to be founded on Article 235 EEC. They had to be adopted by the Council under a specific new legal basis: Article 130s EEC (Art. 192 TFEU). This provision allowed for a shift away from the classical common market integration process towards a much more flexible and decentralized process at the cost of uniform harmonization.[27] However, environmental policy lagged behind the internal market because of the unanimity rule in the Council. In many instances, the unanimity requirement was forcing the Council to decide on the basis of the lowest common denominator. In particular, the unanimity rule hampered the development of a consistent regulatory approach to the release of hazardous substances into surface water.[28]

That aside, the SEA was of major significance for the internal market. First, ex Article 14 EEC provided that the activities of the Community shall include an internal market characterized by the abolition, as between the Member States, of obstacles to the free movement of goods, persons, services, and capital. Second, harmonization was

---

[25] *ADBHU* (n 23), para. 9.   [26] See the discussion in Chapter 5, Sections 4 and 6.
[27] I. von Homeyer, 'The Evolution of EU Environmental Governance' in J. Scott (ed.), *Environmental Protection. European Law and Governance* (Oxford: OUP, 2009) 15.
[28] M. Pallemaerts, *Toxics and Transnational Law* (Oxford: Hart Publishing, 2003).

facilitated, on the one hand, by qualified majority rather than by unanimity[29] and, on the other, by cooperation procedure making the European Parliament a key institutional player. Third, economic integration gathered momentum on account that the SEA took stock of the Commission's willingness to complete the internal market before 1992. As a result, thanks to the implementation of the White Paper, *Completing the Internal Market*,[30] a swathe of directives adopted prior to 1992 removed physical, technical, and fiscal barriers to trade whereas environmental law obviously lagged behind. Moreover, given that the new Article 100a(3) EEC required the Commission's proposal to seek a high level of environmental protection, the genuine internal market basis—Article 100a(1) EEC—has been increasingly used for much of the harmonization of environmental product standards.[31] As discussed in Chapter 3, these institutional discrepancies led to boundary disputes between ex Article 100a(3) EEC and other Treaty provisions, among which was the environmental legal basis. As a result, a number of concerns were voiced regarding the continuous expansion of economic integration to the detriment of other policies, including the new environmental policy.[32]

3.3 From Maastricht to the Lisbon Treaty: the consolidation of EU environmental policy

Subsequently, competences over environmental matters as well as the internal market were expanded in 1992 by the Maastricht Treaty, when the EEC became the EC. Two developments deserve attention.

First, environmental policy made headway through a clearer statement of objectives and, within the Council, the replacement of unanimity by qualified majority voting according to cooperation procedure. Thus, the national veto was dropped from the new Article 175(1) EC, replacing ex Article 130s EEC, although some environmental matters still remain subject to unanimous Council decisions. However, environmental policy was still lagging behind the internal market. Indeed, the new co-decision procedure applied to internal market harmonization (Art. 95 EC, replaced by Art. 114 TFEU) was more favourable to the European Parliament than the cooperation procedure applied to environmental harmonization (Art. 175 EC, replaced by Art. 192 TFEU). Accordingly, in institutional terms, the European Parliament was therefore more keen on the internal market harmonization process than on the environmental one.[33] Furthermore, Member State powers to derogate from internal market measures were clarified, although their powers remain quite limited. As regard other societal values, account must be taken of the fact that the Maastricht Treaty introduced a

---

[29] Given that unanimity was previously required under Art. 100 EEC, common market harmonization was often victim 'to the varying interest and preferences of Member States, and the bargaining and horse-trading, that often led to lowest common denominator decisions'. Eg M. Egan, *Constructing a European Market* (Oxford: OUP, 2001) 66.

[30] White Paper, *Completing the Internal Market*, COM(85) 310.

[31] Von Homeyer (n 27), 11–14.

[32] P. Craig, 'The Evolution of the Single Market' in C. Barnard and J. Scott (eds), *The Law of the Single European Market* (Oxford: Hart Publishing, 2002) 25–7.

[33] Case C-187/93 *European Parliament v Council* [1994] ECR I-2857.

specific competence regarding consumer protection; a competence intricately related to both the internal market and the environment. Indeed, in changing the ways in which their lifestyles impact on the environment, consumers can play a key role.

Second, the Maastricht Treaty has also introduced a general subsidiarity principle applicable to all areas of Community activities,[34] the impact of which would be to decrease in the long run the involvement of the Union in environmental matters.[35]

In 1997, thanks to the replacement under the Treaty of Amsterdam[36] of the co-operation procedure with co-decision, which has a decidedly more democratic character, environmental policy has finally been placed, from an institutional point of view, on an equal footing with internal market policy. Whereas the European Parliament's amendments were previously ignored by the Commission and the Council, thanks to its new legislative powers, the European Parliament sought rather successfully substantial amendments of the Commission's proposals. Nonetheless, the unanimity clause for some environmental competences (land planning, ecotaxes, etc) still remains.

Neither the Treaty of Nice, nor the draft Constitution, nor the Lisbon Treaty (TEU and TFEU)[37] introduced any significant developments to these arrangements.[38]

As will be seen in the following section, the TEU as amended by the Lisbon Treaty has been slightly recasting the concept of sustainable development. For its part, the TFEU simply endorses, as far as environmental protection is concerned, the institutional choices adopted by the framers of the reforms stretching from the SEA to the Treaty of Nice. It should be stressed that the *passerelle* clause which is set out in Article 192(2) TFEU could allow the application of the ordinary legislative procedure to matters that are currently covered by the special legislative procedure. Of particular salience is the fact that a new common energy policy saw the light of the day under the Lisbon Treaty. Pursuant to Article 191(1), fourth indent TFEU, the energy policy has thus to 'promote energy efficiency and energy saving and the development of new and renewable forms of energy'—issues that have so far been harmonized by virtue of environmental competence.[39] Finally, the inclusion of judicial cooperation in criminal matters in the first pillar (Arts 82–89 TFEU) should put an end to the institutional controversies opposing the partisans of the first and third pillar.[40]

Whilst they may not amount to a revolution, these successive adjustments are testament to the growing importance which environmental protection enjoys within the European project, an issue which touches directly on the lives of European citizens, on behalf of whom the EU claims to be acting. As a result, the EU Courts have

---

[34] Prior to the Maastricht Treaty, the subsidiarity principle was applicable by virtue of Art. 130r(2) exclusively to EEC environmental policy.

[35] See the discussion in Chapter 3, Section 2.2.

[36] The Treaty of Amsterdam led to the renumbering of Treaty provisions.

[37] The concept of European Community has been replaced throughout the Treaties by the EU. In addition, the Treaty of Lisbon led to a second renumbering of the provisions embodied in these two Treaties.

[38] Indeed, these arrangements were little changed by the Lisbon Treaty. See M. Lee, 'The Environmental Implications of the Lisbon Treaty' (2008) 22:2 *Env L Rev* 131–8; H. Vedder, 'The Treaty of Lisbon and European Environmental Law and Policy' (2010) 22:2 *JEL* 285–99.

[39] European Parliament and Council Directive 2003/30/EC on the promotion of the use of biofuels or other renewable fuels for transport [2003] OJ L123/43.

[40] See Chapter 3, Section 4.7.

acknowledged the scale of these developments. They have very quickly recognized that environmental protection has become one of the essential objectives of the EU.[41] In so doing, the European Courts have been endorsing the same line of reasoning as both the ICJ[42] and the ECtHR[43] which had also recognized the importance of the environment. Additionally, this brief historical analysis highlights the extent to which the development of environmental policy with other societal values, such as in the areas of health and consumers, has been intricately related to the establishment and functioning of the internal market, even if this may be at its expense.

4. Sustainable Development

4.1 Introductory remarks

The initial task of environmental law was, during the first three decades of its existence, to curb impacts, contamination, and pollution through the harmonization of administrative regulations and practices. In this regard, the law governing listed installations and industrial pollution still occupies a core position within this branch of law.

However, this initial approach sidelined issues concerning, first, the extraction of natural resources—since the potential for exploitation appeared to be unlimited—and, second, the incessantly growing consumption of goods and services. However, the availability of natural resources is not unlimited and the absorption capacity of sinks may quickly be exceeded. The record of environmental policy remained modest precisely as a result of its inability to regulate the exploitation of natural resources and the consumption of goods and services. What, indeed, is the point of equipping cars with new technologies if the number of cars and of kilometres travelled is constantly on the increase? What interest is there in subjecting aviation to a regime of greenhouse gas emission quotas if air transport continues to grow? What interest is there to designate nature sanctuaries around cities if land planning policies fall short of preventing urban sprawl? Conversely, environmental protection measures have been criticized on account that they are at best indifferent, and at worst hostile, to economic development and social aspirations.

At the outset, the concept of sustainable development has been forged in an attempt to reconcile the needs of development with environmental protection. Sustainable development has been defined by the World Commission on Environment and Development (WCED) as 'a development that meets the needs of the present without compromising future generations to meet their own needs'.[44] The underlying idea was

---

[41] Case 240/83 *ADBHU* [1985] ECR 531, para. 13; Case 302/86 *Commission v Denmark* [1988] ECR 4607, para. 8; Case C-213/96 *Outokumpu Oy* [1998] ECR I-1777, para. 32; and Case C-176/03 *Commission v Council* [2005] ECR I-7879, para. 41. See also Opinion AG Misho in Case C-513/99 *Concordia Bus Finlandia* [2002] ECR I-7213, para. 92; and Opinion AG Geelhoed in Case C-230/03 *Commission v Austria* [2005] ECR I-9871, para. 2.

[42] The ICJ held that it had 'no difficulty in acknowledging that the concerns expressed by Hungary for its natural environment in the region' affected by a dam project related to an 'essential interest' of that State (*Gabčíkovo-Nagymaros Project (Hungary v Slovakia)* [1997] ICJ Rep. 41, para. 53).

[43] See *Hamer v Belgium*, 27 November 2007, para. 79.

[44] WCED, *Our Common Future* (Oxford: OUP, 1987) 86.

to strike a balance between, on the one hand, the social and economic advantages of development projects providing jobs and amenities for the present generation and, on the other, the need to conserve a sufficient amount of natural resources for future generations. Since its proclamation in 1987, sustainable development has been gathering momentum from a swathe of international declarations and academic writings. Since then, it has been encapsulated into a flurry of international and national law.[45] Given the challenges related to energy security, rising climate change, food safety, biodiversity loss, illegal immigration prompted by natural disasters, and the limited amount of natural resources that are heavily exploited, the importance of sustainable development is even more obvious today than 20 years ago.

Sustainable development obliges us to rethink environmental law, although according to the academic literature, in international law this concept bears a greater resemblance to a political objective than a legal principle.[46]

Since it is made up of three heads (social, environmental, and economic), sustainable development represents a delicate balancing of competing social, economic, and environmental interests. Indeed, according to the ICJ's case law, 'this need to reconcile economic development with protection of the environment is aptly expressed in the concept of sustainable development'.[47] As a result, sustainable development requires commercial law, competition law, consumer law, environmental law, and worker protection law to interact. Similarly, the dialogue between law and science, economic development and the preservation of natural resources, and the regulation of access to resources and our consumer society, must find the green shoots of a solution under the aegis of this type of rule that is dedicated par excellence to the reconciliation of competing interests. What is more, given that 'environmental law and the law on development stand not as alternatives but as mutually reinforcing', there is a duty under international law 'to prevent, or at least to mitigate' significant harm to the environment.[48]

We are taking the view that acting under the impetus provided by sustainable development, environmental law should intervene at times more upstream and at other times more downstream. We will consider first upstream intervention. Since the exploitation of natural resources is not infinite, it is necessary to exploit them in a sensible manner since it is senseless to squander precious resources. Hence, Article 191(1) TFEU requires 'a prudent and rational use of natural resources'. However, despite much debate and a flurry of political initiatives, the EU still lacks a clear political and legal approach regarding natural resource use.[49] Turning now to

---

[45] M.-C. Cordonier Segger and A. Khalfan, *Sustainable Development Law* (Oxford: OUP, 2004).

[46] V. Lowe, 'Sustainable Development and Unsustainable Arguments' in A. Boyle and D. Freestone (eds), *International Law and Sustainable Development* (Oxford: OUP, 1999) 19; D. French, 'Sustainable Development' in M. Fitzmaurice et al. (eds), *Handbook on International Environmental Law* (Cheltenham: Edward Elgar, 2010) 56.

[47] *Gabčíkovo-Nagymaros Project* (*Hungary v Slovakia*) [1997] ICJ Rep. 7, 140. See also *Arbitration Regarding the Iron Rhine Railway* (*Belgium v Netherlands*), Arbitral Award of 24 May 2005, para. 222, *Pulp Mills on the river Uruguay* (*Argentina v Uruguay*) [2010] ICJ Rep. 7, 177.

[48] *Arbitration Regarding the Iron Rhine Railway* (*Belgium v Netherlands*), Arbitral Award of 24 May 2005, para. 58.

[49] The 2002 6th Environmental Action Programme (6EAP) identified natural resources and waste as one of four key priority areas for the next decade. With the aim of fleshing out the 6th EAP objectives, in 2005, the Thematic Strategy on the Sustainable Use of Natural Resources (COM/2005/0670 final) was adopted by

downstream issues, unfettered consumption of goods and services is the cause of over-exploitation of natural resources and the succession of negative impacts on the environment which this exploitation engenders. Accordingly, sustainable development impinges upon consumption of goods and services.

4.2 Legal status

Despite the success which it has met in international circles, the concept of sustainable development has encountered difficulty establishing itself under Treaty law. At the outset, under the Maastricht Treaty, the Union was called on to promote 'sustainable and non-inflationary growth' rather than 'sustainable development' in its own right.[50] However, with the entry into force of the Treaty of Lisbon, the concept of sustainable development was later recognized as one of the main objectives pursued by the EU. The concept is currently enshrined in Articles 3(3)–(5) and 21(2)(d)–(f) TEU, Article 11 TFEU, as well as Article 37 EUCFR.[51]

The third paragraph of Article 3 TEU runs as follows: 'The Union . . . shall work for the sustainable development of Europe based on balanced economic growth and price stability, a highly competitive social market economy, aiming at full employment and social progress, and a high level of protection and improvement of the quality of the environment. It shall promote scientific and technological advance.' Moreover, pursuant to paragraph 5 of that provision as well as Article 21(2)(d) TEU, sustainable development is one of the cornerstones of EU external policy.

In addition, sustainable development is also encapsulated in both Article 11 TFEU and Article 37 EUCFR without, however, being defined. Under these two provisions, sustainable development is set out as the objective that environmental policy must pursue. Article 11 TFEU (ex Art. 6 EC) provides that: 'Environmental protection requirements must be integrated into the definition and implementation of the Union policies and activities, in particular with a view to promoting sustainable development'. By the same token, by virtue of Article 37 EUCFR 'a high level of environmental protection and the improvement of the quality of the environment must be integrated into the policies of the Union and ensured in accordance with the

---

the Commission alongside a Thematic Strategy on Waste Prevention and Recycling, to take forward these aims. These thematic strategies form the cornerstone of EU natural resources policy to date. More recently, the EU's economic strategy, 'Europe 2020', focuses on resource efficiency ('Resource Efficient Europe'). However, this strategy falls short of explaining how efficiency is to be understood or how it can be achieved. A resource efficiency 'roadmap' to 2050 is expected from the European Commission. Furthermore, few legislative acts on products place emphasis on natural resource management. On a more positive note, the Ecodesign Directive (2009/125/EC) replacing Directive 2005/32/EC includes provisions relating to resources aspects, such as water consumption in the use phase, the quantities of a given material incorporated in the product, or a requirement for minimum quantities of recycled material.

[50] Formerly, sustainability was linked to economic growth. That link was maintained under the Maastricht and the Amsterdam Treaties. Pursuant to the Maastricht Treaty, 'The Community shall . . . promote sustainable and not-inflationary growth respecting the environment' (Art. 2 EC). Similarly, pursuant to the Amsterdam Treaty, sustainable development was linked to economic activities (Art. 2 EC). However, new economic treaties do not enshrine sustainability requirements. Eg the inter-governmental treaty adopted on 1 March 2012 on Stability, Coordination and Governance in the Economic and Monetary Union refers to 'economic growth through enhanced convergence and competitiveness' (Art. 9).

[51] See also the 6th recital of the preamble to the TEU.

principle of sustainable development'. A minor difference must be stressed: the Charter mentions 'policies' and not 'activities'.

Six issues arise for comment here.

First, in contrast to the dissipation and lack of precision in the references to sustainable development in the previous Treaties, this third paragraph of Article 3 TEU expresses the tripartite nature of the concept in much clearer terms. However, Treaty law is silent as regards the equitable allocation of resources both within the present generation and between the present and future generations, as well as other duties such as the right to development.

Second, it should be stressed that sustainable development does not appear in Title XX TFEU on environmental policy but in different provisions of the TEU, in Article 11 TFEU, and in the EUCFR. By introducing a social and economic dimension, sustainable development thus broadly moves beyond traditional environmental issues.[52] What is more, whereas environmental protection involves a defensive stance against the depletion of natural resources and pollution, sustainability entails a proactive approach in requiring the integration of environmental requirements into economic growth.

Third, the fact that sustainable development is encapsulated in three different provisions situated at the apex of the EU legal order does not mean that its legal status is not dogged by controversy.[53] For instance, given that sustainable development has been coined both as an objective and a principle, there was obviously no clear concept of what sustainable development meant from a legal point of view when these various provisions were drafted.[54]

Fourth, the Treaty provisions do not determine the substantive and procedural components of sustainable development. Nonetheless, it could be argued that Articles 11 and 191(1) TFEU already encapsulate some elements, such as the duty to integrate environmental concerns into other policies and the 'rational' utilizations of natural resources.[55]

Fifth, clearly this concept is characterized by a strong degree of indeterminacy. Though few institutions and Member States will contend with the proposition that development should be sustainable, they might disagree on how to flesh out this proposition in individual cases. Given the significance of the social, economic, and environmental value judgements involved in deciding what is sustainable,[56] institutions are indeed endowed with broad discretion in giving effect to Article 3(3) TEU,

---

[52] The somewhat confusing dividing line between sustainable development and traditional economic development is likely to impinge on the choice of legal base. By way of illustration, the Council granted a Community guarantee to the European Investment Bank against losses under loans and loan guarantees for projects outside the Community. In a case regarding the legal base of that decision, the Court of Justice held that the act at issue fostered the sustainable economic and social development of developing countries, notwithstanding the fact that other components of that act concerned economic, financial, and technical cooperation with third countries other than developing countries. As a result, the decision fell under Art. 179 EC (Art. 208 TFEU) as well as under Art. 181a EC (Art. 212 TFEU). See Case C-155/07 *Parliament v Council* [2008] ECR I-8103, para. 67.

[53] As regard international law, see eg P. Birnie, A. Boyle, and C. Redgwell, *International Law and the Environment*, 3rd edn (Oxford: OUP, 2009) 124.

[54] L. Krämer, 'Sustainable Development in EC Law' in H.-C. Bugge and C. Voigt (eds), *Sustainable Development in International and National Law* (Groeningen: Europa Law, 2008) 378.

[55] See the discussion in Section 5.   [56] Birnie, Boyle, and Redgwell (n 53), 126.

Article 11 TFEU, and Article 37 EUCFR. That said, whilst the third paragraph of Article 3 TEU may not impose binding obligations, it nevertheless spells out a political imperative: the 'high level of protection and improvement of the quality of the environment' now has the same status as the objective, for example, of 'economic growth and price stability' (economic pillar) as well as with that of 'full employment and social progress' (social pillar of sustainable development). Given that these three components must be seen as interdependent and mutually reinforcing, the main objective of promoting economic growth and social progress must be viewed from a balanced and sustainable perspective. Since no hierarchy is provided for between these different pillars, they constitute an inseparable whole and cannot therefore be interpreted in isolation from one another. As a result, economic growth cannot be achieved without the promotion of the two other components, and environmental protection should constitute an integral part of that development. By the same token, both environmental and labour protection requirements are likely to reinforce each other. By way of illustration, energy from biofuels should be taken into account only if it fulfils different sustainability criteria.[57]

This interpretation appears to be consistent with settled case law. Account must be taken of the fact that the Court of Justice has already held that the Union has not only an economic but also a social purpose.[58] Accordingly, the rights under the provisions of the Treaty on the free movement of goods, persons, services, and capital must be balanced against the objectives pursued by social policy.[59]

The sixth issue to be addressed is whether sustainable development necessarily enhances environmental protection. In fact, the main attraction of this concept is that 'both sides in any legal argument will be able to rely on it'.[60] The interpretation given by Advocate General Léger to sustainable development in his Opinion in *First Corporate Shipping*, a case on development taking place in protected birds habitats, is testament to a conciliatory approach. Indeed, the Advocate General stressed that 'the concept "sustainable development" does not mean that the interests of the environment must necessarily and systematically prevail over the interests defended in the context of the other policies pursued by the Community ... On the contrary, it emphasizes the necessary balance between various interests which sometimes clash, but which must be reconciled'.[61] In addition, the manner in which Article 3(3) TEU has been

---

[57] Both for third countries and Member States that are a significant source of raw material for biofuel consumed within the EU, the Commission has been called on to issue a report addressing the respect of land use rights and the implementation of various ILO conventions. See European Parliament and Council Directive 2009/30/EC amending Directive 98/70/EC as regards the specification of petrol, diesel, and gas-oil and introducing a mechanism to monitor and reduce greenhouse gas emissions [2009] OJ L140/88, Art. 7b(7).

[58] Case 43/75 *Gabrielle Defrenne v Sabena* [1976] ECR 455, para. 12.

[59] See Case C-438/05 *Viking Line* [2007] ECR I-10779, para. 79; Case C-341/05 *Laval* [2007] ECR I-11767, para. 105; and Case C-319/07 *3F* [2009] ECR I-5963, para. 58.

[60] Birnie, Boyle, and Redgwell (n 53), 116. Under Art. 12 of the Kyoto Protocol, Clean Development Mechanisms (CDM) have to fulfil a sustainability test set out by the receiving State. In spite of their significant environmental impact, large hydroelectric projects in China and India made up more than a quarter of all CDMs and accordingly were deemed to be sustainable. See A. Vassa, *The Effectiveness of the Clean Development Mechanism. A Law and Economic Analysis* (Rotterdam, 2012) 142.

[61] Opinion AG Léger in Case C-371/98 *First Corporate Shipping* [2000] ECR I-9235, para. 54.

drafted does not reflect the postulate that each pillar has to be oriented towards the needs of future generations. As a result, these needs do not necessarily trump the right to economic development. It follows that environmental concerns risk being laid aside in the name of reconciliation stemming from the three-pillar structure.[62] By way of example, in the event of conflict between growth and environmental protection, compromise must be found and necessary environmental measures could be discarded. That aside, it is submitted that sustainable development should not water down basic environmental requirements. In effect, pursuant to Article 3(3) TEU and Article 191(2) TFEU, the tasks of the EU include the requirement to attain a 'high level of protection and improvement of the quality of the environment'. Section 7.2 will provide a detailed analysis of the legal status of the obligation to achieve a high level of environmental protection.

4.3 Case law

So far, the Court of Justice and the General Court have barely referred to sustainable development. By way of illustration, according to the Court of Justice, preventing further accumulation of small arms and light weapons in Africa permits the promotion of sustainable development in the region.[63] More recently, the Greek Council of State sought to ascertain whether the Habitats Directive, interpreted in the light of the objective of sustainable development, could allow the conversion of a natural fluvial ecosystem into a largely man-made fluvial and lacustrine ecosystem, irrespective of the negative impacts on the integrity of sites that are part of the Natura 2000 network. The Court of Justice took the view that the Habitats Directive, and in particular its mechanism allowing projects likely adversely to affect the integrity of a Natura 2000 site interpreted in the light of the objective of sustainable development, permits such a project.[64] Nonetheless, the Court stressed that such a project can be authorized inasmuch as the conditions for granting the derogation were satisfied—conditions which have so far been interpreted rather narrowly.[65]

It is doubtful whether the concept of sustainable development is akin to the general principles of EU law, such as proportionality and subsidiarity, that enable the EU Courts to review the powers of the institutions. However, it may be akin to the concept of constitutional objective found in French and Belgian constitutional law.[66]

4.4 Secondary law

Since 1992, sustainable development issues have become pre-eminent on the policy agenda. For instance, the Europe 2020 Strategy is geared towards a green vision of the

---

[62] G. Winter, 'A Fundament and Two Pillars' in H.-C. Bugge and C. Voigt (eds), *Sustainable Development in International and National Law* (Groeningen: Europa Law, 2008) 28.

[63] Case C-91/05 *Commission v Council* [2008] ECR I-3651, para. 98.

[64] *Nomarchiaki Aftodioikisi Aitoloakarnanias e.a.* (n 8), paras 134–9.

[65] Case C-538/09 *Commission v Belgium* [2011] OJ C211/5, para. 53.

[66] Belgian Constitution, Art. 7bis; French Charter for the Environment, Art. 1st.

economy. As a consequence, a flurry of communications are dealing with strategies related to sustainable development.[67]

Although the establishment of the concept amounts to an important step forward in taking ecological imperatives into account, it still needs to be endowed with a content that measures up to its ambitions and which can actually be applied within the various EU policies likely to contribute to the deterioration of the environment. As far as secondary legislation is concerned, sustainable development and its offshoot, the integration clause,[68] tend to favour the establishment of rules intended to protect the environment beyond the confines of environmental law in more peripheral domains such as research, agriculture, energy, and transport, as well as the internal market. So far, the approach endorsed by the EU institutions has been somewhat patchy.

To make matters worse, since it is not defined under Treaty law, few pieces of secondary law define this concept;[69] and even when the concept is proclaimed, its content has barely been fleshed out. Although the Water Framework Directive 2000/60/EC stresses that water management must promote 'sustainable water use based on a long-term protection of available water resources',[70] it does not impose on the Member States any specific method of defining sustainability. With respect to waste management, when applying extended producer responsibility, Member States shall take into account the three pillars of sustainable development, for example 'the overall environmental, human health and social impacts' as well as 'the need to ensure the proper functioning of the internal market.'[71]

Furthermore, the manner in which some environmental provisions were drafted or are implemented is testament to the ambiguous nature of sustainable development. For instance, Directive 2009/28/EC of 23 April 2009 on the promotion of the use of energy from renewable sources provides striking evidence of this ambiguity. On the one hand, the directive establishes mandatory national targets consistent with a 20 per cent share of energy from renewable sources and a 10 per cent share of energy from renewable sources in transport in EU energy consumption by 2020. On the other hand, it sets out sustainability criteria ensuring that biofuels and bioliquids can qualify for the incentives only when they can be guaranteed not to come from land with high biodiversity value or with high carbon stock.[72] The question is whether these criteria will be

---

[67] Communication from the Commission to the European Parliament, the Council, the European Economic and Social Committee and the Committee of the Regions—Mainstreaming sustainable development into EU policies: 2009 Review of the European Union Strategy for Sustainable Development (COM/2009/0400 final).

[68] See Section 5.

[69] Eg with regard to the conservation of tropical forests, sustainable development is defined as 'the improvement of the standard of living and welfare of the relevant populations within the limits of the capacity of the ecosystems by maintaining natural assets and their biological diversity for the benefit of present and future generations'. See European Parliament and Council Regulation (EC) No. 2494/2000 on measures to promote the conservation and sustainable management of tropical forests and other forests in developing countries [2000] OJ L288/6, Art. 2(4). Clearly, such a definition is extremely broad.

[70] European Parliament and Council Directive 2000/60/EC establishing a framework for Community action in the field of water policy [2000] OJ L327/1, Art. 1(b).

[71] European Parliament and Council Directive 2008/98/EC on waste [2008] OJ L312, Art. 8(3).

[72] Directive 2009/28/EC on the promotion of the use of energy from renewable sources [2009] OJ L140/16, rectial 69 and Art. 17.

sufficient to ward off the negative social and environmental impacts of biofuels production. In effect, the increased production of biofuels is likely to compound deforestation in developing countries and to increase intensive agriculture of biomass crops.

By the same token, the Common Fisheries Policy (CFP) also illustrates the inherent ambiguity of sustainable development. Pursuant to Article 2(1) of Council Regulation (EC) No. 2371/2002 of 20 December 2002 on the conservation and sustainable exploitation of fisheries resources, the general objectives of the CFP consist of ensuring 'exploitation of living aquatic resources that provides sustainable economic, environmental and social conditions' and that the environmental impact of fishing shall be limited.[73] The tri-dimensional aspect of sustainable development and the simultaneous character of the pursuit of those aspects are thus underscored. Needless to say, the fixing of total allowable catch proposed by the Commission on the basis of scientific data has generally been raised by the Council on account that the different interests at stake had to be balanced in the context of sustainable development, among others safeguarding jobs and food security.[74] At first glance, the Council's argument seems compatible with the three-pillar structure of sustainable development. Given that conflicting interests must be weighed, biodiversity concerns are deemed to be merely one aspect of the problem. Admittedly, such a short-term vision has been downgrading environmental concerns at the expense of an ecosystemic approach and the sustainable exploitation of fish stocks.[75]

Another piece of evidence for this are the objectives of the Regional Fund, the Social Fund, and the Cohesion Fund setting out that these funds 'must be pursued in the framework of sustainable development'.[76] However, no indication is given as to how this should be achieved. For instance, the question arises as to what 'sustainable tourism'[77] means as regards land planning, water and energy consumption, ecotourism, transport, coastal zonal management, and a flurry of other indicators.[78]

To sum up, there has been no serious attempt to operationalize this popular piece of EU political jargon and to take measures with a view to reversing unsustainable environmental trends.[79]

---

[73] Council Regulation (EC) No. 2371/2002 on the conservation and sustainable exploitation of fisheries resources [2002] OJ L358.

[74] See N. de Sadeleer and C.-H. Born, *Droit international et de l'UE de la biodiversité* (Paris: Dalloz, 2004) 684, no. 740; J. Wakefield, 'Fisheries: A Failure of Values' (2009) 46 *CML Rev* 439 and 440; Winter (n 62), 28; Krämer (n 54), 379–81.

[75] T. Markus, *European Fisheries Law. From Promotion to Management* (Groeningen: Europa Law, 2009).

[76] Regulation (EC) No. 1083/2006 laying down general provisions on the European Regional Development Fund, the European Social Fund and the Cohesion Fund [2006] OJ L210/25, Art. 17. See also Regulation (EC) No. 1080/2006 on the European Regional Fund [2006] OJ L 210/1, Arts 4, 5(2)(d), 6(2)(b)(d), 9, and 10; Regulation (EC) No. 1081/2006 on the European Social Fund [2006] OJ L210/12, Art. 3(1)(b) and (c); Regulation (EC) No. 1084/2006 on the European Cohesion Fund [2006] OJ L210/79, Art. 2(1).

[77] Regulation (EC) No. 1080/2006 on the European Regional Fund [2006] OJ L210/1, Arts 6(2)(b) and 10.

[78] Krämer (n 54), 392.   [79] Krämer (n 54), 392.

5. Environmental Integration Clause

5.1 Introductory remarks

Environmental protection has more often given way to socio-economic considerations. For instance, in cases involving the overlap of administrative regulations, the solutions adopted by the EU and national courts generally lean in favour of economic development rather than the conservation of natural resources.[80] Nature has thus paid a weighty tribute to the absence of any incorporation of environmental requirements into other policies.[81] As discussed in Section 4, one of the key features of sustainable development is precisely to integrate environmental concerns into socio-economic policies. In other words, curbing unsustainable trends thus requires the integration of environmental requirements across policies such as energy, agriculture and fisheries, forestry, industry, transport, regional development, land use, and land planning. Unless this is achieved, environmental degradation will continue apace. Standing alone, environmental policy has no chance to achieve its objectives.

Although international treaties rarely provide for the obligation to integrate environmental requirements into other policies,[82] principle 4 of the Declaration on Environment and Development provides that 'environmental protection shall constitute an integral part of the development process and cannot be considered in isolation from it'. In the *Iron Rhine* Arbitration, a dispute involving nature conservancy as well as the

---

[80] For the convenience of representation, the impact of transport infrastructures on protected habitats have been chosen. Eg the construction of a highway across a Natura 2000 site in order to alleviate traffic was deemed to be an imperative reason of overriding public interest that justifies, by virtue of Art. 6(4) of the Habitats Directive, encroachments on priority habitats and species (BVerwG A 20.05 of 17 January 2007, BVerwGE 128 1). By the same token, the enlargement of a protected area within an existing industrial plant in order to complete the production of a jumbo jet was deemed to fulfil an imperative reason of overriding public interest on account that 'the German authorities have demonstrated that the project is of outstanding importance for the region of Hamburg and for northern Germany as well as the European aerospace industry' (Commission, C(2000) 1079 of 14 April 2000). In spite of the fact that a number of specimens of the most endangered mammal in Europe, the Iberian lynx (*Lynx iberica*), were killed due to an increase in traffic, the conversion of a by-road into a regional motorway across a national park did not infringe the Habitats Directive's obligations on the protection of that rare species (Case C-308/08 *Commission v Spain* [2010] ECR I-4281). See also G. Garcia Ureta, 'Habitats and Environmental Assessment of Plans and Projects' (2007) 2 *JEEPL* 84–96; L. Krämer, 'The European Commission's Opinions under Article 6(4) of the Habitats Directive' (2009) 21:1 *JEL* 70.

[81] EU policies have been criticized for being inconsistent, in particular in respect of nature conservation. In an infringement case brought by the Commission against France regarding the destruction of the wetlands of the *Marais poitevin*, the French authorities submitted that the Community aid package for intensive agriculture ran contrary to the policy of safeguarding wetlands pursuant to Directive 2009/147/EC on the conservation of wild birds [2009] OJ L20/7 (Wild Birds Directive). In answer to those allegations, the ECJ held that even assuming that that was the case, and a certain lack of consistency between various EC policies was shown to exist, that would not authorize a Member State to depart from its obligations under the Wild Birds Directive (Case 96/98 *Commission v France* [1999] ECR I-8531, para. 40).

[82] Declaration on the Human Environment (Stockholm, 16 June 1972), Principle 14; Declaration on Environment and Development (Rio de Janeiro, 14 June 1992), Principle 4; UN World Charter for Nature (28 October 1982), paras 7 and 8; Convention on Biodiversity (Rio de Janeiro, 5 June 1992), Art. 6(b); Convention to Combat Desertification in Those Countries Experiencing Serious Drought and/or Desertification (Paris, 17 June 1994), Art. 4(2). With respect to integration of more specific nature protection concerns, see the Protocol to the Alpine Convention on Conservation of Nature and the Landscape Protection (Chamberry, 20 December 1994), Art. 4; and Framework Convention on the Protection and Sustainable Development of the Carpathians (Kiev, 22 May 2003), Art. 4(6).

obligation to assess the environmental impacts of the project at issue, principle 4 was regarded as 'a principle of general international law' which applies not only in autonomous activities but also in activities undertaken in implementation of specific treaties between the parties.[83]

As far as EU law is concerned, it was also indispensable, alongside the recognition of sustainable development, to make provision for the decompartmentalization of different policies in line with environmental considerations. Against this background, a number of Treaty provisions require the integration of environmental concerns.

As discussed previously, Articles 3(3) and 21 TEU promote sustainable development: a concept calling for reconciliation of the economic, social, and environmental objectives pursued by the EU.

In addition, by virtue of Articles 13 and 21(3) TEU as well as Article 7 TFEU, the Union ensures consistency between all its policies and activities.[84]

In particular, Article 11 TFEU requires that: 'Environmental protection requirements must be integrated into the definition and implementation of the Union policies and activities, in particular with a view to promoting sustainable development'. Moreover, Article 11 TFEU must be read in combination with Article 37 EUCFR that, in much the same vein, requires the integration of 'a high level of environmental protection and the improvement of the quality of the environment'. That said, it must be noted that with the sole exception of the new energy policy encapsulated in Article 194 TFEU, the other policies impinging upon the quality of the environment—industry, agriculture, transport, tourism, etc—do not contain reference either to the environment or to sustainable development.

5.2 Relationship between Article 11 TFEU and other integration clauses

Before attempting to set out the legal nature of this provision, the following paragraphs will discuss several observations regarding the positioning of Article 11 within the TFEU. In effect, the obligation to integrate environmental requirements is no longer an exclusive priority,[85] as other provisions of the TFEU proclaim the cross-cutting nature of the legitimate interests of EU citizens, whether it be in the areas of culture, regional policy, animal welfare, industry, health, consumer protection, or development cooperation (see Table 1.1).

Conversely, the Treaty drafters have been calling on the EU institutions to integrate societal concerns into hard-core economic policies. Pursuant to Article 114(3) TFEU, the Commission's proposals which have as their object the establishment and functioning of the internal market, must pursue a high level of protection, when they concern health, safety, environmental protection, and consumer protection. Accordingly, health, safety, environmental protection, and consumer concerns have to be fully integrated into the internal market harmonization process.

[83] *Arbitration Regarding the Iron Rhine Railway (Belgium v Netherlands)*, Arbitral Award of 24 May 2005, para. 59.
[84] C. Franklin, 'The Burgeoning Principle of Consistency in EU Law' (2011) YEL 66.
[85] When the environmental integration clause was inserted in ex Art. 130s(1) EEC by the SEA, it was the single horizontal clause.

Table 1.1 TFEU and EUCFR provisions requiring cross-sectoral approaches

EU Policy	TFEU provisions	EUCFR provisions
Equality between men and women	Article 8 TFEU	Article 23 EUCFR
High level of employment	Article 9 TFEU	
Combating discrimination based on sex, racial or ethnic origin, religion or belief, disability, age, or sexual orientation	Article 10 TFEU	Article 21(2) EUCFR
Environment protection	Article 11 TFEU	Article 37 EUCFR
Consumer protection	Article 12 TFEU	Article 38 EUCFR
Animal welfare	Article 13 TFEU	
Culture	Article 167(4) TFEU	Article 151(4) EC
Health	Article 168(1) TFEU	Article 35 EUCFR
Industry	Article 173(3) TFEU	
Regional policy	Article 175 TFEU	
Development cooperation	Article 208(1)(2) TFEU	
Internal market	Article 114(3) TFEU	

Finally, this cross-sectoral approach has been exacerbated by Articles 13 and 21(3) TEU and Article 7 TFEU; provisions that have been placing emphasis upon the 'consistency' between different EU policies and activities. The obligation to ensure consistency not only has a horizontal dimension, but also a vertical one on the account that national policies and Union policy must be mutually consistent.[86] In particular, secondary legislation may require a consistent approach between an EU policy, such as that combating climate change, and national policies.[87] In addition, according to the Court's case law, a national measure hindering a fundamental economic freedom is appropriate to ensure attainment of the objective pursued if it genuinely reflects a concern to attain it in a consistent and systematic manner.[88] Accordingly, in assessing whether an Austrian traffic prohibition is appropriate to attain the environmental protection objectives it pursues, it is 'essentially necessary to determine whether this traffic prohibition can contribute in a *consistent* and *systematic* manner to reducing NO_2 concentrations' along a motorway.[89]

This flurry of cross-sectoral obligations calls for four observations.

First, these TFEU and EUCFR provisions foster a more holistic approach. Indeed, the different integration clauses require decision-makers to take into account, as part of the decision-making process, not only the full range of interests affected by their decision but also a number of interests that have so far not received any degree of priority. It follows that the EU institutions must reconcile the various objectives laid

---

[86] See in particular Art. 181(1) TFEU.

[87] According to recital 23 of Directive 2003/87/EC establishing a scheme for green house gas emission allowance trading within the Community (ETS Directive [2003] OJ L275/32), allowance trading should 'form part of a comprehensive and coherent package of policies and measures implemented at Member State and Community level'. See Case 127/07 *Arcelor Atlantic et Lorraine* [2008] ECR I-9895, para. 9.

[88] Case C-384/08 *Attanasio Group* [2010] I-2025, para. 51; and Case C-169/08 *Presidente del Consiglio dei Ministri* [2009] ECR I-10821, para. 42.

[89] Opinion AG Trstenjak in Case C-28/09 *Commission v Austria* [2010] OJ C49/2, para. 95.

down in both the TEU and the TFEU. Prioritizing one objective should not render the achievement of the other objectives impossible.[90]

Second, one might ask whether all these integration clauses should be placed on an equal footing. The answer must be nuanced.[91] It should be noted that there are subtle differences between the wording of each of these clauses. Whereas the environment must be 'integrated' and the protection of health must be 'ensured', the other interests need only be taken 'into account'[92] or into consideration. Moreover, Article 11 TFEU is the only horizontal clause pursuing one of the objectives spelled out by Article 3(3) TEU. It follows that Article 11 TFEU lays down a stronger commitment than some of the other horizontal clauses.

Third, given this proliferation of cross-cutting concerns, one could ask whether these numerous integration clauses all end up cancelling each other out. This calls for a few words of explanation. There is no doubt that an EU act will never end up addressing all objectives cumulatively at the same time.[93] Sometimes it will emphasize one of them, sometimes another, whilst at other times both at the same time.

Fourth, given that the TFEU does not prioritize a specific clause, one policy objective or requirement could override the other policies. Hence, this flurry of integration clauses brings with it the risk of watering down the integration of environmental requirements and their replacement with good intentions.[94] Given that the EU institutions have wide discretionary powers as to how they shape their different policies, EU environmental policy is not likely to have been given priority over other policy areas. Indeed, it is settled case law that institutions have 'to strike a balance between the relative importance of the environmental objectives and other objectives as they proceed'.[95]

Nonetheless, it will not be possible for action carried out within the ambit of a policy to reject or disregard squarely the other interests in play. Therefore, even though it is not necessary to grant absolute priority to the interests protected by the different integration clauses, the EU institutions should nevertheless take due account of the impact caused by the act considered on lesser priority objectives. Put simply, they cannot remain blind to the concerns expressed by each of these policies. As far as environmental issues are concerned, this is particularly true when the action carried out may imperil key natural resources, endanger endemic or rare species, or cause irreversible damage. These values are too fundamental to be overridden by the

---

[90] See in particular the ECJ case law on CAP objectives. Joined Cases 197–200/80 *Ludwigshafener Walzmühle v Council and Commission* [1981] ECR 3211, para. 41; Case 59/83 *Biovilac v Commission* [1984] ECR 4057, para. 16; Case C-280/93 *Germany v Council* [1994] ECR I-4973, paras 47 and 51; Case C-122/94 *Commission v Council* [1996] ECR I-881, para. 24.

[91] Some authors take the view that there is no hierarchy between these various integration clauses. See H. Vedder, 'The Treaty of Lisbon and European Environmental Law and Policy' (2010) 22:2 *JEL* 289.

[92] Arts 9 and 12 TFEU.

[93] Several EU acts list a host of objectives without organizing them into a hierarchy. Eg in accordance with its Art. 1(a), European Parliament and Council Regulation (EC) No. 1829/2003 on genetically modified food and feed is deemed to ensure concomitantly 'a high level of protection of human life and health, animal health and welfare, environment and consumer interests in relation to genetically modified food and feed, whilst ensuring the effective functioning of the internal market' ([2003] OJ L268/1).

[94] J. Jans, 'Stop the Integration Principle' (2010) 33:5 *Fordham Intl LJ* 1547.

[95] Case C-341/94 *Giani Bettati* [1998] ECR I-4355, para. 35.

objectives of other policy sectors. In a nutshell, all of these integration clauses participate in a common project, namely of ensuring that the actions of the Union are guided by a quality-of-life project both for its inhabitants as well as its workers. These values are, indeed, a counterweight to the project of an essentially economic nature. Finally, a legal systematic argument supports this interpretation: the founding Treaties should be viewed as forming a consistent legal system.[96] Therefore, where possible, 'treaty provisions should be interpreted so as to help, and not hinder, the EU's other policy objectives'.[97]

5.3 Legal status

We now turn to the legal status of Article 11 TFEU. Five issues emerge as of particular importance.

First, having been progressively reinforced by the amendments made to the former EC Treaty,[98] the integration clause embodied in Article 11 TFEU now occupies a symbolic position amongst the introductory provisions of the TFEU.[99] Admittedly, it is important to point out that although the desire of the framers of the Treaty to place this clause in the part dedicated to 'Provisions having general application' is apparently devoid of any legal significance, this does not alter the fact that this logistical choice may have effects with regard to the position of the environment within the hierarchy of values and the resulting balance of interests.[100] As a result, this clause has been coined a 'general principle',[101] a 'legal principle',[102] and even a 'basic principle'.[103]

Second, in spite of the fact that the procedures for its application have not been specified, it should be pointed out that this provision is binding ('must'). Unlike sustainable development, which is a rather ambiguous objective, Article 11 TFEU poses a concrete obligation. Indeed, a literal interpretation of Article 11 TFEU suggests

---

[96] P. Pescatore, *The Law of Integration* (Leiden: Stijhol, 1974) 41.

[97] S. Kingston, 'Integrating Environmental Protection and EU Competition Law: Why Competition Isn't Special' (2010) 6 *ELJ* 781.

[98] The environmental clause has been progressively reinforced. Although the environmental protection requirements were originally 'a component of the Community's other policies' (Art. 130r(2) as it appears in the SEA), later they would have to 'be integrated into the definition and implementation of other Community policies' (according to the same article as it appears in the Treaty of Maastricht), as well as in 'the Community ... activities' (Art. 6 as it appears in the Treaty of Amsterdam). In addition, under the Treaty of Maastricht, the aim of the clause has been specified: integration must be pursued specifically with a view to achieving sustainable development.

[99] M. Wessmaier, 'The Integration of Environmental Protection as General Rule for Interpreting Law' (2001) *CML Rev* 159–77; N. D'Hondt, *Integration of Environmental Protection into other European EU Policies. Legal Theory and Practice* (Groeningen: Europa Law, 2003); D. Grimmeaud, 'The Integration of Environmental Concerns into EC Policies: A Genuine Policy Development?' (2000) *EELR* 207–18; W. Lafferty and E. Hovden, 'Environmental Policy Integration: Towards an Analytical Framework' (2003) 3 *Environmental Politics* 1–22; R. Macrory, *Regulation, Enforcement and Governance in Environmental Law* (Oxford: Hart Publishing, 2010) 567–83; Jans (n 94), 1533–47.

[100] Case C-176/03 *Commission v Council* [2005] ECR I-7879, para. 42.

[101] M. Wessmeier (n 99), 161; Jans (n 94), 1537.

[102] D'Hondt (n 99), 143; N. Hervé-Fournereu, 'Le principe d'intégration des exigences de la protection de l'environnement: essai de clarification juridique' in *Liber amicorum Jean RAUX, Le droit de l'Union européenne en principes* (Rennes: Apogée, 2006) 661.

[103] S. Mahmoudi, 'Integration of Environmental Considerations into Transport' in R. Macrory (ed.), *Reflections on 30 Years of EU Environmental Law* (Groeningen: Europa Law, 2006) 185.

that there is an obligation to 'integrate' and not merely to take into account. In sharp contrast, by virtue of Article 192(3) TFEU, institutions are merely called upon to 'take into account' the different environmental criteria, which are not binding.[104] It follows that EU institutions cannot ignore environmental protection requirements when pursuing other policies.

Third, also known as the principle of integration, the environmental integration clause is called upon to play a greater role, not only due to the fact that it makes it possible to avoid interferences and contradictions between competing policies, but also because it may enhance sustainable development in favouring the implementation of more global, more coherent, and more effective policies.

Fourth, given that 'environmental requirements' have to be integrated, the institutions cannot content themselves with the objectives of that policy. They also have to pay heed to the principles and the criteria guiding that policy.[105]

Fifth, the material scope of Article 11 is particularly broad ('definition and implementation of policies and activities'). This provision not only obliges the EU institutions to intervene, but also encourages them to extend the field of environmental action, given that 'policies and activities' embrace all regulatory and financial measures contemplated under that provision, including measures, programmes, regimes, and not only those specifically entitled 'policies' and 'activities'. In other words, environmental policy should now reach beyond the restricted area to which it is generally confined (listed installations, emission and quality standards, waste management, ecosystem management, etc). Furthermore, integration calls in any event for the abandonment of a vertical organizational model, according to which each policy is confined to a very specific field of action, in favour of a more cross-cutting approach.

However, the binding nature of Article 11 TFEU is hindered by several stumbling blocks. One of its drawbacks stems from the fact that the conceptual tools and the methods of integrating environmental requirements are not spelled out in the TFEU.

So far, many questions are left unanswered. Indeed, this provision refers to the integration of 'environmental policy requirements'. But what should be integrated into other policies: objectives, principles, procedural rights, emission standards, quality targets?

The environmental principles proclaimed in Article 192(2) TFEU[106] could provide the muscle for the obligation to integrate environmental considerations, but the EU Courts appear to be hesitant to head down this path.[107] Pursuant to Article 37 EUCFR, 'a high level of protection' should at least be integrated. But, as emphasized later, the determination of that level will always be mired in controversy. The degree of integration required is not specified at all in the TFEU and, in practice, it may vary substantially depending on the degree of openness of the different public policies which contribute to worsening the quality of the environment.

---

[104] Jans and Vedder (n 12), 17. See the discussion in Section 8.

[105] D'Hondt (n 99), 72–80; Jans (n 94), 1542. As regards the scope of the environmental principles and criteria, see the discussion in Sections 7 and 8.

[106] See the discussion in Section 6.

[107] The CFI took the view that the precautionary principle is 'the corollary of the principle that the requirements of the protection of public health are to prevail over economic interests'. See Case T-74/00 *Artegodan* [2002] ECR II-4945, para. 174.

A further difficulty stems from the fact that the incorporation of environmental requirements is supposed to promote, pursuant Article 11 TFEU, 'in particular... sustainable development' or, by virtue of Article 37 EUCFR, 'the principle of sustainable development'. Hence, integration is not a goal in itself but rather a means by which the EU should achieve a much more ambitious objective. Clearly, since sustainable development tends precisely to reconcile economic, social, and environmental interests, the environmental requirements risk being laid aside in the name of contradicting requirements. The result is at the very least paradoxical: since Article 11 TFEU appears to give priority to environmental protection, the promotion of sustainable development may, by contrast, water down or even weaken the scope of the integration clause.

To sum up, as with the concept of sustainable development, this provision is characterized by a strong degree of indeterminacy.

5.4 Case law

There is, indeed, a question as to the binding nature of Article 11 TFEU: does it set out an objective lacking in binding effects, a standard, or a Treaty obligation, the violation of which is likely to be reviewed by the EU Courts? Besides, there is a further aspect to Article 11 TFEU: it functions as a canon of interpretation. Furthermore, it also functions as a directing principle in that it obliges the EU institutions to define a framework for action with a view to mitigating the pressure put on the environment by other policies. We shall address these issues in the subsequent subsections.

5.4.1 *Judicial review*

The academic literature has underscored the difficulties which the EU Courts could come up against when reviewing the legitimacy of an act of the Council or the Commission regarding energy or rural development against this obligation.[108] Some commentators consider that the violation of Article 11 TFEU could not result in the annulment of the act in question except in exceptional circumstances.[109]

To date, a single measure has been challenged before the EU Courts on the ground that environmental requirements were absent or were insufficiently integrated. In 2004, Austria brought an action for annulment against Regulation (EC) No. 2327/2003 of the European Parliament and of the Council of 22 December 2003 establishing a transitional points system applicable to heavy goods vehicles travelling through Austria. In the context of this action, within the framework of a sustainable transport policy, Advocate General Geelhoed examined, among other things, the compatibility of the regulation with ex Article 6 EC (Art. 11 TFEU). Even though the case was removed from the register, the Advocate General took the view that 'although this provision is drafted in imperative terms,... it cannot be regarded as laying down a standard according to which in defining Community policies environmental protection must

---

[108] Jans and Vedder (n 12), 20.   [109] Macrory (n 99), 558 and 573.

always be taken to be the prevalent interest'.[110] Considering that 'such an interpretation would unacceptably restrict the discretionary powers of the Community institutions and the Community legislature'[111] this provision is 'at most...to be regarded as an obligation on the part of the Community institutions to take due account of ecological interests in policy areas outside that of environmental protection *stricto sensu*. It is only where ecological interests manifestly have not been taken into account or where they have been completely disregarded that Article 6 EC [Art. 11 TFEU] may serve as the standard for reviewing the validity of Community legislation'.[112] At the end of the day, the Court of Justice did not adjudicate the case but if Advocate General Geelhoed's Opinion were to be endorsed by the Court, the judicial review of EU secondary measures integrating environmental protection concerns would then be seriously limited to very exceptional cases, where institutions have 'manifestly' or 'completely' disregarded environmental concerns.

Without doubt, the indeterminate nature of the substantive content of the obligation to integrate environmental requirements means that judicial review is a more sensitive issue; however, this does not mean that review is precluded. We are taking the view that the wording of Article 11 TFEU does not represent an obstacle to review by the EU Courts, even though this review is narrow in scope insofar as the EU Courts generally limit themselves to condemning manifest errors of appraisal or misuse of powers.

Consequently, if it is manifestly clear, with regard to given objectives (scientific or technical), that where a contested measure does not take environmental concerns into account, even though they arise in very concrete terms, the Court will have to annul it. Such a review must, in any event, become more stringent where the institution adopting the contested instrument has not properly stated its reasons for not taking the environmental dimension into account. This would be the case, for instance, of an executive or a delegated act adopted by the Commission by virtue of a legislative act paying heed to the environmental dimension.

That said, in spite of the hurdles claimants are likely to face, Article 11 is not devoid of legal effects.

5.4.2 *Principle of interpretation*

Although judicial review is likely to be limited to whether institutions have committed a manifest error of appraisal or misuse their powers, Article 11 TFEU has been playing a greater role so far as a principle of interpretation.[113] Specifically, where the Court of Justice is called on to rule on hard cases, it resorts to Article 11 TFEU which comes in the form of a principle of interpretation. This can be illustrated by the following cases.

It is settled case law that the integration clause implies in particular that provisions other than Article 192 TFEU may operate as a basis for actions that are partially related to environmental protection. Accordingly, an international agreement providing for an

---

[110] Opinion AG Geelhoed delivered on 26 January 2006 in Case C-161/04 *Austria v Parliament and Council* [2006] ECR I-7183, para. 59.
[111] Opinion AG Geelhoed (n 110).   [112] Opinion AG Geelhoed (n 110).
[113] Case T-212/09 *Denmark v Commission* [2012] OJ C373/2, para. 76.

opt-in procedure for the transfer of chemical products and hazardous pesticides may, in the eyes of the Court, 'be properly approved on the basis of an article such as Article [207 TFEU]' even though 'it pursued, primarily or subsidiarily, objectives of an environmental nature'. Recourse to this type of legal basis may be justified on the basis of Articles 11 and 168(1) TFEU, according to which environmental protection requirements, and requirements relating to the protection of human health, must be integrated into the definition and implementation of Union policies and activities.[114] As a result, Article 11 TFEU broadens the other EU policies' objectives.

By the same token, Article 11 TFEU justifies a broad implementation of the precautionary principle even within policies that do not expressly proclaim it, such as health.[115]

Article 11 TFEU also requires the EU Courts to follow the interpretation that is most favourable to environmental protection when they are required to weigh up ecological interests against economic interests.[116] By way of example, in one of the numerous judgments concerning the traffic in goods travelling along the section of motorway in the Inn Valley in Austria, the Court of Justice upheld the justification for tariff barriers imposed by the Austrian authorities as compatible with imperative requirements relating to environmental protection, on the ground, in particular, that these considerations had to be incorporated into the definition and implementation of the policies and actions of the former Community.[117] Accordingly, preference should be given to the interpretation that is deemed to be the most favourable to environmental requirements.

The Court of Justice also relied on Article 11 TFEU when concluding that a framework decision—an act related to the former third pillar—defining a certain number of environmental offences, for which the Member States were called on to prescribe criminal penalties, had to be replaced by an act adopted on the basis of Article 175 EC (Art. 192 TFEU) and not on the basis of the ex Article 34 TEU.[118]

The General Court also relied implicitly on this clause in order to arrive at the following solutions. The Commission may recognize the compatibility of State environmental aids not only with reference to the framework dedicated to this type of aid, but 'directly on the basis of Article [107(3) TFEU], unless it has explicitly adopted a position on the question at issue in its framework'.[119]

5.5 Secondary law

As an instrument providing legal guidance, since 1993 the integration clause has been the object of an important debate within the EU institutions which have often come across as part of an organization essentially pursuing economic regional integration.

---

[114] Case C-94/03 *Commission v Council* [2006] ECR I-1, para. 26.
[115] See the discussion in Section 7.6.
[116] Opinion AG Jacobs in Case C-379/98 *PreussenElektra* [2001] ECR I-2159, para. 232.
[117] Case C-320/03 *Commission v Austria* [2005] ECR I-9871, para. 73.
[118] Case C-176/03 *Commission v Council* [2005] ECR I-7879, para. 42.
[119] Case T-375/03 *Fachvereinigung Mineralfaserindustrie* [2007] ECR II-121, para. 143. Judgment not available in English.

Reassured by the recommendations of the Cardiff Summit, the European Commission has gradually opened itself up to environmental concerns through the adoption of various communications and strategies. These non-binding instruments thus provide the modus operandi for the integration clause.[120]

There is no shortage of secondary law provisions referring to this obligation. For instance, the objectives of the Regional, Social and Cohesion Funds shall be pursued 'in the framework of sustainable development and the Community promotion of the goal of protecting and improving the environment as set out in [Article 11 TFEU].'[121] However, such statements may be ineffective where they not supplemented with more precise environmental requirements integrated into non-environmental legislation.[122] In this respect, it is worthy of note that the environmental integration clause has been transposed into secondary EU law, in particular through a number of harmonization measures obliging public and private actors to incorporate into their decisions certain basic rules and procedures which have the goal of contributing to environmental protection. In other words, EU secondary law progressively integrates environmental concerns. For convenience, a few examples have been chosen relating to land planning, the Common Agricultural Policy (CAP), transport, State aids, air transport, public tendering, structural funds, and international private law.

Inasmuch as land planning regulations allow the realization of public or private projects, environmental concerns must be taken into account at the earliest stage, when conceiving the land-planning regulation, not at the time of construction. It is certainly more effective first to assess the overall impact of all the roads encapsulated in a highways project than to single out every road without any broader assessment. On this account, Directive 2001/42/EC of the European Parliament and of the Council of 27 June 2001 on the assessment of the effects of certain plans and programmes on the environment subjects the plans and programmes underlying the realization of particular projects to a preliminary environmental assessment procedure.

Furthermore, 'eco-conditionality' or 'cross-compliance' allows the granting of direct payments provided the recipients (farmers, fishermen, etc) abide by specific environmental requirements. The strength of this financial mechanism lies in the economic nature of the sanction it contains, which is the suppression of the advantage granted.[123] So far, agricultural aid has been the favoured field of this mechanism. By way of illustration, Regulation (EC) No. 1782/2003 establishing common rules for direct support schemes under the CAP and establishing certain support schemes for farmers encapsulates such a mechanism. Pursuant to that Regulation, farmers receiving direct

---

[120] See, notably, Commission Communications: Market and Environment. Communication from the Commission to the European Parliament and the Council, COM(99) 263 final; Elements of a Strategy for the Integration of Environmental Protection Requirements into the Common Fisheries Policy, COM(2001) 143 final; Directions towards Sustainable Agriculture, COM (99) 22 final; Integrating Environment and Sustainable Development into Economic and Development Cooperation Policy—Elements of a Comprehensive Strategy, COM(99) 499.

[121] Regulation (EC) No. 1083/2006, Art. 7.

[122] The integration requirement provided the basis for an action of annulment lodged by an Irish NGO against a Commission's decision financing through structural funds the construction of an interpretative centre in a national park. See Case T-461/93 *An Taisce v Commission* [1994] ECR II-733.

[123] B. Jack, *Agriculture and EU Environmental Law* (Farnham: Ashgate, 2009) 70–9.

support of any type are bound by two types of environmental requirement: on the one hand, requirements relating to the respect of secondary environmental legislation; and, on the other, the obligation to maintain their land in 'good agricultural and environment condition'. It emerges from the regulation's genesis that the Council wanted to lend more weight to environmental considerations.[124]

As regards the integration of security and travellers' health considerations in air security policy, Article 6 of Regulation (EC) No. 1592/2002 of the European Parliament and of the Council of 15 July 2002 on common rules in the field of civil aviation and establishing a European Aviation Safety Agency, the legal basis of which is ex Article 80(2) EC (Art. 100 TFEU), sets out a number of measures in order to curb air and noise pollution. Moreover, in accordance with the proportionality principle, Directive 2002/30/EC of the European Parliament and of the Council of 26 March 2002 on the establishment of rules and procedures with regard to the introduction of noise-related operating restrictions at Community airports allows Member States progressively to eliminate the noisiest planes on the basis of an impact study.[125]

As discussed in Part III, the integration clause is also fleshed out in the European Commission's practice aiming to encourage State aids that are deemed to be favourable to environmental protection. Thus, as will be seen later,[126] undertakings may obtain State aids not to comply with existing environmental standards but exclusively in order to improve their environmental performance beyond the regulatory standards.

It is common ground that the choices made by public authorities in relation to tendering, have traditionally been influenced by the cheapest tender, or by other criteria having no link with protection of the environment. However, as soon as it is likely that environmental criteria may prevail over 'the most economically advantageous tender' criterion, it can be expected that every tenderer will integrate these requirements in its tender.[127] In a case relating to the conclusion of a contract concerning the acquisition of eco-friendly buses for the city of Helsinki, Finland, the ECJ referred to ex Article 6 EC (Art. 11 TFEU) to conclude that Council Directive 92/50/EEC of 18 June 1992 relating to the coordination of procedures for the award of public service contracts did not 'exclude the possibility for the contracting authority of using criteria relating to the preservation of the environment when assessing the economically most advantageous tender.'[128] Hence, the Court of Justice took the view that 'when assessing the economically most advantageous tender' the contracting authority could attach a weighting of 45 per cent to the environmental criterion on which it proposed to base the award of contract. The importance given to this criterion did not appear 'to present an obstacle to an overall evaluation of the criteria applied in order to identify the most economically advantageous tender'.[129] In requiring

[124] Opinion AG Trstenjak in Case C-428/07 *Mark Horvath v Secretary of State for Environment* [2009] ECR I-6355, paras 47 et seq.

[125] [2002] OJ L85/40. See Case C-422/05 *Commission v Belgium* [2007] ECR I-4749.

[126] Chapter 12.

[127] S. Arrowsmith and P. Kunzlik (eds), *Social and Environmental Policies in EC Procurement Law* (Cambridge: CUP, 2009); J. J. Pernas García, *Contratación pública verde* (Madrid: La Ley, 2009).

[128] Case C-513/99 *Concordia Bus Finland* [2002] ECR I-7213, para. 57.

[129] Case C-448/01 *ENV AG and Wienstrom GmbH v Austria* [2003] ECR I-4527, para. 42. In this judgment, the Court follows the same reasoning as in *Concordia Bus Finland* which concerned an electricity

environmental criteria in public contracts to be taken into account, the EU lawmaker followed that lead.[130] Given that each year Member State public authorities spend the equivalent of 16 per cent of GDP on the purchase of goods and services, one might expect the progressive greening of public procurement to enlarge markets for environmentally friendly products and services.[131]

Even though the conflict-of-law settlement principle set out in Article 4(1) of Regulation Rome II is that 'the law applicable to a non-contractual obligation arising out of a tort/delict shall be the law of the country in which the damage occurred . . .', Article 7 of the regulation allows the victim of environmental damage 'to base his or her claim on the law of the country in which the event giving rise to the damage occurred'. The victim may thus resort to the law that is most favourable to the protection of his or her interests: the law of the country in which the event giving rise to the damage occurred or the law of the country in which the damage occurred.[132] For water pollution, this mechanism entices the undertaking with a good environmental record, and which is based in an upstream Member State, to take into consideration the higher standards applied in its home State rather than the less comprehensive standards of the downstream Member State in which the damage is most likely to occur.

Given that the exhaustion of natural resources and the damage caused to the environment might thwart efforts aiming at reducing poverty in developing countries, the EU has defined, through environmental criteria, the modes according

supply contract. It should also be noted that the Court accepted an award criterion that did not refer to the physical characteristics or materials of the product (electricity), but instead to the method or process of production (renewable energy).

[130] See European Parliament and Council Directive 2004/18/EC on the coordination of procedures for the award of public works contracts, public supply contracts, and public service contracts ([2004] OJ L351/44), which 'clarifies how the contracting authorities may contribute to the protection of the environment and the promotion of sustainable development' (recital 5, see in particular, Art. 23). Regarding the extent to which contracting authorities can, under Directive 2004/18, make the environmental and social sustainability of the products to be supplied a condition for the award of a contract, see Case C-368/10 *Commission v Netherlands* [2012] OJ C 328. In addition, European Parliament and Council Directive 2006/32/EC on energy end-use efficiency and energy services ([2006] OJ L114/64) obliges Member States to adopt two measures from the group of measures provided in Annex VI, entitled 'List of eligible energy efficient public procurement measures'. By the same token, European Parliament and Council Directive 2009/33/EC on the promotion of clean and energy-efficient road transport vehicles ([2009] OJ L120/5) obliges contracting authorities to take into account the energy and environmental impact of vehicles during their useful life, including energy consumption and CO_2 and other pollutants, when they purchase vehicles for road transport (Art. 5). Finally, European Parliament and Council Regulation (EC) No. 106/2008 on a Community energy-efficiency labelling programme for office equipment ([2008] OJ L39/1) requires EU institutions and Member State authorities to purchase office equipment that meets certain energy efficiency requirements.

[131] See Public Procurement for a Better Environment, COM(2008) 400 final, para. 1.1. This EU strategy has been developed within the framework of the EU Strategy of Sustainable Development and the Action Plan on Sustainable Consumption and Production (2008). In 2005, the Commission contributed to promoting its environmental public procurement strategy by publishing a *Handbook on Environmental Public Procurement* (updated 25 October 2011).

[132] M. Bogdan, 'The Treatment of Environmental Damage in Rome II' in J. Ahern and W. Binchy (eds), *The Rome II Regulation on the Law Applicable to Non-Contractual Obligations* (Leiden/Boston: Martinus Nijhoff, 2009) 219–30; E. Guinchard and S. Lamont-Black, 'Environmental Law—the Black Sheep in Rome II's Drive for Legal Certainty?' (2009) 11 *Env L Rev* 161–72.

to which developing countries may benefit from its financial aid and technical assistance.[133]

These regimes illustrate how the environmental clause has filtered into secondary law. However, one doesn't have to be a genius to acknowledge the extent of the disparity between the discourse of integration and hard facts.[134] Integration discourses in many respects go hand in hand with the replacement of action with good intentions, given the difficulties encountered in modifying policies deeply branded by a production-based ideology, whether it be the CAP[135] or transport policy.[136]

Also, the implementation of contradictory EU policies has the effect of exacerbating environmental problems.

6. Objectives of the EU Environmental Policy

6.1 Introductory comments

In the original Treaty of Rome, the only articles setting out specific objectives were those relating to the CAP and the association of overseas countries and territories. The framers of the Treaties certainly had the intention of enshrining within Treaty law the political guidelines to be followed in Community legislation. Setting these objectives did not fail to have an impact. Very early on, in fact, the Court of Justice established the principle that objectives had legal status on the same footing as the introductory articles to the Treaty.[137]

Starting with the SEA, and even more so after the Maastricht Treaty, numerous specific objectives of increasing detail were incorporated into the Treaties. Taking account of the principle that the EU may only act in accordance with the powers conferred upon it, the stating of objectives has helped to provide the Union's action with an indispensable legal basis. Moreover, given the proliferation of Union policies having their own objectives, the Court of Justice is working on objective criteria, among which are the objectives of the legislation, to rule whether the choice of legal basis for the

---

[133] European Parliament and Council Regulation (EC) No. 2493/2000 on measures to promote the full integration of the environmental dimension in the development process of developing countries [2000] OJ L288/1. This regulation has a double legal basis, consisting in ex Arts 175 and 179 EC (Arts 192 and 209 TFEU).

[134] As regards the lack of integration of environmental concerns in EU development policy, see Special Report No 6/2006 of the Court of Auditors concerning environmental aspects of the Commission's development cooperation, together with the Commission's replies ([2006] OJ C235/1–39). With respect to the use of EU funds jeopardizing a habitat deemed to be protected under the Habitats Direction 92/43/EC ([1992] OJ L206/7), see *An Taisce v Commission* (n 122). With regards to inadquate implementation of environmental requirements in the energy, agriculture, and transport policies, see D'Hondt (n 99), 442–4.

[135] See the first objective of the CAP, namely the increase of the agricultural productivity (Art. 39(1)(a) TFEU).

[136] In the context of 'the establishment and development of trans-European networks in the areas of transport, telecommunications and energy infrastructures' (Art. 170(1) TFEU; ex Art. 154(1) EC), which is a full EU's policy, the 21 priority projects of the trans-European transport network (TEN-T) would cross no less than a thousand sites classified as protected in the Natura 2000 network in accordance with Directive 92/43/EC on the conservation of natural habitats and of wild fauna and flora (Birdlife International, *Hundreds of Nature Sites at Risk from EU Transport Projects*, 2008), even though those sites harbour wildlife species which are extremely sensitive to the cutting effects of road-building.

[137] Case 8/57 *Groupement des hauts fourneaux et aciéries belges HFA* [1958] ECR 245.

contested act is appropriate. In addition, the objectives may also be regarded as a way of guiding the Court of Justice when interpreting the provisions of a directive or a regulation if it has been requested to provide an answer on a reference for a preliminary ruling.[138]

Accordingly, EU environmental law must be analysed in the light of the 'essential'[139] objectives set forth in the TEU and TFEU. By virtue of Article 3 TEU, the EU aims 'to promote... the well-being of its peoples' and, in particular, 'a high level of protection and improvement of the quality of the environment'.

As far as environmental policy is concerned, the competence is defined, since the entry into force of the SEA, in terms of objectives to be achieved, rather than areas of activities to be regulated. Indeed, pursuant to Article 191(1) TFEU, the EU environmental policy pursues four objectives:

- preserving, protecting and improving the quality of the environment,
- protecting human health,
- prudent and rational utilisation of natural resources,
- promoting measures at international level to deal with regional or worldwide environmental problems, and in particular combating climate change.

This provision calls for several observations.

First, by virtue of the extremely general and fluid nature of these four objectives, the EU lawmakers are left with a genuine discretionary power as to the fundamental choices of this policy. In effect, their general wording permits a degree of flexibility as well as adaptability in the aims pursued by the EU legislature when it wishes to provide for common action. For instance, in *Peralta*, the Court of Justice ruled that ex Article 130r (Art. 191(1) TFEU) 'confines itself to defining the general objectives of the Community in environmental matters.' 'Responsibility for deciding what action is to be taken' in order to achieve these goals is conferred on the lawmaker by [Article 192 TFEU]'.[140] Consequently, the priority areas of action are likely to change regularly in accordance with political willingness to ward off environmental risks. Given that the powers to act in environmental matters are so broad, EU environmental competence encompasses almost any environmental measure: biodiversity, water, soil, air, climate, hazardous substances, waste, oil spills, product life-cycle analysis, pesticides, listed installations, noise, impact assessments, procedural rights such as access to information and justice, etc. It thus proves difficult to draw the limits of this protean policy.

Second, whilst the objectives do contribute to delineating the scope of environmental policy, they also mark out its limits. If an act based on Article 192 TFEU fails to pursue one or more of these objectives, it will have to be ruled invalid.

Third, they are listed in a linear fashion. One could ask whether these four objectives are placed on a completely equal footing or whether, by contrast, any hierarchy could

[138] Case C-343/09 *Afton* [2010] ECR I-7027, para. 64; Case C-420/10 *Söll* [2012] OJ C118/3, para. 27.
[139] Case 240/83 *ADBHU* [1985] ECR I-531, para. 13; Case C-195/90 *Commission v Germany* [1992] ECR I-3141, para. 29; Case C-508/04 *Commission v Austria* [2007] ECR I-3787, para. 120; and Case C-487/06 P *British Aggregates v Commission* [2008] ECR I-10515, para. 91.
[140] Case C-379/92 *Peralta* [1994] ECR I-3454, para. 57.

be envisaged. Since there is no hierarchy between them, one objective may prevail over the others;[141] it is not possible to infer any order of priority whatsoever. This therefore means that the EU institutions have to specify and hierarchically classify objectives within each given area of secondary law.[142] However, as noted later, there is no need to conceal the problem of possible contradictions between these objectives. The Court of Justice may therefore resolve any differences between them. Analogous reasoning could be followed regarding the case law of the Court of Justice on the objectives of the CAP.[143] Regarding that policy, nothing precludes the Court of Justice from giving priority to one over another.[144]

Fourth, environmental obligations set out in secondary law have to be read in the light of the objectives spelled out by Article 191(1) TFEU.[145]

Fifth, it should be noted that environmental objectives may also be taken into account by virtue of Article 11 TFEU and Article 37 EUCFR within the context of action conducted in relation to other EU policies.

Finally, it is a matter of regret that the health of consumers, which is placed in jeopardy by numerous pollutants, is not included amongst the objectives of environmental policy.[146] Without doubt, consumer protection law—which is older than environmental law—falls within the area of private law, whilst environmental law is an offshoot of public law. However, as a result of the effect of sustainable development and the integration clause,[147] this boundary is becoming increasingly blurred. Thus, public law is driven to interact with private law in this area. There is no doubt that environmental law, consumer protection law, and health protection law will one day be called upon to form a triple alliance.

A brief discussion of each of these four objectives is warranted to make clear the baseline against which the EU environmental policy unfolds.

---

[141] With respect to Natura 2000 habitats, setting conservation and restoration objectives 'may in fact require decisions to be made on conflicts between various objectives'. Opinion AG Kokott in Case C-241/08 *Commission v France* [2010] ECR I-1697, para. 71.

[142] See, eg, the manner in which the waste management objectives have been classified under the waste hierarchy provided for under Art. 4 of Directive 2008/98/EC on waste [2008] OJ L312/3. With regards to other EU policies, nothing precludes environmental interests from prevailing over economic objectives, such as that of improving plant production (recital 24 of Regulation (EC) No. 1107/2009 concerning the placing of plant production products on the market [2009] OJ L309/1).

[143] Case 5/73 *Balkan Import-Export* [1973] ECR 1091; and Cases 279/84, 280/84, 285/84 & 286/84 *Rau* [1987] ECR I-1069.

[144] The Court has held that 'in pursuing the objectives of the common agricultural policy the Community institutions must secure the permanent harmonization made necessary by any conflicts between those objectives taken individually and, where necessary, give any one of them temporary priority in order to satisfy the demands of the economic factors or conditions in view of which their decisions are made.' See Case 203/86 *Spain v Council* [1988] ECR 4563, para. 10; Case C-311/89 *Joseph Hierl* [1988] ECR I-2079, para. 13.

[145] In much the same vein, CAP obligations have to be read in the light of the objectives spelled out by Art. 39(1) TFEU. See Case C-137/00 *Milk Marque Ltd and NFU* [2008] ECR I-7975, paras 98–9.

[146] Consumer health is one of the objectives of EU consumer policy under Art. 169(1) TFEU. *Afton* is a good case in point regarding the impossibility to draw a dividing line between consumer health and environmental objectives of a measure restricting the use of a chemical additive. See *Afton* (n 138).

[147] See Section 5.

6.2 The environmental objective

The first objective is the only one which concerns the environment, a concept which, as we saw earlier, is somewhat imprecise.[148] The policy must be both reactive ('protection')[149] as well as proactive ('improvement'). As will be seen in the next section, the principle of prevention underpins most of the regulatory devices.

Protection can entail either mitigation or compensatory measures.[150] Moreover, most of the EU measures aiming at protecting wildlife, conserving ecosystems, or managing natural resources are pursuing both a reactive as well as a proactive approach.

As far as a proactive approach is concerned, restoration of a degraded environment has become the thrust of the policy. Numerous illustrations can be found: for instance, given that the water quality is so poor in most of the Member States, the Water Framework Directive 2000/60/EC calls upon the national authorities to 'restore all bodies of surface water,…, with the aim of achieving [in 2015] good surface water status'.[151] By the same token, given that a number of species are on the brink of extinction,[152] Members States are obliged to restore 'at favourable conservation status, natural habitats and species of wild fauna and flora of Community interest'.[153]

Lastly, environmental objectives pursued by the EU lawmaker can be subject to broad interpretation. This may be illustrated by the Court of Justice's case law on the definition of eutrophication.[154]

6.3 The human health objective

6.3.1 *Intertwined issues*

Health-related problems today are no longer confined to the discreet surroundings of medical surgeries or hospitals; they also manifest themselves in real estate, airports, foreign trade, control of foodstuffs, health crises, etc.

---

[148] See Section 2.

[149] However, there is no mention of the issue of conservation, a concept that is understood as the 'series of measures required to maintain or restore the natural habitats and the populations of species of wild fauna and flora at a favourable status' (Council Directive 92/43/EEC on the conservation of natural habitats and of wild fauna and flora [1992] OJ L206/7, Art. 1(a)).

[150] See, eg, Art. 6(4) of Directive 92/43/EEC on the conservation of natural habitats and of wild fauna and flora [1992] OJ L206/7, and the CDM and Joint Implementation provided for under Directive 2003/87/EC establishing a scheme for green house gas emission allowance trading within the Community [2003] OJ L275/2.

[151] European Parliament and Council Directive 2000/60/EC establishing a framework for Community action in the field of water policy [2000] OJ L327/1, Art. 4(1)(ii).

[152] Nearly one in six of Europe's mammal species, a quarter of amphibians, one-fifth of reptiles, and 9 per cent of European butterflies are listed as threatened status in Europe. See the European Red List reviewing the conservation status of *c.* 6,000 European species according to the International Union for Conservation of Nature's regional Red Listing guidelines.

[153] Council Directive 92/43/EEC of 21 May 1992 on the conservation of natural habitats and of wild fauna and flora [1992] OJ L206/7.

[154] The Court held that the term 'eutrophication' defined in Directive 91/271 must be interpreted in the light of the Nitrates Directive's objective, which goes beyond mere protection of aquatic ecosystems. Accordingly, it encompasses a vast number of environmental issues. See Case C-280/02 *Commission v France* [2004] ECR I-8573, paras 13–17; and Case C-390/07 *Commission v UK* [2009] ECR I-214, para. 26.

In addition, the environment plays a crucial role in people's physical, mental, and social well-being. Hence, environmental degradation, through air pollution, noise, chemicals, poor quality of water, and loss of natural areas, is likely to contribute to significant increases in rates of, for example, obesity, diabetes, diseases of the cardio-vascular and nervous systems, and cancer.[155]

It comes as no surprise that environmental and health issues are constantly inter-twined. For example, contamination of bovine animals by the BSE agent has been directly linked to recycling of animal carcasses. Since carcasses may no longer be consumed, they need to be burned, which contributes to an increase in atmospheric pollution. Similarly, when imports from Brazil of soya, a replacement for animal feed, rose considerably, this speeded up the destruction of the Amazonian rainforest.[156] This means that food safety issues and environmental impacts end up becoming entangled. Even the supply of drinking water is, in principle, to be included in considerations relating to human health.[157] This interpenetration has also made reconciliation of health-care concerns with environmental requirements inevitable.

6.3.2 *Secondary law*

Numerous directives—in particular in the areas of air, water, and waste management—also recognize public health protection amongst their objectives. It may even be the case that the EU lawmaker himself favours health protection over environmental protection, placing the former on a higher level in the hierarchy of values.[158] Moreover, the imposition of air quality standards which may not be exceeded, 'with a view especially to protecting human health' creates subjective rights which individuals must be able to rely on before the national courts.[159] As the review of the issue of access to justice has shown,[160] the possibility of relying directly on such rights applies particularly 'in respect of a directive . . . which is designed . . . to protect public health'.[161]

6.3.3 *Case law*

Given their importance, health issues are likely to reinforce environmental regulation. For instance, a standstill approach governing the placing on the market of GMOs

---

[155] EUGLOREH Project, *Report on the Status of Health in the European Union. Towards a Healthier Europe* (2009); European Environment Agency (EEA), *The European Environment 2010. State and Outlook* (Copenhagen: EEA, 2010) 91.

[156] V. Elferink, S. Nonhebel, and A. J. M. Schoot Uiterkamp, 'Does the Amazon Suffer from BSE Prevention?' (2007) 2–4 *Agriculture, Ecosystems & Environment* 467–9.

[157] *Nomarchiaki Aftodioikisi Aitoloakarnanias e.a.* (n 8), para. 126.

[158] Eg by virtue of Art. 4(7)(2) of the Water Framework Directive 2000/60/EC there is no breach of the Water Framework Directive when 'the benefits to the environment and to society of achieving' the environmental objectives as regards the quality of waters 'are outweighed by the benefits of the new modifications or alterations to human health' or 'to the maintenance of human safety' ([2000] OJ L327/1).

[159] Case C-361/88 *Commission v Germany* [1991] ECR I-2567; and Case C-237/07 *Dieter Janecek* [2008] ECR I-6221, para. 37. See the discussion in Chapter 2, Section 2.4.1.

[160] N. de Sadeleer and C. Poncelet, 'Protection Against Acts Harmful to Human Health and the Environment Adopted by the EU Institutions' (2012) *Cambridge Yearbook of EU Law* 177–208.

[161] *Janecek* (n 159), para. 37.

precludes the relaxation of safety requirements. Consequently, since the protection of public health is a fundamental objective of EU novel food regulation, the scope of ambit of an alternative procedure cannot be interpreted in such a way that it amounts to a relaxation of basic safety requirements.[162]

The Court of Justice has already taken the view that health protection objectives may prevail over those relating to nature protection. By way of illustration, a project jeopardizing a wild bird sanctuary protected under the Wild Birds Directive can be authorized insofar as it wards off the risk of floods[163] but, by the same token, irrigation and the supply of drinking water can be of such an importance that such projects can be weighed against the Habitat Directive's objective of conservation of natural habitats and wild fauna.[164]

Public health also occupies, as we shall see later, a preferential position at the level of general arrangements governing the free movement of goods, since Article 36 TFEU lists amongst the legitimate justifications capable of restricting the free movement of goods, the 'the protection of health and life of humans [and] animals'.[165]

Finally, as regard the placing on the market of hazardous substances, it is settled case law that the protection of human health, 'may justify adverse economic consequences' and 'take precedence over economic considerations'.[166]

6.4 The prudent and rational use of natural resources objective

The third objective, the prudent and rational use of natural resources, must be considered in the light of the promotion of sustainable development, which is one of the key tasks of the EU.[167] This objective should encourage lawmakers to place more emphasis on sustainable consumption[168] and, therefore, to bring about an interaction between environmental rules and consumer protection regulations.

---

[162] Case C-236/01 *Monsanto Agricultora Italia* [2003] ECR I-8105, para. 80.

[163] Case C-57/89 *Commission v Germany* [1991] ECR I-883, paras 20–3. As a result, EU law expressly acknowledges that 'human health considerations' may be raised by national authorities with a view to justifying a plan or project likely to jeopardize the integrity of a Natura 2000 site hosting priority species and habitats (Directive 92/43/EEC on the conservation of natural habitats and of wild fauna and flora [1992] OJ L206/7, Art. 6(4)).

[164] *Nomarchiaki Aftodioikisi Aitoloakarnanias e.a.* (n 8), paras 121–2.

[165] See Chapter 5, Section 5.3.

[166] Order in Case C-180/96 R *UK v Commission* [1996] ECR I-3903, para. 93; Case C-320/93 *Ortscheit* [1994] ECR I-5243; Case C-183/95 *Affish* [1997] ECR I-4315, para. 43; Case C-473/98 *Kemikalineinspektionen and Toolex Alpha* [2000] ECR I-5681, para. 38; Case C-262/02 *Commission v France* [2004] ECR I-6569, para. 24; Case C-170/04 *Rosengren and others* [2007] ECR I-407, para. 39; Case C-143/06 *Ludwigs-Apotheke* [2007] ECR I-9623, para. 27; and Case C-141/07 *Commission v Germany* [2008] ECR I-6935, para. 46. With respect to General Court case law, see Case T-13/99 *Pfizer Animal Health v Council* [2002] ECR II-3305, paras 456 and 457; Case T-392/02 *Solvay v Council* [2003] ECR II-4555, para. 122; and Case T-158/03 *Metalaxyl* [2005] ECR II-2425, para. 134.

[167] See Section 4.

[168] Communication from the Commission of 25 June 2008 on the Sustainable Consumption and Production and Sustainable Industrial Policy Action Plan, COM(2008) 397 final.

6.5 The international objective

We now turn to the last objective which is stressing the importance of international cooperation as well as the fight against climate change.[169] Article 191(1) TFEU allows the EU institutions to take action on an international level, which appears to be logical as a large number of problems have a regional, or even universal, dimension. Since the environment takes no notice of borders, regulatory initiatives may therefore transcend the territorial framework of the EU.[170] Therefore, nothing prevents the EU environmental policy from tackling new problems which may be detected outwith the EU. This possibility is expressly recognized by Article 191(4) TFEU.[171] Due to the international impact of a number of EU environmental measures, it is by no means certain that their importance will wane.

Furthermore, the territorial scope of EU secondary law obligations cannot be interpreted narrowly. Article 52(1) TEU provides that the Treaty 'shall apply' to the States listed therein. Since this provision does not make any reference to the territory of the Member States, it cannot be interpreted as limiting the territorial extent of the Treaty exclusively to the areas falling under the sovereignty of the Member States. The field of application of the Treaty, along with that of secondary EU law, may thus extend beyond the territory of the Member States insofar as public international law permits the Member States to exercise limited jurisdiction. This interpretation is of considerable importance from the point of view of the conservation and sustainable use of biodiversity, in particular as regards the continental shelf, fishing areas, and exclusive economic zones (EEZs). This interpretation results, in particular, from the case law of the Court, and more specifically the *Kramer* case, where the Court recognized—with regard to the EU's competence to adopt measures aimed at the conservation of marine biological resources—that the material powers of the EU extended to the high seas.[172] Thus, to the extent that a Member State has competence in relation to the continental shelf or the EEZ, so too does the Union. This judgment was subsequently confirmed in the *Mondiet* case, concerning the validity of a prohibition on the use of drift nets with a length greater than 2.5 kilometres.[173] Similarly, the Court held that the application of the provisions transposing the directive on habitats conservation into national law cannot be limited only to national territory. It should also encompass the EEZ and the territorial sea.[174] It follows that the EU is competent to adopt rules concerning the

---

[169] Prior to the Treaty of Lisbon which introduced the objective of the fight against climate change, the Court of Justice had already held that the use of renewable energy sources for producing electricity was useful for protecting the environment insofar as it contributed to the reduction in emissions of GHGs which are among the main causes of climate change which the European Community and its Member States have pledged to combat (Case C-379/98 *PreussenElektra* [2001] ECR I-2099, para. 73).

[170] The Court of Justice has found that the supervision and control procedures established by Regulation (EEC) No. 259/93 on the supervision and control of shipments of waste within, into and out of the European Community ([1993] OJ L30/1) are intended to protect the environment, not only within the Community but also in third countries to which waste is exported from the EU. See Case C-259/05 *Omni Metal Service* [2007] ECR I-4945, para. 30.

[171] See Chapter 3. [172] Joined Cases 3, 4 & 6/76 *Cornelis Kramer and others* [1976] ECR I-1279.

[173] Case C-405/92 *Mondiet* [1993] ECR I-6133.

[174] Case C-6/04 *Commission v UK* [2005] ECR I-9017, paras 115–17. See also *R v Secretary of State for Trade and Industry, ex p Greenpeace Ltd* [1999].

conservation of biodiversity and the prevention of pollution which fall within the ambit of Article 191 TFEU in any zone where the Member States have jurisdiction, under the terms of public international law, in order to protect the environment outwith their own territory.

Nevertheless, the exercise of extra-territorial jurisdiction in environmental matters must occur in accordance with the rules of international law.[175] With respect to the EU emissions trading schemes (ETS), the Court of Justice stressed in *ATAA* that the ETS Directive lays down a criterion for the greenhouse gases (GHG) allowances scheme to be applicable to operators of aircraft registered in a third State according to which the scheme is applicable when the aircraft is in the territory of a Member State. Accordingly, the EU lawmaker does not infringe either the principle of territoriality or the principle of sovereignty.[176]

7. Principles of the EU Environmental Policy

7.1 Introductory remarks

Article 191(2) TFEU is worded as follows:

> Union policy on the environment shall aim at a high level of protection taking into account the diversity of situations in the various regions of the Union. It shall be based on the precautionary principle and on the principles that preventive action should be taken, that environmental damage should as a priority be rectified at source and that the polluter should pay.

Given that the environmental policy is the only EU policy to proclaim such a cluster of principles, this provision is somewhat exceptional. It thus comes as no surprise that practising lawyers are increasingly asking themselves what type of role these five principles have to play in legal practice. Two observations can be made at the outset.

First, given that most of these five principles were already embodied in international environmental agreements, they did not take root in virgin soil. For instance, prevention and precaution straddle both international and EU law. Nonetheless, there are a number of discrepancies between the two sets of principles. On the one hand, Article 191(2) proclaims principles that are particular to EU environmental law and policy, such as the principle of rectification at source as well as the principle of a high level of environmental protection. On the other hand, that provision does not embody all the principles laid down in international agreements. These are the cases of the principle of common but differentiated responsibility and of the principle of transboundary cooperation.

Second, several principles encapsulated in various directives and regulations, such as the principles of proximity and self-sufficiency of waste management and substitution, have not hitherto been incorporated in Article 191(2) TFEU.

---

[175] Case C-286/90 *Anklagenindighedenc Poulsen and Diva Navigation* [1992] ECR I-6019.
[176] Case C-366/10 *ATAA* [2011] OJ C49/7, para. 125.

Given that these five principles may justify EU and national environmental measures likely to hinder the internal market, we now take a close look at their role. It is the aim of the following subsections to determine the scope of each principle and how they have been fleshed out into more precise legal obligations and interpreted by the EU Courts. However, at this juncture a number of more general issues need to be addressed. The first question to be asked is why the Treaty drafters did not define these principles.

7.1.1 *Absence of definition*

Even though there are various definitions of these five principles in international environmental law, the five principles were not defined by the Treaty framers.

Broadly speaking, the lack of definition could be justified on the ground that their implementation across a wide range of policies is rather contextual. In some instances, the EU institutions have clarified the conditions under which some principles have to be applied.[177] That said, though, several regulations and directives provide for more comprehensive definition, while others are silent. By way of illustration, the General Food Law (GFL) Regulation offers a comprehensive definition of the precautionary principle[178] but neither the Environmental Liability nor the Waste Framework Directive define the polluter-pays principle. Although they are not defined in Treaty law, the EU Courts have also introduced extremely useful clarification on the application of these principles.

7.1.2 *Binding principles*

It is well known that the adoption of environmental measures owes more to political compromise than to tidy application of constitutional principles.[179] This statement does not mean that principles enshrined in the TFEU are devoid of legal effects. On the contrary, in contrast to other rules of indeterminate content, these five principles are mandatory.[180] Indeed, the use in paragraph 2 of the indicative rather than the

---

[177] To fill this gap, in February 2000 the European Commission issued a communication seeking to inform all interested parties of the manner in which the Commission applies or intends to apply the precautionary principle when taking decisions relating to the containment of risk (COM 2001/1).

[178] See Regulation (EC) No. 178/2002 laying down the general principles and requirements of food law, establishing the European Food Safety Authority and laying down procedures in matters of food safety [2002] OJ L31/1, Art. 7 ('GFL Regulation').

[179] C. Lister, *EU Environmental Law* (Chichester: Wiley, 1997) 21.

[180] Most academics regard Art. 192 TFEU principles as binding: G. Winter, 'Constitutionalizing Environmental Protection in the EU' (2002) 2 *YbEEL* 76 and 'The Legal Nature of Environmental Principles in International, EC and German Law' in R. Macrory (ed.), *Principles of European Environmental Law* (Groeningen: Europa Law, 2004) 19–22 et seq.; A. Epiney, *Umweltrecht in der Europäischen Union* (Cologne: Heymanns, 1997) 108; and 'Environmental Principles' in Macrory (n 103), 21; C. Hilson, 'Rights and Principles in EU Law: A Distinction without Foundation' (2008)15 *MJ* 209; contra L. Krämer, '30 Years of EC Environmental Law: Perspectives and Prospectives' (2002) 2 *YbEEL* 163; and *EC Environmental Law*, 6th edn (London: Sweet & Maxwell, 2007) 15; E. Fisher, *Risk Regulation and Administrative Constitutionalism* (Oxford: Hart Publishing, 2007) 212. See also M. Doherty, 'Hard Cases and Environmental Principles: An Aid to Interpretation?' (2002) 3 *YbEEL* 157–68; and 'The Judicial Use of the Principles of EC Environmental Policy' (2002) 2 *Env L Rev* 251–63.

conditional confirms that such principles are binding.[181] As a result, EU institutions have to abide by these principles.[182] It follows that EU measures not complying with these principles are likely to be subject to judicial review, although the EU Courts leave to the institutions a rather broad margin for discretion, provided a number of formal conditions are met. In addition, as discussed later, Member States are obliged to apply these principles when carrying out action in the environment field that has been harmonized by secondary EU law.[183]

One further point is worth making here. The unclear meaning of some principles alone is not sufficient to deny their legal effect. Indeed, their meaning has been crystallized through the sheer number of judgments that will be briefly discussed in the following text. Nevertheless, given their generality, these principles always allow for the possibility of accommodation. As will be seen, there is some discretion in the way in which they can be fleshed out in more concrete measures. In other words, the EU institutions are able to envision different regulatory devices with the aim of implementing these principles. That said, the discretion may become non-existent where a principle such as precaution has been fleshed out in a comprehensive authorization scheme.[184]

7.1.3 *The status of the principles in the Member State legal orders*

The fact that the EU environmental policy has given rise to a large number of directives prompts the question whether Article 192(2) principles apply at national level.[185]

Several hypotheses could be advanced by way of answer but the following distinctions should be made. A distinction must be drawn between areas covered by secondary law and those which are not. Furthermore, a second distinction should be drawn between principles that are explicit in EU secondary legislation and those that are implicit.

First, we shall address the issue of the impact of these principles in areas that have not been harmonized. Given that they are addressed to EU institutions, these principles cannot constrain national authorities and are therefore devoid of direct effect. As a result, Member State actions may not, in principle, be reviewed on the

---

[181] This provision reads: 'Union policy on the environment ... shall aim (and) ... shall be based on ...'

[182] In *Artegodan*, the General Court held that the precautionary principle constituted 'a general principle of EU law requiring the competent authorities to take appropriate measures' (*Artegodan* (n 107), para. 184). Against this background, the principle 'requires', pursuant to the rules applying to the re-authorization of a medicinal product, 'the suspension or the withdrawal of marketing authorisation when new scientific evidence give rise to serious doubt as to the efficacy and the safety of the product' (para. 192). In *Pfizer*, the General Court observed that a public authority can, by reason of the precautionary principle, be *required* to act even before any adverse effects have become apparent (Case T-13/99 *Pfizer* [2002] ECR II-3305, para. 444). However, pursuant to Art. 7(1) of the GFL Regulation, the Community may adopt precautionary measures ([2002] OJ L31/1).

[183] Case C-127/02 *Waddenzee* [2005] ECR I-7405, para. 44.

[184] Case T-229/04 *Sweden v Commission* [2007] ECR II-2437.

[185] At the outset, several authors took the view that these principles were not justiciable before national courts. See J. Holder, 'Safe Science? The Precautionary Principle in UK Environmental Law' in J. Holder (ed.), *The Impact of EC Environmental Law in the UK* (Wiley: Chichester, 1997) 131.

basis of these principles if they have not been fleshed out expressly or implicitly in secondary law.[186]

Second, it should be borne in mind that few areas of national law fall outside the scope of EU obligations. In effect, Member States are bound by a swathe of directives and regulations aiming at protecting the environment. The question arises whether the Member State authorities could eschew the Treaty principles in implementing environmental directives. The answer is straightforward: in areas that have been harmonized by directives or regulations, the Treaty's environmental principles may apply both directly and indirectly to Member States through secondary legislation. Hence, two hypotheses can be distinguished.

On the one hand, the principles may apply in an autonomous manner to national authorities if the latter are obliged to implement EU directives that recognize one or more of the principles contained in Article 192(2) TFEU.[187] There are relevant examples to illustrate this situation. The GFL Regulation expressly states that the precautionary principle applies to measures adopted at the national level.[188] Likewise, in both Directive 2001/18/EC on the deliberate release of GMOs and Regulation 1107/2009 on the placing on the market of plant protection products, the precautionary principle is explicitly mentioned.[189] In this connection, national authorities are called on to conduct risk assessments of GMOs and plant protection products due to the extent of lingering uncertainties. By the same token, when applying the waste hierarchy, the Member States 'shall take into account' a cluster of principles, among which 'the general environmental protection principles of precaution and sustainability...'[190]

On the other, the Article 192(2) TFEU principles can implicitly underpin the whole regulatory framework contemplated by the EU lawmaker. In effect, where a principle enshrined in that provision is not explicitly set out either in the operative provisions or in the recitals of the preamble to a directive or a regulation it may still apply to Member States. Admittedly, Article 4(3) TEU obliges the Member States to 'take all appropriate measures...to ensure fulfilment of the obligations arising out of this Treaty or resulting from action taken by the institutions of the Union' and 'facilitate the achievement of the Union's tasks' as well as 'abstain from any measure which could jeopardize the attainment of the objectives' of the Treaty. Article 4(3) thus imposes on national authorities

---

[186] Case C-378/08 *Agusta* [2010] ECR I-1919, para. 46. See also *R v Secretary of State for Trade and Industry, ex p Duddridge and others* (1995) *Env L Rev* 151 and *JEL* 7. In *Duddridge*, a case where a decision to lay an underground high-voltage electrical cable close to a school, the applicants argued that the Secretary of State was under a duty imposed by the EC Treaty to apply the precautionary principle. Although the risk assessment of the link between exposure to an electromagnetic field and the increased risk of leukaemia among children was inconclusive, the High Court declined to interpret English law by referring to the EC principle. The precautionary principle was deemed to be merely a 'principle' but neither a 'rule' nor a binding Treaty obligation. Attention must be drawn to the fact that it was not disputed whether the Environmental Impact Assessment Directive 2011/29/EU had to apply to the installation of the power cable ([2012] OJ L26/1).

[187] N. D'Hondt, 'Environmental Law Principles and the Case Law of the Court of Justice' in M. Sheridan and L. Lavrysen (eds), *Environmental Law Principles* (Brussels: Bruylant, 2000) 141–55.

[188] Food Safety Regulation (EC) No. 178/2002 ([2002] OJ L31/1), recital 16.

[189] Directive 2001/18/EC on the deliberate release of GMOs [2001] OJ L106/1, recital 8 and Art. 1; Regulation 1107/2009 concerning the placing of plant production product [2009] OJ L309/1, Art. 1(4).

[190] Directive 2008/98/EC on waste [2008] OJ L312/3, Art. 4(2).

wide-ranging obligations of environmental protection, preservation, and conservation, in order to implement the principles of prevention and precaution.[191] Moreover, the national authorities are called on strictly to interpret the environmental obligations stemming from secondary law, irrespective of whether the directives or regulations encapsulate these principles. For instance, with respect to the assessment and authorization procedures within Natura 2000 sites laid down in the Habitats Directive, account must be taken of the principle of precaution referred to in Article 192(2) TFEU although the principle is not mentioned as such in that directive.[192]

Lastly, in order to justify the proportionality of their measures hindering the free movement of goods, Member States may invoke the precautionary principle.[193]

7.1.4 *Environmental principles: shield or sword?*

A principle enshrined in Article 191(2) TFEU is likely to be viewed as a double-edged sword.

On the one hand, the EU lawmaker may justify the validity of its regulatory measures in the light of the Article 192(2) TFEU principles. By way of illustration, the preventive and remediation measures flowing from the environmental liability directive are justified by the polluter-pays principle.[194] Accordingly, in actions for annulment brought by private parties pursuant to Article 263 TFEU against an EU measure aiming to limit health or environmental risks, the institutions have regularly been invoking principles such as precaution to justify the soundness of their measures.

On the other hand, in infringement cases brought by virtue of Article 258 TFEU by the European Commission against Member State health and environmental measures on the grounds that they are hindering—for instance, free trade in goods—the national authorities may invoke the principles as a shield in order to justify the validity of the measures.[195] Clearly, there has been increasing use of the precautionary principle by Member States to derogate from the principle of free movement of goods where the matter has not been harmonized or with a view to departing from internal market harmonization by virtue of Article 114(4) and (5) TFEU.[196] Thus, to some extent EU secondary law may encourage the use of a principle as a shield.[197]

---

[191] A. Doyle and T. Carney, 'Precaution and Prevention: Giving Effect to Article 130r Without Direct Effect' (1999) 8 *EELR* 44.

[192] In *Waddenzee*, the Court of Justice assessed the validity of a Dutch project in the light of the EU precautionary principle (Case C-127/02 *Waddenzee* [2004] ECR I-7405, para. 44).

[193] Opinion AG Geelhoed in Case C-121/00 *Walter Hahn* [2001] ECR I-9193, para. 51; and Opinion AG Misho in Case C-6/99 *Greenpeace France* [2000] ECR I-1676, para. 202. See the discussion in Chapter 5, Section 7.3.

[194] European Parliament and Council Directive 2004/35/CE on environmental liability with regard to the prevention and remedying of environmental damage [2004] OJ L43/56, Art. 1. See Case C-378/08 *Raffinerie Méditerrannée* [2010] ECR I-1919, para. 57.

[195] J. Zander, *Different Kinds of Precaution* (Cambridge: CUP, 2010) 113.

[196] Case C-3/00 *Denmark v Commission* [2003] ECR II-2643; and Joined Cases T-366/03 & T-235/04 *Germany v Austria* [2005] ECR II-4005. See the discussion in Chapter 7, Section 3.

[197] By way of illustration, pursuant to Regulation (EC) No. 1107/2009, 'Member States shall not be prevented from applying the precautionary principle where there is scientific uncertainty as to the risks with regard to human or animal health or the environment posed by the plant protection products to be

It appears that the EU Courts are at their most deferential in cases in which the Commission invokes the precautionary principle. However, the grounds for judicial review will be set much higher when Member States invoke the same principle with a view to justifying measures which are restrictive of trade.[198]

7.2 The principle of a high level of environmental protection

7.2.1 *Legal status*

Pursuant to Article 3(3) TEU, Article 191(2) TFEU, and Article 37 EUCFR, EU policies shall aim at attaining a high level of environmental protection. With respect to measures related to the establishment and the functioning of the internal market, Article 114(3) TFEU lays down a similar obligation. Given that these obligations present a number of challenges for lawyers, some introductory thoughts on the matter are set out in the following text.

First, unlike the prevention or the precautionary principles, none of these provisions proclaim, as such, a 'principle' of a high level of environmental protection. That said, the EU Courts as well as several commentators have qualified this obligation as a principle.[199]

Second, since the requirement laid down by Article 3(3) TEU, Article 191(2) TFEU, and Article 37 EUCFR no longer concerns protection alone but also an 'improvement of the quality of the environment', this obligation has a dynamic nature. EU institutions are therefore expected to adopt a more interventionist than conservative stance. In other words, they are not only required to avoid degradation of the environment, but must also seek to improve its quality as well as their citizens' standard of living.

Third, nothing is said of the ways in which the EU should achieve such a high level of environmental protection: although Article 191(2) TFEU lists a number of other principles that could enhance the level of protection. As a result, both the Court of Justice and the General Court have combined the obligation to achieve a high level of environmental protection with the principles of prevention and precaution.[200] By the same token, in *Tatar v Romania*, the ECtHR stressed that the precautionary principle could be seen as a basis for the obligation to attain a high level of environmental protection.[201] In addition, other principles laid down in Article 191 also oblige the EU institutions to attain a high level of protection. These include the standstill principle[202]

---

authorized in their territory.' See European Parliament and Council Regulation (EC) No. 1107/2009 concerning the placing of plant protection products on the market [2009] OJ L309/1, Art. 1(4).

[198] Opinion AG Poiares Maduro in Case C-41/02 *Commission v Netherlands* [2004] ECR I-11375, para. 30; Opinion AG Kokott in *Afton* (n 138), para. 74.

[199] D. Misonne, *Droit européen de l'environnement et de la santé: l'ambition d'un niveau élevé de protection* (Louvain: Anthémis, 2010); N. de Sadeleer, 'The Principle of a High Level of Environmental Protection in EU Law' in C. Zetterberg and L. Gipperth (eds), *Festskrift G. Michanek and J. Darpö* (Uppsala: Iustus, 2013).

[200] Cases C-418 & 419/97 *ARCO Chemie Nederland* [2000] ECR I-4475, paras 36–40; and Case C-252/05 *Thames Water Utilities* [2007] ECR I-3883, para. 27.

[201] *Tatar v Romania*, 27 January 2009, para. 120.

[202] Art. 2(4) OSPAR Convention (Council Decision of 7 October 1997, OJ [1998] L104/1); European Parliament and Council Directive 2000/60/EC establishing a framework for Community action in the field

as well as the ALARA (as low as reasonably achievable) principle[203] which are likely to enhance the level of protection. Furthermore, the idea of a common heritage requires, first, a stringent implementation of the obligations laid down in the Birds Directive[204] and, second, that ecological criteria guiding the classification of Natura 2000 bird sites should not be offset by economic considerations.[205]

Fourth, insufficient attention has hitherto been given to the level of stringency of EU measures in the light of this principle. Regardless of whether it relates to the internal market by virtue of Article 114(3) TFEU or environmental policy by virtue of Article 3(3) TEU and Article 191(2) TFEU, the wording of the obligation to seek a high level of environmental protection is perplexing. For instance, a measure proposed by the Commission may appear at the same time draconian in the eyes of the Member States where environmental policy is more lenient, and yet insufficient for other Member States. There is a question whether the EU should strive for maximal protection,[206] zero tolerance, or even zero risk.[207] Does it follow from these Treaty provisions that the level of protection must be calculated at the highest conceivable level? Or should lawmakers make do with an intermediate level of protection? The uncertainty in the scope of this obligation does not, however, mean that the EU institutions enjoy absolute discretion in this regard. It is beyond question that a non-existent or low level of protection would violate this Treaty law obligation.[208]

Nonetheless, with respect to the harmonization taking place in the environmental realm, a minimum degree of flexibility would appear to be permissible by virtue of Article 191(2) TFEU in view of the differences between regional situations. In addition,

---

of water policy [2000] OJ L327/1, Arts 4(9) and 11(6). Under certain circumstances, loss of protected habitats can be authorized provided that compensatory measures are carried out (Council Directive 92/43/ EEC on the conservation of natural habitats and of wild fauna and flora [1992] OJ L206/7, Art. 6(4)). As regards the prohibition of relaxation of health standards applicable to herds of domestic animals likely to be affected by transmissible spongiform encephalopathies, see Case T-257/07 P, order of 28 September 2008 and Case T-257/07 P II, order of 30 October 2008, paras 86 and 89.

[203] Pursuant to Art. 15 of the Convention on Nuclear Safety (17 June 1994), approved by Commission Decision 1999/819/Euratom of 16 November 1999 concerning the accession to the 1994 Convention on Nuclear Safety by the European Atomic Energy Community (OJ [1999] L318/20), 'Each Contracting Party shall take the appropriate steps to ensure that in all operational states the radiation exposure to the workers and the public caused by a nuclear installation shall be kept as low as reasonably achievable and that no individual shall be exposed to radiation doses which exceed prescribed national dose limits.'

[204] It is clear on reading Art. 2 of the Birds Directive that 'ecological, scientific and cultural requirements' take precedence over 'economic and recreational requirements', the latter playing only an ancillary role (Case C-247/85 *Commission v Belgium* [1987] ECR 3029; and Case C-262/85 *Commission v Italy* [1987] ECR 3073). Furthermore, given that birds and habitats are considered a 'common heritage', Member States are being called upon accurately to transpose the directive's obligations. See Case C-247/85 *Commission v Belgium* [1987] ECR 3029, para. 9; Case C-38/99 *Commission v France* [2000] ECR I-10941, para. 53; Case C-6/04 *Commission v UK* [2005] ECR I-9017, para. 25; and Case C-508/04 *Commission v Austria* [2007] ECR I-3787, para. 57.

[205] Case C-44/95 *Regina* [1996] ECR I-3805, paras 23–5.

[206] With respect to the health and safety of workers, employers have 'to ensure that the risk from a hazardous chemical agent to the safety and health of workers at work is eliminated or reduced to a minimum' (Council Directive 98/24/EC on the protection of the health and safety of workers from the risks related to chemical agents at work [1998] OJ L131/11, Art. 6(1)).

[207] In the field of food safety, the EU lawmaker has endeavoured to find a zero risk approach (Case C-286/02 *Bellio Flli* [2004] ECR I-3465). With respect to consumer protection, see Cases C-305/03 & C-229/04 *Schulte* [2005] ECR I-9215.

[208] A. Epiney, 'Environmental Principles' in Macrory (n 180), 28; D. Misonne (n 199), 63, 167, and 399.

pursuant to Article 191(3) TFEU, the quest for high protection levels is tempered by the obligation to take into account differences between situations in various regions of the EU. Similarly, the ability of Member States to adopt enhanced protection measures pursuant to Article 193 TFEU[209] indicates that the benchmark need not necessarily be the highest possible. This seems to be logical: certain countries suffer from drought whilst others are prone to flooding and species endangered within the territory of one Member State are not necessarily under threat elsewhere.[210]

Reasoning by analogy, from the point of view of the establishment of the internal market, Article 27 TFEU, along with the provisions of Article 114(10) TFEU, confirm that it is not necessarily mandatory to obtain the highest level of protection.

However, this variation brings with it the risk of weakening protection levels. Due to the absence of uniform protection, one may fear à la carte exceptions and the toning down of obligations as a function of geographic area.[211]

Finally, in the absence of harmonization and to the extent that uncertainties continue to exist in the current state of scientific research, it is for the Member States to decide on their intended level of protection of human health and life.[212]

7.2.2 *High level of environmental protection and of other societal values*

At this point a number of legal issues relating to the implementation of similar obligations encapsulated in the TFEU and EUCFR will be enumerated (see Table 1.2). Indeed, public health and consumer protection policies reiterate this qualitative requirement[213] and, moreover, the EU is called on to promote a 'high level of employment'.[214] Conversely, the internal market policy must fully integrate these various concerns since, by virtue of Article 114(3) TFEU, the internal market Commission's proposals must pursue a high level of protection when they concern health, safety, environmental protection, and consumer protection.[215]

Be it for workers, patients, consumers, or the environment, the requirement to attain a 'high level of protection' has barely attracted any attention and has been the object of

---

[209] Chapter 7, Section 2.

[210] See Annex IIB to Directive 2009/147/EC on the conservation of wild birds [2009] OJ L20/7.

[211] The Waste Packaging Directive is a good case in point in this respect. Eg, because of their specific situation, some Member States in Southern Europe may decide to postpone the attainment of recycling targets (European Parliament and Council Directive 94/62/EC on packaging and packaging waste [1994] OJ L365/10, Art. 6(5)).

[212] See Case 174/82 *Sandoz* [1983] ECR I-2445, para. 16; Case C-192/01 *Commission v Denmark* [2003] ECR I-9693, para. 42; and Case C-24/00 *Commission v France* [2004] ECR I-1277, para. 49.

[213] By virtue of Art. 168(1) TFEU 'a high level of human health protection shall be ensured in the definition and implementation of all Union policies and activities' whereas pursuant to Art. 169(1), 'in order to promote the interests of consumers and to ensure a high level of consumer protection', the Union shall contribute to safeguard various consumers' interests. In addition, Arts 35, 37, and 38 EUCFR require the achievement of a high level of health, environmental protection, and consumer protection.

[214] Art. 9 TFEU.

[215] However, in *Schulte* the Court of Justice held that the requirement for a high level of protection contained in ex Art. 95(3) EC (Art. 114(3) TFEU) was not directly applicable to national authorities, irrespective of its implementation under secondary law. This obligation was therefore not directly binding on the Member States. See Cases C-350/03 & C-229/04 *Schulte* [2005] ECR I-9215, para. 61, noted by E. Jerry (2007) 44 *CML Rev* 501–18.

Table 1.2 TFEU and EUCFR provisions requiring a high level of protection

Values	EU-TFEU provisions	EUCFR provisions
Environment	Article 3(3) EU, Articles 114 (3) and 191 TFEU	Article 37
Health	Articles 114(3) and 168 TFEU	Article 35
Consumers	Articles 114(3) and 169 TFEU	Article 38
Worker safety	Article 114(3) TFEU	—
Employment	Article 9 TFEU	—

only a few commentaries in the academic literature. These obligations have often been classed in the category of declarations of intent. They are considered at best as policy principles devoid of any binding force, or as a guarantee of legitimacy which is automatically placed on draft regulations, directives, and decisions.

There is initially a strong doctrinal resistance to the idea that the EU Courts may control compliance with the requirement for a high level of protection irrespective of the subject matter. It is argued that it is not a matter for the Courts to interfere with the margin of appreciation that is naturally reserved to the EU institutions. This is claimed to undermine the very idea of the separation of powers. Strictly speaking, institutions not the Courts are called on to determine the optimal level of protection. Accordingly, the obligation to improve living and working standards which is incumbent upon the Member States in the area of social protection has been interpreted as being of a general and policy nature.[216]

By way of illustration, in a case concerning the safety of working conditions, with an evident environmental element since the danger threatening the health of workers came from petrol vapours emitted by service stations, the Court of Justice held that it was not a matter for the Court to review the proportionality of a duty to reduce the use of a carcinogen at a place of work, without linking that requirement to the outcome of a risk assessment.[217] Admittedly, it is not for the Court of Justice to interfere with the verification of more stringent measures (more stringent thresholds, reductions in time limits, or extensions to the scope of application, etc) than those which form the subject matter of Community action. Review of the proportionality of these measures is a matter for the national courts.

That said, these obligations to attain a high level of protection are likely to become interpretative principles where a conflict between economic and antagonist societal objectives arises. The need to guarantee a high level of protection for health had already led the Court of Justice to emphasize the efficacy of a directive adopted pursuant to Article 114 TFEU in order to justify its compatibility with the general principles of EU law. For instance, in *Tobacco II*, the Court of Justice held that in situations where there is a risk of divergence resulting from differing levels of protection at the national level, the common goal of achieving a high level of protection for health means that it is necessary to harmonize national regulations.[218] Similarly, only a prohibition on the

---

[216] Case C-126/86 *Gimenez-Zaera* [1987] ECR I-3697; and Case C-72/91 *Sloman-Neptune* [1993] ECR I-887.

[217] Case C-2/97 *Borsana* [1998] ECR I-8597, para. 40.

[218] Case C-380/03 *Germany v European Parliament and Council* [2006] I-11573, paras 40–1.

marketing of tobacco for chewing will guarantee complete efficacy with regard to the pursuit of a high level of health protection, going beyond economic interests.[219] In other words, an effective policy of prevention will contribute to achieving a high level of protection. This assertion, made with reference to public health, is of course capable of applying to the environment.

7.2.3 *Secondary law*

If Article 3(3) TEU, Article 191(2) TFEU, and Article 37 EUCFR are not to be rendered ineffective, they must be fleshed out with more precise regulatory devices. As regards the place of the obligation to seek a high level of environmental protection in secondary law five issues arise for comment.

First, whilst it has taken care to do so rather sparingly for the polluter-pays and the precautionary principles, the EU lawmaker has not hesitated to proclaim the need for a high level of protection under a number of secondary law obligations.[220] For instance, compliance with this obligation is a prerequisite for the admissibility of State aids in environmental matters: in order to raise the level of environmental protection beyond that provided under national law, only aids which encourage such protection may benefit from an exemption.[221]

Second, the achievement of this principle is betrayed by a relatively heterogeneous terminology: 'significant improvement', 'adequate level of protection', 'optimal protection', 'good conservation status', 'good chemical and ecological status of water', and so on. Similarly, environmental law abounds with expressions that are testament to a search for optimization or excellence: best available technologies, energy efficiency, resource efficiency, etc.

Third, the lack of precision as to the meaning of these terms can lead to significant variations in their implementation. For instance, the obligation not to endanger human health or the environment while managing waste, which is laid down in the Waste Framework Directive, does not specify the actual content of the measures which must be taken by the Member States.[222] Nevertheless, it is settled case law that this provision is binding on the Member States as to the objective to be achieved, whilst leaving them a margin of discretion in assessing the need for such measures.[223]

---

[219] Case C-434/02 *Arnold André* [2004] ECR I-11825; and Case C-210/03 *Swedish Match* [2004] ECR I-11893, paras 56 and 57.

[220] The former IPPC 2008/1/EC Directive ([2008] OJ L24/8) refers at least ten times to the obligation to achieve a high level of protection. Such an obligation can require the promotion of 'high quality recycling' pursuant to Art. 11(1) of Directive 2008/98/EC on waste [2008] OJ L312/3.

[221] Environmental State Aids Guidelines 2008, paras 5.2.1.3 and 171; General Block Exemption Regulation (EC) No. 800/2008 [2008] OJ L214/3, Art. 8(1). See N. de Sadeleer, 'State Aids and Environmental Measures' (2012) *Nordic Journal of Environmental Law* 3–13.

[222] European Parliament and Council Directive 2006/12/EC on waste [2006] OJ L114/9, Art. 4(1); Directive 2008/98/EC on waste [2008] OJ L312/3, Art. 13. See Case C-236/92 *Comitato di Coordinamento per la Difesa della Cava* [1999] ECR I-485.

[223] Case C-365/97 *Commission v Italy* [1999] ECR I-7773, para. 67; Case C-420/02 *Commission v Greece* [2004] ECR I-11175, para. 21; and Case C-297/08 *Commission v Italy* [2010] ECR I-1749, para. 96.

Fourth, EU secondary law is not always consistent.[224] What level of harm or impact should lead to regulatory intervention varies significantly from one regulation to another. Whereas several chemical regulations squarely prohibit the use of chemical substances, companies may under the REACH Regulation place on the market hazardous chemicals the risks of which can be 'adequately controlled'.[225]

A fifth issue emerges as being of particular importance. Most of the EU measures aiming to protect the environment, Art. do not seek an absolute level of protection.[226] The following illustrations are testament to the restricted approach endorsed by the EU lawmaker. For instance, EU institutions or national authorities are called upon to eliminate or to prevent the occurrence of:

- an '*unacceptable effect* on the environment' of residues of plant protection products;[227]

- the '*serious risk* to human or animal health or to the environment' of seeds treated with plant protection products;[228]

- 'a *serious risk* to human health, animal health or the environment' must be demonstrated in order to 'suspend or modify urgently an authorisation' on the placing on the market of genetically modified food and feed.[229] Moreover, 'the expressions "likely" and "serious risk" must be understood as referring to a significant risk which clearly jeopardises human health, animal health or the environment'. That risk must be established on the basis of new evidence based on reliable scientific data.[230] Departing from its previous case law, the Court of Justice did not invoke precaution at all with a view to softening these requirements.[231]

Similarly, Member States are obliged to assess 'projects likely to have *significant* effects on the environment'.[232]

It follows that insignificant risks are likely to fall outwith the ambit of a number of EU regulatory schemes.

---

[224] N. de Sadeleer, *Commentaire Mégret. Environnement et marché intérieur* (Brussels: ULB, 2010) 331–3.

[225] Regulation (EC) No. 1907/2006 concerning the Registration, Evaluation, Authorisation and Restriction of Chemicals [2006] OJ L396/1, Art. 57(2).

[226] However, under legislative acts regarding health protection EU intervention is not subject to a specific threshold. See, in particular, Food Safety Regulation (EC) No. 178/2002 [2002] OJ L31/1, Art. 7(1). Under that provision, with a view to ensuring a high level of health protection, 'provisional risk management measures' may be adopted in order to prevent 'the possibility of harmful effects on health'. No threshold has been set for the significance of these effects.

[227] European Parliament and Council Regulation (EC) No. 1107/2009 concerning the placing of plant protection products on the market [2009] OJ L309/1, Art. 4(2)(b).

[228] Regulation (EC) No. 1107/2009, Art. 49(2) (n 227).

[229] European Parliament and Council Regulation (EC) No. 1829/2003 on genetically modified food and feed [2003] OJ L268/1. See Cases C-58–68/10 *Monsanto* [2011] OJ C311/8.

[230] *Monsanto* (n 229), paras 69 and 76.

[231] *Monsanto Agricultora Italia* (n 162), para. 112. See M. Weimer, 'The Right to Adopt Post-Market Restrictions of GM Crops in the EU' (2012) *EJRR* 447 and 451.

[232] Directive 2001/42/EC on the assessment of the effects of certain plans and programmes on the environment [2001] OJ L197/30, Art. 2(1).

By the same token, the EU Courts are also requiring the EU institutions and the Member States to assess whether the environment risk is real or significant. There are various examples in the case law.

- 'A *significant deterioration* in the environment over a protracted period without any action being taken by the competent authorities' may be an indication that the Member State has exceeded the discretion conferred by a framework directive on environmental protection.[233]

- National measures restricting the trade in wild mammals and birds bred in captivity can be justified inasmuch as there is a '*real risk*' to animal welfare and biodiversity.[234]

- 'The *significant environmental effects* caused by the incorrect implementation of the urban wastewater directive must be substantiated by a certain amount of evidence'.[235]

- Another illustration of the threshold regarding the significance of the risk is the case law on eutrophication of water within the meaning of Council Directive 91/271/EEC concerning urban wastewater treatment.[236] Eutrophication is characterized by, among other conditions, an '*undesirable*' disturbance to the balance of organisms present in the water, which 'must be considered to be established where there are *significant adverse effects* on flora or fauna'.[237] It follows that an accelerated growth of algae is not sufficient, as such, to demonstrate such 'undesirable disturbance'. Hence, the Commission bears the brunt of the burden of proof to demonstrate 'loss of ecosystem biodiversity, nuisances due to the proliferation of opportunistic macroalgae and severe outbreaks of toxic or harmful phytoplankton'.[238]

Finally, it should be recalled that Article 8 ECHR is engaged where the alleged nuisance is 'sufficiently serious' adversely to affect the applicant's right to private and family life.[239]

That said, environmental directives can also be more ambitious. For instance, the scope of waste law encompasses every waste irrespective of whether it is subject to 'ecologically responsible treatment'.[240] Likewise, all threats to Natura 2000 habitats are subject to a preventive regime.

---

[233] Case C-365/97 *Commission v Italy* [1999] ECR I-7773, para. 68; Case C-420/02 *Commission v Greece* [2004] ECR I-11175, para. 22; Case C-297/08 *Commission v Italy* [2010] ECR I-1749, para. 101; and Case C-37/09 *Commission v Portugal* [2010] ECR I-76, para. 38.

[234] Case C-219/07 *Andibel* [2008] ECR I-4475, para. 36; Case C-100/08 *Commission v Belgium* [2009] ECR I-140, para. 100.

[235] Case C-508/03 *Commission v UK* [2006] ECR I-3969, para. 78; and Case C-390/07 *Commission v UK* [2009] ECR I-214, para. 46.

[236] [1991] OJ L135, Art. 40.

[237] Case C-280/02 *Commission v France* [2004] ECR I-8573, paras 22 and 23; and Case C-390/07 *Commission v UK* [2009] ECR I-214, para. 36.

[238] C-390/07 *Commission v UK* [2009] ECR I-214, paras 36 and 38.

[239] *Mileva v Bulgaria*, 25 November 2010, para. 91. See the discussion in Chapter 2, Section 4.3.2.1.

[240] Cases C-418/97 & C-419/97 *Arco Chemie* [2004] ECR I-4475, para. 67. In this judgment, the Court dismissed the reasoning of AG Alber who proposed excluding from the concept of waste any substances which did not 'pose a danger typical of waste' (para. 109).

Table 1.3 Regulatory responses according to the level of gravity of environmental harm

Unknown probability of serious or irreversible damage	Precautionary measures aiming at achieving a high level of environmental protection
Probability of a significant risk	Preventive measures aiming at achieving a high level of environmental protection
Insignificant risks	Variable scenarios depending on the scope of the directives and regulations

Table 1.3 highlights the different regulatory approaches according to the level of gravity of environmental harm.

7.2.4 *Case law*

7.2.4.1 Reviewing the legality of EU acts

Since they are binding on the EU institutions, environmental and health measures may be subject to review in the light of this requirement. The Court of Justice has held that when adopting the prohibition on the use and marketing of hydrochlorofluorocarbon (HCFC), 'the Community legislature did not infringe the requirement of a high level of protection laid down in Article 130r(2) EC since no manifest error of assessment had been committed when determining the level of protection'.[241] In stressing that the requirement is compulsory, the Court departed from Advocate General Léger's Opinion. The Advocate General considered that the obligation to aim at a high level of protection 'must … be interpreted as a recommendation addressed to the Community legislature, under which the latter is called upon to ensure that the policy already being pursued is constantly improved'.[242] On the other hand, in 1999 Advocate General Cosmas asserted his view that the level of protection in environmental matters is binding on the legislator when it acts on the basis of ex Article 130r EC (Art. 192 TFEU). As a result, an EU measure that does not meet 'that qualitative criterion' could be annulled.[243]

Account must be taken of new case law developments regarding the placing on the market of chemical substances. In the *DecaDBE* case, the Court of Justice held that the prohibition on the use of certain hazardous substances in electrical and electronic equipment implies, in accordance with the requirement for a high level of protection, that the Commission may 'grant exemptions only in accordance with carefully defined conditions' and that the conditions for exemption be interpreted strictly.[244] In this case, the fact that the directive had been enacted on the basis of Article 95 EC (Art. 114 TFEU) did not have the effect of exempting the Commission from the requirement to respect the obligation for a high level of protection under Articles 152 and 174 EC (Arts 168 and 191(1) TFEU).

---

[241] Case C-341/95 *Safety Hi-Tech SRL* [1998] ECR I-4355, para. 53.
[242] Opinion AG Léger in Case C-341/95 *Safety Hi-Tech SRL* [1998] ECR I-4355, para. 67.
[243] Opinion AG Cosmas in Case C-318/98 *Fornasar* [2000] ECR I-4785, para. 32.
[244] Cases C-14/06 & 295/06 *Parliament and Denmark v Commission ('décaBDE')* [2008] ECR I-1649, paras 74 and 75.

However, with regard to the validity of the entry into force of protection regimes, the Court of Justice does not require an immediate optimal level of protection. Given that the implementation of EU protective measures may be carried out gradually, the most stringent option does not prevail immediately. For instance, the prohibition of a substance which depletes the ozone layer does not necessarily entail the outlawing of other gases, even if the general application of the measure would have permitted a higher level of protection.[245] Similarly, the subjection of certain polluting plants to the EU ETS does not imply the immediate extension of this regime to all installations emitting such gases.[246] To conclude, the Court appears to be satisfied with an intermediate level of protection, in particular at the initial stage of the implementation of a new regulatory approach.

The obligation to achieve a high level of environmental protection also impinges on the manner in which the lawmaker complies with the principle of proportionality. In this respect, *Afton* is a case in point. The Court was asked to rule on whether an EU limit for the presence of a metallic additive likely to cause air pollution in fuel complied with the principle of proportionality. The Court stressed that 'the European Union legislature could justifiably take the view that the appropriate manner of reconciling the high level of health and environmental protection and the economic interests of producers of the substance' was to limit its content 'on a declining scale while providing for the possibility...of revising those limits on the basis of the results of assessment'.[247]

7.2.4.2 An interpretative principle of the scope of EU environmental regimes

The obligation to seek a high level of protection is also an interpretative principle as regards the validity of EU legislation. By way of illustration, the harmonization of criminal penalties in the context of the first pillar was justified by Advocate General Ruiz-Jarabo Colomer with reference to the obligation to achieve a high level of protection and to improve the quality of the environment, as provided for under ex Article 2 EC (Art. 3(3) TEU).[248] The registration of 'monomer substances' is confirmed by the objectives of the REACH Regulation, 'which consist in ensuring a high level of protection of human health and the environment'.[249]

7.2.4.3 An interpretative principle of the environmental obligations placed on Member States

The scale necessary in order to be successful in establishing an effective policy on the environment, taken together with the ongoing concern to eliminate barriers to the free movement of goods and services, evidently call for the adoption of harmonized rules. Indeed, harmonized rules have the advantage of putting all of the Member States on an

---

[245] Case C-341/95 *Safety Hi-Tech SRL* [1998] ECR I-4355, para. 47.
[246] Case C-127/07 *Arcelor Atlantique et Lorraine* [2008] ECR I-9895, para. 32.
[247] *Afton* (n 138), para. 64.
[248] Opinion AG Ruiz-Jarabo Colomer in Case C-176/03 *Commission v Council* [2005] ECR I-7879, para. 72.
[249] Case C-558/07 *SPCM and others* [2009] ECR I-5783, para. 35.

equal footing and requiring them to contribute equally to the financial costs resulting from the regulatory obligations.

One further point is worth making here. In contrast to the areas of health and consumer and employment protection, a number of environmental issues are distinctly less tied to concerns over the functioning of the internal market. Admittedly, with respect to wildlife, water, soil, air, and ecosystem protection, a high level of environmental protection may be achieved, independent of the need to eliminate technical barriers to the free movement of goods. Additionally, where the harmonization is, in principle, minimal in nature (Art. 193 TFEU), nothing prevents the Member States which so wish from reinforcing the EU standards of protection.[250]

However, since the harmonization process is replete with rather loose requirements and opt-out clauses, Member States are likely to be encouraged to follow the lowest common denominator. As has been seen in the fight against global warming, the possibility offered to the Member States to determine for themselves the number of allowances to allocate to each industrial sector concerned, has led national authorities to be very generous to their own industries.[251] As a result, derogatory regimes are likely to encourage some Member States to depart from the obligation to seek a high level of environmental protection.

Be that as it may, it is clear from the case law that the obligation to achieve a high level of protection inevitably impinges on the margin of appreciation of the authorities called upon to implement EU environmental law. According to the Court of Justice's case law, this is an interpretative principle. The following cases are illustrative of the ways in which the obligation can tilt the balance in favour of more rigorous interpretation of environmental regimes.

- This may be illustrated by the case law on the concept of waste. The term 'to discard' an object or substance liable to become waste and, accordingly, the scope of the framework directive on waste, must be interpreted not only in the light of the objectives set forth by the lawmaker, but also in the light of the obligation to achieve a high level of protection.[252] This means that the concept of waste cannot be interpreted restrictively.

- By the same token, the concept of biocide cannot be interpreted restrictively. Given that Directive 98/8 governing the placing of biocidal products on the market takes 'as a condition a high level of protection for humans, animals and the environment', such a level of protection could be seriously jeopardized if classification as biocidal products were to be interpreted too narrowly. Consequently, the directive's scope of application encompasses not only 'those products containing one or more active substances and having a direct chemical or biological effect on the target harmful organisms', but also 'products which...

---

[250] Art. 193 TFEU. See the discussion in Chapter 7, Section 2.
[251] A. Brohé, N. Eyre, and N. Howarth, *Carbon Markets* (London: Earthscan, 2009) 120–2; J. de Sépibus, 'Scarcity and Allocation of Allowances in the EU Emissions Trading Scheme—A Legal Analysis', NCCR Trade Working Paper 2007/32, 36.
[252] Cases C-418 & 419/97 *ARCO Chemie Nederland* [2000] ECR I-4475, paras 36–40; Case C-252/05 *Thames Water Utilities* [2007] ECR I-3883, para. 27.

contain one or more active substances but exert only an indirect chemical or biological effect on those organisms'.[253]

- Given that the precautionary principle is one of the foundations of the high level of environmental protection, nature conservation requirements must be strictly interpreted.[254]

- In a similar vein, under the framework directive on waste, national water regulations applicable to domestic wastewater discharged from sewage works can be imposed as an alternative to EU waste law inasmuch as they guarantee a level of protection equivalent to that resulting from the application of EU waste law.[255]

- The determination of the relevant control procedure is also likely to be influenced by the principle. Regulation No 1013/2006 on shipments of waste establishes various procedures and control regimes for the shipment of waste depending, inter alia, on the origin, destination, and route of the shipment, and on the type of waste shipped. A German court asked the Court of Justice whether Regulation No 1013/2006 was to be interpreted as meaning that the export to Lebanon of catalyst waste is prohibited. The case arose from the fact that catalysts fall within two different categories, one of which means that export of the waste concerned is prohibited, whereas the other means that a special control procedure is to be implemented by the country of destination. Advocate General Bot took the view that where there is uncertainty regarding the treatment of waste being exported outside the EU, 'it is necessary to choose the narrowest approach, making it possible to limit shipments of waste: namely, the prohibition of exports. That is also the best approach for attaining the objective of protecting human health and the environment, which Regulation No 1013/2006 is designed to achieve.'[256] The Court of Justice endorsed that line of reasoning.[257]

- *Inter-Environnement Wallonie* raises similar issues, but in the context of an entirely different set of facts. The effects of a regional programme concerning the protection of waters against pollution caused by nitrates, adopted in accordance with Nitrates Directive 91/676, can be exceptionally maintained by a national court in spite of its annulment for reasons linked to the violation of another environmental directive.[258] In effect, the programme at issue had not been subject to a strategic impact assessment pursuant to Directive 2001/42. To justify the maintenance of the protective effects of the programme, the Court of Justice stressed that annulling the illegal order could result 'in a lower level of protection of waters against pollution caused by nitrates from agricultural sources, given that this would run specifically counter to the fundamental objective of that directive, which is to prevent such pollution'.[259]

---

[253] *Söll* (n 138), para. 27.
[254] Case C-127/02 *Waddenzee* [2004] ECR I-7405, para. 44; and Opinion AG Sharpston in Case C-258/11 *Peter Sweetman* [2012] OJ C156, para. 51.
[255] Case C-252/05 *Thames Water Utilities* [2007] ECR I-3883.
[256] Opinion AG Bot in Case C-405/10 *Garenfeld* [2011] OJ C25/14, para. 69.
[257] *Garenfeld* (n 256), para. 47.
[258] Cases C-105/09 & C-110/09 *Terres Wallones et Inter-Environnement Wallonie* [2012] ECR I-5611, para. 58.
[259] Case C-41/11 *Inter-Environnement Wallonie* [2012] OJ C118/6, para. 61.

However, this requirement to achieve a high level of environmental protection cannot be relied on by the Member States in order to circumvent the obligations resulting from the implementation of environmental directives. Support for this proposition may be found in the following case. The Commission initiated an infringement action against Spain due to its failure to implement the former Integrated Pollution Prevention and Control (IPPC) Directive correctly, in particular with regard to its failure to require administrative authorization for existing listed installations. Spain had argued that this directive only had the goal of achieving a high level of environmental protection and not a maximum level. Since 88.53 per cent of installations existing in Spain would be operated in accordance with the directive on expiry of the time limit set in the Commission's reasoned opinion, the Spanish authorities argued that a high level of environmental protection had been achieved. The Court of Justice dismissed this argument on the ground that the directive required 'complete and total implementation' by the Member States.[260]

That said, the obligation to seek a high level of environmental protection can also be invoked by Member State authorities when enacting measures likely to hinder the free movement of goods. It hardly needs to be pointed out that the free movement of waste may be affected by waste management measures which may differ substantially from one Member State to another. In its *EU-Wood* judgment, the Court of Justice considered a German export measure in the light of the obligation to achieve a high level of protection pursuant to ex Article 2 EC (Art. 3(3) TEU). The Court accepted that the most stringent national criteria may prevail within the context of controls over the cross-border movement of waste. In order to appreciate the risks which the waste recovery operation in another country entails, the German competent authority of dispatch was entitled, in accordance with a teleological interpretation of the regulation in the light of the obligation to seek a high level of protection, to rely on the standards applicable to the recovery of waste within its national territory, even where its own standards were stricter than those in force in the Member State of destination (Italy).[261] The Court thereby accepted an extra-territorial application of the most stringent standards.

7.3 The polluter-pays principle

7.3.1 *Genesis*

Given a name that is almost a slogan and the seeming clarity of its underlying logic, the polluter-pays principle easily wins approval. Its main function is to internalize the social costs borne by public authorities for pollution prevention and control. Accordingly, the principle serves as an economic rule according to which a portion of the profits accruing to polluters as the result of their activities must be returned to the public authorities responsible for inspecting, monitoring, and controlling the pollution these activities produce. However, as it attaches a price to the right to pollute, the redistributive function has attracted criticism that is not entirely unfounded. Consequently, it is seen as accepting environmental degradation as inevitable, provided that

---

[260] Case C-48/10 *Commission v Spain* [2010] ECR I-151, para. 26.
[261] Case C-277/02 *EU-Wood-Trading* [2004] ECR I-11957, para. 47.

the polluter pays: 'I pay, therefore I pollute'. For the polluting firm, however, a charge merely represents a supplementary tax. The result is to perpetuate pollution as long as charges cover the costs of the regulatory tasks relating to pollution control and abatement. Moreover, the purely distributive function may be subject to an even more fundamental criticism. To speak of a polluter is to evoke ecological damage, which in turn means that such damage has already taken place—that is, prevention is no longer of any use.

Of course, such criticisms must be nuanced.

First, polluter-pays and preventive principles could be viewed as constituting two complementary aspects of a single reality. Put at the service of prevention, the polluter-pays principle should no longer be interpreted as allowing a polluter who pays to continue polluting with impunity. The true aim of the principle would then be to institute a policy of pollution abatement by encouraging polluters to reduce their emissions instead of being content to pay charges. Indeed, the principle aims to correct market failure: the costs of pollution should be reflected in the price of services and products and be borne by the polluters and not society at large. This would create an incentive for producers to place environmentally friendly products on the market.

Second, whatever the importance or quality of preventive or redistributive measures, the risk of environmental degradation remains. Indeed, setting emission thresholds or establishing funds necessarily leads to degradation of water, soil, and air. One should therefore consider whether civil liability would be fertile ground for adding a new dimension to the principle: a curative function. If civil liability guarantees a form of redistribution *ex post*, it differs from the classical distributive function in that it is more individual than collective in character.

7.3.2 *Recognition within EU law*

The polluter-pays principle has gradually commanded recognition as one of the pillars of the EU's environment policy. It has successively been invoked to address distortion of competition, to prevent chronic pollution, and, finally, to justify the adoption of fiscal measures or strict liability regimes. The procedures for applying the principle were specified in Recommendation 75/436/Euratom, ECSC, EEC of 3 March 1975 regarding cost allocation and action by public authorities on environmental matters, which broadly takes up the rules elaborated by the OECD. Subsequent to the Recommendation of 3 March 1975, the polluter-pays principle recurred in all subsequent Environmental Action Programmes and in the EC Guidelines relating to State aids for the protection of the environment.[262]

Despite the recognition of the principle under Article 192(2), the TFEU in making public funds available for environmental measures departs from the logic of the internalization of the externalities. First, the Cohesion Fund established under Article 177 TFEU co-finances environmental projects in the poorer Member States. Second, Article 192(5) TFEU provides for national public intervention in the form of

---

[262] Information from the EC Commission: EC Guidelines 94/C 72/03 on State Aid for Environmental Protection, replaced by EC Guidelines 2001/C 37/03 on State Aid for Environmental Protection.

temporary financial support where an act adopted under Article 192(1) TFEU involves costs deemed to be disproportionate.

The polluter-pays principle also appeared in secondary EC legislation throughout the 1970s and was expressly taken up in several waste management directives.[263] In condemning a prohibition on the export of waste oils outside France as incompatible with Article 34 TFEU, the Court of Justice rejected the economic argument invoked by the French authorities that an export ban was needed to avoid bankrupting recycling firms, since under the EC Waste Oils Directive Member States 'may, without placing restrictions on exports, grant to such undertakings "indemnities" financed in accordance with the principle of "polluter-pays".'[264] However, EU directives dealing with atmospheric pollution, water protection, nature protection, and noise do not expressly refer to the principle. Relatedly, the Habitat Directive recognizes that 'the polluter-pays principle can have only limited application in the special case of nature conservation'.[265]

We must now consider whether this principle is really capable of bringing about changes to two redistributive legal instruments: taxation (instrument of prevention *ex ante*) and civil liability (instrument of remediation *ex post*).

7.3.3 Ex ante *application of the principle: environmental charges*

7.3.3.1 Internalizing environmental costs

The main function of the polluter-pays principle is to internalize the social costs borne by public authorities for pollution prevention and control.[266] At this stage, the principle serves as an economic rule according to which a portion of the profits accruing to polluters as the result of their activities must be returned to the public authorities responsible for inspecting, monitoring, and controlling the pollution these activities produce. It is generally recognized that the polluter-pays principle implies setting up a system of charges by which polluters help to finance public policy to protect the environment.[267]

In obliging Member States to implement this environmental principle when carrying out pricing policy, several EU directives embrace this redistributive function in line with

---

[263] Several waste management directives recall that the principle must be respected when setting out economic instruments (Directive 75/439/EEC on the disposal of waste oils [1975] OJ L194/23, Directive 94/62/EC on packaging and packaging waste [1994] OJ L365/10).

[264] Case C-172/82 *Inter-Huiles* [1983] ECR I-555, para. 18.

[265] Eleventh recital of the preamble to Council Directive 92/43/EEC on the conservation of natural habitats and of wild fauna and flora [1992] OJ L206/1.

[266] H. C. Bugge, *Forurensnings-Ansvaret* (Oslo: Aschehoug, 1999); N. de Sadeleer, *Environmental Principles* (Oxford: OUP, 2002) 35; and 'The Polluter-Pays Principle in EU Law. Bold Case Law and Poor Harmonisation', *Pro Natura. Festskrift til H.-C. Bugge* (Oslo: Universitetsforlaget, 2012) 405–19. Directive 2011/76/EU amending the directive on the charging of heavy goods vehicles for the use of certain infrastructures (the Eurovignette Directive [2011] OJ L269/1) links the polluter-pays principle to the 'user pays' principle. See recital 3.

[267] According to the terms of the 1975 Council Recommendation regarding cost allocation and action by public authorities on environmental matters, this is in fact the most appropriate instrument for carrying out the polluter-pays principle. The Commission Communication of 26 March 1997 on taxes, fees and environmental charges in the Single Market considers that 'such levies could constitute an adequate means for implementing the polluter-pays principle, by including environmental costs in the price of goods and services.' See COM(97) 9 final.

the polluter-pays principle. Article 10 of Directive 1999/31/EC on the landfill of waste has given concrete expression to the principle by requiring that the cost of waste disposal include all operation costs, including financial guarantees and restoration of the site once it ceases to be used for disposal.[268] By the same token, Article 9 of Directive 2000/60/EC establishing a framework for Community action in the field of water policy has also given concrete expression to the principle, by requiring that 'Member States shall take account of the principle of recovery of the costs of water services, including environmental and resource costs'. In addition, Member States were required to ensure by 2010 that water-pricing policies provide adequate incentives for the efficient use of water resources, thereby contributing to the environmental objectives of the directive.

As regards taxation, the polluter-pays principle throws up more questions than it answers.[269]

7.3.3.2 Who should pay pollution charges?

Identifying the person who must pay pollution charges has given rise to a great deal of controversy, since generally more than one identifiable individual contributes to pollution. Can the authority charge each person who has contributed to the harm, no matter how small their share, on the ground of equity? Or, for the sake of efficiency, is it preferable to charge the person who is best placed to pay? With respect to the scope of Article 10 of Directive 1999/31/EC on the landfill of waste, the Court held in *Pontina Ambiente* that all the costs of operating a landfill must be borne by the holders of the waste deposited in the site for disposal.[270] Although nothing precludes a Member State from introducing a levy on waste to be paid by the landfill operator, it can do so only on condition that the fiscal provision in question is accompanied by measures to ensure that the levy is actually reimbursed by the holders of the waste 'within a short time so as not to impose excessive operating costs on the operator on account of late payment' by those holders, thereby undermining the 'polluter pays' principle.[271] The fact that Article 10 does not impose on the Member States any specific method of financing the cost of a landfill does not deprive that obligation of being unconditional and sufficiently precise to have direct effect.[272]

7.3.3.3 How much must the polluter be charged?

By the same token, determining the basis of a charge has also sparked controversy. According to the principle of proportionality, polluters must pay in proportion to the damage they cause. As a result, activities that are the most harmful to the environment should pay the highest charges. *Standley* is a textbook example of the fact that the polluter-pays principle is the expression of a general principle of EU law: the principle of proportionality. With regard to charges related to the protection of waters against pollution caused by nitrates from agricultural sources, that were exclusively paid by farmers, the Court was asked to rule on whether the Nitrates Directive infringes the

---

[268] Case C-172/08 *Pontina Ambiente* [2010] ECR I-1175, para. 36; Case C-97/11 *Amia SpA* [2012] OJ C200/2.
[269] De Sadeleer (n 266), 44–9.   [270] Case C-172/08 *Pontina Ambiente* [2010] ECR I-1175, para. 37.
[271] *Pontina Ambiente* (n 270), para. 38.   [272] *Amia SpA* (n 268), paras 35 and 37.

polluter-pays principle laid down in Treaty law. The claimants argued that farmers were being singled out to bear the cost of reducing the concentration of nitrates in waters to below the threshold of 50 mg/l even though agriculture is acknowledged to be only one source of nitrates, while no financial demands were being made on other sources. Referring to the polluter-pays principle, the Court of Justice judged that:

> the (Nitrates) Directive does not mean that farmers must take on burdens for the elimination of pollution to which they have not contributed; ... the Member States are to take account of the other sources of pollution when implementing the Directive and, having regard to the circumstances, are not to impose on farmers costs of eliminating pollution that are unnecessary. Viewed in that light, the polluter-pays principle reflects the principle of proportionality ...[273]

According to this case law, Member States cannot impose on farmers costs of eliminating pollution that are 'unnecessary': they must also take into account other sources of pollution.[274] Following that reasoning, the costs charged to some categories of economic agents arising from the designation of a protected area should not be superior to the costs of the pollution generated by those agents.[275] It follows that where the polluter is an industrial plant located upstream, it would run contrary to the principle to charge exclusively the farmers downstream. This demonstrates clearly how a principle laid down in the TFEU may influence the interpretation of an act of secondary legislation and consequently determine national administrative practices.

However, applying proportionality to charges in a rigorous manner may prove a relatively complex operation owing to the multiple parameters which must be taken into account—among them, the nature of the nuisance, the hazards it presents, the means available to remedy its harmful effects, and the cost of meeting an environmental quality objective, including the administrative costs directly linked to carrying out anti-pollution measures. Put simply, flexibility is needed in applying the principle. In this respect, *Futura Immobiliare* is illustrative of the ways in which the tax basis has to be calculated in accordance with the principle. The Court was asked to decide whether waste management charges could be calculated on the basis of the economic activity or the surface area of the undertaking, instead of the amount of waste produced and collected. The Court held that the principle did not preclude Member States from varying the contribution of each category of taxpayers 'in accordance with their respective capacities to produce urban waste'.[276] As a result, some categories of undertakings—such as hotels—can be treated less favourably than households provided that this distinction 'is based on objective criteria ... such as their waste-production capacity or the nature of the waste produced'.[277] As a result, national authorities are endowed with 'broad discretion' when determining the manner in which an environmental charge must be calculated.[278]

---

[273] Case C-293/97 *Standley* [1999] ECR I-2603, paras 51–2.   [274] *Standley* (n 273), para. 52.

[275] According to the Opinion of AG Léger, the Directive had to be interpreted as requiring Member States to impose on farmers only the cost of pollution for which they were responsible, and he explicitly added 'to the exclusion of any other cost' (Opinion of 8 October 1998, Case C-293/97 *Standley* [1999] ECR I-2603, para. 98).

[276] Case C-254/08 *Futura Immobiliare* [2009] ECR I-06995, para. 52.

[277] *Futura Immobiliare* (n 276), para. 54.   [278] *Futura Immobiliare* (n 276), para. 55.

In *Amia SpA*, the Court held that all costs incurred by the operator of a landfill site (interest on those sums for which the waste holder is liable, levies, etc) fall within the scope of Article 10 of the directive on landfills.[279]

Lastly, in applying charges which are distinctly higher than the costs they are intended to cover, national authorities may be tempted to penalize undesirable behaviour. Although these charges are incentive enough to oblige consumers to change their behaviours, they are consistent with the polluter-pays principle as well as the principle of prevention.

7.3.3.4 Allocation of charge revenues

Allocating the revenue from charges also gives rise to a number of questions. EU directives and recommendations do not indicate whether the sums collected should be set aside in a special fund for financing environmental policy or whether they should be paid into the general State budget.[280] The redistributive function generally assigned to charges argues in favour of the first option. Since a financial transfer from polluters to public authorities is intended to spare the community from having to assume environmental liability, the proceeds of charges should primarily be allocated to the tasks of prevention, control, monitoring, and clean-up carried out by public authorities. In the event that charge revenue exceeds total expenditure, Recommendation 75/432 states that 'the surplus should preferably be used by each government for its national environmental policies.' Clearly, allocating charge revenues to a dedicated fund does not conform to the principle of universality, according to which tax revenues should not be used for specific expenditure.

The question also arises whether public authorities may assign part of the charges back to the polluters themselves. Recommendation 75/432 authorizes such mechanisms under certain conditions. Strictly applied, financial intervention by Member States in support of certain private investments should not be considered contrary to the polluter-pays principle.[281] Methods for Member State financing have, moreover, been specified in several European Commission Communications. However, national authorities can intervene in as much as their measures are consistent with State aids law.

7.3.4 Ex post *application of the principle: civil liability*

7.3.4.1 Introductory remarks

More or less unnoticed, the polluter-pays principle has shifted from the public sphere to civil liability.[282] Indeed, there is an increasing tendency in international circles to ascribe a curative dimension to the polluter-pays principle.[283]

---

[279] *Amia SpA* (n 268), paras 35 and 37.
[280] Art. 9(2) of the amended Eurovignette Directive ([2011] OJ L269/1) requires the allocation of revenues and charges to specific sectoral investments.
[281] See the discussion in Chapter 12.
[282] As to the scope of that environmental principle, see de Sadeleer (n 266), 21–60; and 'Polluter Pays, Precautionary Principles and Liability' in G. Betlem and E. Brans (eds), *Environmental Liability in the EU* (Cambridge: Cameron & May, 2006) 89–102.
[283] In a 1991 Recommendation on the Use of Economic Instruments in Environment Policy, the OECD Council admitted that a 'sustainable and economically efficient development of environmental resources' required internalizing the costs of preventing and controlling pollution as well as of the damage itself (C(90)

Accordingly, environmental liability has been considered as a way of implementing the polluter-pays principle.[284] If this principle were not to be applied to cover the costs of restoration of environmental damage, either the environment would remain unrestored or the State, and ultimately the taxpayer, will have to pay for it. Therefore, a first objective is making the polluter liable for the damage he has caused. If polluters need to pay for damage caused, they will cut back pollution up to the point where the marginal cost of abatement exceeds the compensation avoided. Thus, environmental liability results in prevention of damage and in internalization of environmental costs. Nonetheless, a number of questions remain unanswered. Who is the liable party (the polluter, the producer, the waste holder, the consumer, etc)? Which damage or type of pollution should he compensate? To what extent should he pay? A comprehensive analysis of three cases is provided—*Agusta*, *van de Walle*, and *Mesquer*—in which the Court of Justice was asked to answer some of those questions.

7.3.4.2 Environmental Liability Directive

This line of reasoning, according to which environmental liability results in the principle of internalization of environmental costs, found echo in Directive 2004/35/EC on environmental liability with regard to the prevention and remedying of environmental damage. Pursuant to Article 1, the directive is underpinned by the polluter-pays principle;[285] however, it should be noted that the directive does not establish a genuine liability regime given that, on the one hand, compensation for private parties is expressly excluded[286] and, on the other, the directive straddles the divide between civil and administrative law.[287] In *Agusta*, the Court of Justice held that a strict liability regime does not in itself run contrary to the polluter-pays principle which applies to Directive 2004/35/EC.[288] Nonetheless, reasoning by analogy with *Standley*, the Court expressed the view that in spite of the strict liability regime, operators subject to the liability regime are not required to bear the costs of remedial action 'where they can prove that the environmental damage was caused by a third party and occurred despite the fact that appropriate safety measures were in place, since it is not a consequence of the "polluter pays" principle that operators must take on the burden of remedying

---

177 (final), OECD, 1991). Similarly, the preamble to the 1993 Lugano Convention on civil liability for damage resulting from activities dangerous to the environment (not in force) (Lugano, 21 June 1993) 'has regard to the desirability of providing for strict liability in this field, taking into account the "polluter-pays" principle'.

[284] COM(2000) 66 final, 9 February 2000.

[285] In addition, the preamble to that directive stresses that 'the prevention and remedying of environmental damage should be implemented through the furtherance of the "polluter-pays" principle' and that, according to this principle, the 'operator should bear the cost of the necessary preventive or remedial measures' (2nd and 18th recitals of the preamble).

[286] Arts. 2(1) and 3.

[287] N. de Sadeleer, 'La directive 2004/35/CE relative à la responsabilité environnementale: avancée ou recul pour le droit de l'environnement des Etats membres?' in B. Dubuisson and G. Viney (eds), *Les responsabilités environnementales* (Brussels/Paris: Bruylant/LGDJ, 2005) 732.

[288] Case C-378/08 *Agusta* [2010] ECR I-01919, para. 70. See S. Casotta and C. Verdure, 'Recent Developments Regarding the EU Environmental Liability for Enterprises: Lessons Learned from Italy's Implementation of the "Raffinerie Mediterranee" Cases' (2012) *EEELR* 156–64.

pollution to which they have not contributed'.[289] In other words, the strict liability regime does not preclude the demonstration of the link of causation.

7.3.4.3 Waste Framework Directive

In both *van de Walle* and *Mesquer*, the Court of Justice applied the principle to waste liability cases relating to the clean-up of sites polluted by hydrocarbons. It should be noted that in the case of a contaminated site, it is not always easy to identify who has actually caused the pollution—the person in charge of the installation, the manufacturer of the defective plant, the owner of the property, and the licence-holder or his representatives may be liable for pollution. This question becomes even more complex in the case of diffuse pollution, where multiple causes produce single effects and single causes produce multiple effects.

The Court has been asked to rule on whether the producers of oil products from which the waste emanated might be held liable for the costs of cleaning up environmental damage resulting from accidental oil spills. In particular, the Court was asked, with respect to the financial costs of the waste disposal, to determine the scope of Article 15 of the former Waste Framework Directive 75/442/EC (WFD) that provided that, in accordance with the 'polluter pays' principle, 'the holder' of the waste (first indent) or 'the previous holders or the producer of the product from which the waste came' (second indent) must bear the costs of disposing of the waste. It should be pointed out that under the former WFD the concept of 'holder' (first indent) embraced both 'the producer of waste' and 'the natural or legal person who is in possession of it'.

These two judgments enhance the enforceability of the principle where it has been fleshed out in specific EU obligations.

In *van de Walle*, the Court was asked to decide whether the WFD's obligations were applicable to a petroleum company which produces hydrocarbons and sells them to a manager operating one of its service stations under a contract of independent management excluding any relationship of subordination to the company.[290] In order to answer the question whether Texaco could be deemed to be the holder of the waste, the Court of Justice emphasized the need to interpret Article 15 of the directive in the light of the polluter-pays principle.

At the outset, the Court stressed that the WFD draws a dividing line between, on the one hand, 'practical recovery or disposal operations, which it makes the responsibility of any "holder of waste", whether producer or possessor' and, on the other hand, 'the financial burden of those operations, which, in accordance with the principle of polluter pays, it imposes on the persons who cause the waste, whether they are holders or former holders of the waste or even producers of the product from which the waste came.'[291]

---

[289] *Agusta* (n 288), para. 67.
[290] Case C-1/03 *van de Walle* [2004] ECR I-7613. See case notes by N. de Sadeleer (2008) 3 *CML Rev* 16; McIntyre (2005) 17 *JEL* 109. In reaction to this judgment, the EU lawmaker explicitly excluded land and unexcavated contaminated soil from the scope of the new Waste Framework Directive (Directive 2008/98/EC on waste [2008] OJ L312/3, Art. (2)(1)(b)).
[291] Case C-1/03 *van de Walle* [2004] ECR I-7613, para. 58.

As a matter of principle, that is the service station manager 'who, for the purpose of his operations, had them in stock when they became waste and who may therefore be considered to be the person who "produced" them within the meaning of Article 1(b) of [the] Directive'.[292] Nevertheless, an oil company selling hydrocarbons to the manager of a petrol station can, under certain circumstances, be considered to be the holder of the land contaminated by hydrocarbons that accidentally leak from the station's storage tanks, even where the petrol company does not own or 'hold' them.[293] In other words, the 'polluter' should be the person who causes the waste and thereby the pollution. The Court of Justice left it to the national court to determine whether the poor condition of the service station's storage facilities and the resultant leak of hydrocarbons could be attributed to a disregard of the contractual obligations by the petroleum undertaking which supplied the service station. The channelling of liability is thus foreclosed if the producer of the products from which the waste came can prove that it has acted in accordance with its contractual obligations.

Oil spills at sea raise interesting liability issues. In *Mesquer*, in adjudicating the issue of whether French oil companies could be charged for the cleaning up of heavy fuel accidentally discarded by a tanker operated by a Maltese company, the Court of Justice ensured a correct application of the 'polluter pays' principle, which cannot be emasculated by limitation or exemption systems resulting from international agreements to which the EU is not party.[294]

What deserves attention here is that the international agreements applicable to the compensation for damage caused by the discharge of hydrocarbons are, at first glance, far more favourable to oil companies than to victims. This is because, on the one hand, they channel liability to the oil tanker owner,[295] which has the effect of paralysing any compensation claims for third parties where the owner is insolvent. On the other hand, even if this limitation of liability is countered by the intervention of a compensation fund—such as the International Oil Pollution Compensation Funds (IOPCF)—this intervention remains limited.[296] The limitation can, as such, result in neither the shipowner nor IOPCF bearing any part of the costs of waste disposal resulting from damage due to pollution by hydrocarbons at sea. This leads to the financial burden being placed on the general public, which seems to run contrary to the logic of the polluter-pays principle. In sharp contrast to these international agreements, the WFD obligation regarding waste disposal costs was not subject to any limitation.

Both Advocate General Kokott and the Court of Justice reached the conclusion that, even if it was in principle the shipowner who held the waste,[297] the producer of heavy fuel oil as well as the seller and the oil tanker charterer could be held liable for waste disposal costs, on the ground that they could be deemed to have contributed in some

---

[292] *Van de Walle* (n 291), para. 59.   [293] *Van de Walle* (n 291), para. 60.

[294] Case C-188/07 *Mesquer* [2009] ECR I-4501. See case note by N. de Sadeleer (2009) 21:2 *JEL* 299.

[295] International Convention on Civil Liability for Oil Pollution Damage (Brussels, 29 November 1969), Art. III. In channelling the liability exclusively to the owner of the oil tanker, the Convention insulates the seller-charterer from civil liability.

[296] International Convention on the Establishment of an International Oil Pollution Compensation Fund (1992).

[297] Case C-188/07 *Mesquer* [2009] ECR I-4501, para. 74.

way to the causal chain which led to the shipwreck which was the origin of the spillage.[298] Indeed, that financial obligation is thus imposed on the 'previous holders' or the 'producer of the product from which the waste came' 'because of their contribution to the creation of the waste and, in certain cases, to the consequent risk of pollution'.[299] As a result, the liability for damage caused by waste disposal cannot only be channelled to the sole owner of the vessel, who generally speaking is more often insolvent than the companies chartering said ship. On the contrary, it will be possible in accordance with the polluter-pays principle to regard the seller-charterer as a previous holder of the waste.[300] That said, the producer may only be made liable, in accordance with the 'polluter pays' principle, insofar as the latter has 'contributed by his conduct to the risk that the pollution caused by the shipwreck will occur'.[301]

In shifting the channelling of the liability, the Court of Justice was nonetheless surrounded by opposing norms with, on the one hand, international agreements limiting the liability of oil companies and, on the other hand, Article 15 of the former WFD, which does not provide for any limitation on the liability of the waste holder.[302] The Court considered that Article 15 WFD did not prohibit Member States, in accordance with the two international agreements, from laying down limitations and exemptions of liability in favour of the shipowner or the charterer.[303] There was therefore no incompatibility between EU law and international law.

However, taking into account that the cost of disposal of the waste may not be borne by IOPCF, or cannot be borne because the ceiling for compensation for the accident has been reached, or 'that, in accordance with the limitations and/or exemptions of liability laid down, the national law of a Member State,..., prevents that cost from being borne by the ship-owner and/or the charterer' the Court reached the conclusion that such a national law will have to be interpreted in such a way in order to ensure that the full costs are borne by the producer.[304]

Practically speaking, if the damage caused by the oil spill exceeds the ceiling for compensation provided under the international regime, the Member State is called on to give precedence to the EU waste liability scheme interpreted in the light of the polluter-pays principle to ensure that the costs are borne by the producer of the oil from which the waste emanated. As a result, Member States cannot limit the scope of

---

[298] Opinion AG Kokott in Case C-188/07 *Mesquer* [2009] ECR I-4501, para. 147; Case C-188/07, para. 78.

[299] *Mesquer* (n 298), para. 77.   [300] *Mesquer* (n 298), para. 78.

[301] *Mesquer* (n 298), para. 82. The criterion of 'contribution to the risk that the pollution might occur' is somewhat lower than the threshold to be met in *van de Walle*, the direct causal link or the negligent behaviour of the operator.

[302] However, by not concluding these international instruments, the EC was not bound by the obligations therein, whereas the majority of Member States, including France, were parties to those instruments. See *Mesquer* (n 298), para. 85.

[303] *Mesquer* (n 298), para. 81. The fact that these limitations and exemptions stemming from international law would have the effect of passing on to the general public a substantial part of the environmental liability was, according to AG Kokott, in accordance with the 'polluter pays' principle (Opinion, para. 142).

[304] *Mesquer* (n 298), para. 82. In so doing, the Court of Justice departed somewhat abruptly from the Opinion of AG Kokott in considering that a correct transposition of Art. 15 of the directive implied that national law must ensure that further costs 'be borne by the producer of the product from which the waste thus spread came'.

their EU secondary law obligations interpreted in the light of the polluter-pays principle, even though they will have to disregard their international obligations. In short, EU waste law and hence the polluter-pays principle takes precedence over international law. Obviously, the outcome would have been different if the EU had been a party to that international convention.

As a result of *van de Walle* and *Mesquer*, the willingness of the Court to channel liability to the oil producers, provided that their conduct has given rise to the waste, has been somewhat softened under the new WFD of 2008.[305] In any event, Member States may still under the new regime channel liability along the production chain of the waste. The case law must be approved for the following reasons.

First, for reasons of economic efficiency and administrative simplicity, the law need not necessarily adhere to reality, and it is sometimes preferable to apply the qualification of polluter or waste holder to a single person rather than a number of people.[306] In particular, Recommendation 75/436 regarding cost allocation and action by public authorities on environmental matters provides that the costs of pollution could be charged 'at the point at which the number of economic operators is least and control is easiest'. Consequently, the polluter may be the agent who plays a determining role in producing the pollution rather than the person actually causing the pollution (eg the producer of pesticides rather than the farm worker).[307]

Second, in shifting the channelling of the liability towards the most solvent party—the oil-producing company or the seller-charterer—the Court ensures that the clean-up of the oil spillage will take place.

Third, given that the liability is not channelled towards the least solvent party—the holder of the waste—all the parties involved in the chain of operation are enticed, in accordance with the principle of prevention, to monitor closely their respective activities.

7.4 The principle of prevention

Curative measures may remediate environmental damage, but they come too late to avert it. In contrast, preventive measures do not depend on the appearance of ecological problems; they anticipate damage or, where it has already occurred, try to ensure that it does not spread. In any event, common sense dictates timely prevention of environmental damage to the greatest extent possible, particularly when it is likely to be irreversible or too insidious or diffuse to be effectively dealt with through civil

[305] Under Art. 14(1) of the new WFD 2008/98/EC, 'in accordance with the polluter-pays principle, the costs of waste management shall be borne by the original waste producer or by the current or previous waste holders' and no longer by 'the previous holders or the producer of the product from which the waste came'. However, pursuant to the second para. of that article, 'Member States may decide that the costs of waste management are to be borne partly or wholly by the producer of the product from which the waste came and that the distributors of such product may share these costs'.
[306] De Sadeleer (n 266), 41–2.
[307] The fact that the hydrocarbons were accidentally spilled does not exclude the obligation to decontaminate the land in the light of the polluter-pays principle. Indeed, the OECD Recommendation of 5 July 1989 on the Application of the Polluter-Pays Principle to Accidental Pollution confirms the intention to apply the principle to accidental as well as chronic pollution and thereby to require potential polluters to contribute financially to preventive measures adopted by public authorities.

liability or when reparation would be extremely expensive.[308] Given that prevention is a bedrock principle of international environmental law,[309] it comes as no surprise that it has long been the Cinderella of EU environmental law. Furthermore, prevention is a flagship principle of other EU policies, such as workers' safety, that have close links to environmental policy.[310]

However, its outline is difficult to discern; it gives rise to so many questions that any attempt at interpretation calls for constant clarification. We may, for example, ask whether a preventive measure presupposes complete knowledge of the risk to be reduced, if all forms of damage must be foreseen, if intervention should take place at the level of the source of the damage or of its effects, and whether it is preferable to monitor the progress of damage or to intervene when it occurs.

Nonetheless, the proliferation of preventive mechanisms found in EU secondary law—environmental impact assessments,[311] notification procedures,[312] adequate control of risks,[313] exchange of data on the impact of harmful activities,[314] etc—gives substance to this principle. In effect, these regulatory devices play a crucial role in preventing environmental harm and therefore give substance to the principle. With respect to waste management, prevention prevails over other operations such as re-use, recycling, recovery, and disposal.[315] Likewise, a procedure for authorization to be obtained prior to setting up a large retail establishment is appropriate for achieving the objectives relating to town and country planning and environmental protection pursued by regional authorities. In truth, the damage that would be caused if the authorization scheme were not to be applied could not be repaired after the project is complete. Against this background, the Court of Justice stressed the soundness of the preventive approach: 'adoption of measures a posteriori, if the setting up of a retail establishment already built should prove to have a negative impact on environmental

---

[308] EEA, *The European Environment. State and Outlook* (Copenhagen: EEA, 2005) 19.

[309] *Arbitration Regarding the Iron Rhine Railway* (*Belgium v Netherlands*), Arbitral Award of 24 May 2005, para. 58. In *Pulp Mills on the River Uruguay*, the ICJ held that environmental impact assessment (EIA) 'has gained so much acceptance among States that it may now be considered a requirement under general international law to undertake an EIA where there is a risk that the proposed industrial activity may have a significant adverse impact in a transboundary context'. Eg *Pulp Mills on the River Uruguay* (*Argentina v Uruguay*) [2010] ICJ Rep. 7, para. 204.

[310] Council Directive 89/391/EEC on the introduction of measures to encourage improvements in the safety and health of workers at work [1989] OJ L183/1, Arts 1(2) and 3(d).

[311] European Parliament and Council Directive 2001/42/EC on the assessment of the effects of certain plans and programmes on the environment [2001] OJ L197/30; Council Directive 92/43/EEC on the conservation of natural habitats and of wild fauna and flora [1992] OJ L206/1, Art. 6(3).

[312] European Parliament and Council Regulation (EC) No. 1013/2006 on shipments of waste [2006] OJ L190/1; European Parliament and Council Regulation (EC) No. 689/2008 concerning the export and import of dangerous chemicals [2008] OJ L204/1.

[313] REACH Regulation, Art. 57(1).

[314] Directive 2001/42/EC on the assessment of the effects of certain plans and programmes on the environment [2001] OJ L197/30, Art. 7.

[315] Directive 2008/98/EC on waste [1998] OJ L312/3, Art. 4(1). In sharp contrast, as regards packaging waste, the Court took the view that re-use should be placed on an equal footing with recycling. See Case C-309/02 *Radlberger and Spitz* [2004] ECR I-11763, para. 33; and Case C-463/01 *Commission v Germany* [2004] ECR I-11705, para. 40.

protection, appears a less effective and more costly alternative to the system of prior authorisation'.[316]

Furthermore, pursuant to the case law of the ECtHR, Member States have positive obligations by virtue of Article 8 ECHR to take appropriate measures to avoid serious interference with the right to private life.[317] In addition, the ECtHR took the view that Article 2 ECHR entails 'a primary duty on the State to put in place a legislative and administrative framework designed to provide effective deterrence against threats to the right to life'.[318]

Finally, the companion principle of standstill may go hand in hand with prevention.

7.5 The principle that environmental damage should, as a matter of priority, be remedied at source

In refining the preventive principle, the principle of rectification at source is grounded in common sense. Damage should as a priority be rectified by taking action at source rather than by using end-of-the-pipe technologies. There is no shortage of regulatory devices fleshing out this principle. The fact that the best environmental policy consists of preventing the creation of pollution or nuisances at source, rather than subsequently trying to counteract its effects explains why so many projects are subject to authorization and environmental impact assessments. As regards waste management, this principle entails that 'it is for each region, municipality or other local authority to take appropriate steps to ensure that its own waste is collected, treated and disposed of and that that waste must therefore be disposed of as close as possible to the place where it is produced, in order to limit as far as possible the transportation of waste'.[319] Even if one of the regions of a Member State lacks the infrastructure needed to meet its waste disposal needs, such 'serious deficiencies at regional level are likely to compromise the national network of waste disposal installations'.[320] Moreover, under Article 16(1)(2) of Directive 2008/98, Member States are to take appropriate measures to establish an 'integrated and adequate network of waste disposal installations', in order to enable the Union as a whole to become self-sufficient in waste disposal and recovery of waste and to enable 'the Member States to move towards that aim individually'.[321] With the aim of encouraging rationalization of waste management, Member States must establish waste management plans. Accordingly, pursuant to the principle of proximity enshrined in Article 16(3) of Directive 2008/98, the network of installations must enable waste to be disposed of in the nearest appropriate installation.[322] These plans should include location criteria governing the location of waste disposal sites. Some of

---

[316] Case C-400/08 *Commission v Spain* [2011] ECR I-1915, para. 92.

[317] See the discussion in Chapter 2, Section 4.3.

[318] *Oneryildiz v Turkey*, 18 June 2002, para. 90.

[319] See Case C-155/91 *Commission v Council* [1993] ECR I-939, para. 13; and Case C-297/08 *Commission v Italy* [2010] ECR I-1749, para. 67.

[320] Case C-297/08 *Commission v Italy* [2010] ECR I-1749, para. 68.

[321] Case C-494/01 *Commission v Ireland* [2005] ECR I-3331, para. 154; and Case C-286/06 *Commission v Spain* [2008] ECR I-8025, para. 57.

[322] Case C-480/06 *Commission v Germany* [2009] ECR I-04747, para. 37.

these criteria should relate, inter alia, to the distance of such sites from inhabited areas.[323] Lastly, the new Directive 2010/75/EU on industrial emissions is meant to give 'priority to intervention at source, ensuring prudent management of natural resources'.[324]

7.6 The precautionary principle

7.6.1 *Genesis*

Known at the start of the 1990s by only a few specialists of environmental law, the precautionary principle has experienced a meteoric rise within the space of a decade and, as a result, has been able to establish itself as a new general principle of international law. It has not only come to occupy an uncontested position in international but also in EU law as well as in several European countries, to the point where it overshadows the principle of prevention. Furthermore, the precautionary principle has been applied increasingly often in a wide array of areas ranging from classical environmental issues (nature, water, air, . . .) to wider areas such as food safety (mad cow disease, the spread of GMO, . . .) as well as health issues (the French HIV blood-contamination scandal, health claims linked to phthalates in PVC toys and endocrine disruptors, among other issues).[325]

This introductory section will not reopen a full discussion on the meaning of this principle, other than to recall its function as the expression of a philosophy of anticipated action, not requiring that the entire corpus of scientific proof be collated in order for a public authority to be able to adopt a preventive measure. In so doing, the principle lowers the hurdles faced by regulatory agencies tackling risks permeated with uncertainty. While there are multiple definitions of this principle in international and national law, every enunciation of the principle contains the elements of an anticipatory regulatory approach in the face of uncertainty. In a nutshell, precaution epitomizes a paradigmatic shift. Whereas, under a preventive approach, the decision-maker intervenes provided that the threats to the environment are tangible, pursuant to the precautionary principle authorities are prepared to tackle risks for which there is no definitive proof that there is a link of causation between the suspected activity and the harm or whether the suspected damage will materialize. In such a situation, decision-makers cannot determine the threshold levels to which preventive action appears to be subject in order to avoid or to minimize the occurrence of the risk. In other words, precaution means that the absence of scientific certainty—or, conversely, the scientific uncertainty—as to the existence or the extent of a risk should henceforth no longer delay the adoption of preventative measures to protect the environment. That said,

---

[323] Joined Cases C-53/02 & C-217/02 *Commune de Braine-le-Château and others* [2004] ECR I-3251, para. 34; and *Commission v Spain* (n 321), paras 49 and 50. It must be kept in mind that mandatory minimum distance requirements, such as those between roadside service stations, are likely to restrict freedom of establishment. See Case C-384/08 *Attanasio Group* [2010] ECR I-2025.

[324] Directive 2010/75/EU on industrial emissions [2010] OJ L134/17, 2nd recital.

[325] The precautionary principle is seen by the Court of Justice as constituting 'an integral part of the decision-making processes leading the adoption of any measure for the protection of human health'. *Monsanto Agricultora Italia* (n 162), para. 133.

given that few activities take place in the realm of either total certainty or total uncertainty, the distinction between the two principles is more an issue of a sliding scale rather than of substance.[326]

The precautionary principle has quickly developed into one of the foundations of the high level of environmental protection in the EU and as an obligation laid down by the TFEU.[327] As a result, precaution has slowly but inexorably been permeating numerous crevices of EU law, either through the declaration of public policy objectives (soft law), directives and regulations (hard law), or judicial interpretation (case law). From an academic perspective, much ink has been spilled over its status at the EU level.[328]

Praised by some, disparaged by others, the principle is not unfamiliar with contro- versy. Moreover, discussions about its status and functions have greatly intensified with respect to World Trade Organization (WTO) trade issues. Indeed, much of the recent debate has focused on the question whether the principle fosters protectionism by justifying arbitrary standards that developing countries cannot meet and, as a result, jeopardizes innovation.

It is submitted that the significance of the principle lies in its challenge to traditional legal systems, many of which are permeated by the need for certainty. It should be noted that an operator's civil liability can be incurred provided that the victim is able to shed light on the link of causation between the operator's behaviour and the ensuing damage. A WTO member is able to enact a food safety measure provided that its regulatory choice is based on clear scientific evidence resulting from a risk assess- ment.[329] This presupposes continuous recourse to scientific expertise, with experts

---

[326] Eg bans on asbestos or tobacco smoking in the 1950s and 1960s would have involved both precaution and prevention. Nowadays these risks are well known. Henceforth, such bans are justified by the principle of prevention.

[327] Case C-127/02 *Waddenzee* [2004] ECR I-7405, para. 44.

[328] I. Cheyne, 'Taming the Precautionary Principle in EC Law: Lessons from Waste and GMO Regula- tion' (2007) 4:6 *JEEPL* 468–84; G. Corcelle, 'La perspective communautaire du principe de précaution' (2001) 450 *RMC* 447; A. Alemanno, 'Le principe de précaution en droit communautaire' (2001) *RDUE* 917–40; W. T. Douma, *The Precautionary Principle. Its Application in International, European and Dutch Law*, Phd thesis, Groeningen (2002); J. Scott and E. Vos, 'The Juridification of Uncertainty: Observations on the Ambivalence of the Precautionary Principle in the EU and the WTO' in Ch. Joerges and R. Dehousse (eds), *Good Governance in Europe's Integrated Market* (Oxford: OUP, 2002) 253–86; J. Scott, 'The Precautionary Principle before the European Courts' in Macrory (n 180), 51–72; A. Szajkowska, 'The Impact of the Definition of the Precautionary Principle in EU Food Law' (2010) 47 *CML Rev* 173–96; Zander (n 195), 76–151; M. Weimer, 'Applying Precaution in EU Authorisation of Genetically Modified Products—Challenges and Suggestions for Reform' (2010) 16:5 *ELJ* 624–57. See also N. de Sadeleer in the following: 'Le statut juridique du principe de précaution en droit communautaire: du slogan à la règle' (2001) 1 *CDE* 79–120; 'The Precautionary Principle in EC Health and Environmental Law' (2006) 12 *ELJ* 139–72; *Implementing the Precautionary Principle: Approaches from the Nordic Countries, the EU and USA* (London: Earthscan, 2007); 'The Precautionary Principle Applied to Food Safety' (2009) 1 *EJCL* 147–70; 'The Precautionary Principle as a Device for Greater Environmental Protection: Lessons from EC Courts' (2008) 18:1 *RECIEL* 3–10; and 'The Precautionary Principle in EU Law' (2010) 5 *Aansprakelijkheid Verzekering en Schade* 173–84.

[329] See Art. 5(1)(2) Sanitary and Phytosanitary (SPS) Agreement. *European Communities—DS 26 Measures concerning meat and meat products (hormones)*, Appellate Body, Doc. WT/DS 26 & 48/AB/R (16 January 1998), para. 186; *Australia—DS 21 Measures concerning the importation of salmonids*, Appel- late Body, Doc. WT/DS18/AB/R (20 October 1998), para. 129. Attention should be drawn to the fact in interpreting Art. 5(7) of the SPS Agreement, the WTO Appellate Body took the view in *Japan—Measures affecting the importation of apples* that the application of the safeguard clause enshrined in that provision, which was previously deemed to reflect the precautionary principle, 'is triggered not by the existence of scientific uncertainty, but rather by the insufficiency of scientific evidence' (*Japan—Measures affecting the*

being able to provide flawless data to both courts and decision-makers. However, at first glance precaution provides for the possibility of acting while uncertainties have not yet been cleared. This requires a few words of explanation.

7.6.2 *Uncertainty as a triggering factor*

The precautionary principle came to centre stage in the field of environment policy in response to the limitations of science in assessing complex and uncertain ecological risks. Indeed, environmental risks and, in particular, global risks confront assessors with serious difficulties: uncertainty is a persistent feature both of understanding the chain of causation[330] as well as predicting the outcomes. Scientific uncertainty exists whenever there is no adequate theoretical or empirical basis for assigning probabilities to the occurrence or the extent of a risk. As far as environmental risks are concerned, there is indeed a strong deficit in predictive capability. In fact, the distance in time and space between sources and damages, the cumulative and synergistic effects, the unpredictable reactions of some ecosystems (potential resilience), and the large scale of impacts compound the methodological difficulties in assessing these risks.[331]

Clearly, uncertainty is not a clear-cut concept. In fact, a whole range of different types of uncertainty exist, ranging from lack of full evidence, lack of causal mechanisms, incorrect assumptions, extrapolation uncertainty, inconclusiveness, indeterminacy, and ambiguity, all the way to complete ignorance.[332] The following examples are illustrative of the ways in which uncertainty pervades the risk assessment process:

- insufficiency: for instance, the various scientific disciplines involved in assessing the risk are not sufficiently developed to explain the cause-and-effect relationship;[333]

- inconclusiveness: the realities of science dictate that scientists, whatever the quality of their investigations, will never be able to eliminate some uncertainties;[334] for instance, there may be too many unpredictable variables to enable the identification of the relative influences of each factor;

---

importation of apples, Appellate Body, Doc. WT/DS245/AB/R, para. 184). In contrast, in situations in which the data available have been sufficient to allow for diverging scientific assessments, Art. 5(7) SPS has not been considered to apply. See Zander (n 195), 93; E. Vecchione, 'Is It Possible to Provide Evidence of Insufficient Evidence? The Precautionary Principle at the WTO' (2012) *Chicago J Intl L* 153–78. As a result, under the SPS Agreement, a safeguard measure cannot be triggered by uncertainty but exclusively by insufficient results.

[330] Eg the French food safety agency (AFSSA) claimed that there exist more than 40 possible causes that might explain the observed trends of honeybee decline. See AFSSA, *Weakening, Collapse and Mortality of Bee Colonies* (2008).

[331] J. Kasperson, 'Introduction: Global Environmental Risk and Society' in J. Kasperson and R. Kasperson (eds), *Global Environmental Risk* (London: Earthscan, 2001) 4.

[332] T. Christoforou, 'The Regulation of GMOs in the EU: The Interplay of Science, Law and Politics' (2004) 41 *CML Rev* 703.

[333] Typical in this respect is recital 32 of Regulation (EC) No. 1829/2003 on GM food and feed recognizing that, in some cases, scientific risk assessments cannot provide all information on which a risk management decision should be based ([2003] OJ L268/1). In *Dupont de Nemours*, the General Court took into consideration the 'gaps in basic knowledge' of the impacts of endocrine disruptive substances. These gaps 'prevented international experts from being able to recommend suitable standard tests for regulatory purposes'. Case T-31/07 *Dupont de Nemours* [2013] OJ C156, para. 170.

[334] A quantitative risk assessment exercise performed by 11 different teams in the EC came up with 11 different results that differed a million fold. See S. Contini, A. Amendola, and I. Ziomas, *Benchark Exercise*

- imprecision: could be caused by the fact that the data used in the analysis of risks are not available or are out of date, or that assessors face information gaps, measurement errors, contradictions, indeterminacy, ambiguity, etc.

Table 1.4 indicates the ways in which state of knowledge is likely to underpin the rationale of preventive and precautionary regulatory measures.

7.6.3 Risk analysis

At the outset, it should be stressed that the principle is located within the broader context of the principle of risk analysis, which comprises a two-step process: risk assessment and risk management.[335] The point here is not to delve into the highly complex world of risk analysis; it is merely to emphasize some of the key issues arising in the discussion of the implementation of a precautionary measure. The first two stages are essential as they aim, on the one hand, to ensure as rigorous as possible a scientific basis for managing the risk (risk assessment) and, on the other hand, to recognize a margin of autonomy for the body authorized *in fine* to make a decision on the risk (risk management).[336] The distinction between the phases of assessment and

Table 1.4 Level of knowledge and precautionary approach

	Situation	State of knowledge	Rationale of regulatory measures
Risk	Activities that are known to impair natural habitats or ecosystems	Risk assessments highlight the level of impact and determine the probability of occurrence of the risk	**Prevention:** measures aiming at reducing known hazards
Uncertainty	Antibiotic growth promoters or endocrine disruptors	Given insufficient, inconclusive, or imprecise information, it is impossible to assess the impact and to determine the probability	**Precaution:** measures aiming at reducing plausible hazards
Ignorance	Discovery in 1974 of the depletion of the ozone layer caused by an apparently harmless class of chemicals, CFCs	'Unknown' impact and 'unknown' probability	**Precaution:** measures taken to anticipate the occurrence of 'surprises'

on Major Hazard Analysis (Ispra, European Commission Joint Research Center, 1991). By the same token, different models for assessing carcinogenicity can result in cancer predictions that differ by a factor of 100 or more when extrapolated to low doses. Eg M. Shapiro, 'Toxic Substances Policy' in O. Portney (ed.), *Public Policies for Environmental Protection* (Washington DC, Resources for the Futures, 1990) 218. Given 'the uncertainty inherent in assessing the public health risks posed by the use of food additives', the Court of Justice acknowledges the possibility of conducting legitimately different risk assessments yielding different scientific evidence. See Case C-3/00 *Denmark v Commission* [2003] ECR I-2643, para. 63.

[335] Communication from the Commission on the precautionary principle of 2 February 2000 (COM(2000) 1).

[336] In this respect, Regulation (EC) No. 178/2002 establishing the general principles of food legislation distinguishes in particular between assessment which 'shall be based on the available scientific evidence and undertaken in an independent, objective and transparent manner' (Art. 6(2)) and management which must bear in mind the risk evaluation, 'other factors legitimate to the matter under consideration', and the precautionary principle (Art. 6(3)) ([2002] OJ L31/1).

management thus meets a dual requirement: the need to base a political decision on scientific facts and the need to maintain the autonomy of politics vis-à-vis the results of scientific assessments.[337]

Therefore, a brief discussion of the concepts of risk assessment and risk management is warranted to make clear the baseline against which the precautionary principle has to be applied.[338]

Although the precautionary principle acknowledges the limits of a traditional scientific approach, it does not, however, discard genuine scientific research. Verification of the serious nature of a hypothesis should be undertaken using a specific technique known as risk assessment providing specific evidence 'which, without precluding scientific uncertainty, makes it possible reasonably to conclude on the basis of the most reliable scientific evidence available and the most recent results of international research that the implementation' of precautionary measures is necessary.[339] According to the EU Courts,[340] a scientific risk assessment requires 'the identification of the biological, chemical and physical agents liable to give rise to adverse health effects which may be present in a given food or group of foods and which call for scientific assessment in order better to understand them'.[341] In addition, risk assessment must be entrusted to experts who will provide the institutions with scientific advice which must be based on the principles of excellence, independence, and transparency.[342]

Nonetheless, as indicated previously, it may be impossible to carry out a full risk assessment because such investigations operate at the frontiers of scientific knowledge. In fact, scientists do not have an answer for everything. Their investigations do not always allow for an identification of the risks in a convincing manner. Indeed, in many cases, their assessments will demonstrate that there is a high degree of scientific and practical uncertainty. In particular, in fields marked by uncertainty they must acknowledge the limits of their knowledge or, where appropriate, their ignorance. As will be seen later, it is precisely at this stage that the precautionary principle comes into play.

---

[337] Opinion AG Mischo in *Commission v Denmark* (n 212), para. 92.

[338] On the relationship between the scientific process of risk assessment and a political process of risk management, see eg C. Noiville and N. de Sadeleer, 'La gestion des risques écologiques et sanitaires à l'épreuve des chiffres. Le droit entre enjeux scientifiques et politiques' (2001) 2 *RDUE* 389–449; T. Christoforou, 'Science, Law and Precaution in Dispute Resolution on Health and Environmental Protection: What Role for Scientific Experts?' in *Le commerce international des OGM* (Paris: Documentation française, 2002) 213–83; E. Fisher, 'Framing Risk Regulation: A Critical Reflection' (2013) 4:2 *EJRR* 125–32.

[339] *Monsanto Agricoltura Italia* (n 162), para. 113.

[340] The emphasis placed on risk assessment is likely to lead to closing the gap between the EU Courts' interpretation of the principle and its application by the WTO Dispute Settlement Body with respect to the SPS Agreement. See E. Stockes, 'The Role of Risk Assessment in Precautionary Intervention: A Comparison of Judicial Trends in the EC and WTO' (2007) 4:6 *JEEPL* 461.

[341] *Pfizer* (n 182), para. 156; Case T-70/99 *Alpharma v Council* [2002] ECR II-3495, para. 169; *Monsanto Agricoltura Italia* (n 162), para. 179; *Dupont de Nemours* (n 333), para. 142. See to that effect, inter alia, Art. 3(9)–(14) of Regulation (EC) No. 178/2002 of the GFL Regulation ([2002] OJ L31/1) and points 5.1.1 and 5.1.2 of and Annex III to the Communication from the Commission on the precautionary principle of 2 February 2000 (COM(2000) 1).

[342] *Pfizer* (n 182), paras 157 and 159.

Additionally, the risk is not only a question for the experts. It takes on a distinct individual meaning once situated within its political, social, and economic context. Accordingly, when the risk assessment procedure is completed, a *risk management* decision must be taken by politicians, taking into account both the legislative requirements and the economic, political, and normative dimensions of the problem.[343] Risk management, in contrast to risk assessment, is the public process of deciding how safe is safe. Indeed, 'societal, economic, traditional, ethical and environmental factors as well the feasibility of controls' might appear as factors legitimizing the regulation of a specific risk.[344] In addition, to refuse to run a risk is often to accept other risks. Therefore, the decision-maker may find himself confronting competing scenarios.[345]

Against this background, decision-makers can choose to err on the safe side even though the available scientific evidence does not prove full evidence of harm. In other words, a risk management measure can be decided despite the fact that the risk assessors were unable to determine the probability of the occurrence of the risk. Admittedly, precaution aims to bridge the gap between scientists working at the frontiers of scientific knowledge and decision-makers willing to act to determine when and how safe is safe enough.

That said, although unpredictable risks are rising, authorities tend to linger in the face of uncertainty and react only to crisis events: they characteristically err towards belated and costly measures.[346] Admittedly, 'paralysis by analysis' is not uncommon. This can be explained by the fact that damage to the environment is likely to be more controversial than damage to health. Whereas one usually agrees that activities endangering human health should be restricted or banned, people usually disagree whether ecosystems, ecosystemic processes, species of plants and animals, or micro-organisms deserve any kind of protection.

7.6.4 *Secondary law*

The principle has steadily expanded its dominion in the field of secondary law. It has been fleshed out in a broad range of measures ranging from notification procedures,[347]

---

[343] According to the Communication on the precautionary principle, the determination of what constitutes an 'acceptable' level of risk for society is an eminently *political* responsibility.

[344] Regulation (EC) No. 1829/2003 on GM food and feed ([2003] OJ L268/1) provides that as risk assessments cannot provide all the information on which a risk management decision should be based, 'other legitimate factors relevant to the matter under consideration' may be taken into account (Art. 6(6)). By the same token, Art. 6(3) of the GFL Regulation (EC) No. 178/2002 states that risk management 'shall take into account the results of risk assessments' as well as 'other factors legitimate to the matter under consideration' ([2002] OJ L31/1). Likewise, the EU Courts acknowledge the possibility of including 'consumers' concerns' in the balancing process. Eg Cases T-344 & 345/00 *LEVA & Pharmacia Enterprises v Commission* [2003] ECR II-229, para. 66.

[345] There is no shortage of illustrations of risk trade-offs. Eg CFCs were banned under the 1987 Montreal Protocol on Substances that Deplete the Ozone Layer (Montreal, 16 September 1987) and replaced by other gases known as HCFCs, which are mildly damaging to the ozone layer. However, the concentrations of ozone-friendly HCFCs are rising rapidly. Given that their warming effect is 2,100 times that of carbon dioxide, they seriously compound the risk of climate change.

[346] EEA, *Late Lessons from Early Warnings: the Precautionary Principle 1896–2000* (Copenhagen: EEA, 2001) 168.

[347] According to the Court of Justice, observance of the precautionary principle is reflected in the GMO notifier's obligation immediately to notify the competent authority of new information regarding the risks

prior authorization schemes,[348] restrictions on the use or sale of products,[349] and safeguard clauses[350] to bans.[351] Moreover, the uncertainty surrounding the causes and effects of GMOs and chemical substances has served to favour recognition of the principle.[352] For instance, the obligation to register monomers 'satisfies the precautionary principle' as referred to in the REACH Regulation.[353] Hence, the burden of proof as regard the safety of these substances has been shifted to their applicants.[354]

In accordance with the integration clause, the principle also applies in the area of fisheries[355] and where the institutions take measures to protect human health under the CAP.[356] This diversity of application indicates the potential of a principle, born of environmental law, which is being called upon to govern health law as well as consumer law.

However, secondary law is far from being perfect: several EU legislations refer to the principle whereas legislations on similar topics may ignore it. By way of illustration, the REACH Regulation refers to the principle[357] whereas the Classification, Labelling and Packaging of Substance and Mixtures Regulation does not mention it.

Lastly, the European Commission produced a Communication in February 2000 that seeks to inform all interested parties—and in particular the European Parliament, the Council, and the Member States—of the manner in which that institution applies or intends to apply the principle when faced with taking decisions relating to the containment of risk.[358]

of the product it has placed on the market and the competent authority's obligation immediately to inform the Commission and other Member States of this information. See *Greenpeace France* (n 193), para. 44.

[348] Communication from the Commission on the Precautionary Principle (COM(2000) 1).

[349] *Greenpeace France* (n 193), para. 44; Case C-77/09 *Gowan* [2010] ECR I-13533, para. 79; and *Dupont de Nemours* (n 333), para. 181.

[350] According to case law, 'the safeguard clause must be understood as giving specific expression to the precautionary principle'. See *Greenpeace France* (n 193), para. 55; *Monsanto Agricoltura Italia* (n 162), para. 110; and Case C-36/11 *Pioneer Hi Breed Italia* [2003] OJ C355/5, paras 51–5.

[351] The proportionality principle does not preclude the adoption of bans of hazardous substances in the light of the precautionary principle. See Case T-13/99 *Pfizer Animal Health v Council* [2002] ECR II-3305, para. 457.

[352] I. Cheyne, 'Taming the Precautionary Principle in EC Law: Lessons from Waste and GMO Regulation' (2007) 4:6 *JEEPL* 468–84. However, as a matter of practice, the European Commission appears to have failed to apply the principle in a balanced way, veering to the extremes of either a genuine science-based decision or somewhat politicized rhetoric. See M. Weimer, 'Applying Precaution in EU Authorisation of Genetically Modified Products—Challenges and Suggestions for Reform' (2010) 16:5 *ELJ* 624–57.

[353] *SPCM and others* (n 249), para. 54.

[354] The Communication from the Commission on the Precautionary Principle stresses that precautionary action 'must, in certain cases, include a reversal of the burden of proof'. As regards GMOs, Directive 2001/18/EC requires applicants to carry out an environmental risk assessment of the GMO being proposed for authorization ([2001] OJ L106/1). By the same token, EU chemicals legislation has moved in a similar direction in requiring applicants to collect, elaborate, and present the scientific and factual data about their substances. See the REACH and Classification, Labelling and Packaging Regulations.

[355] Council Regulation (EC) No. 2371/2002 on the conservation and sustainable exploitation of fisheries resources under the Common Fisheries Policy [2002] OJ L358/59, Art. 2(1). See Case C-453/08 *Karanikolas* [2010] ECR I-7895, para. 45.

[356] Case C-157/96 *National Farmers' Union and others* [1998] ECR I-2211, para. 64; Case C-180/96 *UK v Commission* [1998] ECR I-2265, para. 100; *Gowan* (n 349), para. 72.

[357] REACH Regulation, Arts 1 and 3 as well as recitals 9 and 69.

[358] Communication from the Commission on the Precautionary Principle (COM(2000) 1), para. 2. The communication was intended to build a consensus among the Directorates General, paving the way for a common position among EU institutions and a common understanding between Member States. While the

7.6.5 *Case law*

7.6.5.1 EU Courts confronted with the principle

Given that the precautionary principle is binding on the EU institutions, it can be invoked in an action for annulment by the applicant (eg by an institution or a private party) before the Court of Justice or the General Court to contend with the validity of secondary legislation (mostly, in the field of environmental protection, consisting of directives and regulations). The applicant may therefore argue before the EU Courts that the lawmaker has wrongly failed to apply the principle. The fact that such a Treaty principle has been infringed will constitute a ground for annulment. So far, the principle has mainly been invoked in lawsuits dealing with health and safety issues. Nonetheless, environmental cases are highlighting a new role for the principle as a means of controlling the discretion of the EU institutions.

Moreover, the extent to which national authorities are bound by the principle has been addressed in many preliminary ruling requests by virtue of Article 267 TFEU and action for infringement by virtue of Articles 258–260 TFEU. Therefore, it comes as no surprise that the EU Courts have been regularly asked to rule on the precautionary principle.

Although EU lawmakers are reluctant to define the principle, the EU courts have endorsed such an anticipatory approach. The jurisprudential definition of the precautionary principle runs as follows: 'where there is uncertainty as to the existence or extent of risks to human health, protective measures may be taken without having to wait until the reality and seriousness of those risks become fully apparent'.[359] That said, the status of the principle is still dogged by controversy. Whereas the Court of Justice has been more careful in speculating about the nature of the principle,[360] the General Court took the view in *Artegodan* that that precaution was a general principle of EU law.[361]

In looking at the EU Courts' case law, one needs to draw a line between the health and food safety cases[362] and genuine environmental cases (climate change, waste

communication is typically a soft law instrument, it is not devoid of legal consequences. Indeed, applying the principle of equal treatment, the EU judiciary can ascertain whether an EU measure is consistent with the guidelines that the institutions have laid down for themselves by adopting such a communication. See Case T-13/99 *Pfizer Animal Health v Council* [2002] ECR II-3305, para. 123.

[359] See *National Farmers' Union and others* (n 356), para. 63; *UK v Commission* (n 356), para. 99; *Monsanto Agricoltura Italia* (n 341), para. 111; *Gowan* (n 356), para. 73; Case C-333/08 *Commission v France* [2010] ECR I-757, para. 91; and *Afton* (n 138), para. 62. See also *Pfizer* (n 358), para. 139.

[360] AG Kokott took the view that a legislative measure adopted on the basis of Art. 114 TFEU cannot be directly assessed according to whether it observes the precautionary principle. See Opinion AG Kokott in *Afton* (n 138), para. 54. That reasoning was implicitly endorsed by the Court of Justice.

[361] Due to its highly abstract nature and particularly broad scope of application, the precautionary principle could then be defined 'as a general principle of [EU] law requiring the competent authorities to take appropriate measures to prevent specific potential risks to public health, safety and the environment, by giving precedence to the requirements related to the protection of those interests over economic interests'. Joined Cases T-74, 76, 83–85, 132, 137 & 141/00 *Artegodan* [2002] ECR II-4945, para. 184; and *Dupont de Nemours* (n 333), para. 134.

[362] In fact, over the past years, the precautionary principle has regularly been invoked before the EU Courts in major food safety and drugs cases. The case law has not only managed to extend the scope of application of the precautionary principle to all policies involving scientific uncertainty, but has also introduced extremely useful clarification of the application of the principle, in particular in the domain

management, water and nature conservation). With respect to health issues, where scientific knowledge is far more advanced than it is in the environmental sector, various rules of secondary law define the precautionary principle further in connection with the Commission's implementing powers.[363] It is in this area that the case law has been particularly developed.

The stricter approach endorsed by the EU Courts with respect to the health and food safety cases can be explained by the fact that those cases chiefly deal with the placing on the market of products (GMOs, food additives, medicinal products) where a fundamental principle of Treaty law, the free movement of goods, is at stake.[364] Whereas in the environmental cases, the Courts have to balance economic freedoms—that is, the right to property, the freedom to pursue a trade or business—vis-à-vis an EU public interest—that is, the objective of a high level of health protection—in the latter cases the Courts have to weigh an EU public interest—free movement of goods enshrined in Articles 34–36 TFEU—against a national public interest—the willingness to depart from EU harmonized standards according to Article 114(4) and (5) TFEU or to maintain a measure impinging upon trade according to Article 36 TFEU or the rule of reason.[365]

Conversely, with respect to environmental cases, the obligation to take account of the most salient scientific findings does not warrant strict rules of evidence.[366] In effect, the uncertainties are far more important in this field given the difficulty of predicting the reactions of ecosystems to ecological risks. Ecosystems are subject to chaotic fluctuations that are not adequately modelled, nor even understood in traditional scientific terms.[367] In addition, the environmental cases so far decided by the Court of Justice deal mostly with the interpretation of provisions of several environmental directives, rather than with the functioning of the internal market and the fundamental principle of free movement of goods.

It is also important to note that the intensity of review exercised by the EU Courts varies extensively. In effect, one needs to draw a line between, on the one hand, lawsuits brought by a private party against a directive, a regulation, or a decision and, on the other hand, actions for infringement of EU law brought by the Commission against the Member States. With respect to cases regarding actions for annulment, the precautionary principle generates a review test of adequacy of scientific evidence

---

of public health. See N. de Sadeleer, 'The Precautionary Principle in EC Health and Environmental Law' (2006) 12 *ELJ* 139–72; A. Szajkowska, 'The Impact of the Definition of the Precautionary Principle in EU Food Law' (2010) 47 *CML Rev* 173–96.

[363] It should at this point be noted that in contrast to EU food safety and chemicals regulations where the principle is expressly defined (GFL Regulation, Art. 7; See Szajkowska (n 362), 173), few environmental directives or regulations specifically mention the precautionary principle in their operative provisions (REACH Regulation, Art. 1; Regulation 1107/2009, Art. 1(4)).

[364] Opinion AG Poiares Maduro in *Commission v Netherlands* (n 198), para. 30. According to the AG, 'the discretion that Member States are allowed as regards recourse to the precautionary principle is increasingly restricted the further they depart from scientific analysis and the more they rely on policy judgment', in particular in cases of lack of data on account of the novelty of the product or a lack of resources in conducting scientific research (para. 33). The Court of Justice did not address that issue.

[365] Case C-120/78 *Rewe-Zentral* ('*Cassis de Dijon*') [1979] ECR I-649.

[366] Opinion AG Kokott in *Afton* (n 138), para. 34.

[367] B. Wyne, 'Uncertainty and Environmental Learning' (1992) 2 *Global Environmental Change* 111–27.

supporting the contested measure. In contrast, in adjudicating references for a preliminary ruling, the Court of Justice resorts to precaution as an interpretative principle.[368]

We shall restrict ourselves to commenting on the environmental cases ranging from
wildlife conservation measures to chemical management issues, although several of
them overlap to some extent with health issues. As will be seen, relying explicitly or
implicitly upon the precautionary principle, the Court of Justice departs from a literal
interpretation of obligations laid down in secondary law. Moreover, the cases commented on in this section are testament to the binding effect of the principle as regards
Member State measures.

7.6.5.2 Reviewing the scientific evidence needed to adopt precautionary measures

Questions arise as to in which category of foreseeability we should range anticipated
risks on the basis of the precautionary principle. Should the principle apply to all
suspected risks? Does the adoption of a measure require a minimum set of indications
showing that the suspected risk is well founded, or are public authorities relieved of all
proof requirements when confronted by an important risk? Is there an obligation for
scientists to disclose all uncertainties?

The EU Courts' as well as the EFTA Court's reply to these questions is that a
preventative measure cannot properly be based on a purely hypothetical consideration
of the risk, founded on mere conjecture which has not been scientifically verified.[369]
Accordingly, a generalized presumption of a health risk must be supported by scientific
evidence explaining the need to adopt a pre-marketing authorization scheme.[370] In this
way, the European Courts exclude from the scope of application of the principle such
risks qualified as residual—that is, speculative risks founded upon purely speculative
factors and with no basis in science. It follows that there must exist a threshold of
scientific plausibility.

However, the concept of hypothetical risk is fraught with controversy. As has been
held by the Court of Justice, this concept must not be interpreted too broadly. In *Solvay
Chemicals*, the Court of Justice held that a Council decision highlighting the difficulties
faced by scientists in determining the extent of a risk did not amount to a 'purely
hypothetical risk'.[371] Likewise, the restrictions placed on the use of an active substance
of a plant protection product cannot be considered to be based on purely hypothetical
considerations when the EU institutions work on different items of evidence, such as
scientific studies and reports and the ongoing work of the OECD.[372]

Basic scientific knowledge is thus required. For instance, the principle cannot be
invoked by the Commission with a view to softening the standards of proof as regards
water that in the near future may become eutrophic. Given that the Commission must

---

[368] E. Scotford, 'Mapping the Article 174(2) EC Case Law: A First Step to Analysing Community
Environmental Law Principles' (2008) 8 *YbEEL* 20–41.

[369] *Pfizer* (n 358), para. 143; see also *Monsanto Agricoltura Italia* (n 162), para. 106; *Commission v
Denmark* (n 212), para. 49; *Commission v Netherlands* (n 198), para. 52; *Monsanto* (n 229), para. 77; Case
E-3/00 *EFTA Surveillance Authority v Norway* (2000–01) EFTA Ct. Rep. 73, para. 29.

[370] *Commission v France* (n 359), para. 97.

[371] *Solvay v Council* (n 166), para. 135.

[372] *Gowan* (n 356), para. 78.

demonstrate 'a certain amount of evidence' in respect of the Nitrates Directive's criteria and of the existence of the relationship of cause and effect, the likelihood of eutrophication is insufficient.[373] That said, the Commission does not have to provide irrefutable evidence that the criteria are fulfilled.

Scientific issues are also gathering momentum with respect to the complex relationship between internal market rules and environmental policy. For instance, paragraph 5 of Article 114 TFEU authorizes the Member States, insofar as certain conditions are fulfilled, to 'introduce' more stringent measures than those provided for by an EU measure related to the functioning of the internal market.[374] These measures must be based on 'new scientific evidence'. The question arose as to whether an Austrian province could ban GMOs on its territory with the aim of protecting nature as well as organic farming pursuant to that paragraph. The European Commission contended that the scientific evidence gathered by the Austrian authorities in the light of the precautionary principle was not 'new scientific evidence' in the sense of paragraph 5 of Article 114 TFEU. Advocate General Sharpston took the following view in her Opinion: 'Having regard to...the precautionary principle,..., no amount of precaution can actually render that evidence or that situation new. The novelty of both situation and evidence is a dual criterion which must be satisfied before the precautionary principle comes into play.'[375] The Court of Justice dismissed the appeal lodged by the Austrian authorities, claiming that the General Court had not erred in law by stating that the findings of the European Food Safety Authority concerning the absence of scientific evidence demonstrating the existence of a specific problem had been taken into consideration by the Commission.[376] In other words, the principle does not prevail over the obligation for the Member State to bear the burden of the proof as regards the novelty of the scientific evidence.

This prompts the question of the quality or the severity of the scientific knowledge needed to adopt precautionary measures. No easy answer can be given. At first glance, the open-textured term 'reasonable grounds for concerns' set out in the Commission guidelines leaves a wide margin of discretion to the EU institutions. By the same token, the Court of Justice and the General Court alike have expressed the view that 'where it proves to be impossible to determine with certainty the existence or extent of the alleged risk because of the insufficiency, inconclusiveness or imprecision of the results of studies conducted, but the likelihood of real harm to public health persists should the risk materialise, the precautionary principle justifies the adoption of restrictive measures'.[377] Nevertheless, there are no further indications in relation to the manner in

---

[373] Case C-390/07 *Commission v UK* [2009] ECR I-214, para. 28.
[374] See Chapter 7, Section 3.2.
[375] Opinion AG Sharpston in Joined Cases C-439/05 P & C-454/05 P *Land Oberösterreich and Republic of Austria v Commission of the European Communities* [2007] ECR I-7441, para. 134.
[376] *Land Oberösterreich and Republic of Austria v Commission of the European Communities* (n 375), para. 64.
[377] *Commission v Denmark* (n 212), para. 55; *Commission v Netherlands* (n 198), para. 54; *Commission v France* (n 359), para. 93; *Gowan* (n 356), para. 76; *Afton* (n 138), para. 61; and *Dupont de Nemours* (n 333), para. 142. Moreover, these criteria are listed in the Commission's communication on the precautionary principle, COM/2001/1, 10.

which these three criteria should be interpreted.[378] It must also be kept in mind that
any scientific advice is surrounded by some degree of uncertainty. Is it impossible to
determine more precisely the thresholds needed to trigger the adoption of precautionary measures?[379]

Attention should be drawn to the fact that the lessons that can be drawn from the
case law on food safety[380] cannot be applied, as such, to environmental cases.[381] As
stressed by Advocate General Kokott, with respect to subject areas where the precautionary principle has not been defined further in connection with the Commission's
implementing powers, 'the obligation to take account of the latest scientific findings
does not... warrant strict rules of evidence'.[382]

Moreover, the EU institutions 'may disregard the conclusions' drawn by experts.[383]
For example, in *Mondiet* the Court held that precautionary measures do not have to be
in complete conformity with scientific opinion.[384] In *Gowan*, the Court held that in
restricting the period during which a hazardous substance can be placed on the market,
the Commission and the Council were not bound by the national report on the
substance and the opinion of the EU scientific committee that validated the report.
The institutions thus remain entitled to adopt different risk management measures
from those proposed by the rapporteur.[385]

Nonetheless, in so doing, the institutions 'must provide specific reasons for their
findings by comparison with those made in the opinion and its statement of reasons
must explain why it is disregarding the latter.' Consequently, as a matter of procedure,
'the statement of reasons must be of a scientific level at least commensurate with that of
the opinion in question'.[386]

7.6.5.3 Discretionary power, high level of protection, and precautionary principle

As regards actions for annulment, it needs merely to be noted that the EU Courts are
fully aware of the difficulties of regulating either in controversial cases or where action
is urgently required. On that basis, they rightly show themselves to be seldom inclined
to penalize institutions for any errors which they may have committed in their desire to
safeguard the general interest. Hence, review must be limited to cases in which the

---

[378] The criteria might differ. Whereas it is settled case law that EU institutions might act whenever the
'scientific evidence is insufficient, inconclusive or uncertain', under Art. 6(2) of the 1995 UN FAO Code of
Conduct for Responsible Fisheries and the 1995 UN Agreement on Straddling Fish Stocks and Highly
Migratory Fish Stocks, the obligation to endorse a precautionary approach reads: 'States shall be more
cautious when information is uncertain, unreliable or inadequate'.

[379] R. von Schomberg, 'The Precautionary Principle' in W. S. Bainbridge (ed.), *Leadership in Science and
Technology* (London: Sage, 2011).

[380] For a systematic analysis of this case law, see N. de Sadeleer, 'The Precautionary Principle in EC
Health and Environmental Law' (2006) 12 *ELJ* 139–72.

[381] In order to fulfil the scientific requirements laid down in the case law, it is not necessary that a
precautionary measure refers expressly to the precautionary principle. See *Solvay v Council* (n 166), para. 124.

[382] AG Kokott in *Afton* (n 138), para. 34.

[383] Eg the Commission can depart from the scientific opinion of the European Food Safety Authority
insofar as it can justify such departure appropriately. See *Pfizer* (n 166), paras 199–200.

[384] *Mondiet* (n 173), para. 31.

[385] *Gowan* (n 356), para. 60; and *Dupont de Nemours* (n 333), para. 269. Regarding the validity of a
decision based on US studies, see Case T-368/11 *Polyelectrolyte* [2013] nyr, paras 45–8.

[386] *Pfizer* (n 166), para. 199.

institutions are required to undertake a scientific risk assessment and to evaluate highly complex scientific and technical facts.[387] As discussed later, the review must be circumscribed to (1) the compliance with the relevant procedural rules, (2) the accuracy of the statement of facts, and (3) the existence of a manifest error of appraisal or misuse of powers.[388]

Regarding health and environmental risks, the Courts have stressed that the institutions enjoy wide discretion in determining the scope of precautionary measures according to the nature, severity, and scope of the risk involved. Indeed, where the EU institutions are called upon to make 'complex assessments', they enjoy a wide margin of discretion when they adopt risk management measures.[389] As a result, the EU judiciary has shown restraint as it is not entitled to substitute its own assessment of the facts for that of the institutions on which the Treaty confers sole responsibility.[390] In this respect, when invoking the principle or the idea of precaution, the Court of Justice[391] and the General Court[392] have on various occasions in the past rejected lawsuits founded on manifest errors of appraisal committed by the institutions when taking decisions which were not fully justified in the light of prevailing scientific knowledge.

This analysis can be taken a little further. At the outset, one could take the view that the undefined principle offers no guidance about actions to take in the face of uncertainty. Therefore, one is driven to the conclusion that the precautionary principle does not determine a general level of protection; it simply makes it easier for the institutions to enact preventive measures. Hence, it may be argued that the decision to invoke the principle will depend 'as a general rule on the level of protection chosen by the competent authority'.[393] On this matter, the General Court has held that: 'it is for the [EU] institutions to determine the level of protection which they deem appropriate for society'.[394] Accordingly, it is by reference to that level of protection that the institutions may be required to take preventive measures in spite of any existing scientific uncertainty. Therefore, determining the level of risk deemed unacceptable 'involves the [EU] institutions in defining the political objectives to be pursued under the powers conferred on them by the Treaty'.[395]

---

[387] *Pfizer* (n 166), para. 169.   [388] *Gowan* (n 356), para. 56.

[389] *UK v Commission* (n 166), para. 97; *Artegodan* (n 107), para. 201; *Solvay Chemicals* (n 166), para. 126; *Gowan* (n 356), paras 55 and 82; *Afton* (n 138), para. 28; and *Polyelectrolyte* (n 385), para. 29.

[390] *Pfizer* (n 166), para. 169.

[391] See Case 174/82 *Sandoz* [1983] ECR 2445, para. 17; Case C-331/88 *Fedesa* [1990] ECR I-4023, para. 9; *UK v Commission* (n 166), paras 99 and 100; and Case C-127/95 *Norbrook Laboratories Ltd* [1998] ECR I-1531.

[392] See Case T-199/96 *Laboratoires pharmaceutiques Bergaderm SA* [1998] ECR II-2805, paras 66 and 67. In *Pfizer* (n 166) and *Alpharma* (n 341), the General Court noted that 'the legislature has a discretionary power which corresponds to the political responsibilities given to it by [Art. 40 TFEU] Article 34 of the EC Treaty and [Art. 49 TFEU]' (para. 412). The Court concluded that the adoption of the regulation in question did not constitute a manifestly inappropriate measure for the achievement of the pursued objective. See also Case T-257/07 R *France v Commission* [2007] ECR II-4153, para. 67.

[393] *Artegodan* (n 361), para. 186; *Solvay* (n 166), para. 125.

[394] *Pfizer* (n 166), para. 151; and *Dupont de Nemours* (n 333), paras 137 and 145.

[395] *Pfizer* (n 166), para. 151.

This reasoning is not devoid of legal consequences. In practice, this means that the fact that the decision-maker paid little heed to the level of protection would limit any subsequent recourse to the principle. Conversely, giving protection of health or the environment precedence over economic considerations at an early stage would enhance the principle. As this review of the implementation of the high level of protection has shown, the level set out by the lawmaker is likely to vary significantly as it can be set either in qualitative terms or in quantitative terms. This wide discretion entails the risk that at the end of the day a low level of protection could belittle recourse to the principle. That said, this discretion is far from absolute. Indeed, with respect to the enactment of precautionary environmental measures, the institutions are obliged to seek a high level of environmental protection.[396] In particular, environmental and health protection take precedence over economic interest.[397]

However, precautionary measures 'must not aim at zero risk' as this may be deemed to be disproportionate.[398] Nevertheless, nothing precludes the EU institutions from endorsing a 'zero tolerance' policy with regard to certain risk factors for which the producer cannot adduce proof that they are acceptable.[399] In particular, the concept of zero tolerance may, through the precautionary principle, result in the total ban of a substance provided that its potential risk is supported by scientific data.[400]

In any event, case law provides the most striking evidence of the role of the principle in justifying ambitious environmental measures. In this connection, the judgment in *Armand Mondiet* provides a good illustration of the role that the precautionary principle can play in justifying secondary legislation enacted in the face of uncertainty. In this case, the regulation at issue aimed to protect cetaceans taken accidentally against a background of scientific uncertainty.[401] A shipowner challenged EC Regulation 345/92[402] forbidding the use of tangle nets of over 2.5 kilometres in length, on the ground that no scientific data justified this measure and that it did not conform to the only information available although the regulation provided that conservation measures should be drawn up 'in view of the information that was available'.[403] The Court of Justice took the view that in the exercise of its powers, the Council could not be forced

---

[396] *Gowan* (n 356), para. 71.

[397] *Solvay* (n 166), para. 125; Case T-177/02 *Malagutti* [2002] ECR II-830, para. 186; *Artegodan* (n 107), para. 186.

[398] Communication of the European Commission, no. 6.3.1, para. 18. *Pfizer* (n 166), para. 145; *Alpharma* (n 341), para. 158.

[399] Case C-121/00 *Hahn* [2002] ECR I-9193, para. 93; *Solvay* (n 166), para. 97.

[400] Taking account of the genuine risk that the intake of fluoride in food supplements will exceed the upper safe limit established for that mineral, a Member State may set the maximum amount of fluoride which may be used in the manufacture of food supplements at zero. Case C-446/08 *Solgar Vitamin's France* [2010] ECR I-03973, para. 47.

[401] Case C-405/92 *Armand Mondiet* [1993] ECR I-6133.

[402] Regulation (EEC) No. 345/92 amending for the eleventh time Regulation (EEC) No. 3094/86 laying down certain technical measures for the conservation of fishery resources (no longer in force) [1992] OJ L42/15.

[403] AG Gulmann concurred with the Commission's argument that 'it is sometimes necessary to adopt measures as a precaution'. In order to conserve tuna stocks, for which insufficient scientific data existed, total allowable catch (TAC) had been based on that principle (Opinion AG Gulmann in *Armand Mondiet* (n 401), para. 28).

to follow particular scientific opinions.[404] It therefore follows that the Council did not make any manifest error of appraisal by banning certain tangle nets despite the uncertainty involved.

Unlike waste management policy, the regulatory approach regarding the safety of chemicals is afflicted with rather cumbersome, time-consuming, and expensive scientific assessments.[405] In fact, chemicals policies are designed with a general preference for a certainty-seeking regulatory style in which formal, science-based, and standardized risk assessment has been singled out as the predominant tool for decision-making relating to chemicals. Although chemicals assessment procedures have called for absolute certainty, data are nonetheless incomplete and results may be unclear or contradictory. As it is difficult to establish causal links between exposure to chemicals and health or environmental effects, there is generally a significant degree of uncertainty in estimates of the probability and magnitude of effects associated with a chemical agent. As the result of limited knowledge, experts are not always able to provide conclusive evidence of a threat to human health and the environment. It follows that the precautionary principle has been at the core of the negotiations of the REACH Regulation and Regulation (EC) No. 1107/2009 concerning the placing of plant protection products, both of which proclaim the precautionary principle.[406] Besides, both the General Court and the Court of Justice have endorsed a closer look at the Commission's attempts to relax somewhat the level of safety requirements in the area of active substances found in plant protection products and chemicals.

Against that backdrop, the principle can shed new light on the duty to place on the market only products not endangering human health. In this respect, the *Paraquat* judgment handed down by the General Court on 11 July 2007 is a case in point. Paraquat is an active substance used in plant protection products. Such active substances can be listed under Annex I to former Directive 91/414[407] on plant protection products inasmuch as the use of the products, 'in the light of current scientific and technical knowledge', will not have any harmful effects on animal health. Adjudicating an action for annulment lodged by Sweden against a European Commission decision listing Paraquat under Annex I to Directive 91/414/EC in spite of the hazards entailed by the use of the active substance, the General Court stressed that the safety requirement had to be interpreted 'in combination with the precautionary principle'. It follows that 'in the domain of human health, the existence of solid evidence which, while not resolving scientific uncertainty, may reasonably raise doubts as to the safety of a

---

[404] *Armand Mondiet* (n 401), paras 31–6.

[405] C. F. Cranor, *Toxic Torts. Science, Law, and The Possibility of Justice* (Cambridge: CUP, 2010) 9–13.

[406] REACH Regulation, Art. 1 and European Parliament and Council Regulation (EC) No. 1107/2009 concerning the placing of plant protection products on the market and repealing Council Directives 79/117/EEC and 91/414/EEC [2009] OJ L309/1, Art. 1(4). In addition, the EU is party to the Stockholm Convention on Persistent Organic Pollutants (POPs) that lays down the precautionary approach as its main objective (preamble, eighth recital; and Arts 4 and 8(7)) (Stockholm, 22 May 2001) and to the London International Maritime Organization (IMO) Convention on the Control of Harmful Anti-Fouling Systems on Ships, which establishes a precautionary mechanism to prevent the potential future use of other harmful substances in anti-fouling systems (Art. 6(3) and (5); preamble, fifth recital) (London, 5 October 2001).

[407] Directive 91/414/EEC concerning the placing of plant protection products on the market [1991] OJ L230/1. This directive has been replaced by Regulation (EC) No. 1107/2009.

substance, justifies, in principle, the refusal to include that substance in Annex I to Directive 91/414'.[408]

Another recent case raises some of the same issues, but in the context of an entirely different procedure. The European Parliament and Denmark sought review before the Court of Justice of a general exemption granted by the European Commission for the use of a hazardous chemical substance, deca-BDE, used as a flame retardant in electrical and electronic equipment. The applicants argued that the conditions laid down by the Community legislature in Article 5(1) of Directive 2002/95 of 27 January 2003 on the restriction of the use of certain hazardous substances in electrical and electronic equipment had not been met. They claimed that the decision at stake ran counter to the objective pursued by that legislature of establishing the principle of the prohibition of the components referred to in that directive. In analysing the preamble, the Court reached the conclusion that the intention of the legislature was to prohibit hazardous products referred to in the directive and to grant exemptions 'only in accordance with carefully defined conditions'.[409] The Court expressed the view in *obiter dictum* that:

> Such an objective, in compliance with [Article 168 TFEU], according to which a high level of human health protection is to be ensured in the definition and implementation of all Community policies and activities, and in compliance with [Article 192(2) TFEU], according to which EU policy on the environment is to aim at a high level of protection and is based on the principles of precaution and preventive action justifies the strict interpretation of the conditions for exemption.[410]

In this second judgment, the precautionary principle was not applied by the Court of Justice as a ground for annulment, but as an interpretative principle supporting a strict interpretation of the basic safety requirements laid down by the EU lawmaker.

Finally, these two judgments have thrown into relief the willingness of both the General Court and the Court of Justice to investigate in detail the scientific evidence underlying contested decisions. Therefore, these judgments are markedly at odds with previous case law according to which judicial review of scientific evidence has to be limited.[411]

7.6.5.4 Justification of restrictions on economic freedoms

The precautionary principle can lower the scientific hurdles national regulators face while trying to protect environmental values to the detriment of certain economic freedoms, such as the free movement of goods. Against this background, bans,[412] safeguard clauses,[413] pre-market system,[414] restrictions on marketing licences,[415] and

---

[408] Case T-229/04 *Sweden v Commission* [2007] ECR I-2437, paras 161 and 224.
[409] *Sweden v Commission* (n 408), para. 170.
[410] Cases C-14/06 and C-295/06 *European Parliament v Commission* [2008] ECR I-1649, paras 74–5.
[411] Zander (n 195), 115.
[412] The time limit placed on the marketing of a substance does not amount to a ban on account that nothing precludes the renewal of the authorization. See *Gowan* (n 356), para. 84.
[413] *Monsanto Agricoltura Italia* (n 162), para. 106.   [414] *Gowan* (n 356), para. 74.
[415] There is no inconsistency between the grant of a temporary authorization and the simultaneous pursuit of the same authorization. See *Solvay* (n 166), para. 108.

registration of chemicals,[416] can be seen as expressing the principle. What is more, recourse to the principle does not necessarily imply urgency.[417] The manner in which precaution is likely to justify these limitations on economic freedoms can be illustrated by the following cases.

The *Toolex* judgment provides striking evidence of the use of the precautionary principle in the resolution of a conflict between undertakings and a Member State, which departed from EU harmonized standards.[418] Interestingly, the case does not refer to the principle specifically, but does apply the anticipative approach in the face of the uncertainty behind the principle. The *Toolex* case arose from a challenge to the Swedish decision to ban the chemical substance trichloroethylene, which had been classified as a category 3 carcinogen under Directive 67/548/EEC[419] on the classification of dangerous substances.[420] Although the Swedish ban was tantamount to a measure having effect equivalent to a quantitative restriction within the meaning of Article 34 TFEU,[421] the Court of Justice took the view that it was compatible with the Treaty insofar as it was necessary for the effective protection of the health and life of human beings despite scientific uncertainties surrounding the effects of exposure to the chemical.[422] In other words, the lingering uncertainties regarding the impact of this hazardous substance used in industry did not preclude the Swedish authorities from regulating it, and, as a result, from restricting the free movement of goods in that country; although that substance could be freely traded within the EU.

Another case in point is *Bluhme*, where the Court of Justice ruled that a Danish wildlife measure prohibiting the import of any species of bee other than the endemic population *Apis mellifera mellifera* into a Baltic island was justified under Article 36 TFEU, notwithstanding the lack of conclusive evidence establishing both the exact nature as a matter of taxonomy of the endemic population and its risk of extinction.[423]

A final illustrative example is that of listing wild animals that can be traded. According to Court of Justice case law, an application to include a species of mammal on a national 'positive' list of protected species that cannot be subject to trading may be refused by the competent national authorities only if the holding of specimens of that species poses a genuine risk to the protection of the environment or other imperative requirements such as animal welfare.[424] This requirement appears necessary to comply with the free movement of goods. An application to have a species included on the list of species of mammals that may be held or traded may be refused by the competent authorities only on the basis of a full assessment of the risk posed to the environment. Nevertheless, the precautionary principle leaves the Member States some room for manoeuvre in order to cope with uncertain scientific issues, such as how to determine

---

[416] *SPCM and others* (n 249), para. 54. [417] *Solvay* (n 166), para. 135.
[418] Case C-473/98 *Toolex* [2000] ECR I-5681. [419] [1967] OJ 196/1.
[420] Several scientists contended that classification owing to the hazards entailed from use of the substance in question. Given that the EC committee was unable to reach agreement on an evaluation of that substance (Opinion AG Mischo in *Toolex* (n 418), para. 63), the Swedish Government decided to ban the substance on the ground that its use endangered workers' health and, consequently, endorsed a more stringent approach than the one contemplated at the EU level.
[421] See Chapter 6, Section 3.2.2. [422] See *Toolex* (n 418), para. 47.
[423] Case C-67/97 *Bluhme* [1998] ECR I-8033.
[424] As regards the technique of positive list, see Chapter 5, Section 7.3.

the negative impact of trading a mammal species on the conservation of their wild population. In that regard, the Court of Justice has taken the view that: 'Where it proves impossible to determine with certainty the existence or extent of the risk envisaged because of the insufficiency, inconclusiveness or imprecision of the results of the studies conducted, but the likelihood of real harm to human or animal health or to the environment persists should the risk materialise, the precautionary principle justifies the adoption of restrictive measures.'[425]

7.6.5.5 Member States are bound by a purposive interpretation of their environmental obligations

Pursuant to Article 258 TFEU, the European Commission regularly brings Member States before the Court of Justice for failure to implement EU directives and regulations aimed at protecting the environment. In addition, pursuant to Article 267 TFEU, national courts refer questions to the Court for preliminary rulings as to the validity and the scope of EU environmental directives and regulations. In these cases, the Court is confronted with competing interpretations. Whether the action is for infringement of EU law or whether it is a request for preliminary ruling, the defendant Member States usually support a somewhat narrow interpretation of EU environmental obligations, whereas national NGOs and the European Commission lean towards a purposive interpretation of the obligations at stake.

The following cases illustrate the manner in which the principle buttresses a purposive interpretation of the obligations placed on State authorities.

(i) GMOs

In *Greenpeace*, a case concerning marketing approval for genetically modified maize, the Court of Justice held that the principle of precaution implies that the former EC Directive 90/220/EEC relating to the placing on the market of GMOs should be interpreted in such way that gives full weight to environmental protection requirements.[426] Although the precautionary principle was not supposed to affect the interpretation of the directive's requirements regarding the obligation on the national authorities to give their consent to GM products already authorized by the Commission, the Court held that:

> the system of protection put in place by Directive 90/220/EEC, ..., necessarily implies that the Member State concerned cannot be obliged to give its consent if in the meantime it has new information which leads it to consider that the product for which notification has been received may constitute a risk to human health and the environment.[427]

In English, the mood, verb tense, and construction of the obligation laid down in the directive to grant consent all constituted an a priori invitation to the Court to recognize that the French State was bound (*compétence liée*) by the decision of the European

---

[425] Case C-219/07 *Nationale Raad van Dierenkwekers en Liefhebbers VZW* [2008] ECR I-4475, para. 38.
[426] *Greenpeace France* (n 193).   [427] *Greenpeace France* (n 193), para. 45.

Commission to allow commercialization of genetically modified maize.[428] Nevertheless, the precautionary principle allowed the Court of Justice to reach a far more nuanced solution, by recognizing the right of a Member State to oppose the placing on the market of GMOs on the ground of the emergence of new risks. In this decision, the precautionary principle took the form of an interpretative principle of law, which served to correct the effect of a provision the meaning of which could nevertheless be directly established. In other words, the principle of precaution appears capable of modifying the meaning of even a relatively clear text in favour of greater environmental protection in the face of uncertainty.[429]

(ii) Waste

A further example is the differentiation between waste and product, which has been the subject of much heated academic debate as well as litigation in EU law.[430] Pursuant to Article 192(2) TFEU, EU environmental policy aims at a high level of protection and must be based, in particular, on the precautionary principle and the principle that preventive action should be taken.[431] It follows that the concept of waste cannot be interpreted restrictively. In a similar fashion, the Court, in *Lirussi and Bizzaro*, used both the preventive and precautionary principles as interpretative devices in determining the scope of the obligations regarding the legal regime applicable to temporarily stored waste.[432]

(iii) Biodiversity

As far as biodiversity is concerned, attempts to conserve habitats and their species must grapple with a wide range of uncertainty as well as ignorance.[433] The difficulties are compounded by the lack of sufficient data as well as the fact that modelling the functioning of ecosystems and understanding the complex relationship between human activities and the state of preservation of ecosystems and species remain complex.[434] Indeed, there are still major gaps in the understanding of how ecosystems

---

[428] *Greenpeace France* (n 193), paras 28–30.

[429] Account must be taken of the fact that *Codacons* is markedly at odds with the *Greenpeace* judgment. In a preliminary reference, the ECJ took the view that the exception from the Regulation's labelling requirements in the case of foodstuffs where the concentration of GM food was less than 1 per cent had to be applied strictly as regards infant food. In particular, the Court stressed that there was no indication from the wording, the context, or the purpose of the exception regime that labelling requirements should apply to infant food. Moreover, this interpretation could not be called into question 'on the basis of the precautionary principle' that was found to be applicable exclusively as part of the decision-making process. See Case C-132/03 *Codacons* [2005] ECR I-4167, paras 56–64.

[430] G. Van Calster, *Handbook of EU Waste Law* (Richmond: Richmond Law & Tax, 2006) 9–32; N. de Sadeleer, 'Waste, Products and By-Products' (2005) 1:4 *JEEPL* 46; N. de Sadeleer, 'EC Waste Law or How to Juggle with Legal Concepts. Drawing the Line between Waste, Residues, Secondary Materials, By-Products, Disposal and Recovery Operations' (2005) 2:6 *JEEPL* 46.

[431] Cases C-418/97 & C-419/97 *ARCO Chemie Nederland* [2000] ECR I-4475, para. 39; Case C-9/00 *Palin Granit Oy* [2002] ECR I-3533, para. 23; Case C-1/03 *Paul Van de Walle* [2004] ECR I-7613, para. 45; and see N. de Sadeleer, 'Note under Case C-1/03' (2006) 43:1 *CML Rev* 207–23.

[432] Joined Cases C-175/98 & C-177/98 *Lirussi and Bizzaro* [1999] ECR I-6881.

[433] R. Cooney and B. Dickson (eds), *Biodiversity & the Precautionary Principle* (London: Earthscan, 2005).

[434] P. Opdam, M. Broekmeyer, and F. Kistenkas, 'Identifying Uncertainties in Judging the Significance of Human Impact on Natura 2000 Sites' (2009) 12 *Env Science & Policy* 912–21.

and species interact and react against new threats. In some cases, uncertainties cannot be reduced by gathering more accurate data; that is to say, uncertainty is intractable. Accordingly, in adjudicating a number of nature protection cases, the Court of Justice endeavoured to find a precautionary approach. In so doing, the Court implicitly took into consideration the precautionary obligation flowing from the Convention on Biological Diversity, a mixed international agreement.[435]

Another illustrative example is a judgment concerning wild birds. In *Association pour la protection des animaux sauvages et préfet de Maine-et-Loire et préfet de La Loire-Atlantique*, the Court of Justice favoured a determination of the close of the hunting season in a manner that guaranteed the optimal level of protection for avifauna.[436] It judged that in the absence of 'scientific and technical data relevant to each individual case'—that is, in cases of uncertainty—Member States should adopt a single date for closing the season, equivalent to 'that fixed for the species which is the earliest to migrate' and not 'the maximum period of migratory activity'. This means that as long as a degree of uncertainty remains concerning the timing of pre-mating migration of migratory birds, the strictest method of determining the close of the hunting season should override methods attempting to accommodate hunting interests on the basis of scientific approximation.

By ruling against Spain in *Marismas de Santoña* for not having protected wetlands of importance for certain species of migratory birds, in conformity with the Wild Birds Directive,[437] the Court of Justice again adopted a precautionary approach. As no reduction in the number of protected birds had been observed, the Spanish authorities disputed that the destruction of a valuable ornithological site violated the requirements of the Directive. Their argument was rejected on the ground that the obligation to preserve the natural habitats in question applied whether or not the population of protected birds was decreasing in those areas.[438] In so ruling, the Court of Justice considered the context of uncertainty resulting from the fact that destruction of a natural habitat does not necessarily translate into an immediate decline in its animal populations:

> The obligations on Member States ... exist before any reduction is observed in the number of birds or any risk of a protected species becoming extinct has materialised.[439]

Also, in a landmark decision the Court of Justice assessed the validity of Dutch environmental impact assessment regulation on fishing activities taking place within

---

[435] The Preamble to the UN Convention on Biological Diversity (CBD, Rio de Janeiro, 5 June 1992) provides that 'where there is a threat of significant reduction or loss of biological diversity, lack of full scientific certainty should not be used as a reason for postponing measures to avoid or minimize such a threat'. Although this statement is not binding on the ground that it is encapsulated in the preamble to the agreement and not its operative provisions, it is not, however, devoid of legal effects. See Case C-67/97 *Bluhme* [1998] ECR I-8033, paras 36 and 38.

[436] Case C-435/93 *Association pour la protection des animaux sauvages et préfet de Maine-et-Loire et préfet de La Loire-Atlantique* [1994] ECR I-67, para. 21.

[437] Directive 79/409/EEC codified by Directive 2009/147/EC on the conservation of wild birds [2009] OJ L20/7.

[438] Case C-355/90 *Commission v Spain* [1993] ECR I-6159, para. 28.

[439] *Commission v Spain* (n 438), para. 54.

special protection areas for birds in the sea of Wadden. In order for the project to be authorized, Article 6(3) of the Habitats Directive[440] provides for a specific environmental impact assessment procedure of plans or projects 'likely' to affect a conservation site.[441] According to the Court, since the impact study regime covers plans and projects 'likely' to affect a site, the wording of the provision implies that the conductor of the study must be able to identify, according to the precautionary principle, even that damage that is still uncertain.[442] In addition, the Habitats Directive's authorization regime requires that the competent authority ensures that the project at stake will not adversely affect the integrity of the site concerned. As a result, the authorization can only be given when the assessment demonstrates the absence of risk for the integrity of the site. 'Where doubt remains as to the absence of adverse effect on the integrity of the site', the Directive requires, in line with the precautionary principle, the competent authority to refrain from issuing the authorization.[443] Although it is likely to restrict economic and property rights, this authorization criterion 'integrates the precautionary principle'.[444] Conversely, a less stringent criterion would not be as effective in ensuring the fulfilment of the conservation objectives set forth by the EU lawmaker.[445] In accordance with the logic of the precautionary principle, authorities can, if necessary, order additional investigations to remove any uncertainty.[446] Of course, one should note that the strict interpretation endorsed by the Court of Justice is a consequence of the manner in which the authorization regime of projects endangering threatened habitats has been formulated by the EU lawmaker.

(iv) Concluding remarks

Clearly, in all these cases the Court resorted to the precautionary principle as an interpretative aid; hence, this case law mirrors a trend in purposive reasoning.[447] Moreover, the ways in which the principle is interpreted by the EU Courts may result in the imposition of far-reaching obligations on the national authorities.[448]

8. Criteria of the EU Environmental Policy

Pursuant to Article 192(3) TFEU, EU institutions must take several criteria into account when drafting an environmental measure based on Article 192 TFEU:

– available scientific and technical data,
– environmental conditions in the various regions of the Union,

---

[440] Directive 92/43/EC on the conservation of natural habitats and of wild fauna and flora [1992] OJ L206/7.

[441] For a description of this procedure, see N. de Sadeleer, 'Habitats Conservation in EC Law: From Nature Sanctuaries to Ecological Networks' (2005) 5 *YbEEL* 215.

[442] Case C-127/02 *Waddenzee* [2004] ECR I-7405, para. 44.   [443] *Waddenzee* (n 442), para. 57.

[444] *Waddenzee* (n 442), para. 58.   [445] *Waddenzee* (n 442).

[446] Opinion AG Kokott in *Waddenzee* (n 442), paras 99–111.

[447] Doherty (n 180), 76; Scotford (n 368), 23.

[448] Scott (n 328), 55. It should be noted, however, that recourse to the environmental principles will not inevitably imply the most far-reaching interpretation. In *Dusseldorp*, the Court found that the principles of self-sufficiency and proximity did not apply in relation to waste for recovery as opposed to waste for disposal. See Case C-203/96 *Dusseldorp* [1998] ECR I-4075, para. 50.

- the potential benefits and costs of action or lack of action,
- the economic and social development of the Union as a whole and the balanced development of its regions.

These requirements deserve further analysis. First, account must be taken of the available scientific data.[449] The requirement to take scientific data into account must be understood in dynamic terms, since it is necessary to follow the constant development in scientific and technical data. This obligation applies in particular to the procedure governed by Article 114(5) and (6) TFEU.[450]

As a matter of course, it is a truism to assert that science underpins the development of environmental policy.[451] However, the key role of scientific experts gives rise to controversy. Whereas experts have scientific legitimacy, they have neither democratic legitimacy nor political responsibilities.[452] Moreover, should scientific evidence be the decisive criterion in setting up standards? Or should that evidence be weighed against economic, ethical, and social considerations?[453] At first glance, no easy answers can be given. It is to be noted that although the EU must take into account 'available scientific data', it is not however obliged, in accordance with the precautionary principle, to obtain compelling evidence regarding the emergence of the environmental risks which it intends to combat before being able to take action.[454] The case law on the procedures for authorization to place plant protection products on the market provides the most striking evidence of the fact that science alone is not sufficient in the risk management process. Having regard to the complex scientific assessments that the Commission must make when it is called on to assess the risks posed by the use of active substances pursuant to Directive 91/414, the Commission must be allowed a wide discretion. Nonetheless, the exercise of that discretion is not excluded from review by the Court. The EU Courts must verify whether that institution has examined, carefully and impartially, all relevant facts of the individual case, facts which support the conclusions reached.[455] Nonetheless, the institutions may disregard the conclusion drawn from the official scientific body of opinion provided they can appropriately justify such a departure.

Second, the requirement that regional environmental conditions must be taken into consideration is a reminder that the environment in the EU is marked by its diversity. Indeed, environmental conditions as well as pressures on the ecosystems vary

---

[449] Similarly, the Technical Barriers to Trade (TBT) Agreement requires that members shall ensure that the risks countered by their technical regulations are assessed in the light of 'available scientific and technical information'.

[450] Case C-405/07 P *Commission v Netherlands* [2008] ECR I-8301, para. 61; *Afton* (n 138), para. 49. See the discussion in Chapter 7, Section 4.

[451] Experts conducting EIA on the impacts of projects on Natura 2000 sites must show a high level of competence with respect to nature conservation issues. See Case C-127/02 *Waddenzee* [2004] ECR I-7405, para. 54.

[452] *Pfizer* (n 166), para. 201.

[453] F. Francioni and M. Montini, 'Integration Scientific Evidence in Environmental Law: the International Dimension' in A. Biondi et al. (eds), *Scientific Evidence in the European Environmental Rule-Making* (The Hague: Kluwer Law, 2003) 17.

[454] See the discussion in Section 7.6.

[455] See, inter alia, Case C-269/90 *Technische Universität München* [1991] ECR 1-5469, para. 14; and *Gowan* (n 356), paras 56–7.

tremendously between rural and urban areas, between Northern and Southern Europe, between rich and poor Member States, between low-lying and mountainous countries, and between inland and coastal regions.[456] By way of illustration, thanks to its short and fast-flowing rivers and the adjacent seas and oceans, the UK is endowed with a significant natural advantage compared to other continental Member States. Accordingly, classical pollution problems from industries located along estuaries or the coast are less likely to arise than in the Benelux countries, for instance. Even the consequences of climate change are expected to vary considerably across the EU.[457] However, one should be wary of an approach favouring differentiation of standards to the detriment of uniform standards which are 'easier to formulate and cheaper to administer and to enforce'.[458]

Third, the framers of EU environmental legislation are also required to weigh up the costs and benefits which may result from action or inaction, a requirement which consists in an expression of the proportionality principle.[459] Rising concerns in the 1990s of the impact of EU environmental measures on the competitiveness of national undertakings explain to some extent why this cost–benefit analysis came to the fore. Although this requirement is peculiar in Treaty law to environmental policy, the Commission has combined in one single evaluation the impact assessments relating inter alia to social, economic, and environmental aspects for 'major items of draft legislation'.[460] That said, one should be aware that the assessment of the costs incurred by environmental regulations remains a tall order: their outcomes are significantly influenced by the methods applied and the assumptions made. As a result, there are significant differences between *ex ante* and *ex post* estimates of these costs, the former usually being overestimated.[461] That said, EU institutions are left with a large degree of

---

[456] Eg in the calculation of external-cost charges under the Eurovignette Directive Member States are allowed to multiply the values by a factor of up to two in mountain areas. See Annex IIIb.

[457] WHO, JRC, EEA, *Impact of Europe's Changing Climate-2008 Indicator-Based Assessment* (EEA Report, 4/2008); EEA, *The European Environment. State and Outlook 2010* (n 155), 38.

[458] J. Scott, *EU Environmental Law* (London: Longman, 2001), 37.

[459] As far as a cost–benefit analysis is concerned, the General Court considered in *Pfizer* that such an instrument was a particular expression of the principle of proportionality in cases involving risk management. *Pfizer* (n 166), para. 468.

[460] The institutions have made a certain number of commitments as to the *assessment of the impact* of their legislative and policy initiatives. See Commission communication on the Action Plan Simplifying and improving the regulatory environment, COM(2002) 278 final, 7; Commission communication on Implementing the Community Lisbon Programme: A strategy for the simplification of the regulatory environment, COM(2005) 535 final, 10. In accordance with para. 27 of the Interinstitutional Agreement on Better Law-Making ([2003] OJ C381/1), the Commission has to 'take due account in its legislative proposals of their financial or administrative implications, for the Union and the Member States in particular'. Lately, the Commission communication on Smart Regulation in the European Union (COM(2010) 543) makes the commitment that evaluation will become standard practice for legislations subject to modification. This communication suggests that the European Parliament and the Council should, as co-legislators, systematically discuss Commission impact assessments.

[461] P. Ekins and M. MacLeod, 'Conclusions and Recommendations' in M. MacLeod et al. (eds), *Understanding the Costs of Environmental Regulation in Europe* (Cheltenham: Edward Elgar, 2009) 230. Moreover, cost–benefit analysis has been subject to lively criticism in American academic writing to the extent that it is likely to ignore so-called 'incommensurables', ie values which cannot be expressed in financial terms. In fact, while it is possible to calculate with precision the financial losses which result from the application of a precautionary measure, the financial benefits for the protection of human health flowing from the application of the precautionary measure are more difficult to evaluate. What price is to be

discretion relating to the means of assessing the economic costs entailed by the implementation of proposed regulatory measures. In this respect, it should be pointed out that the different commitments of the EU institutions offer substantial leeway. Moreover, according to case law, the requirements linked to the protection of human health should undoubtedly be given greater weight than economic considerations.[462]

Fourth, the effectiveness of an environmental protection measure depends not only on the diversity of regional situations but also on the special economic and social nature of certain regions, which leaves scope for some adjustments in the form of temporary exceptions in accordance with Article 192(5) TFEU. Consequently, taking into account economic and social facts may also result in the adoption of specific financial support mechanisms for particular regions.

To sum up, these four requirements are framed in broad terms and, as a matter of practice, they play a subordinate role.[463] Whilst it is obliged within the ambit of its environmental policy to achieve a high level of protection and to apply the various environmental Treaty principles, the EU need only 'take into account' these four criteria.[464] Therefore, the fact that it does not take into account one or more of the criteria does not constitute a sufficient basis for the annulment of the act.

9. Conclusions

It was the aim of this chapter to lay particular emphasis on the real teeth of the objectives and the principles laid down under Article 192(1) and (2) TFEU.

First, the objectives of environmental policy set out in Article 191(1) TFEU have proved to be particularly far-reaching, especially when compared with those of transport policy. They play a key role in justifying Article 192 TFEU as the legal basis for a host of environmental measures. Moreover, the objectives may also be regarded as a way of guiding the Court of Justice in interpreting the provisions of a directive or a regulation if it has been requested to provide an answer to a reference for a preliminary ruling.

Second, the five principles enshrined in Article 191(2) TFEU have a guiding-oriented role not only a theoretical or political one. On the one hand, they enrich the formulation and implementation of environmental law. They can be invoked by the EU institutions as a justification for adopting stringent regulatory regimes. Conversely, they can also be used by the Member States to derogate from the free movement of

---

put on human life? See F. Ackerman and L. Heinzerling, *Priceless* (New York/London: The New Press, 2004); C. R. Sunstein, *Risk and Reasons* (Cambridge: CUP, 2002).

[462] Case C-183/95 *Affish* [1997] ECR I-4315, para. 43; *Alpharma* (n 341), para. 356; and *Artegodan* (n 107), para. 173. In its communication on the precautionary principle, the Commission acknowledges that protection of health and the environment should be put before economic concerns.

[463] L. Krämer, *EC Environmental Law* (n 180), 29.

[464] In much the same vein, Art. 39(2) TFEU lists the criteria which must be taken into account in the CAP. Thus, CAP obligations have to be read in the light of these criteria. *Milk Marque Ltd and NFU* (n 145), paras 98–9. Similarly, Art. 94 TFEU that requires that 'any measures taken within the framework of the Treaties in respect of transport rates and conditions shall take account of the economic circumstances of carriers' has not been subject to a strict interpretation. See Joined Case C-184/02 & C-223/02 *Spain and Finland v Parliament and Council* [2004] ECR I-7789, para. 56.

goods. On the other hand, by more clearly defining the limits within which public administrations exercise their discretionary powers, they provide them with a more coherent orientation and consequently legitimize their actions. Lastly, by freeing courts from the constraints of an overly literal interpretation of texts, they have also an interpretative function. Accordingly, they may play a determinative role by helping courts to understand the specific value of environmental protection measures. All in all, given their mixed policy and legal nature, these principles play a dual role of influencing legal outcomes while preserving policy discretion and thus shifting away from the classical 'rule/principle' divide adopted in the literature on legal theory.[465]

In sharp contrast, the four requirements set out in Article 191(3) TFEU play an ancillary role.

This points to the conclusion that the objectives and the principles play a key role in carving out an environmental general interest. In effect, restrictions brought to basic rights, such as property or economic activities, with a view to protecting the environment can be justified provided, on the one hand, that those restrictions correspond to objectives of general interest and, on the other hand, that they do not constitute an intolerable interference impairing the very substance of the rights guaranteed. With respect to the first condition—restrictions corresponding to objectives of general interest—it is sufficient to observe that the conservation of biodiversity,[466] waste management,[467] water protection,[468] and prevention of climate change[469] have been recognized by the Court of Justice as pursuing an objective of general interest restricting basic rights. As regards the second condition—restrictions do not constitute an intolerable interference impairing the very substance of the rights guaranteed—the preventive and precautionary principles enable the judiciary to endorse a broad interpretation of an array of environmental obligations ranging from waste management to wildlife conservation. As a result, measures impairing fundamental freedoms might be justified in the light of these principles.

---

[465] Scotford (n 368), 1–47.
[466] Case C-67/97 *Bluhme* [1998] ECR I-8053, para. 33.
[467] Case C-302/86 *Commission v Denmark* [1988] ECR I-4607, para. 9.
[468] Case C-293/97 *Standley* [1999] ECR I-2603, para. 54.
[469] Case C-379/98 *Preussen Elektra* [2001] ECR I-2099, para. 54.

2

The Right to Environmental Protection in Treaty Law, in the ECHR, and in the EUCFR

1. Introduction

Until the Treaty of Lisbon entered into force in December 2009, Treaty law did not contain a list of fundamental rights, let alone a right regarding the environment. The EU legal order, which was initially characterized largely by its economic objective, was constructed around a series of fundamental freedoms—freedom of movement of goods, services, persons, and capital; and freedom of competition—that may conflict with fundamental rights such as the freedom of expression[1] or the right to judicial protection. Consequently, the market integration rationale has dominated the 'genetic code' of ancillary policies, such as social, consumer, and environmental policies.[2] The absence of the recognition of a genuine environmental right has had important effects. In contrast to undertakings that may rely on the economic 'fundamental principles'[3] enshrined in the TFEU before their national courts, individuals are not in a position to invoke the provisions of Treaty law that are dedicated to the protection of the environment.

Although human rights and environmental law have historically developed in parallel, they now intersect with increasing frequency. As Judge Weeramantry stressed: 'The protection of the environment is . . . a vital part of contemporary human rights doctrine, for it is [an indispensable requirement] . . . for numerous human rights such as the right to health and the right to life itself.'[4] Arguably, the quality of the human environment goes hand in hand with basic human rights.

In this regard, it is important to note three major legal developments that have taken place at the European level.

The first development, in Article 6(3) TEU, states that fundamental rights result from constitutional traditions common to Member States. In this regard, a number of Member State constitutions have been modified with a view to enshrining a constitutional right to environmental protection. That right is coined either as a State duty to preserve the environment[5] or as a substantive right to environmental protection. Among the diverse formulations used to assert such a fundamental right are: 'healthy environment',[6] 'balanced and health-friendly environment',[7] 'favourable environment',[8] or 'environment suitable for the development of the person'.[9]

---

[1] Case C-112/02 *Schmidberger* [2003] ECR I-5659.

[2] M. Poiares Maduro, 'The Double Constitutional Life of the Charter of Fundamental Rights of the EU' in T. Hervey and J. Kenner (eds), *Economic and Social Rights under the EU Charter of Fundamental Rights* (Oxford: Hart Publishing, 2003) 285.

[3] The Court of Justice has defined the TFEU free movement provisions as 'fundamental freedoms'. Case C-112/02 *Schmidberger* [2003] ECR I-5659, para. 51; Case C-320/03 *Commission v Austria* [2005] ECR I-9871, para. 63.

[4] *Gabčíkovo-Nagymaros Project (Hungary v Slovakia)* [1997] ICJ Rep. 492 (Separate Opinion of Judge Weeramantry, at para. A(b)).

[5] Under other constitutions that do not mention the existence of an individual right, the State is under a duty to adopt measures to protect the environment. See Estonian Constitution, Art. 34; Greek Constitution, Art. 24; Italian Constitution, Art. 117; Portuguese Constitution, Art. 66; Latvian Constitution, Art. 115; Lithuanian Constitution, Art. 53; Luxembourg Constitution, Art. 11bis; and Romanian Constitution, Art. 135(2)(e).

[6] Belgian Constitution, Art. 23; Bulgarian Constitution, Art. 55; Croatian Constitution, Art. 69; Hungarian Constitution, Art. 18; Slovenian Constitution, Art. 72; Dutch Constitution, Art. 21; Finnish Constitution, Sct 20.

[7] French Constitutional Charter for the Environment, Art. 1.

[8] Slovakian Constitution, Art. 44(1).   [9] Spanish Constitution, Art. 45.

Why does the recognition of an environmental right in a national constitution matter? First, proclaiming respect for the environment as a fundamental right amounts to elevating a new value to the apex of the national legal order. As a result, this value stands 'above a mere policy choice that may be modified or discarded at will'.[10] Second, such a right is not deprived of legal effects; a constitutional right will be given precedence over inferior legal and executive norms. In addition, it will justify the constitutionality of environmental rules that can no longer be trumped by other fundamental rights.

Since then, these constitutional provisions have provoked controversy, given that they do not fit neatly into a single category.[11] In view of the role that the State plays in protecting the environment, the provisions depart significantly from the 'hand-off' attitude[12] that underpins first-generation human rights (ie civil and political rights). Indeed, the provisions call for affirmative action by the State. Moreover, these environmental rights straddle the second generation (economic, social, and cultural rights) and third generation of human rights (solidarity rights).[13]

The second development is in the EUCFR that has been endowed, since December 2009 in accordance with Article 6(1) TEU, with the status of Treaty law. In addition, for two decades, the ECtHR has, to some extent, carved out environmental duties from a number of rights enshrined in the ECHR, which, in virtue of Article 6(3) TEU, constitute 'general principles of the Union's law'.

Finally, although the United Nations Economic Commission for Europe (UNECE) Convention on Access to Information, Public Participation in Decision-Making and Access to Justice in Environmental Matters—a mixed agreement that was adopted on 25 June 1998 in Aarhus (Aarhus Convention)[14]—does not explicitly state that any environmental right exists per se,[15] it nonetheless paves the way, through the use of various procedural rights, to the objective of an adequate environment for every person.[16]

In view of all these developments, the question arises as to whether individuals could rely on the implicit and explicit environmental duties embodied in these instruments in cases that fall within the scope of EU law. In other words, despite the absence of individually justiciable rights to a clean environment in the TEU and TFEU, should the European Court of Justice and the national courts consider the EUCFR, ECHR, and the Aarhus Convention obligations while adjudicating environmental cases?

---

[10] D. Shelton, 'Introduction' in D. Shelton (ed.), *Human Rights and the Environment*, vol. I (Cheltenham: Edward Elgar, 2011) x.

[11] A. Boyle, 'Human Rights or Environmental Rights? A Reassessment' (2007) *Fordham Env L Rev* 471.

[12] J. L. Sax, 'The Search for Environmental Rights' (1990) 6 *J Land Use & Env L* 94.

[13] It should be noted that Art. 37 EUCFR is included under the Chapter 'Solidarity'.

[14] Council Decision 2005/370/EC on the conclusion, on behalf of the European Community, of the Convention on access to information, public participation in decision-making and access to justice in environmental matters [2005] OJ L124/1.

[15] The preamble to the Convention proclaims that every person has the right to live in a healthy environment, a right that is connected with the obligation to protect the environment. Pursuant to Art. 1, its goal is to protect the right of every person of present and future generations to live in an environment adequate for health and well-being.

[16] O. W. Pedersen, 'European Environmental Human Rights and Environmental Rights: A Long Time Coming' (2008) 21:73 *Georgetown Int'l Env L Rev* 100.

This chapter is divided into three sections. In the absence of directly applicable rules of Treaty law concerning environmental protection, it is a matter for the EU legislature to organize the protection of individuals, where appropriate, by way of sufficiently clear and precise provisions that may be directly applicable. The second section of this chapter is dedicated to the issue of access to justice with respect to the implementation of EU environmental law. Section 3 provides an in-depth analysis of Article 37 EUCFR. The third and final section explores how the ECHR could improve the implementation of EU environmental law.

2. The Issue of Standing With Regard to the Right to Environmental Protection

2.1 Introductory note

After decades of fleshing out lofty environmental slogans into a broad range of legal instruments, the time has come to enforce these rules more effectively with a view to halting ongoing environmental degradation. The courts are among the most powerful of all the institutions involved in enforcement of this branch of law.[17] Although their core business is to resolve disputes, the courts may play a key role in developing principles and substantive standards, as discussed previously.[18] As far as EU environmental law is concerned, given the high level of decentralization, it is the myriad State authorities, including the courts, that enforce the EU protective standards, rather than the EU institutions. Moreover, it should be borne in mind that Article 4(3) TEU calls upon Member States to 'facilitate the achievement of the Union tasks and refrain from any measure which could jeopardise the attainment of the Union's objectives', and that Article 197 TFEU links the proper functioning of the EU to the effective implementation of its law at the national level.[19]

Hence, not only the Court of Justice but also 'the national courts and the tribunals of the Member States' are the guardians of the EU legal order and the judicial system of the EU.[20] It is therefore up to the national courts to ensure judicial protection of individual rights under EU law.[21] However, national procedural law has shown an amazing variety of approaches, ranging from *actio popularis* to very restrictive standing requirements, such as the impairment of an individual legally granted right.[22] As a result, standing requirements remain a major procedural hurdle that many public interest litigants are unable to overcome.

---

[17] H. McLeod-Kilmuray, 'Lowering Barriers to Judicial Enforcement' in LeRoy Paddock et al. (eds), *Compliance and Enforcement in Environmental Law* (Cheltenham: Edward Elgar, 2011) 289.

[18] See the discussion in Chapter 1, Sections 4 to 7.

[19] P. Nicolaides and M. Geilmann, 'What is Effective Implementation of EU Law?' (2012) 19:33 *MJ* 83–420 *MJ* 39–74.

[20] Opinion 1/09 [2011] OJ C211/2, para. 66.

[21] A. Rosas, 'The National Judge as EU Judge: Opinion 1/09' in P. Cardonnel, A. Rosas, and N. Wahl, *Constitutionalising the EU Judicial System. Essays in Honour of Pernilla Lindh* (Oxford: Hart Publishing, 2012) 118.

[22] German administrative law requires a 'subjective-public right' (*Subjectiv-öffentliches Recht*). See §42(2) VwGO (Code of Administrative Court Procedure).

In the following sections we discuss the extent to which the principle of effective judicial protection and the implementation of the Aarhus Convention call into question national procedural autonomy regarding standing.

2.2 Expansion of litigation rights under the Aarhus Convention

In the absence of any option to rely on a true EU constitutional right to environmental protection, individual rights may emerge in accordance with Article 52(5) EUCFR through the intermediation of EU secondary law.[23] Although EU secondary environmental law has not hitherto encapsulated a substantive right of individuals to a clean environment, several environmental directives do provide propitious breeding grounds for procedural rights.

Thus, instead of vague principles, individuals may invoke a series of procedural rights, particularly those that guarantee the implementation of the Aarhus Convention. The EU, as well as all its Member States, are parties to this mixed agreement, the provisions of which now form an integral part of the legal order of the EU.[24] In short, the Aarhus Convention requires the contracting parties to implement information, participation, and litigation rights for individuals and environmental non-governmental organizations (NGOs). Access to justice is linked to the participatory and information rights. While a complete discussion on all the procedural rights encapsulated in that international agreement and in EU secondary law is beyond the scope of this section, it is possible to give careful consideration to standing.[25]

Although the focus of this Convention is strictly procedural in content,[26] it already influences the case law of both the EU Courts and the ECtHR.[27] For instance, Articles 9(2) and 2(5) of the Convention oppose a narrow interpretation of standing before national courts.[28]

2.2.1 *Article 9(2) of the Aarhus Convention*

On the one hand, Article 9(2) provides for a right 'to challenge the substantive and procedural legality of any decision, act, or omission' relating to projects and activities listed under Article 6. The review should be open to all members of the public inasmuch as they have 'a sufficient interest' or, alternatively, 'maintain impairment of a right'. It must be noted that these conditions have to be interpreted 'consistently with the

---

[23] N. de Sadeleer, 'Enforcing EUCHR Principles and Fundamental Rights in Environmental Cases' (2012) 81 *NJIL* 39–74.

[24] See Case C-240/09 *Lesoochranárske zoskupenie* [2011] ECR I-9967, para. 30. The Court of Justice therefore has jurisdiction to issue preliminary rulings concerning the interpretation of such an agreement.

[25] Lack of space precludes discussion of the review procedure under Art. 9(1) in relation to requests for information.

[26] P. Birnie, A. Boyle, and C. Redgwell, *International Law and the Environment*, 3rd edn (Oxford: OUP, 2009) 274.

[27] M. Pallemaerts (ed.), *The Aarhus Convention at Ten; Interactions and Tensions between Conventional International Law and EU Environmental Law* (Groeningen: Europa Law, 2009).

[28] CEb, no.193593, 28 May 2009, *Vzw Milieufront Omer Wattez*.

objective of giving the public concerned wide access to justice'. Of importance is that the interest of any environmental NGO shall be deemed to have been impaired.

Against this background, significant legislative developments took place after the entry into force of the Aarhus Convention, particularly with a view to expanding access to justice before the national courts. In line with the Convention, the EU lawmaker has thus improved the standing of environmental NGOs, the key result of which has been their recognition in both the Court of Justice[29] and the ECtHR case law.[30]

In accordance with several environmental directives, individuals and NGOs may challenge before their national courts administrative decisions likely to be inconsistent with EU environmental requirements. A prime example would be Directive 2004/35/EC,[31] under which interested third parties may institute a review procedure against an administration which will not enact preventive or remedial measures against environmental damage. By the same token, the directive on freedom of access to environmental information confers a right to access 'to any applicant'.[32] This directive also holds, in its Article 6, that applicants may bring administrative or judicial proceedings against the acts or omissions of a public authority.

A further example is Article 10a of the Environmental Impact Assessment (EIA) Directive, the purpose of which is to incorporate Article 9(2) of the Aarhus Convention into EU law.[33] The article makes provision for review procedure before a court of law for the members of the public concerned, on condition that they have a 'sufficient interest' or, alternatively, that they demonstrate the 'impairment of a right'.[34] Unlike natural or legal persons, NGOs promoting environmental protection *always* have the status of 'the public concerned' provided that they comply with 'any requirements

---

[29] Directive 2003/35 which has been given effect in the EU legal order to the Aarhus Convention makes particular reference to the role of NGOs in promoting environmental protection. In AG Sharpston's view, 'the Århus Convention and Directive 85/337, as amended by Directive 2003/35, have deliberately chosen to reinforce the role of non-governmental organisations promoting environmental protection. They have done so in the belief that such organisations' involvement in both the administrative and the judicial stages not only strengthens the decisions taken by the authorities but also makes procedures designed to prevent environmental damage work better'. Opinion of AG Sharpston in Case C-263/08 *Djurgården-Lilla Värtans Miljöskyddsförening* [2009] ECR I-9967, paras 40, 61, and 64.

[30] With respect to Art. 6(1) ECHR, the ECtHR held that 'les ONG jouent un rôle important, notamment en défendant certaines causes devant les autorités ou les juridictions internes, particulièrement dans le domaine de la protection de l'environnement' (text only available in French). Case *Collectif national d'information et d'opposition à l'usine Melox—Collectif stop Melox and Mox v France*, 28 March 2006.

[31] Environmental Liability Directive [2004] OJ L143/56.

[32] European Parliament and Council Directive 2003/4/EC on public access to environmental information and repealing Council Directive 90/313/EEC [2003] OJ L41/26, Art. 3(1).

[33] With respect to EIAs, Art. 10a requires Member States to grant standing either (a) to bodies which have sufficient interest, or (b) to those which 'are maintaining the impairment of a right'.

[34] As regards standing before national courts, both Art. 9(2) of the Aarhus Convention and Art. 10 of Directive 2003/35/EC expressly leave to the parties the decision to require either 'a sufficient interest' or the demonstration of 'an impairment of a right, where administrative procedural law of a Member State requires this as a precondition'. See Art. 9(2) of the Aarhus Convention and Art. 10a of the EIA Directive (Directive 85/337, as amended by Directive 2003/35). What constitutes sufficient interest or impairment of a right shall be determined by the Member States, consistent with the objective of giving the public concerned wide access to justice. In other words, the national rules implementing the provision relating to access to justice set out in the EIA Directive are to be strictly interpreted, since the Aarhus Convention's main objective is to widen standing. Moreover, according to Art. 10(a), fith indent, those procedures must 'be fair, equitable, timely and not prohibitively expensive'.

under national law'. Consequently, NGOs acting for the protection of the environment are deemed, pursuant to Article 10(a), third intend, to 'have an automatic right of access to justice'.[35]

Although it is for the Member States to determine what amounts to an NGO promoting environmental protection,[36] the vagueness of the terms of Article 10a does not confer an unlimited discretion to the Member States. In *Djurgården-Lilla Värtans Miljöskyddsförening* the Court of Justice had to verify whether Sweden had exceeded that discretion. The Court found that this provision applies at least to 'a provision of national law which reserves the right to bring an appeal against a decision on projects which fall within the scope of that directive solely to environmental protection associations which have at least 2000 members'.[37] Accordingly, the members of the public concerned 'must be able to have access to a review procedure to challenge the decision by which a body attached to a court of law of a Member State has given a ruling on a request for development consent, regardless of the role they might have played in the examination of that request'.[38] Put differently, the criteria NGOs are required to meet must be consistent with the objective of providing the public concerned with a wide access to justice.

By the same token, Article 9 of the Aarhus Convention and Article 10a of the EIA Directive would lose all effectiveness if the mere fact that an illegal project is adopted by an illicit legislative act 'were to make it immune to any review procedure for challenging its substantive or procedural legality'.[39]

The conclusion follows that those various procedural obligations must be interpreted in the light of, and having regard to, the objectives of the Aarhus Convention.[40]

2.2.2 *Article 9(3) of the Aarhus Convention*

In addition to the Article 9(2) review procedure, Article 9(3) confers on 'members of the public' the right to administrative or judicial review of 'acts and omissions by private persons and public authorities which contravene provisions of its national law relating to the environment'. The scope of this third paragraph is much broader than that in the previous paragraph. Indeed, this enforcement review procedure is not restricted to a limited number of administrative acts related to specific activities of listed installations, but encompasses all material acts and omissions.[41]

Fewer legislative developments took place at EU level with a view to fleshing out this review procedure. Given adamant opposition from several Member States, a proposal

---

[35] Opinion AG Sharpston in Case C-263/08 *Djurgården-Lilla Värtans Miljöskyddsförening* [2009] ECR I-9967, paras 42 and 43.

[36] See R. Moules, *Environmental Judicial Review* (Oxford: Hart Publishing, 2011) 108–11.

[37] *Djurgården-Lilla Värtans Miljöskyddsförening* (n 35), para. 52.

[38] *Djurgården-Lilla Värtans Miljöskyddsförening* (n 35), para. 39.

[39] Cases C-128–131/09, C-134/09 & C-135/09 *Boxus* [2011] OJ C362/2, para. 53.

[40] Case C-115/09 *Trianel Kohlekraftwerk Lünen* [2011] OJ C141/26, para. 41. Regarding the interpretation of the scope of protection of the confidentiality of public proceedings in the light of Art. 4(4) of the Aarhus Convention, see Case C-204/09 *Flachglas Torgau* [2012] OJ C98/2, para. 61.

[41] L. Lavrysen, 'The Right to the Protection of a Healthy Environment' at the World Congress on Justice, Governance and Law for Environmental Sustainability (Rio de Janeiro, 2012) 28.

for a directive on access to justice in environmental matters[42] has never seen the light of day. Regulation (EC) No. 1367/2006 of the European Parliament and of the Council of 6 September 2006 on the application of the provisions of the Aarhus Convention on Access to Information, Public Participation in Decision-Making and Access to Justice in Environmental Matters to Community institutions and bodies (Aarhus Regulation) establishes a two-stage right of access to justice: first, an application for an internal review of administrative acts by the NGO and, second, the possibility for the latter to apply to the Court of Justice.[43]

The fact that Article 9(3) has not yet been incorporated into EU law[44] is compounded by its absence of direct effect. To conclude, a general right to standing for the purpose of enforcing environmental law is still absent. Nonetheless, the national courts are called on to interpret, to the fullest extent possible, the procedural rules relating to the conditions to be met in order to bring administrative or judicial proceedings in accordance with the objectives of that provision and the objective of effective judicial protection of the rights conferred by EU law, so as to enable an environmental protection organization to challenge before the national courts a decision liable to be contrary to EU environmental law.[45]

2.3 Standing of individuals and environmental NGOs in national courts

Should enforcement of environmental law be left entirely in the hands of national authorities? The answer to that question is clearly negative. Given that environmental law suffers from a lack of enforcement, suits lodged by citizens dissatisfied with inaction by national agencies are of utmost importance for the following reasons. The recognition of a substantive right to a clean environment would be of limited value if the beneficiaries had no possibility of invoking this right before their national courts.[46] Indeed, there is little point in granting participation rights in decision-making unless they can be enforced in the courts. Moreover, if there are no rights conferred on third parties to challenge inadequate compliance by national administrations of EU environmental law under a particular directive, 'the enforcement armoury is lessened'.[47]

---

[42] COM(2003) 624.

[43] Commission Decision 2008/50/EC laying down detailed rules for the application of European Parliament and Council Regulation (EC) No. 1367/2006 on the Aarhus Convention as regards requests for the internal review of administrative acts [2006] OJ L264/13. See P. Wennerås, *The Enforcement of EC Environmental Law* (Oxford: OUP, 2007) 216–50; J. H. Jans, 'Did Baron von Munchhausen Ever Visit Århus?' in R. Macrory (ed.), *Reflections on 30 Years of EU Environmental Law* (Groeningen: Europa Law, 2006) 477–84; M. Pallemaerts, *Compliance by the EC with its Obligations on Access to Justice as a Party to the Århus Convention* (IEEP Report, 2009) 45; A. Garcia Ureta, *Aspectos sobre el acceso a la justicia en el Convenio de Aarhus y su incidencia sobre el Derecho comunitario* (Oñati: Europar Ikerten Taldea, 2005) 63–88; N. de Sadeleer and C. Poncelet, 'Protection Against Acts Harmful to Human Health and the Environment Adopted by the EU Institutions' (2012) *Cambridge Yearbook of EU Law* 177–208.

[44] *Lesoochranárske zoskupenie* (n 24).   [45] *Lesoochranárske zoskupenie* (n 24), para. 51.

[46] E. Enamorca, 'Division of Competence between Member States and the EC' in J. Jans (ed.), *The European Convention and the Future of European Environmental Law* (Groeningen: Europa Law, 2003) 30.

[47] C. Hilson, 'Community Rights in Environmental Law: Rhetoric or Reality?' in J. Holder (ed.), *The Impact of EC Environmental Law in the UK* (Chichester: Wiley & Sons, 1994) 58.

In spite of the legislative improvements resulting from the implementation of the Aarhus Convention in EU law, the Member States retain much leeway in tailoring the standing requirements in accordance with the principle of procedural autonomy.[48] In the absence of harmonization rules, procedural law remains the domain of Member States. Indeed, it is for the domestic legal system of each Member State to lay down detailed procedural rules governing actions for safeguarding the rights which individuals derive from EU law.[49] As a result, proceedings initiated by private individuals and environmental NGOs in the national courts have not met with success. Restrictions imposed on the interest to sue, the duration of court proceedings, and the financial risk to which applicants expose themselves create obstacles to the invocation of an EU law provision incorrectly transposed before the national courts.[50] To make matters worse, the interest to sue is in particular subject to the rider that the majority of EU environmental rules have less the goal of creating procedural rights than of putting in place procedures which enable the national administrations to reconcile environmental protection with economic development.[51]

The upshot of these difficulties is that the weak enforcement of EU environmental law is deemed to be one of the main weaknesses of environmental protection within the EU.[52] It should be noted that the majority of environmental directives appear as paper tigers due to hesitancy, or even bad faith, on the part of certain national authorities and the difficulties encountered by the Commission in pursuing infringements before the Court of Justice.[53]

2.4 Procedural autonomy and private enforcement

Given the number of hurdles applicants have to overcome at national level, the question arises whether the Member States' procedural autonomy as regards standing in environmental issues is likely to be undermined by the principle of effective judicial protection and *effet utile*.

To answer this question calls for a closer analysis of *Rewe/Comet* case law,[54] where the Court of Justice drew a dividing line between:

---

[48] This principle is subject to two limitations. On the one hand, in accordance with the principle of non-discrimination, the national rules applying for legal proceedings based on EU law may not be less favourable than those which apply in purely national cases. On the other, in accordance with the principle of effectiveness, the exercise of rights granted by EU law 'may not be rendered almost impossible or excessively difficult'. Case C-33/76 *Rewe v Comet* [1976] ECR 1523, para. 5; Case 45/76 *Comet* [1976] ECR 2043, para. 14; Case 68/79 *Hans Just* [1980] ECR 501, para. 25; and Case 199/82 *San Giorgio* [1983] ECR 3595, para 14.

[49] *Lesoochranárske zoskupenie* (n 44), para. 47.

[50] N. de Sadeleer, G. Roller, and M. Dross, *Access to Justice in Environmental Matters and the Role of NGOs; Empirical Findings and Legal Appraisal* (Groeningen: Europa Law, 2005) 7; J. Ebbesson (ed.), *Access to Justice in Environmental Matters in the EU* (The Hague: Kluwer Law, 2002).

[51] See the discussion in Chapter 4, Section 5.4.

[52] See the discussion in Chapter 4, Section 6.5. Brief mention should be made of the fact that the situation has worsened with the accession in 2004 and 2007 of a number of new Member States that lack sufficient resources to enforce environmental law.

[53] Wennerås (n 43), 251–308.

[54] Case C-33/76 *Rewe v Comet* [1976] ECR 1523; Case 222/84 *Johnston* [1986] ECR 1651, para. 18; Case C-432/05 *Unibet* [2007] ECR I-2271, para. 37; and Case C-279/09 *DEB* [2010] ECR I-13849, para. 29.

- on the one hand, where [EU] law confers personal or individual rights on individuals, the national courts are called upon to protect these rights in virtue of the principle of cooperation;[55] hence, these individuals can rely on their rights in national courts,

- on the other, in the absence of [EU] rules on the matter, it is 'for the domestic legal system of each Member State to designate the courts having jurisdiction and to determine the procedural rights which citizens have from the direct effect of [EU] law'.[56] It follows that anyone who has an interest in a controversy involving the application of EU law should not have standing unless national law so provides.

Therefore, one could be tempted to distinguish between environmental directives that expressly grant rights to citizens in fleshing out the Aarhus Convention's obligations and those that do not explicitly confer such rights. It is, in this context, important to stress that in spite of a few procedural directives, the majority of EU environmental regulatory measures do not confer rights on citizens.

However, as will be discussed, the principle of procedural autonomy according to the *Rewe/Comet* case law is far from absolute. Secondary law obligations have been construed by the Court of Justice either as conferring rights on individuals or as pre-empting contrary national law irrespective of the conferral of rights. Broadly speaking, the following cases reflect a shift towards emphasizing judicial remedies in the field of environmental protection.

The discussion in this section will be structured in the following manner. First, we will consider directives focusing on improvement of the quality of the environment. Second, we shall move on to directives enshrining procedural rights. Lastly, we shall address the particularities of directives aiming at nature protection.

2.4.1 *Health protection*

Do citizens of the Union enjoy a right to a clean environment in accordance with environmental quality standards[57] set out in various technical directives? The Court of Justice has accepted that, when directives oblige Member States to comply with quality standards aiming to improve the health of individuals, the latter may rely on them before their national courts. This interpretation was developed in cases concerning directives imposing the respect of air and quality values.[58] In particular, the Court of Justice took the view that 'whenever the exceeding of limit values could endanger human health, the "persons concerned" must be in a position to rely upon the EU mandatory thresholds in order to ascertain their rights'.[59] Although they are not

---

[55] Ex Art. 10 EC; new Art. 4(3) TEU.   [56] *Rewe v Comet* (n 54).   [57] Chapter 4, Section 5.5.

[58] Case 131/88 *Commission v Germany* [1991] ECR 825; Case 361/88 *Commission v Germany* [1991] ECR 2567, para. 16; Case C-58/89 *Commission v Germany* [1991] ECR I-4983, para. 14; Case C-59/89 *Commission v Germany* [1991] ECR I-2607; and Case C-237/07 *Janecek* [2008] ECR I-6221, para. 37. See S. Prechal and L. Hancher, 'Individual Environmental Rights: Conceptual Pollution in EU Environmental Law' (2002) 2 *Yb Eur Env L* 89–115.

[59] Case C-361/88 *Commission v Germany* (n 58), para. 16.

sufficiently precise and unconditional to exhibit direct effect, such directives had to be implemented in such a way that 'individuals can rely on their provisions before national courts'. Indeed, as stressed by the Court of Justice, 'where the directive is intended to create rights for individuals the persons concerned can ascertain the full extent of their rights and, where appropriate, rely on them before their national courts'.[60] Hence, these directives indirectly confer on citizens personal rights regarding their health. In other words, they have to be implemented by legislation, rather than administrative guidelines, in a manner that is sufficiently binding. Only if the directives are implemented in that way can citizens avail themselves of environmental protection rights in the national courts.

Thus, in the landmark judgment of *Janecek*, the Court of Justice underscored that the persons 'directly concerned by a risk that the limit values or alert thresholds may be exceeded' have the right to rely, before their national courts, on the obligation to ensure respect of those standards, which oblige the latter to dismiss a restrictive interpretation of the *locus standi*.[61] In particular, the Court of Justice stressed that the directive at issue was tailored to control and reduce air pollution and thus to protect 'public health'.[62]

In sum, where national authorities do not abide by EU protective obligations, individuals whose health is likely to be endangered, are entitled to rely on harmonized EU standards of an imperative nature. It thus follows that national law must guarantee effective judicial protection to persons whose health might be affected by the incorrect application of EU law.

However, the creation of such rights is likely to be an exception; in fact, with few exceptions, it is rare for environmental directives to confer rights on individuals or associations of individuals. For example, rules which provide for the communication of national reports to the European Commission do not give rise to any right.[63] In addition, account must be taken of the fact that the rights conferred by the Court in the cases commented on previously are anthropocentric in focus. It follows that only those 'whose health may be affected enjoy personal rights under these directives'.[64] Last but not least, the Court's case law has been circumvented by new legislative developments. In effect, the EU lawmaker has recently carved out quality standards in such a way that 'their enforcement by private persons and bodies become impossible'.[65]

---

[60] Case C-361/88 *Commission v Germany* (n 58), para. 15.

[61] *Janecek* (n 58), para. 39. See J. Jans, 'Harmonization of National Procedural Law via the Back Door? Preliminary Comments on the ECJ's Judgment in *Janecek* in a Comparative Context' in M. Bulterman et al. (eds), *Views of European Law from the Mountain. Liber Amicorum P. J. Slot* (Alphen: Wolters Kluwer, 2009) 273–4.

[62] The concept of 'public health' is distinct from the concept of 'human health' mentioned in Art. 191(1) TEU. See L. Krämer, note on Case C-237/07 *Janecek* (2008) 5:3–4 *JEEPL* 400–1.

[63] Case 380/87 *Enichem Base* [1989] ECR 2492, paras 23 and 24.

[64] Hilson (n 47), 56.

[65] L. Krämer, 'Environmental Justice in the European Court of Justice' in J. Ebbesson and P. Okowa (eds), *Environmental Law and Justice in Context* (Cambridge: CUP, 2009) 209.

2.4.2 *EIA*

Conferring rights on persons likely to be affected by illegal pollution due to the unwillingness of State authorities to ensure compliance with EU harmonized standards does not go far enough. Given that environmental protection is much more than impairment of health, an exclusive anthropocentric approach will not suffice to address major environmental problems such as biodiversity losses, ozone layer depletion, and climate change. Therefore, the question arises whether more favourable standing conditions are likely to flow from directives that are not restricted to human health protection. In that respect, the directive on the assessment of the effects of certain public and private projects on the environment[66] (EIA Directive) clearly confers participatory and information rights on citizens, irrespective of health issues.

Since *Kraaijeveld*, it is settled case law, on the one hand, that the national authorities are not endowed with an unfettered margin of discretion when they select projects submitted to an EIA and, on the other, that individuals may rely on the EIA obligations before their national courts. In other words, even though EIA procedures provide national authorities with some room for manoeuvre, national courts are nonetheless called upon to verify whether the authorities have exceeded the limits of their discretion. In so doing, the national courts are required to interpret national law 'as far as possible' in conformity with EU requirements. The Court of Justice's reasoning is based on the assumption that the effectiveness of such a directive 'would be diminished if individuals were prevented from relying on it in legal proceedings and if national courts were prevented from taking it into consideration as a matter of Community law in determining whether the national legislature, in exercising its choice as to the form and methods for implementing the directive, had kept within the limits of its discretion set by the directive'.[67]

Linster is a good illustration of proceedings in which the EIA Directive was relied on irrespective of the direct effect of that directive. In that case, the national court referred a question to the Court of Justice for a preliminary ruling on whether it could verify the legality of a procedure for the expropriation in the public interest of immovable property belonging to a private individual, taking into account the EIA Directive which had not yet been fully transposed despite the expiry of the time limit laid down for that purpose. In particular, the national court asked the Court of Justice whether such a finding involved an appraisal of the direct effect of the directive.

In his opinion in *Linster*, Advocate General Léger made clear that: 'In such proceeding [juridical review of national measures] which are simultaneously "vertical" and "objective" (non-personal), in which the pleas put forward by a party against a public body do not seek directly to obtain recognition of an individual right, the question of direct effect tends to be eclipsed by that of primacy'.[68] The Advocate General went on to

---

[66] European Parliament and Council Directive 2011/92/EU on the assessment of the effects of certain public and private projects on the environment [2012] OJ L26/1.

[67] Case C-72/95 *Kraaijeveld* [1996] ECR I-5403; Case C-435/97 *WWF* [1999] ECR I-5613, para. 69.

[68] Opinion AG Léger in Case C-287/98 *Linster* [2000] ECR I-6917, para. 73. Such an interpretation was endorsed in similar cases by AG Elmer in Case C-72/95 *Kraaijeveld* [1996] ECR I-5403, paras 69–72; and AG Kokott in Case C-127/02 *Waddenzee* [2004] ECR I-7405, para. 140.

stress that 'where the national court is faced with a provision which leaves Member States genuine discretion, it has the task, taking account of the objective being sought by the injured party, of verifying that the public body whose decision is being challenged has kept within the limits of the powers which it was left under the directive'.[69] The Court of Justice did not go on to assess whether the directive at issue exhibited direct effect. It held that the discretion left to the Member State did not 'preclude judicial review of the question whether it has been exceeded by the national authorities'.[70]

Accordingly, the issue of private enforcement of EU environmental law is distinct from the recognition of subjective rights. In ensuring the reviewing of the legality of national legislations that have failed to ensure compliance with EU procedural obligations, the Court of Justice focused on the effectiveness of EU law. Thus, the 'approach of exclusion' of the national rule not implementing the EU directive must prevail over the 'approach of substitution'.[71]

To sum up, the justification for allowing individuals to rely on EU procedural obligations for the purposes of challenging the legality of national decisions rests on the principle of supremacy rather than the concept of direct effect.[72] Put differently, rights are not a precondition for supremacy of EU secondary law.

In *Christopher Mellor*, the Court of Justice again held that in spite of the margin of discretion left by the EIA Directive to the Member States, the national courts are nonetheless called upon to verify whether the authorities exceeded the limits of their discretion. 'Third parties, as well as the administrative authorities concerned, must be able to satisfy themselves that the competent authority has actually determined, in accordance with the rules laid down by national law, that an EIA was or was not necessary'. Furthermore, they 'must be able to ensure, if necessary through legal action, compliance with the competent authority's screening obligation. That requirement may be met... by the possibility of bringing an action directly against the determination [of the administration] not to carry out an EIA'.[73]

It follows that the persons interested or directly concerned by the projects subject to an EIA should also be able to rely on EU obligations before their national courts. Their *locus standi* to challenge an alleged failure correctly to apply particular provisions of environmental legislation should not be dependent on showing a particular or specific link with human health.[74]

In these cases, the Court of Justice placed emphasis on an 'objective control of legality' (*un recours objectif*). In this context, one should talk about objective rights (French: *droits objectifs*; German: *Objektives Recht*) rather than subjective rights (French: *droits subjectifs*; German: *Subjectives Recht*).[75] It therefore follows that not only the individuals affected by the illegal projects but also other interested parties can

---

[69] *Linster* (n 68), para. 74.   [70] *Linster* (n 68), para. 37.
[71] J.-V. Louis and T. Ronse, *L'ordre juridique européen* (Brussels: Helbing & Lichtenhahn/Bruylant/ LGDJ, 2005) 303–4. The line between the 'objective of exclusion' and the 'objective of substitution' is far from theoretical. See Opinion AG Léger in *Linster* (n 68), para. 78.
[72] Wennerås (n 43), 20.
[73] Case C-75/08 *Christopher Mellor* [2009] ECR I-3799, paras 57 and 58.
[74] Opinion AG Sharpston in Case C-115/09 *Trianel Kohlekraftwerk Lünen* [2011] OJ C204/6, para. 39.
[75] Attention should be drawn to the fact that both the Aarhus Convention and the directives implementing it encapsulate the objective legal protection regime as well as the subjective approach.

rely before their national courts on the provisions of the EIA Directive. As a result, a broader interpretation of the concept of interested party should prevail over a narrow interpretation of requirements of standing. This interpretation is completely in line with new case law developments concerning Article 10a of the EIA Directive.

Finally, German administrative law provides that an action challenging an administrative measure will be admissible only if the administrative measure affects the claimant's rights. In so doing, such requirements preclude environmental NGOs from relying on infringement of environmental law that primarily concerns the general public and not the protection of individual rights. In *Trianel Kohlekraftwerk Lünen*, the Court went on to say that the German *Schutznorm* theory was too restrictive regarding the wide access of justice for environmental NGOs and was therefore at odds with Article 10a.[76]

2.4.3 *Nature protection*

A final issue must be addressed. In line with the *Rewe/Comet* case law, one could argue that despite the fact that nature protection NGOs have a genuine interest in the correct enforcement of EU nature protection law, the national lawmaker is not required to confer on them enforceable rights of litigation. This reasoning is based on the assumption that the nature conservation directives do not confer any rights either on humans or on wild species. That said, nothing precludes the national lawmaker from granting standing to nature protection NGOs.

Accordingly, the few EU directives on nature protection[77] confer on individuals neither participatory nor litigation rights. However, the absence of such rights did not prevent the Court of Justice from paving the way to improve legal remedies. In the *Waddenzee* case, the Court stressed that the effectiveness of secondary law would be undermined:

> In particular, where the Community authorities have, by directive, imposed on Member States the obligation to pursue a particular course of conduct, the useful effect of such an act would be weakened if individuals were prevented from relying on it before their national courts, and if the latter were prevented from taking it into consideration as an element of Community law in order to rule whether the national legislature, in exercising the choice open to it as to the form and methods for implementation, has kept within the limits of its discretion set out in the directive.[78]

In *Lesoochranárske zoskupenie*, the referring court asked whether an environmental protection association, where it wishes to challenge a decision to derogate from a

---

[76] *Trianel* (n 74), para. 51. This interpretation has been supported by different authors. See A. Schwerdtefeger, '*Schutznorm*theorie and Aarhus Convention. Consequences for German law' (2007) *JEEPL* 270–7; Jans (n 61), 274; de Sadeleer, Roller, and Dross (n 50), 204; E. J. Lohse, 'Surprise? Surprise!— Case C-115/09 (*Kohlekraftwerk Lünen*)—A Victory for the Environment and a Loss for Procedural Autonomy of the Member States' (2012) 18:2 *EPL* 249–68; B. Wegener, 'European Rights of Action for Environmental NGOs' (2011) *JEEPL* 315–28; and case note (2012) 49 *CML Rev* 787–93.

[77] N. de Sadeleer and C.-H. Born, *Droit international et communautaire de la biodiversité* (Paris: Dalloz, 2004) 481–581.

[78] Case C-72/95 *Kraaijeveld* [1996] ECR I-5403, para. 56; Case C-127/02 *Waddenzee* [2004] ECR I-7405, para. 66.

system of full protection of a species of Community interest—the brown bear—put in place by the Habitats Directive, may derive a right to bring proceedings under EU law, having particular regard to the provisions of Article 9(3) of the Aarhus Convention. The Court held that Article 9(3) of the Aarhus Convention did not contain any clear and precise obligation capable of directly regulating the legal position of individuals on the ground that 'that provision is subject, in its implementation or effects, to the adoption of a subsequent measure'.[79] Nonetheless, given that the Convention's provisions, 'are intended to ensure effective environmental protection',[80] the Court expressed the view that 'if the effective protection of EU environmental law is not to be undermined, it is inconceivable that Article 9(3) of the Aarhus Convention be interpreted in such a way as to make it in practice impossible or excessively difficult to exercise rights conferred by EU law.'

As a result, 'it is for the national court, in order to ensure effective judicial protection in the fields covered by EU environmental law, to interpret its national law in a way which, to the fullest extent possible, is consistent with the objectives laid down in Article 9(3) of the Aarhus Convention.'[81]

This line of reasoning is completely in line with the *Kraijeveld* case law. Private enforcement does not depend upon the willingness of the EU lawmaker to protect claimant's individual interests. Even if the Habitats Directive does not protect human health, citizens or NGOs who have merely a general interest in the proper enforcement of that directive can invoke it before the national courts.[82]

3. Article 37 EUCFR

3.1 Introduction

By virtue of Article 6(1) TEU, 'the Union recognises the rights, freedoms and principles set out in the Charter . . . which shall have the same legal value as the treaties'.

Environmental protection is not absent in the Charter. A specific provision, Article 37, provides for a duty to protect the environment. That provision reads: 'A high level of environmental protection and the improvement of the quality of the environment must be integrated into the policies of the Union and ensured in accordance with the

---

[79] *Lesoochranárske zoskupenie* (n 24), para. 45.

[80] *Lesoochranárske zoskupenie* (n 24), para. 46.

[81] *Lesoochranárske zoskupenie* (n 24), paras 49 and 50. Regarding the impact of this judgment on Swedish administrative case law where previously only the government was empowered to represent the public interest, see Y. Epstein and J. Darpö, 'The Wild Has No Words: Environmental NGOs Empowered to Speak for Protected Species as Swedish Courts Apply EU and International Environmental Law' (2013) *JEEPL* 250–61.

[82] The Court of Justice thus departed from AG Kokott's Opinion which stressed that 'there is no evidence to suggest that rights of an individual are established. The objective of protection laid down by Article 6(2) and (3) of the Habitats Directive is to conserve habitats and species within areas which form part of Natura 2000. Unlike in the case of rules on the quality of the atmosphere or water, the protection of common natural heritage is of particular interest but not a right established for the benefit of individuals. The close interests of individuals can be promoted only indirectly, as a reflex so to speak'. Opinion AG Kokott in Case C-127/02 *Waddenzee* [2004] ECR I-7405, para. 143.

principle of sustainable development'. That provision stands alongside similar provisions in the area of consumer protection and health care.[83]

Given that Article 37 has been drafted more as a policy requirement rather than as an individual right, it is known as one of the *parents pauvres* of the Charter.[84] Nonetheless, the wording of the article requires some clarification in terms of its material and personal scope.

3.2 Rights or principles?

At the outset, it is important to draw a distinction between rights and principles, although the dividing line between the two concepts is a fine one.[85]

Several EUCFR provisions clearly embody rights.[86] By way of illustration, Article 31 (1) relating to working conditions states that 'every worker has the right to working conditions which respect his or her health, safety and dignity'. In sharp contrast to that provision, Article 37 asserts the requirement to integrate a 'high level' of environmental protection into the different EU policies and actions. In so doing, such a 'principle'[87] merely reiterates the programmatic statement embodied in Article 11 TFEU.[88] Article 37 is careful not to specify any beneficiary of the environmental policy and confers any right in the sense of an individual entitlement guaranteed to the victims of pollution.[89]

Therefore, Article 37 cannot be placed on an equal footing with other economic rights, such as the freedom to conduct a business or the right to property, which can be invoked directly.[90]

---

[83] Whereas the first sentence of Art. 35 embodies an individual entitlement to 'access preventive health care', the second sentence requires that 'a high level of human health protection shall be ensured in the definition and implementation of all Union policies and activities.' In much the same vein, Art. 38 EUCFR states that: 'Union policies shall ensure a high level of consumer protection.' The right of access to preventive health care and the right to benefit from medical treatment are deemed to be 'far too general'. As a result, Art. 35, first sentence EUCFR 'does not enshrine an individual right that could be invoked before the Court of HR'. Eg Network of Independent Experts on Fundamental Rights, *Commentary on the Charter of Fundamental Rights of the EU* (June 2006), 308. See also T. Hervey, 'The "Right to Health" in European Union Law' in Hervey and Kenner (n 2), 202.

[84] A. Kiss, 'Environmental and Consumer Protection' in S. Peers and A. Ward (eds), *The EU Charter of Fundamental Rights: Politics, Law and Policy* (Oxford: Hart Publishing, 2004) 247.

[85] C. Hilson, 'Rights and Principles in EU Law: A Distinction without Foundation?' (2008) 15:2 *MJ* 193–215.

[86] See in particular Arts 2(1), 3(1), 6, 7, 8(1), 10(1), 11(1), 12(1), 14(1), 15(1), (2), 17(1), 24(1), 28, 29, 30, 31(1), (2), 33 (2), 35, first sentence, 39(1), 40, 41(1)–(3), 42, 43, 44, 45, and 47 EUCFR.

[87] The explanations accompanying the Charter ascertain that Art. 37 contains a principle. By the same token, the European Parliament underlined that Art. 37 is 'a political objective, and not a legally binding right'. Eg European Parliament, *Freedom, Security and Justice: an Agenda for Europe*. According to the interpretation of the EU Network of Independent Experts on Fundamental Rights, Art. 37 enshrines 'a principle and not a right'. See EU Network of Independent Experts on Fundamental Rights (n 83), 318. However, explanations accompanying the Charter do not shed light on the legal status of Art. 35, second sentence and Art. 38 (Bureau of the Convention, *Explanations relating to the Charter*, 2000).

[88] Chapter 1, Section 5.

[89] The drafters of Art. 37 came to grips with the scope of that provision. They decided to reiterate the Treaty law obligations rather than proclaiming a genuine environmental right. In addition, the drafters discarded any references to procedural rights such as information and participatory rights (EU Network of Independent Experts on Fundamental Rights (n 83), 315).

[90] Arts 16 and 17 EUCFR.

Little guidance has been provided as to the legal status of the Charter's principles. Article 52(5) EUCFR is the key provision for distinguishing the scope of the principles from the Charter's rights. Paragraph 5 of Article 52 states that principles 'may be implemented by legislative and executive acts taken by institutions, bodies, offices and agencies of the Union, and by acts of Member States when they are implementing Union law'. As regards the principles' legal effects, paragraph 2 stresses that they 'shall be judicially cognisable only in the interpretation' of the measures enacted with a view to fleshing them out as well as 'in the ruling on their legality'. Several lessons can be drawn from Article 52(5) EUCFR.

Pursuant to Article 6(1), third subparagraph TEU, 'the rights, freedoms and principles in the Charter shall be interpreted . . . with due regard to the explanations referred to in the Charter'. In this connection, the explanations accompanying the Charter stress that the principles 'do not . . . give rise to direct claims for positive action by the Union's institutions or Member States authorities'.[91] Consequently, the principles cannot be invoked to oblige EU or Member State authorities to adopt an environmental or health measure when none exist.[92] Given that the principles cannot provide a basis for claims for new regulatory actions, Article 265 TFEU, which provides for an action for failure to act, and similar national remedies are inapplicable. As discussed previously, the Court of Justice's case law on the enforceability of EU environmental obligations is more favourable to applicants than the EUCFR principles.[93]

On the other hand, while the legal effects of the principles may be weak, they are not absent. Accordingly, courts cannot ignore principles.[94]

First, the principles are likely to come in the form of a source of interpretation. Along the same lines, Article 11 TFEU—a provision that encapsulates the environmental integration clause—already operates as an interpretative principle.[95] Consequently, courts are called upon to interpret EU obligations consistently in accordance with the environmental principle.[96]

Second, given that the EUCFR principles are not effective per se, they require the adoption of implementing measures if they are to become fully fledged. Therefore, they become 'judicially cognisable' where EU and national courts are called upon to review the legality of EU and national implementing acts. As a result, Article 37 can be invoked inasmuch as it is fleshed out into more concrete measures adopted either by the EU institutions or by the national authorities.[97] Admittedly, violations of Article 37 may be invoked by applicants within the context of annulment proceedings pursuant to Article 263 TFEU. In other words, the EU Courts may apply such a provision to quash an EU measure or to invalidate a national implementing measure that falls short of

---

[91] EU Network of Independent Experts on Fundamental Rights (n 83), 315.

[92] Hilson (n 85), 200.

[93] As discussed previously, the Court of Justice held in *Janecek* that an individual can contest his national agency's failure to act by requesting the drawing up of an air pollution action plan for the area in which he resides. See Case C-237/07 *Janecek* (n 58).

[94] By the same token, the courts cannot ignore Art. 38 EUCFR. See EU Network of Independent Experts on Fundamental Rights (n 83), 315.

[95] Chapter 1, Section 5.

[96] T. Hervey and J. V. McHale, *Health Law and the European Union* (Cambridge: CUP, 2004) 409.

[97] EU Network of Independent Experts on Fundamental Rights (n 83), 315.

implementing the EUCFR principle. Given that environmental requirements must be integrated into other EU policies, even a measure adopted based on Article 114 TFEU can be criticized for failing to be consistent with Article 37.[98]

3.3 Positive and negative duties

The discussion on the review of Articles 3(3) TEU and 11 as well as Article 191(2) TFEU has shown that there is indeed strong doctrinal resistance to the idea that the Courts may review compliance with the requirement for a high level of protection. This is claimed to undermine the very idea of the separation of powers. In addition, the imprecise nature of such provisions might render them non-justiciable. Furthermore, the EU institutions enjoy wide discretion in fleshing out these duties, subject to limited judicial review.

In view of these criticisms, it remains to be seen whether a claim based on the violation of Article 37 would be successful. In effect, by providing for a relatively fuzzy objective, such as the quest for a high level of environmental protection and improvements to its quality, that provision is limited to requiring public authorities to take action, while specifying that such action calls for the integration of environmental requirements into all Union policies according to the model of the 'principle of sustainable development'.[99] Whereas Article 11 TFEU holds that the integration must be implemented 'with a view to promoting sustainable development', Article 37 requires that environmental concerns be integrated 'in accordance with the principle of sustainable development'. Hence, sustainable development is raised to a principle conditioning the integration of environmental concerns. Such requirements may be surprising: sustainable development has precisely the effect of undermining the scope of public authorities' initiatives, since it implicitly calls for environmental requirements to be weighed against social and economic interests.[100]

This is not to say that Article 37 duties may not determine, let alone affect, the outcome of a case. One should not underestimate the interpretive function of such a principle that could be used to fill the gaps in existing legislation.[101]

3.4 Personal scope

The Charter's principles are to be implemented, pursuant to Article 51(1), by the 'institutions and bodies'[102] responsible for the 'policies of the Union' 'with due regard to the principle of subsidiarity'. Admittedly, principles impose obligations incumbent upon the EU institutions and agencies, which are the only bodies entitled to assess the scope and nature of their initiatives.

---

[98] EU Network of Independent Experts on Fundamental Rights (n 83).
[99] One could argue that sustainable development amounts at most to a solidarity right.
[100] See the discussion Chapter 1, Section 4.
[101] K. Hectors, 'The Chartering of Environmental Protection' (2008) *EEELR* 172.
[102] The French version of Art. 21(1) EUCFR adds the concept of '*organismes*'.

That said, it is important to remember that, pursuant to Article 51(1)(5), the Charter also 'binds' the Member States 'when they are implementing Union law'. Thus, where the Member States implement EU law, be it internal market law or CAP law, they are subject to the principles set out in the EUCFR. In other words, the Charter is applicable where EU law is applicable. However, it is not always easy to draw the line between national rules that fall within and outside the scope of EU law.[103] The link between the national measure and EU law may be too indirect or hypothetical. As an example, in 2010 the Court of Justice held that a municipal land planning development scheme fell outside the scope of EU law, which meant that EUCFR provisions were inapplicable.[104] As far as environmental policy is concerned, since the core of national environmental policy is grounded on provisions of secondary law,[105] Article 37 is likely to impact upon large parts of environmental law at a national level.

4. ECHR Rights With Regard to the Right to Environmental Protection

Since it satisfies the characteristics of a Union governed by the 'rule of law',[106] the EU has by virtue of Article 6(3) TEU enhanced the status of fundamental rights within the EU legal order in relying on constitutional rights as well as the rights embodied in the ECHR. These rights are qualified 'as general principles'. According to the case law of the ECJ, respect for human rights is a condition of the lawfulness of EU acts.[107] Moreover, measures which are incompatible with the observance of those human rights are not accepted in the EU.[108]

As far as environmental protection is concerned, Article 6(3) TEU brings the case law of the ECtHR on nuisances even more firmly within EU law. It is the aim of this last section to assess whether ECHR case law is likely to reinforce EU and national environmental law in providing new remedies for the victims of pollution.

4.1 Absence of a specific environmental right

Two issues arise for comment here. On the one hand, the key role of environmental protection measures in today's society has been recognized by the ECtHR.[109] As a result, national environmental policy measures are pursuing an objective of general interest likely to restrain fundamental rights enshrined in the ECHR. Accordingly, fundamental rights do not override environmental protection measures. By way of illustration, planning regulations that interfere with the right of peaceful enjoyment of

---

[103] A. Rosas and L. Armati, *EU Constitutional Law* (Oxford: Hart Publishing, 2010) 148.
[104] Case C-339/10 *Estov Ivanova and Kemko International EAD* [2010] OJ C13/16.
[105] See the discussion in Chapter 4.   [106] Art. 2 TEU.
[107] Opinion 2/94 [1996] ECR I-1759, para. 34.
[108] Case C-112/00 *Schmidberger* [2003] ECR I-5659, para. 73; Joined Cases C-402/05 P & C-415/05 P *Kadi* [2008] ECR I-6381, para. 284.
[109] *Fredin v Sweden*, 18 February 1991, para. 14.

private property are clearly a legitimate aim 'in accordance with the general interest' for the purpose of the second paragraph of Article 1 of the First Protocol.[110]

On the other hand, as was the case for the original EEC Treaty, the ECHR, adopted in 1950, was drafted at a time when environmental law did not yet exist. Although with the introduction of subsequent amendments, environmental questions came to take on increasing importance under EU Treaty law, no right to the conservation of nature or the environment was included under the rights and freedoms guaranteed by the ECHR.[111] For this reason, the Strasbourg Court still refuses to grant preferential status to 'environmental human rights'.[112] In the Court's view, 'neither Article 8 nor any of the other Articles of the Convention are specifically designed to provide general protection of the environment as such; to that effect, other international instruments and domestic legislation are more pertinent in dealing with this particular aspect'.[113]

However, despite the absence of an adequate regulatory framework to condemn violations of protection thresholds or the failure to implement court orders requiring the cessation of harmful or hazardous activities, the ECtHR has nevertheless ended up indirectly guaranteeing a minimum level of environmental protection.[114] In fact, a constructive and dynamic interpretation of the ECHR has permitted these concerns of a novel nature gradually to filter into the interpretation of first generation human rights. As a result, a right to basic environmental protection can be derived from existing human rights, such as the right to life (Art. 2), the right to a fair trial (Art. 6), the right to private and family life and the home (Art. 8), the freedom of expression and information (Art. 10), as well as the freedom of assembly and association (Art. 11).

Although the essential core of the decisions issued by the ECtHR is based on Article 8, the other provisions cited also deserve attention. In addition, since the ECtHR rules on circumstances with highly specific facts, it is at times difficult to infer any definitive conclusions from its judgments.

4.2 Right to life

Although environmental degradation, and in particular poor air quality, still cause hundreds of thousands of premature deaths in Europe,[115] the right to life enshrined in Article 2 has not been a particularly fruitful source of case law. Since, in the view of the

---

[110] *Hakansson and Sturesson v Sweden*, 15 July 1987; *Fredin v Sweden*, 18 February 1991; *Pine Valley Development Ltd and others v Ireland*, 29 November 1991, paras 54 and 57; *Jacobsson v Sweden*, 15 October 1995; *Buckley v UK*, (n 164). Moreover, it is settled case law that given the importance of land planning and environmental policies, State authorities are endowed with a greater margin of discretion than in cases where civil rights are involved. *Depalle v France*, 29 March 2010, para. 81.

[111] *Fadeyeva v Russia*, 9 June 2005, para. 68; *Kyrtatos v Greece*, 22 May 2003, para. 52.

[112] *Hatton and others v UK*, 2 February 2001, para. 122.

[113] *Kyrtatos v Greece* (n 111), para. 52.

[114] M. Dejeant-Pons and M. Pallemaerts, *Droits de l'Homme et environnement* (Strasbourg: Conseil de l'Europe, 2002); D. Garcia San José, *La protection de l'environnement et la Convention européenne des droits de l'homme* (Strasbourg: Conseil de l'Europe, 2005); M. Pâques, 'L'environnement, un certain droit de l'homme' (2006) 1 *APT* 38–66; and F. Haumont, 'Le droit fondamental à la protection de l'environnement dans la CEDH' (2008) *Amén-Envt* 9–55.

[115] European Environmental Agency, *Europe's Environment. The Fourth Assessment* (Copenhagen: EEA, 2007) 73.

ECtHR, there has not been any opportunity to examine complaints concerning the violation of Article 2 where it has already ruled on an application introduced on the basis of Article 8. Accordingly, few judgments have ruled on the extent of this provision.[116] When the inappropriate management of a landfill causes the death of local residents, the inadequate nature of the regulatory framework is liable to result in violation of Article 2.[117] The positive obligation to take all necessary measures to protect life therefore means that a preventive policy must be implemented. As regards the procedural aspect of Article 2, both judicial proceedings as well as criminal law remedies must comply with the requirements of the positive obligation for the law to safeguard life.[118] Without doubt, one of the difficulties concerns the fact that the threshold of severity necessary in order to apply this provision is higher than that required under Article 8, since the interference must result in death, even if it was not caused intentionally or unlawfully.[119]

Additionally, the manner in which the competent authorities act in response to a major risk is likely to violate Article 2 in its procedural aspect. That would be the case in the absence of an adequate judicial response to a major hazard.[120]

4.3 Right to private and family life and the home

Pollution results from a complex mix of corporate and governmental conduct: although a listed installation causes the pollution, it does so under the oversight of State authorities. Whether the pollution is caused directly by the State or whether responsibility for it is the result of an absence of adequate regulation of private industry,[121] the protection of the right to respect for private life and home has given rise in recent years to a particularly rich seam of case law on environmental matters, even though this provision does not make any claim to protect the environment.[122] The following subsections will examine the level of protection offered under Article 8 ECHR, the interferences that are actionable under that provision, the scope of State obligations, and the justifications which may permit the interference.

---

[116] *Guerra v Italy*, 19 December 1998, para. 62; *Taskin and others v Turkey*, 10 November 2004, para. 140; *Luginbühl v Switzerland*, 17 January 2006; *Ockan v Turkey*, 28 March 2006, para. 57; *Tatar v Romania*, 27 January 2009, para. 72.

[117] *Oneryildiz v Turkey*, 18 June 2002. This arrest was confirmed after a transfer to the Grand Chamber by *Oneryildiz v Turkey*, 30 November 2004.

[118] *Oneryildiz v Turkey* (n 117), paras 92–6.

[119] *LCB v UK*, 9 June 1998, para. 39. In that case, the Court considered that Art. 2 had not been infringed, given the absence of proof concerning the causal link between the exposure of the applicant's father to radiation during nuclear tests and her leukaemia.

[120] *Kolyadenko v Russia*, 9 June 1998, para. 203.

[121] Inasmuch as environmental damage may be authorized directly by the granting of an administrative authorization or indirectly due to the absence of adequate measures, Art. 8 may also be applied to pollution caused by individuals or private undertakings. As a result, the violation of Art. 8(1) may arise from a failure to regulate private undertakings. See notably *Ruano Morcuende v Spain*, 6 September 2005; *Fadeyeva v Russia* (n 111), para. 89; *Moreno Gómez v Spain*, 16 November 2004, para. 57; *Tatar v Romania* (n 116), para. 87; *Dées v Hungary*, 9 November 2010, para. 23.

[122] *Fadeyeva v Russia* (n 111), para. 68.

4.3.1 *Scope*

Article 8 is undeniably framed in anthropocentric terms, according to which the environment deserves to be protected only because it is used by humankind. Accordingly, the destruction of a marshland cannot be analysed as a restriction on the private or family life of local residents. However, even if the Court considers that the damage caused to the environment does not interfere with the applicants' private and family lives, this does not preclude that the destruction of a forest in the vicinity of the applicants' houses could have indirectly affected the applicants' well-being.[123]

Moreover, only the private sphere of the victims of environmental pollution is protected. In principle, the case law is not particularly favourable to NGOs, which cannot claim that they have been the victims of a violation of Article 8.[124]

According to ECtHR case law, both the private life sphere and the protection of the applicant's home are likely to be affected by environmental impairment. The majority of cases adjudicated thus far have been lodged by claimants complaining of an invasion of their home caused by environmental pollution. Interference with domicile may be caused by airport activity (*Hatton*), a waste-treatment plant (*Lopez Ostra*), mining activities (*Taskin* and *Dubetska*), lack of appropriate enforcement of waste management law (*Di Sarno*), nightclubs (*Moreno Gómez*), a motorway (*Dées* and *Grimkovskaya*), or electromagnetic emissions from a transformer located next to the claimant's home (*Ruano Morcuende*).

On the other hand, in other cases only private and family life was at stake, with no link to the applicant's home. In adjudicating these cases, the ECtHR has widened the territorial scope of Article 8. In that respect, *McGinley and Egan* was a good case in point. The case concerned information requested by the applicants about the risks involved during nuclear tests by British soldiers.[125]

4.3.2 *Types of interference in the domicile or private life of the applicants*

With regard to the nature of the damage, the ECtHR accepts, due to the particularly broad spectrum of ecological problems, that they are not only material or corporeal; they may also be non-material or incorporeal. As a consequence, noise pollution,[126] atmospheric emissions,[127] smells,[128] radiation,[129] and concerns over increases in allegedly harmful emissions also amount to interference in the domicile or the private life of applicants.[130]

---

[123] *Kyrtatos v Greece* (n 111), para. 53.
[124] *Asselbourg and 78 Others and Greenpeace Luxembourg v Luxembourg*, 29 June 1999, para. 4.
[125] *McGinley and Egan v UK*, 9 June 1998.
[126] The Court and the former Commission have had to deal with a swathe of cases concerning noise nuisance. A summary of these can be found in paras 92 and 93 of *Mileva v Bulgaria*, 25 November 2010. See in particular *Moreno Gómez v Spain* (n 121).
[127] *Fadeyeva v Russia* (n 111).
[128] *Lopez Ostra v Spain*, 9 December 1994, para. 58.
[129] *Ruano Morcuende v Spain*, 17 January 2006.
[130] *Guerra and others v Italy*, 19 February 1998, para. 57.

Although the Court has condemned States on the ground that they have illegally interfered with varied aspects of private life (well-being, peace of mind,...), in the majority of cases it is the health of the victims that is at issue, most often due to exposure to hazardous substances. Since the damage may be caused by the anguish and anxiety felt by a victim due to the continuation of an unlawful situation, the concept of health is interpreted broadly.[131] Finally, by not requiring that the victims' health has been seriously jeopardized by State action causing such interference, the Court appears to view the situation of victims favourably.

4.3.2.1 Significance of the interference

There must in any event be a 'direct and sufficient link' between the impugned situation and the applicants' home or private and family life. Whether it comes in the form of exposure to a polluting substance or to noise pollution, the interference must directly affect his home, or his private or family life.[132]

In spite of the extremely varied situations which could risk damage alleged to harm health, the protection conferred by Article 8 applies in the event that the interference exceeds 'a minimum level of severity'.[133] *A contrario*, there would be no arguable claim under Article 8 if the effect is negligible 'in comparison to the environmental hazards inherent to life in every modern city'.[134] Although the requirement of the severity of harm has been established, little has been said with regard to its extent.[135]

Since it is a relative concept, the evaluation of this 'minimum level of severity' will depend on all of the circumstances of the case, such as frequency, intensity, repetition, duration, ability of the authorities to enforce environmental law, location of the pollution, and level of existing environmental degradation.[136] Given that the cases adjudicated so far are marked by significant geographic and substantive diversity, a detailed examination of the manner in which some of these criteria have been applied should be carried out.

First, it is common sense that the higher the *level of harm* entailed by the activity, the higher the likelihood of deleterious effects on the person. In this connection, a sufficiently close link with private and family life may also be established where the

---

[131] *Egan*, (n 125), para. 99; *Giacomelli v Italy*, 2 November 2006, para. 104; *Tatar v Romania* (n 116), para. 122.

[132] *Fadeyeva v Russia* (n 111), para. 68.

[133] *Fadeyeva v Russia* (n 111), paras 69–70; *Giacomelli v. Italy* (n 131), para. 76; *Mileva v Bulgaria* (n 126), para. 90; *Grimkovskaya v Ukraine*, 2 July 2011, para. 58; *Maile and Hardy*, 14 February 2012, para. 187. See also *Downs v Secretary of State for Environment, Food, and Rural Affairs* [2009] 3 *CMLR* 46.

[134] *Maile and Hardy* (n 133), para. 188.

[135] The following sources of pollution were deemed to be characterized by a certain degree of gravity. The smells, noises, and smoke caused by a waste-treatment plant interfere with the right enshrined in Art. 8(1) (*Lopez Ostra v Spain* (n 128), para. 51). By the same token, nightclubs and bars exceeding municipal noise thresholds infringe Art. 8(1) (*Moreno Gómez v Spain* (n 121)). This is also the case in a steel plant exceeding air quality standards (*Fadeyeva v Russia* (n 111), para. 70) as well as municipal traffic exceeding significantly statutory thresholds (*Dées v Hungary* (n 121), para. 23; *Grimkovskaya v Ukraine* (n 133), para. 61). On the other hand, pollution caused by an urban development does not appear to be sufficiently serious to be taken into account under Art. 8 (*Kyrtatos v Greece* (n 111), para. 54; see also *Luginbühl v Switzerland* (n 116), para. 2).

[136] *Fadeyeva v Russia* (n 111), para. 69.

dangerous effects of the disputed activity have been examined within the context of an environmental impact report.[137]

Second, the *distance* between the source of the pollution and the applicant's home may vary significantly. In the majority of cases, the hazardous installation is located a short distance from the applicant's home,[138] with the Court appearing to be reluctant to apply Article 8(1) where the source of the pollution is some distance away from the victim's home.[139]

Third, although a single activity may cause the harm, environmental damage may also be caused by numerous sources. Accordingly, the *cumulative effects* of different sources of pollution may significantly deter the applicant from enjoying his rights guaranteed by Article 8.[140]

Fourth, the *regulatory context*—planning permission, hazardous substances consent, etc—may be taken into consideration to demonstrate a close link between potential industrial risks and the applicant's private life and home.[141]

Fifth, where concentrations of toxic pollutants exceed regulatory thresholds, the pollution becomes potentially dangerous to the health and well-being of the applicant. As a result, the fewer the *appropriate enforcement* measures of the activities entailing the risk, the greater the likelihood of a deleterious impact on human beings.[142] Therefore, the ECtHR generally assumes that Article 8(1) has been violated where the exposure or environmental quality thresholds have been exceeded.[143] That said, the mere fact that the source of pollution is unlawful is not sufficient to ground the assertion that the applicants' rights under Article 8 have been interfered with.[144] In fact, the issue of proper enforcement of domestic environmental or land planning law has not been approached as 'a separate and conclusive test but rather as one of many aspects which should be taken into account in assessing whether the State has struck a fair balance'.[145]

Sixth, the longer the illegality persists, the greater the likelihood of environmental harm.[146] For instance, the repetition over a period of several years of noise pollution in excess of the thresholds authorized during night hours will infringe the rights protected under Article 8.[147]

---

[137] *Taskin and others v Turkey* (n 116), paras 17, 19, and 21; *Lemke v Turkey*, 5 June 2007, para. 36; *Giacomelli v Italy* (n 131); *Grimkovskaya v Ukraine* (n 133), para. 61.

[138] *Moreno Gómez v Spain* (n 121).

[139] *Atanasov v Bulgaria*, 2 December 2010, para. 76. However, the Court held in another mining case that the fact that the victim of pollution lived 50km from the polluting gold mine was sufficient to establish a strong link with his private and family life. See *Lemke v Turkey* (n 137), para. 36 (text only available in French).

[140] *Grimkovskaya v Ukraine* (n 133), para. 62.

[141] *Maile and Hardy* (n 133), paras 191–2.

[142] *Dubetska v Russia*, 10 February 2011, paras 151–4.

[143] *Moreno Gómez v Spain* (n 121); *Dubetska v Russia* (n 142), para. 151.

[144] *Mileva v Bulgaria* (n 126), para. 91.

[145] F. McManus, note on *Gómez v Spain* (2006) 8 *Env L Rev* 227.

[146] *Dubetska v Russia* (n 142), para. 147; *Di Sarno v Italy*, 10 January 2012, para. 112.

[147] *Moreno Gómez v Spain* (n 121).

In this connection, the ECtHR has had regard to the *judgments* of domestic courts that have found statutory violations,[148] and even to those of the Court of Justice.[149]

Last, the particular *sensitivity* of the applicant may reinforce the sufficiently direct nature of the link.

4.3.2.2 Burden of proof and scientific uncertainty

As a matter of principle, the ECtHR requires that the applicant produces 'reasonable and convincing evidence of the likelihood that a violation affecting him personally would occur; mere suspicion or conjecture is insufficient in this regard.'[150] Applicants must overcome major hurdles in order to prove their allegations 'beyond reasonable doubt', particularly where there is no scientific assessment of the impact of the interference on their health[151] or where the assessment is biased.

Similarly, the ECtHR has taken the view that the 'minimum level of severity' threshold is not exceeded when the health risks remain purely speculative, irrespective of the fact that the applicant is particularly sensitive to electromagnetic radiation.[152] By way of illustration, given that the risks posed by mobile phone antennae are still embroiled in controversy, these risks remain speculative. According to the Court, one cannot, for now, call on the State to enact more stringent standards for the sake of particularly vulnerable persons. In so doing, by categorically excluding the possibility that the risk of a future violation may confer on the individual applicant the status of 'victim', the Court does not follow a precautionary logic.

However, in *Tatar*, when confronted with contradictory scientific assessments concerning the impact on health of sodium cyanide, the ECtHR referred to the precautionary principle when condemning the superficial nature of the investigation into the risks incurred by the local population, which had been carried out prior to the issue of the authorization for a gold mine.[153]

4.3.3 *State's margin of appreciation*

4.3.3.1 The balance

In addition to demonstrating the serious nature of the damage, the applicant must overcome a second obstacle: his right to respect for private and family life is tempered by the application, when reviewing the interference, of the principle of the margin of appreciation and the proportionality principle. Provided that the State respects the conditions laid down thereunder ('in accordance with the law', necessity and

---

[148] *Taskin and others v Turkey* (n 116), paras 12 and 111–14; *Ockan v Turkey* (n 116), para. 40.

[149] *Di Sarno v Italy* (n 146), para. 108.

[150] *Asselbourg and 78 Others and Greenpeace Luxembourg v Luxembourg* (n 124), para. 1; *Bernard and 47 other physical persons as well as Greenpeace Luxembourg v Luxembourg*, 29 June 1999, para. 1. In *Fadeyeva*, the ECtHR stressed that there was 'a very strong combination of indirect evidence and presumptions' which made it possible to conclude that the applicant was suffering from prolonged exposure to hazardous pollutants. See *Fadeyeva v Russia* (n 111), paras 80–8.

[151] *Grimkovskaya v Ukriane*, 21 July 2011, para. 60.

[152] *Luginbühl v Switzerland* (n 116). Here, the margin of appreciation granted to the State goes against the precautionary principle.

[153] *Tatar v Romania* (n 116), esp. paras 109–20.

proportionality of the interference), Article 8(2) permits infringement of the right to a clean environment, as inferred from the first paragraph.

Although it enjoys a broad margin of appreciation in the complex sphere of environmental policymaking,[154] the State must strike a fair balance between the objectives pursued by the interference and respect of the applicants' right to private and family life and home.[155] The question therefore arises as to what extent *the interference is acceptable.*

When called on to assess the correct balance, the State will by definition find itself in a favourable position. Its margin of appreciation is especially broad[156] where environmental rights are not granted special status.[157] This means, for example, that the fair balance struck between the rights of those residing in the vicinity of airports and the economic well-being of the country is generally weighed against the residents.[158]

The ECtHR has shown itself to be more sensitive to efforts undertaken by the State than to the status of the victim.[159] Where the State has done all it can to avoid the interference, the Court will take the view that Article 8 has not been infringed.[160] Accordingly, the interference with the right to respect for private life and home, consisting in the right to sleep at night, is more easily justified than in matters regarding sexual preference, where the margin of appreciation left to the State is particularly reduced.[161]

4.3.3.2 Limits to the State's margin of appreciation

The search for a fair balance is not, however, an absolute science. The extent of the margin of appreciation is subject to three limits.

In the first place, the State has a positive duty to enact adequate measures to secure the applicants' rights. Thus, the State authorities are required to put in place a preventive regulatory framework under which the standards are adapted 'to the specific features of the activity concerned, and in particular to the level of risk which may result'.[162] The enactment of a significant number of regulatory measures makes it possible to ensure respect for a fair balance: prior assessment of risks, application of maximum exposure thresholds, measures to mitigate impacts, proper enforcement,

---

[154] *Grimkovskaya v Ukraine* (n 133), para. 65.

[155] If it is lawful for the State to oversee worker protection and social welfare, it should not however do so to the detriment of protection of health and the environment. Economic and social interests cannot prevail per se over Art. 8.

[156] On the extent of the margin of appreciation in environmental matters, see particularly: *Hatton and others v UK* (n 112), paras 97 et seq.; *Oneryildiz* (n 117), para. 107; *Fadeyeva v Russia* (n 111), para. 102; *Giacomelli v Italy* (n 131), para. 80.

[157] *Oneryildiz v Turkey* (n 117), para. 107; *Fadayeva v Russia* (n 111), para. 104.

[158] *Pauwell and Rayner v UK*, 21 February 1990, para. 45; and *Hatton and others v UK* (n 112), paras 124–8.

[159] *Luginbühl v Switzerland* (n 116) (text only available in French). In this case, the Court held that: 'compte tenu de l'état du débat scientifique actuel' on the noxiousness of mobile phone antennae and considering that 'les efforts entrepris par les autorités compétentes pour suivre le développement scientifique en la matière et pour réexaminer périodiquement les valeurs limites applicables', the Swedish authorities could not exceed their margin of appreciation by granting building licences for mobile phone antennae, irrespective of the applicant's vulnerability to electrosmog.

[160] *LCB v UK* (n 119), para. 27.   [161] *Dudgeon v UK*, 22 October 1981, para. 52.

[162] Case *Budayeva v Russia*, 20 March 2008; *Tatar v Romania* (n 116), para. 88.

partial compensation to victims,[163] etc. However, the State enjoys a certain margin of appreciation in tailoring the measures intended to protect Article 8 rights.[164]

Second, the interference will not be permitted where public authorities do not adhere to the law. Accordingly, in most instances where rulings are made against the States, the ECtHR points to a flagrant breach of environmental regulations.[165] The defendant State cannot expect to persuade the Court that it is striking a fair balance between the needs of the community and the applicants' rights by not enforcing domestic regulation.[166] In several cases, the ECtHR has highlighted the absence of law enforcement, and in particular the fact that national court decisions ordering the closure of the plant in question were ignored by the relevant administrative authorities.[167] It is inevitable that where the severity of the damage is assessed with reference to the breach of pollution exposure standards, the interference will always be illegal. Indeed, these regulatory standards are deemed to afford citizens a minimum level of protection. Hence, an individual right of action to enforce those minimum standards might arise.

Third, with a view to guaranteeing a fair balance, the ECtHR has imposed the requirement to comply with obligations of a procedural nature, the content of which is inspired by the Aarhus Convention. For example, the absence of an environmental impact study on the exploitation of a plant for the treatment of hazardous waste and the refusal by the authorities to comply with the national court's judgments condemning the irregular nature of the contested activity demonstrate that the State has not been able to strike a fair balance between the interest of the community in removal of a waste-treatment plant and the enjoyment, by residents adjacent to the plant, of their right to respect for the home and private and family life.[168] Similarly, the resumption of mining activities liable to cause pollution must first be subject to 'the conduct of investigations and studies of an appropriate nature to prevent and evaluate in advance' their effects on the environment.[169]

Moreover, the ECtHR has enshrined, expanding the scope of Article 8, the rights to information and to challenge domestic decisions pursuant to Article 9(2) of the Aarhus Convention. It has also underscored the importance for the public of being able to gain access to these studies in order, on the one hand, to evaluate the danger to which they are exposed and, on the other hand, to permit opponents to initiate court proceedings in the event that their observations have not been sufficiently taken into consideration. The deprivation of these procedural guarantees of all effectiveness

---

[163] Compensation, even partial, may constitute a measure likely to ensure the correct balance. See Eur. Comm. HR, *S v France*, 17 May 1990.

[164] *Buckley v UK*, 25 September 1996, paras 74–7; *Taskin and others v Turkey* (n 116), para. 116; *Giacomelli v Italy* (n 131), para. 80; and *Dées v Hungary* (n 121), para. 23.

[165] *Hatton v UK* (n 112), para. 120; *Fadeyeva v Russia* (n 111), paras 83–4. *A contrario*, in the absence of a noise threshold exceeding the WHO recommended thresholds, wind turbines located near second homes are not likely to interfere significantly with the private and family life of the applicants (*Fägerskiöld v Sweden*, 28 February 2008).

[166] Birnie, Boyle, and Redgwell (n 26), 285.

[167] *Taskin and others v Turkey* (n 116); *Lemke v Turkey* (n 137), paras 124–5.

[168] *Giacomelli v Italy* (n 131).

[169] *Lemke v Turkey* (n 137), para. 44; *Tatar v Romania* (n 116), para. 116.

entails a violation of Article 8, although this provision does not lay down any express procedural condition.[170]

However, procedural guarantees are not unlimited. Whilst a decision to authorize the exploitation of an activity violating the right enshrined by Article 8 will necessarily entail appropriate investigations and studies being conducted, the fact remains that a decision may be taken even though the authority does not have 'comprehensive and measurable data... in relation to each and every aspect of the matter to be decided'.[171] The national authority may therefore accept the interference on the basis of incomplete information.

4.3.4 *Complaint under Article 8 ECHR of the right to be informed of environmental hazards*

As far as access to information is concerned, Article 8 takes precedence over Article 10. Accordingly, the State is also subject, pursuant to Article 8, to a positive obligation to provide information regarding environmental risks to which the public is exposed.[172] The ECtHR considers that this amounts to an essential procedural guarantee in order to strike a fair balance between private life and State interference.[173] In addition, such procedural requirement stems from the Aarhus Convention.[174]

Interpreted in its procedural dimension, this provision may also come to the assistance of those whose private and family life is disrupted by the stress and anxiety arising from exposure to a particular risk of pollution. This obligation is all the more pressing where the authorities dispose of information which would have permitted the residents to evaluate those risks and to take appropriate action in order to protect themselves.[175]

In this regard, Article 8 requires[176] that 'an effective and accessible procedure be established which enables such persons to seek all relevant and appropriate information',[177] failing which the article will be violated. Similarly, the right to the protection of health set out in Article 11 of the European Social Charter is breached when the authorities do not 'enter into fair and genuine consultations with those exposed to environmental risks' about the risks of pollution to which they are exposed due to the exploitation of lignite.[178] Therefore, a decision which interferes with private life is not admissible unless it is taken at the conclusion of a transparent decision-making process involving public inquiries, the provision of information, and so on. On the other hand, where there are faults in the decision-making process, the ECtHR may rule that Article 8 has been violated by the State.

---

[170] *Hatton v UK* (n 112), para. 128; *Taskin and others v Turkey* (n 116); and *Giacomelli v Italy* (n 131), para. 82.
[171] *Hatton v UK* (n 112), para. 128; *Taskin v Turkey* (n 116), para. 118; *Maile and Hardy* (n 133), paras 219 and 231.
[172] *Taskin v Turkey* (n 116), para. 119; *Giacomelli v Italy* (n 131), para. 83; *Tatar v Romania* (n 116), para. 113; *Di Sarno v Italy* (n 146), para. 107.
[173] *Maile and Hardy* (n 133), para. 249.   [174] *Di Sarno v Italy* (n 146), para. 107.
[175] *Guerra v Italy* (n 116), para. 60.   [176] *Tatar v Romania* (n 116), para. 116.
[177] *McGinley and Egan v UK*, 26 November 1996, para. 101.
[178] European Comm. of Social Rights, *Fondation Maranyopoulos v Greece*, 6 December 2006, para. 217.

In contrast, in other cases the ECtHR has accepted that the State has complied with its positive obligation by creating a special procedure according to which the applicants could have gained access, had they taken advantage of it, to information of such a nature as to allay their fears of a violation of their right to respect for their private and family life resulting from their exposure to the risk of radiation.[179]

4.3.5 *Is Article 8 ECHR likely to enhance a right to a decent environment?*

It is therefore clear from the case law that either the absence of a legal framework or a failure to comply with the rules—both substantive (emissions thresholds) as well as procedural (information, participation by the public)—will entail a violation of Article 8. However, the case law is open to criticism. First of all, it must be observed that the right to private life is not protected where the substantive protection standards prove to be inadequate, which is generally the case. This could lead the authorities to conduct themselves in a cynical manner: at best, the State would no longer regulate pollution; at worst, it would set particularly relaxed emissions values which would never be exceeded. Since no regulatory violation could be averred, Article 8 rights would not operate in favour of victims. It could, however, be stated in response to these criticisms that the regulatory framework must forestall damage in an effective manner, as required by the case law of the ECtHR.[180]

As regards the procedural aspect, the added value of the ECHR is unclear beyond the procedural rights contained in the Aarhus Convention as well as the national and EU regulations issued in accordance with it.

By specifying procedures for the implementation of the right to participate, legislative advances of the past few years (eg the general obligation to provide active information) appear to be markedly more significant than the relatively fluid contributions of Strasbourg case law. At this stage, it should be pointed out that the right enshrined in Article 8 has far from established a lead on legislative developments at the international and EU level.

4.4 Right to a fair trial

The difficulty in relying on Article 6 in environmental cases is due to the fact that the challenge, which must be real and serious, must concern a 'civil right'.[181]

This led the ECtHR to disregard the provision in the following cases. A right to participation in the decision-making process relating to the construction of a road cannot be inferred from the provision, which applies exclusively to judicial proceedings and not to administrative proceedings.[182] By the same token, the Court held that the challenge to a permit to operate nuclear power plants was not of a civil nature on the ground that there was not a sufficiently close connection between the operating

---

[179] *McGinley and Egan v UK* (n 177), paras 101–2.
[180] *Budayeva v Russia* (n 162); *Tatar v Romania* (n 116), para. 88.
[181] *Association des amis de Saint-Raphaël et Frejus v France*, 29 February 2000.
[182] *Smits, Kleyn and Hal v Netherlands*, 3 May 2003.

standards of the plant and the right to physical protection of the applicants, who were not able to establish the existence of a precise and imminent threat.[183] Finally from this perspective, the link between the decision to extend the operation of a nuclear power plant and the right to bodily integrity was considered too tenuous and too distant.

In other cases, the Strasbourg Court has held that Article 6(1) was liable to be violated; this was the case in a challenge brought against an administrative authorization to store waste, on the ground that the authorization interfered with the rights of owners of adjacent land to use drinking water drawn from that land.[184] Since Article 6(1) grants the citizen the right to have court orders enforced within a reasonable time, the failure to enforce a court order requiring cessation of the operations of a hazardous activity, as well as the unlawful resumption of that activity with a view to circumventing a judicial decision, resulted in a violation.[185] The restriction of access to environmental information may also amount to an infringement of Article 6(1) where the respondent State has prevented the applicant from gaining access to documents which are essential in order to establish his right.[186]

The ECtHR went one step further in adjudicating that proceedings for annulment initiated by an NGO against an authorization permitting the expansion of a nuclear plant, which had not been subject to public inquiry, called into question rights of a civil nature pursuant to Article 6(1). The Court relied on the following argument: given that the NGO's application was instigated in order to 'defend the general interest against that which it perceives as an activity that is hazardous for the general public', there was a sufficient connection with a civil right within the meaning of Article 6(1).[187] Moreover, the ECtHR underscored that a more restrictive interpretation will not match the expectations of modern society, 'where environmental NGOs play a key role'.[188] Finally, it is clear that a local NGO, even though it defends the general interest, also defends the individual interest of its members against the risks created by a landfill.[189]

4.5 Freedom of expression

The two aspects of Article 10—the 'right to receive' information and the right to express ideas—may be called into question by the State. Although the right to information, as well as the corresponding obligation on the authorities to collect it, constitutes one of the pillars of environmental law, Article 10 has been systematically set aside by the ECtHR in environmental cases in favour of Article 8.[190] Furthermore,

---

[183] *Balmer—Schafroth v Switzerland*, 26 August 1997; *Athanassoglou and others v Switzerland*, 6 April 2000.

[184] *Zander v Sweden*, 25 November 1993, para. 27.

[185] *Taskin and others v Turkey* (n 116); *Öneryiltiz v. Turkey* (n 117); *Lemke v Turkey* (n 137), para. 53.

[186] *McGinley and Egan v UK* (n 125), para. 86.

[187] *Collectif national d'information et d'opposition à l'usine Melox—Collectif stop Melox and Mox v France*, 28 March 2006, para. 4 (text only available in French).

[188] *Collectif national d'information et d'opposition à l'usine Melox* (n 187).

[189] *L'Erablière v Belgium*, 24 February 2009.

[190] *Guerra and others v Italy* (n 130), para. 53. This provision 'cannot be construed as imposing on a State...positive obligations to...disseminate information of its own motion'. See *Roche v UK*, 19 October 2005, para. 172.

the applicant must provide evidence that the activity regarding which he is seeking information is of a hazardous nature. On the other hand, the ECtHR will more readily hold that there has been a violation of freedom of expression where it may be jeopardized by legal proceedings for defamation instigated against certain activists and environmental protection associations known for their uncompromising stance on controversial issues.

The following cases merit attention:

- the prohibition on a scientist from mentioning in the media the dangers of a new technology for human health;[191]
- the arrest of eco-warriors peacefully demonstrating against hunting;[192]
- the censorship of a report on seal hunting as well as the ruling for its authors to pay damages;[193]
- the sentencing of an NGO criticizing the behaviour of a municipal councillor favouring illegal building projects in protected areas;[194]
- the finding of public defamation against an elected politician who criticized a senior civil servant for his statement concerning the absence of danger from a radioactive cloud;[195]
- the sentencing of people publicly contesting road developments even though the remarks made contained an element of subjectivity.[196]

4.6 Freedom of assembly and association

References to this provision are somewhat atypical; however, mention should be made of two cases concerning, first, arrangements seeking compulsorily to include land-owners in a hunting association, despite their moral opposition to hunting[197] and, second, to the prohibition on a public meeting by an environmental protection association[198] which was censured under the terms of Article 11 ECHR.

5. Conclusions

At first blush, the EU legal order is far from being perfect from an environmental rights perspective. Consequently, much water will need to flow under the bridge before a right to a clean environment is written in stone in European constitutional law.

That said, the trend towards recognizing a human right to a decent environment grows increasingly stronger with the proclamation of such a right in a number of

---

[191] *Hertel v Switzerland*, 25 August 1998.
[192] *Steel and others v UK*, 23 September 1998.
[193] *Bladet Tromseu and Stensaas v Norway*, 20 May 1999.
[194] *Vides Aizsardzibas Klubs v Latvia*, 27 May 2004.
[195] *Mamère v France*, 7 November 2006.
[196] *Almeida Azevedo v Portugal*, 23 January 2007; *Lombardo and others v Malta*, 24 April 2007.
[197] *Chassagnou and others v France*, 29 April 1999, para. 117; *Schneider v Luxembourg*, 10 July 2007, para. 82.
[198] *Zeleni Balkni v Bulgaria*, 12 April 2007.

national constitutions. Account must be taken of the fact that under Article 6(2) TEU the Union is called on to respect fundamental rights resulting from the constitutional traditions common to all Member States. The recognition of these rights is likely to enhance the appropriate enforcement of protective standards. Indeed, if individuals were accorded the opportunity to avail themselves of their constitutional right to a clean environment through private enforcement proceedings, weak public enforcement would thereby be offset.

In addition, given the binding nature of the Charter, Article 37 is likely to become a benchmark for judicial review of legislative and executive EU acts[199] as well as national measures implementing EU environmental obligations. The relevance of Article 37 has to be enhanced through development of secondary law. In this connection, a number of procedural rights have emerged through the intermediation of EU secondary law with a view to fleshing out some of the obligations of the Aarhus Convention. For instance, in fleshing out the Article 37 requirements into more concrete measures, the lawmaker is likely to award specific rights to the victims of environmental damage. Pursuant to Article 52(5) EUCFR, the ways in which these rights are implemented is subject to review in the light of the previously mentioned principles.

It is also worthy of note that the Court of Justice has shown less deference to national laws on standing. Standing requirements which are too stringent prevent access to justice and, as a result, weaken private enforcement of environmental law. With a view to improving the enforcement of environmental law, the Court has clearly been broadening the scope of rights beyond the directives that aim at protecting human health. In so doing, the Court has taken stock of the fact that in seeking vindication of the correct implementation of EU protective standards, citizens and NGOs have become central figures in modern environmental law. Indeed, they contribute to effective enforcement of environmental law in national courts irrespective of health issues.

Finally, although EU law does not specify a self-executing right to environmental protection, such a right emerges in the wake of the fundamental rights enshrined by the ECHR. Nevertheless, it should be remembered that this case law amounts to a greening of the existing first generation of human rights, rather than forging a new generation of human rights. In other words, this case law falls short of guaranteeing a full right to environmental protection.

---

[199] Hervey and McHale (n 96), 407.

3

Competences, Powers, and Legal Bases

1. Introduction

It has always been a tall order to specify with exactitude the division of competence between the EU and the Member States. Given their cross-cutting nature, the exercise of competence relating to environmental issues has been dogged with controversy. In fact, the allocation of competence between the EU and the Member States tends to be not so much a separation but rather an intermingling of powers.[1] Accordingly, their relationship is more dynamic than static.

It is the aim of this chapter to explore some of the key issues relating to the allocation of environmental competence to the EU. This issue is clearly of central importance. Given that the EU environmental policy straddles a number of other competences, among which the internal market, agriculture, transport, energy, and animal welfare, environmental shared competence interacts constantly with both exclusive and complementary competences listed under Articles 3 and 6 TFEU.

For the sake of clarity, we will distinguish internal competence (Section 2) from external competence (Section 3). Indeed, on an international level, Article 191(4) TFEU emphasizes the shared nature of environmental external competence, as the EU and the Member States each intervene 'within their respective spheres of competence'. As discussed later, this shared competence has implications for the nature of the agreements concluded by the EU.[2]

Whilst the expansion of EU regulatory action aimed at environmental protection dates back to the early 1970s, it has however suffered—following the entry into force of the SEA—from differences of interpretation regarding the legal basis on which legislation adopted in this area is grounded. Section 4 will set out the procedures relating to the legal basis on which measures pursuing environmental objectives are grounded. The relations between Article 192 TFEU with the other legal bases will also be described.

2. Nature of Internal Environmental Competence

2.1 Shared competence

The EU does not have exclusive competence for protecting the environment. Pursuant to Article 4(2)(e) TFEU, the environment has been classified among the 11 shared competences: alongside the internal market, consumers protection, transports, etc.

---

[1] L. Brinkhorst, 'Subsidiarity and European Community Environmental Policy. A Pandora's Box' (1991) *EELR* 20.
[2] Opinion 2/00 [2001] ECR I-9713, para. 47; and Case C-459/03 *Commission v Ireland* [2006] ECR I-4635, para. 92.

Consequently, by virtue of Article 2(2) TFEU, the EU has the power to legislate and to adopt legally binding acts in the environmental area.

As a starting point for analysis of the question of the meaning of shared competence, focus should be placed on Article 2(2) TFEU that reads: 'When the Treaties confer on the Union a competence shared with the Member States in a specific area, the Union and the Member States may legislate and adopt legally binding acts in that area. The Member States shall exercise their competence to the extent that the Union has not exercised its competence. The Member States shall again exercise their competence to the extent that the Union has decided to cease exercising its competence.'

It is important to make six observations in this context.

First, both the EU and the Member States may act in order to protect the environment. However, Member States exercise their competence only if the EU has not exercised its own competence. Member State intervention can be envisioned, first, when the EU has not yet activated its powers, second, when the EU decides to repeal existing legislation without replacing it with new legislation,[3] or when the legislation has been annulled by an EU Court.[4]

Second, if the EU has not taken action, the Member States maintain their competence, provided that they act in accordance with EU law.[5]

- As the following example shows, the absence of EU legislation does not allow the Member States to regulate the use of products as they wish. In accordance with the principle of subsidiarity, the EU legislature has chosen, thus far, to leave enactment of the rules by which to ensure the coexistence of genetically modified crops and neighbouring traditional agricultural crops to the Member States.[6] As long as no decision has been adopted with respect to the coexistence of different categories of crops at the EU level,[7] Member States are empowered to decide on coexistence measures. However, in spite of the ability to lay down national, regional, or local coexistence rules, a Member State is not entitled to make the cultivation of genetically modified organisms (GMOs) subject to a specific national authorization based on considerations of protection of health or the environment.[8] In particular, national authorities are called upon to give consideration to the substantive and procedural conditions provided for in the different EU regulations and directives covering the placing on the market of GMOs and seeds.[9]

---

[3] It should be noted, however, that whenever the EU has acquired new competences regarding the protection of the environment, it has never given them up. That said, the Council and the Parliament have watered down several obligations deemed to be too strict, in particular regarding waste management and nature conservation.

[4] R. van Ooik, 'The European Court of Justice and the Division of Competence in the EU' in D. Obradovic and N. Lavranos (eds), *Interface between EU Law and National Law* (Groeningen: Europa Law, 2007) 24.

[5] Case C-114/01 *AvestaPolarit Chrome Oy* [2003] ECR I-8725, para. 57.

[6] Opinion AG Bot in Case C-442/09 *Bablok* [2011] OJ C311/7, para. 4.

[7] See, eg, Commission Recommendation of 13 July 2010 on guidelines for the development of national measures to avoid the unintended presence of GMOs in conventional and organic crops [2010] OJ C200/1.

[8] Case C-36/11 *Pioneer Hi Bred Italia* [2012] OJ C355/5, para. 69.

[9] See Cases C-58–68/10 *Monsanto* [2011] OJ C311/8, para. 76.

- With respect to the fundamental freedom of free movement of goods, as long as the EU lawmaker has not pre-empted the position in this area, Member States may justify their restrictive measures by invoking either one of the reasons provided for in Article 36 TFEU or a mandatory requirement. Conversely, Member States may no longer rely on these exceptions if the area has already been fully harmonized.

Third, given the sheer breadth of the objectives set out in Article 191(1) TFEU[10] and the zeal of the EU institutions to harmonize an array of environmental issues, it comes as no surprise that national competences are constantly diminishing. It follows that where the subject matter has already been harmonized under secondary law, Member States cannot pursue their own environmental policy. In such a case, the Member States must simply implement secondary law. If they do not do so, infringement proceedings may be brought against them before the Court of Justice for failure to fulfil their EU obligations.

Fourth, the real limits of national environmental competence are based on the manner in which the EU has exercised its own competence. However, as discussed in Chapter 4, the position of EU secondary law is much more complex. Unless the subject matter has already been completely harmonized, the Member States remain free to intervene provided that their regulatory measures are consistent with the economic freedoms of the TFEU. In this context, account must also be taken of the fact that EU legislation is not only minimal but also often incomplete. Thus, where a criterion necessary for the implementation of a directive adopted on the basis of Article 192 TFEU has not been defined in the directive, such definition falls within the competence of the Member States and they have broad discretion, in accordance with Treaty rules, when laying down national rules to develop or give concrete expression to EU obligations.[11] Moreover, the scope of several pieces of environmental legislation is far from complete. In this connection, one example will suffice: given that the 'Forest Focus' Regulation No. 2152/2003 does not seek to effect complete harmonization, it is not designed to establish common rules for governing all activities concerning the management of forest areas. Accordingly, EU law does not preclude any other definition of what constitutes the forests that Member States seek to make subject to any action programme other than those governed by the 'Forest Focus' Regulation.[12]

Fifth, although an area may be subject to harmonization, Member States still retain much leeway. Although Article 192 TFEU is silent on the choice of regulatory instruments, directives have always been preferred to regulations, and framework directives preferred to detailed directives.[13] Indeed, the majority of environmental legislation is 'predicated upon broadly drawn principles and objectives' and follows the principle of subsidiarity by setting mainly general targets for protection.[14] In particular, with respect to management of ecosystems, the need for uniform rules seems less pressing

---

[10] See the discussion in Section 4.3.1.

[11] See, to that effect, Case C-254/08 *Futura Immobiliare and others* [2009] ECR I-6995, paras 48, 52, and 55; and Case C-378/08 *Agusta* [2010] ECR I-01919, para. 55.

[12] Case C-82/09 *Dimos Agiou Nikolaou* [2009] ECR I-03649, para. 26.

[13] See the discussion in Chapter 4, Section 4.2.

[14] J. Scott, 'International Trade and Environmental Governance: Relating Rules and Standards in the EU and the WTO' (2004) 15:2 *EJIL* 309.

than for the establishment of the internal market. In addition, Member States can also depart from EU harmonized standards since this legal discipline is rife with specific escape and safeguard clauses. These highly fluid pieces of legislation charge the national authorities with the programming of implementing measures. Against this background, they are endowed with much latitude to frame their own policy. Consider, for sake of illustration, the review of the decisions adopted by the Commission on the validity of national allocation plans for greenhouse gas (GHG) emission allowances by virtue of Emissions Trading Scheme (ETS) Directive 2003/87/EC.[15] The General Court held that according to the principle of subsidiarity, 'in a field, such as that of the environment governed by [Articles 191–193 TFEU], where the [EU] and the Member States share competence, the [EU], . . . , has the burden of proving the extent to which the powers of the Member State and, therefore, its freedom of action, are limited' with respect to the obligation to implement through proper regulatory instruments the obligations laid down in Directive 2003/87/EC.[16]

Finally, even in situations where the EU lawmaker has already pre-empted the field, the Member States still retain residual competence. Indeed, following the adoption of EU measures, they have the right by virtue of Article 13 TFEU to retain or to introduce more stringent protection measures.[17] As a result, minimum harmonization has been recognized as the modus operandi of environmental policy. Given that minimum harmonization expresses a preference for regulatory differentiation that mirrors subsidiarity,[18] minimum EU environmental standards allow diverging national standards.[19]

2.2 Shared competence and subsidiarity

Since environmental policy is not vested exclusively in the EU, the principle of subsidiarity enshrined in Article 5(3) TEU applies.[20] Moreover, subsidiarity comes further to the fore in the environmental field than in other policies such as the internal market. Indeed, in sharp contrast to the harmonization of the internal market where Member States are usually unable to achieve the economic goals pursed by harmon-

---

[15] [2003] OJ L275/32.

[16] Case T-374/04 *Germany v Commission* [2007] ECR II-4431, para. 78; and Case T-263/07 *Estonia v Commission* [2009] ECR II-03463, para. 52.

[17] Case C-6/03 *Deponiezweckverband Eiterköpfe* [2005] ECR I-2753. See Chapter 7, Section 2.

[18] F. De Cecco, 'Room to Move? Minimum Harmonization and Fundamental Rights' (2006) 43 *CML Rev* 10.

[19] D. Freestone and H. Somsen, 'The Impact of Subsidiarity' in J. Holder (ed.), *The Impact of EC Environmental Law in the UK* (Chichester: Wiley & Sons, 1994) 87.

[20] Case C-114/01 *AvestaPolarit Chrome* [2003] ECR I-8725, para. 56. It should be recalled that the principle of subsidiarity was at the outset enshrined in Art. 130r(4) EEC and was thus restricted to environmental policy. However, the Court of Justice never ruled on that requirement. However, although agriculture falls under the area of shared competence (Art 4(2) d TFEU), the decision to include an active substance in annex I of Directive 91/414 on pesticide fall within the exclusive competence of the Community authorities. It follows that the measure adopted in the exercise of that competence is not covered by application of the principle of subsidiarity. See Case T-420/05 R *Vischim v Commission* [2006] ECR II-3841, para. 223; Case T-334/07 *Denka International v Commission* [2009] ECR II-4205, para. 200; and Case T-31/07 *Dupont de Nemours* [2013] OJ C 156, para. 205.

ization,[21] environment policy entails constant cooperation between all institutional players.

In a nutshell, the aim of the principle of subsidiarity is not to allocate powers, but rather to regulate the use of powers.[22] In particular, the focus is on whether the EU is the most appropriate decision-maker. EU 'action' must satisfy two tests. First, the EU institutions have to demonstrate that the objectives of the proposed action cannot be sufficiently achieved by the Member States 'either at central level or at regional and local level' (sufficiency test). Second, they should also demonstrate that the proposed action, by reason of its scale or its effects, 'can be better achieved at Union level'. According to this second test, the lawmaker is required to demonstrate that the proposed action has an added value in terms of effectiveness (value-added test).

Five separate, albeit related, issues must be distinguished.

The first concerns the objectivity of these two tests. Neither of them establish objective points of comparison.[23] As regard environmental protection, what is 'better' is embroiled in controversy. Does it mean more effective, more protective, more democratic, more social, cheaper, more consistent with internal market obligations or with international obligations, etc? At first glance, no easy answer can be given.[24] That said, there are a number of good reasons to support the view that EU environmental measures easily pass the hurdle of subsidiarity. Several arguments can be mustered in this regard.

On the one hand, there is no doubt as to the Member States' inability to solve environmental issues having a transboundary nature, such as ozone depletion, climate change, biodiversity, air and water pollution, and so on. As a result, regulating these issues should be a matter for the EU and not chiefly for the Member States.

On the other hand, subsidiarity does not preclude the EU lawmaker from regulating issues that do not have a cross-frontier element, such as urban noise, household waste, or contaminated land remediation. Given the significant discrepancies between the Member States regarding the stringency of their environmental policies, EU harmonization ensures that a level playing field exists in all Member States in a way which ensures a high level of environmental protection. In the absence of such a common regulatory approach, the efforts made by the most zealous Member States would easily be frustrated by the passivity of the others.

In addition, it is likely that unilateral measures would exacerbate the distortion of competition and create new barriers to free trade.

The second issue concerns judicial review of legislative powers exercised in this area. Since the EU Courts carry out a marginal review action whenever the institutions have to address complex issues, the Court of Justice has until now never declared void an EU legislative act on the ground that it contradicts subsidiarity. Accordingly, it is likely to reject the claim that existing environmental legal acts violate the principle. In this

---

[21] Case C-58/08 *Vodafone* [2010] ECR I-4999, paras 77 and 78.

[22] A. Estrella, *The EU Principle of Subsidiarity and Its Critique* (Oxford: OUP, 2002) 91; N. de Sadeleer, 'Principle of Subsidiarity and the EU Environmental Policy' (2012) 9:1 *JEEPL* 63–70.

[23] Estrella (n 22), 95.

[24] L. Krämer, *EC Environmental Law*, 6th edn (London: Sweet & Maxwell, 2007), 19.

respect, it is sufficient to observe that with respect to measures regarding safety at work, public health, and food safety, claims according to which these measures could have been better achieved at national level have been rebutted.[25] This prompts the question whether subsidiarity is no more than a mere pre-legislative requirement.

Nevertheless, with the entry into force of the Lisbon Treaty, 'ineffective' *ex post* judicial review has been supplemented by *ex ante* political control that is likely to increase the accountability of the EU's lawmaking bodies.[26] Brief mention should also be made of the fact that pursuant to Article 5(3) TEU and Protocol No. 1 on the Role of National Parliaments in the EU, national parliaments may consider all legislative proposals for compatibility with subsidiarity. Clearly, some parliaments may have a strong interest in ensuring that the EU abides by the principle. What is more, Article 8 of the Protocol confers on the Court of Justice jurisdiction to hear actions for the annulment of EU acts based on the principle of subsidiarity brought by Member States on behalf of their national parliaments or a chamber thereof. That said, whether this review mechanism will lead to closer national checks on the exercise of EU competence as regards the protection of the environment remains to be seen.

The third issue concerns the political impact of subsidiarity. Although it is doubtful whether this principle could become a serious ground for review of environmental measures, EU environmental policy bears the mark of subsidiarity. First, the policy is highly decentralized since control of its implementation is left, by virtue of Article 192(4) TFEU, to the Member States. In particular, the enforcement of EU harmonized measures is entirely left to the Member States.[27] This means that decisions whether to grant a licence for operating a plant, conducting an EIA, regulating waste, designating protected areas, protecting vulnerable species, or prosecuting environmental crimes are matters for national, regional, and even local authorities not for the Commission. Hence, it is appropriate that the Member States establish control and oversight regimes in order to apply the policing measures associated with the conservation of environmental protection[28] and in order to punish infringements.[29] Given that the mechanics of enforcement are likely to diverge significantly between Member States, the adequacy of enforcement still remains a major issue. As the Guardian of the Treaties, the European Commission only exercises a relatively marginal level of control over the proper implementation of EU secondary law.[30]

---

[25] Case C-84/94 *UK v Council (Working Time Directive)* [1996] ECR I-5755; Case C-491/01 *British American Tobacco* [2001] ECR I-11453; Case C-154/04 *Alliance for Natural Health* [2005] ECR I-6541.

[26] M. Dougan, 'The Treaty of Lisbon 2007: Winning Minds, not Hearts' (2008) 45 *CML Rev* 659.

[27] Given the absence of genuine liability rules and legal remedies, private enforcement is still far less prominent.

[28] European Parliament and Council Recommendation 2001/331/EC providing for minimum criteria for environmental inspections in the Member States [2001] OJ L118/41.

[29] See European Parliament and Council Directive 2008/99/EC on the protection of the environment through criminal law [2008] OJ L328/28, replacing Council Framework Decision 2003/80/JAI on the protection of the environment by criminal law. The Framework Decision was nullified in 2005 in Case C-176/03 *Commission v Council* [2005] ECR I-7879.

[30] Given that the Commission does not have investigative powers of its own in the environmental area, it is largely reliant on the information provided by complainants, by public or private bodies, by the press, or by the Member State concerned. See Case C-494/01 *Commission v Ireland* [2005] ECR I-3331, para. 43, Case C-135/05 *Commission v Italy* [2007] ECR I-3475, para. 28; and Case C-297/08 *Commission v Italy*

By the same token, the financing of environmental projects is, by virtue of Article 192(4) TFEU, also a matter for the Member States. Remarkably enough, although the social and economic pillars of sustainable development dispose of funds made available for these purposes,[31] the title dedicated to the environment does not make any provision for structural financing. Moreover, the significance of the socio-economic funds dwarfs the LIFE Programme that is deemed to be one of the spearheads of EU environmental funding.[32] Furthermore, other programmes of importance to the protection of the natural environment depend on the willingness of the Member States to provide matched funding. Although contributions to the agri-environmental schemes, provided for under Regulation (EC) No. 1698/2005 on rural development, may be as low as 15 per cent—unlike the first pillar of the Common Agricultural Policy (CAP), these schemes are subject to co-financing—this appears to be sufficient deterrent for financial intervention by the State.[33]

Another practical observation must be made: the intent to repatriate in the name of subsidiarity some legislation on water protection has not been successful.[34] Indeed, not a single piece of major environmental legislation has been repealed thus far. Instead, subsidiarity-led thinking has been an exercise of simplification and deregulation of existing environmental legislation.

A last issue regarding the personal scope of the principle should be addressed. One school of thought argues that subsidiarity is not exclusively related to the EU Member State dimension. In addition to this vertical dimension (who is the appropriate decision-maker?), the horizontal dimension of the principle has to be emphasized (what is the appropriate instrument).[35] Accordingly, self-regulation should be promoted owing to the rhetoric of subsidiarity. Therefore, subsidiarity signals not only a shift away from detailed harmonization and towards a more flexible regulatory style characterized by vague objectives leaving ample room for manoeuvre but also a shift towards negotiated rule-making through soft law instruments. Such interpretation is open to doubt.[36] It is submitted that the view that the question of whether

[2010] ECR I-1749, para. 101. With respect to the ineffectiveness of enforcement, see R. Williams, 'The European Commission and the Enforcement of Environmental Law: An Invidious Position' (1994) 14 *Yb Eur L* 351; P. Weneraas, *The Enforcement of EC Environmental Law* (Oxford: OUP, 2007) 251–308; L. Krämer, 'The Environmental Complaint in EU Law' (2009) 6:1 *JEELP* 13–35; P. Frassoni, 'Is the Commission Still the Guardian of the Treaties?' (2009–10) 1 *RAE-LEA* 45–57.

[31] Council Regulation (EC) No. 2012/2002 establishing the European Union Solidarity Fund [2002] OJ L311/3.

[32] Launched in 1992, LIFE has financed 3,115 projects contributing in €2.2 billion to the protection of the environment. The latest Financial Instrument for the Environment (LIFE +) was adopted through Regulation (EC) No. 614/2007 concerning the Financial Instrument for the Environment (LIFE +) [2007] OJ L149/1. See Communication from the Commission, Mid-term review of the LIFE + Regulation, COM (2010) 516 final.

[33] B. Jack, *Agriculture and EU Environmental Law* (Farnham: Ashgate, 2009).

[34] A. Weale et al., *Environmental Governance in Europe* (Oxford: OUP, 2000) 359, 461.

[35] B. E. Olsen, 'The Subsidiarity Principle and its Impact on Regulation' in B. E. Olsen and K. E. Sorensen (eds), *Regulation in the EU* (Copenhagen: Thomson-Sweet & Maxwell, 2006) 57.

[36] N. de Sadeleer, 'Particularités de la subsidiarité dans le domaine de l'environnement' (2012) 80 *Droit et Société* 73–90.

environmental goals could be better achieved by self-regulation or by deregulation falls within the scope of the principle of proportionality and not subsidiarity.[37]

2.3 Interaction with other competences

2.3.1 *Introductory comments*

The dividing of various subject areas into different categories of competence matters significantly since this categorization determines the extent to which the EU has the power to legislate. By virtue of shared competence in that area, environmental policy stands out from policies subject to exclusive competence by virtue of Article 3 TFEU as well as complementary competence listed under Article 6 TFEU. However, as discussed previously, the concept of environment must be understood broadly and flexibly.[38] The fact that environmental competence is rather broad does not mean that the EU institutions may encroach upon exclusive or complementary competences. Given that the EU environmental policy also embraces health issues, the management of natural resources, and territorial management, and to some extent worker protection, other areas classified as having shared competence are likely to interact with environmental policy. It is necessary to draw a dividing line between these different areas.

2.3.2 *Interaction with exclusive competence*

Competence over environmental policy is shared, which marks it out from other EU policies with exclusive competence. Article 3(1) TFEU lists a restricted number of areas that fall within the scope of exclusive EU competence, several of which have little connection with environmental issues. That said, whenever exclusive competence interacts with environmental issues, the border with shared competence in this area is somewhat blurred. This is particularly so with the Common Commercial Policy (CCP) that we will address in the following section. Furthermore, under the terms of Articles 3 and 4 TFEU, it should be noted that 'the conservation of marine biological resources under the common fisheries policy' falls exclusively under EU competence, whilst the environment—which includes the conservation of natural resources and biodiversity—is included in shared competences, alongside agriculture, fishing, energy, consumer protection, and common safety concerns in public health.

2.3.3 *Interaction with other shared competences*

2.3.3.1 Health issues

The fact that environmental policy takes account of health protection raises the problem of its delineation with regard to other EU policies, given that health, alongside

---

[37] G. Winter 'Constitutionalizing Environmental Protection in the EU' (2002) 2 *YbEEL* 86.
[38] See the discussion in Chapter 1, Section 2.

Table 3.1 Categorization of competences relating to health and the environment   t-

Environment	Article 4(2)(e)TFEU	Shared competence
Common concerns	Article 4(2)(k)TFEU	Shared competence
in public health matters		
Protection and improvement of human health	Article 6(a)TFEU	Supplementary competence

he environment, is a cross-cutting concern permeating, by virtue of Articles 168(1) TFEU and 35 EUCFR, all other EU policies.[39]

Account must be taken of the fact that there are significant differences between environmental and health policies. First, it should be noted that on an institutional level the framers of the EC Treaty and later the TFEU did not put environmental policy on an equal footing with health policy. In fact, the means of action differ substantially on an institutional level. On the one hand, pursuant to Article 4(2)(e)–(k) TFEU, both competences as regards health aspects of the environmental policy and the 'common safety concerns in public health matters' are shared. On the other, the genuine 'protection and improvement of human health' is deemed to be a complementary competence by virtue of Article 6(a) TFEU (see Table 3.1).

Moreover, this imbalance is accentuated where there is a need to create exceptions to rules harmonizing the internal market, as new measures may be taken in order to curb an environmental risk, but not a strictly health-related concern (Art. 114(5) TFEU).[40]

2.3.3.2 Worker protection issues

The boundary problems we have seen in the previous subsection are all the more evident in relation to 'social policy', for the aspects defined in the TFEU on account that it encompasses the 'improvement in particular of the working environment to protect workers' health and safety'.[41] Indeed, the relationship between environmental policy and health and safety policy for workers is not easy to trace. The working environment focuses on working conditions. That said, several worker protection directives aim at reducing risks relating to exposure to biological agents and chemicals at work.[42] In so doing, they oblige the Member States to abide by rather similar safety obligations to the ones stemming from the environmental directives adopted under Article 192 TFEU. Moreover, the principle of substitution stands astride both environmental and worker protection.[43]

Furthermore, whilst the health and safety of workers is generally subject to measures different from those taken in order to protect residents living near industrial installations, it may however occur that the same instrument lays down internal control

---

[39] However, certain matters such as food safety do not fall within the ambit of environmental policy. See Opinion AG Darmon in Case 62/88 *Greece v Council* [1990] ECR I-1527.

[40] Chapter 3, Section 3.2.   [41] Arts 4(2) and 153(1)(a) TFEU.

[42] European Parliament and Council Directive 2000/54/EC on the protection of workers from risks related to exposure to biological agents at work [2000] OJ L262/21; European Parliament and Council Directive 2004/37/EC on the protection of workers from the risks related to exposure to carcinogens or mutagens at work [2004] OJ L229/23.

[43] Case C-473/98 *Kemikalieinspektionen and Toolex* [2000] ECR 5681, para. 45.

measures concerning worker protection at the same time as external control measures applying to listed installations. Given that it straddles both worker and neighbourhood protection against major accident hazards involving dangerous substances, the Seveso III Directive is a good case in point.[44]

2.3.3.3 Energy issues

Given the absence from the former EC Treaty of a chapter specifically dedicated to energy policy, certain measures promoting renewable energy were adopted on the basis of Article 175 EC (Art. 192 TFEU).[45] This gap has finally been filled by the Treaty of Lisbon. Pursuant to Article 4(2)(i) TFEU, energy has been placed on an equal footing with the other ten categories of shared competence. As a consequence, Article 194(1) TFEU stresses that the Union policy on energy interacts both with 'the establishment and functioning of the internal market and with regard for the need to preserve and improve the environment'. Admittedly, much emphasis has been placed on interaction with environmental policy.[46] One of the four objectives to be pursued is the 'promotion of energy efficiency and energy saving and the development of new and renewable forms of energy'. Given the emphasis placed on climate change under Article 192(1) TFEU, energy measures aiming at preventing climate change should be adopted by virtue of both Articles 192(1) and 194(2) TFEU.

2.3.4 *Interaction with animal welfare*

Article 13 TFEU brings into the limelight animal welfare issues. Although the concept of environment must be distinguished from that of 'animal welfare', its boundaries are not always easy to draw. Some environmental directives enacted on the basis of ex Article 130s EEC (Art. 192 TFEU) contribute to animal welfare.[47] Moreover, Member States justify some measures having equivalent effect to a quantitative restriction on both biodiversity and animal welfare imperative requirements.[48]

2.3.5 *Interaction with supporting, coordinating, and supplementary competences*

A variety of 'supporting', 'coordinating', and 'complementary' competences are bought together in one category under Article 6 TFEU. These competences allow the EU to intervene merely to flank national policies without limiting the national authorities'

---

[44] European Parliament and Council Directive 2012/18/EU on the control of major-accident hazards involving dangerous substances [2012] OJ L197/1.

[45] European Parliament and Council Directive 2001/77/EC on the promotion of electricity produced from renewable energy sources in the internal electricity market [2001] OJ L283/33.

[46] P. Thieffry, 'Les politiques européennes de l'énergie et de l'environnement: rivales ou alliées?' (2009–10) 4 *RAE-LEA* 783–809; K. Kulovesi, E. Morgera, and M. Munoz, 'Environmental Integration and Multi-Faceted International Dimensions of EU Law: Unpacking the EU's Climate and Energy Package' (2011) 48 *CML Rev* 829–91.

[47] Council Directive 1999/22/EC relating to the keeping of wild animals in zoos [1999] OJ L94/24.

[48] Case 100/08 *Commission v Belgium* [2009] ECR I-140, paras 91–3.

freedom of action. In effect, these competences share a common feature, namely the prohibition of harmonization.[49]

The fact that some of these competences do interact with environmental policy should not be overlooked. First, the management of environmental emergencies and other disasters overlaps with civil protection.[50] Pursuant to Article 196(1)(a) TFEU, Member State action at national, regional, and local levels aiming at preventing risk stemming from natural or man-made disasters within the Union has been classified under Article 6(f) TFEU as a complementary competence. Second, by virtue of Article 195(1), the Union complements the action of the Member States in the tourism sector, which is categorized under Article 6(d) TFEU as a complementary competence. Both areas overlap: whereas touristic infrastructures have impacted significantly on the natural environment,[51] ecotourism provides funds for ecological conservation.

3. Nature of External Environmental Competence

3.1 Introductory remarks

A central feature of EU environmental law is its multi-level character. Even if EU environmental policy were to succeed in reducing pollution in the EU, the European environment would still suffer from polluting sources located outside its Member State territories. Conversely, to fuel its economic development, the EU is becoming increasingly dependent on imports of natural resources. It follows that environmental problems associated with the extraction and processing of many materials and natural resources are shifting from the EU to the respective exporting countries.[52] Thus, the EU cannot conduct its environmental policy in isolation.

In its early years, the EU concluded a significant number of international agreements in the area of environmental protection. Given the absence of a specific competence, these agreements were concluded on the basis of the Community's implicit external competences.[53] Since the entry into force of the Single European Act (SEA), according to a combined reading of the last sentence of Article 191(1) and Article 191(4) TFEU, the EU has enjoyed express competence to conclude international agreements in

---

[49] Pursuant to Art. 2(5) TFEU, legally binding acts adopted on the basis of the provisions relating to exclusive competences shall not entail harmonization of Member State laws or regulations. With respect to tourism and civil protection policies, this prohibition is repeated in Art. 195(2) TFEU as well as Art. 196(2) TFEU making it crystal-clear.

[50] By way of illustration, as the frequency and intensity of disasters—eg extreme weather events—affecting Member States and third countries have risen due to climate change, the Civil Protection Mechanism has become a major tool for responding to these disasters. See COM(2008) 130.

[51] The impact of touristic infrastructure on the conservation of habitats protected under Natura 2000 sites may be illustrated by the following cases: Case 304/05 *Commission v Portugal* [2004] ECR I-5901; Case C-304/05 *Commission v Italy* [2007] ECR I-7495; and Case T-461/93 *An Taisce v Commission* [2007] ECR II-733.

[52] European Environment Agency (EEA), *The European Environment 2010. State and Outlook* (Copenhagen: EEA, 2010) 69.

[53] The Community was able to acquire exclusive competence in the environmental field through internal regulation according to the *ERTA* principle. See *ERTA* and Opinion 1/94 [1994] ECR I-5267, para. 77.

the area of environmental protection with third countries and international organizations.[54]

Paragraph 4 reads: 'Within their respective spheres of competence, the Union and the Member States shall cooperate with third countries and with the competent international organisations. The arrangements for Union cooperation may be the subject of agreements between the Union and the third parties concerned.' The material scope of Article 191(4) TFEU is determined in the same way as the EU's internal competences, in the light of the objectives and the principles enshrined in Article 191(1)–(2) TFEU.[55]

Among roughly the one thousand international agreements to which the EU is a party, about one hundred international agreements which relate, directly or indirectly, to the protection of the environment are to be found. As will be seen, the external competence of the Union over environmental matters is shared with the Member States and is therefore not exclusive.[56]

Brief mention should be made here that environmental issues are also at the core of the Union's external action. Pursuant to the objectives of the environmental policy listed in Article 191(1) TFEU, the EU aims at solving 'regional and worldwide problems'. Moreover, in accordance with Article 3(5) TEU, 'in its relations with the wider world, the Union shall... contribute to... the sustainable development of the Earth'. Moreover, pursuant to Article 21(2)(f) TEU a 'high degree of cooperation' is needed, inter alia, in order to 'help develop international measures to preserve and improve the quality of the environment and the sustainable management of global natural resources, in order to ensure sustainable development'.

3.2 Express competence and implied external powers

As a starting point it may be said that this division of external competences appears to be beyond doubt since Article 4(2)(e) TFEU stipulates that competence over environmental matters shall be shared. In addition, pursuant to Article 191(4) TFEU, 'within their respective spheres of competence, the Union and the Member States' are competent to conclude international agreements in the area of environmental protection with third countries and international organizations. Accordingly, external competence in this area is not exclusive, but rather shared between the EU and the Member States.[57]

As a result of this explicit competence of the EU to enter into agreements regarding environmental protection, there is no need to rely on the doctrine of implied powers. Hence, the EU's external competence in the environmental field is not contingent on

---

[54] With a few exceptions (1973 Washington Convention on International Trade in Endangered Species of Wild Fauna and Flora (CITES)), most international environment agreements provide for the accession of regional economic integration organizations.

[55] J. H. Jans and H. Vedder, *European Environmental Law*, 4th edn (Groeningen: Europa Publishing, 2012), 60. See the discussion in Chapter 1, Section 6.

[56] *Commission v Ireland* (n 2), para. 92, noted by P. J. Cardwell and D. French (2007) 19:1 *JEL* 121–9; Opinion AG Poiares Maduro in Case C-246/07 *Commission v Sweden* [2010] ECR I-3317, para. 28; Case C-240/09 *Lesoochranárske zoskupenie* [2011] ECR I-9967, para. 35.

[57] *Commission v Ireland* (n 2).

the prior adoption of EU legislation covering the area of law which would be likely to be affected in the event of participation by the Member States in procedures for the conclusion of the agreement concerned, in accordance with the principle set out by the Court in paragraph 17 of *ERTA*.[58] Similarly, nothing prevents the EU from concluding such agreements in areas which have only partially been subject to EU harmonization.[59]

Nonetheless, only agreements concerning environmental protection matters are subject to the arrangements of Article 191(4) TFEU. Where the agreement falls under an explicit external competence because it does not fall within the ambit of paragraph 4 of that provision, it must comply with the *ERTA* case law. This would be the case if an agreement in the area of public health contemplated, as an ancillary matter, research into the impact of endocrine disruptors. In the same vein, certain international agreements on biodiversity which touch on areas covered by other EU policies may fall under *ERTA* case law.[60]

3.3 Limits to the Member States' external powers

The right of Member States to exercise concurrent external powers is restricted by the principle of exclusivity and the duty of loyal cooperation, in particular in areas touching upon the internal market.

3.3.1 *Principle of exclusivity*

The second subparagraph of paragraph 4 merits special note. This subparagraph is worded as follows: 'The previous subparagraph shall be without prejudice to Member State's competence to negotiate in international bodies and conclude international agreements'. It is not easy to reconcile this sentence with the preceding subparagraph. There is a question whether this subparagraph could be interpreted as authorizing the Member States to negotiate international agreements even at the risk of affecting EU harmonization rules. This interpretation would go against the principles set out in *ERTA*,[61] which negotiators have precluded.[62]

The following interpretation is more convincing. The Member States are empowered to exercise their international competences insofar as their action does not affect the common rules laid down by the EU. In other words, when negotiating, concluding, and implementing such international agreements, the Member States are required not to impinge upon the measures adopted at EU level where the latter result from complete harmonization. This means that the external competence of the Member States in

---

[58] Case C-239/03 *Commission v France* [2004] ECR I-9325, para. 30, noted by P. J. Kuijper (2005) 45 *CML Rev* 1491–500. The principle was reiterated in *Kramer*, a case concerning fisheries conservation. See Joined Cases 3, 4 & 6/76 *Cornelis Kramer and others* [1976] ECR I-1279. Art. 3(2) TFEU fleshes out the principle.

[59] Opinion 2/00 (n 2), para. 44; *Commission v France* (n 58), para. 30; and *Commission v Ireland (Mox Plant)* (n 2), para. 95.

[60] Ph. Léger (ed.), *Commentaire article par article des Traités UE et CE* (Geneva: Helbing & Lictenhahn, 2000) 121–1365.

[61] *ERTA* (n 53), para. 17.

[62] Indeed, a declaration added to the Final Act of the SEA stressed that this subpara. did not affect the *ERTA* case law.

environmental protection matters is limited by the manner in which the EU has exercised its internal competence in that field.[63]

It is necessary to be aware that EU environmental law follows a twofold approach: one relating to ecosystems, listed installations, waste, water sewage, etc; the other relating to the harmonization of product standards.

On the one hand, as evidenced in Chapter 4, much emphasis has been placed on minimum harmonization. Against this background, the EU is not likely to acquire exclusive competence over the majority of environmental rules adopted pursuant to Article 192 TFEU.[64] Indeed, wherever harmonization is minimum or incomplete, which is generally the case in matters concerning nature, water, and the atmosphere, the conclusion of agreements by the Member States will not be liable to affect common EU rules. In this connection, it should be noted that in the *Mox Plant* case, the Court of Justice held that where EU competence is restricted to setting minimum rules, the existence of these common rules does not deprive Member States from their right to conclude an international agreement which itself imposes such standards.[65]

However, exclusive competence acquired through the application of the *ERTA* case law, now codified in Article 3(2) TFEU, is likely to be more usual with respect to product standards where it is subject to maximal and complete harmonization (Art. 114 TFEU).[66]

The absence of EU exclusive competence has practical implications. For instance, nothing prevents a Member State party to the Baltic Sea Convention from proposing to outlaw the discharge of dangerous substances in the marine environment in accordance with that convention, even if secondary EU legislation does not expressly prohibit the discharge of that substance. There is no risk of this international obligation having any effect on EU 'common rules' or altering their scope. This interpretation is sound. As stressed by Advocate General Poiares Maduro, 'the distribution of competences operated by the Treaty is biased towards action: neither Member States nor the Community can block the other from pursuing a higher level of protection of the environment'.[67] Accordingly, all action in this area must be understood as introducing minimum harmonized standards, which in no way prevent further action by the Member States.

3.3.2 *Duty of loyal cooperation*

Although the competence is shared, the Court of Justice has played its part in limiting the cacophony: Member State action is limited by the duty of loyal cooperation

---

[63] Léger (n 60), 125–1366.

[64] Opinion AG Poiares Maduro in *Commission v Sweden* (n 56), para. 30. See also Jans and Vedder (n 55), 63–4; P. Wennerås, 'Towards an Ever Greener Union? Competence in the Field of the Environment and Beyond' (2008) 45 *CML Rev* 1674.

[65] *Commission v Ireland (Mox Plant)* (n 2), paras 70–1. See A. Dashwood, 'Mixity in the Era of the Treaty of Lisbon' in C. Hillion and P. Koutrakos (eds), *Mixed Agreements Revisited* (Oxford: Hart Publishing, 2010) 361.

[66] See the discussion in Section 4.4.

[67] Opinion AG Poiares Maduro in *Commission v Sweden* (n 56), para. 29.

enshrined in Article 4(3) TEU.[68] The Court of Justice has held that where competence is shared, it is essential to ensure close cooperation between the EU and the Member States 'both in the process of negotiation and conclusion and in the fulfilment of the commitments entered into'.[69] In particular, the implications of the duty of loyal cooperation are twofold.

First, the Member States are called upon to cooperate in good faith with the EU institutions in the course of the decision-making process. With respect to the assessment of the environmental impacts of a nuclear plant, the Court has stated that a Member State has a duty to inform and consult the EU institutions prior to engaging in individual action.[70] They are required to do so even if they believe that the subject matter falls outwith the scope of EU law, in case there is a risk of impinging on the EU's competence.[71]

Second, Member States have to refrain from taking individual action, at least for a reasonable period of time, until a conclusion to the cooperation process with the EU institutions has been reached.[72] By way of illustration, the unilateral proposal made by Sweden to list an additional chemical substance in an annex to the Stockholm Convention on Persistent Organic Pollutants, had the consequence of splitting the international representation of the EU and compromising the common position not to propose, at that time, to list the substances at issue.[73] Given that such a unilateral measure was 'likely to compromise the principle of unity in the international representation of the Union and its Member States and weaken their negotiating power with regard to the other parties to the Convention concerned', the Court found that it was in breach of the duty of loyal cooperation under Article 4(3) TEU which applies to shared external competences. In dissociating itself from a concerted common strategy within the Council,[74] Sweden was likely to jeopardize the exercise of EU competence in a specific area of environmental international law. Moreover, the infringement of that duty was independent of the fact that there were no common rules that were liable to be affected within the meaning of the *ERTA* case law.[75] As a result, the Members States are

---

[68] Terminology is confusing. In *Commission v Sweden* (n 56), the Court of Justice used the terms 'duty of cooperation in good faith' as well as 'duty of genuine cooperation' whereas the AG used the term 'duty of loyal cooperation'. Art. 4(3) TEU refers to the 'principle of sincere cooperation'. On this duty, see A. C. Hillion, 'Mixity and Coherence in EU External Relations: The Significance of the Duty of Cooperation' in Hillion and Koutrakos (n 65), 87–115; and 'Mixity and Coherence in EU External Relations: the Significance of the 'Duty of Cooperation' (CLEER Working Papers, 2009).

[69] *Commission v Sweden* (n 56), para. 73; Opinion AG Poiares Maduro in *Commission v Sweden* (n 56), para. 49.

[70] *Commission v Ireland* (n 2), para. 179.

[71] P. J. Cardwell and D. French, 'Who Decides? The European Court of Justice's Judgment on Jurisdiction in the MOX Plant Dispute' (2007) 19:1 *JEL* 125.

[72] Opinion AG Poiares Maduro in *Commission v Sweden* (n 56), para. 49.

[73] *Commission v Sweden* (n 56), paras 91–101. See E. Neframi, 'The Duty of Loyalty: Rethinking its Scope through its Application in the Field of EU External Relations' (2010) 47 *CML Rev* 323–59; G. De Baere, 'O, Where is Faith? O, Where is Loyalty ? Some Thoughts on the Duty of Loyal Co-operation and the Union's External Environmental Competences in the Light of the *PFOS* Case' (2011) 36 *ELR* 405–19; J. van Zeben, 'The Principle of Unity under Article 10 EC and the International Representation of the Union and its Member States' (2010) 3 *EJRR* 304.

[74] *Commission v Sweden* (n 56), para. 91.   [75] Para. 61.

called upon to cooperate with the decision-making process within the context of an international legal framework.

Additionally, where shared competences have been exercised by the EU, the Member States are obliged: (a) to refer matters to the EU Courts and to respect the exclusive jurisdiction of the Court of Justice to rule on all disputes relating to the interpretation and application of EU law; and (b) not to carry out procedures within the ambit of arrangements regulating disputes contained in mixed agreements (arbitration) without having previously informed or consulted the competent EU institutions.[76] Nevertheless, the judicial monopoly of the Court of Justice no longer applies where the States are in agreement over the very principle of the application of EU law. In fact, where there are no disputes regarding the application or interpretation of EU law, nothing prevents the Member States from submitting their disputes to international arbitration.[77]

3.4 Procedural requirements

As far as procedural requirements are concerned, it should be noted that the conclusion of agreements between the EU and one or more States or international organizations is governed by Article 218 TFEU. The eighth paragraph of this provision lays down similar voting procedures in the Council for the conclusion of external agreements as well as for the adoption of corresponding internal rules. Pursuant to Article 218(8) TFEU, if the agreement relates to an area for which the special legislative procedure is required when adopting internal rules, the Council must decide unanimously. Otherwise, it rules by qualified majority voting (QMV).[78] This may be illustrated by the *Danube River Convention* case. This international agreement, approved by the EU, has the goal principally of protecting and improving the quality of river water, despite the fact that it regulates the use of waters in the Danube basin in quantitative terms.[79] Consequently, the Court of Justice held that the improvement of water quality fell within the field of application of paragraph 1 (QMV) and not paragraph 2 (unanimous voting) of ex Article 175(2) EC (Art. 192 TFEU).[80] As a result, the logic of 'communautarisation' superseded the logic of 'intergouvernmentalism'.

---

[76] *Commission v Ireland* (n 2), para. 93. See N. Lavranos, 'The Scope of Exclusive Jurisdiction of the Court of Justice' (2007) 32 *EL Rev* 83.

[77] In the *Iron Rhine* Arbitration, with regard to the limits of its jurisdiction drawn from Art. 344 TFEU, the Arbitral Tribunal found itself in a position analogous to that of a domestic tribunal within the EU. Accordingly, the relevant questions of interpretation of EU law would have to be submitted to the Court of Justice. See *Arbitration Regarding the Iron Rhine Railway (Belgium v Netherlands)*, Arbitral Award of 24 May 2005, paras 103, 119, and 143. Commentators have voiced doubts about the validity of this interpretation. See Cardwell and French (n 71), 128; P. d'Agent, 'De la fragmentation à la cohésion systémique: la sentence arbitrale du 24 mai 2005 relative au "Rhin de fer" in *Droit du pouvoir, Pouvoir du droit. Mélanges J. Salmon* (Brussels: Bruylant, 2007) 113.

[78] Given that international environmental agreements are mixed, the requirement of QMV is somewhat illusory, since the agreement at issue must be ratified by all Member States.

[79] This approach should have meant that the Council decided unanimously pursuant to ex Art. 175(2) EC (Art. 192(2) TFEU), which required that these procedures be used for the adoption of measures relating to 'the management of water resources'.

[80] Case C-36/99 *Spain v Council* [2001] ECR I-279, paras 60–74.

3.5 Mixed agreements and their internal effects

3.5.1 *The practice of mixed agreements*

In practice, all environmental agreements to which the EU is a contracting party, including those concluded both before and after the entry into force of the SEA, are classified in the academic literature as 'mixed agreements' since they were concluded both by the EU as well as by the Member States.[81] However, the mere fact that the EU is not a party to an agreement does not have the effect of binding the latter where it has not exercised the competences previously held by the Member States. This doctrine applies even if all the Member States are party to the international agreement.[82]

Thus, these agreements are negotiated, concluded, implemented, and managed jointly by the EU and the Member States. In particular, the mixed representation at the conferences of parties guarantees the participation of both the EU and its Member States in the decision-making process. However, mixity entails rather complex negotiations and delays the entry into force of the agreement. Furthermore, according to some authors, the rather cumbersome and time-consuming mixed representation has hampered the EU's capacity to become a global actor on the international scene.[83] The visibility of the EU has been blurred by the presence at the conferences of parties of the Member States, the Commission, and the Member State holding the presidency. In addition, the rigidly defined EU common position is at odds with the flexibility needed in international negotiations.[84] Whether the new political role conferred on the High Representative would be able to pacify this conflictive exercise of concurrent competences remains to be seen.

3.5.2 *Mixed agreements as ground for reviewing the legality of EU measures*

It is now necessary to address the issue of the binding effect of mixed agreements which have the same status in the EU legal order as purely EU agreements insofar as their provisions fall within the scope of EU competence.[85] Given that the agreements concluded by the EU have primacy over secondary EU legislation,[86] the conclusion of an international agreement has the effect of binding both the EU and the Member States by virtue of Article 216(2) TFEU.

---

[81] A. Rosas, 'Mixed Union–Mixed Agreements' and L. Granvik, 'Incomplete Mixed Environmental Agreements of the EU and the Principle of Bindingness' in M. Koskenniemi (ed.), *International Law Aspects of the EU* (The Hague: Kluwer Law, 1998) 125, 255; P. Okowa, 'The EC and International Environmental Agreements' (1995) 15 *Yb EL* 169–92.

[82] Case C-188/07 *Mesquer* [2008] ECR I-4501, para. 85.

[83] T. Fajardo del Castillo, 'Revisiting the External Dimension of the Environmental Policy of the EU: Some Challenges Ahead' (2010) 4:4 *JEEPL* 365–90.

[84] Eg under several mixed agreements the EU is not to exercise its right to vote if any of its Member States exercise their right to vote and vice versa. See G. Loibl, 'The Role of the European Union in the Formation of International Environmental Law' (2002) 2 *YbEEL* 240.

[85] Case C-213/03 *Etang de Berre* [2004] ECR I-7357, para. 25.

[86] Case C-61/94 *Commission v Germany* [1996] ECR I-3989, para. 52; and Case C-311/04 *Algemene Scheeps Agentuur Dordrecht* [2006] ECR I-609, para. 25.

It follows that the compliance of EU secondary law with these international obligations may be subject to review before the EU Courts. Moreover, the very fact that a
treaty, such as that on biological diversity, contains provisions which do not have direct
effect does not preclude the ability of the Courts to review compliance with the
obligations incumbent upon the EU as a party to that agreement.[87]

In cases involving preliminary references questioning the validity of EU legal acts in
the light of international treaty law, the Court of Justice may carry out a review
provided that, first, the EU is bound by the agreement and, second, 'only where the
nature and the broad logic of the latter do not preclude this and, in addition, the treaty's
provisions appear, as regards their content, to be unconditional and sufficiently precise'
as to confer on persons subject to EU law the right to rely thereon in legal proceeding in
order to contest the legality of an EU act.[88] These conditions are applied restrictively.

As regards the second condition, the Court of Justice is keen to take into consideration the broad logic of international environmental agreements. In *Etang de Berre*, the
Court of Justice held that the recognition of the direct effect of an obligation laid down
in the Protocol for the Protection of the Mediterranean Sea against Pollution from
Land-Based Sources to subject discharges of dangerous substances to the issue of an
authorization, could only serve the purpose of that Protocol. Such recognition reflects
'the nature of the instrument, which is intended, inter alia, to prevent pollution
resulting from the failure of public authorities to act.'[89] However, the logic of other
environmental agreements makes it impossible to recognize some of their provisions as
having direct effect even if they do lay down a clear and precise stipulation. For
instance, in *Intertanko* the Court held that the broad logic of the Montego Bay
Convention on the Law of the Sea, as revealed in particular by its aim, preamble, and
terms, precluded examination of the validity of EU measures in the light of its
provisions.[90] Nevertheless, according to *Intertanko*, in accordance with the customary
principle of good faith and the requirement of loyal cooperation, the provisions of
secondary EU legislation falling within the scope of the agreement must be interpreted
'taking into account' the latter.[91] Moreover, as the Court found in *Mesquer*, this
obligation to take into account international law must be interpreted narrowly and
cannot go as far as to circumscribe the scope of cost-allocation arrangements provided
for under secondary law.[92]

The third condition is fulfilled where the provision relied upon contains 'a clear and
precise obligation which is not subject, in its implementation or effects, to the adoption

---

[87] Case C-437/98 *Netherlands v Parliament and Council* [2001] ECR I-7079, paras 53–4.
[88] See Case C-308/06 *Intertanko* [2008] ECR I-4057, paras 54–65, noted by P. Eckhout (2009) 46 *CML
Rev* 2041–57; and J. Makowiak (2009) 45:2 *RTDE* 396. See also F. Dopagne, 'Arrêt "Intertanko": l'appréciation de la validité d'un acte communautaire au regard de conventions internationales' (2008) 152 *JDE*
241–3; Wennerås (n 64), 1719–22; J. Gonzalez Gimenez, 'Regimen Comunitario de la contaminacion por
descargas procedentes de buques: la relacion con las normas internacionales y la sentencia del TJCE sobre el
asunto Interkanko' (2009) *RDCE* 915–44.
[89] Para. 45.   [90] *Intertanko* (n 88), para. 48.
[91] *Intertanko* (n 88), para. 52. However, the Court did not reiterate the formula which it uses with regard
to the principle of interpretation for conformity with directives.
[92] *Mesquer* (n 82), para. 85.

of any subsequent measure'.[93] Given that many international obligations are couched in vague, flexible, hortatory terms rather than prescriptive language, this condition, as is clear from the following examples, is not easily fulfilled.

- In *ATAA*, the Court of Justice took the view that the Kyoto Protocol provisions on the reduction of GHG emitted by aviation were not unconditional and sufficiently precise to provide a basis for challenging the validity of the EU Directive on aviation.[94]

- By the same token, in *Lesoochranárske zoskupenie*, the Court held that Article 9(3) of the Aarhus Convention had no direct effect on the ground that it does not contain 'any clear and precise obligation capable of directly regulating the legal position of individuals.'[95] Nonetheless, with a view to safeguarding rights which individuals derive from the mixed agreement and EU secondary law, the Court expressed the view that the provision at issue could not be interpreted by national courts in such a way as to make it in practice impossible or excessively difficult to exercise rights conferred by EU law.[96] Applying the doctrine of consistent interpretation may in such a case lead to a similar result as would have direct effect.[97]

3.5.3 *Interpretation of mixed environmental agreements*

Where a case is brought before the Court of Justice for a preliminary ruling, the Court has jurisdiction to define the obligations which the EU has assumed and those which remain the sole responsibility of the Member States in order to interpret the mixed agreement. Accordingly, the Court of Justice has jurisdiction to give preliminary rulings on the validity and interpretation of mixed agreements falling within the competence of the EU.

However, it is not easy to draw the boundaries between the respective spheres of competence.[98] Indeed, as a matter of practice, the declarations deposited by the EU while concluding the agreements do not clearly allocate the powers between the EU and the State authorities. Where a provision can apply both to situations falling within the scope of national law and to situations falling within the scope of EU law, provided that the EU 'has exercised its powers and adopted provisions to implement obligations deriving from' the mixed agreement, the Court of Justice is best placed to interpret whether a particular provision of a mixed agreement has direct effect.[99] Indeed, in

---

[93] Case 12/86 *Demirel* [1987] ECR 3719, para. 14; *Etang de Berre* (n 85), para. 39; and *Lesoochranárske zoskupenie* (n 56), para. 4.

[94] Case C-366/10 *ATAA* [2011] OJ C49/7, para. 77.

[95] *Lesoochranárske zoskupeni* (n 56), para. 45.

[96] *Commission v Sweden* (n 56), para. 49.

[97] A. Rosas, 'The European Court of Justice and Public International Law' in J. Wouters, A. Nollkaemper, and E. de Wet (eds), *The Europeanisation of International Law* (The Hague: Asser Press, 2008) 76.

[98] M. Montini, 'EC External Relations on Environmental Law' in J. Scott (ed.), *Environmental Protection. European Law and Governance* (Oxford: OUP, 2009) 140; T. Fajardo del Castillo, *La politica exterior de la Union Europea en materia de medio ambiente* (Madrid: Tecnos, 2005) 80.

[99] *Lesoochranárske zoskupenie* (n 56), para. 34, case note (2012) 49 *CML Rev* 782.

order to forestall future differences of interpretation, that provision should be interpreted uniformly.[100]

Although the subject matter has not yet been subject to EU legislation, it still 'may fall within the scope of EU law if it relates to a field covered in large measure by it'.[101] In a case concerning whether an environmental protection association may be a 'party' to administrative proceedings concerning the protection of a species protected under the Habitats Directive, the Court expressed the view that the dispute fell within the scope of EU law and that it had jurisdiction to interpret whether Article 9(3) of the Aarhus Convention had direct effect.

Conversely, where the EU has not legislated within the particular 'sphere' of the mixed agreement, it is for the national courts to interpret the provisions of the mixed agreement and to determine whether they should be construed as having direct effect within a particular Member State's legal order.[102]

3.5.4 *Obligations placed on Member States*

Once environmental mixed agreements have been concluded by the EU, they form an integral part of the EU legal order. Accordingly, the EU as well as the Member States are jointly responsible for fulfilling the obligations owed to third States. By breaching a mixed agreement, a Member State can trigger EU responsibility. Moreover, the obligations resulting from the mixed agreement are applicable to the Member States, despite the absence of EU secondary rules. This is in particular the case as regards an obligation to authorize pollution from land-based sources in fresh water, included in a mixed agreement—the Protocol to the Barcelona Convention for the Protection of the Mediterranean Sea against Pollution, since those discharges had not been subject to specific EU legislation and, as a result, fell under France's own competence.[103] However, the duty to comply with international law has seldom led the European Commission to initiate infringement proceedings against the Member States failing to do so.[104]

By the same token, as long as it is worded in clear, precise, and unconditional terms, the requirement for such a mixed agreement to subject the discharge of pollutants into surface water to an authorization procedure has direct effect.[105] Interestingly, the Court stressed in *Etang de Berre* that direct effect 'can only serve the purpose of the Protocol...and reflect the nature of the instrument, which is intended, *inter alia*, to prevent pollution resulting from the failure of public authorities to act'.[106] This case law underscores the Court's willingness to ensure the enforcement of mixed agreements at a domestic level.

---

[100] *Lesoochranárske zoskupenie* (n 56), para. 42.   [101] *Lesoochranárske zoskupenie* (n 56).
[102] *Lesoochranárske zoskupenie* (n 56), para. 40.
[103] *Commission v France* (n 58), para. 30. See P. J. Kuijper, 'International Responsibility for EU Mixed Agreements' in Hillion and Koutrakos (n 65), 210.
[104] Remarkably enough, there has been one case adjudicated by the Court of Justice on the correct implementation of CITES. See Case C-182/89 *Commission v France* [1990] ECR I-4337.
[105] *Etang de Berre* (n 85).   [106] *Etang de Berre* (n 85), para. 45.

In concluding mixed environmental agreements, the EU usually passes their obligations on to its Member States in the form of directives or regulations. As a matter of practice, where the international agreement lays down trade-related measures, the EU generally adopts regulations. Although these regulations enhance a homogeneous application of international environmental law, they do not always deprive Member States from enacting more stringent measures.[107]

3.6 Concluding remarks

In sum, the developments noted previously mean that the division of competences regarding the external competence of the EU in environmental protection matters manifests itself in three stages.[108]

First, since the EU has exercised its express shared competence over external relations in the environmental sector, there is no longer any need to invoke the theory of the exercise of internal competence in order to justify the conclusion of an agreement. This is the case where the object and purpose of the mixed agreement essentially relate to environmental matters.

Second, where the object and goal of an agreement do not necessarily relate to the environment within the meaning of Article 191 TFEU, but to other matters, Article 191(4) TFEU no longer applies. Where there is no other explicit external competence, the agreement must be concluded, in accordance with *ERTA* case law, on the basis of an implicit external competence. Moreover, where an area of law has been completely harmonized (which is often the case for instruments regulating the internal market that contribute to environmental protection pursuant to Art. 114(3) TFEU), competence may become exclusive, having regard to the risk of implications for secondary law.

Third, where harmonization is minimal, which is often the case for instruments the main objective of which is protection of the environment, the Member States may conclude international agreements which touch on EU harmonization rules. In the event of disputes between the Member States, the latter must respect the obligations applicable to them pursuant to Article 4(3) TEU (duty of cooperation) and Article 344 TFEU (obligation to respect the exclusive competence of the Court of Justice to rule on all disputes concerning the interpretation and application of EU law).

4. Choice of Legal Bases

4.1 Introductory remarks

Few sectors of EU law still elude the growing reach of environmental concerns. Hence, whilst before the entry into force of the Lisbon Treaty the majority of rules which aim

---

[107] European Parliament and Council Regulation (EC) No. 850/2004 on persistent organic pollutants [2004] OJ L158/7.

[108] I. Macleod, D. Hendry, and S. Hyett, *The External Relations of the European Communities* (Oxford: OUP, 1996) 327.

to protect the environment fell under the aegis of the first pillar (formerly the Treaty establishing the European Community), the two other pillars have not remained untouched by this cross-cutting issue. The frameworks put in place for military operations, which fall under the Common Foreign and Security Policy (formerly the second pillar; currently Title V EU), have impacts on the environment.[109] Similarly, the need to combat environmental crime effectively has resulted in the policy for Police and Judicial Cooperation in Criminal Matters (formerly the third pillar; currently Arts 82–89 TFEU) opening itself up to this issue.[110] Furthermore, by virtue of the integration clause enshrined in Article 11 TFEU,[111] measures taken in order to protect the environment have progressively merged with an array of other policies. Due to their cross-cutting nature, environmental questions are much broader and interact constantly with different EU policies, the legal bases of which have proliferated as a result of successive revisions to the founding Treaties. To some extent, these other EU policies also contribute to improving environmental protection.

It must not be lost from view that each piece of EU legislation must be founded on one or more legal basis set out in the TEU and TFEU. The byzantine structure of Treaty law with its diversification of legal bases likely to provide for specific competences to address environmental challenges remains the subject of ongoing debate. Indeed, given the cross-cutting nature of environmental issues, the choice of legal base for the adoption of an environmental measure is far from self-evident. As emphasized later, identification of the act's centre of gravity may prove particularly difficult.

On the one hand, the competence to protect the environment is not limited in advance by reference to a particular subject matter defined *ratione materiae* but rather by a flurry of broad objectives encapsulated in Article 191(1) TFEU. Given the general nature of these objectives and the imprecision of the concept environment, it is difficult to lay down the exact limits of the areas covered by the policy.[112] As a result, genuine environmental measures adopted by virtue of Article 192 are likely to encroach on other EU policies.

On the other hand, not all the provisions which are closely, or remotely, related to the environment are likely to be adopted by virtue of the provisions laid down in Title XX TFEU, a title that is entirely devoted to environmental protection. Indeed, the proliferation of legal bases in the environmental field has not been blocked by Article 192 TFEU, a provision regulating the decision-making of environmental measures. In effect, it is settled case law that this genuine environmental legal basis does not alter the

---

[109] According to the 2007 Annual Report of the Council to the European Parliament on the main aspects and basic choices of the CFSP, 'energy security, climate change and the scarcity of resources will continue to grow in importance within the CFSP context'. See European Communities, Council document on the main aspects and basic choices of the Common Foreign and Security Policy (CFSP) presented to the European Parliament in application of para. G (para. 43) of the Interinstitutional Agreement of 17 May 2006 (2007) 13.

[110] See in particular Case C-176/03 *Commission v Council* (n 29); and Case C-440/05 *Commission v Council* [2007] ECR I-9097.

[111] See the discussion in Chapter 1, Section 5.

[112] See, by analogy, the protean nature of other EU policies, such as economic and social cohesion. See Opinion AG Poiares Maduro in Case C-166/07 *Parliament v Council* [2009] ECR I-7135, para. 81.

competences which the EU holds under the terms of other provisions contained in either the TEU or the TFEU.

Needless to say, the choice of legal basis of legislation aiming at protecting the environment represents a critical juncture in relations between institutions, as well as relations between the Member States and the EU.

First, in defining the scope of EU's intervention, the legal base enables the EU to exercise its legislative competence in a given field.[113] Moreover, the basis chosen determines not only which institution has competence to take action but also the procedure to follow and the objective pursued. It also determines the types of act that can be adopted.[114]

Just as the powers of the Commission, the Parliament, and the Council are capable of varying considerably depending on the procedure used, they can also end up expressing contradicting preferences as regards the choice to be made between the different legal bases provided for.[115] Indeed, the choice between a basis which requires unanimity within the Council and a basis which requires only a qualified majority is fundamental,[116] as too is the choice between a basis implying an ordinary legislative procedure (OLP) and a special legislative procedure (SLP).[117] Admittedly, an incorrect choice of legal basis does not therefore constitute a purely formal defect. Although the Treaty of Lisbon has generalized to some extent the OLP, situations in which the special legislative procedure applies remain sufficiently numerous to result in institutional conflicts. Unsurprisingly, given that the choice of legal base shapes the decision-making process and influences its political outcomes, the institutions seek to choose the legal basis that provides the procedure most advantageous to them.[118] The fact that such a choice is deemed to be of constitutional importance is likely to guarantee institutional equilibrium.

---

[113] Art. 5(1) TEU provides that 'The limits of Union competence are governed by the principle of conferral'. Accordingly, competence is conferred on the EU by a swathe of Treaty provisions in order to achieve objectives particular to those provisions, read in the light of the general objectives of the EU. As a result, the legal base occupies centre stage inasmuch as it identifies the competence under which EU institutions act.

[114] K. St C. Bradley, 'The European Court and the Legal Basis of Community Legislation' (1998) *EL Rev* 379; N. Emiliou, 'Opening Pandora's Box: the Legal Basis of Community Measures Before the Court of Justice' (1994) *EL Rev* 488; B. Peter, 'La base juridique des actes en droit CEE' (1994) 378 *RMC* 324; L. Defalque et al., *Libre circulation des personnes et des capitaux. Rapprochement des législations. Commentaire J. Mégret* (Brussels: IEE, 2007) 225–40; D. Chalmers and A. Tomkins, *EU Public Law* (Cambridge: CUP, 2007) 140; D. Chalmers, G. Davies, and G. Monti, *European Union Law* (Cambridge: CUP, 2010) 95; C. Kohler and J.-C. Engel, 'Le choix approprié de la base juridique pour la législation communautaire: enjeux constitutionnels et principes directeurs' (2007) *Europe* 4–10; Jans and Vedder (n 55), 59–94; N. de Sadeleer, 'Environmental Governance and the Legal Bases Conundrum' (2012) *YEL* 1–29.

[115] R. Barents, 'The Internal Market Unlimited: Some Observations on the Legal Basis of EU Legislation' (1993) 30 *CML Rev* 85; H. Cullen and H. Charlesworth, 'Diplomacy by Other Means: the Use of Legal Basis Litigation as a Political Strategy by the European Parliament and Member States' (1999) 36 *CML Rev* 1243.

[116] If QMV prevails, recalcitrant Member States opposing the adoption of the proposed measure could be sidelined.

[117] Art. 289(1)–(2) TFEU. With respect to environmental policy, some acts have to be taken by the Council unanimously (Art. 192(2) TFEU) whereas others by a qualified majority (Art. 192(1) TFEU). Accordingly, as regards environmental policy, the role of the European Parliament varies considerably: it can be placed on an equal footing with the Council or it can merely be consulted by the Council.

[118] Chalmers, Davies, and Monti (n 114), 95.

In a recent case regarding the validity of a Council position to be adopted on behalf of the EU in a body established by CITES, the Court of Justice placed particular emphasis on the obligation to indicate the legal basis of a legal act. The indication is justified in the light of the principle of the allocation of powers, the duty to preserve the prerogatives of the EU institutions, the obligation to state reasons, and the requirement of legal certainty.[119]

Second, although the inter-institutional power struggles have abated to some extent with the generalization of the general legislative procedure, the antagonism between Member States and the EU is still alive.[120] In effect, when regulating activities impairing the environment, the EU does not act in a policy vacuum. Indeed, as regards the vertical division of competence, the choice significantly affects the room for manoeuvre left to the Member States. Using Article 207 TFEU as the legal base for a regulation regulating trade in hazardous substances implies that the act is a matter of exclusive competence.[121] Conversely, using Article 192(1) TFEU to adopt such an act implies that the act is a matter of shared competence.[122] In addition, in accordance with Article 193 TFEU, where the legal base is Article 192 Member States cannot be prevented 'from maintaining or introducing more stringent protective measures' inasmuch as these measures are compatible with the Treaties.

This fourth section unfolds in seven subsections. Before embarking on an analysis of the conflicts between environmental policy and other EU policies, it is necessary to recall in Section 4.2 the principles which govern the choice of legal bases and the review by the Court of its exercise. Section 4.3 examines the different legal bases encapsulated in Article 192 TFEU. Sections 4.4 to 4.8 cover conflicts between environmental policy and the internal market, the CCP, the CAP, criminal law, and nuclear law. Underpinning this analysis of the case law is the view that environmental issues are progressively addressed within a broad range of EU policies. This evolution is testament to the influence of the key objective of sustainable development.

4.2 Principles governing review by the Court of Justice of the choice of legal bases

When confronted with a draft act, the instinctive reaction of lawyers from the institutions, bodies, and organisms of the EU is to search for the legal base which could serve as its foundation. Similarly, judges and advocates general share the same instinct when examining applications and preliminary references concerning such acts. It is hence through the practice of substantive law that one achieves an awareness of the importance of this issue. The question is especially important since disputes concerning the legal bases of environmental acts are far from limited in number.

The choice of the legal base is not a purely formal question, but rather one of substance, being a matter of 'constitutional significance'[123] that is regularly ruled on by

---

[119] C-370/07 *Commission v Council* [2009] ECR I-8917, paras 37, 39, 46, and 48. It should be noted that AG Kokott stressed in addition to these obligations the principle of transparency (paras 37 and 38).
[120] Wennerås (n 64).   [121] Art. 3(1)(e) TFEU.   [122] Art. 4(2)(e) TFEU.
[123] Opinion 2/00 (n 2), para. 5.

the Court of Justice. It is settled case law that 'the choice of the legal base for a measure may not depend simply on an institution's conviction as to the object pursued'.[124] Instead, the determination of the legal base is amenable to judicial review, which includes in particular the aim and the content of the measure.[125]

If it is established that the act simultaneously pursues different objectives or has several components that are inextricably linked, and if one of these is identifiable as the main or predominant purpose or component whereas the other is merely incidental, it will have to be founded on a single legal base, namely that required by the main or predominant purpose or component—the centre of gravity of the act—rather than its effects.[126] Accordingly, the act concerned should in principle be adopted on one sole legal base, *namely that required by the main or predominant purpose or component.* It is therefore necessary to define precisely the scope of each legal base which is likely to found the proposed measure and to distinguish the core objectives and components from those which are ancillary. By way of example, the mere fact that the act contributes simultaneously to the internal market and environmental policy is insufficient to take it outwith the core of one of these EU policies.

However, it may be the case that the twin objectives and the two constituent parts of the act are 'inseparably' or inextricably linked without one being secondary and indirect in relation to the other. In such a case, it is impossible to apply the predominant aim and content test. Exceptionally, the Court of Justice accepts that such a measure must be founded on the corresponding legal bases and the applicable legislative procedures respected.[127] In other words, this will call for recourse to a dual or multiple legal base, provided that the corresponding procedures are compatible.

The fact that EU action may have a different legal base poses barely any difficulties where the procedures are identical. By way of illustration, the novel food regulation is founded on three legal bases: Articles 43, 114, and 168(4) TFEU.[128] By the same token, in order to adopt an act promoting the use of renewable energy with the aim of combating climate change—objectives laid down under Articles 191(1) and 194(1)—the legislature ought to have recourse to both Articles 192(1) and 194(2) TFEU, both of which require recourse to the OLP.

However, where there are differences between the procedures, the decision-making process becomes much more complex. In effect, the compatibility of the procedures may raise difficulties, both with regard to the rules governing the majority within the Council and with regard to the participation of the European Parliament, which for

---

[124] Case C-300/89 *Commission v Council* ('*Titanium Dioxide*') [1991] ECR I-2867, para. 10.

[125] See, inter alia, *Titanium Dioxide* (n 124), para. 10; Case C-269/97 *Commission v Council* [2000] ECR I-2257, para. 43; Case C-211/01 *Commission v Council* [2003] ECR I-8913, para. 38; and Case C-338/01 *Commission v Council* [2004] ECR I-4829, para. 54.

[126] See, inter alia, Case C-155/91 *Commission v Council* [1993] ECR I-939, paras 19 and 21; Case C-36/98 *Spain v Council* [2001] ECR I-779, para. 59; Case C-211/01 *Commission v Council* (n 125), para. 39; Case C-281/01 *Commission v Council* [2002] ECR I-12049, para. 57; Case C-338/01 *Commission v Council* (n 125), para. 55; and Case C-91/05 *Commission v Council* [2008] ECR I-3651, para. 73.

[127] *Titanium Dioxide* (n 124), para. 13; Case C-336/00 *Huber* [2002] ECR I-7699, para. 31; Case C-281/01 *Commission v Council* (n 126), para. 35; Case C-211/01 *Commission v Council* (n 125), para. 40; Case C-91/05 *Commission v Council* (n 126), para. 75; and Opinion 2/00 (n 2), para. 23.

[128] European Parliament and Council Regulation (EC) No. 1829/2003 on genetically modified food and feed [2003] OJ L268/1.

certain procedures is merely consulted whilst for others is actively involved as a co-legislator. Therefore, no dual legal base is possible *where the procedures laid down for each legal base are incompatible with one another.*[129] This relative strict view entails the risk that in some cases it would not be possible to give priority to the OLP.[130] As a result, recourse to the SLP is likely to encroach upon Parliament's rights whereas the use of other legal bases may *involve greater participation by the Parliament inasmuch as they provide for the adoption of a measure by the ordinary legislative procedure.*[131] In particular, this would undermine 'the fundamental democratic principle that the people should participate in the exercise of power through the intermediary of a representative assembly.'[132] In addition, the use of two different legal bases is also liable to affect the Member States' right to enact more stringent measures.[133]

The case law has recently undergone a certain change in emphasis. Aware of such difficulties, the Court of Justice has held that *an act could be based on the dual legal base* inasmuch as it is not impossible from the point of view of legislative technique.[134] However, that situation is deemed to be exceptional.[135] It follows that it is only where the procedures are incompatible from the point of view of legislative technique that a dual legal base is impossible and a choice has to be made between them.

That said, the difficulties raised by recourse to a dual legal base may also encourage the institutions to split the act into two distinct acts, one based on the legal base that is more favourable for the European Parliament and the other on a base which is less favourable for it or one that leads to minimal harmonization and the other to maximal harmonization. However, this dissociation may compromise consistency of EU action.[136]

4.3 The environmental legal bases

4.3.1 *Measures under Article 192(1) TFEU: ordinary legislative procedure*

Following the entry into force of the Treaty of Amsterdam, the co-decision procedure from the first paragraph of Article 175 EC (Art. 192 TFEU) has been brought into line

---

[129] *Titanium Dioxide* (n 124), paras 17–21; Joined Cases C-164/97 & C-165/97 *Parliament v Council* [1999] ECR I-1139, para. 14; Case C-338/01 *Commission v Council* (n 125), para. 57; Case C-94/03 *Commission v Council* [2006] ECR I-1, para. 52; Case C-178/03 *Commission v Parliament and Council* [2006] ECR I-107, para. 57; and Case C-155/07 *Parliament v Council* [2008] ECR I-8103, para. 37.

[130] Case C-155/07 *Parliament v Council* (n 129).

[131] Case C-178/03 *Commission v European Parliament and Council* (n 129); Case C-155/07 *Parliament v Council* (n 129), para. 37.

[132] *Titanium Dioxide* (n 124), para. 20; and Case C-65/93 *Parliament v Council* [1995] ECR I-643, para. 21.

[133] Wennerås (n 64), 70.

[134] Case C-155/07 *Parliament v Council* (n 129), para. 79. Regarding the combination between the OLP referred to in Art. 159(4) EC (Art. 175 TFEU) and the requirement that the Council should act unanimously in accordance with Art. 308 EC (Art. 352 TFEU), see Case C-166/07 *Parliament v Council* [2009] ECR I-7135, para. 69, noted by T. Corteau (2011) 48:4 *CML Rev* 1271–96. According to Cremona, the Court takes the view that safeguarding the Parliament's rights by using the OLP does not undermine the Council's right to be the sole lawmaker. See M. Cremona, 'Balancing Union and Member State Interests: Opinion 1/2008, Choice of Legal Base and the Common Commercial Policy under the Treaty of Lisbon' (2010) 35 *EL Rev* 686.

[135] Case C-411/06 *Commission v Parliament* [2009] ECR I-7585, para. 49.

[136] See Opinion AG Kokott in Case C-155/07 *Parliament v Council* (n 129), para. 89.

with the provisions governing the completion of the internal market. Following the entry into force of the Treaty of Lisbon, pursuant to Article 192(1) TFEU measures of secondary law aiming at environmental protection must now be adopted in accordance with the OLP that is replacing the co-decision procedure.[137] However, there is a formal difference between the standard procedure regulated by Article 192 TFEU and that governed by Article 114 TFEU, a legal basis which takes on considerable importance with regard to the impact of products on the environment. Article 192 TFEU stipulates that the Committee of the Regions be consulted, a requirement flowing from the regional impact of EU environmental policy.[138] In substantive terms, it should be noted that Article 114 TFEU provides that the Council adopt 'measures for the approximation of provisions laid down by law', whereas Article 192 TFEU enables the Council and the Parliament to 'decide what action is to be taken by the EU in order to achieve the objectives referred to in Article 191 TFEU'. The generic term 'action' covers the adoption of regulations, directives, and decisions; EU lawmakers hence dispose of a significant margin of appreciation with regard to the choice of technique most appropriate for harmonization, which may be made in accordance with the specific circumstances in the area of environmental matters. Finally, Article 193 TFEU authorizes the Member States to take more stringent protection measures than those decided by the Council, which Article 114 TFEU does not, in principle, allow.[139]

4.3.2 *Measures under Article 192(2) TFEU: special legislative procedure*

The SLP[140] or, in other words, the requirement for unanimity within the Council following consultation with the European Parliament, is maintained for a certain number of sectors regarded as sensitive. First, decisions regarding 'provisions primarily of a fiscal nature' are subject to a SLP. Second, and surprisingly, several important aspects relating to quality of life are not covered by the OLP. These include 'measures affecting town and country planning, quantitative management of water resources or affecting, directly or indirectly, the availability of those resources, and land use, with the exception of waste management'. Finally, 'measures significantly affecting a Member State's choice between different energy sources and the general structure of its energy supply' also fall within the scope of the SLP.

However, a *passerelle* clause empowers the European Council to apply the OLP instead of the SLP. As a result, it will imply the introduction of QMV in Council instead of unanimity and place the Parliament on an equal footing with the Council. The *passerelle* clause does not require the prior approval of national parliaments.[141]

---

[137] Arts 289 and 294 TFEU.

[138] The Treaty of Lisbon reflects a shift towards greater recognition of the role of regional and local self-government. On the one hand, in accordance with Art. 4(2) TEU the Union is called upon to respect the national identities of regional and local self-government, on the other, the new wording of Art. 5(3) TEU on the subsidiarity principle refers to the various levels of government within a Member State: central, regional, and local.

[139] Chapter 7, Section 2.   [140] Arts 192(2) and 289(2) TFEU.

[141] However, in its *Lisbon* judgment, the German Federal Constitutional Court prescribed positive confirmation of the use of the *passerelle* clause by the German parliament. Judgment of 30 June 2009, 2BvE 2/08, 2BvE 5/08, 2BvR 1010/08, 2BvR 1022/08, 2BvR 1259/08, 2BvR 182/09.

Due to the fact that paragraph 2 has been worded in an extremely convoluted manner, the extent of these exceptions is difficult to determine. This calls for a closer analysis of the boundaries of these exceptions.

4.3.2.1 Fiscal provisions

Decisions regarding 'provisions primarily of a fiscal nature' are not subject to the OLP. This exception goes hand in hand with other TFEU provisions requiring unanimity on fiscal matters.[142] In cases where the principal goal of the measure is redistributive, the action must therefore be taken unanimously under the terms of paragraph 2; on the other hand, where the fiscal aspects are simply ancillary to the legislative act, the principal objective of which is to protect the environment, the OLP will apply. The requirement for unanimity prevented in particular the adoption of an EU tax on CO_2 emissions in the particularly sensitive area of taxation.

4.3.2.2 Land use

As regards 'measures affecting town and country planning, ..., and land use', it should be noted that the SLP applies to large areas traditionally reserved to the Member States.[143] This exception is justified by the fact that land use and land planning are primarily a national, regional, or even local issue. However, the dividing line between environmental policy *stricto sensu* and that of town and country planning is particularly difficult to identify. Clearly, the interpretation of these terms raises significant difficulties.

Land use decisions have a significant environmental dimension: in allocating areas for housing, industrial activities, infrastructure, and agriculture, these decisions reduce the available natural space, thus significantly impinging upon the conservation of habitats and species. In the eyes of regional and local authorities, town and country planning undoubtedly amounts to environmental law tools *lato sensu*.[144]

Also, in numerous regions of Europe, land is so built up that natural areas occupy nothing more than insignificant portions of land. Given population density in continental Europe, it is without doubt a limited resource, which must accordingly fall under the aegis of the SLP.

However, this expansive interpretation of the SLP would jeopardize the more democratic nature of the OLP. An expansive interpretation of the special procedure should, it is submitted, be precluded. Insofar as contemporary town and country

---

[142] Arts 113 and 194(3) TFEU.

[143] In spite of its impact on planning activities across the EU, the European Spatial Development Perspective (ESDP)—a framework for policy guidance to improve cooperation between EU sectoral policies—is part of the social and economic cohesion policy rather than the environmental policy. Moreover, the ESDP is merely an intergovernmental, non-binding instrument serving as a framework for decision-making by the Member States, their regional and local authorities, as well as the Commission. See J. Holder, 'Building Spatial Europe: An Environmental Justice Perspective' in Scott (n 98), 100–1.

[144] In AG Léger's view, measures which must be adopted on the basis of Art. 191 TFEU in conjunction with Art. 192(2), first subpara., second indent TFEU 'are those whose aim is the preservation or improvement of the quality of the physical, social or cultural human environment. They concern in particular town and country planning, and the establishment of transport and communication networks adapted to changing lifestyles'. See Opinion AG Léger in *Spain v Council* (n 126), para. 106.

planning rules now place more of an emphasis on 'qualitative aspects' than quantitative ones, with a view to promoting sustainable development, the harmonization of these measures must be governed by the OLP. In other words, town and country planning today has more a qualitative than a quantitative aspect.

The proposal made here will be illustrated with reference to various examples. A number of environmental directives directly impinge upon the ways in which planning competences are exercised. The most important are the Environmental Impact Assessment (EIA), Strategic Emissions Assessment (SEA), Landfill, Birds, and Habitats directives.[145] For instance, the establishment of the Natura 2000 network affects both town and country planning as well as land use. There is a question as to whether the harmonization measures taken in order to safeguard habitats should be covered by the SLP but it is important, it is submitted, to distinguish between principal and ancillary matters. Since this legal regime has the principal objective of safeguarding species threatened with extinction, it has more a qualitative than a quantitative dimension.[146] Moreover, given that they harbour endangered species at a continental level, the areas designated as habitats under the directive are ecologically important from an EU perspective rather than from a national point of view. Therefore, such a regulatory approach rightly falls within the ambit of the OLP.

Following the same line of argument, whilst Directive 2007/60/EC on the assessment and management of flood risks[147] was indeed adopted according to the former co-decision procedure, it cannot be denied that flood hazard maps and flood risk maps determine the concept of territorial management. As far as such cartography is concerned, lawmakers have sought to prevent polluting activities from being exploited in areas subject to flooding hazards. In other words, this planning does have an environmental dimension. Thus, it involves more the assessment and management of risks than territorial management *stricto sensu*.

To further complicate matters, paragraph 2 of Article 192 TFEU also covers 'land use, with the exception of waste management'. Consequently, waste management is subject to the OLP. By laying down criteria governing the establishment of installations for the disposal of waste, various directives adopted pursuant to Article 192(1) TFEU exercise a not insignificant influence on the choices to be made in the area of town and country planning and land use.[148]

4.3.2.3 Quantitative management of water resources

We now turn to the exception relating to 'quantitative management of water resources or affecting, directly or indirectly, the availability of those resources'. The wording of paragraph 2 resulted from the desire to clarify, when amending the Treaty of Nice, the scope of the earlier text as interpreted by the Court of Justice in 2001 in the

---

[145] M. Purdue, 'The Impact of EC Environmental Law on Planning in the UK' in J. Holder (n 19), 231; F. Haumont, *Droit européen de l'aménagement du territoire et de l'urbanisme* (Brussels: Bruylant, 2007).
[146] Opinion AG Léger in *Spain v Council* (n 126), para. 106.
[147] Directive 2007/60/EC on the assessment and management of flood risks [2007] OJ L288/27, Art. 6.
[148] Council Directive 1999/31/EC on the landfill of waste [1999] OJ L182/1.

Danube case.[149] The fact that the Convention on cooperation for the protection and sustainable use of the river Danube regulated the use of water from the Danube basin and their management in quantitative terms should *ipso facto* have led the Council to rule unanimously under the SLP. However, the Court held in *Council v Spain* that it was the measures regulating the 'quantitative aspects' of the use of water resources that were covered by the initial expression. In the eyes of the Court, it followed from the general economy of the Danube Convention that its main objective was the protection and improvement of water quality, 'although it also refers, albeit incidentally, to the use of those waters and their management in its quantitative aspects'.[150] This interpretation therefore confirmed the view that the Council had been right in ruling by qualified majority and was not required to vote unanimously under Article 192(1) TFEU. Accordingly, whenever an act gives greater emphasis to qualitative than to quantitative management, it falls within the scope of Article 192(1) TFEU.

4.3.2.4 Energy

When it comes to assessing the scope of the adjective 'significant' (para. 2(c)), in view of the interpretative difficulties which this standard raises, the Court of Justice will have to rule on the procedure from square one by virtue of its more democratic character. Despite their significant impacts on the Member States' choices regarding energy resources, various acts regarding the fight against global warming fall under environmental policy.[151] In laying down relatively modest objectives, these acts did not call into question the energy options set at a national level.

4.3.3 *Decisions under Article 192(3) TFEU: ordinary legislative procedure*

Under the terms of Article 192(3) TFEU, 'general action programmes setting out priority objectives to be attained' must also be adopted in accordance with the OLP, after consulting the Economic and Social Committee and the Committee of the Regions. This paragraph clearly underscores the importance the Treaty drafters have been accorded to subject the environment policy programming to legislative debate. Given that they are adopted in accordance with the OLP, these programmes have greater legitimacy than Commission communications.[152] It should be noted that most of the other policy programmes are not subject to such democratic debates—although the sixth programme was adopted by way of a decision, this instrument was distinct from the decisions taken pursuant to Article 249 EC (Art. 288 TFEU). Admittedly, the addressees of such decisions are not specified and its obligations are general on this

---

[149] *Council v Spain* (n 126), para. 50.   [150] *Council v Spain* (n 126), para. 74.

[151] Council Decision 94/69/EC concerning the conclusion of the United Nations Framework Convention on Climate Change [1994] OJ L33/11; European Parliament and Council Directive 2001/77/EC on the promotion of electricity produced from renewable energy sources in the internal electricity market [2001] OJ L283/33. By virtue of Art. 194(3) the adoption of tax measures on energy is also subject to the SLP.

[152] With the exception of research and trans-European networks (Arts 172 and 182 TFEU), no other EU policy programmes are subject to the OLP.

point, which means that they are not capable of having legal effects. These decisions have more of a political than a legal nature.[153]

Lastly, account should be taken of the fact that the first four programmes set out specific proposals for legislation that the European Commission was intent on later submitting to the Council. In so doing, the Commission provided an occasion to discuss the new outlines of its policy. In emphasizing 'shared responsibility' rather than the adoption of new legislations, the fifth action programme represented a significant change in direction from its predecessors.

4.4 Environment and internal market

As the historical analysis in Chapter 1 has evidenced, the rise of environmental policy was undeniably born out of concern to avoid distortions of competition between undertakings. To give the national authorities free rein to enact unilateral product and operating standards would entail the risk of a race to the bottom between States keen to attract polluting installations to the place where the cost of pollution is lowest. This would result in a generalized reduction of protection levels. Against this backdrop, a significant number of product-oriented directives were adopted on the basis of ex Article 100a EC (Art. 114 TFEU) within the perspective of the completion of the internal market.

However, some pieces of legislation may pursue inextricably and equally associated environmental and internal market objectives. This is particularly the case for operating standards. Although the impact of such measures on the functioning of the internal market may be attenuated in contrast to product-related standards, it is nonetheless still there.[154] In effect, national environmental operating standards are likely to place domestic industries at a competitive disadvantage. The variation of these standards can influence decisions by companies regarding plant location.[155] This is well illustrated by the case of the Titanum Dioxide Directive, a piece of legislation setting out rules prohibiting or requiring the reduction of waste discharges into soil and water. The Court held that this directive had to be adopted under ex Article 100a EC (Art. 114 TFEU) on the grounds, among others, that the third paragraph of that provision required internal market legislation to seek a high level of environmental protection.[156]

---

[153] M. Pallemaerts et al., *Drowning in Process? The Implementation of the EU 6th Environmental Action Programme* (London: IEEP, 2006). However, the fact that the Sixth Environment Action Programme, which was based on ex Art. 175 EC (Art. 192 TFEU), thematically shows numerous points of contact with European Parliament and Council Regulation (EC) No. 304/2003 concerning the export and import of dangerous chemicals ([2003] OJ L63/1) impinges upon the choice of Art. 192 TFEU as the proper legal base of the Regulation. Accordingly, the Court held that the regulation at issue was 'primarily an instrument of environmental policy, not an instrument of commercial policy'. See Opinion AG Kokott in Case C-178/03 *Commission v Parliament and Council* (n 129), paras 38–9.

[154] A. Weales et al., *Environmental Governance in Europe* (Oxford: OUP, 2000) 35.

[155] Eg there is a strong concern among undertakings subject to the EU GHG emission scheme about the costs incurred by the auctioning of allowances. See ETS Directive 2003/87/EC, Art. 13(1). So far, the impact of environmental concerns on the location of polluting industries has been rather limited in scale since environmental costs generally represent a small proportion of the overall production costs.

[156] *Titanium Dioxide* (n 124). See N. de Sadeleer, 'Le droit communautaire de l'environnement, un droit sous-tendu par les seuls motifs économiques?' (1991) 4 *Amén-Env* 217; K. St C. Bradley, 'L'arrêt dioxyde de

The Court's reasoning was underpinned by other conclusive arguments. The harmonization of operating standards requires the elimination of distortions of competition likely to be generated by excessively stringent environmental standards. In addition, the internal market procedure was at that time markedly more democratic than that laid down in Article 130s. The *Titanium Dioxide* judgment seemed to be inexorably pushing the whole sphere of environmental policy, as well as other policies such as health and consumer protection, into the purview of the internal market and strengthening total harmonization.

However, the lessons of the *Titanium Dioxide* judgment could apply only in cases where environmental protection was inextricably linked to completion of the internal market. In all other cases, the operative criterion had to remain the centre of gravity. In subsequent litigation on the legal bases of the Waste Framework Directive[157] and of the regulation of transfrontier waste shipments,[158] the Court took the opposite view. In spite of the fact that these acts secured the internal market objectives of free movement of waste, they were rightly based on Article 130s EC (Art. 192 TFEU). As a result, the mere fact that these pieces of legislations were likely to affect the internal market[159] was insufficient to justify the legal base being constituted by Article 100a EC. It is worthy of note that in sharp contrast to the *Titanium Dioxide* case, there was no question in the two subsequent cases of indissociably linked objectives and content but of prevailing environmental objective and content. This case law was approved on the ground that extending the rationale of the *Titanium Dioxide* judgment to other environmental measures would have rendered the Treaty provisions on environmental protection nugatory. The consequences of invalidating these acts would have been particularly irksome for those Member States which wished to maintain or to develop a more ambitious environmental policy.

In the light of this case law, it is possible to trace the dividing line between the provisions governing, respectively, the internal market and the environment. On the one hand, acts which have a direct impact on the internal market, and in particular

titane, un jugement de Salomon' (1992) 5–6 *CDE* 609; J. Robinson, 'The Legal Basis of EC Environmental Law' (1992) 4:1 *JEL* 109; P. Pilitu, 'Commentaire sous l'affaire C-300/89' (1991) *Foro it.* 369; T. Schroër, 'Mehr Demokratie statt umweltpolitischer Subsidiarität?' (1991) 4 *EuR* 356; U. Everling, 'Abgrenzung der Rechtsanleichung zur Verwicklung des Binnenmarktes nach Art. 100 A EWVG durch der Gerichtshof' (1991) *EuR* 179; C. Barnard, 'Where Politicians Fear to Tread?' (1992) *EL Rev* 127; A. Sawandono, 'Beginsel van democratie versus milieu' (1992) *NJB* 63; L. Krämer, 'Article 100A or 130S as a Legal Basis for Community Measures: Case C-300/89—Titanium Dioxide', *European Environmental Law Casebook* (London: Sweet & Maxwell, 1993) 21.

[157] Case C-155/91 *Commission v Council* (n 126). See N. de Sadeleer, 'Legal Basis of EC Environmental Legislation' (1993) 2 *JEL* 291; J. Bouckaert, 'Artikel 130S EEG als juridische basis voor afvalrichtlijn' (1993) 4 *TMR* 226; D. Geradin, 'The Legal Basis of the Waste Directive' (1993) 5 *EL Rev* 418. Case C-187/93 *European Parliament v Council* [1994] ECR I-2857.

[158] Case C-187/93 *European Parliament v Council* (n 157).

[159] Given that waste management is usually caught between genuine environmental concerns and the free movement of goods, it has always been difficult to draw the dividing line between the measures that ought to be adopted pursuant to Art. 192 TFEU and those related to the functioning of the internal market. The Packaging Directive 94/62/EC ([1994] OJ L365/10) is a good case in point. In increasing the collecting and recycling of discarded materials above EU thresholds, national authorities are likely to give a competitive advantage to their domestic recycling industries. Cheaper recycled products can therefore inundate other Member State markets where recycling operations are more costly. In so doing, the import of recycled products is likely to hamper these Member States from developing their own recycling facilities. Accordingly, this directive was founded on the internal market legal base.

those which lay down product standards, must be adopted in accordance with Article 114 TFEU. Accordingly, acts addressing the environmental risks of chemical substances,[160] GMOs,[161] biocides,[162] motor vehicles,[163] objects or substances likely to become waste,[164] as well as acts encouraging the ecodesign of products[165] have been founded exclusively on Article 114 TFEU.[166] It may also occur that certain provisions which do not directly relate to products are adopted on the basis of this provision.[167] In a nutshell, the establishment and the functioning of the internal market may be a contributory factor in developing EU environmental policy.

On the other side of the dividing line, a residual category embraces all acts for which an analysis of the aim and the content of the measure shows that they seek to achieve a high level of environmental protection and that they at most affect the establishment of the internal market on an ancillary basis. Despite their direct or potential impact on the functioning of the internal market, these acts should be adopted on the basis of Article 192 TFEU.[168] This is the case of directives aiming at protecting wildlife, different ecosystems, soils, marine, underground as well as surface water, air, and climate.[169] In addition, acts regulating pollution emitted by listed installations and waste management[170] have also been adopted on the basis of this provision.

However, in practice, it is not easy to sketch out the dividing line between these two types of provision.[171] Furthermore, in spite of their impact on the functioning of the internal market, several acts which regulate the placing on the market of products end up falling within the fold of environmental policy.[172]

---

[160] Regarding chemical substances, see among others: REACH Regulation [2006] OJ L396/1; European Parliament and Council Regulation (EC) No. 1272/2008 on classification, labelling and packaging of substances and mixtures [2008] OJ L373/1.

[161] With respect to GMOs, see European Parliament and Council Directive 2001/18/EC on the deliberate release of GMOs [2001] OJ L106/1; European Parliament and Council Regulation (EC) No. 1830/2003 concerning the traceability and labelling of genetically modified organisms and the traceability of food and feed products produced from genetically modified organisms [2003] OJ L268/24.

[162] European Parliament and Council Directive 98/8/EC concerning the placing of biocidal products on the market [1998] OJ L123/1.

[163] European Parliament and Council Directive 2006/40/EC relating to emissions from air-conditioning systems in motor vehicles [2006] OJ L161/12.

[164] Packaging Directive 94/62/EC [1994] OJ L365/10.

[165] European Parliament and Council Directive 2005/32/EC establishing a framework for the setting of ecodesign requirements for energy-using product [2005] OJ L121/29.

[166] Recourse to Art. 114 TFEU does not preclude the possibility of adopting an act on other legal bases such as Arts 43 and 168(4) TFEU. See European Parliament and Council Regulation (EC) No. 1107/2009 concerning the placing of plant protection products on the market [2009] OJ L309/1.

[167] European Parliament and Council Directive 2000/14/EC on the noise emission in the environment by equipment for use outdoors [2000] OJ L162/1.

[168] Case C-155/91 *Commission v Council* (n 126); and Case C-187/93 *European Parliament v Council* (n 157), paras 24–6.

[169] For an overview of the different acts founded on Art. 192 TFEU, see N. de Sadeleer, *Commentaire Mégret. Environnement et marché intérieur* (Brussels: ULB, 2010) 247–329.

[170] However, product-related waste standards—packaging, hazardous substances in technical equipment—are based on Art. 114 TFEU.

[171] According to L. Krämer, as regards the regulation of hazardous substances, the dividing line between the two provisions is somewhat blurred. See Krämer (n 24), 82.

[172] European Parliament and Council Directive 1999/94/EC relating to the availability of consumer information on fuel economy and CO_2 emissions in respect of the marketing of new passenger cars [1999] OJ L12/16; European Parliament and Council Regulation (EC) No. 443/2009 setting emission performance

But regardless of the appropriateness of this choice, it is the very nature of the integration process of the Member States that is at stake. By authorizing the mainten-ance or adoption of more binding measures with the endorsement of the Commission, Article 114 TFEU avoids the spectre of the creation of a multi-speed Europe on environmental issues. As was seen in the *Titanium Dioxide* case, this argument could be justified on economic grounds; differentiated policies could be a source for distortion of competition. Due to their implementation in a disorderly fashion, national initiatives also risk turning out to be largely ineffective, as pollution does not respect international borders. However, for acts adopted with this legal base, considerations relating to the internal market become predominant, whilst the political objective of guaranteeing optimum protection for the environment fades into the background.

On the other hand, recourse to Article 192 TFEU permits integration of a political nature to be pursued that consists in attainment of basic benchmarks common to the 28 Member States. Here, since environmental objectives are predominant, consider-ations regarding the internal market become secondary.

Nevertheless, the choice remains a delicate one. Is environmental protection best assured through the adoption of uniform legislation? Or is it necessary to guarantee this protection through minimum harmonization rules relying on Article 192 TFEU? One could answer these questions by stating that since they are reached on the basis of a consensus between 28 Member States, maximum harmonization rules adopted pursuant to Article 114 TFEU do not authorize the States to seek an absolute level of protection, even though in the wake of the Treaty of Amsterdam, the Council and the Parliament must endeavour to attain a high level of protection.[173] However, through the mediation of minimum harmonization rules, Article 192 TFEU leaves untouched the Member States' powers to adopt a higher level of protection than that set by the EU harmonization rule, even where this mechanism may result in the emergence of European environmental law à la carte.[174] Indeed, air, water, and soil quality, and emission standards are likely to differ from one Member State to another. Moreover, Member States with a low environmental profile are likely to argue for the adoption of EU harmonization standards lacking vigour, arguing that the more ambitious Member States could always work on more stringent standards in accordance with Article 193 TFEU.[175]

This all throws up a number of questions. Are the fears that economic cohesion may be undermined by more stringent national rules overstated? Should we conceive of environmental policy exclusively in terms of market unity? Does the fundamental nature of commitments and the importance of ecological challenges not imply, by contrast, that the Member States may move forward by adopting, if necessary, more stringent rules than the EU harmonization rule? In the final analysis, perhaps this is

---

standards for new passenger cars as part of the Community's integrated approach to reduce CO_2 emissions from light-duty vehicles [2009] OJ L140/1.

[173] See the discussion in Chapter 1, Section 7.2.
[174] Art. 193 TFEU. See the discussion in Chapter 7, Section 2.
[175] L. Krämer, *EC Environmental Law*, 6th edn (London: Sweet & Maxwell, 2007) 87.

simply just a false dichotomy. One might be inclined to agree, if one considers that the Member States currently limit themselves to transposing directives adopted on the basis of Article 192 TFEU, without however seeking to apply reinforced protection measures.[176]

That said, new developments are taking place: the lawmaker has drawn a distinction in some directives between different provisions, some of them falling under Article 114 TFEU and others under Article 192 TFEU.[177] As far as provisions based on Article 192 TFEU are concerned, it would be possible to adopt more stringent measures in accordance with Article 193 TFEU. As far as provisions based on Article 114 TFEU are concerned, Member States are called on to comply with paragraphs 4 to 6 of that provision.[178]

4.5 Environment and CCP

The question arises as to whether an EU external measure concerning other policies, such as international trade, is likely to fall outside the scope of Article 192 TFEU merely because, in accordance with Article 11 TFEU, it takes account of environmental protection requirements. Or, conversely, should an environmental measure seeking to facilitate trade be adopted on the basis of the legal base relating to the environmental policy? So far, the Court of Justice has been reluctant to draw strict demarcation lines between these competing legal bases.

One difficulty stems from the fact that numerous environmental multilateral agreements (EMAs) regulating trade in certain products sometimes invoke trade mechanisms in order to sanction States which do not respect their international obligations.[179] Put simply, these trade-related measures can prohibit or restrict imports of goods on the ground that the exporting country does not comply with the international

---

[176] J. H. Jans, 'Gold Plating of European Environmental Measures?' (2009) 6:4 *JEEPL* 417–35.

[177] Although the aim and content of the measure favour environmental protection, the legislature succeeds in isolating the provisions which are covered by Art. 114 TFEU. See, eg, European Parliament and Council Directive 2009/28/EC on the promotion of the use of energy from renewable sources ([2009] OJ L140/16) which is based on Art. 175(1) EC (Art. 192 TFEU) and Art. 95 EC (Art. 114 TFEU) in relation to some provisions setting out product standards (Arts 17, 18, and 19). See also European Parliament and Council Directive 2006/66/EC on batteries and accumulators and waste batteries and accumulators [2006] OJ L266/1; and European Parliament and Council Regulation (EC) No. 842/2006 on certain fluorinated greenhouse gases [2006] OJ L161/1.

[178] Art. 114 TFEU leaves Member States markedly less leeway than Art. 192 TFEU, since national authorities cannot maintain or introduce more stringent measures than those encapsulated in secondary law unless expressly authorized by the Commission. See Chapter 7, Section 3.

[179] The EU is party to several multilateral environmental agreements that rely on trade-related measures designed to ensure compliance: the Basel Convention on the Control of Transboundary Movements of Hazardous Wastes and their Disposal (Basel, 22 March 1989, Council Decision 97/640/EC [1997] OJ L272/45); the Montreal Protocol on Substances that Deplete the Ozone Layer (Montreal, 16 September 1986, Council Decision 88/540/EC [1998] OJ L297/8); the Kyoto Protocol (Kyoto, 11 December 1997, Council Decision 2002/358/EC [1997] OJ L130/1); the Cartagena Protocol on Biosafety (Cartagena, 29 January 2000); and the Stockholm Convention on Persistent Organic Pollutants (Stockholm, 22 May 2001, Council Decision 2006/507/EC [2006] OJ L209/1). It should be noted that unlike the Member States the EU is not a party to the Convention on International Trade in Endangered Species (CITES) (Washington DC, 3 March 1973) which allows punitive trade restrictions to be imposed on non-complying parties.

agreement. Whilst the goal of these international agreements is clearly not to promote trade, this nevertheless does not prevent commercial aspects from constituting an anchor point for environmental policy.

By virtue of Article 3(1)(f) TFEU, the EU's powers are exclusive in the area of CCP. Insofar as CCP instruments need not necessarily promote or facilitate commercial exchanges, Article 207 TFEU does not prevent EU lawmakers from placing restrictions on the importation or exportation of certain goods.[180]

Consequently, the demarcation between the CCP and environmental policy may be marked out in the following manner. Council decisions to conclude agreements with a main environmental goal and an ancillary goal related to foreign trade must be founded on Article 192 TFEU, which is the case for the majority of agreements in this area.[181] Conversely, where EU law is intended 'essentially to...promote, facilitate or govern trade',[182] it is necessary to found it on Article 207 TFEU.

Nevertheless, there is no lack of boundary disputes. In fact, the inclusion in international agreements of trade measures motivated by non-trading interests is likely to erode the scope of the CCP. In addition, in Advocate General Kokott's view, 'the more players there are on the European side at international level, the more difficult it will be to represent effectively the interests of the Community and its Member States outwardly, in particular vis-à-vis significant trading partners'.[183] Anxious to guarantee a uniform EU position with regard to the external world, the Commission tends to conclude agreements on the back of the CCP with a view to depriving the Member States of their external prerogatives. Conversely, as guarantor of Member State sovereignty, the Council on the other hand seeks to limit the exclusive competences of the EU. Moreover, under EC arrangements, the decision-making weight of the European Parliament has been decisive in environmental matters, whilst it was almost non-existent in CCP matters. Finally, the choice of the environmental legal base has a significant bearing on the Member States' room for manoeuvre to enact more stringent measures. Whereas a decision concluding an international agreement founded on Article 192 TFEU allows the Member States capacity to adopt more stringent measures by virtue of Article 193 TFEU, this is not the case where agreements are founded on Article 207 TFEU.

---

[180] Footnote 28 in Opinion AG Kokott in Case C-178/03 *Commission v European Parliament and Council* (n 129).

[181] See Opinion 2/00 (n 2), para. 44; *Commission v Ireland* (n 2), para. 90. As a matter of practice, see the following agreements: the Vienna Convention for the Protection of the Ozone Layer (Vienna, 22 March 1985) and the Montreal Protocol (Montreal, 16 September 1986, Council Decision 88/540 [1988] OJ L297/8); UN Convention on Biological Diversity (Rio de Janeiro, 5 June 1992, Council Decision 93/626 [1993] OJ L309/1); United Nations Framework Convention on Climate Change (Rio, 9 May 1992, Council Decision 94/69 [1994] OJ L33/11); Convention on Environmental Impact Assessment in a Transboundary Context (Espoo, 25 February 1991); and Helsinki Convention on the Protection and Use of Transboundary Watercourses and International Lakes (Helsinki, 17 March 1992, Council Decision 95/308 [1995] OJ L186/42). The decision ratifying the Montego Bay Convention on the Law of the Sea was founded on Arts 37, 113, and 174(1) EC (Arts 43, 207, and 192(1) TFEU). Arts 145–7 as well as Arts 192–243 of this convention deal with environmental protection.

[182] Opinion 2/00 (n 2), para. 5.

[183] Opinion AG Kokott in Case C-13/07 *Commission v Council*, withdrawn, para. 72.

Less to be expected was that the Court's judgments on this matter would follow such a tortuous path, leaving commentators distinctly unsure as to the respective weight to be given to aspects relating to the CCP, and those related to environmental protection.

In *Greek Chernobyl I*, a case concerning the conditions for importing agricultural products originating in third countries following the nuclear accident at Chernobyl power station, the Court of Justice confirmed the applicability of the CCP legal base[184] when adopting a regulation governing imports of agricultural products originating in third countries following the accident.[185]

The Court's opinion regarding the conclusion of the Cartagena Protocol on Biosafety to the Convention on Biological Diversity made it possible to clarify the dividing line which separates the CCP from environmental policy. In some respect, Opinion 2/00 reflects the transfer to the international stage of the internal trade versus environment conflict that led to the *Titanium Dioxide* and *Waste Directives* cases commented on previously.[186] Since this agreement had the goal of regulating, or even preventing, trade in GMOs, it falls within the ambit of environmental competence (shared competence).[187] In effect, this Protocol is essentially intended to avoid biotechnological risks and not, as argued by the Commission, to facilitate or to regulate commercial exchanges. The Court gave particular consideration to the Treaty framework within which the Protocol was negotiated, that is, the Convention on Biological Diversity. The Commission's argument concerning the practical difficulties related to the implementation of the mixed agreements was not considered to have sufficient weight in order to tip the balance in favour of the CCP legal base.[188] In effect, any practical difficulties associated with joint participation cannot affect the allocation of shared competence.

On the other hand, the opposite solution was reached regarding Council Decision 2001/469/EU of 14 May 2001 concerning the conclusion, on behalf of the EC, of an agreement between the government of the United States of America and the EC on the coordination of energy efficient labelling programmes for office equipment. The Council replaced Article 133 EC (Art. 207 TFEU), which had been proposed by the Commission, with Article 175(1) EC (Art. 192(1) TFEU). In applying the centre of gravity test, the Court nonetheless found that the CPP objectives were predominant, due to the fact that the programme did not contain any new energy efficiency requirements.[189] Although the Court confirmed the centre of gravity test, it introduced at the same time the test of 'direct and immediate effects on trade'.[190]

---

[184] Ex Art. 133 EC.　　[185] Case C-62/88 *Greece v Council* (*'Chernobyl I'*) [1990] ECR I-1527.
[186] See the discussion in Section 4.4.
[187] Opinion 2/00 (n 2); (2003) *CML Rev* 15. See K. St C. Bradley and M. Moore, 'Case Law of the European Court of Justice' (2003) 3 *YbEEL* 527–30; C. Maubernard, 'L'intensité modulable des compétences externes de la CE et de ses Etats membres' (2003) 39:2 *RTDE* 230–46.
[188] As a result, an agreement was concluded with the aim of allocating the tasks between the European Commission and the Member States. Whereas the Commission was competent to negotiate trade-related matters, the Presidency took charge of the residual matters. See C. Bail, J. Decaestecker, and M. Jorgensen, 'European Union' in C. Bail, R. Falkner, and H. Marquard (eds), *The Cartagena Protocol on Biosafety* (London: Royal Institute of International Affairs, 2002) 170–1.
[189] Case C-281/01 *Commission v Council* (n 126), para. 43.
[190] Case C-281/01 *Commission v Council* (n 126), paras 40–1.

In two judgments issued on 10 January 2006 on the choice of legal base of acts concerning the export and import of dangerous chemicals,[191] the Court of Justice however accepted the possibility of grounding a Council decision concluding, on behalf of the EC, the Rotterdam Convention on the Prior Informed Consent procedure for certain hazardous chemicals and pesticides, and the Parliament and Council regulation transposing the provisions of that international convention, respectively on Articles 133 and 175(1) EC (Arts 207 and 192 TFEU), since the 'commercial and environmental components' of the instruments were 'indissociably linked'.[192] Indeed, even though 'the protection of human health or of the environment was the most important concern in the mind of the signatories of the Convention', the trade element of the convention was not merely ancillary by virtue 'of direct and immediate effects on trade'.[193] In so doing, the Court combined the centre of gravity test with the test of 'direct and immediate effects on trade'. Given that in contrast to the Cartagena Protocol, the Rotterdam Convention focuses almost exclusively on trade issues of chemical management, the Court could reach a different conclusion than in the previous case.[194] Accordingly, it is insufficient to rely exclusively on the environmental objectives of the agreement without paying heed to the convention's obligations relating to import and export of chemicals. Also, the Court dismissed Advocate General Kokott's Opinion, arguing in favour of the applicability of the environmental legal base on the ground that the recourse to a dual legal base was precluded since the procedures provided for under each of these two bases were incompatible.[195] On a procedural level, the Court found that recourse to a dual legal base was possible, first since the Council ruled by qualified majority and, second, because 'recourse to Article 133 EC jointly with Article 175(1) EC is likewise not liable to undermine the Parliament's rights'.[196] The Court concluded that the combination of legal bases did not involve any encroachment on Parliament's rights, which had in any event been consulted. In contrast to the *Titanium Dioxide* case,[197] the procedures were therefore not incompatible. However, the Court did not address the issue of Member States' residual competence. In this connection, it should be noted that Article 207 TFEU does not encapsulate a clause similar to Article 193 TFEU, a provision allowing Member States to enact more stringent measures.

At this stage, it is difficult to set out the practical implications of the judgments of 10 January 2006. Although the Court acknowledges the possibility of combining exclusive and shared competence, it does not answer the question how these competences should be handled in practice. One is left with little guidance with respect to this issue.

---

[191] Case C-94/03 *Commission v Council* (n 129); Case C-178/03 *Commission v European Parliament and Council* (n 129), noted by D. Simon (2006) *Europe* 12–13; D. Langlet (2006) 18:3 *JEL* 495–504; and P. Koutrakos (2007) 44 *CML Rev* 171.

[192] Case C-94/03 *Commission v Council* (n 129), para. 51; and Case C-178/03 *Commission v European Parliament and Council* (n 129), para. 44.

[193] Case C-94/03 *Commission v Council* (n 129), paras 43 and 42.   [194] Langlet (n 191), 500.

[195] Opinion AG Kokott in Case C-178/03 *Commission v European Parliament and Council* (n 129), para. 61.

[196] In fact, although ex Art. 133 EC, read in conjunction with Art. 300(3) EC did not formally provide for the Parliament's participation, ex Art. 175 EC by contrast was premised on Parliament's involvement.

[197] Case C-300/89 *Commission v Council* [1991] ECR I-2867.

One could ask whether the Rotterdam Convention must still be regarded as a mixed agreement, or whether it falls under the exclusive competence of the EU by virtue of its ties with the CPP.[198] Like other EMAs, the Rotterdam Convention was concluded jointly by the EU and the Member States. Accordingly, the Member States participate in the agreement alongside the EU. Practical difficulties in the management of the shared competence cannot in themselves justify full exclusivity.[199] However, a closer analysis of the new acts implementing the Rotterdam Convention highlights that the EU enjoys to a great extent an exclusive competence. Indeed, the implementation of the international agreement leads to total harmonization of this field. In particular, the annex to the new Council decision on the conclusion of the Rotterdam Convention[200] declares that, 'in accordance with Article 133 of the Treaty, the European Community has exclusive competence on common commercial policy, concerning, in particular, trade in goods.' Replacing Council Regulation (EC) No. 304/2003, which was annulled by the Court of Justice in Case C-178/03 as it was based solely on Article 175(1) of the Treaty, Regulation (EC) No. 689/2008 concerning the export and import of dangerous chemicals[201] implements the Rotterdam Convention.[202] Under that regulation the Commission is to decide on behalf of the EU whether to permit the import into the Community of each chemical subject to the Prior Informed Consent (PIC) procedure. Moreover, as regards the participation of the EU in the convention, the Commission acts as the single contact point with the Secretariat and other parties to the Convention as well as with other countries.[203] Put simply, although the Commission works in close cooperation with the Member States, it is nevertheless the common designated authority for the participation of the EU in the convention.[204]

As a result, the conclusion of the Rotterdam Convention by the Member States does not enable them to adopt more stringent measures governing the export of chemical substances which diverge from the comprehensive harmonized EU law provisions adopted pursuant to Article 114 TFEU, except in accordance with Article 114(5) TFEU. In any event, the judgments of 10 January 2006 represent a change in emphasis from the cautious reading of the extent of the external competences to the EU in the area of the CCP.[205]

---

[198] See Council Decision 2006/730/EC on the conclusion, on behalf of the European Community, of the Rotterdam Convention on the Prior Informed Consent Procedure for certain hazardous chemicals and pesticides in international trade [2006] OJ L229/25.

[199] By virtue of Rule 44 of the rules of procedure for the Conference of the Parties to the Rotterdam Convention, a regional economic integration organization shall not exercise its right to vote if any of its Member States exercises its right to vote, and vice versa (UNEP/FAO/RC/COP.1/33).

[200] Council Decision 2006/730/EC on the conclusion, on behalf of the European Community, of the Rotterdam Convention on the Prior Informed Consent Procedure for certain hazardous chemicals and pesticides in international trade [2006] OJ L299/23. That Decision is founded on Arts 133 and 175(1) EC (Arts 207 and 192(1) TFEU) in order to reflect the impact of provisions on both trade and environmental issues.

[201] Regulation (EC) No. 689/2008 ([2008] OJ L204/1) is founded on Arts 133 and 175(1) EC (Arts 207 and 192(1) TFEU).

[202] Art 1(1)(a).   [203] Fifth recital of the preamble.

[204] Communication of the Commission, Technical Guidance Notes for Implementation of Regulation (EC) No. 689/2008 [2011] OJ C65/1.

[205] D. Simon (2006) *Europe* 12–13.

A further twist in this case law is the judgment on the validity of the legal base of Regulation (EC) No. 1013/2006 on the transfrontier movement of waste.[206] In the proceedings initiated by the Commission against that regulation, the applicant argued that since shipment of waste also has a commercial dimension, and the new regulation increased this dimension, the act concerned had to be based on both Articles 175 and 133 EC (Arts 192 and 207 TFEU). The Commission route had not been followed by the European Parliament and the Council on the ground that the act concerned essentially related to waste management and not the facilitation of trade in waste. Applying the principles in this area, according to which the choice of legal base is based on objective elements associated with the purpose and content of the act, and given that where the act pursues multiple goals it is necessary to take account of the principal goal, the Court of Justice rejected the Commission's annulment action. Essentially, the Court held that the contested regulation pursued an environmental objective as its principal goal. This finding was made on various grounds: out of the 42 recitals setting out the justification for the regulation, only two referred to the internal market, the implementation of which may be furthered by the common trade policy.[207] The content of the various mechanisms for controlling transboundary movements of waste also confirms the environmental justification. The fact that waste may originate from or be destined for third countries did not imply that the regulation was trade related, as argued by the Commission. The Court found that the regulation did not treat such waste differently.[208] In this way, the regime applicable to transfers of waste with third countries was based on the same type of environmental control mechanism as that governing transfers within the Union. The Court went on to assert that an EU act falls within exclusive competence in the field of the CCP insofar as it relates specifically to international trade, in that it is essentially intended to promote, facilitate, or govern trade and has direct and immediate effects on trade in the products concerned.[209] It follows from this judgment that recourse to a dual legal base remains the exception rather than the rule.

In line with the case law on the Rotterdam Convention, in some cases EU measures are based jointly on Articles 207 and 192 TFEU.[210] In other cases, a distinction can also be drawn between different provisions, some of them falling under Article 207 and others under Article 192 TFEU.[211] Last but not least, since the entry into force of the TFEU, inter-institutional tensions should subside. Admittedly, procedures for the

[206] European Parliament and Council Regulation (EC) No. 1013/2006 on shipments of waste [2006] OJ L190/1.

[207] Case C-411/06 *Commission v Parliament* [2009] ECR I-7585, para. 52.

[208] Case C-411/06 *Commission v Parliament* (n 207), para. 60.

[209] Case C-411/06 *Commission v Parliament* (n 207), paras 71–2.

[210] Regulation (EEC) No. 3254/91 prohibiting the use of leghold traps in the Community and the introduction into the Community of pelts and manufactured goods of certain wild animal species originating in countries which catch them by means of leghold traps or trapping methods which do not meet international humane trapping standards [1991] OJ L308/1; Regulation (EC) No. 689/2008 concerning the export and import of dangerous chemicals [2008] OJ L204/1.

[211] In isolating in the act the provisions covered by Art. 192 from the other provisions, the legislature should be able to draw a clear distinction between measures falling within exclusive competence and those falling within shared competence conferred on the Community by Art. 192 TFEU. See Opinion AG Poiares Maduro in Case C-411/06 *Commission v Parliament* [2009] ECR I-7585, para. 13.

adoption of acts falling under these two policies are the same, namely the OLP, albeit with minor procedural differences.[212]

4.6 Environment and CAP

So far, environmental protection has not numbered among the concerns of the CAP, the objective of which is still today of an exclusively economic or social nature. Needless to say, the objectives of Article 39 TFEU require, at the very least, serious grooming. The first, focusing on 'productivity', certainly does not meet current needs since it completely conceals concerns relating to the protection of the environment, consumers, and public health, to mention only the most obvious. Again, from an environmental point of view, this objective entirely disregards the more modern functions of agriculture, such as the nature protection function, improvement of the countryside, as well as tourism. Article 39 TFEU also disregards this multi-functional purpose of agriculture which the Union thus seeks to defend and to promote within the ambit of the World Trade Organization (WTO).[213] The integration clause would thus be nothing more than a last resort which would not make it possible to call into question productivity-focused objectives with regard to agriculture as pursued under Article 39 TFEU. This old-fashioned vision of agriculture is all the more striking since in an increasing number of legal systems agricultural law takes account of environmental and public health concerns.[214]

The Court of Justice has relaxed this apparent rigidity within the texts.[215] The broad interpretation of the objectives of the CAP within the context of the protection of public health has thus opened the way for the adoption of measures of an environmental nature on the base only of former Article 37 EC, that has been replaced by Article 43 TFEU. The CAP has thus provided an anchor point which measures intended to protect the environment could latch on to. Furthermore, the Court of Justice has ruled that various anticipatory protective health measures adopted either by the Commission or by the Council on agriculture could be justified by the precautionary principle encapsulated in the title on the environment.[216] The environment has therefore become a fully-fledged element of agriculture,[217] even though the procedure contemplated under the EC Treaty paid much less attention to the democratic role played by the European Parliament than the TFEU.

This means that regulations pursuing simultaneously objectives of agricultural policy and environmental protection, such as a regulation which limits the use of

[212] Pursuant to Art. 192(1) TFEU, the legislature is called on to consult the Economic and Social Committee and the Committee of the Regions which is not the case under Art. 207(2) TFEU.
[213] C. Blumann (ed.), *Commentaire J. Mégret. Politique agricole commune et politique de la pêche* (Brussels: ULB, 2011) 34.
[214] B. Jack, *Agriculture and EU Environmental Law* (Farnham: Ashgate, 2009).
[215] Case C-405/92 *Mondiet* [1998] ECR I-6133.
[216] Case C-180/96 P *UK v Commission* [1996] ECR 3903, para. 93; Case C-352/98 P *Bergaderm* [2000] ECR I-5291, para. 53. See N. de Sadeleer, *Environmental Principles* (Oxford: OUP, 1992) 119–21.
[217] *Huber* (n 127), para. 33; Case C-61/09 *Landkreis Bad Dürkheim* [2010] ECR I-09763, para. 47; Case C-152/09 *Grootes* [2010] ECR I-11285, para. 47; Case T-212/09 *Denmark v Commission*, [2012] OJ C373/2, para. 79. See also Opinion AG Trstenjak in Case C-428/07 *Horvath* [2009] ECR I-06355, para. 55.

driftnets and a regulation on agricultural production methods compatible with the requirements of the protection of the environment, are rightly covered by the CAP.[218] On the other hand, where an act specifically forms part of environmental policy, it must be adopted on the basis of Article 192 TFEU, even if it pursues the goal of improving agricultural production. This is the case for measures to protect forests against fires and atmospheric pollution.[219] The Court dismissed the view that agricultural policy objectives had any priority over those on environmental policy.

Since the entry into force of the Treaty of Lisbon, these tensions should subside, partially because the competences of the European Parliament have been enhanced as the adoption of acts falling under the CAP are subject to the OLP (Art. 43(2) TFEU).[220]

However, the integration clause encapsulated in Article 11 TFEU does not under any circumstances entail that it is acceptable to incorporate all environmental requirements into the CAP. In this regard, it is certain that it is not possible to integrate safeguarding mechanisms[221] or the exceptions provided for in relation to environmental policy into the CAP.

4.7 Environment and criminal law

Under the terms of the EC Treaty, the adoption of technical harmonization rules by the Council acting by qualified majority in co-decision with the European Parliament (first pillar) represented a significant break with the previous arrangements for unanimous voting within the Council (third pillar). Two judgments concerning the fight against pollution have clarified the extent of the Council's competences in criminal matters before these were transferred to the first pillar following the entry into force of the Treaty of Lisbon.[222] In spite of the changes introduced by the new Treaty, these judgments continue to arouse interest on a theoretical level.

Since criminal matters fell exclusively under the third pillar, the EC was not competent to harmonize criminal environmental law although most of the national rules were fleshing out EC secondary law obligations. As a result, the Council adopted Framework Decision No. 2003/80 on the protection of the environment through criminal law, in particular with a view to countering the designs of the European Commission which had proposed the adoption of a directive with a legal base in Article 175 EC (Art. 192 TFEU). In a judgment handed down by the Grand Chamber on 13 September 2005, the Court accepted the Commission's submission, holding that it may

---

[218] *Mondiet* (n 215), paras 25–7; and *Huber* (n 127), paras 25–7.
[219] Joined Cases C-164/97 & C-165/97 *European Parliament v Council* [1999] ECR I-1139.
[220] With respect to the CAP, the difficulty in drawing the dividing line between the scope of the OLP and the *sui generis* procedure conferring on the Council the power 'to adopt measures on fixing prices, levies, aid and quantitative limitations' (Art. 43(2)(3) TFEU) should not be underestimated. Indeed, the structure of that provision seems to suggest that para. 2 should be interpreted as the main procedure whereas para. 3 should be seen as an exception likely to be interpreted narrowly. See R. Mögele and F. Erlbacher (eds), *Single Common Market Organisation—Article-by-Article Commentary of the Legal Framework for Agricultural Markets in the EU* (Munich/Oxford: C.H. Beck/Hart Publishing, 2011) 39–41.
[221] Art. 192(5) TFEU.　　[222] Art. 83 TFEU.

adopt harmonization measures 'in relation to the Member States' criminal law' within the ambit of the first pillar.[223]

Following this first judgment, a second case concerning proceedings for annulment was introduced by the Commission under Framework Decision No. 2005/667 of 12 July 2005 to strengthen the criminal law framework for the enforcement of the law against ship-source pollution, a framework decision which the Court of Justice annulled two years later.[224]

In these two cases, the Court annulled the framework decisions in their entirety, 'being indivisible'.[225]

By undermining the foundations of the third pillar, the Court asserted the indispensable nature of the policies contemplated under the first pillar when these permit the adoption of measures 'in relation to the Member States' criminal law'. Having regard to the large-scale initiatives by the Member States in tandem with the Council as well as the highly contrasting positions adopted by the EC institutions regarding the extent of their prerogatives over criminal law matters, these two judgments have profoundly shaken up the European institutional realm.

In these two cases, the Court appears to have taken account of the need to reinforce the effectiveness of the protection given to the numerous harmonization rules, 'non-compliance with which may have serious environmental consequences'.[226]

In its judgment of 13 September 2005, the Court placed the emphasis on the obligation to achieve a high level of protection for this policy, the obligation to incorporate environmental considerations, the need to achieve an essential objective of the European Community, the existence of a specific EU policy in environmental matters, as well as obligations classified as 'essential', 'fundamental', and 'transversal'.[227] It follows from the 'transversal and fundamental' nature of environmental policy that it exercises an attractive force, thus justifying incursions by Community lawmakers into areas of competence reserved to the third pillar.

By the same token, in its judgment of 23 October 2007, the Court emphasized the fact that environmental protection 'must be regarded as an objective which also forms part of the common transport policy'.[228]

After having reviewed the classical criteria within its case law concerning disputes relating to the legal base, such as the determination of the centre of gravity of the measure in question in the light of its purpose and content, the Court recalled that although 'as a general rule, neither criminal law nor the rules of criminal procedure fall within the Community's competence', this reservation does not however prevent 'the

---

[223] Case C-176/03 *Commission v Council* (n 29), noted by D. Simon (2005) *Europe* 13. See H. Labayle, 'L'ouverture de la boîte de Pandore. Réflexions sur la compétence de la Communauté en matière pénale (2006) 3–4 *CDE* 379–428; D. Pichoustre, 'La compétence pénale de la Communauté' (2006) 12 *JTDE* 15; S. Peers, 'The European Community's Criminal Competence: The Plot Thickens' (2008) 33 *EL Rev* 399; M. Hedeman-Robinson, 'The EU and Environmental Crime' (2008) 20 *JEL* 279; Wennerås (n 64), 49–50.

[224] Case C-440/05 *Commission v Council* (n 110).

[225] Case C-176/03 *Commission v Council* (n 29), para. 54; and Case C-440/05 *Commission v Council* (n 110), para. 74.

[226] Case C-440/05 *Commission v Council* (n 110), para. 69.

[227] Case C-176/03 *Commission v Council* (n 29), paras 41 and 42.

[228] Case C-440/05 *Commission v Council* (n 110), para. 60.

Community legislature...from taking measures which relate to the Member States' criminal law', subject to a number of conditions.[229]

It follows from these two cases that it was not, however, possible to harmonize any criminal law provision whatsoever within the ambit of the first pillar. In accordance with the case law, three conditions must be satisfied.

In the first place, 'the application of effective, proportionate and dissuasive criminal penalties by the competent national authorities' must constitute 'an essential measure' for combating serious environmental offences.[230]

Second, the adoption of measures concerning criminal law must 'ensure that the rules which it lays down on environmental protection'[231] or 'in the field of maritime safety'[232] are fully effective. Thus, criminal legislation may only be an ancillary element of existing Community legislation, and a criminal law concerning the environment or transport cannot exist autonomously.

Finally, whilst the first judgment did not rule on the question whether Community law may go as far as to impose a minimum threshold for sanctions, leaving to national authorities the task of setting the precise level of penalty, the Court took a clear stance on this question in its judgment of 23 October 2007: the determination of the type and level of criminal penalties to be applied does not fall within the Community's sphere of competence.[233]

Due to the fact that the Lisbon Treaty provides for the incorporation of the third pillar into the first, it will be necessary to see whether this case law will have an effect on the future exercise by the Council and European Parliament of their competences in criminal matters.

4.8 Environment and nuclear law

Neither the objectives nor the obligations laid down in the 1957 EURATOM Treaty refer to the protection of the environment. This absence of reference does not preclude the adaptation of nuclear law to environmental concerns. Although the European Atomic Energy Community (EAEC) Treaty does not contain a title relating to nuclear energy production installations, the provisions of Chapter 3, Title II of that Treaty, entitled 'Health and safety', have been interpreted broadly with a view to providing for the protection of public health in the nuclear sector. Hence, the Commission has regulated various aspects relating to health protection against the dangers of ionizing radiation for the general public.[234] Moreover, the purpose of its Article 37 is to prevent the possibility of radioactive contamination of the water, soil, or air of another Member State.[235]

---

[229] Case C-176/03 *Commission v Council* (n 29), para. 47; Case C-440/05 *Commission v Council* (n 110), para. 66.

[230] Case C-176/03 *Commission v Council* (n 29), para. 48; Case C-440/05 *Commission v Council* (n 110), para. 66.

[231] Case C-176/03 *Commission v Council* (n 29), para. 48.

[232] Case C-440/05 *Commission v Council* (n 110), para. 69.

[233] Case C-440/05 *Commission v Council* (n 110), para. 70.

[234] See, inter alia, Case C-29/99 *Commission v Council* [2002] ECR I-11221, para. 78; Case C-115/08 ČEZ [2009] ECR I-10265, para. 105.

[235] Case 187/87 *Land de Sarre and others* [1988] ECR 5013, paras 12–16; Case C-61/03 *Commission v UK* [2005] ECR I-2477, para. 39; Case C-115/08 ČEZ (n 234), para. 104.

That said, the choice of legal base of acts relating to systems for authorization, monitoring, inspection, and intervention in the event of a radiological emergency has been open to debate. In the aftermath of the nuclear accident at Chernobyl, the Council adopted by a qualified majority on the basis of Article 113 EEC (Art. 207 TFEU) a regulation on the conditions governing imports of agricultural products originating in third countries. Challenging that choice, Greece claimed that, by basing the contested regulation on Article 113 EEC, the Council infringed the EEC and EAEC Treaties on the ground that the regulation was concerned exclusively with protection of the health of the general public. Accordingly, the regulation should have been based on Article 31 EAEC or on Articles 130r and 130s EEC (Art. 192 TFEU). Both the aim and content of the impugned regulation pointed to the rule's primary purpose being to regulate trade between the Community and non-member countries, thus more properly falling within the scope of the CCP.[236]

In a further example, in *Chernobyl II* the European Parliament contended that Regulation No. 3954/87 laying down maximum permitted levels of radioactive contamination of foodstuffs and feeding stuffs following a nuclear accident was not legitimately based on Article 31 EAEC. In view of the prohibition on marketing contaminated goods, the European Parliament argued that this piece of legislation was an internal market measure which should therefore have been based on Article 100a EC (Art. 114 TFEU). However, the Court of Justice held that, according to its objective and its content, the regulation had 'only the incidental effect of harmonizing the conditions for the free movement of goods'.[237] The significance of this judgment lies in the fact that not every harmonization of national product standards should fall within the scope of Article 114 TFEU.

4.9 Concluding remarks

By virtue of their cross-cutting nature, environmental questions constantly interact with the internal market (Arts 114–118 TFEU), transport (Title VI TFEU), CCP (fifth part, Title II TFEU), public health policy (Title XIV TFEU), consumer protection (Title XV TFEU), trans-European networks (Title XVI TFEU), industry (Title XVII TFEU), economic and social cohesion (Title XVIII TFEU), as well as development (fifth part, Title III, Chapter 1 TFEU). Other policy areas thus do not remain untouched by the Treaty obligations to foster sustainable development and to integrate environmental requirements. As a result of this, the application of the centre of gravity test founded on identifying the main and incidental aims and content of the measure is becoming more challenging. Therefore, alongside the harmonization of legislation with a view to facilitating the establishment of the internal market, there is constant interaction between environmental policy and most policies mentioned in the TFEU. In order to achieve sustainable development in accordance with Article 3(3) TEU, these various EU policies must adopt an environmental dimension.

---

[236] *Chernobyl I* (n 185), para. 16.
[237] Case C-70/88 *Parliament v Council* [1991] ECR I-4561; p. 159, noted by N. de Sadeleer (1992) 3 *Amén-Env* 104.

As discussed previously, the question whether a measure aiming at protecting the environment should be based on Article 192 TFEU is anything but an academic exercise. The choice of the proper legal base has significant repercussions for institutional equilibrium and on the leeway enjoyed by Member States in implementing EMAs as well as secondary law. In effect, the legal base chosen can be of importance both for setting the content of the EU measure and its implementation in the national law of the Member States. Although a single base is still preferable to multiple bases, it comes as no surprise that the Court of Justice's resistance to dual or multiple legal bases is diminishing. Indeed, there is no shortage of acts founded on different legal bases. Although the *raison d'être* of a host of product-oriented and trade-oriented measures is clearly one of improving the state of the environment, they simultaneously pursue environmental and trade objectives which are inseparably linked without one being ancillary to the other.

Whether the proliferation of legal bases is likely to improve the environment remains to be seen but there is no shortage of grey area in which environmental competence ends and other competences begin to unfold. Accordingly, other institutional actors—Directorates-General of the Commission, parliamentary committees, Council configurations—than the traditional environmental protagonists[238] would be

Table 3.2 Legal bases of legislation contributing to protection of the environment

Policies	Scope of the measures	Legal bases	Procedures	Illustrations
CAP	Production and trading in agricultural products	Art. 43 TFEU (Art. 37 EC)	OLP or SLP	Chapter 1, Title II of Regulation (EC) No. 1782/2003 establishing common rules for direct support schemes under the common agricultural policy
Transport	Common Transport Policy	Art. 91(1) TFEU	OLP	'Eurovignette' Directive 2011/76/EU
	Maritime and air transport	Art. 100 TFEU (Art. 80 EC)	OLP	Directive 2002/30/EC on the introduction of noise-related operating restrictions at Community airports; Regulation 417/2002/EC on the accelerated phasing-in of double hull
Approximation of provisions on indirect taxation	Harmonization of indirect taxes	Art. 113 TFEU (Art. 93 EC)	SLP	Proposed Directive on CO_2 taxation
Energy	Renewable forms of energy	Art. 194(1)c TFEU	SLP	Directive 2010/30 on the information of the production of energy; Directive 2010/31 on the energy performance of buildings

---

[238] See Chapter 4, Section 3.

Internal market	Establishment and functioning of the internal market	Art. 114 TFEU (Art. 95 EC)	OLP	Product standards regarding chemical substances, biocides, GMOs, etc
CCP		Art. 207(4) TFEU (Art. 133(4) EC)	OLP	Regulation (EC) No. 2173/ 2005/EC establishing a licence scheme for the import of timber into the EC
Health	Veterinary and phytosanitary measures	Art. 168(4)(b) TFEU (Art. 152(4)(b) EC)	OLP	Regulation (EC) No. 1774/ 2002/EC laying down health rules concerning animal by-products not intended for human consumption
Environment	General measures	Art. 192(1) TFEU (Art. 175(1) EC)	OLP	Quality standards, emission standards, operating standards, listed installation authorization schemes
	Harmonization touching upon Member States' residual powers	Art. 192(2) TFEU (Art. 175(2) EC)	SLP	Provisions primarily of a fiscal nature, town and country planning, quantitative management of water resources, land use
	General policy programmes	Art. 192(3) TFEU (Art. 175(3) EC)	OLP	Sixth action programme
Environment and CCP		Arts 192(1) and 207(4) TFEU (Arts 175(1) and 133(4) EC)	OLP	Regulation (EC) No. 842/2006/ EC on certain fluorinated greenhouse gases; Regulation 689/2008/EC concerning the export and import of dangerous chemicals
Environment and development cooperation		Arts 192(1) and 209 TFEU (Arts 175 and 179 EC)	OLP	Regulation (EC) No. 2494/ 2000/EC on measures to promote the conservation and sustainable management of tropical and other forests in developing countries
Environment and, incidentally, internal market		Art. 192(1) as well as for a number of provisions Art. 114(1) TFEU	OLP	Directive 2009/28/EC on the promotion of the use of energy from renewable sources
Internal market and CCP		Arts 114 and 207(4) TFEU	OLP	Council Decisions on the conclusion of the agreements prohibiting the use of leghold traps
Agriculture, internal market, and health		Arts 43(2), 114, and 168(4)(b) TFEU	OLP	Regulation (EC) No. 1107/ 2009/EC concerning plant protection products
Agriculture, CCP, and environment		Arts 43(2), 207(4), and 192 (1) TFEU	OLP	Council Decision 98/392/EC concerning the conclusion of UNCLOS

eager to be involved in the decision-making process. In spite of the improvements made by the Lisbon Treaty, conflicting views on identifying the centre of gravity of measures linked to the aim of environmental protection are likely to continue. Needless to say, Case C-411/06 on the legal base of the regulation on the transfrontier movement of waste precludes all hope of a much-awaited agreement on this matter. Perhaps the frontline victim of such drawn-out conflict is the credibility of EU environmental governance.

Table 3.2 highlights the key legal bases of acts which, directly or indirectly, contribute to the protection of the environment and provides illustrations of various legal instruments pertaining to specific EU policies.

4

General Overview of EU Secondary Environmental Law

1. Introduction

Clearly, EU environmental law has a considerable impact on national policies, so much so that some even speak of a true *ius commune*. First created in the early 1970s, environmental law currently embraces more than two hundred directives and a dozen regulations.[1] As almost 8 per cent of EU legislation is dedicated to the protection of the environment, this body of legislation has over time become relatively substantial, and national experts estimate that almost 80 per cent of their environmental law is in one way or another shaped by EU obligations.[2] Indeed, the scope of environmental law is striking. EU legal acts cover nearly all aspects of that policy, ranging from listed installations and pollution control, through waste management and nature conservation, to procedural requirements. It must also be added that the transposition of EU secondary law is a matter not 'simply' for 28 national legislatures, but rather around one hundred regional authorities, as jurisdiction over environmental matters has generally been devolved to sub-federal bodies such as regions and Länder. As a result, EU legal acts are binding on all the authorities of the Member States, that is to say, not merely the national courts but also all administrative bodies, including decentralized authorities, and those authorities are required to apply them.[3]

As is the case for national provisions which transpose or apply EU legislation, the latter rules themselves are difficult to master.

At first sight, given the technical and disparate nature of an area of law which ranges from climate change to genome diversity within a species population, the provision of such an overview certainly appears to be a tall order. For example, although global warming upsets the division of wild species and their natural habitats, nature's own conservation measures without doubt do not have much do to with emissions trading schemes (ETS) which aim to reduce CO_2 and other greenhouse gas (GHG) emissions.

Moreover, harmonization measures have been piled one on top of the other without any global vision. In contrast to certain Member States which have enacted environmental codes—Sweden, France, etc—EU law is still made up of disparate legal frameworks,[4] as is clear from the differences between the legal instruments employed as well as the diversity of legal basis.[5]

Furthermore, environmental law by no means aspires to stability: the instruments discussed in the following are subject to constant adaptation not only to scientific and technical progress, but also to decisions taken on an international level. Hemmed in by the principles of legal certainty, legislation is not well equipped to deal with this evolutionary dimension.

---

[1] Considering the spread of environmental preoccupation in many polities, no figure can genuinely be put forward. L. Krämer, *EC Environmental Law*, 6th edn (London: Sweet & Maxwell, 2007) 7.

[2] Eg Communication of the Commission on the midterm review of the Sixth Community Environmental Programme, COM(2007) 225 final, 3. As for the 12 States which joined the EU after 2004, the whole of their environmental law results from the implementation of secondary law obligations. See Krämer (n 1) 451. Most secondary law acts oblige national authorities regularly to inform the Commission of the implementation of the obligations. Those obligations were codified by Council Directive 91/692/EEC standardizing and rationalizing reports on the implementation of certain Directives relating to the environment ([1991] OJ L377/48).

[3] See, to that effect, Case C-103/88 *Costanzo* [1989] ECR I-1839, paras 30–3; Case C-243/09 *Fuß* [2010] ECR I-9849, para. 61 and the case law cited therein; and Case C-97/11 *Amia SpA* [2012] OJ C200/2, para. 38. See also K. Lenaerts and N. Cambien, 'Regions and the European Courts: Giving Shape to the Regional Dimension of Member States' (2010) 35 *EL Rev* 609.

[4] Sector-based codifications have taken place, notably in the sectors of water (Directive 2000/60/EC [2000] OJ L327/1), air (Directive 2008/50/EC [2008] OJ L152/1), waste (Directive 2008/98/EC [2008] OJ L312/3), and listed installations (Directive 2011/75/EU [2011] OJ L239/1).

[5] See Chapter 3, Section 4.

Language as much as style is also an obstacle.[6] Acting on the back of a phalanx of specialist associations, environmental law has, as a new area of law, given rise not only to principles specific to it—polluter pays, precautionary principle, etc—but also a jargon or blossoming of the most diverse acronyms—BAT, CBA, CDM, EIA, EMAS, ETS, GMOs, ILUC, IPPC, MAPP, SAC, SEA, SPA, WEEE, etc.[7]

Finally, due to the progressive integration of environmental considerations into various sectors—Common Agricultural Policy (CAP), transport, energy, foreign trade, cooperation and development, tourism, etc—EU law is called upon to become even more diversified and complex.[8]

As will be seen, Sections 2 and 3 discuss the validity of a flurry of national environmental measures that usually transpose EU obligations. In order to understand the rationale of these measures, Chapter 4 offers lawyers who are not specialists in environmental law an overview of the most important rules of EU secondary law no matter whether they were adopted pursuant to Article 192 or Article 114 TFEU. Hence, this chapter does not have the goal of furnishing an exhaustive inventory of the rules applicable in the numerous sectors of environmental protection law. Strictly speaking, it shall be limited, first, to setting out the principle sectors and, second, to highlighting the impact of EU law on the policing powers of the national authorities and, accordingly, on the practices of undertakings and their right to move goods and services freely within the internal market. Hence, this chapter will not address questions of comparative or international law unless this is necessary in order to understand the issue.

The discussion within this chapter will be structured in the following manner.

Given that EU secondary law addressing environmental issues is deeply embedded in its economic, social, and political context, the scope of this area of law cannot be grasped without first making an effort to understand the various factors which condition the emergence of a policy evolving on the back of ecological crises, technological innovation, and economic opportunities. These different factors are brought into the fold in Section 2.

The specific nature of certain institutional aspects, and particularly comitology and agencies, are underlined in Section 3.

---

[6] Examination of the various official language version of a technical annex to the EIA Directive shows that a procedural concept is likely to be subject to various interpretations. Given these divergences, 'one must go to the purpose and general scheme of the directive'. See Case C-72/95 *Kraaijeveld and others v Gedeputeerde Staten van Zuid-Holland* [1996] ECR I-5403, paras 29–30. By the same token, the phrase 'likely to have [an] effect' used in the English-language version of Art. 6(3) of the Habitats Directive appears to be stricter than those used in other versions. It follows that each of those versions suggests that the test is set at a lower level than under the English-language version. See Opinion AG Sharpston in Case C-258/11 *Peter Sweetman* [2012] OJ C156, para. 48.

[7] Best Available Techniques (BAT), Cost–Benefit Analysis (CBA), Clean Development Mechanisms (CDM), Environmental Impact Assessment (EIA), Eco-Management and Audit (EMAS), Emissions Trading Scheme (ETS), Genetically Modified Organisms (GMOs), Indirect Land Use (ILUC), Integrated Pollution Prevention and Control (IPPC), major-accident prevention policy (MAPP), Special Area for Conservation (SAC), Strategic Environmental Assessment (SEA), Special Protection Area (SPA), and Waste Electrical and Electronic Equipment (WEEE).

[8] See Chapter 1, Section 5 and Chapter 3, Section 4.

Section 4 will sketch out a schema of the various forms of EU acts and instruments addressing environmental protection. This is followed, in Section 5, by analysis focusing on different policy sectors.

A final section deals with the challenges facing the growth of environmental law.

Most of the directives and regulations mentioned were adopted by the EC and not by the EU. For the sake of simplicity, the EC lawmaker is described as the 'EU' irrespective of when the measures were adopted.

2. Factors Influencing Environmental Law

2.1 Introductory remarks

In order to be able to navigate through the maze of this broad-sweeping branch of the EU, it is necessary to throw light on its main sources of influence. This exercise is all the more important as legal rules cannot be read in 'clinical isolation' from other disciplines such as science, economics, sociology, and political sciences. Moreover, a consideration and balancing of these different factors within the context of the decision-making process and, therefore, during judicial review of the proportionality and subsidiary nature of EU law, is set to become increasingly important in future.[9]

2.2 Science

First and foremost, the history of environmental law has been marked by a paradoxical relationship with science. Although this field of the law emerged in the early 1970s as a reaction to unlimited economic growth and progress by the over-powerful 'creator-man' who ended up destroying his own environment, science nonetheless occupies a central role. In particular, Articles 114(3) and (5) and 191(3) TFEU are testament to the key role played by scientific analysis in the adoption of secondary acts.

In order to explain the influence of science on EU secondary law, three factors need to be highlighted.

At first sight, science is the only credible tool for the pursuit of an environmental policy worthy of the name; it offers decision-makers and the population at large a snapshot of the state of the planet. And there are naturally scientists who uncover, identify, and pose ecological problems which need to be answered by the law. There are also experts who warn the general public of crises, even though the gap between scientists and the uninitiated can turn out to be baffling.

There are always sciences which take on a predominant role during the framing of environmental protection rules. Furthermore, scientific concepts progressively filter in through the drafting of legislation. The incorporation into legislation of the concepts of

---

[9] According to the Court of Justice, the discretion left to the EU institutions 'presupposes the taking into consideration of all the relevant factors and circumstances of the situation the act was intended to regulate'. See Case C-310/04 *Spain v Council* [2006] ECR I-7285, para. 122, noted by X. Groussot (2007) *CML Rev* 761–85. For an example of marginal review due to the 'complex economic and ecological assessments' carried out by the Commission in its control of national allocation plans for the allocation of GHG emission allowances, see Case T-374/04 *Germany v Commission* [2007] ECR II-4431, para. 81.

system,[10] ecosystem,[11] natural habitat,[12] species,[13] and sub-species[14] is testament to this. Similarly, arrangements inspired by ecological considerations, such as biogeographical regions[15], or transfrontier hydrographic basins,[16] transcend national boundaries and overturn traditional administrative divisions. Expressed in the form of technical prohibitions, discharge thresholds, or chemical concentrations, these technical standards put interdisciplinarity to the test. Hence, risk assessment currently occupies a central position in the drafting of regulations concerning chemical substances and genetically modified organisms (GMOs).[17]

Since health and environmental measures may mask protectionist measures, the EU Courts have elevated scientific assessment to a decisive criterion.[18] Indeed, it is always science which intervenes, at times decisively, during the course of annulment procedures for product safety regulations.[19] Even human rights no longer fall beyond the remit of scientific debate.[20]

That said, even though environmental law draws substantial inspiration from scientific facts, this does not affect its status as a legal discipline or, in other words, as a technique for managing the social order that is capable of regulating conflicts with its own conceptual tools.[21] Thus, the concepts of species, sub-species, GMOs, substances, and pollutants have a regulatory scope which does not necessarily follow the contours of scientific definitions. A striking example of this is that pollen contained in honey must be classified as an 'ingredient'.[22]

In addition, science can also be a killjoy, as the constant need to adapt legal rules to the evolution of scientific knowledge means that the lawmaker ends up continuously taking the rules intended to protect the environment back to the drawing board.[23]

---

[10] Framework Convention on climate change (Rio de Janeiro, 9 May 1992), Art. 1(3).

[11] Convention on Biological Diversity (Rio de Janeiro, 5 June 1992), Art. 1; European Parliament and Council Directive 2008/56/EC establishing a framework for community action in the field of marine environmental policy (Marine Strategy Framework Directive) [2008] OJ L164/19, Art. 1(2)(a).

[12] Council Directive 92/43/EEC on the conservation of natural habitats and of wild fauna and flora [1992] OJ L206/7, Art. 1(b).

[13] Council Regulation (EC) No. 338/97 on the protection of species of wild fauna and flora by regulating trade therein [1997] OJ L51/3, Art. 2(s). Despite the concept of species being embroiled in controversy, the Court of Justice did not hesitate to define it as being 'the totality of all individual beings which form a reproducing community'. See Case C-507/04 *Commission v Austria* [2007] ECR I-5939, para. 235.

[14] Case C-202/94 *G. Van der Feesten* [1996] ECR I-355.

[15] Council Directive 92/43/EEC on the conservation of natural habitats and of wild fauna and flora [1992] OJ L206/7–50, Arts. 1(c)(iii) and 4(2).

[16] European Parliament and Council Directive 2000/60/EC establishing a framework for EU action in the field of water policy [2000] OJ L327/1, Art. 2(13), (14), and (15).

[17] See the discussion of the precautionary principle in Chapter 1, Section 7.6.3.

[18] Scientific proof seems to take on more weight in sanitary disputes before the WTO Dispute Settlement Body. See A. Alemanno, *Trade in Food* (London: Cameron & May, 2007).

[19] Case T-229/04 *Sweden v Commission* [2007] ECR II-2437.

[20] *Tatar v Romania*, 27 January 2009, para. 104 (ECHR).

[21] E. Naim-Gesbert, *Les dimensions scientifiques du droit de l'environnement* (Brussels: Bruylant-VUB Press, 1999).

[22] Case C-442/09 *Bablok* [2011] OJ C311/7, para. 74.

[23] By requiring a periodical review of protection measures, substantive law is not outdone. Thus, the Kyoto Protocol must be periodically reviewed by the Conference of the Parties 'in the light of the best available scientific information...' See Kyoto Protocol to the United Nations Framework Convention on Climate Change (Kyoto, 11 December 1997), Art. 9. By the same token, measures contributing to the safety

The duration, content, rigour, and precision of legislation—and by extension legal certainty—may suffer from the constant adaptation of law to scientific facts.

From another point of view, an overzealous recourse to science has the effect of restricting the ambit of judicial review: limiting itself to ascertaining the existence of the scientific facts underlying a decision, rather than assessing them, the Courts need not resolve the complex problems, and may rely on the enlightened assistance of experts.[24] For instance, implementation of a precautionary measure should start with as complete a scientific assessment as possible and, where possible, identifying at each stage the degree of uncertainty attached to the results of evaluation of available scientific information.[25] On the ground that it may not substitute its assessment for that of the administrative authorities, the Court's remit is marginal, and only decisions that are manifestly unreasonable in the light of the conclusions of a scientific study are liable to be annulled.[26]

In fact, as the following examples show, the EU Courts have tended to extend their control of the scientific basis of EU acts.

- First and foremost, since it is 'of the utmost importance' scientific advice must be based on the principles of excellence, independence, and transparency.[27]

- The fact that a complete examination was not made of all the representative uses of a pharmacological product in order to assess the effect of the substance on wildlife means, in the eyes of the General Court, that the scientific dossier did not contain sufficient evidence.[28]

Similarly, national measures have to be backed by undisputable scientific facts.

- The proportionality of a national measure refusing to include a wild species in a 'positive list' with a view to marketing it requires from the Member States a 'specific analysis' of the risks on the basis of scientific studies.[29]

- The risks resulting from the export of dangerous waste to Member States which apply less stringent regulations 'must be measured, not by the yardstick of general considerations, but on the basis of relevant scientific research'.[30]

- An administrative measure adopted in order to counter the risk of the accidental introduction of exotic pathogenic organisms calls for 'an in-depth evaluation ... carried out on the basis of the most reliable scientific data and the most recent results from international research'.[31]

---

of food adopted in accordance with the precautionary principle must regularly be reviewed according to new scientific developments (GFL Regulation [2002] OJ L31/1, Art. 7(2)).

[24] Case C-341/95 *Safety Hi-Tech* [1998] ECR I-4355, para. 54.   [25] COM(2001) 1.

[26] Case C-180/96 *UK v Commission* [1998] ECR I-2265, para. 97; Case T-74/00 *Artegodan* [2002] ECR II-4945, para. 201; Case T-392/02 *Solvay Chemicals* [2003] ECR II-4555, para. 126; Case C-77/09 *Gowan* [2010] ECR I-13533, paras 55 and 82; and Case T-31/07 *Dupont de Nemours* [2013] OJ C156, paras 125 and 156.

[27] Case T-13/99 *Pfizer* [2002] ECR II-3305, para. 158; and *Dupont de Nemours* (n 26), para. 141.

[28] *Sweden v Commission* (n 19) paras 232–5.

[29] Case C-510/99 [2001] *Tridon* ECR I-7777, para. 58; and Case C-219/07 *Andibel* [2008] ECR I-4475, para. 41.

[30] Case C-277/02 *EU-Wood-Trading GmbH* [2004] ECR I-11957, para. 50.

[31] Case C-249/07 *Commission v Netherlands* [2008] ECR I-174, para. 51.

- The Member States are required to adopt conservation measures in favour of endangered bird species using the most up-to-date scientific data.[32]

- In order to preserve classified habitats from development or other activities likely to alter their ecological integrity, Article 6(3) of the Habitats Directive provides for a *sui generis* 'prospective impact study' of the environmental effects applicable to 'any plan or project . . . likely to have a significant effect thereon, . . .' Accordingly, the assessment is not deemed to be appropriate where reliable and updated data are lacking.[33] It flows from that that the experts conducting the assessment must show a high level of competence with respect to nature conservation issues.

- However, the principle of the independence of scientific experts may be called into question. When asked whether an authority responsible for drawing up a development plan may be designated as the sole scientific authority to be consulted under the Strategic Environmental Assessment (SEA) Directive,[34] the Court of Justice held that the directive did not prevent the authority from wearing two hats.[35] It follows that whilst the obligation to consult must be functionally separated, it need not be institutionally separated. By adopting such a minimalist approach to the obligation to consult provided for under the directive, the Court departed from the opinion of Advocate General Bot. It is clear that the Court's reading of the SEA Directive does not satisfy the objective of transparency in the national decision-making process pursued by the EU legislature. Indeed, it is the contribution of external expertise to that of the authority that creates and fuels debate, results in constructive criticism, and even offers alternative solutions to the planned project. Requesting the authority adopting the plan or the programme to be an independent expert in the procedure to which it is a party may appear to be somewhat schizophrenic.

Nevertheless, public authorities do not always have a monopoly over scientific knowledge. For instance, a review of the classification by national authorities of natural habitats for wild birds may be made by reference to scientific inventories drawn up by NGOs.[36]

Finally, as is clear from the following examples, there may be a considerable gap between the warnings issued by scientists and the risk management measures taken to counteract significant risks.

- Although British health and safety inspectors had been highlighting the danger for workers of exploiting asbestos since the start of the twentieth century,[37] it was

---

[32] Case C-355/90 *Commission v Spain* [1993] ECR I-4221, para. 24; and Case C-418/04 *Commission v Ireland* [2007] ECR I-10947, para. 47.

[33] Case C-127/02 '*Waddenzee*' [2004] ECR I-7405, para. 54; Case C-404/09 *Commission v Spain* [2011] OJ C25/3, para. 100; and Case C-43/10 *Nomarchiaki Aftodioikisi Aitoloakarnanias e.a.* [2012] OJ C355/2, para. 128.

[34] European Parliament and Council Directive 2001/42 on the assessment of the effects of certain plans and programmes on the environment [2001] OJ L197/30.

[35] Case C-474/10 *Seaport* [2011] OJ C362/10.

[36] Case C-3/96 *Commission v Netherlands* [1998] ECR I-3031; and Case C-418/04 *Commission v Ireland* [2007] ECR I-10947, paras 51 and 55.

[37] D. J. Gee and M. Greenberg, 'Asbestos: from "Magic" to "Malevolent Mineral"' in *Late Lessons from Early Warnings: the Precautionary Principle 1896–2000* (European Environment Agency, Environmental Issue Report 22, 2001) 53.

necessary to wait until 19 March 1987 before the EU lawmaker adopted the first directive on the prevention and reduction of environmental pollution by asbestos[38] and until 26 July 1999 for the use of this ore to be banned completely by the EU.[39]

- In 1982, the European Commission identified 129 dangerous substances which should be subject, as a matter of priority, to harmonized water discharge standards in accordance with Water Framework Directive 76/464/EEC; only 17 of them were regulated during the course of the 1980s.

- Although the Intergovernmental Panel on Climate Change emphasized in its report of 2007 that a 0.2°C increase per decade could result in serious disruptions,[40] the Kyoto Protocol to the United Nations Framework Convention on Climate Change of 11 December 1997, to which the EU is a party, provides for a reduction of total GHG emissions 'by at least 5 per cent below 1990 levels in the commitment period 2008 to 2012' (Art. 3), which, in the eyes of the majority of the scientific community, is clearly insufficient to halt global warming.

2.3 Economy

Since environmental law may have a chilling effect, which can at times be significant, on commercial and industrial investments and may, depending on the circumstances, result in the delocalization of businesses, environmental policies give rise to serious doubts in the private sector. Consequently, the Commission proposal at the end of 2007 to reduce CO_2 emissions from cars to 120mg/m^3 per km,[41] unleashed the wrath of the German authorities anxious to protect their car industry, whilst it caused less hostility from French and Italian car manufacturers whose lighter vehicles were able to comply with the proposed thresholds. In 2012, the Commission's proposal further to reduce CO_2 emissions again faced strenuous opposition from the German car industry.[42] Nonetheless, environmental law contributes to the creation of new markets—such as recycling, green energy, green certification, etc—which guarantee the emergence of technologies that make more efficient use of natural resources and energy.

The Treaty takes this into account, since in elaborating its environmental policy, the EU must take into account, by virtue of Article 191(3) TFEU, 'the potential benefits and costs of action or lack of action'. Accordingly, new legal acts should only be adopted following a comparison between the costs of a policy and the consequences of inaction. Obviously, this is often an extremely delicate balancing act: the costs of the

---

[38] Council Directive 87/217/EEC on the prevention and reduction of environmental pollution by asbestos [1987] OJ L85/40.

[39] Commission Directive 1999/77/EC adapting to technical progress for the sixth time. Annex I to Council Directive 76/769/EEC on the approximation of the laws, regulations and administrative provisions of the Member States relating to restrictions on the marketing and use of certain dangerous substances and preparations (asbestos) [1991] OJ L207/18.

[40] IPCC, *Climate Change 2007. The Physical Science Basis: Summary for Policymakers* (Geneva: IPCC, 2007) 10.

[41] COM(2007) 856 final.

[42] D. Keating, 'Porshe Proposals Fuel Noisy Traffic Debate' (Sept 2012) *European Voice* 8.

implementation of a new regulation may be calculated, whilst it is harder to quantify the benefits in terms of quality of life and the management of ecosystems.[43]

However, EU law remains wrought with contradictions: although granting State aids may enhance the optimal level of environmental protection, such subsidies at first sight contradict the polluter-pays principle enshrined in Article 191(2) TFEU.[44]

That said, there is no choice but to accept the fact that EU law is already characterized by economic considerations, as is shown by the following examples.

- REACH Regulation, which was subject to more than 40 economic impact studies, provides for the intervention of a Committee for Socio-Economic Analysis, which formulates an opinion on every measure intended to control or prohibit the placing on the market of dangerous substances.[45]

- The Water Framework Directive requires the Member States to follow a 'pricing policy' with a view to encouraging users to use water resources 'efficiently'.[46]

- Public authorities may only require the use of best available techniques (BAT) in the exploitation of large industrial facilities provided that they are determined 'under economically and technically viable conditions, taking into consideration the costs and advantages'.[47]

- Member States may use economic instruments, for example by adopting differentiated tax rates, in order to promote the collection of used batteries.[48]

- The ETS Directive, which implements the Kyoto Protocol, established for the first time a trading market in GHG emissions allowances from certain industrial sectors. The purpose of the ETS Directive is to establish an efficient European market in GHG emission allowances, with the least possible diminution of economic development and employment. Accordingly, the reduction of GHG emissions 'must be achieved, in so far as possible, while respecting the needs of the European economy'.[49]

- Finally, the Commission now requires the subjection of all draft legislation included in its working programme to an *Integrated Impact Assessment*, which has the goal of analysing the ecological, economic, and social impact of draft regulations.[50]

---

[43] Few ecosystem services have explicit prices. Services such as crops, livestock, fish, or water are most likely to be priced in markets on the account that they are directly consumed. See TEEB, *The Economics of Ecosystems and Biodiversity. Mainstreaming the Economics of Nature* (Malta: Progress Press, 2010).

[44] Chapter 12, Section 3.3.4.　　　[45] REACH, Arts 64 and 71.

[46] European Parliament and Council Directive 2000/60/EC establishing a framework for EU action in the field of water policy [2000] OJ L327/1, Art. 9 (1) and (2). See H. Unnerstall, 'The Principle of Full Recovery in the EU Water Framework Directive. Genesis and Content' (2007) 19:1 *JEL* 29–42.

[47] European Parliament and Council Directive 2008/1/EC concerning integrated pollution prevention and control (IPPC) [2008] OJ L24/8, Art. 2(12)(b); European Parliament and Council Directive 2010/75/EU on industrial emissions [2010] OJ L334/17, Arts 3(10)(b) and 11(b).

[48] European Parliament and Council Directive 2006/66/EC on batteries and accumulators and waste batteries and accumulators [2006] OJ L266/1, Art. 9.

[49] Case T-178/05 *UK v Commission* [2005] ECR II-4807, para. 60.

[50] Commission Communication COM 2002/276 on Impact Assessment (COM(2002) 276 final); Commission Communication, Better Regulation for Growth and Jobs in the European Union, COM(2005) 97 (March 2005).

2.4 Civil society

The absence of a genuine environmental policy is likely to wreak havoc. By way of illustration, inhabitants of Campania, exasperated by the accumulation of waste, ignited fires in piles of refuse, which was harmful for their own health.[51] In addition, for a long time the solitary exercise of power related to the administrative tradition of secrecy has created considerable inertia against the participation of the general public in technical and technological choices which may cause harm to the environment.

Thanks to the 1998 Aarhus Convention on Access to Information, Public Participation in Decision-Making and Access to Justice in Environmental Matters, environmental law increasingly adopts an informatory and participatory perspective.[52] As a result, a number of EU legislations have increased transparency, participation, and accountability with respect to environmental issues. In particular, efforts have been undertaken with a view to improving the quality of information on the environmental performance of products and undertakings. When better informed of the risks, the public are able to make their views heard without coming up against a wall of secrecy. Moreover, in numerous areas (eg operating permits, the placing on the market of substances which pose health and environmental risks,[53] and public procurement[54]) various forms of participation (eg public inquiries or prior consultation) are now a matter of course. A final example is the directive on environmental liability under which environmental NGOs are the watchdog of both the authority and the operator in relation to environmental damage.[55]

As is well known, environmental policy has always been at the forefront of legal developments: the participation provided under environmental law has led to Treaty law advances which we all know. For instance, the principle of transparency as stated in Articles 1 and 10 TEU and Article 15 TFEU 'enables citizens to participate more closely in the decision-making process and guarantees that the administration enjoys greater legitimacy and is more effective and more accountable to the citizen in a democratic system'.[56] Similarly, the right to information in environmental matters preceded the

---

[51] Case C-297/08 *Commission v Italy* [2010] ECR I-1749, para. 103. See also *Di Sarno v Italy*, 10 January 2012.

[52] W. Howarth, 'Aspirations and Realities under the Water Framework Directive: Proceduralisation, Paticipation, and Practicalities' (2009) 21:3 *JEL* 391–417.

[53] European Parliament and Council Directive 2001/18/EC on the deliberate release into the environment of genetically modified organisms [2001] OJ L106/1, Art. 7(4).

[54] By virtue of Directive 2004/18, contracting authorities may use eco-labels to define specifications in terms of performance or functional requirements in the conditions of tender, inasmuch as these eco-labels were adopted by national authorities after consulting all stakeholders, among whom were consumers as well as environmental organizations. See European Parliament and Council Directive 2004/18/EC on the coordination of procedures for the award of public works contracts, public supply contracts and public service contracts [2004] OJ L351/44, Art. 23(6).

[55] European Parliament and Council Directive 2004/35/EC on environmental liability with regard to the prevention and remedying of environmental damage [2004] OJ L143/56, Arts 12 and 13.

[56] Case C-41/00 P *Interporc v Commission* [2003] ECR I-2125, para. 39; Case C-28/08 P *Commission v Bavarian Lager* [2010] ECR I-6055, para. 54; and Joined Cases C-92/09 & C-93/09 *Volker und Markus Schecke GbR* [2010] ECR I-11063, para. 68.

recognition of free access to administrative information held by the EU institutions.[57] By guaranteeing a right to information as well as participatory rights, the EU has thus been able to make up for the democratic deficit within decision-making.

2.5 International challenges

Whereas at the outset harmonization was conceptualized as a response to problems (above all, concerning industrial pollution) common to six Member States (eg harmonized rules for waste oil, transfrontier movements of hazardous waste, etc), problems rapidly took on a continental dimension (transfrontier pollution, Palearctic migratory species, regional seas, etc) if not, indeed, a planetary dimension (stratospheric ozone depletion, climate change, etc). The depletion of biodiversity, the greenhouse effect, the thinning of the ozone layer, and the contamination of international waters are problems of global reach which call for responses on an international level. Following its progressive enlargement to 28 Members, the EU has inevitably become a major player on the international scene. Likewise, development cooperation is increasingly associated with a requirement of sustainable development.[58]

Closely related to the key role played by the EU in international fora is the issue of implementing international environmental law into EU law. Given that the EU is a party to a host of international environmental agreements, it comes as no surprise that several EU arrangements are permeated by international mechanisms. By way of illustration, EU harmonization of legislation governing waters included in particular the goal of ensuring compliance with international agreements.[59] Similarly, international hydrographic districts must be established with the help of existing structures created by international agreement.[60] By the same token, policies to combat global warming depend, for reasons largely stemming from competitive forces in the market, on an international legal framework (eg negotiations on a replacement for the Kyoto Protocol). Accordingly, the EU ETS Directive is closely linked to the mechanisms provided for under the Kyoto Protocol.[61] Lastly, conditions as regards standing, participation, as well as access to information have been eased due to the implementation of the Aarhus Convention of 25 June 1998.[62]

---

[57] At first, this right was established for national authorities in accordance with Council Directive 90/313/EEC on the freedom of access to information on the environment ([1990] OJ L158/56). Then, on the basis of ex Art. 251 EC (Art. 294 TFEU), this right was extended to the EU institutions in accordance with European Parliament and Council Regulation (EC) No. 1049/2001 regarding public access to European Parliament, Council and Commission documents ([2001] OJ L145/43).

[58] Art. 21(2)(d) TEU. See R. Williams, 'EU Development Cooperation, Sustainable Development, and the Convention on Europe. From Dislocation to Consistency?' (2005) 4 *YbEEL* 303–76.

[59] European Parliament and Council Directive 2000/60/EC establishing a framework for EU action in the field of water policy [2000] OJ L327/1, Art. 1(e).

[60] Case C-32/05 *Commission v Luxembourg* [2006] ECR I-11323, paras 66–72.

[61] ETS Directive 2003/87/EC, Art. 11(a) and (b).

[62] Case C-115/09 *Trianel Kohlekraftwer Lünen* [2011] OJ C204/6, para. 39. See E. J. Lohse, 'Surprise? Surprise!—Case C-115/09 (*Kohlekraftwerk Lünen*)—A Victory for the Environment and a Loss for Procedural Autonomy of the Member States' (2012) *EPL* 249–68. Case C-240/09 *Lesoochranárske zoskupenie* [2011] ECR I-9967, para. 51, case note (2012) *CML Rev* 767–92.

As with the problem of the chicken and the egg, we no longer know whether EU law originates from international law or vice versa. In any event, as is clear from the origins of the precautionary principle—a creation of German administrative law, which subsequently became part of international law, then also EU law, thus applying to all Member States—the relations between different legal spheres are particularly complex. EU law has even ended up 'renationalizing' environmental policy, both by offering an extremely broad margin of discretion to national authorities, and also by virtue of the conceptual ambiguities littered throughout the texts.[63]

Moreover, as the *ATAA* case shows, the potential risk of conflict between EU law and international law is real.[64]

One last point needs to be made: although pollution does not recognize boundaries, EU secondary law seems to have neglected the coordination of national policies.[65] Environmental policy is, above all, a national matter.[66]

3. Institutional Aspects

3.1 Institutions

Though the EU institutions do not have any special features of note with regard to the environment, a brief discussion of this issue is warranted to make clear the baseline against which EU secondary law unfolds.[67]

The European Council has been increasingly active in addressing climate change issues.[68] As far as the Council of the Union is concerned, the Environment Council meets in principle once every three months and includes the ministers or secretaries of state with responsibility for environmental protection. Given that environmental policy is closely related to other regulatory issues, environmental questions may also be considered by the Council when sitting in another configuration or even, if they take on a political dimension, within the General Affairs configuration of the Council.[69] As the Presidency among the 28 Member States rotates every six months, the country in charge is likely significantly to shape the political agenda: as a matter of course, Council

---

[63] See Sections 6.1 and 6.2.   [64] Case C-366/10 *ATAA* [2011] OJ C49/7, paras 46–111.

[65] See, however, the obligations of cooperation or coordination in matters of evaluation of the impacts of transboundary projects (European Parliament and Council Directive 85/337/EC on the assessment of the effects of certain public and private projects on the environment [1985] OJ L175/40, Art. 7), of the crossing of thresholds of atmospheric pollution due to transboundary pollution (Council Directive 96/62/EC on ambient air quality assessment and management [1996] OJ L296/55–63, Art 8(6)), of international river basin districts (European Parliament and Council Directive 2000/60/EC establishing a framework for EU action in the field of water policy [2000] OJ L327/1, Art. 3(3), (5), and (6)), and of common plans to fight against transboundary air pollution (European Parliament and Council Directive 2008/50/EC on ambient air quality and cleaner air for Europe [2008] OJ L152/1, Art. 25).

[66] See European Parliament and Council Directive 2000/60/EC establishing a framework for EU action in the field of water policy [2000] OJ L327/1, Art. 13(4).

[67] As regards the integration of environmental concerns in the institutions' organization, see Krämer (n 1) 37–51.

[68] See, eg, ETS Directive 2003/87/EC, Art. 10(a) and (13).   [69] Art. 16(6) TEU.

positions mirror the national interests of the Member States.[70] Since the beginning of this policy, conflicts which oppose the 'green' Member States to the others have not abated.[71] Moreover, the watering down of a number of Commission proposals, ranging from chemicals to the greening of CAP, is testament to the competitive concerns embedded in the Council.[72] COREPER plays an important role in the preparation of the Council's business[73] and may set up specific working groups for areas related to environmental policy.

The European Parliament boasts a Committee on Environment, Public Health and Food Safety (ENVI). Given that most EU measures aiming at protecting the environment must be adopted in accordance with the ordinary legislative procedure (OLP),[74] the Parliament's powers have been greatly enhanced. Like the European Commission, the Parliament can be viewed as a supranational body, whereas the Council of the Union is more intergovernmental.

Since it is responsible for submitting legal acts to the Council and to the Parliament as well as for controlling the proper application of environmental law by Member States, the European Commission occupies a central position within the institutional framework. In 1978, the Commission set up a Directorate-General with responsibility for this portfolio and a commissioner has been granted specific responsibility for questions relating to that area. In 2009, due to the specific features of the climate policy, another commissioner was placed in charge of a specific policy concerning the fight against global warming. Acting under the authority of these two commissioners, two Directorates-General fulfil an essential administrative role. That aside, the role of the Commission in enforcing environmental law should not be overlooked.[75]

The ambiguity contained in the sheer number of directives and regulations adopted over the last decade seems to be the result of numerous political compromises struck during the legislative drafting procedure. These ambiguities are rooted in the elaboration of draft texts by the Commission Services. Whilst permanent contact between the EU administrative authorities and the lobbies offers an antidote to the famous technocratic drift, a practice of which Brussels bureaucrats are often accused, they also give rise to concessions on the level of protection sought. In addition, the OLP, which is frequently used,[76] nurtures a culture of compromise. Whereas transactions within the European Parliament are the result of ideological differences, settlements reached in the Council reflect differences in national interests. The culmination of this evolution is

---

[70] Weales et al. have stressed that 'agendas and priorities were established on the basis of one-off preferences of national governments'. See A. Weales et al., *Environmental Governance in Europe* (Oxford: OUP, 2000) 42.

[71] A. Héritier et al., *Ringing the Changes in Europe: Regulatory Competition and Transformation of the State* (Berlin/New York: de Gruyter, 1996).

[72] The sharpest illustration is the watering down in 2012 of the Commission's proposal to make one-third of CAP direct payments conditional on specific environmental criteria. Member States favoured greater flexibility as regards the 'green' measures to be chosen.

[73] Art. 240(1) TFEU.

[74] Arts 114(1), 192(1), and 194(2) TFEU. See the discussion in Chapter 3, Section 4.3.1.

[75] M. Hedemann-Robinson, *Enforcement of EU Environmental Law* (London: Routledge-Cavendish, 2007).

[76] Arts 114(3) and 192(1) TFEU. See the discussion in Chapter 3, Section 4.3.1.

that compromises must necessarily be struck by a 'trilogue' or within the Conciliation Committee.[77]

Certain less well-known institutional arrangements, such as the competences of committees and agencies operating in this area, will be discussed in the next two sections.

3.2 Scientific committees and comitology

It is important at the outset to distinguish between 'expert groups' created by the Commission itself and the committees (or 'comitology'). The latter provide expertise to the Commission with a view to advising it in preparing and implementing its policy, whereas comitology committees assist the Commission in the exercise of the implementing powers that have been conferred upon it by basic legal acts.

Given the importance of the place occupied by science, the policy pursued by the Commission must be clarified in the light of independent and impartial scientific opinion.[78] Moreover, a Scientific Committee on Health and Environmental Risks (SCHER) may be called upon to give opinions to the Commission on health and environmental risks relating to pollutants and other biological and physical factors or changing physical conditions which may have a negative impact on health and the environment.[79] On the other hand, the Commission has not established a committee of experts on the conservation of ecosystems which would be in a position to address broader ecological problems.

Whilst they may play a significant role in the growth of environmental policy, these committees do not fall within the ambit of comitology *stricto sensu*. Indeed, the executive competences delegated to the Commission were overseen by several types of committee which operated for a number of years in accordance with so-called comitology procedures.[80]

Comitology makes it possible to establish a dialogue between the EU executive and the national administrations, a technique which offers clear advantages both for the Commission as well as for the Member States. On the one hand, the Commission avails

---

[77] Art. 294(10)–(12) TFEU.

[78] See, notably, the Scientific Review Group put in charge of studying all questions of scientific matters relating to the trade in wild exotic species (Council Regulation (EC) No. 338/97 on the protection of species of wild fauna and flora by regulating trade therein [1997] OJ L51/1, Art. 18(1)) and the ORNIS Committee concerning the protection of birds.

[79] The tasks of this committee are set in the Annex I.2 to Commission Decision 2008/721/EC setting up an advisory structure of Scientific Committees and experts in the field of consumer safety, public health, and the environment ([2008] OJ L241/21).

[80] Council Decision 1999/468/EC laying down the procedures for the exercise of implementing powers conferred on the Commission [1999] OJ L184/4. Amended by Council Decision 2006/512/EC [2006] OJ L200/11. See the following doctrinal analyses: C. Joerges and E. Vos, *EU Committees* (Oxford: Hart Publishing, 1999); T. Christiansen and E. Kirchner (eds), *Committee Governance in the EU* (Manchester: Manchester University Press, 2000); M. Andenas and A. Türk (eds), *Delegated Legislation and the Role of Committees in the European EU* (The Hague: Kluwer Law, 2000); G. Roller, 'Komitologie und Demokratieprinzip' (2003) 3 *Kritische Vierteljahresschrift für Gesetzgebung und Rechtswissenschaft* 249–78; C. F. Bergström, *Comitology* (Oxford: OUP, 2005); C. Demmke, 'Comitology in the Envrionmental Sector' in M. Andenas and A. Türk (eds), *Delegated Legislation and the Role of the Committees in the EC* (London: Kluwer, 2000).

itself of the scientific and technical expertise that is indispensable in order for it to carry out its tasks. On the other hand, since they are made up of national civil servants, these committees control the executive tasks of the Commission. Finally, these committees also help the Commission better to devise the technical rules which the national civil servants will subsequently have to apply. After the sectors of energy and transport as well as undertakings, environmental policy is the sector which has generated the most committees. In 2010, out of a total of 259 committees, 32 committees attached to the Environment Directorate General and four working on climate change were operating according to Comitology Decision 1999/468/EC.[81]

With the entry into force of the Lisbon Treaty, comitology underwent significant change. A distinction has been drawn, first, between legislative and non-legislative acts and, second, between delegated and implementing acts. Indeed, Articles 290 and 291 TFEU provide for two possible means for the EU lawmaker to confer powers on the Commission. The lawmaker may either 'delegate' to the Commission the power to adopt acts of a quasi-legislative nature (Art. 290 TFEU) or confer implementing powers of an executive nature on the Commission (Art. 291 TFEU).

The first innovation relates to the possibility granted by the EU lawmaker to empower the Commission to adopt 'non-legislative acts of general application to supplement or amend certain non-essential elements of the legislative act' in accordance with Article 290 TFEU. Accordingly, a delegation of power is possible only in a legislative act, irrespective of whether the legislative act was adopted jointly by the Parliament and the Council. This is a sharp departure from previous practice on account that previously the Commission had to consult a committee in order to get an opinion. That obligation has been abolished in favour of much greater control by the EU lawmaker. Indeed, both the European Parliament and the Council may decide to revoke the delegation or to veto the Commission's proposal (Art. 290(2) TFEU).

It should also be noted that the definition of delegated acts in Article 290(1) is very similar to that of acts that are subject to the regulatory procedure with scrutiny (RPS).[82] In both cases the acts in question are of general application and seek to amend or supplement certain non-essential elements of the legislative instrument.[83] In particular, the term 'supplement' encapsulated in Article 290 TFEU blurs the dividing line between delegated acts and implementing acts.

The second innovation should attract the attention of environmental lawyers. Article 291(2) TFEU provides that 'where uniform conditions for implementing legally binding Union acts are needed', legislative acts shall confer implementing powers on the Commission. In contrast to the delegated acts, the implementing acts 'execute the legislative act without amendment or supplementation'.[84]

---

[81] The majority of these committees operated under several procedures. European Commission, Report from the Commission on the working of Committees during 2010, COM(2011) 879 final.

[82] The entry into force of the new Comitology Regulation does not affect the RPS referred to in Art. 5a of Comitology Decision 1999/468/EC. Accordingly, the RPS will continue to apply to all basic acts which make reference to it until those acts are formally amended.

[83] Communication from the Commission on the Implementation of Article 290 of the Treaty on the Functioning of the European Union, COM(2009) 673 final, para. 2.1.

[84] P. Craig, 'Delegated Acts, Implementing Acts and the New Comitology Regulation' (2011) 5 *EL Rev* 672.

Pursuant to Article 291(3) TFEU, the European Parliament and the Council, in accordance with the OLP, enacted Regulation 182/2011 that lays down 'the rules and general principles concerning mechanisms' for comitology.[85] This regulation enables Member States to exercise control of the implementing powers exercised by the Commission by virtue of Article 291(2) TFEU. In contrast to delegated acts, here we find the traditional comitology structure, albeit with significant changes.[86] The five procedures (advisory, management, regulatory, safeguard, and RPS) set out in Council Decision 1999/468/EC are replaced by just two basic procedures (advisory and examination). Consequently, former regulatory and management procedures are abolished.[87] Comitology has thus been simplified.[88]

The committees falling within the ambit of the new comitology can be classified according to the following schema.

Advisory committees have no power other than that to give an opinion to the Commission, and the latter need only take it into consideration.[89] In contrast to examination committees, these committees operate prior to the decision-making stage.

On the other hand, the *examination committees*, combining elements of the former management and regulatory committees, operate after the framework acts have been adopted. These committees are competent to examine acts of general scope designed to implement basic acts as well as specific implementing acts with a potentially important impact, among which are acts relating to 'the environment, security and safety, or protection of the health or safety, of humans, animals or plants'.[90] The Commission has to seek a qualified majority in favour of its proposal in order to be empowered to adopt the implementing act. If the committee is unable to obtain a qualified majority for or against the proposal, the Commission is called upon to reconsider and resubmit its proposal to the committee. Indeed, the Commission's proposal cannot be adopted if it is not in accordance with the opinion of the committee, except in very exceptional circumstances. Moreover, in case the committee votes by qualified majority against the Commission's proposal, the Commission is not empowered, as it was previously, to forward it to the Council[91] and must forward its

---

[85] European Parliament and Council Regulation (EU) No. 182/2011 laying down the rules and general principles concerning mechanisms for control by Member States of the Commission's exercise of implementing powers [2011] OJ L55/13. Regulation (EU) No. 182/2011 thus repealed Council Decision 1999/468/EC.

[86] EIPA, *Delegated & Implementing Acts. The New Comitology* (Maastricht: EIPA, 2011) 15.

[87] Account must be taken of the fact that there were no criteria for choosing between regulatory and management committees. It was therefore a matter for EU legislative bodies. Should the EU lawmaker decide to disregard them, they will have to give reasons for their choice (Council Decision 1999/468/EC, Art. 2(2)). In contrast to the former management procedure, the regulatory procedure envisaged a more important role for the Council and provided, subject to certain conditions, for the intervention of the European Parliament. The Court of Justice has reviewed the discretion of the EU institutions. The Commission, which viewed the management procedure more favourably, has on two occasions—LIFE Programme and Forest Focus—challenged the regulatory procedure chosen by the Council and the Parliament on the ground that these institutions had disregarded the criteria laid down in Decision 1999/468/EC. See Case C-378/00 *Commission v Parliament and Council* [2003] ECR I-937; and Case C-122/04 *Commission v Parliament and Council* [2006] ECR I-2001.

[88] Regulation (EU) No. 182/2011 [2011] OJ L55/13, recitals 8 and 9.

[89] Regulation (EU) No. 182/2011, Art. 4(1) and (2).

[90] Regulation (EU) No. 182/2011, Art. 2(2)(b)(iii).

[91] The saga of placing GMOs on the market is interesting on more than one account. In the vast majority of cases, regulatory committees disagreed with the Commission's proposals for the marketing of GMOs. As

proposal to the Appeals Committee.[92] Henceforth, the European Parliament and the Council have the right of scrutiny that enables them to pass a non-binding resolution if they believe that the proposed measure exceeds the implementing powers provided for in the basic act.

With respect to environmental issues, the new examination committees are called upon to play a key role on the ground that they take action especially in relation to measures concerning the protection of the health or safety of humans, animals, or plants. Since their remit covers authorization procedures for products that pose a risk, such as GMOs, these committees should still exercise considerable powers. Whilst it is normally a matter for the Commission to implement legislative acts, the legislative instruments discussed later specify the extent of the executive competences thereby conferred on the Commission, as well as the manner in which it must exercise them.

To conclude, the choice between delegated powers and implementing powers is not a purely academic exercise: the attitude of the institutions remains a matter of political strategy rather than of strict legal analysis. In fact, the role of the European Parliament is dwarfed by the Article 291 procedure.[93] Given that most of the national representatives taking part in the advisory and examination committees report to their ministers, the Council is likely to be much more favourable towards supporting implementing procedures rather than delegated procedures, notwithstanding the fact that it has no formal veto. Accordingly, the Council is likely *de facto* to seek to regain ground that it had lost *de jure* with the new comitology procedures. Table 4.1 summarizes the institutional advantages and drawbacks of each category.

One last point may be worth making here. To make matters more complex, 'Comitology' Regulation (EU) No. 182/2011 of 16 February 2011[94] did not have the effect of abrogating the RPS introduced by Council Decision 2006/512/EC.[95] The RPS

the Commission could not obtain the approval of these committees, which were decided by qualified majority, the proposals were sent to the Council. Generally speaking, the Council was divided. In accordance with Council Decision 1987/373/EEC ([1987] OJ L197/33), the Commission's draft could only be rejected by unanimity. Given that several Member States supported the placing on the market of GMOs, it was impossible for the Council to reject the proposal. As a result, the Commission was able to grant the licences despite strong objections from a majority of Members States. See, eg, Commission Decision 1997/98/EC ([1997] OJ L31/69). See M. Lee, *EU Regulation of GMOs* (Cheltenham: Edward Elgar, 2008) 71. Under Council Decision 1999/468/EC, this extreme scenario was removed. The Council was empowered to reject the Commission's proposal by qualified majority; however, the Council was unable to reach such a majority either for or against the proposal. It followed that the Commission was still empowered to authorize the placing of the market of GMOs. As a result, several Member States had recourse to safeguard clauses (Directive 2001/18/EC, Art. 23) in order to prevent the marketing of GMOs authorized by the Commission. The Commission and the Council strongly disagreed on the validity of such safeguarding clauses. See M. Weimer, 'Applying Precaution in EU Authorisation of GM Products—Challenges and Suggestions for Reform' (2010) 16:5 *ELJ* 624–57.

[92] Regulation (EU) No. 182/2011, Art. 6.
[93] C. Blumann, 'Un nouveau départ pour la Comitologie' (2012) *CDE* 38; J. Bast, 'New Categories of Acts after the Lisbon Reform: Dynamics of Parliamentarization in EU Law' (2012) 19 *CML Rev* 913.
[94] European Parliament and Council Regulation (EU) No. 182/2011 laying down the rules and general principles concerning mechanisms for control by Member States of the Commission's exercise of implementing powers [2011] OJ L55/13.
[95] Although Regulation (EU) No. 182/2011 introduced considerable changes to existing comitology mechanisms, nonetheless the RPS 'shall be maintained for the purposes of existing basic acts making reference thereto'. See Art. 12(2) and recital 21.

Table 4.1 Non-legislative acts

	Delegated acts	Implementing acts
Lawmaking process regarding the adoption of environmental protection acts	EP (absolute majority); Council (qualified majority) Case-by-case approach (objectives, scope, duration, conditions)	EP (absolute majority); Council (qualified majority)
Nature of the powers conferred to the Commission	Quasi-legislative nature	Executive nature
Material conditions	'[N]on-legislative acts of general application to supplement or amend certain non-essential elements of the legislative act'	'[W]here uniform conditions for implementing legally binding Union acts are needed'
Formal condition	The word 'delegated' is inserted in the title of the act	The word 'implementing' is inserted in the title of the act
Comitology	Absence of committees	Advisory and Examination committees If the Examination Committee votes by qualified majority against the proposal, the Commission may forward the act to the Appeals Committee
Ex post **supervisory role of conferring institutions**	Right of veto: EP and Council may object to the delegated act on any ground	Right of scrutiny: EP and Council may pass non-binding resolution
Revocation	EP and Council may revoke the delegation	No revocation

covers the adoption of measures with a general scope designed to amend non-essential elements of a basic instrument adopted by co-decision (eg amendments to the field of application of the instrument due to the addition of new appendices). Several environmental directives make reference to that procedure.[96] Furthermore, RPS allows the Council and Parliament to carry out a prior check, irrespective of whether a negative or positive opinion is given.[97]

---

[96] This procedure was added to a number of environmental directives (water, waste management, eco-design . . .). Eg, Council Regulation (EU) No. 333/2011 establishing criteria determining when certain types of scrap metal cease to be waste under Directive 2008/98/EC on waste management ([2011] OJ L94/2) has been adopted by the Council in accordance with the regulatory procedure with scrutiny. Since the committee had not issued its opinion on the measures proposed by the Commission, the Council adopted the regulation concerned under the 1999 'Comitology' Decision. The European Parliament did not object to the measures proposed.

[97] This procedure was added in a number of environmental directives (water, waste management, eco-design . . .). In May 2010 the Council made use of its right of veto on draft measures in one environmental case. It opposed the adoption of a draft Commission Directive related to the use of organic solvents in certain paints and varnishes and vehicle refinishing products. The draft measure was consequently not adopted.

3.3 Agencies

The agencies, which are distinct from EU institutions and endowed with legal personality and financial autonomy, are EU public law bodies which, by virtue of the specific missions conferred on them concerning technical and scientific issues, play an increasingly important role in the protection of the environment which complements that of the European Commission.

It should be noted that these various agencies, the competences of which touch on environmental matters, were not created under the Treaty but, rather, under the terms of regulations adopted either by the Council or by the two branches of the legislature. On an institutional level, there is a question over the practicability of a fragmentation of these administrative structures. There is no doubt that these agencies are largely controlled by the Commission which has the power to propose directors for nomination, is consulted in relation to working plans, and places representatives on their management boards. However, since at the same time one of their goals is the pursuit of a policy of decentralization and geographic dispersion, they undoubtedly undermine the centralizing role of the Commission.

With respect to environmental protection, a swathe of functions are conferred on the agencies. By way of illustration, the regulatory decisions in chemicals policy, such as those relating to the registration, authorization, restrictions, classification, and labelling under the REACH and CLP Regulations,[98] are backed by opinions of the European Chemicals Agency (ECHA), whereas the placing on the market of GMOs and pesticides is subject to the opinion of the European Food Safety Agency (EFSA). Moreover, the European Environment Agency (EEA) provides for regular surveys of the state of the environment. Table 4.2 illustrates the main environmental tasks performed by several EU agencies.

Clearly, these agencies enjoy an undeniable advantage, including scientific expertise, independence, and autonomy from EU procedures.

Table 4.2 Agencies endowed with environmental tasks

Agencies	Framework regulations	Environmental tasks
European Environmental Agency (EEA)	Regulation 1210/90/EEC	Information on the state of the environment
European Food Safety Agency (EFSA)	Regulation 178/2002/EC	Scientific opinion on risk assessment regarding food and feed safety
Community Fisheries Control Agency (CFCC)	Regulation 2847/93/EEC	Coordination of fisheries control and inspection activities
European Aviation Safety Agency (EASA)	Regulation 1592/2002/EC	Environmental certification of aircraft and related products
European Chemicals Agency (ECHA)	Regulation 1907/2006/EC	Implementation of REACH
European Maritime Safety Agency (EMSA)	Regulation 1406/2002/EC	Marine pollution preparedness and response

[98] European Parliament and Council Regulation (EC) No. 1907/2006 concerning the Registration, Evaluation, Authorisation and Restriction of Chemicals (REACH) [2006] OJ L396/1; and European

It is important to consider whether the decisions adopted by these agencies may be subject to internal and judicial review.

First, the decisions or omissions of these agencies may be subject to an internal review procedure.[99]

Second, with respect to judicial review, the situation varies.[100] Whilst certain decisions adopted by the ECHA concerning the assessment of files may be subject to an appeal before an appeal board and thereafter before the General Court,[101] opinion given by the scientific committee of EFSA cannot be treated as an act falling within the ambit of Article 263 TFEU, since it is a preparatory instrument which does not produce binding legal effects capable of affecting the applicants' interests by bringing about a distinct change in their legal position.[102]

That said, in the event that the Agency's scientific opinion is defective, there is a knock-on effect on the legality of subsequent decisions taken by the Commission, which are subject to review before the Courts. Even though the General Court has found that it cannot substitute its opinion for the opinion given by a scientific committee, it nonetheless oversees the functioning of the committee in question, the compliance of its opinion with EU law, and the reasons given for its decisions.[103]

The question also arises as to whether the decision taken by the Commission or by the Council, where it departs from the Agency's opinion, is likely to be annulled. In this connection, it should be noted that the General Court requires any institution wishing to disregard scientific opinion 'to provide specific reasons for its findings by comparison with those made in the opinion', and the justification 'must be of a scientific level at least commensurate with that of the opinion in question'.[104] Since the Commission does not have the same type of scientific expertise as the agencies, it would appear to be difficult to circumvent such a requirement.[105] Consequently, the Commission rarely disregards EFSA's scientific opinions.

4. Legal Acts, Self-Regulation, and Case Law

4.1 Introductory comments

Environmental policy enshrined in Title XX TFEU is based on both legal acts as well as non-legal instruments. Moreover, the institutions encourage non-institutional actors

---

Parliament and Council Regulation Regulation (EC) No. 1272/2008 on classification, labelling and packaging of substances and mixtures [2008] OJ L353/1.

[99] European Parliament and Council Regulation (EC) No. 1367/2006 on the application of the provisions of the Aarhus Convention on Access to Information, Public Participation in Decision-making and Access to Justice in Environmental Matters to Community institutions and bodies [2006] OJ L264/13, Arts 2(1)(c) and 10(1).

[100] M. Chamon, 'EU Agencies between *Meroni* and *Romano* or the Devil and the Deep Blue Sea' (2011) 48 *CML Rev* 1071–2.

[101] REACH Regulation, Arts 91–4. See Case T-96/10 *Rütgers Germany GmbH and Others v ECHA* [2013]; Case T-95/10 *Cindu Chemicals BV and Others v ECHA* [2013].

[102] Case T-311/06 *FMC Chemical and Arysta Lifesciences v EFSA* [2008] ECR II-88, paras 67 and 68; and Case T-397/06 *Dow AgroSciences v EFSA* [2008] ECR II-90, paras 59 and 60.

[103] Case T-74/00 *Artegodan v Commission* [2002] ECR II-4945.

[104] Case T-123/03 *Pfizer v Commission* [2004] ECR II-1631, para. 199.

[105] A. Alemano and S. Mahieu, 'The EFSA before the European Courts' (2008) 5 *European Food and Feed L Rev* 325.

to negotiate agreements. It is the aim of this fourth section to address the issue of this flurry of legal acts as well as the variety of soft law instruments (atypical legal acts) that are adopted alongside binding legal acts. Also, the case law is of paramount importance.

4.2 Legal acts

Neither Article 192 nor Article 114 TFEU specify that a particular legal act should be used in order to harmonize environmental measures. Accordingly, environmental policy is based on the five legal acts listed in Article 288 TFEU (directive, regulation, decision, recommendation, and opinion). At present, a somewhat haphazard method has influenced the choice of these legal instruments in the environmental field.

It should at the outset be noted that in environmental matters there has always been a mismatch with traditional legal categories. Some directives are so precise and restrictive that they end up looking like regulations.[106] By contrast, other directives framed in more fleeting terms—such as the draft framework directive on soils—bear more resemblance to declarations of intent.

As a result of an EU policy in favour of subsidiarity, EU environmental law consists more of directives than regulations. Accordingly directives, and more specifically framework directives, spearhead EU harmonization. The provisions of these framework directives are generally worded in very general terms, whilst regulations may be extremely precise.[107] By prescribing broad objectives but leaving the choice of implementation to Member State authorities, framework directives are well tailored to take into account the diversity of administrative and legal culture in the EU. In so doing, the lawmaker increases the discretion of national authorities in the choice of form and appropriate means for implementing EU law. In tolerating—let alone encouraging—administrative diversity, these directives keep uniformity at bay. Clearly, the extent of such discretion compounds the difficulties faced by the European Commission in verifying the compliance of EU environmental law in 28 Member States.

The Court of Justice has, for example, held that when national courts review the legality of measures to combat agricultural pollution, they must take account of the discretionary power of the Member States, which is presupposed by the complex nature of the assessments concerning the impact of the spreading of nitrates.[108] Similarly, Member States are endowed with broad discretion when they are required to ensure that their land-use policies take into consideration the need to maintain appropriate distance between Seveso establishments and buildings for public use.[109]

---

[106] See Council Directive 67/548/EEC on the approximation of laws, regulations and administrative provisions relating to the classification, packaging and labelling of dangerous substances ([1967] OJ 196/1) and Council Directive 76/769/EEC relating to restrictions on the marketing and use of certain dangerous substances and preparations ([1976] OJ L262/201), which are very detailed insofar as they guarantee the good functioning of the internal market.

[107] See the degree of precision reached by European Parliament and Council Regulation (EC) No. 1013/2006 on the shipment of waste ([2006] OJ L190/1) and European Parliament and Council Regulation (EC) No. 2037/2000 on substances that deplete the ozone layer ([2000] OJ L244/1).

[108] Case C-293/97 *Standley* [2004] ECR I-2603, para. 37.

[109] Case C-53/10 *Franz Mücksch* [2011] OJ C319/5, paras 40–1.

That said, this discretion is by no means unfettered. As will be discussed, in a swathe of cases, the Court of Justice has interpreted rather narrowly the Member States' room for manoeuvre.[110]

Nonetheless, given the importance conferred on subsidiarity, directives are likely to remain dominant in the environmental realm.

Let us turn to the issue of regulations, which for a long time played a secondary role.[111] As far as internal market policy is concerned, regulations have been privileged as a means of enhancing a level playing field for traders, in particular with regard to harmonization of the placing of certain goods posing environmental and health risks on the market and control of the import, export, or transfer of goods involving ecological risks—chemical products, GMOs, etc. Indeed, the preference of regulations based on Article 114 TFEU could be explained by the fact that the more flexible nature of a directive entails a genuine risk of market fragmentation. There have been developments in recent years, principally in the area of product safety where regulations have been more prevalent. For instance, chemicals (REACH and CLP Regulations), pesticides, and GMOs have been harmonized thanks to the adoption of regulations. Given that these sectors are product-related, it comes as no surprise that the EU institutions have lately favoured regulations adopted pursuant to Article 114 TFEU. Where these regulations require Member States to establish enforcement agencies and to develop enforcement policy, these are not self-executing.

Regulations have also been adopted under Article 192 TFEU with the aim of formalizing voluntary forms of participation for businesses—see, for example, the regulations on eco-labels or on environmental audits and where it is necessary to implement obligations flowing from international agreements to which the EU is a party.[112] On occasion, a choice has been made, within the context of environmental policy, for regulations aiming to set out product standards or to ban the import of species threatened with extinction.[113] Moreover, in some cases directives are amended, or even completed, by regulations.[114] On the other hand, the EU lawmaker has never used regulations to ensure the protection of water or the air, or the regulation of noise.

---

[110] See Section 4.5.

[111] Under ex Art. 100 EEC, the use of a directive was the only means by which the Council could enact legislation regarding the establishment of the common market. Prior to the SEA, most legislative acts were adopted pursuant to that provision. See Chapter 1.

[112] Regulation (EC) No. 2037/2000 on substances that deplete the ozone layer, see earlier in this chapter; Regulation (EC) No. 1013/2006 on the shipment of waste, see earlier in this chapter; Regulation (EC) No. 338/97 on the protection of species of wild fauna and flora by regulating trade therein, see earlier in this chapter.

[113] Council Regulation (EEC) No. 348/81 on common rules for imports of whales or other cetacean products [1981] OJ L39/1; Council Regulation (EEC) No. 3254/91 prohibiting the use of leghold traps in the EU and the introduction into the EU of pelts and manufactured goods of certain wild animal species originating in countries which catch them by means of leghold traps or trapping methods which do not meet international humane trapping standards [1991] OJ L308/1.

[114] See European Parliament and Council Regulation (EC) No. 166/2006 concerning the establishment of a European Pollutant Release and Transfer Register and amending Council Directives 91/689/EEC and 96/61/EC [2006] OJ L33/1; European Parliament and Council Regulation (EC) No. 850/2004 on persistent organic pollutants and amending Directive 79/117/EEC [2004] OJ L158/1. See also Art 19(3) of European Parliament and Council Directive 2003/87/EC establishing a scheme for greenhouse gas emission allowance trading within the EU ([2003] OJ L275/32–46) empowering the European Commission to enact regulations.

So far, decisions have also been adopted in order to establish an organ, finance environmentally friendly projects, harmonize administrative forms,[115] reject national plans for the allocation of GHG emission allowances,[116] determine the ecological criteria for the award of an EU label,[117] lay down the BAT for listed installations,[118] and to authorize State aids intended to cover investments to combat pollution or agreements with anti-competition effects.[119]

On the other hand, the institutions have shown themselves to be less fond of recommendation and opinion. Whilst recommendations have regularly been adopted by the OECD or by the Council of Europe in environmental matters,[120] this instrument has not been privileged by the Commission, which is generally able to ensure the adoption of its proposals for environmental law directives.[121] Finally, express provision has been made for certain advisory procedures, particularly regarding the recycling of packaging waste[122] and the conservation of natural habitats.[123]

4.3 Atypical acts

The EU increasingly acts through a melange of resolutions, declarations of intent, Green and White Papers, action plans and programmes, codes of conduct, and contracts—all somewhat spellbinding instruments which replace action with the mere shadow of action. As is the case for international environmental law, EU law hence abounds with instruments of ambiguous legal status. This soft or 'muffled' law is viewed not

---

[115] See eg: Commission Decisions 94/741/EC concerning questionnaires for Member States' reports on the implementation of certain Directives in the waste sector [1994] OJ L296/42; and Commission Decision 94/774/EC concerning the standard consignment note referred to in Council Regulation (EEC) No. 259/93 on the supervision and control of shipments of waste within, into and out of the European Community [1993] OJ L310/70.

[116] European Parliament and Council Directive 2003/87/EC establishing a scheme for greenhouse gas emission allowance trading within the Community [2003] OJ L275/32–46, Art. 9(2).

[117] European Parliament and Council Regulation (EC) No. 1980/2000 on a revised EU eco-label award scheme [2000] OJ L237/1–12.

[118] The Commission is empowered by Art. 13(5) of European Parliament and Council Directive 2010/75/EU on Industrial Emissions ([2010] OJ L334/17) to adopt decisions encapsulating the conclusions of the best available technique documents which are non-binding.

[119] For examples, see Part III.

[120] Recommendation of the OECD Council of 21 April 2004 on material flows and resource productivity.

[121] See Commission Recommendation 1999/125/EC on the reduction of CO_2 emissions from passenger cars ([1999] OJ L40/49) and the recommendations taken relating to the automotive sector on the reduction of CO_2 emissions (see Section 5); and Commission Recommendation 96/733/EC concerning Environmental Agreements implementing EU directives [1996] OJ L333/59 (see later). Likewise, given that Member States may take appropriate measures to avoid the unintended presence of GMOs in other products (Directive 2001/18/EC, Art. 26a), the Commission has adopted two successive recommendations on the development of national strategies and best practices to ensure the coexistence of genetically modified crops with conventional and organic food. See Opinion AG Bot in Case C-36/11 *Pioneer Hi Bred Italia* [2012] OJ C355/5, paras 3–7. Though not constituting binding sources as such, recommendations are likely to have relevance for national disputes insofar as national courts are bound to take them into account when they are likely to shed light on binding legislation (Case C-322/88 *Grimaldi* [1989] ECR I-4407).

[122] European Parliament and Council Directive 94/62/EC on packaging and packaging waste [1994] OJ L365/10–23, Art. 6(6).

[123] A. García Ureta, 'Habitats Directive and Environmental Assessment of Plans and Projects' (2007) 2 *JEEPL* 84–96.

only as a precursor to legislative action, but also even as ersatz law. Moreover, non-regulatory instruments are used both prior to as well as after the adoption of regulations.

Prior action, such as non-regulatory instruments—action programmes, Green and White Papers—acts as a warning signal sent to the various 'actors' of the adoption of future regulations. Consequently, non-regulatory instruments, such as communications, are widespread: the Commission sets out its guidance. Finally, when adopting its resolutions, the Council adopts a position in relation to Commission communications.

Certain legislative acts expressly provide at the outset for the adoption by the Commission of guidance documents on the implementation of specific provisions, such as those regarding the allocation of GHG emission allowances.[124] Similarly, the Industrial Emission Directive provides for guidance documents on BAT applying to listed installations that are prepared by a 'forum' composed of Member State representatives, industry representatives, and environmental NGOs.[125] Moreover, the European Commission also adopts interpretation guides in order to inform the Member States of the scope of specific legal arrangements. By way of illustration, with a view to providing Member States with clarification on the ways in which several provisions of the Habitats Directive have to be applied in different sectors—mining, dams, etc—the Commission has adopted several guides on the compatibility of development projects within Natura 2000 areas.[126] As a matter of law, such guidance documents must be in line with Court of Justice case law.

All these instruments by definition lack binding force since they are not included in the list of EU instruments endowed with this characteristic.[127] Nevertheless, whilst guidance documents do not have self-standing binding force in relation to third parties, the Commission may not disregard them without stating its reasons, at the risk, depending on the circumstances, of violating general principles of EU law.[128] After all, the EU Courts do not hesitate to seek support for their reasoning in atypical acts. Indeed, there are various examples in the case law illustrating the extent to which the EU Courts are prone to rely on soft law instruments to adjudicate hard cases.

- In *Chemische Afvalstoffen Dusseldorp*, the Court of Justice based its reasoning on a Council resolution in order to determine the scope of the principle of self-sufficiency in relation to the treatment of waste.[129]

[124] See ETS Directive 2003/87/EC, Art. 9(1), first indent; and Communication COM(2003) 830 final of 7 January 2004.
[125] IE Directive 2010/75/EU, Art. 13(3).
[126] See the many interpretation guides seeking to define the scope of obligations relating to nature conservation.
[127] L. Senden, *Soft Law in EC Law* (Oxford: Hart Publishing, 2004); N. de Sadeleer and I. Hachez, 'Hiérarchie et typologie des actes juridiques de l'UE' in N. de Sadeleer et al. (eds), *Les innovations du traité de Lisbonne* (Brussels: Bruylant, 2011) 45–132. Nonetheless, the fact that participation of undertakings in the Energy Star labelling programme is not mandatory cannot affect that the decision approving the agreement must be based on the Common Trade Policy legal basis (ex Art. 133 EC; Art. 227 TFEU). See Case C-281/01 *Commission v Council* [2002] ECR I-12049, paras 43–4.
[128] As for the obligation to take into account the recommendations establishing guidelines concerning the ETS (COM(2003) 830 final), see Case T-374/04 *Germany v Commission* [2007] ECR II-4431, paras 111 and 112.
[129] See Case C-203/96 *Chemische Afvalstoffen Dusseldorp* [1998] ECR I-4075, para. 31. See, eg, Opinion AG Bot in Case C-362/06 P *Sahlstedt e.a. v Commission* [2009] ECR I-2903, para. 97.

- Concerning the legal effects of a Commission communication confirmed by a Council resolution which listed dangerous substances that must be subject to a system of administrative authorization, the Court of Justice recognized that the substances in question 'belong scientifically to the families and groups of substances in List I' of Directive 76/464/EC.[130]

- In a similar vein, Advocate General Bot laid emphasis on recourse to Natura 2000 interpretation guides in order to specify the scope of obligations concerning the conservation of natural habitats. In particular, he stressed that these documents had the effect of limiting the Member States' margin of appreciation, which shows how far a decision of the Commission on listing protected habitats was capable of directly affecting, within the meaning of Article 230(4) EC (Art. 263(4) TFEU), the owners of the land concerned.[131] However, the Court of Justice did not endorse this line of reasoning.[132]

4.4 Self-regulation and co-regulation

Self-regulation has enjoyed, in environmental matters, a success similar to that of deregulation. This approach has been seen as a response to deficiencies both of administrative regulation and economic instruments.[133] As a result, it has been advocated as a remedy for the administrative model. Replacing the rigour and weight of binding norms with the pragmatism and flexibility of negotiated rules, the conclusion of agreements has in particular been branded by industry as a means of avoiding State intervention. As a result, concerted action has, since the beginning of the 1990s, undergone unprecedented expansion. In fact, environmental agreements are likely to cover many sectors of environmental policy such as product waste-related agreements (recycling of end-of-life vehicles, batteries), product-related agreements (phase out, product improvement, packaging, and labelling), as well as GHG reduction and energy efficiency targets.

That said, the concept of environmental agreement is not generally defined in precise terms.[134] This term in fact embraces regulatory techniques that are highly varied with regard to the resulting level of binding force. A distinction may be drawn here between co-regulation and self-regulation, although this distinction is somewhat artificial.[135]

Co-regulation agreements are those which are concluded between either the EU institutions or national authorities and business federations. In other words, the undertakings' self-commitment is expressly recognized by the State authorities. In

---

[130] Case C-207/97 *Commission v Belgium* [1999] ECR I-275.

[131] Opinion AG Bot in *Sahlstedt* (n 129), para. 97. See N. de Sadeleer and C. Poncelet, 'Protection Against Acts Harmful to Human Health and the Environment Adopted by the EU Institutions' (2012) *Cambridge Yearbook of EU Law* 177–208.

[132] *Sahlstedt* (n 129).

[133] E. Rehbinder, 'Self-Regulation by Industry' in G. Winter (ed.), *European Environmental Law* (Aldershot: Dartmouth, 1995) 240–2.

[134] See the definition given by European Parliament and Council Directive 94/62/EC on packaging and packaging waste [1994] OJ L365/10–23, Art. 3(12).

[135] In fact, some of the environmental agreements are concluded without any intervention by public authorities, whilst the conclusion of other agreements is encouraged by public authorities, either EU or national.

EU law, these agreements have been defined as 'the mechanism whereby a [EU] legislative act entrusts the attainment of the objectives defined by the legislative authority to parties which are recognised in the field...'[136] Accordingly, draft agreements concluded by the parties have to be forwarded by the Commission to the lawmaker. In accordance with its responsibilities, the Commission will verify whether those draft agreements comply with EU law. In contrast to genuine self-regulation, the authorities remain the key actors representing the public interest. In addition, given that agreements with private business may lead to unsatisfactory results, the authorities are likely to have the last word.

It should be noted that a number of agreements have been concluded under the aegis of the European Commission. Although the Treaty does not allow the institutions to conclude agreements with private individuals, the Commission may make it known that it is favourably disposed towards such agreements. Confronted with the threat of the adoption by the EU of new legislative acts looming on the horizon, business federations have accordingly concluded 12 agreements relating to CFCs, detergents, energy efficiency, etc.[137] The procedure is simple: the Commission takes note of the commitment signed by the business federations, tacitly undertakes not to initiate regulatory initiatives, and makes a recommendation to the Member States encouraging them not to stand in the way of the implementation of the agreement. The most well known and controversial of these agreements is that concluded between the federations of car manufacturers, which undertook to apply measures reducing CO_2 emissions— below the threshold of 140gm/km[138]—an approach which has not borne fruit.[139] In competition law matters, voluntary agreements concluded by federations of car manufacturers have been approved by the Commission on the ground that they did not impose precise targets on each producer, only a common target, each undertaking being free to choose the technologies and to set its own emissions thresholds.[140]

As far as the Member States are concerned, since 1992 the European Commission has strongly encouraged them to promote the conclusion of this type of agreement.[141] Additionally, obligations laid down in environmental directives may be implemented

---

[136] Interinstitutional Agreement on better law-making (2003/C 321/01) [2003] OJ L321/1, para. 18.

[137] See the list of those agreements in G. Schnabl, 'The Evolution of Environmental Agreements at the Level of the EU' in E. Croci (ed.), *The Handbook of Environmental Voluntary Agreements* (Vienna: Springer, 2005) 104–6.

[138] In 1999 and 2000, the Commission endorsed the three agreements concluded by business federations regrouping car manufacturers (ACEA—European Automobile Manufacturers' Association; JAMA—Japanese Automobile Manufacturers' Association; and KAMA—Korean Automobile Manufacturers' Association). The reduction targets relating to CO_2 were endorsed by the Commission. See Communication from the Commission, Results of the review of the EU Strategy to reduce CO_2 emissions from passenger cars and light-commercial vehicles, COM(2007) 19 final.

[139] Given that the car industry was unable to reach its own objectives as set out in these three agreements, on February 2007 the Commission acknowledged the need to replace this conciliatory approach by a genuine regulatory approach. As a result, the Commission proposed the Council and the European Parliament adopting a regulation setting emission performance standards for new passenger cars as part of the EU's integrated approach to reduce CO_2 emissions from light-duty vehicles. See European Parliament and Council Regulation (EC) No. 443/2009 setting emission performance standards for new passenger cars [2009] OJ L140/1–15.

[140] 28th Report on Competition Policy (1998), para. 167.

[141] European Commission, 'Towards sustainability' Programme of policy and action in relation to the environment and sustainable development, COM(92) 23 final.

through such agreements. This is indeed the case in the field of nature protection as well as the area of waste management.[142]

In contrast, *self-regulation* agreements are concluded by businesses or federations of businesses without either the involvement or the endorsement of public authorities. However, this type of voluntary initiative does not imply that the institutions have adopted any particular stance.[143] In EU law, these agreements have been defined as 'the possibility for economic operators, the social partners, non-governmental organisations or associations to adopt amongst themselves and for themselves common guidelines at European level (particularly codes of practice or sectoral agreements)'.[144]

So far, numerous agreements have been concluded exclusively by businesses—codes of conduct—without reference to any requirement imposed by State authorities. Various examples of such agreements will be given in Part III of the book. The Commission has also made recommendations to the Member States to encourage 'voluntary agreements and other forms of self-regulation'.[145] Hence, some agreements concluded exclusively between undertakings are likely to follow encouragement from national public authorities. It follows that the 'self-commitment' of undertakings or their federations can be the result of negotiations commenced on a State's initiative. It comes as no surprise that EU environmental law encourages this practice.[146]

Irrespective of their degree of success or failure, these voluntary agreements are a long way from winning unanimous support. In the first place, freedom of contract does not really apply: not only are the parties not placed on an equal footing, but also the bargaining procedure is administered within a legislative framework. Are they legally binding on the parties or merely informal gentlemen's agreements? This means that it is difficult to classify such agreements in legal terms, as they may be classified both as unilateral administrative acts requiring beneficiaries to comply with specific obligations, as well as administrative contracts, declarations of intent, and so on.... Furthermore, the academic literature has criticized the confidential manner in which they are drafted, the absence of any legal basis, the inability to sanction non-compliance with the obligations contained therein, and the difficulties encountered by third parties

---

[142] Therefore, return, collection, and recovery systems of packaging waste must be 'open to the participation of the economic operators of the sectors concerned and to the participation of the competent public authorities' (European Parliament and Council Directive 94/62/EC on packaging and packaging waste [1994] OJ L365/10–23, Art. 7(1)). See also European Parliament and Council Directive 2000/53/EC on end-of-life vehicles [2000] OJ L269/34, Art. 10(3). Likewise, conservation measures within the Natura 2000 network may be contractual (Council Directive 92/43/EEC on the conservation of natural habitats and of wild fauna and flora [1992] OJ L206/7–50, Art. 6(1)).

[143] Interinstitutional Agreement on better law-making (n 136), para. 22.

[144] Interinstitutional Agreement on better law-making (n 136).

[145] See European Commission, 'Towards sustainability' (n 141).

[146] The REACH Regulation encourages undertakings to exchange their data on the impact of chemical substances in view of preventing useless testing (REACH Regulation 1907/2006, Art. 25(1)). See also Directive 2005/32/EC on ecodesign [2005] OJ L191/29, recitals 16–18. Similarly, the WEEE Directive (waste electrical and electronic equipment) encourages 'cooperation between producers and recyclers...to promote the design and production of EEE, notably in view of facilitating re-use, dismantling and recovery of WEEE, its components and materials' (European Parliament and Council Directive 2012/19/EU on waste electrical and electronic equipment [2012] OJ L197/38, Art. 4). Authorities may also require the participation of private operators in collecting systems (European Parliament and Council Directive 2006/66/EC on batteries and accumulators and waste batteries and accumulators [2006] OJ L266/1, Art. 8(2)(a) and (b)).

in invoking the obligations resulting from them before the courts. The bypassing of the legislative process is clear: a negotiated agreement between the Commission and economic operators sidelines the other institutions.

To date, the Court of Justice has only once examined the compatibility of national agreements with EU law. The Court held that even if voluntary agreements concluded between different business circles of packaging producers already complied with the reduction programmes provided for under EU law, it was still necessary for the projected reductions in the quantity of waste packaging to be specified and to be subject to periodical revision.[147]

4.5 Case law

Consulted both by the national courts as well as by the Commission, the EU Courts have rapidly become an unavoidable reference point within this area of law.[148] As a result of the tangled web of contradictory rules, which is riddled with ambiguities, the EU Courts are not only the guardian of the temple of law, but have also turned into the architect. Indeed, the protection of the environment today plays a key role within EU litigation.[149] Evidence of this can be found in the significant number of landmark judgments dealing with environmental protection. The judgments regarding free movement of goods (*Walloon Waste*[150]), the choice of legal basis for environmental measures (*Titanium Dioxide*[151]), and the imposition of both a lump sum and a penalty payment for failure to comply with a judgment finding a breach of EU fishery law[152] have attracted widespread attention.

So far, most Court of Justice judgments have dealt with infringement proceedings, sometimes accompanied by requests that a party be ordered to pay a lump sum or a penalty payment,[153] or alternatively preliminary references. The bad faith of certain national authorities in the correct application of EU law justifies recourse to infringement proceedings by virtue of Article 258 TFEU. Interim measures are, on the other hand, practically unknown.[154]

---

[147] Case C-255/93 *Commission v France* [1994] ECR I-4949.

[148] Several books give quite an expansive overview of European case law: W. Douma (ed.), *European Environmental Case Law* (The Hague: Asser Instituut, 2002); L. Krämer, *Casebook on EU Environmental Law* (Oxford: Hart Publishing, 2002); and G. Bandi (ed.), *The Environmental Jurisprudence of the European Court of Justice* (Budapest: Szent Istvan Tarsulat, 2008). See also F. Jacobs, 'The Role of the European Court of Justice' (2006) 18:2 *JEL* 185–205.

[149] For the year 2011, on 535 cases completed by judgments handed down by the Court of Justice 35 concerned environmental issues (Court of Justice *Annual Report 2011*, Luxembourg, 106). See also L. Krämer, 'Statistics on Environmental Judgments by the EC Court of Justice' (2006) 18:3 *JEL* 407–21.

[150] Case C-2/90 *Commission v Belgium* [1992] ECR I-4431.

[151] Case C-176/03 *Commission v Council* [2005] ECR I-7879.

[152] Case C-304/02 *Commission v France* [2005] ECR I-6263.

[153] Art. 260(2) TFEU. See P. Weneraas, 'A New Dawn for Commission Enforcement under Articles 226 and 228 EC' (2006) 43 *CML Rev* 31–62.

[154] Even though the Court of Justice hands down its judgments long after the occurrence of ecological damage, the European Commission seems reluctant to put an end to the ecological harm resulting from incorrect implementation of EU secondary law by using the emergency interim proceeding pursuant to Arts 278 and 279 TFEU. In fact, the first emergency interim proceeding was unsuccessful (Case C-197/03 P *Commission v Germany* [1989] ECR I-2849). See, however, the orders concerning the conservation of nature (Case C-197/03 R *Commission v Poland* [2008] unpublished; and Case C-76/08 R *Commission v*

It is principally the directives concerning EIAs, nature protection, procedural obligations stemming from the Aarhus Convention, and the management of waste which make up the hard core of litigation brought before the Court of Justice pursuant to Article 258 TFEU.[155]

Besides, the increasingly frequent recourse by the EU lawmaker to catch-all formulae can account for the growing importance of preliminary references pursuant to Article 267 TFEU. Even though most of the obligations laid down in framework directives provide for relatively fuzzy obligations, the Court has nonetheless gradually been able to uncover their full potential, thanks to a teleological and systematic interpretation of these texts, thereby causing the objectives of nature conservation or the preservation of the environment to prevail over more literal interpretations.[156] Accordingly, the purpose of the directive at issue is the determining factor for how to interpret technical concepts.[157]

The stage is therefore set for the Court of Justice to play the role of a counterweight: the low level of binding force of the EU legal arrangements has been compensated for by the *effet utile* of the directive. Consequently, the adequacy of national legislation on remedies has been called into question.[158] Moreover, in an attempt to guarantee the effectiveness of the conservation regimes for vulnerable ecosystems, the Court has accordingly circumscribed the margin of appreciation of the national authorities in relation to the following operations:

- the choice of projects covered by Annex II of EIA Directive 85/337/EEC[159] codified by Directive 2011/92/EU;[160]
- the choice of plans and programmes covered by SEA Directive 2001/42/EC;[161]

Malta [2008] ECR I-64). This pusillanimity to resort more regularly to emergency interim proceedings contrasts sharply with the assiduous resort to interim proceedings where a national measure aiming at protecting the environment jeopardizes the free movement of goods. See the different judgments handed down by the Court of Justice with respect to the conformity of an Austrian regulation on atmospheric pollution restricting the movement of some heavy goods vehicles on a Tyrolean motorway: Case C-320/03 P *Commission v Austria* [2003] ECR I-7929; Case C-320/03 P *Commission v Austria* [2003] ECR I-11665; and C-320/03 P *Commission v Austria* [2005] ECR I-3593.

[155] Since 1976, the Court of Justice has handed down 152 judgments in cases relating to waste management.

[156] In much the same vein, in *Massachusetts v Environmental Protection Agency* (127 S Ct 1438 (2007)), the US Supreme Court held that the EPA had the authority to regulate greenhouse gases taking into account the Air Pollution Act's broad and inclusive language implying that Congress had empowered the Agency to respond to new environmental risks.

[157] As regards the interpretation of the scope of technical projects laid down in the annex to the EIA Directive, the Court of Justice held that 'the purpose of the directive would be undermined if some projects could escape an environmental impact assessment, though they were likely to have significant effects on the environment'. Case C-72/95 *Kraaijeveld* [1996] ECR I-5403, para. 39.

[158] Case C-41/11 *Inter-Environnement Wallonie* [2012] OJ C118/6; Case C-201/02 *Wells* [2004] ECR I-723, para. 67.

[159] Opinion AG Elmer in Case C-72/95 *Kraaijeveld* [1996] ECR I-5403.

[160] European Parliament and Council Directive 2011/92/EU on the assessment of the effects of certain public and private projects on the environment [2012] OJ L26/1.

[161] Case C-427/07 *Commission v Ireland* [2009] ECR I-6277, para. 42; and Case C-295/10 *Valciukiene* [2011] OJ C331/5, para. 46; Case C-567/10 *Inter-Environnement Bruxelles* [2012] OJ C133/8.

- the designation of sites intended to guarantee the favourable conservation of habitats or endangered species, which must comply with scientific criteria;[162]
- the designation of areas vulnerable to pollution from nitrates of agricultural origin;[163]
- the designation of bathing waters.[164]

In the same way, the Court of Justice has classified contaminated soils and polluted waters as waste where such matters appear by definition to be precluded from the scope of the Waste Framework Directive.[165] Finally, it has also made adjustments to theories on direct effect[166] and consistent interpretation.[167]

For several years, environmental law has no longer been the privileged domain of the Court of Justice. Indeed, the growth in litigation on Commission decisions regarding more restrictive national measures pursuant to Article 114(4) and (5) TFEU,[168] national plans for the allocation of GHG allowances,[169] the prohibition of the placing on the market of substances which pose a risk, and State aids in environmental matters has brought to the fore the case law of the General Court.

Finally, as discussed in Chapter 1, the EU Courts have not hesitated to 'judicialize' principles, such as the polluter-pays principle, the principle of substitution, the precautionary principle, and a high level of environmental protection, even if it means elevating some of them to the status of a general principle. Endorsed by the General Court as a general principle,[170] the precautionary principle represents an undeniable interest in justifying the adoption of numerous measures intended to protect both the human[171] and natural[172] environments adopted in the face of uncertainty. By contrast, as only a limited number of environmental directives confer subjective rights on individuals, the Court of Justice has not yet been confronted with the question whether the principle of the responsibility of the Member States, in accordance with the *Francovich* case, could be extended to this area of law.[173]

---

[162] N. de Sadeleer and C. H. Born, *Droit international et communautaire de la biodiversité* (Paris: Dalloz, 2002) 496–9.

[163] Case C-258/00 *Commission v France* [2002] ECR I-5959.

[164] Case C-56/90 *Commission v UK* [1993] ECR I-4109, case note (1993) 6:1 *JEL* 125.

[165] Case C-1/03 *Van De Walle* [2004] ECR I-7613, case note (2006) 43 *CML Rev* 207–23.

[166] Case C-72/95 *Kraaijeveld* [1996] ECR I-5403; Case C-201/02 *Wells* [2004] ECR I-723, para. 67; and *Amia SpA* (n 3) paras 34–5.

[167] *Amia SpA* (n 3) paras 29–30.

[168] Joined Cases C-439/05 P & C-454/05 P *Land Oberösterreich and Republic of Austria v Commission* [2007] ECR I-7441.

[169] Case T-263/07 *Estonia v Commission* [2009] ECR II-3463; Case T-183/07 *Poland v Commission* [2009] ECR II-152; Case T-369/07 *Latvia v Commission* [2011] ECR II-1039; Case T-237/09 *Région wallonne v Commission* [2012] OJ C193/27; Case C-6/08 *US Steel Košice* [2008] ECR I-96; Case C-504/09 P *Commission v Poland* [2012] OJ C151/2. See C. Poncelet, 'The Emission Trading Scheme Directive: Analysis of Some Contentious Points' (2011) *EEELR* 245–55.

[170] Cases T-74, 760, 83–85, 132, 137 & 141/00 *Artegodan* [2002] ECR II-4945.

[171] Case C-473/98 *Toolex* [2000] ECR I-5681.

[172] Case C-127/02 *Waddenzee* [2004] ECR I-7405; and Case C-258/11 *Peter Sweetman* [2012] OJ C156, para. 41.

[173] Regarding the issue of procedural requirements laid down in several environmental acts, some authors consider that the condition laid out in the *Francovich* case law that relates to the rights conferred on private persons is fulfilled. See J.-V. Louis and T. Ronse, *L'ordre juridique de l'UE* (Brussels/Helbing: Bruylant/LGDJ, 2005) 321.

On the other hand, EU environmental law is primarily based on decentralized enforcement. Sad to say, national courts have generally been less rash than the EU Courts, and the concepts of *effet utile* and loyal cooperation are often ignored. As far as judicial cooperation is concerned, the situation is varied. Indeed, whilst certain administrative courts regularly refer preliminary questions to the Court of Justice,[174] others rarely bother to make preliminary references regarding the interpretation of EU environmental law obligations.[175] This means that certain supreme courts display a certain reticence in complying with the obligation to make preliminary references in the name of the *acte clair* theory set out in the *CILFIT* judgment.[176]

5. Instruments Specific to EU Environmental Law

5.1 Introductory remarks

Hemmed in by national practices, EU law has not proved to be particularly original. Sometimes it draws inspiration from techniques commonly applied by the national authorities—operating permits, process standards, emission ceilings, discharge thresholds, etc—whilst at other times it mirrors international mechanisms—emission allowance trading schemes established within the ambit of the Kyoto Protocol. That said, despite consensus on the need to safeguard the environment, there has been no shortage of disputes over the nature and scope of the EU instruments aiming to protect the environment. In addition, the appearance of successive waves of new regulatory instruments has resulted in a veritable mutation of environmental law both on the EU as well as the national level. Section 5 does not describe all EU instruments: to do so, several additional volumes would be required. Focusing on some key features of environmental legislation, this section merely highlights the breadth of this transformation.

5.2 From administrative law to a legal branch in its own right

When confronted with environmental legislation, lawyers experienced in well-established legal disciplines may easily lose themselves in a web of conjecture. This branch of the law inevitably comes across as an unidentified discipline.

---

[174] The numerous bodies acting in the environmental field in an administrative capacity, but not as a judicial authority, are not entitled to refer questions for a preliminary ruling. Regarding the interpretation of Council Recommendation 1999/519/EC on the limitation of exposure of the general public to electromagnetic fields, the Court of Justice ruled that it clearly lacked jurisdiction to rule on a reference for a preliminary ruling sent by a Swedish municipal environmental protection and health board that was acting in its capacity as an administrative authority. See Case C-344/09 *Dan Bengtsson* [2011] OJ C211/6, paras 23–4.

[175] Even though the implementation of the EIA Directive 85/337/EEC (codified by Directive 2011/92/EU) was recognized as deficient, the Spanish courts never considered it necessary to question the Court of Justice on this matter, notwithstanding the plethora of disputes caused by the weak implementation of this directive. It was necessary to wait for an administrative court from Madrid to question the Court in January 2007, ie nine years after the end of the transposition period of the Directive (3 July 1988), to allow the Court of Justice to answer the first preliminary reference referred by a Spanish court in an environmental case (Case C-142/07 *Ecologistas en Accion-CODA* [2008] ECR I-6097).

[176] In Belgium, the reluctance of the Cour constitutionnelle to make preliminary references in complex cases relating to the environment (CA, 92/2006, 7 June 2006, paras B.13 and B.24) has been overcome (*Inter-Environnement Bruxelles* (n 161); Case C-182/10 *Solvay* [2012] OJ C98/5).

For many years, administrative law has been the main source of environmental law. Hence, this branch of law has been hitherto practised mostly by administrative lawyers and not by lawyers specialized in economic law or in civil or common law.[177] Indeed, the preference of the EU lawmaker initially resulted in a regulatory approach, following in the footsteps of models conceptualized at State level. As a result, EU law has expanded the policing powers of the administrations, powers which are authoritarian in nature.[178]

Furthermore, given that the territorialization of environmental legislation is all too apparent, this branch of law is strongly intertwined with land planning law which is part of national administrative law.[179] Indeed, most directives relating to water,[180] the air,[181] noise,[182] hazardous plants,[183] and nature protection[184] entail a delineation of specific areas which act as a framework for the application of technical rules adapted to the management of these issues or the protection of these environments. Therefore, protection rules only apply to areas that have been subject to a prior designation by a Member State.[185] Table 4.3 highlights the extent to which environmental measures are entangled with land planning requirements.

Alongside duties of oversight, policing powers allow the national authorities to impose prohibitions, grant authorizations for activities which would normally be prohibited, to encourage or require the taking of particular action, and to verify compliance with the obligations created.[186] These obligations are generally associated

---

[177] Having favoured an approach based on civil liability, the Commission supported an administrative liability scheme, which led to the adoption by the European Parliament and the Council, on 21 April 2004, of Directive 2004/35/EC on environmental liability (ELD) with regard to the prevention and remedying of environmental damage [2004] OJ L143/56.

[178] The administrative policing powers (French: *pouvoirs de police*) can be defined as powers conferred on the administrative authorities by means or by virtue of a legislative act, which allow them to restrict, with a view to ensuring public order, the rights and freedoms of individuals.

[179] C-400/08 *Commission v Spain* [2011] OJ C152/2.

[180] Designation of vulnerable areas to nitrates is required under Article 3(2) of Council Directive 91/76/EEC concerning the protection of waters against pollution caused by nitrates from agricultural sources [1991] OJ L375/1.

[181] Establishment of areas where concentrations of ozone sulphur dioxide, nitrogen dioxide, and oxides of nitrogen, particulate matter, lead, benzene, and carbon monoxide are exceeded is required under Art. 4 of European Parliament and Council Directive 2008/50/EC on ambient air quality and cleaner air for Europe [2008] OJ L152/1.

[182] Strategic noise mapping is required under Art. 7 of European Parliament and Council Directive 2002/49/EC relating to the assessment and management of environmental noise [2002] OJ L189/2168.

[183] Under the Seveso III Directive (European Parliament and Council Directive 2012/18/EU on the control of major-accident hazards involving dangerous substances [2012] OJ L197/1), land-use planning policies shall ensure that appropriate distances between hazardous establishments and residential areas are maintained (Art. 13(2)(a)). Regarding the distances set out under the Seveso II Directive, see *Franz Mücksch* (n 109).

[184] In order to fulfil its objective of the conservation of biodiversity, the Habitats Directive 92/43/EC provides for the constitution of a 'coherent ecological network', called Natura 2000. The ecological coherence of this network rests mainly on Member States' site selection procedures based on ecological criteria. With respect to wild birds, Member States are called upon to designate 'special protection areas' (SPAs) whereas they have to designate 'special conservation areas' with a view to protecting other types of habitat. See N. de Sadeleer, 'Habitats Conservation in EC Law: From Nature Sanctuaries to Ecological Networks' (2005) 5 *YbEEL* 215–52.

[185] However, the habitats preventive regime applies prior the designation of Natura 2000 sites. See Case C-117/03 *Dragaggi* [2005] ECR I-167, para. 29; Case C-244/05 *Bund Naturschutz* [2006] ECR I-8445, para. 46; and *Commission v Spain* (n 33), paras 156–7.

[186] Council Directive 96/82/EC on the control of major-accident hazards involving dangerous substances as amended by Directive 2003/105/EC [2003] OJ L345/97.

Table 4.3 EU environmental designated areas

Directive	Subject matter	Type of designated areas
91/271/EEC	Urban waste treatment	Sensitive areas
91/676/EEC	Nitrates	Vulnerable zones (NVZ)
92/43/EC	Habitats	Special area for conservation (SAC)
2006/7/EC	Bathing waters	Bathing waters
2008/50/EC	Ambient air quality	Zones and agglomerations
2009/147/EC	Birds	Special protection area (SPA)
2012/18/EU	Major accident hazards involving dangerous substances	Appropriate distances between Seveso establishments and residential areas

with criminal and administrative sanctions.[187] Exercised by the administrative authorities themselves, these powers are rarely confined to private operators. Administrative policing sets aside, in principle, private law contracts. Traditionally, national authorities were given infamously wide powers of discretion to ensure compliance with the broad obligations laid down in the legislation. Nevertheless, a confrontational stance appeared to be counter-productive. Using an iron fist in a velvet glove,[188] they tended to enforce environmental law by cooperation, negotiation, conciliation, and compromise instead of resorting immediately to prosecution.

However, due to the Environmental Liability Directive (ELD), national administrations no longer have carte blanche to decide whether to exercise their powers. In effect, given that it places primary responsibility on the operator to identify and subsequently to carry out preventive and remediation environmental measures, the ELD has called into question this conciliatory relationship between the authorities and the operators. In particular, authorities are called upon to require preventive or remedial action by operators,[189] which have the duty to act in response to any governmental orders.[190] In addition, operators' liability has markedly increased.[191] To conclude, the ELD's emphasis to drive enforcement is likely, on the one hand, to diminish the room for manoeuvre left to the enforcement authorities and, on the other, to enhance the effectiveness of the preventive principle.

At the end of the twentieth century, the command-and-control approach has to an ever increasing extent been criticized for being burdensome, inefficient, and jeopardizing innovation. The calling into question of an interventionist policy against a political backdrop characterized by neo-liberalism led first to the simplification of the *acquis* and, second, a diversification of the instruments for intervention.[192]

---

[187] IE Directive 2010/75/EU, Art. 79; European Parliament and Council Directive 2008/99/EC on the protection of the environment through criminal law [2008] OJ L328/28.

[188] R. Macrory, 'Integrated Prevention and Pollution Control: The UK Experience' in C. Backes and G. Betlem (eds), *Integrated Prevention and Pollution Control—The EC Directive From a Comparative Legal and Economic Perspective* (London: Kluwer Law, 1998) 60.

[189] ELD, Arts 5(3) and 6(2).   [190] ELD, Arts 5(4) and 6(3).

[191] However, the extent of the deterrent effect of the regime is subject to the defences available to the operator. See Art. 8(3)(4).

[192] In its Fifth Environmental Action Programme, the Commission called for the reshaping of environmental law and stressed the need to adopt a swathe of new policy instruments ranging from voluntary covenants to co-auditing schemes.

Traditional regulatory mechanisms have thus been supplemented by tax incentives, mechanisms encouraging businesses to become aware of their responsibilities—eco-audits,[193] and economic measures such as State aids or carbon markets.[194] In contrast to so-called regulatory instruments, economic instruments are flexible in nature in that they allow addressees to choose between several alternatives, such as the choice between a tax break or payment of an eco-tax. Similarly, in providing for a collective emissions standard for groups of installations, emissions trading markets may be distinguished from the model of individual permits setting emissions thresholds for each installation. When they purchase emission allowances, buyers achieve savings on technological investment just as the sellers turn a profit through the sale. As a result, the success of emissions trading schemes is dependent on the need to purchase an increasingly limited number of quotas, within the context of supply and demand mechanisms. Finally, while economic instruments offer undertakings a relatively high degree of flexibility, they still fall within the realm of an interventionist environmental policy. Accordingly, they cannot be associated with deregulation.[195]

However, for some of these instruments such as eco-taxation and emissions trading schemes, the efforts made at EU level amount more to a catalogue of good intentions—Green Papers or recommendations—than harmonization.[196] Hence, with the exception of the EU carbon market, which in any event does not cover more than a limited number of facilities,[197] economic instruments have barely moved on at EU level. Moreover, the recourse to so-called economic instruments or tax instruments simply puts a new face on State interventionism, paving the way for flexibility gains by industry.

In sum, due to its use of a variety of regulatory instruments with different legal status, environmental law nowadays has a composite nature. The relations between this branch of law and the more traditional disciplines do, in fact, vary. In some respects, environmental law is like a toolbox containing a host of tools stemming from other branches of law. Indeed, the framers of environmental legislation constantly draw inspiration from private law, public law, and criminal law, without forgetting tax law, and even reshape these classical instruments in order to internalize the costs of pollution. This means that for certain directives it is not always clear whether a particular provision forms part of public or private law.[198] To cite another example, the *ČEZ* case straddled civil and public law. This case concerned the validity of an action for cessation of actual or potential nuisance caused to land by the activities of a nuclear power plant situated on the territory of the Czech Republic. The action was

---

[193] European Parliament and Council Regulation (EC) No. 761/2001 allowing voluntary participation by organisations in a Community eco-management and audit scheme (EMAS) [2001] OJ L114/1.

[194] ETS Directive 2003/87/EC.

[195] E. Rhebinder, 'Environmental Agreements. A New Instrument of Environmental Policy', European University Institute, Jean Monnet Chair Paper RSC No. 97/45, 1997.

[196] See the Commission Green Paper on market-based instruments for environment and related policy purposes (COM(2007) 388).

[197] ETS Directive 2003/87/EC, Annex I. See Case C-127/07 *Arcelor* [2008] ECR I-9895.

[198] Given that it mirrors a shift from a civil liability regime to an administrative responsibility regime, the ELD 2004/35/EC is testament to the transformation of classical liability regimes.

Table 4.4 Instruments particular to the environmental policy

Legal branches	Instruments	Incorporation into EU law
Administrative law	Impact assessment (EIA and SEA)	EIA Directives 2011/92/EU; SEA Directive 2001/42/EC
	Licensing	IE Directive 2010/75/EU; Seveso
	Prevention and remediation measures	Directive; WFD 2008/98/EC; Environmental Liability Directive 2004/35/EC
Criminal law	Offences punishable by appropriate criminal penalties	Directive 2008/99/EC
Civil law	Strict liability	Absent at EU level
Tax law	Eco-taxes or ecobonus	Absent at EU level

brought before an Austrian court by the Land Oberösterreich acting as a private party as well as by other Austrian landowners.[199]

Table 4.4 highlights the extent to which different legal branches are likely to influence EU regulatory outcomes.

5.3 From sectoral to transectoral approaches

As is the case for national law, EU environmental law has since the outset adopted a sectoral perspective, and the majority of its directives are limited to:

- a specific industrial sector (waste-treatment facilities, incinerators, co-incineration plants, cement factories, chemical plants, sewage treatment plants, installations using organic solvents, port facilities, landfills, etc);
- one element of the environment (surface water, underground water, air, soils, habitats, etc);
- a group of products or substances (waste, GMOs, hazardous substances, fuels, pesticides, biocides, etc).

As a whole, EU law tends more to regulate pollution caused by specific sources (facilities which pose a significant risk) than more diffuse pollution (agricultural pollution, emissions caused by air transport, pesticides discarded by farmers), as well as the sacred cows (structural funds) which EU institutions have generally not dared to attack.[200] Whilst it may be targeted, this sectoral approach has the drawback of being too compartmentalized. The absence of a holistic vision, particularly as far as the regulation of pollution sources is concerned, entails the risk of a transfer of pollution from one sector to another. What is the point of limiting the production of waste if this ends up increasing sewage?

---

[199] Questions arose as to whether there was an obligation to tolerate actual or potential nuisance caused by the nuclear plant or whether the authorization issued in the Czech Republic did not have to be taken into account. The Court of Justice left many questions unanswered, such as whether there was a reciprocal relationship between these two branches of law. See Case C-115/08 *ČEZ* [2009] ECR I-10265, noted by M. Möstl in (2010) 47 *CML Rev* 1221–3.

[200] L. Krämer, 'L'apport de la CE au droit de l'environnement' in CEDRE (ed.), *Quel avenir pour le droit de l'environnement?* (Brussels: FUSL-VUB, 1996) 458.

Table 4.5 Overview of EU environmental instruments

Transversal instruments
Impact assessment of projects, plans, and programmes
Access to information—Participation—Access to justice

Nuisances	Ecosystems
Listed installations	*Air*
IED, SEVESO I, II, and III	Environmental quality standards (EQS)
	Emission limit values (ELV)
	Programmes
	Product standards (CFC, fuels, vehicles, etc)
Waste	*Water*
Product standards (batteries, packaging, WEEE)	EQS
	ELV
Operating standards (landfills, incinerators)	Programmes
Waste management operations (sorting, recycling, etc)	
Transfrontier movements	
Hazardous substances	*Soils*
Chemical substances,	EQS
pesticides, biocides, asbestos	ELV
	Programmes
Noise	*Wildlife*
Product standards	Species and habitats protection
EQS	Deliberate release of GMOs
ELV	
Programmes	

Economic instruments
Eco-label—Eco-audit
Voluntary agreements
Cap-and-trade schemes

Nonetheless, after around 20 years, thanks to the EIA and SEA Directives on impact assessments,[201] as well as integrated pollution control,[202] a trans-sectoral perspective is tentatively emerging. Clearly, these horizontal directives cut across traditional administrative boundaries; however, it is important to point out that these instruments are still exceptions. Therefore, the resorption of certain pollutants of industrial origin through the contribution of EU law should not mask a deterioration in pollution of diffuse origin, such as photochemical pollution, endocrine disruptors, or the eutrophication of aquatic environments.[203]

Table 4.5 draws a distinction between harmonization measures related to transsectoral approaches and those adopting sectoral approaches. For sectoral approaches,

[201] EIA Directive 2011/29/EU on the assessment of the effects of certain public and private projects on the environment [2012] OJ L26/1; and European Parliament and Council Directive 2001/42/EC on the assessment of the effects of certain plans and programmes on the environment OJ [2001] L197/30–7.
[202] European Parliament and Council Directive 2008/1/EC concerning integrated pollution prevention and control [2008] OJ L24/8–29; and European Parliament and Council Directive 2010/75/EU on industrial emissions OJ [2010] L334/17.
[203] EEA, *The European Environment 2010. State and Outlook* (Copenhagen: EEA, 2010).

a further distinction has been drawn between rules intended to limit nuisance and those which aim to protect the receptor media.

5.4 Regulatory techniques: technical thresholds, legal standards, and standardization

It is the aim of this subsection to explore the specificies of the three main regulatory techniques: technical thresholds, legal standards, and standardization.

All noise, pollution, nuisances, or attacks on the natural environment cannot be prohibited because, were this to be done, life within society would become impossible. The only viable solution therefore involves authorizing polluting activities and requiring compliance with thresholds over which the impact of the activity is considered to be unacceptable. Therefore, since a certain level of environmental pollution can be sustained without significant damage, certain limits have been set on the exercise of economic activities with regard to their technical characteristics and the ability of the ecosystems and human beings to withstand them. It follows that environmental law resembles more an approach accompanying a process of industrial, agricultural, and urban development that is already well established, rather than a move to call it into question. In fact, the aim is not to eliminate pollution but, rather, to contain its most serious consequences.

Consequently, most EU harmonization measures are therefore based on thresholds which may not be exceeded. A multitude of provisions outlaw or regulate airborne, water, and soil pollutants; other provisions set out product standards, process standards, concentrations of substances, upper limits, decibel levels, etc.

Against this background, the threshold technique plays an essential yet controversial role in EU environmental law. Thresholds entail three obvious advantages. First, they are in principle set in line with scientific criteria. Experts, who play an essential role, are accordingly consulted in order to identify the threshold above which pollution becomes problematic, and as a result should be prohibited by EU law. Second, recurring throughout the various instruments authorizing polluting activities, respect for these thresholds is particularly well guaranteed since an infringement is an automatic result of any failure to respect them. Whether they are qualitative or quantitative, the thresholds thus set a dividing line between what is lawful and what is unlawful. Third, their harmonization on an EU level is particularly valued by the economic operators responsible for the creation of nuisances, since the adoption of uniform standards limits distortion in competition resulting from decisions taken on a case-by-case basis, which creates uncertainty. Hence, thresholds are likely to buttress legal certainty and enhance the smooth functioning of the internal market.

In spite of their benefits, thresholds do not, however, offer absolute environmental protection. The protection level offered by setting pollution thresholds essentially remains the result of political compromise, which proves to be particularly problematic since it is science itself which proves to be uncertain. Indeed, their scientific foundation is likely to be undermined where the threshold results from a compromise between industry and public authorities. Clearly, thresholds considered under environmental law do not always reflect the experts' recommendations.[204] In effect, the level of protection is more the result of a pragmatic approach and a search for possibilities rather than a desire to implement in detail the scientific experts' recommendations. With hindsight, it appears that this approach to pollution control has turned out to be little more than a sticking plaster on a weeping sore. Moreover, the technique of compartmentalizing the regulations that apply to different media makes it possible for them to be circumvented.[205]

On the other hand, environmental law does not rely exclusively on precise technical standards. Regardless of whether it has national, international, or EU status, environmental law cannot consist of a mass of technical rules incomprehensible to lawyers. In addition to its general principles, entire fields of environmental law are bursting with legal standards: that is, terms or phrases which refer to a state of affairs or a quality, the identification of which requires an assessment by the addressee. Thus, the impact of certain projects or programmes may only be evaluated insofar as they have 'significant' effects on the environment.[206] In the same vein, the general principles governing the basic obligations of the operator of a listed installation are couched in vague, flexible, open-textured, and hortatory terms rather than prescriptive language. The operator thus has to apply the 'best available techniques' with the aim of not causing 'significant pollution' and using energy efficiently.[207] No guidance is provided as to the meanings of 'significance' and 'efficiency'. Further, Member States can derogate from their obligations to protect wild species inasmuch as there is 'no other satisfactory solution'.[208] One is left with little guidance as to the meaning of the term 'satisfactory'.[209] In each case, the content of the obligation remains intentionally indeterminate in order to allow national authorities to differentiate between extremely disparate situations.

Lastly, we turn to standardization[210] that has been applied to certain fields touching on environmental protection issues.[211] Accordingly, framework directives lay down requirements termed 'essential',[212] in particular regarding safety requirements which

[204] Even the threshold to limit the global mean temperature increase since the pre-industrial era to less than 2°C provides no guarantee for avoiding all adverse climate change impacts. See EEA (n 203) 27.
[205] Case C-142/07 *Ecologistas en Accion-CODA* [2008] ECR I-6097, para. 20.
[206] EIA Directive 2011/92/EU, Art. 1; Directive 2001/42/EC, Arts 1 and 3; Habitats Directive 92/43/EEC on the conservation of natural habitats, Art. 6, para. 1; Convention on Environmental Impact Assessment in a Transboundary Context (Espoo, 25 February 1991), Art. 1.
[207] IE Directive 2010/75/EU, Art. 11(b), (c), and (f).
[208] Wild Birds Directive 2009/147/EC, Art. 9(1); Habitats Directive 92/43/EC, Art. 16(1).
[209] Case C-10/96 *LRBPO* [1996] ECR I-6675; Case C-342/05 *Commission v Finland* [2007] ECR I-4713, para. 45; and Case C-76/08 *Commission v Malta* [2009] ECR I-8213, para. 48.
[210] See Council Resolution 85/C 136/01 on a new approach to technical harmonization and standards [1985] OJ C136/1; Council Resolution 2000/C 141/01 on the role of standardization in Europe [2000] OJ C141/1; Council Resolution 2003/C 282/02 on the Communication of the European Commission 'Enhancing the Implementation of the New Approach Directives' [2003] OJ C282/3.
[211] European Parliament and Council Directive 94/62/EC on packaging and packaging waste [1994] OJ L365/10–23, Art. 9.
[212] EU legislation harmonizing the conditions for the marketing of products 'shall restrict itself to setting out the essential requirements determining the level of the protection' of public interest, among which are environmental interests. See European Parliament and Council Decision 768/2008/EC on a common framework for the marketing of products [2008] OJ L218/82, Art. 3(1). However, 'where health

products must satisfy in order to be placed on the market. It is then a matter for the standardization bodies—CEN, CENELEC—to adopt the technical specifications 'drawing up the technical specifications needed for the production and placing on the market of products conforming to the essential requirements established by the Directives'. Although technical specifications maintain their status as voluntary rules,[213] products manufactured in accordance with them are presumed to comply with the essential requirements laid down in the directives.

Resolution of 7 May 1985 on the 'new approach' stipulates that safeguard procedures must be incorporated into the directives in order to enable both the Commission and the Member States to challenge measures drafted by standards bodies.[214] The 'new approach' has recently been reinforced by Decision No 768/2008/EC of the European Parliament and of the Council of 9 July 2008 on a common framework for the marketing of products,[215] which constitutes a non-binding 'general framework of a horizontal nature' intended for use as a basis for the elaboration of sectoral directives or the revision of existing directives, in respect of the conditions for the marketing of products, through to the requirements laid down by sectoral harmonization directives.[216]

---

and safety, the protection of consumers or of the environment, other aspects of public interest, or clarity and practicability so require, detailed technical specifications may be set out in the legislation concerned'. See recital 8.

[213] Annex II to the Council Resolution 85/C 136/01 ([1985] OJ C136/1) setting out that they 'are not mandatory'.

[214] By way of illustration, the Packaging Directive 94/62/EC ([1994] OJ L365/10) authorizes a Member State or the Commission, where they consider that the standards established by the European Committee for Standardization (CEN) 'do not entirely meet the essential requirements' concerning the manufacturing and composition, the reusable nature, and the recoverable nature of packaging, to bring the matter before the Committee set up by Directive 83/189/EEC (*not* Directive 98/34/CE, which is the committee the CEN consults). In the light of the Committee's opinion, the Commission may withdraw the standards adopted by the CEN. Thus, taking up the criticisms of Denmark and Belgium which contested the validity of several standards proposed by the CEN regarding packaging requirements on the ground that they diluted the notion of prevention by favouring incineration, contrary to the essential requirements set out in Annex II to the Directive, the Commission decided not to publish several standards proposed by the CEN. See Commission Decision 2001/524/EC relating to the publication of references for standards EN 13428:2000, EN 13429:2000, EN 13430:2000, EN 13431:2000, and EN 13432:2000 in the Official Journal of the European Communities in connection with Directive 94/62/EC on packaging and packaging waste [2001] OJ L190/21.

[215] By way of contributing to the internal market dynamic, three legal acts were adopted in 2008, among which was Decision 768/2008/EC on a common framework for the marketing of products [2008] OJ L218/82. In addition to the creation of a common framework for the marketing of products, Regulations (EC) Nos 764/2008 and 765/2008 respectively set out prescriptions relating to the accreditation of evaluating organisms and proceedings concerning the application of technical national rules in not harmonized fields ([2001] OJ L218/21). This legislative package reinforces the taking in hand of Member States while facilitating implementation of the principle of mutual recognition. Despite the different techniques used, those three legal acts form a coherent body aiming to enhance the free movement of industrial products within the internal market. See R. Kovar, 'Le législateur communautaire encadre le régime de la mise des produits dans le marché intérieur' (2009) 44:2 *RTDE* 289–311.

[216] With the purpose of guaranteeing better homogeneity, those directives will have to comply with the precepts laid down in this decision. As far as the protection of non-trading interests is concerned, only the essential requirements establishing the level of this protection can be fixed by the EU lawmaker (recital 8, and Art. 3). It is only in the case where it is not possible to fix essential requirements that detailed specifications can be set out in the relevant EU legislation. Preference is thus given to bringing national requirements together rather than in reaching total harmonization.

5.5 Listed installations and products

The fight against nuisances, pollution, and the risks created both by products and listed installations is centred around four types of provision (emissions, immissions, procedural, and product standards) (Table 4.1).

- *Environmental quality standards (EQS)*, or quality targets, means 'the set of requirements which must be fulfilled at a given time by a given environment or particular part thereof'.[217] These standards provide guarantees of the quality of environmental receptors (water, air, soil) striking a balance between the conservation of natural resources and the presence of pollutants.

- *Emission limit values (ELV)*, or disposal standards, limiting the direct or indirect release of substances, vibrations, heat, noise, and other pollutants emitted by fixed polluting facilities (plants, facilities, industries) or diffuse sources into air, water, or land. These standards are 'expressed in terms of certain specific parameters, concentration and/or level of an emission, which may not be exceeded during

Table 4.6 Typology of environmental standards

	EQS	ELV	Process standards	Product standards
Objective	Set of requirements which must be fulfilled at a given time by a given environment (air, water, soils)	Standards expressed in terms of certain specific parameters, concentration and/or level of an emission, limiting the pollutants emitted by fixed polluting facilities with a view to protecting ecosystems and human health	Ensure that plant operations are conducted in a safe, effective, and professional manner, in accordance with safety requirements	Standards setting limits on pollution or nuisance levels
Addressees	Authorities	Plant operator	Plant operator	Producer and importer of the substance or the product
Level of stringency	Low	Inasmuch as the operator does not exceed the ELVs, he is free to choose the technology	The operator is called on to apply BATs	Standards not to be exceeded both as regards the product's composition as well as its emissions
Sanctions	Administrative measures	Administrative and criminal sanctions	Administrative and criminal sanctions	Administrative and criminal sanctions

---

[217] European Parliament and Council Directive 2010/75/EU on industrial emissions [2010] OJ L344/17, Art. 1(6).

one or more periods of time'.[218] ELVs should be set in order to avoid EQS being exceeded.[219]

- *Operating standards* call for the improvement of industrial techniques, particularly through the use of new technologies. They are guided by the principle of the reduction of pollution at source.

- *Product standards* are those which set limits on pollution or nuisance levels and may not be exceeded both as regards the product's composition as well as its emissions.

Table 4.6 compares the different regulatory techniques.

Finally, EU environmental law can also be conveniently divided into two headings: listed installations and products. Table 4.7 summarizes the techniques applied by public authorities with respect to both listed installations and products.

Table 4.7 Listed installations and products

Legal instruments	Listed installations	Products
Legal bases	Article 192 TFEU	Article 114 TFEU
Instruments	Framework directives	Regulations regulating the placing on the market or the use of hazardous products and substances
Integration	Decentralization	Centralization at EU level
Principles	Prevention, precaution, and rectification at source	Prevention, precaution, and substitution
Ex ante assessments	SEA and EIA	Substance risk assessments
Authorization	Licensing authorization No installation is operated without a permit	No product can be placed on the market without prior authorization
Restrictions	Process standards likely to be underpinned by EQS	Restrictions on the sale or the use of hazardous products and substances
Participation	Public inquiry Guidance documents on BAT	Prior public inquiry
Information for the public	Emergency plans (Seveso) Access to information Pollutants register	Information regarding the environmental risks through labelling
Control	From cradle to grave	Life-cycle approach
State aids	Restricted to investments aiming at increasing the level of environmental protection	Prohibited, but R&D
Ex post measures	Site closure subject to specific remedial measures	End-of-life, by-products, and waste management requirements

---

[218] Directive 2010/75/EU, Art. 3(4) and (5).

[219] The articulation between the two techniques is somewhat haphazard. In Joined Cases C-165–167/09 *Stichting Natuur en Milieu and others* [2011] OJ C211/4, the Court looked into the question of the interpretation of IPPC Directive 2008/1/EC ([2008] OJ L24/8), which establishes the principles that govern the procedures and conditions for granting permits for the construction and operation of large industrial installations, and of Directive 2001/81/EC ([2001] OJ L309/22), which introduces a system of national emission ceilings for certain pollutants (SO_2 and NO_x). The Court held that, when granting an environmental permit for the construction and operation of an industrial installation, the Member States are not obliged to include among the conditions for granting that permit the national emission ceilings for SO_2 and NO_x laid down by Directive 2001/81/EC.

6. Challenges Faced by EU Environmental Law

6.1 A law of unresolved compromises

In its various guises, this branch of law is one of unresolved compromises. The EU institutions and the Member States are continuously mediating to resolve tensions between opposing interests, which are only partially appeased; they are never totally eliminated. Often the law does not have the goal of settling conflicts of interest: it limits itself to putting in place more or less refined procedures for treating such conflicts.

Since most human activities have an impact on the environment, the policies implemented in order to protect it seek more to regulate them rather than eliminate them completely. For example, different impact assessment procedures or arrangements for the granting of permits do not aim to eliminate pollution but to balance economic growth with the expectations of the public for a clean environment. As a result, sectoral measures only rarely contain absolute prohibitions on polluting or on harming the environment. In the absence of a power to remove nuisances, it is limited to the bounds of the acceptable. And where the law enacts a regime of prohibitions, it is generally subject to compromise, be it the prohibition of chemicals or the prohibition to exceed emission thresholds for industrial pollutants.[220] The courts are therefore constantly called upon to weigh up and decide between the interests at play, in particular with the assistance of the principle of proportionality.

The same applies to EU legislation. The first generation of directives with their clear content now belong to a 'paradise lost'. When drafting them, their framers did not have to give consideration, on the one hand, to the fact that the Commission would one day have to oversee the effective application of these legal acts and, on the other hand, the judicial activism of the Court of Justice which has placed emphasis on the *effet utile* of environmental directives, the direct effect of some of their provisions, as well as the obligation for national courts to interpret national law in conformity with the directives. The consequences of a judgment declaring that a Member State has breached an environmental directive now require negotiators to exercise caution, since it has meant that the drafting of a preamble to a directive has been transformed into a veritable free-for-all. Negotiators therefore tend to sit on the fence and adopt formulae that are open to more than one interpretation, and in relation to which each may vindicate their own point of view. Obviously, the ambiguities flowing from late-night compromises struck either in the Council or in the Parliament run counter to the principle of legal certainty.[221]

At best, there has been an abdication of legislative power as a result of the conferral of powers to the Commission; at worst, where a particular legislative act turns out to be too restrictive, it gives rise to remedial operations, as was the case for the watering down of the protection regime for wild bird habitats after the *Leybucht* judgment.[222]

---

[220] REACH Regulation, Art. 60(4). With respect to the possibility of national authorities setting out less stringent emission values than those set out in the BAT conclusions, see IE Directive 2010/75/EC, Art. 15(4).

[221] B. Beijen, 'The Implementation of European Environmental Directives: Are Problems Caused by the Quality of the Directives?' (2011) *EEELR* 150–63.

[222] Case C-57/89 *Commission v Germany* [1991] ECR I-883.

There is a question whether the quality of EU law has become inversely proportional to the number of texts that have been enacted. Without doubt, secondary legislation has now drawn close to international environmental law with its fuzzy objectives, domino legal mechanisms, etc. Finally, compromise texts raise the spectre of judicial activism which may be required to untangle the web of contradictory legislation.

6.2 Opposing logics of deceleration/flexibility and acceleration/stringency

Two opposing logics of deceleration/flexibility and acceleration/stringency conflict head-on.

On the one hand, it is when the legal bases for EU action are at their firmest—where the legal principles underlying this branch of law are enunciated by the Courts when ruling on hard cases—and when the values are most clearly proclaimed in both the TEU and TFEU that legislative output in environmental protection matters slows down—in accordance with the principle of subsidiarity and the fixation with concerted action. This branch of law appears to be the sacrificial victim to recent political developments—Better Regulation, Smart Regulation, etc—under which, according to the logic of deregulation, the law was called upon to climb down from its pedestal in order to engage with market requirements.[223]

First, since the early 1990s there has been a marked reduction of proposed environmental legislation. Second, the reduction in quantity of legislation went in parallel with a reduction of the binding character of new EU secondary law obligations. Third, there has been a marked tendency not to set out common environmental standards, such as emission values. In particular, there has been no willingness to fix limit values for discharges of hazardous substances into waters. The obvious expression of this trend has been the IPPC and Industrial Emissions (IE) Directives in which standardized emission limit values have been replaced by BAT. As a result, the fixing of emission values has not been decided at EU level but at national, and even, local level.[224]

Against the backdrop of the far-reaching calling into question of the traditional functions of the State, environmental law no longer takes the form of a system of unilateral constraints which impose on social actors a definition of the common good or the general interest. Public law constraints are simply one of many instruments, the role of which is in any event called into question. Nevertheless, a new form of regulation appears to be taking the place of the 'hard law' advocated by the partisans of State regulation. Self-regulation mechanisms (eco-auditing, eco-labelling) or contractual agreements (referred to in the jargon as *negotiated environmental* agreements) have the wind in their sails.[225]

---

[223] Until the Fifth Environmental Action Programme, environmental policy was primarily addressed to the EU level with legislation. The fifth programme reversed that trend in fostering other instruments complementing the traditional command and control approach. Even though the different strategies and communications aiming at promoting better regulation are deemed to encompass all EU legislation, environmental law has been considerably affected by this exercise of legislative simplification. See also I. Lynch-Fannon, 'Legislative Policy, Law and Competitiveness' (2009) 15:1 *ELJ* 98–120.

[224] IE Directive 2010/75/EC, Art. 15(3).

[225] As such, the eco-label (European Parliament and Council Regulation (EC) No. 66/2010 on the EU Ecolabel [2010] OJ L37/1) is based on a voluntary scheme rather than on a classical regulating scheme. See also the discussion in Part III, Introduction.

On the other hand, the growth in environmental harmonization did not take place in a smooth fashion. When confronted with problems of an unprecedented scope, such as climate change and the depletion of the ozone layer, EU law moves rapidly apace. Indeed, EU institutions intervene in certain sectors with all their strength, as shown by the gamut of new legislation on renewable energy, pesticides, climate change, chemical substances, and so on. In particular, the sector related to climate change is undergoing speedy developments. Therefore, in spite of the fact that the carbon market constitutes a 'new and complex system' calling for a 'progressive approach', it is destined to see significant developments over the coming years.[226] By contrast, more well-established sectors have trouble making progress—regulation of the disposal of dangerous substances in water—due to reticence on the part of certain national authorities. Finally, entire sectors—maritime law, land planning—have been completely neglected on the ground that these areas of law fall within the purview either of international or national law.

6.3 Opposing logics of market integration and environmental protection

From another perspective, secondary legislation is also torn between the need to find solutions to the problems facing Member States and the requirements of the internal market.

On account of its economic foundations, the EU seeks above all to guarantee the functioning of the internal market. Yet the market is by its very nature not particularly susceptible to strong State regulation, which generally calls for the implementation of policies with the goal of protecting vulnerable environmental media such as aquatic ecosystems undergoing radical changes due to eutrophication, or species threatened with extinction. Although the Lisbon Treaty called for a more nuanced approach, Treaty law remains strongly wedded to a hierarchy of values favouring economic integration. Whereas the functioning of the internal market benefits from the direct effect of economic rights, the achievement of the objective of a heightened level of environmental protection by virtue of Article 3(3) TEU, Article 191(1) TFEU, and Article 37 EUCFR is dependent, in the first place, on the determination of EU institutions to reach this target by way of appropriate regulatory arrangements and, second, the goodwill of national authorities to free the financial and human resources necessary to guarantee the effectiveness of secondary legislation. Moreover, the subsidiarity test relating to environmental policy is decidedly more pronounced than it is in relation to internal market policy.

6.4 Opposing legal cultures

The fact that successive enlargements have led to the abandonment of the style of the Romano-Germanic family of legal systems has hardly helped matters. The Franco-German regulatory hierarchy model has been replaced by an Anglo-Saxon style

---

[226] Case C-127/07 *Arcelor* [2008] ECR I-9895, paras 60 and 61.

procedural model which is particularly marked in matters relating to the protection of the water and the air. There is no doubt that this new approach has been able to impose itself because it is less easy to identify a common denominator when dealing with 28 legal systems rather than 15. Both the differences between the various legal cultures as well as the changes in ecological conditions on a continental scale have contributed to making secondary legislation less readable.

6.5 Enforcement

Given that Article 197 TFEU refers to an 'effective implementation of Union law by the Member States',[227] another issue touches on the question of inefficacy of EU environmental law. Here it is necessary to face hard facts: the main weakness of EU rules is, as recognized by the Commission, their lack of efficacy, with directives appearing as paper tigers due to the hesitancy, criminal activities,[228] or even bad faith, on the part of certain national authorities and the difficulties encountered by the European Commission in pursuing infringements before the Court of Justice. Evidence of this can be found in the first three orders for 'dual infringement' issued against a Member Sate pursuant to Article 260 TFEU due to non-compliance with a Court of Justice judgment concerning environmental directives.[229] In certain cases, the bad faith is such that the Court condemns the Member States for 'generally and persistently failing to fulfil its obligation to ensure a correct implementation' of the directives.[230] The fact that 10 per cent of parliamentary questions and 35 per cent of petitions processed by the Committee on Petitions address the issue of the incorrect application of secondary law is testament to the lack of proper enforcement of EU environmental law.[231]

Despite the delays, omissions, and inadequacies of national regimes, Court rulings condemning national failings are not frequent. There are various reasons which account for a certain degree of impunity.

To begin with, proceedings initiated by individuals before national courts have not met with success. Restrictions imposed on the interest to sue, the duration of court proceedings, and the financial risk to which applicants expose themselves create obstacles to the invocation before the national courts of an incorrectly transposed EU law provision.[232] The interest to sue is in particular subject to the rider that the majority

---

[227] P. Nicolaides and M. Geilmann, 'What is Effective Implementation of EU Law?' (2012) 19:3 *MJ* 383–99.

[228] The presence of criminal activity in the waste management sector cannot justify the failure by that Member State of fulfilling its obligations under Directive 2006/12/EC (Case C-263/05 *Commission v Italy* [2007] ECR I-11745, para. 51; Case C-297/08 *Commission v Italy* [2010] ECR I-1749, para. 84).

[229] As regards the transposition of waste management directives, see Case C-387/97 *Commission v Greece* [2000] ECR I-5047. As regards the transposition of the bathing waters directive in Spain, see Case C-278/01 *Commission v Spain* [2003] ECR I-14141. With respect to fisheries, see *Commission v France* (n 152).

[230] With respect to waste management, see Case C-494/01 *Commission v Ireland* [2005] ECR I-3331, para. 139. As regards fisheries, see *Commission v France* (n 152), para. 39.

[231] Communication on implementing European Community Environmental Law (COM(2008) 773/4, p. 10).

[232] N. de Sadeleer, G. Roller, and M. Dross, *Access to Justice in Environmental Matters and the Role of NGOs* (Groeningen: Europa Law, 2005).

of environmental rules at an EU level has less the goal of creating individual rights than of putting in place procedures which enable national administrations to reconcile environmental protection with economic development. This has two consequences. First, the monopoly on the implementation of EU legislation has the effect of removing control by the courts.[233] Second, given the failure to establish individual rights, private parties and environmental NGOs are not in a position to benefit from the procedural guarantees (principle of effectiveness, availability of remedies, precise and clear implementation of directives[234]) progressively put in place by the Court of Justice.

The second problem relates to the Commission, as Guardian of the Treaties, and the hope that it may pursue these infringements relentlessly. Here too there are numerous pitfalls.[235] First, the Commission is not sufficiently well informed. Since it does not have any general powers of inspection, nor a body of inspectors, the control exercised by the Commission over the national authorities is largely based on reports transmitted by the Member States on the one hand,[236] and on complaints made by the victims of violations of EU law on the other. Moreover, the commencement of infringement proceedings is invariably due to the incorrect transposition of directives rather than to flagrant violations of EU law—destruction of protected habitats, illegal use of rubbish dumps, etc—or the absence of any policy worthy of the name—for example, in the area of waste management. Besides, the Commission does not have the human resources to pursue all of the infractions that are notified to it. Hence, although the number of infringement proceedings has increased, the cases dealt with within the ambit of infringement procedures represent merely the tip of the iceberg.[237]

The third hurdle relates to the fact that the doctrines of direct effect, consistent interpretation, and State liability are subject to important limitations. First, the direct effect doctrine cannot apply to broadly framed obligations that are usually laid down in environment directives.[238] In addition, directives do not have horizontal effect.[239]

---

[233] By virtue of Art. 23 of Directive 2010/75/EU on Industrial Emissions, Member States are called upon to set up a system of environmental inspections of listed installations.

[234] Case C-204/09 *Flachglos Torgau* [2012] OJ C98/2, para. 60.

[235] P. Wennerås, *The Enforcement of EC Environmental Law* (Oxford: OUP, 2007), 75–169, 251–304; N. de Sadeleer and C. Poncelet, 'Chronique de jurisprudence. Droit de l'environnement, 2009–2012' (2012) *CDE* 489–586.

[236] The Commission is likely to take into account national case law as well as reports of national jurisdictions, such as the Greek Council of State. See Case C-103/00 *Commission v Greece* [2002] ECR I-1147.

[237] Enforcement of wildlife protection obligations is a good case in point. Although the status of most EU protected species is deemed to be unfavourable (EEA (n 203)), the Commission has brought only a few actions for infringements. See Case C-103/00 *Commission v Greece* [2002] ECR I-1147 (sea turtle *Caretta caretta*); Case C-117/00 *Commission v Ireland* [2002] ECR I-5335 (red grouse); Case C-209/02 *Commission v Austria* [2002] ECR I-1211 (corncrake); Case C-518/04 *Commission v Greece* [2006] ECR I-42 (vipers); Case C-342/05 *Commission v Finland* [2007] ECR I-4713 (wolves); and Case C-340/10 *Commission v Cyprus*, 2012/C 133/09 (snakes).

[238] L. Krämer, 'The Implementation of EC Environmental Directives within Member States: Some Implications of the Direct Effect Doctrine' (1991) 3:1 *JEL* 39; J. Holder, 'A Dead End for Direct Effect? Prospects for Enforcement of EC Environmental Law by Individuals' (1996) 8:2 *JEL* 313. There are various examples in the case law. See Case C-236/92 *Comitato di Coordinamento per la Difesa della Cava* [1994] ECR I-485, para. 14; and Case C-240/09 *Lesoochranárske zoskupenie* [2011] ECR I-9967, para. 51.

[239] See to this effect, in particular, Case C-103/88 *Fratelli Costanzo* [1989] ECR I-1839. Account must be taken, however, of the fact that in *Wells*, the Court admitted that an individual is entitled to invoke the direct effect of EIA Directive 85/337 (codified by Directive 2010/75/EC). Accordingly, this would not

Second, the doctrine of consistent interpretation cannot lead to *contra legem* interpretation.[240] Moreover, that doctrine is unlikely to be invoked in the absence of at least some framework of national legislation to interpret. Third, the *Francovich* doctrine is essentially restricted to compensation whilst environment protection requires a preventive approach. Furthermore, that doctrine can be applied inasmuch as EU law confers rights on individuals, which is hardly the case in environmental law.

This inability to ensure the proper application of EU law by civil society raises a real fundamental problem. In addition to being the arbiters of opposing interests, national administrations are not the anointed owners of the environment which, as a *res communes*, belongs to everyone. Although environmental protection concerns us all, control over the transposition and application of these obligations has hitherto involved a binary relationship (Commission–Member States), rather than a threefold one (civil society–Commission–Member States). Under these circumstances, the reconciliation between economic development and environmental protection, within the context of a policy of sustainable development, turns out to be a vain hope.

We therefore need to speak of a law (*droit*) *of* the environment and not of a right (*droit*) *to* environmental protection.

That said, trade-related directives based on Article 114 TFEU have a better chance of being transposed at some stage rather than environmental directives based on Article 112 TFEU.[241] Indeed, with respect to environmental standards applying to products, the pressure of the market is a strong deterrent for national authorities to avoid non-compliance. Foreign competitors already complying with the harmonized standards have a positive interest in ensuring compliance across the internal market.

7. Conclusions

Painting a portrait of EU environmental law is certainly a challenge. However, at this stage of our reflections it is possible to sketch out an overview without making too many compromises.

(i) An initial observation points to the disparate nature of this area of law. This brief overview of the EU regulations and directives has given us the impression of a largely unfinished edifice, consisting of an array of disparate rules, scattered throughout different sectoral regimes, and with legislation varying widely between them. Despite the existence of a host of programmes, the scope and pace of legislations has resulted from an ad hoc approach rather than a coherent policy. Moreover, the protection regimes are tied to instruments enacted in accordance with different policies, adopted in accordance with specific procedures, pursuing distinctive goals and elaborated

---

amount to 'inverse direct effect' depriving another individual or individuals, such as the owners of a quarry, of their rights. Indeed, 'mere adverse repercussions on the rights of third parties, even if the repercussions are certain, do not justify preventing an individual from invoking the provisions of a directive against the Member State concerned'. See Case C-201/02 *Wells* [2004] ECR I-723, para. 57.

[240] Case C-8/81 *Becker* [1982] ECR 53.

[241] D. Toshkov, 'Embracing European Law: Compliance with EU Directives in Central and Eastern Europe' (2008) 9:3 *European Union Politics* 372–402.

without any general overview. Besides which, EU law is also dependent on international legal developments. Although the EU has moved steadily forwards in some
areas, it has laboured for long periods to achieve only modest gains in other areas.[242]
Therefore, the structuring of EU legislation is inspired less by the model of the
symmetrical arrangement of French-style gardens familiar to the seventeenth-century
landscape gardener André Le Nôtre, and rather more by the composition of a typical
English park. This diversity can end up leaving national authorities, businesses, and
civil society utterly nonplussed. Furthermore, as is the case with other sectors of public
law, the EU legislation discussed in this chapter has diverged, has been delegated to
contract-based solutions, and has become proceduralized. These tendencies increase
the weight of rules drawn up more by technical experts than by lawyers.

This 'Balkanization' of secondary law is a result both of the variety of legal bases as
well as the diverse nature of harmonization measures. Whereas, in accordance with the
White Paper on European Governance, the EU lawmaker relied on Article 192 TFEU
when adopting directives enacted in order to protect ecosystems or to regulate certain
types of pollution, on the other hand the lawmaker invoked Article 114 TFEU when
adopting regulations governing the placing on the market of products or substances
which are harmful to the environment. However, the parallels stop there, as there has
been an increasing tendency to diversify the acts, where regulations modify directives
and vice versa.

Furthermore, the obligation contained in Article 11 TFEU to take environmental
considerations into account within other policies exacerbates the proliferation of rules
of any kind which are more or less directly related to environmental protection. Due to
the many overlaps and mutual intermingling of these rules, different aspects of EU law
which touch on environmental matters are hardly set in stone; this gives rise to
recurrent boundary disputes. Since integration erases any claim to freedom of action,
this discipline looks more like a crossroads than a walled garden.

There is a question whether it is even possible to rationalize EU law in this area;
which would appear to be somewhat difficult, in view of the articulation of the various
policies and their legal bases. Although EU secondary law is the lynchpin around which
national law unfolds, national transpositions are, however, often belated. Once
adopted, national regulations may differ significantly in their form and substance. As
a result, environmental law still differs significantly from one Member State to another,
and even from one region to another. As a result, centrifugal forces begin to pull harder
than their centripetal opposites.

(ii) A second point to be made is that the EU regulatory approach to protect the
environment is still incomplete. In fact, unlike the Member States, the EU is not
capable of regulating every environmental issue, and nor does it seek to be able to do
so. The need to comply with the principle of subsidiarity prevents the Union from
harmonizing in areas of law where the Member States are better placed to enact
legislation: mobile phone masts, nuisances created by small industrial facilities, town

---

[242] C. Lister, *EU Environmental Law* (Chichester: Wiley, 1996) 17.

planning, etc. Additionally, the very nature of harmonization in the area of shared competence is flexible. There is no doubt that certain matters fall rather significantly within the purview of subsidiarity (small sized listed installations, green urban belt, urban sprawl, heritage, etc) whilst other sectors have been almost completely harmonized (movement of waste, hazardous product authorizations, restrictions on the placing on the market or use of chemical substances, etc).

(iii) Third, one should also bear in mind that this is a branch of law which struggles to keep abreast of the times. Whilst the formal aspect may be unsatisfactory, what about the substance? Here there is also a risk of losing ourselves in conjecture. Even though one could dispute the fact that EU policy follows the principle of the lowest common denominator, once again it is necessary to face hard facts. The policy is not particularly innovative, given that it generally limits itself to incorporating the *acquis* of certain Member States. Accordingly, in spite of the accumulation of directives and regulations, along with the resulting national rules, the pressure on ecosystems continues to grow, natural spaces have been seriously diminished, natural habitats are shrinking, species are disappearing at a worrying rate, chemical substances are continuing to accumulate, coasts are ever more smothered in concrete, and so on. The gap between the rules and the problems which the law is supposed to regulate has never been so marked.

One might plausibly hope that this discipline is driven more by the desire to anticipate new risks—GMOs, nanotechnology, etc—than by the need to make up for past mistakes—contaminated soils. However, various aspects of this policy adopt a more reactive than proactive approach. The catalogue of gloom-laden directives— Seveso, Erika, floods, etc—amplifies this feeling of a law of catastrophes. Undoubtedly, for new risks this branch of law is progressing at snail's pace.

Furthermore, one might expect that this great variety of rules will remain in step with the state of the art in science. However, measures to combat global warming, to promote the conservation of biodiversity, or to protect consumers against the risks posed by toxic chemical substances generally fall well short of what scientists call for. The law also bears its own responsibility for this. A hot topic amongst politicians, the precautionary principle—resulting from the need to take into account uncertainty identified by scientists—has keenly felt the difficulties of making its mark in a legal world generally branded with the badge of certainty.

As far as the economic dimension of harmonization measures is concerned, we are still waiting three decades later for the integration into the prices of goods and services of externalities in accordance with the polluter-pays principle. Similarly, the issue of environmental policy funding, a responsibility of the Member States by virtue of Article 192(4) TFEU, has not received sufficient attention. Due to the scarcity of financial means made available by the EU LIFE Fund, the Member States do not take this serious policy seriously enough. In spite of the fact that it embraces hundreds of directives, from an economic point of view, it amounts to little more than a flat-footed colossus.

Finally, acting in the spirit of the principle of subsidiarity, the EU lawmaker is now more inclined to use framework directives of a programmatic nature in order to protect various ecosystems such as the marine environment. By increasing the margin of appreciation of the Member States, these new directives accentuate the differences between the respective national approaches. Harmonizing measures are therefore limited to the objectives, and there are various ways to achieve them. Without doubt, this development takes account of the fact that it is harder today to harmonize national legislations than it was in the past. Indeed, the environmental problems confronting the 28 Member States are markedly different from those encountered by the nine heavily industrialized countries which made up the EEC at the outset of its environmental policy. Moreover, the more this branch of law has a tendency to fragment and dissipate, the greater the importance of the clarifications from the Court of Justice, following preliminary references, on the *effet utile* of these directives.

PART I

CONCLUSIONS

Whereas primary institutional law has not ceased to develop since the SEA, the same may also be said of environmental concerns which, following in the wake of the amendments made to the original Treaties, have filtered into broader or even more cross-cutting concepts. Thus, the consecration of sustainable development, the obligation to integrate environmental concerns into other policies, the consolidation of the legal bases of a policy dedicated to environmental protection, the assertion of policy principles, and the growth in power of the European Parliament in areas such as the CAP and the CCP, which are hardly detached from environmental concerns, are likewise elements mitigating in favour of recognition of a fundamental value of the system of EU law. All these provisions underscore the essential nature of environmental protection. Moreover, we have attempted to establish that both the TFEU as well as the EUCFR reinforce the interdependence between health, consumer, and environmental policies. This interdependence also entails the diffusion of key norms, such as precaution. Furthermore, these three policies relativize the hard core of the EU's economic integration.

The recognition of the environmental objective as an essential value is not neutral. The scope of the obligations under secondary law and of national provisions transposing this secondary law must be interpreted with reference to the principles and requirements laid down in the Treaties. On the ground that it amounts to an objective of general interest for the EU, both the Court of Justice as well as the ECtHR have accepted that this new aspect to the general interest authorizes public authorities to impose policing measures liable to restrict the scope of economic rights or even of fundamental rights.

Whilst for a long time, environmental law tried hard to stand out from the crowd, after the Lisbon Treaty there was a genuine decompartmentalization of the guiding concepts of sustainable development, integration, and the high level of protection. As has been shown, these concepts now strive to apply beyond the confines of environmental policy. Accordingly, they have a vertical dimension in that they are incorporated into national legal systems, and a horizontal dimension in that they transcend the boundaries of the policies pursued by the Union.

Given their degree of indeterminacy, the interpretation of these three concepts is particularly arduous. The guiding concepts described in this part are not only vague but also ambiguous. First and foremost, they do not specify the means to be used in order to achieve the vague objectives they set out. At the end of the day, it all depends on the goodwill of the legislature that is called upon to flesh out these highly general obligations into specific rules. The will of the Member States to concretize the obligations contained in secondary law through more precise arrangements is also vital. These concepts are also ambiguous. If we refer to sustainable development, there is there less a question of hierarchization than of the conciliation of interests. If we consider Article 11 TFEU, it will be appreciated that its scope is diluted by a mass of other integration clauses. Furthermore, the determination of an optimum level of protection is the stumbling block of primary law.

Nonetheless, the vague and ambiguous nature of these three concepts does not mean that they are shorn of legal effect. Indeed, a careful analysis of case law has made it possible to clarify the scope of these key provisions. There is no doubt that they are obligations that the courts must take into account. On one hand, these provisions may be used to interpret other provisions of the Treaties of or secondary law, on the other, violations may be subject to judicial review.

Title XX of the TFEU on the environment authorizes the legislature to take action within a context delineated by objectives, principles, and criteria. Nonetheless, we have observed that this Title also has its drawbacks, and a range of fundamental principles have not been enshrined. Moreover, we may assuredly not encounter the concepts of uncertainty, irreversibility, ecological damage, favourable state of conservation, good environmental status, and eco-system based management which are likely to translate into a new conceptual dimension capable of granting environmental policy its claim to noble status. In addition, no fundamental environmental right is established.

In addition, the economic freedoms guaranteed under the Treaties and the EUCFR take precedence over Articles 191 et seq. TFEU. On the one hand, it must be acknowledged that Articles 34 and 35 TFEU prohibit measures limiting the free movement of goods, Article 101 TFEU outlaws anti-competition agreements between undertakings, whilst Article 107 TFEU in principle prohibits State aids. They may therefore all be directly relied upon by litigants. On the other hand, Articles 191–193 TFEU, on the basis of which environmental policy is articulated, are framework provisions without direct effect. What is more, the EUCFR enshrines economic rights whilst it is less bold as regards environmental and consumer rights. Put simply, these are 'principles' the legal effects of which are less far-reaching than the 'rights' enshrined in the Charter.

Chapter 2 could not disregard the question of fundamental rights which, with the entry into force of the Lisbon Treaty, have witnessed remarkable advances in the EU legal order. Whilst the Treaties have not enshrined a fundamental right to environmental protection, such a right emerges timidly from a whole range of legislative provisions and developments within case law. Nonetheless, it must be admitted that the justiciability of environmental law is inversely proportional to the essential nature this policy is recognized as having both by the Court of Justice as well as the ECtHR. The principles enshrined in the EUCFR are formulated in a similar manner to the corresponding provisions of the TFEU. The provisions commented upon here take care to assert that 'every person has the right . . .' Moreover, the exclusive recourse to human rights, as interpreted by the ECtHR, to protect the environment appears to be dissatisfactory. Proof of the violation of Article 8 ECHR requires the demonstration of a hazard that is often decidedly more serious—serious harm, intoxication, profound psychological unease, etc—than that which could be invoked in administrative or civil litigation, such as the passing of a risk threshold or the lack of administrative authorization. Also, environmental protection extends considerably beyond the private sphere. The lack of a protocol to the ECHR unequivocally enshrining the right of all to a healthy environment thus hits cruelly home. If the ECHR thus appears to be scant consolation, the positive obligation on the States to put in place a preventive framework tailored to the risks and completed by procedural obligations could contribute to limiting the discretionary power of the States.

A great deal of attention was paid in Chapter 3 to the nature of both the internal and external environmental competences. Shared competence as well as subsidiarity have always been central to environmental policy. However, we stressed the boundary problems arising between this shared competence and a swathe of other competences. Regarding the powers conferred on the EU, the environmental legal base does have its drawbacks. Special legislative procedures remain applicable to important aspects of environmental policy, and decision-making criteria are muddled. In particular, the discussion dedicated to the choice of a suitable legal basis for adopting a legislative act with objective and content relating to the protection or improvement of the environment illustrates the cross-cutting nature of the issue. The acts aiming directly or indirectly at protecting the environment are not derived from one single policy but, rather, spurred on by Article 11 TFEU, from a dozen. Indeed, nothing prevents the inclusion of environmental requirements into legislation adopted in other areas of EU law. However, one is left with little guidance as to how to determine the proper legal base.

Secondary law is required to complete the framework built by the Treaties. Only legislation which is consistent, ambitious, and coherent can provide a response, within the context of the internal market, to the multiple, evolving, and complex problems related to cross-border pollution. However, we are facing a largely unfinished work, consisting of an array of disparate rules, scattered throughout a swathe of sectoral regimes. We have also observed the extent to which legal systems are particularly inter-related; the EU is a party to the WTO and sooner or later will accede to the ECHR. Hence, various legal orders have an effect on the EU, and therefore indirectly on the Member States.

PART II

RESPECT OF TREATY PROVISIONS ON FREE MOVEMENT OF GOODS, SERVICES, AND ESTABLISHMENT

Part II Introduction

Focusing since the early 1970s on the regulation of 'point-sources' of pollution (listed installations, discharges into water, landfills, brownfields, etc), environmental policy at both the national and international level gradually shifted through the 1990s towards the control of diffuse pollution. Indeed, there was growing awareness that the traditional focus on production processes was no longer appropriate to safeguard the environment. In spite of the fact that industrial and energy production remains an important source of pollution emissions, the growth in emissions has been consumption-related. In effect, the rise in consumption of products and services has increased pressure on the environment. Throughout their life cycle, all products cause environmental degradation in some way. Depending on their composition, their production method, and how they are transported, used, consumed, re-used, recycled, or discarded, products can become a source of pollution.

However, they can be conceived in such a way as to avoid negative secondary effects. Against this background, the environmental impacts of products have been progressively regulated. For instance, regulations set out the sulphur or lead content of petrol, the list of chemical substances which may not be sold, as well as imposing restrictions relating to the composition of packaging, the phosphate content of detergents, and the maximum noise level for some types of appliance. Most of these standards are still set at a national level, although most of them are derived from EU law. Moreover, in addressing one particular environmental effect, specific product policy is shifting environmental problems from one medium to another. Accordingly, the sectoral product regulatory approach did not succeed in halting the sharp increase of diffuse pollution.

With the aim of promoting sustainable patterns of production and consumption, public authorities have developed an integrated product policy (IPP) that, as opposed to specific product policy, addresses the whole life cycle of a product, from extraction of natural resources, through their design, manufacture, assembly, marketing, distribution, sale, and use to their eventual disposal as waste. The life-cycle approach takes into consideration the whole product system from cradle to grave. At the Member State level, a few States—notably the Nordic countries, the Netherlands, and Austria—articulated at the beginning of this millennium comprehensive policies on products and the environment. By the same token, EU institutions have started to pay heed to a more comprehensive product-oriented environmental policy with a view to enhancing sustainable production and consumption.[1]

More recently, as a result of 'post-industrialization' or 'deindustrialization', the service sector has begun to replace the industrial sector as the leading area of the economy in the EU. Given that producing services tends to require relatively less natural capital and more human capital than producing agricultural or industrial goods, the expanding service sector is putting less pressure on the environment.[2] However, national measures intended to protect the environment could conflict with the free movement of services.

At the same time, the process of economic integration which, since the inception of the EU, has been based on the principles of free trade within a common market, later renamed the internal market, has been gathering momentum. Given the different product regulatory approaches being developed across the EU, there has been fear of the emergence of new barriers to free trade. For some, a neo-protectionist policy underlies national and regional measures regulating products and services for the protection of the environment. Indeed, better protection of the environment through limiting the placing on the market or the use of hazardous products and substances could constitute a plausible motive for reinforcing the competitiveness of national undertakings. Moreover, disparities in the stringency of national environmental regulations frequently lead to demands for protection against 'unfair' competition.

Additionally, such a strategy can become all the more insidious with the use of measures that make no distinction between domestic and imported goods. Should such domestic rules be swept aside by the free movement of goods and services, considered by the Court of Justice as 'one of the fundamental principles of the Treaty'[3] and by most academic authors as a major component of the European integration process? Given that the Treaty provisions on free movement have to be construed broadly, are the Courts called upon to interpret narrowly those environmental measures caught by the TFEU provisions on free movement of goods and services?[4]

There are two ways in which to ascertain the compatibility of environmental measures taken by Member States with fundamental economic freedoms, such as free movement of goods and services: positive and negative harmonization. Either the measure will be assessed only in the light of secondary legislation as in the case of

---

[1] Commission, Green Paper on Integrated Product Policy, COM(2001) 68 final. Several existing measures (the EU Eco-label, the Packaging and Packaging Waste Directive, etc) already form elements of an EU IPP.

[2] World Bank, *Beyond Economic Growth. Meeting the Challenges of Global Development* (Washington DC, World Bank, 2000) 53.

[3] See, eg, Case 265/95 *Commission v France* [1997] ECR I-6959.

[4] See by analogy, the narrow interpretation of Art. 36 TFEU endorsed by the Court of Justice in a number of areas. Eg Case 229/83 *Commission v Italy* [1985] ECR 1; Case 229/83 *Leclerq* [1985] ECR 135; Case 113/83 *Commission v Ireland* [1981] ECR 1625; and Case 13/68 *Salgoil* [1968] ECR 453.

complete harmonization, or it will be observed that the measure goes beyond the scope of existing directives and regulations, and its lawfulness will be assessed directly in the light of Treaty law. We shall briefly examine the major difficulties arising from such compatibility, regarding national legislation that draws inspiration from administrative, tax, and even criminal law.

First, in the absence of harmonization through directives or regulations, or if harmonization by EU measures adopted usually on the basis of either Article 192 or 114 TFEU (ex Arts 175 or 95 EC) is not deemed to be complete, the provisions of the TFEU on free movement of goods (Arts 28, 30, 34, 35, and 110 TFEU; ex Arts 23, 28, 29, and 90 EC) and of services (Art. 56 TFEU; ex Art. 49 EC) are applicable. These provisions prohibit Member States from restricting free movement (*negative harmonization*). The scope of these rules tends to differ according to the legal category to which they belong: to each barrier to the free movement of goods and services there is a corresponding prohibition governed by specific rules. Moreover, the TFEU provisions on free movement are mutually exclusive.[5] In particular, it should be noted that the distinction between goods and services is a fine one: on the one hand, both are normally the subject of commercial transactions; on the other, goods are tangible whereas services are not.[6] It is settled case law that, where a national measure relates to both the free movement of goods and another fundamental freedom, such as the free movement of services, the Court will in principle 'examine it in relation to one only of those two fundamental freedoms, if it appears that one of them is entirely secondary in relation to the other and may be considered together with it'.[7]

It follows that the assessment of the consistency of national environmental measures with regard to TFEU provisions requires constant classification of the measures at stake, which may lead to problems regarding hybrid national measures, such as measures combining taxation and technical aspects.

Second, it should be borne in mind that the regulation of products and services impairing the environment is often governed by rules adopted by the EU institutions (*positive harmonization*), within the framework provided for in the TFEU.[8] In such a

---

[5] Eg it is settled case law, as regards the free movement of persons, that any restriction on individual economic freedom must be justified whereas the case law on goods does not require the justification of any market rule. The question whether to bring the case law on free movement of goods in line with the case law on free movement of persons has been dogged by controversy, as much about the reasoning as about the concrete results. Several authors take the view that these freedoms should be harmonized. See C. Barnard, *The Substantive Law of the EU*, 3rd edn (Oxford: OUP, 2010) 148; Opinion AG Poiares Maduro in Joined Cases C-158/04 & C-159/04 *Alfa Vita* [2006] ECR I-8153. According to other authorities, there are limits to the suggestion of merging these freedoms into a single concept. See A. Rosas, 'Life after *Dassonville* and *Cassis*: Evolution but not Revolution' in M. Poiares Maduro and L. Azoulai (eds), *The Past and Future of EU Law: The Classics of EU Law Revisited on the 50th Anniversary of the Treaty of Rome* (Oxford: Hart Publishing, 2010) 433 and 444; P. Oliver, *Oliver on Free Movement of Goods in the European Union*, 5th edn (Oxford: Hart Publishing, 2010) 11.

[6] Case C-390/99 *Canal Satélite Digital v Spain* [2002] ECR I-607. See also, generally, P. Oliver, 'Goods and Services: Two Freedoms Compared' in *Mélanges en l'honneur de M. Waelbroeck* (Brussels: Bruylant, 1999) 1378; and Oliver (n 5) 11 and 32.

[7] See Case C-275/92 *Schindler* [1994] ECR I-1039, para. 22; Case C-20/03 *Burmanjer* [2005] ECR I-4133, para. 35; and Case C-108/09 *Ker-Optika* [2010] ECR I-12213, para. 43.

[8] The starting point for EU environmental policy related to the need to adopt harmonized environmental product standards with a view to warding off the risk of market fragmentation resulting from disparate national regulation. Since the late 1960s, a considerable body of EU legislation, ranging from

case, the free discretion of national authorities will be limited as harmonization deepens. If secondary law is not necessary to the implementation of free movement of goods and services within the internal market, it remains complementary to it. For instance, harmonization on the basis of Article 114 TFEU of rules on the marketing of many products—such as dangerous substances, fertilizers, insecticides, biocides, GMOs, cars, trucks, aircraft, watercraft, or electric and electronic equipment—creates a precise legal framework limiting Member States' ability to lay down their own product standards. The advantage of such harmonization is undeniable for producers and distributors, since it allows the setting, on the scale of the internal market, of environmental standards which then govern the marketing of products and their free circulation within that market. Given that positive harmonization determines more precisely the room for manoeuvre left to the Member States than a changeable adjudicatory approach, it has been preferred to negative harmonization.

As a matter of principle, internal market harmonization precludes Member State regulatory autonomy. It should be noted that many directives and regulations the legal base of which is Article 114 TFEU, aim to facilitate freedom of trade, as well as protecting non-merchant interests. However, the situation is not made simple. On the one hand, Article 114(4)–(10) TFEU allows Member States to provide reinforced protection; on the other hand, entire segments of environmental secondary law favour minimal over full harmonization. This is notably the case of acts adopted on the basis of Article 192 TFEU.[9] There is undeniably some degree of regulatory flexibility for the adoption of such national measures regulating products to the detriment of total harmonization. But, as discussed, this latitude is contained within limits which are not always particularly clear.[10]

Thus, despite the efforts of secondary law, environmental protection levels still vary significantly from one Member State to another. Yet, if legislation in the recipient State is less permissive than that of the exporting State, the former will hinder free circulation of goods and services even if it does not provide for any difference of treatment between domestic and imported products and services. It is therefore necessary constantly to examine the justification and proportionality of any domestic measure that differs from those of other Member States.[11]

The purpose of Part II is not to revisit the controversies arising from the interpretation of different provisions of the TFEU on free movement of goods and services, or the freedom of establishment, but rather to explore the ways in which they apply to a broad range of environmental measures. That said, both the fragmentation of the

---

GMOs to motor vehicles, has developed. See L. Krämer, *EC Environmental Law*, 6th edn (London: Sweet & Maxwell, 2007) 224–70; N. de Sadeleer, *Commentaire Mégret. Environnement et marché intérieur* (Brussels: ULB, 2010) 207–47.

[9] Eg several waste management directives based on Art. 192 TFEU lay down product requirements.

[10] See the discussion in Chapter 3, Section 4.4 and in Chapter 4, Section 4.2.

[11] If a Member State provides for less restrictive rules than those in another Member State, this does not imply, by itself, that more restrictive rules will be disproportionate or therefore incompatible with EU law (Case C-294/00 *Gräbner* [2002] ECR I-6515, para. 46; Case C-277/02 *EU-Wood-Trading* [2004] ECR I-11957, para. 47). Indeed, the choice by one Member State of a system of protection different from that of another Member State may not have any influence on evaluation of the necessity and proportionality of the contested provisions (Case C-67/98 *Zenatti* [1999] ECR I-7289, para. 34 and *Gräbner* para. 47).

principle of free movement into different categories and the array of regulatory measures hindering free movement require a thorough analysis of case law solutions after a restatement of general principles. Undoubtedly, the characterization of environmental measures is a complex issue. As will be seen, the Court of Justice's case law covers a gamut of cases ranging from wildlife conservation to energy efficiency and, to make matters more complex, that case law oscillates between severity and leniency. In addition, due to the close link between objectives of environmental protection and objectives of public health, the relevant case law concerns both types of objectives, notably cases on free movement of hazardous products such as biocides and pesticides. Attention should also be drawn to the fact that assessment of the room for manoeuvre left to the Member States as regards environmental protection requires a grasp of landmark cases such as *Dassonville, Cassis de Dijon, Keck,* and *Trailers.* Conversely, genuine environmental cases like *Walloon Waste, Danish Bottles, Bluhme, Dusseldorp,* and, more recently, *Swedish Watercraft* have become quite familiar to internal market experts. Finally, to make matters even more complex, many fundamental questions regarding the scope of various TFEU provisions that are covered in Part II remain unresolved.

Given that the large body of environmental product legislation that complements free trade Treaty provisions has already been considered in Chapter 4, these product directives and regulations are not analysed in Part II although there is, indeed, a clear link between Part II and that chapter.

The structure of this part will be the following, taking into account the interconnected character of primary and secondary law.

As the free movement of goods is the most controversial principle as far as environmental measures are concerned, Chapter 5 examines the scope of Member States' powers, both fiscal and regulatory, in the absence of harmonization and in the light of the sometimes disparate case law of the Court of Justice.

Chapter 6 concerns the impact of freedom of establishment and the free movement of services on domestic environmental measures.

Finally, Chapter 7 focuses on the ability for Member States, by virtue of Article 114 or 193 TFEU, to adopt more stringent environmental protective measures than those enacted at EU level.

The Treaty of Lisbon has not modified the TFEU provisisons discussed in Part II apart from renumbering them for a third time. For the sake of convenience, the new numbering will be used.

5

Free Movement of Goods

1. Introduction

A dividing line must be drawn between fiscal and non-fiscal barriers to the free movement of goods. Indeed, when faced with a measure hindering inter-State trade, the practitioner will have to distinguish the prohibition of charges having equivalent effect to customs duties and of discriminatory internal taxation (either Arts 34 and 35 TFEU; ex Arts 28 and 29 EC or Arts 110 and 111 TFEU; ex Arts 90 and 91 EC) from quantitative restrictions on imports or exports or any other measures having equivalent effect (Arts 34 and 35 TFEU). The provisions on services and State aid will be examined further in later chapters.[1]

Because of the autonomous character of the EU legal order, the classification of the contested rule under national law bears no relevance to its classification under EU law,

---

[1] See the discussion in Chapter 6 and Chapter 12.

and therefore need not be taken into account. A measure adopted by a Member State will be contrary to the TFEU the moment it infringes one of the aforementioned rules, even if it is compatible with other such rules.

Tariff and non-tariff obstacles to trade in goods are examined in brief in the following two sections.

1.1 Tariff barriers to the free movement of goods

In spite of the extension of the ordinary legislative procedure (OLP), fiscal harmonization, given its sensitive nature, is still subject in accordance with Article 113 TFEU to decision-making that has not changed since the Treaty of Rome. Indeed, by way of derogation from the OLP, environmental 'provisions primarily of a fiscal nature' in accordance with Article 192(2)(a) TFEU as well as 'excise duties and other forms of indirect taxation' pursuant to Article 113 TFEU have to be enacted by the Council acting unanimously in accordance with a special legislative procedure (SLP) and after consulting the European Parliament. In fact, the SLP has precluded the adoption of a system of EU environmental taxes. For instance, in 1992 and 1995 the Council dismissed the few attempts made by the Commission regarding an environmental eco-tax on energy.[2] Therefore, in sharp contrast to the harmonization of product standards with a view to enhancing the internal market by virtue of Article 114 TFEU, the harmonization of eco-taxes made no headway.[3]

Given the absence of harmonization in the field of environmental taxation, Member States have significant freedom to carry out their own tax policy. This can be illustrated by the following example. In implementing the user-pays principle and the polluter-pays principle, the amended directive on the charging of heavy goods vehicles for the use of certain infrastructures[4] harmonizes external-cost charges relating to the costs of air and noise pollution.[5] As a result, Member States remain free to determine their external-cost charges relating to nature conservation and climate change. Hence, in the absence of harmonization, they are empowered to tax whatever products they wish and at whatever rate they wish.[6]

As a result, the Member States' environmental tax policy has been pulled in different directions. For instance, tax bases[7] as well as tax rates vary considerably across

---

[2] COM(97) 30 final [1997] OJ C139/14.
[3] There are only a few exceptions. Eg, by virtue of Art. 15(1)(b) of Council Directive 2003/96/EC restructuring the Community framework for the taxation of energy products and electricity ([2003] OJ L283/51), Member States may apply exemptions or reductions in the level of taxation on electricity produced by environmentally friendly processes.
[4] European Parliament and Council Directive 1999/62/EC amended by European Parliament and Council Directive 2011/76/EU amending Directive 1999/62/EC on the charging of heavy goods vehicles for the use of certain infrastructures [2011] OJ L269/1.
[5] Directive 1999/62/EC, Art. 7(c).
[6] Eg in *Futura Immobiliare* the Court noted that national authorities are endowed with 'broad discretion' when determining the manner in which an environmental charge must be calculated (Case C-254/08 *Futura Immobiliare* [2009] ECR I-6995, para. 55).
[7] Environmental taxes include among others greenhouse gases, air and water emissions, packaging, landfill waste, aggregates, batteries, pesticides, and fertilizers.

Member States.[8] Moreover, current environmental taxes are generally designed on a case-by-case approach. Originally, environmentally related taxes were intended to raise revenue for financing a number of environmental expenditures ranging from water treatment to clean up of contaminated soils. However, they have increasingly been used to influence consumer as well as undertakings' behaviour without the intention of raising revenue.[9]

That said, in spite of strong economic arguments in its favour and the proclamation of the polluter-pays principle,[10] the use of environmental taxes at national level is still not widespread: rather, their share is growing relatively slowly.[11] Moreover, they do not generally appear to be part of a broader strategy of environmental tax reform (ETR). Although there is no evidence on the impact of environmental taxes on the competitiveness of national industries, concerns over such impact have often been voiced as a reason to restrain further developments as regard regulatory taxes.[12]

Against this background, the EU Commission is committed towards ensuring an ETR 'shifting the tax burden from welfare-negative taxes, (e.g. on labour), to welfare-positive taxes, (e.g. on environmentally damaging activities, such as resource use or pollution)'. As well as discouraging environmentally damaging behaviour, such a reform could help to alleviate the possibly adverse competitiveness effects of environmental taxes on specific sectors.[13] Nonetheless, the Commission considers that it is for Member States to strike the right balance between incentives and disincentives in their tax systems, while respecting overall fiscal constraints and fiscal neutrality.[14]

Account must be taken of the fact that environmental taxes levied either to raise revenue or to influence undertakings and consumer behaviour may afford protection to domestic products. In ensuring that tax policy does not serve protectionist interests, several provisions of the TFEU are likely to prohibit the adoption of fiscal instruments aimed at protecting the environment. By way of illustration, given that there is no 'EU eco-tax' on beverage containers or on batteries, national measures establishing such exo-taxes must be assessed in the light of primary legislation. In other words, it is necessary to ascertain that they are compatible with Treaty law. Accordingly, the fiscal autonomy of Member States is far from absolute, even in the absence of EU harmonization.

Sections 2 and 3 address two separate categories of provisions limiting the use of tariff charges, even if such charges pursue protection of the environment. Found in Title II on free movement of goods, the first of these categories contains Articles 28 and

---

[8] Member States make very different use of environmental taxes: eg in 2006 the share was more than 10 per cent in Denmark, the Netherlands, and Malta, while it was less than 6 per cent in Belgium, Spain, France, Sweden, and Austria. Eg Communication from the Commission on the 2008 Environment Policy Review, COM(2009) 304, 55.

[9] Nonetheless, the majority of environmental taxes still focus on raising revenue rather than on changing environmentally harmful behaviour. Eg ECOTEC, *Study on Environmental Taxes and Charges in the EU and its Member States* (Brussels: ECOTEC, 2008).

[10] See Chapter 1, Section 7.3.   [11] See Chapter 1, Section 7.

[12] European Environment Agency (EEA), *Environmental Taxes: Recent Developments in Tools for Integration* (Copenhagen: EEA, 2000) 10.

[13] Eg Green Paper on market-based instruments for environment and related policy purposes, COM (2007) 140 final.

[14] Green Paper (n 13).

30 TFEU, which prohibit Member States from adopting customs duties on imports or exports or charges having equivalent effect to customs duties (CEE). Finding its basis in Article 110 TFEU, the second category condemns internal taxation of a discriminatory nature.

When faced with a fiscal measure, the practitioner will have to distinguish the prohibition of CEEs—Articles 28 and 30 TFEU—from discriminatory internal taxation—Article 110 TFEU. The financial character of the measure brings it within the scope of the aforementioned provisions, excluding it from the category applicable to 'measures having equivalent effect' (MEEs) to 'quantitative restrictions' on imports pursuant to Article 34 TFEU and following. The practitioner must also examine whether the contested taxation could be deemed to infringe Article 56 TFEU providing for the free movement of services.[15] Furthermore, the practitioner will have to determine whether the use of revenue from a charge or from an internal due amounts to State aid within the meaning of Article 107 TFEU.

Whereas the Court of Justice has often adjudicated cases concerning MEEs resulting from national, regional, or local measures on the protection of the environment,[16] it has seldom had to resolve questions concerning the compatibility of environmental taxes with inter-State trade obligations. Nevertheless, such questions are of great practical significance, because of the risk of potential conflict between domestic tax mechanisms relating to the protection of the environment—soon to become widespread due to the impetus that the fight against climate change has recently seen—and primary EU law ensuring free inter-State trade of goods. Furthermore, upholding the polluter-pays principle in both EU and domestic legal orders[17] should prompt Member States to employ fiscal means more often to reduce the release of greenhouse gases (GHGs) or to influence the behaviour of producers and consumers, through taxing products causing damage or by awarding tax relief to less hazardous products.[18]

1.2 Non-tariff barriers to the free movement of goods

Where the measure is not deemed to be a fiscal barrier to trade, it may fall under the prohibition of MEEs—Article 34 TFEU—and on exports—Article 35 TFEU.

The analysis of these two provisions will be structured in the following manner.

Section 4 examines the personal, material, and territorial scope of these two provisions. Given that the prohibition to adopt or maintain MEEs is far from absolute, Section 5 examines the three exceptions to Articles 34 and 35 TFEU. Although these exceptions to a fundamental principle must be interpreted restrictively, the Court did not always review environmental and health justifications invoked by the Member

---

[15] See the discussion in Chapter 6.   [16] See the discussion in Sections 4–6.

[17] Even though the Court of Justice should ensure respect for this principle in tax cases brought before it, the Court rarely invokes the principle. In condemning the export prohibition of waste oils outside France for non-conformity with Art. 36 TFEU it refuted the economic argument of the French authorities on the ground that the EU directive gave them the power to 'grant to such undertakings "indemnities" financed in accordance with the principle of "polluter pays"' (Case 172/82 *Inter-Huiles* [1983] ECR I-555, para. 13).

[18] See Communication of 26 March 1997 on Environmental Taxes and Charges in the Single Market, COM(97) 9 final. See also the Sixth Environmental Action Programme, Art. 3(1)(c).

Table 5.1 Tariff and non-tariff barriers to the free movement of goods

Tariff barriers to the free movement of goods	
Customs duties	Articles 28–30 TFEU
Charges having an equivalent effect thereto	Articles 28–30 TFEU
Discriminatory internal taxation	Article 110 TFEU
Non-tariff barriers to the free movement of goods	
Quantitative restrictions	Articles 34 and 35 TFEU
Measures having an equivalent effect to quantitative restrictions	Articles 34 and 35 TFEU
Exemptions to the prohibition of quantitative restrictions and measures having an equivalent effect to quantitative restrictions	Article 36 TFEU

States so strictly. In Section 6 attention turns to the extra-territorial dimension of these justifications. The justifications underlying measures running counter to Articles 34 and 35 TFEU are likely to be accepted provided that they are adequate to protect the interest at stake and that they cannot be replaced by less restrictive measures. In this respect, Section 7 offers a detailed examination of the manner in which the principle of proportionality is applied in environmental cases.

Finally, Section 8 is dedicated to preventive internal market procedures regarding information procedures that do complete primary law and are likely to restrict Member States' room for manoeuvre regarding their own product policy.

Given that to each barrier to the free movement of goods and services there is a corresponding prohibition governed by specific rules, Table 5.1 lists the provisions that will be discussed in this chapter.

2. Prohibition of Customs Duties and of Charges Having Equivalent Effect (Arts 28 and 30 TFEU)

2.1 Functions and scope of Articles 28 and 30 TFEU

The removal of tariff barriers was emphasized as a form of action of the EU in ex Article 3(1)(a) EC, repealed and replaced, in substance, by Article 3(a) TFEU and as an internal element of the customs union, upon which the EU is built in accordance with Article 28 TFEU. Articles 28 and 30 TFEU prohibit Member States from applying customs duties on inter-State imports and exports as much as CEEs, notably 'customs duties of a fiscal nature'.

Due to a lack of definition within the Treaty, the Court defined the concept of CEEs in broad terms to avoid the emergence of new forms of customs duties.[19] It is settled case law that a CEE covers 'any pecuniary charge, however small and whatever its designation and mode of application, which is … unilaterally imposed on domestic or

---

[19] Case 2/62 *Commission v Luxembourg* [1962] ECR 425.

exported goods by reason of the fact that they cross a frontier of one of the Member States and which are not customs duty in the strict sense'.[20]

Customs duties and CEEs are necessarily protectionist and discriminatory, as they are levied on the crossing of borders. There is an absolute prohibition on such charges, as opposed to the rules applicable to internal taxation that are caught by Article 110 TFEU or to MEEs.[21] Hidden protectionist tariffs, disguised as lawful pecuniary charges, are therefore prohibited. Environmental protection cannot justify such charges.[22] Moreover, there is no *de minimis* rule: neither the minimal character of the duty[23] nor the absence of discriminatory or protectionist effects[24] has any bearing on this prohibition. The same applies to the absence of competition between the imported product and domestic products.[25] Finally, none of the following elements can alter classification as a CEE:[26] the form of taxation, its purpose, its description,[27] the method of levying, and the use of revenue. As such, in the case of an environmental tax, the use of the revenue for financing environmental policy has no bearing on classification with respect to Article 28 TFEU.

As far as environmental charges are concerned, the Court has held that the following national measures are CEEs: an internal due meant to finance a public body promoting energy saving,[28] the obligation for waste exporters to contribute to a fund for the return of illegally exported waste,[29] a local tax on marble excavated in the territory of a municipality,[30] and an environmental tax on the use of pipelines,[31] irrespective of the environmental purpose of these charges.

Furthermore, associations of undertakings sometimes impose on economic operators costs incurred exclusively on public authorities for services they provide, by means of private contracts. Articles 28 and 30 TFEU may apply to such cases, despite the fact that the State receives no benefit from the CEE.[32]

Finally, the Court condemns not only charges on the trade of products between Member States, pursuant to Articles 28 and 30 TFEU, but also on any charge bearing the characteristics of a customs duty within Member States, even if such charges are

---

[20] Case C-90/94 *Haahr Petroleum* [1997] ECR I-4085, para. 20; Case C-213/96 *Outokumpu Oy* [1998] ECR I-1777, para. 20; Case C-387/01 *Weigel* [2004] ECR I-4981, para. 64; and Joined Cases C-393/04 & C-41/05 *Air Liquide* [2006] ECR I-5293, para. 51.

[21] Case 7/68 *Commission v Italy* [1968] ECR 423. See L. Gormley, *EU Law of Free Movement of Goods and Customs Union* (Oxford: OUP, 2009) 384–6.

[22] See, by analogy, Case C-7/68 *Commission v Italy* [1968] ECR 423; Case C-29/72 *Marimex* [1972] ECR 1309; Case C-78/76 *Steinike* [1977] ECR 595; and Case C-158/82 *Commission v Denmark* [1983] ECR 3573.

[23] Case 24/68 *Commission v Italy* [1969] ECR 193, para. 14.

[24] *Commission v Italy* (n 23), para. 201; Joined Cases 2 & 3/69 *Sociaal Fonds voor de Diamantarbeiders* [1969] ECR I-211, para. 222.

[25] *Sociaal Fonds* (n 24); and Case T-115/94 *Opel Austria* [1997] ECR II-39, para. 121.

[26] Case C-45/94 *Ayuntamiento de Centa* [1995] ECR I-4385, para. 28.

[27] The prohibition contained in Art. 30 TFEU applies to all charges regardless of classification: internal tax consultancy fees.

[28] Joined Cases C-79–83/90 *Compagnie commerciale de l'Ouest* [1992] ECR I-1873.

[29] Case C-221/06 *Stadtgemeinde Frohnleiten* [2007] ECR I-9643.

[30] Case C-72/03 *Carbonati Apuani v Carrara* [2004] ECR I-8027.

[31] Case C-173/05 *Commission v Italy* [2007] ECR I-4917, para. 42.

[32] Case C-16/94 *Dubois* [1995] ECR I-2421; Case C-293/02 *Jersey Produce Marketing Organisation* [2005] ECR I-9543, para. 5; and Case C-517/04 *Koornstra* [2006] ECR I-5015, para. 15.

merely local or regional.[33] Discrimination resulting from the existence of internal frontiers within a Member State are thus prohibited. Such a prohibition is justified on the ground that individual entities of federal States could otherwise adopt taxation on the internal movement of products and thus create surreptitious barriers to free movement, 'at least as serious as a charge levied at the national frontier'.[34]

2.2 Boundary between Articles 28 and 30 TFEU and other Treaty provisions

There is a strong contrast between the difficulty in defining the scope of Articles 34 and 35 TFEU with respect to fields reserved to other provisions of the TFEU and the simplicity of the principle of prohibition of any new customs duty or CEE.

2.2.1 *Scope of Articles 28 and 30 TFEU and Article 34 TFEU, respectively*

A tariff charge under Articles 28–30 TFEU may not be simultaneously governed by the system of Article 34 TFEU, or as a consequence benefit from the exemptions provided for in Article 36 TFEU.[35] Furthermore, Article 34 TFEU has a general character compared to Article 30 TFEU.[36] Accordingly, the concept of a CEE does not encompass non-tariff barriers governed by Article 34 TFEU, even if they become apparent on payment of charges.

2.2.2 *Scope of Articles 28–30 TFEU and Article 110 TFEU, respectively*

Whereas CEEs are unilaterally imposed and concern 'domestic or foreign goods by reason of the fact that they cross a frontier', taxation to which Article 110 TFEU refers, of similar domestic and imported goods, is imposed within a Member State.

The provisions prohibiting CEEs pursuant to Articles 28–30 TFEU may not be cumulatively applied with that on discriminatory internal taxation falling within the ambit of Article 110 TFEU.[37] The reason these provisions are mutually exclusive is that while Member States may adopt taxes and charges within their general system of internal taxation inasmuch as they are not discriminatory, customs duties and CEEs are categorically prohibited.

---

[33] Case C-163/90 *Legros* [1992] ECR I-4625, paras 16 and 17; Joined Cases C-363, 407, 408, 409, 410, & 411/93 *Lancry* [1994] ECR I-3975; Joined Cases C-485/93 & C-486/93 *Simitzi* [1995] ECR I-2655, para. 21; Case C-72/03 *Carbonati* [2004] ECR I-8027; and Case C-293/02 *Jersey Produce* [2005] ECR I-9543. See P. Oliver and S. Enchelmaier, 'Free Movement of Goods: Recent Developments in the Case Law' (2007) 44 *CML Rev* 651–6.
[34] Case C-163/90 *Legros* [1992] ECR I-4625, para. 16.
[35] Case 74/76 *Iannelli & Volpi* [1977] ECR I-557; Case 32/80 *Kortmann* [1981] ECR I-251; and Joined Cases C-79–83/90 *Compagnie commerciale de l'Ouest* [1992] ECR I-1873.
[36] *Iannelli* (n 35); Case 252/86 *Bergandi* [1988] ECR I-1343.
[37] Case 10/65 *Deutschmann v Germany* [1965] ECR I-469; Case 57/65 *Lütticke* [1966] ECR I-205; Case C-266/91 *Celbi* [1993] ECR I-4337, para. 9; Case C-90/94 *Haahr Petroleum* [1997] ECR I-4085, para. 19; Case C-234/99 *Nygard* [2002] ECR I-365, para. 17; Case C-387/01 *Weigel* [2004] ECR I-4981, para. 6; and Joined Cases C-393/04 & C-41/05 *Air Liquide Industries Belgium* [2006] ECR I-5293, para. 50.

Regarding environmental charges, case law has shed some light on the line to draw between the scope of, respectively, Articles 28–30 and Article 110 TFEU.

On the validity of a Finnish general system of taxation on electric energy according to production method, the Court held that the contested charge taxed electricity independently of its origin, be it domestic or imported.[38] Article 30 TFEU does not apply merely because of the fact that imported electricity is taxed at the time of importation while electricity of domestic origin is taxed at the time of production. As the charge is applicable similarly to electricity produced on national territory and to imported electricity, at the same marketing stage, Article 110 TFEU is applicable.[39]

By the same token, as it taxes waste dumping, regardless of the waste's domestic or foreign origin, an environmental tax on waste dumped in Austrian landfills is not levied at the time the frontier of the taxing State is crossed.[40]

However, given the pursued objective, ensuring neutrality between imported and national goods, and the complementary nature of Article 110 TFEU, the line between the two regimes is particularly thin.[41] In principle, Article 30 TFEU prohibits measures affecting imported products and not national products. However, case law has considered that this provision may, under certain circumstances, apply to measures that are applicable without distinction to both national and imported products.[42] For this, the result of the fiscal charge must lead to a *de facto* taxation of only foreign not domestic goods. Practically speaking, only the imported products have to be taxed. The difference lies in the fact that the CEE burdens only imported goods, whereas internal taxation falling within the scope of Article 110 TFEU applies to both domestic and imported products.[43] The course of the line drawn between the two regimes therefore depends on the administration of revenue of the charge, an appraisal that befalls the national court.[44]

That said, the benefits resulting from tax revenue for domestic products might only compensate part of the financial burden. In such a case, it is a discriminatory internal tax under Article 110 TFEU. Levying such a tax is prohibited for the amount administered to compensation for taxed domestic products.[45]

With respect to environmental charges, one must thus distinguish between two hypotheses. If the tax revenue is returned to domestic products only, thereby fully

---

[38] Case C-213/96 *Outokumpu Oy* [1998] ECR I-1777, para. 23.

[39] *Outokumpu Oy* (n 38), para. 25.

[40] Case C-221/06 *Stadtgemeinde Frohnleiten* [2007] ECR I-9643, para. 28.

[41] Opinion AG Jacobs in Case C-90/94 *Haahr Petroleum* [1997] ECR I-4885, para. 38.

[42] Case C-77/76 *Cucchi* [1977] ECR 987; Case C-105/76 *Interzuccheri* [1977] ECR 1029. Accordingly, to constitute a CEE, a duty must fulfil three conditions: first, it has the sole purpose of financing activities for the specific advantage of the taxed domestic product; second, the taxed product and the domestic product benefiting from the tax must be the same; and, third, the charges imposed on the domestic product are made good in full.

[43] Case 78/76 *Steineke & Weinlig* [1977] ECR I-595, para. 28; Case 32/80 *Kortmann* [1981] ECR I-251, para. 18; and Case 193/85 *Co-Frutta* [1987] ECR I-2085, para. 9.

[44] It should be added that the allocation of tax revenue to domestic producers falls within the scope of Art. 107 TFEU as does State aid (repayment of tax levy). See Joined Cases C-79–83/90 *Compagnie commerciale de l'Ouest* [1992] ECR I-1873, para. 32. See also Chapter 12.

[45] Case 78/90 *Compagnie commerciale de l'Ouest* [1992] ECR I-1847; Case C-266/91 *CELBI* [1993] ECR I-4337; Case C-72/92 *Scharbatke* [1993] ECR I-5509; Case C-347/95 *Fazenda Publica* [1997] ECR I-4911; and Case C-28/96 *Fazenda Publica v Fricarenes SA* [1997] ECR I-4939.

compensating the levied tax, it is a CEE and must therefore be prohibited in accordance with Article 30 TFEU. If, on the contrary, the tax revenue finances a public awareness campaign (eg promoting the purchase of environmental goods) and does not neutralize charges burdening domestic products, Article 110 TFEU is applicable.

2.3 Permissible charges

The Court of Justice has held that a charge escapes classification as a CEE in three situations:

> if it relates to a general system of internal dues applied systematically and in accordance with the same criteria to domestic products and imported products alike..., if it constitutes payment for a service in fact rendered to the economic operator of a sum in proportion to the service..., or again, subject to certain conditions, if it attaches to inspections carried out to fulfil obligations imposed by Community law.[46]

Attention should be drawn to the fact that these three situations do not fall within the definition of a cutoms duty or a CEE at all.[47] As we will be dealing with the first exemption—charges falling within the scope of a system of general exemption—in the next section, we will consider the two other exceptions.

2.3.1 *Payments for genuine administrative services actually rendered to the importer or the exporter*

First, when a pecuniary charge is required in return for a service in favour of the importer or exporter, it is an internal due, not a CEE. It should be noted that national law distinguishes between taxes or charges (German: *Steuer*; Danish: *Skat*; French: *impôt*; Spanish: *impuestos*; Portuguese: *imposto*; Dutch: *belasting*) from a pecuniary charge required in return for a service (German: *gebürhen*; Danish: *gebyr*; French: *redevance*; Spanish: *tasas*; Portuguese: *taxa*; Dutch: *heffing*). Whereas the revenue of charges goes to the general budget, pecuniary charges are a payment in return for a clearly identified service or cost. As a result, the revenue of pecuniary charges required in return for a service is not connected with the general budget. Moreover, under constitutional law a pecuniary charge required in return for a service can be adopted by the government whereas the lawmaker is called upon to implement a charge.

In truly exceptional circumstances,[48] three conditions must be met for the due to escape the clutches of Articles 28 and 30 TFEU. Given the strictness of these restrictions, the Court seldom qualifies a pecuniary charge in payment for a genuine administrative service rendered to the importer or the exporter.

The first condition is that there must be no obligation to resort to the service subject to the charge.[49] In other words, performance of the service may not be imposed, which

---

[46] Case 18/87 *Commission v Germany* [1988] ECR 5427, para. 6.
[47] C. Barnard, *The Substantive Law of the EU*, 3rd edn (Oxford: OUP, 2007) 67–8.
[48] Opinion AG van Gerven in Case 340/87 *Commission v Italy* [1989] ECR I-1483, para. 10.
[49] Case 266/81 *SIOT* [1983] ECR I-731.

is rarely the case for services performed by public undertakings in a monopoly or quasi-monopoly position.

Next, the benefit must not only be provided actually and individually to the economic operator,[50] but must also provide it with a tangible benefit. When the service provided is linked to fulfilment of a mandatory formality, there is no real benefit. The Court of Justice was able to apply this requirement to a waste management scheme in the following case. Despite an obligation of secondary law for Member States to reimport illegally exported waste into their territory,[51] the fee due by the German exporters to a solidarity fund, a fee which was computed on the basis of the amount and nature of the exported waste, was held to be contrary to Article 30 TFEU, in that 'compliance by the Federal Republic of Germany with an obligation which Community law imposes on all the Member States in pursuit of a general interest, namely protection of health and the environment, does not confer on exporters of waste established in its territory any specific or definite benefit'.[52] As a result, the costs incurred by environmental inspection of goods crossing a border must be borne by the regulatory agencies.

Finally, fees must amount to a sum proportionate to the real cost of the service provided.[53] In this connection, two examples will suffice.

In its judgment of 27 February 2003 on the validity of a German fund to cover the reimportation costs of illegally exported waste, the Court of Justice underlined the absence of a direct link between the amount of the contribution paid by waste transporters and the real cost of the act of returning the waste to domestic territory.[54]

In the second example, *Escalier and Bonnarel*, the Court was more flexible as regards the proportionality of a charge. Given that a pesticide to be introduced as a parallel import may be used in circumstances differing from those of the reference product, the national simplified marketing authorization procedure may entail costs for the competent authorities which differ from one case to another. Consequently, State authorities may charge for services relating to such parallel imports rendered to farmers. However, to respect the principle of proportionality, 'the amount of the charges imposed ... must have some correspondence to the costs incurred by the control or the administrative steps needed for the examination of the marketing authorisation application'.[55] Conversely, a charge which bears no relation to the costs incurred by the control of or the administrative steps needed for examination of the authorization application is inconsistent with the principle of proportionality. However, the Court took the view that the principle of proportionality did not preclude 'an appraisal of such costs as a fixed sum'.[56]

---

[50] The service cannot benefit a wider group of persons or the economy as a whole. Case 340/87 *Commission v Italy* (n 48), para. 16.

[51] See Art. 26(2)(a) of Regulation 259/93 now replaced by Arts 22–24 of European Parliament and Council Regulation (EC) No. 1013/2006 on shipments of waste [2006] OJ L190/1.

[52] Case C-389/00 *Commission v Germany* [2003] ECR I-2001, para. 35.

[53] Case 170/88 *Ford España* [1989] ECR I-2305; and Case C-111/89 *Bakker Hillegom* [1990] ECR I-1735, paras 12–16.

[54] Case C-389/00 *Commission v Germany* (n 52), para. 45.

[55] Joined Cases C-260 & 261/06 *Escalier and Bonnarel* [2007] ECR I-9717, para. 49.

[56] *Escalier and Bonnarel* (n 55).

2.3.2 *Charges for inspections required by EU law*

A second exception applies to controls permitted by EU secondary law. Accordingly, the charge levied for a control imposed by secondary law is not a CEE inasmuch as it attaches to inspections carried out to fulfil obligations imposed by EU law in the general interest of the EU. By contrast, charges for inspections required by national law do consitute a CEE. As a result, Member State authorities cannot charge the importer to cover the inspection even if the inspection is justified under Article 36 TFEU.[57]

In addition, these inspections must be compulsory and uniform for all products concerned in the EU. Furthermore, they must promote the free movement of goods. Lastly, the fees must not exceed the actual costs of the inspection in connection with which they are charged.[58] To illustrate, under Article 29 of Regulation (EC) No. 1013/2006 on shipments of waste, Member States may charge 'appropriate and proportionate administrative costs of implementing the notification and supervision procedures and usual costs of appropriate analyses'.[59]

3. Prohibition of Discriminatory Internal Taxation (Art. 110 TFEU)

3.1 General considerations

3.1.1 *Functions and scope of Article 110 TFEU*

Member States have significant freedom to carry out their tax policy unless it has been harmonized at EU level. Therefore fiscal measures adopted at national level benefit from a presumption of legitimacy in the light of EU law. However, if Member States retain sovereignty in their fiscal matters, they must not discriminate against foreign producers. As such, even if a charge is not a CEE under Articles 28 and 30 TFEU, it may still be contrary to Article 110 TFEU (ex Art. 90 EC), which prohibits Member States from imposing 'on the products of other Member States any internal taxation... in excess of that imposed directly or indirectly on similar domestic products' or 'of such a nature as to afford indirect protection to other products'. The fact that waste for disposal has no market value does not imply that it is not covered by the concept of 'products' within the meaning of Article 110 TFEU. Indeed, waste for disposal, even if it has no intrinsic commercial value, may nonetheless give rise to commercial transactions in relation to the disposal or deposit thereof.[60]

Aiming to eliminate 'all forms of protection which might result from the application of discriminatory internal taxation against products from other Member States, and to guarantee absolute neutrality of internal taxation as regards competition between

---

[57] Barnard (n 47), 44; A. G. Toth, *The Oxford Encyclopaedia of European Community Law*, vol. II (Oxford: OUP, 2005) 7.

[58] Case 46/76 *Bauhuis* [1977] ECR I-5; Case 89/76 *Commission v Netherlands* [1977] ECR I-1355; and Case 18/87 *Commission v Germany* [1988] ECR I-5427.

[59] Regulation (EC) No. 1013/2006 [2006] OJ L190/21.

[60] Case C-221/06 *Stadtgemeinde Frohnleiten* [2007] ECR I-9643, paras 36–8.

domestic and imported products',[61] Article 110 TFEU is therefore a necessary complement to the aforementioned provisions on the removal of barriers to free movement of goods. An environmental levy is thus consistent with Article 110 TFEU if the core conditions of the provision are met.

The scope of Article 110 TFEU is extremely broad. Whereas the first paragraph of the provision prohibits discrimination between 'similar' products, the second paragraph prohibits taxation of products aiming at affording protection to 'other' products. Together these two paragraphs encompass a broad range of tax regimes ranging from those taxing effectively identical products to those taxing marginally substitutable products.[62]

The scope of the provision must be further detailed. According to settled case law, 'pecuniary charges resulting from a general system of internal taxation applied systematically, in accordance with the same objective criteria, to categories of products irrespective of their origin or destination fall within Article 110 TFEU'.[63] The Court defined the concept of 'internal taxation' broadly, encompassing 'all taxation which is actually and specifically imposed on the domestic product at all earlier stages of its manufacture and marketing or which correspond to the stage at which the product is imported from other Member States'.[64] The concepts of 'discrimination' (para. 1) and of 'protection' (para. 2) encompass all rules on tax base, tax rate, or the procedure for collection.[65] The differentiation at national level between direct and indirect taxation therefore has no bearing on EU law. Article 110 TFEU is applicable, regardless of the fact that a tax might be levied by a public body other than the State or assigned to a specific end use.[66]

If Article 110 TFEU only seems to mention taxation of imported products, it follows from case law that it also applies to export charges.

Case law also provides that EU law does not prohibit the effects of double taxation found notably in the field of transboundary movement of waste, even if the removal of such effects would be preferable for the free movement of goods.[67]

3.1.2 *The boundary between Article 110 TFEU and other TFEU provisions*

3.1.2.1 Exclusivity of Article 110 TFEU

Article 110 TFEU overlaps with a number of other Treaty provisions, among others Articles 28–30 TFEU that prohibit any pecuniary charge imposed on goods by reason of the fact that they cross a border. The difficulties involved in distinguishing CEEs and internal taxation were addressed in the previous section.

---

[61] Case 356/85 *Commission v Belgium* [1987] ECR 3299.   [62] Toth (n 57), 712.

[63] Joined Cases C-393/04 & C-41/05 *Air Liquide Industries Belgium* [2006] ECR I-5293, para. 50.

[64] Case 28/67 *Firma Malkerei—Zentrale Westfalen v Lippe GmbH* [1968] ECR 229.

[65] Case 55/79 *Commission v Ireland* [1980] ECR 481; Case 15/81 *Schul* [1982] ECR 1409; Case 68/96 *Grundig Italiana* [1998] ECR I-3775; and Case 228/98 *Doumias* [2000] ECR I-577.

[66] Case 74/76 *Ianelli and Volpi* [1977] ECR I-557, para. 19; and Case 222/82 *Lewis* [1983] ECR I-4083.

[67] Case 142/77 *Larsen* [1978] ECR I-1543, paras 32–6.

Although Article 110 TFEU encompasses taxes on the use of products, it does not overlap with Treaty provisions on services.[68] The distinction between electricity as a product and a service is clear: an environmentally differentiated tax on electricity falls within the scope of Article 110.[69]

Nor does Article 110 TFEU overlap with Article 34 TFEU. Indeed, the normative content and applicability conditions of Articles 34 and 110 TFEU differ greatly. As such, the definition of the respective scope of these provisions is far from theoretical. Because of its narrower scope, Article 110 TFEU is considered to be a *leges speciales* of Article 34 TFEU, the application of which is residual.[70] On another note, one may not derogate from Article 110 TFEU, even for 'an overriding requirement relating to the public interest' (hereinafter 'mandatory requirement'), whereas Article 34 TFEU can be the subject of two types of exemption.[71]

While Article 110 TFEU is by definition 'fiscal in purpose',[72] Article 34 TFEU is concerned with non-fiscal barriers. In other words, for the contested domestic measure to fall within the scope of Article 110 TFEU, its main objective must be fiscal and therefore redistributive. In sharp contrast, Article 34 TFEU is concerned with non-fiscal barriers. Although the Court seems to exclude the application of Article 34 TFEU to fiscal measures, not all pecuniary measures escape its grasp; as is the case for pecuniary measures hindering importation and exportation of products.[73] Nevertheless, the Court has considered that when fiscal and non-fiscal provisions can be distinguished within the contested national legislation, the domestic measure must be examined with regard to Articles 34 and 110 TFEU, respectively.[74]

3.1.2.2 Eco-taxes

In this respect, one might wonder if economic instruments such as eco-taxes could be deemed as technical barriers. Eco-taxes have been defined by the General Court as

> an autonomous fiscal measure which is characterised by its environmental objective and its specific tax base. It seeks to tax certain goods or services so that the environmental costs may be included in their price and/or so that recycled products are rendered more competitive and producers and consumers are oriented towards activities which better respect the environment.[75]

If eco-taxes are more dissuasive than redistributive, should they be assimilated to product standards and therefore fall within the scope of Article 34 TFEU? In other words, if they succeed in stopping consumption of goods because of their harmful character, would this new form of taxation *de facto* be the same as a ban on the marketing of these products?

In answering these questions, it must be kept in mind that the line to be drawn between Article 110 TFEU and Article 34 TFEU is a fine one, in particular in cases where domestic charges are so high that they are likely significantly to affect inter-State

---

[68] Case C-213/96 *Outokumpu Oy* [1998] ECR I-1777.   [69] *Outokumpu Oy* (n 68).
[70] Case 27/67 *Fink-Frucht* [1968] ECR I-327.   [71] See Section 5.   [72] Toth (n 57), 708.
[73] Case 45/87 *Commission v Ireland* [1988] ECR I-4929, para. 16.
[74] Case 32/80 *Kortmann* [1981] ECR 251; and Case C-47/88 *Commission v Denmark* [1990] ECR I-4509.
[75] Case T-210/02 *British Aggregates Association* [2006] ECR II-2789, para. 114.

trade. In *Commission v Denmark*, the Court pointed out that in the absence of comparable domestic production, the prohibition in Article 110 TFEU did not apply. As a result, the only possibility of appraising an adverse effect of the manifest overtaxation of vehicles on the free movement of goods is 'by reference to the general rules contained in Article [34 TFEU] et seq. of the Treaty'.[76] However, it appears that this was the only case in which the Court alluded to the possibility of applying what is now Article 34 TFEU to exceptionally high internal taxation.

In his Opinion in *Danske Bilimportører*, Advocate General Jacobs considered that a 'manifestly excessive' tax—a Danish tax on cars amounting to 200 per cent of the value of the car, even though Denmark had no car production of its own—'could exceptionally be assessed under Article 34'.[77] The Advocate General concluded that it was 'totally incompatible with the aims of the internal market for a Member State to be able to tax certain imported goods to such an extent that the flow of intra-Community trade is appreciably affected'.[78] Nevertheless, he reached the conclusion that the Danish tax fell outside the scope of Article 34 TFEU. The Court endorsed the Advocate General's reasoning.

One could also invoke the judgment on Danish bottles to uphold the application of Article 34 TFEU to pecuniary measures that form barriers to importation; in this case, a deposit arrangement was imposed for the placing on the market of certain bottles—a pecuniary measure par excellence—and the Court examined its conformity with Article 34 TFEU.[79] However, this argument seems unconvincing, in that the contested system was a deposit system, not a tax system. The distinction between purely regulatory taxes and redistributive taxes is more delicate than it would at first appear to be.[80]

Finally, it is in this context important to stress that Member States endorse rather subtle approaches as regards eco-taxation. In fact, the level at which tax rates are set out is more incitative than prohibitory. These taxes encourage either undertakings or consumers to modify their behaviour. As a result, tax rates do not preclude consumers from purchasing the most polluting products; they make them less attractive than more environmentally friendly products.

To conclude, contrary to the case law on Articles 34 and 36 TFEU, 'in the absence of discriminatory or protective effect', Article 110 TFEU does not condemn the excessive character of the level of taxation that Member States could impose on particular goods.[81] Nothing, therefore, prohibits heavier taxation of products causing harm to

---

[76] Case C-47/88 *Commission v Denmark* (n 74). See P. Oliver, *Oliver on Free Movement of Goods in the European Union*, 5th edn (Oxford: Hart Publishing, 2010) 101–2.

[77] Opinion AG Jacobs in Case C-383/01 *De Danske Bilimportører* [2003] ECR I-6523, para. 42.

[78] *De Danske Bilimportører* (n 77), para. 76.

[79] Case 302/88 *Commission v Denmark* [1988] ECR I-46, para. 13. See the discussion in Subsection 7.3.2.

[80] J. H. Jans and H. Vedder, *European Environmental Law*, 4th edn (Groeningen: Europa Publishing, 2012) 227. According to Krämer this situation would be exceptional in that the tax amount would have to be prohibitively large. See L. Krämer, *EC Environmental Law*, 6th edn (London: Sweet & Maxwell, 2007) 124.

[81] Case 140/79 *Chemial Farmaceutica* [1981] ECR I-1; Case C-132/88 *Commission v Greece* [1990] ECR I-1567, para. 17; Case C-47/88 *Commission v Denmark* [1990] ECR I-4509, para. 10; and Case C-383/01 *De Danske Bilimportører* [2003] ECR I-6523, para. 38.

the environment with the aim of encouraging the consumer to switch to less hazardous products.

3.2 Goods which are similar (Art. 110(1) TFEU)

3.2.1 *Scope*

While the prohibition contained in Articles 28 and 30 TFEU is unconditional—custom duties as well as CEEs are wholly illegal—Article 110 TFEU only condemns the infringement of the general principle of non-discrimination.[82] A charge infringing Article 110 TFEU will therefore be illegal only in part, inasmuch as it exceeds the real or potential burden on similar domestic products. The first paragraph of this provision reads:

> No Member State shall impose, directly or indirectly, on the products of other Member States any internal taxation of any kind in excess of that imposed directly or indirectly on similar domestic products.

This paragraph prohibits Member States from taxing products of other Member States more heavily than similar domestic products. In other words, it prohibits the creation of fiscal discrimination. As a result, it governs the hypothesis where there is a domestic product similar to the imported product.

There is therefore infringement of this paragraph when taxation of the imported product and the domestic product results, even occasionally, in greater taxation of the imported product.[83] It follows that the imported products cannot be subject to less favourable fiscal treatment than the one accorded to the 'like' domestic products. The scope of this requirement concerns not only rates but also provisions on tax base and on the procedure for tax collection.[84]

As a result, if they have identical environmental qualities, imported products must obtain the same benefits as domestic products privileged by tax relief. By way of illustration, a Member State may not grant tax benefits to low-emission vehicles while refusing to grant them to foreign vehicles fulfilling the same criteria as the beneficiary domestic vehicles. Such taxation is contrary to Article 110 TFEU. Exemption from a consumer tax specifically relating to anti-pollution technology must therefore be applicable to all types of motor vehicle.[85]

3.2.2 *Appraisal of similarities between domestic and imported products*

Any type of discrimination towards foreign goods is prohibited under paragraph 1 of Article 110, provided that there is a similarity between the domestic and imported products. If this is not the case, the courts have to assess whether the imported and

---

[82] Case 78/76 *Steinike & Weinlig* [1977] ECR I-595.
[83] Case 45/75 *Rewe-Zentrale* [1976] ECR I-181, para. 15; and Case 327/90 *Commission v Greece* [1992] ECR I-3033, para. 12.
[84] Case 55/79 *Commission v Ireland* [1980] ECR 481.
[85] Case C-375/95 *Commission v Greece* [1997] ECR I-5981, para. 43.

domestic products compete, in which case the second paragraph applies.[86] There is similarity, a key concept, if either the relevant products fall into the same category of taxation, customs duties, or statistics, or if consumers perceive them as being usable in a similar manner.[87]

The relevant criterion in this regard is the interchangeability of products. It is necessary to ascertain whether products have sufficient properties in common to be considered an alternative choice for the consumer. The assessment of discrimination requires, in principle, the existence of a comparative element between national production and its competitors. Failing such national production, the measure in question would appear to fall outside the scope of Article 110 TFEU—it must then be ascertained whether it falls within Article 34 TFEU—although the position of the Court of Justice is not settled in that regard.

In certain environmental cases there is little discussion regarding the similarity between products of different tax arrangements. For instance, the origin of contaminated land matters very little: be it from polluted sites identified with precision through field surveys pursuant to Austrian law or be it from the territory of other Member States that do not have the same type of legislation: contaminated land is a category of 'waste similarly intended for disposal by means of long-term depositing' and the two types of contaminated land are thus 'similar products'.[88] Furthermore, although primary law provides for the principle that environmental damage should as a priority be rectified at source,[89] which is in line with the proximity principle and the principle of self-sufficiency, one may not differentiate between polluted land identified by use of a national register and polluted land originating from abroad.[90]

However, such comparison is likely to become much more difficult with respect to other cases. In the eyes of environmentally sensitive consumers, eco-minded consumption, which has flourished in certain Member States, increases the differences between products fulfilling a similar function. It should also force courts to evaluate the degree of similarity in a new light. Is a vehicle equipped with a catalytic converter similar to competing products without that technology? Can a recyclable battery be put on the same footing as a disposable battery? Is a disposable bottle that cannot be reused different from a reusable bottle that will not become waste? Are sustainably harvested fish dissimilar to other fish? Are all these products close substitutes?

Generally speaking, the Court endorses a broad interpretation of the term 'similar' within the meaning of paragraph 1.[91] If one applies the traditional case law of the Court, environment-friendly qualities within the same range of products would not suffice to eliminate similarity between the products. By way of illustration, a tax system exempting catalyst-equipped motor vehicles from an environmental tax and taxing

---

[86] See Section 3.3.

[87] Case C-45/75 *Rewe* [1976] ECR 181; Case 106/84 *Commission v Denmark* [1986] ECR 833, para. 12; and Case C-302/00 *Commission v France* [2002] ECR I-2055, paras 24–8. For a full account, see Barnard (n 47), 50; Toth (n 57), 713.

[88] Case C-221/06 *Stadtgemeinde Frohnleiten* [2007] ECR I-9643, para. 59.

[89] Art. 191(2) TFEU. See the discussion in Chaper 1, Section 7.5.

[90] *Stadtgemeinde Frohnleiten* (n 88), paras 60–9.

[91] P. Kapteyn and P. Verloren Van Themaat, *Introduction to the Law of the European Communities*, 3rd edn (The Hague: Kluwer, 1998) 605.

vehicles without catalysts would thus be contrary to Article 110(1) TFEU if the domestic industry mainly produces 'clean' cars. Indeed, the anti-pollution tax would then mostly target foreign vehicles and would be likely to reduce the number of imports.

But is it possible to review the legality of eco-taxes in applying traditional case law, which takes the view that whisky and cognac,[92] wine and beer,[93] and dark and light tobacco cigarettes[94] are similar. If these products satisfy identical social needs— quenching one's thirst, smoking—one cannot deny that consumers' expectations differ significantly as regards environmental issues.

So far, the Court has not yet settled the matter of whether, within the framework of selective taxation regarding the environment, products considered by consumers as similar but having different environmental impacts could be taxed differently according to their contribution to pollution, without however falling within the scope of Article 110(1) TFEU.[95] When analysing a Greek system taxing imported second-hand vehicles more heavily than those bought within its borders, the Court of Justice held that imported second-hand vehicles could be compared with second-hand vehicles bought in Greece without stating whether these vehicles should be considered as like or competing products.[96]

It should be noted that in most Member States consumers' expectations are increasingly a function of the environment-friendly quality of available products. In this regard, the EU eco-label scheme merits special note in that it promotes those products that have a high level of environmental performance.[97] In particular, it provides consumers 'with accurate, non-deceptive, science-based information on the environmental impact of products'.[98] In addition, account must be taken of the fact that the Commission considers that evaluation of similarity must take into account the objective of environmental protection. As such, one should consider 'whether goods with the same function but with different environmental properties due to content or differences in production methods could be regarded as being different goods'.[99] Even if it has the same function as a competing product, a product with an eco-label has different environmental properties from competing products.[100] Therefore, if one takes the view that these products impair the environment differently, one might conclude that they

---

[92] Case 168/75 *Commission v France* [1980] ECR 347.

[93] Case 356/85 *Commission v Belgium* [1987] ECR 3299, para. 10; and Case C-167/05 *Commission v Sweden* [2008] ECR I-2127, para. 43.

[94] Case C-302/00 *Commission v France* [2002] ECR I-2055, paras 24–8.

[95] On this, see A. Haagsma, 'De milieuheffing in Europees-rechtelijk perspectief' (1980) *SEW* 512 et seq. and 529. In a case concerning the prohibition on use of asbestos in France, the Dispute Settlement Body of the WTO held that 'the complaining Members', in this instance Canada, must 'establish that despite the pronounced physical differences there is a competitive relationship between the products such that . . . the products are "like" under Article III:4 of the GATT 1994'. See Report of the Appellate Body of 15 March 2001 *European Communities—Measures Affecting Asbestos and Asbestos-Containing Products* WT/DS 135/ R 2001, paras 118 and 121. Communication of the Commission of 26 March 1997, Environmental Taxes and Charges in the Single Market, COM(97) 9 final, 8.

[96] Case C-375/95 *Commission v Greece* [1997] ECR I-5981.

[97] European Parliament and Council Regulation (EC) No. 66/2010 on the EU Ecolabel [2010] OJ L27/1.

[98] Regulation (EC) No. 66/120, first recital.

[99] Commission Communication (n 95), I-8.   [100] Commission Communication (n 95).

fulfil different consumer needs. Finally, one should also expect case law to evolve on this matter, due to the integration clause embodied in Article 11 TFEU.[101]

3.3 Goods which are in competition (Art. 110(2) TFEU)

Although they might not be considered similar to domestic goods under paragraph 1, courts will nonetheless have to examine whether imported products falling within the scope of the tax system are competing with 'other' domestic products. In order to ward off indirect fiscal protectionism, the second paragraph of Article 110 TFEU provides that:

> Furthermore, no Member State shall impose on the products of other Member States any internal taxation of such a nature as to afford indirect protection to other products.

This paragraph has a complementary function with respect to the previous paragraph, in that it prohibits overt discrimination between domestic products and similar imported products.[102] It applies, therefore, to cases where there is no similar domestic product, by prohibiting indirect protectionist taxation. Although their relationship may appear somewhat remote, 'other domestic products' can indeed compete to some degree with imported products. As yet, no judgment has concerned the application of this paragraph to environmental taxation.

3.4 Differentiated system of taxation

3.4.1 *States*

Member States retain a large measure of sovereignty in the field of taxation. Indeed, Article 110 TFEU does not prohibit them from adopting differentiated taxation for similar products, inasmuch as they aim to achieve legitimate economic and social objectives. In order to be admissible, the charge must be part of a general taxation regime which applies the same criteria to domestic and foreign products and which is impartially warranted by the objective pursued. The tax must have the same effect on all taxpayers, be they national or foreign and the amount of tax cannot be greater for imported products. Similarly, the tax base and the means of collecting the tax must be identical. As a result, such differentiation is only compatible with EU law if it meets the following requirements:[103]

- it must pursue aims compatible with the requirements of the Treaties and of secondary law;
- it must be based on objective criteria;
- its rules and implications must avoid all types of discrimination.

---

[101] See the discussion in Chapter 1, Section 5.

[102] Case 27/67 *Fink-Frucht* [1968] ECR 327; Case 168/78 *Commission v France* [1980] ECR 347; and Case C-252/86 *Bergandi* [1988] ECR I-1343. In cases where it is difficult to determine whether goods are 'like' or 'competitive' products, the Court avoids choosing between the two tests.

[103] Case 196/85 *Commission v France* [1987] ECR I-1597, para. 6; and Case C-90/94 *Haahr Petroleum* [1997] ECR I-4085, para. 29.

The Court's case law contains certain clarifications as regards the validity of systems of differentiated taxation pursuing environmental goals.

3.4.2 *First condition: legitimacy of the aim pursued*

The Court accepts that differentiated taxation systems may pursue aims that are compatible with the requirements of the TFEU and of secondary law. The Court thus considered that the compatibility of green electric power-production methods with the environment was an important goal of the EU's energy policy.[104]

However, the Court of Justice has not always adopted such a clear stance on environmental objectives. While Greece justified a heavier taxation system for vehicles of high cylinder capacity due to the pollution they create, the Court only referred to 'the social circumstances prevailing in Greece and to some extent in Europe as a whole' without analysing the environmental argument presented by Greece.[105] Nonetheless, the Court should easily recognize environmental protection as a ground justifying tax arrangements that differentiate between products according to their environmental impact on the basis of objective criteria.

To illustrate, if a Member State taxes more heavily yet without discrimination products generating non-recyclable waste, it will not be deemed contrary to Article 110 TFEU, as it pursues objectives of environmental policy encapsulated in Article 191(2) TFEU, such as the prevention principle, and will not be deemed contrary to secondary EU law.[106]

3.4.3 *Second condition: objectivity of the differentiating criteria*

This requirement will be met if the differentiated tax policy on goods[107] or energy[108] is based on distinctions linked to the nature of the raw materials used or to the power-production processes. The same applies to consumer tax exemptions for regenerated oils[109] and to a progressive tax based on the cylinder capacity of taxed motor vehicles.[110] It follows that an exemption from consumption tax in favour of regenerated oils, and imposition of a progressive tax according to the number of cylinders of motor vehicles, also have to be based on objective criteria.

These criteria must be in conformity with secondary law. Tax differentiation based on environmental criteria will therefore not be permitted if secondary EU law prohibits

---

[104] Case C-213/96 *Outokumpu Oy* [1998] ECR I-1777, para. 33. The environmental aim may even appear to be more important if the preamble to a directive underlines the importance attached to the environmental incidence of methods of production (Opinion AG Jacobs, para. 58).

[105] Case C-132/88 *Commission v Greece* [1990] ECR I-1567, paras 9 and 16. Moreover, the ECJ held that Art. 110 TFEU does not allow it to censure excessive Member State taxation adopted on grounds linked to social policy (para. 17).

[106] See, eg, Directive 2008/98/EC on waste, Art. 4.

[107] Case 46/80 *Vinal* [1981] ECR I-77, para. 13.　　[108] *Outokumpu Oy* (n 104), para. 31.

[109] Case 21/79 *Commission v Italy* [1980] ECR I-1.

[110] Case C-132/88 *Commission v Greece* [1990] ECR I-1567; and Case C-113/94 *Casarin* [1995] ECR I-4203. See also Case C-47/88 *Commission v Denmark* ECR I-4509.

the adoption of such measures. This may be illustrated by the following case. A fiscal distinction between mineral oils of primary distillation and those stemming from a regeneration process was deemed to be in conformity with Article 110 TFEU, in that the directive on waste oils did not aim to harmonize national systems on excise duties and other forms of indirect taxation.[111]

Carbon taxes warrant special attention. Border tax adjustments and trade tariffs have been suggested for addressing concerns over competitive losses due to one country introducing a carbon tax which another country does not. Border tax adjustments would account for emissions attributable to imports from nations without a carbon price. The object of such a tax would be to offset the competitive advantage entailed by the absence of a similar taxation scheme in the exporting State. Given that the tax relates to the conditions under which products—cement, steel, etc—are made, it is non-product-related. Nonetheless, in line with *Otokumpu* case law, such a scheme is likely to fall within the scope of Article 110 TFEU.[112] That said, EU law does not restrict the freedom of each Member State to establish a tax system which differentiates between certain products 'on the basis of objective criteria, such as the nature of the raw materials used or the production processes employed'.[113]

3.4.4 *Third condition: absence of discrimination*

Respecting the first two conditions does not obviate the risk of discriminatory fiscal treatment. Assume, for instance, that a Member State imposes a higher carbon tax on cement made with coal than on cement produced with another source of energy. Assume that this tax pursues a legitimate objective and is based on objective technical criteria. The fulfilment of these two criteria does not preclude the risk that the tax at issue may treat imported cement less favourably than domestic low-carbon cement. In that event, it may infringe Article 110 TFEU on the ground that the effects of differentiated taxation must avoid all forms of discrimination, direct or indirect, towards imports and must avoid protection of domestic production.[114] It follows that although Article 110 TFEU is not intended to prevent a Member State from introducing new taxes or from changing the rate or basis of assessment of existing taxes, these powers to make tax arrangements are limited by the principle of non-discrimination.[115] In other words, environmental measures must not be enacted in such a way that gives rise to discrimination against imported products. Where the tax concerned is discriminatory in nature, 'the fact that the purpose of and reason for the tax may be environmental in nature or seek to reduce pollution has no bearing on any finding of infringement.'[116]

---

[111] Case 21/79 *Commission v Italy* (n 109), para. 18.
[112] D. Berlin, *Commentaire Mégret. Politique fiscale* (Brussels: ULB, 2012) 91–2.
[113] *Outokumpu Oy* (n 104), para. 30.
[114] Case 319/81 *Commission v Italy* [1983] ECR I-601, para. 13; Case 106/84 *Commission v Denmark* [1986] ECR 833, para. 22; and *Outokumpu Oy* (n 104), para. 30.
[115] Case C-402/09 *Ioan Tatu* [2011] OJ C160/8, paras 50–2.
[116] Opinion AG Sharpston in *Ioan Tatu* (n 115), para. 38.

In this respect, the Greek tax system applicable to second-hand vehicles imported into Greece, and intending to discourage registration of vehicles that were old, dangerous, and polluting and thus to encourage the use of new vehicles with 'anti-pollution technology', is a flagrant example. The tax system was found to infringe the principle of non-discrimination embodied in Article 110 TFEU, despite a seemingly legitimate objective.[117] By the same token, the objective of protection of the environment underpinning a Romanian tax scheme on second-hand cars which took the form of preventing the use of particularly polluting vehicles had to be achieved more comprehensively and consistently by imposing the pollution tax on all vehicles of that type in use in Romania.[118]

Unlike proportional taxes where the rate is the same regardless of the taxable amount, progressive taxes provide for a rate that increases as the taxable amount increases, due to the level of harm caused by the taxed activity or product. Gradual taxes can be globally progressive or can increase in stages. If the latter, separate and increasing rates will be applied at each stage, and the most harmful products will be in the most highly taxed category. As such, a small change in taxable amounts can lead to a large difference in taxation. Consequently, the taxpayer is wary of these taxation techniques, fearing that the purchase of more polluting products will lead to heavier taxation.

It may be that only imported products are to be found in the most highly taxed category. Hence, such schemes may impose a higher burden on similar or competing foreign products. However, the Court of Justice has held that such a system cannot be found to be discriminatory only on the basis that products from other States are classified as the most highly taxed products insofar as the distinction is based on objective and non-discriminatory criteria.[119] On the taxation of motor vehicles, a major component in the fight against global warming, it should be noted that the Court validated progressive taxation of vehicles on the basis of cylinder capacity, systems that *de facto* taxed imported vehicles with a larger cylinder capacity. The justification of such systems was that it was always possible for consumers to opt for vehicles in a lower tax bracket, which come from both domestic and foreign markets.[120] Progressive taxation of powerful cars produced abroad is thus possible only insofar as the taxation scheme does not favour national production.[121]

One might wonder whether differentiated taxation, with overriding reasons relating to environmental protection, could be valid despite having potentially negative effects on imported products.

In *Commission v Italy*, Advocate General Mayras suggested an answer to this question. Having reached a preliminary conclusion that divergence between national laws may lead to disparities in the taxes charged on home-produced regenerated oils and similar imported products which may affect the functioning of the common market and distort competition, he continued: 'None the less removal of those disparities must in no circumstances have the result of adversely affecting the protection of

---

[117] Case C-375/95 *Commission v Greece* [1999] ECR I-5981, para. 29.   [118] *Ioan Tatu* (n 115).

[119] Case 140/79 *Chemial Farmaceuti* [1981] ECR I-1, para. 18; Case C-200/85 *Commission v Italy* [1990] ECR I-1567; Case C-132/88 *Commission v Greece* [1990] ECR I-1567, para. 18; and Case C-113/94 *Casarin* [1995] ECR I-4203, para. 24.

[120] Case C-132/88 *Commission v Greece* (n 119), para. 20; and *Casarin* (n 119), para. 24.

[121] Case C-421/97 *Tarantik* [1992] ECR I-3633.

the environment'.[122] However, the Court considered that problems of comparison between Italian and foreign oils to extend tax relief to regenerated oils from abroad should be set aside.[123] If these difficulties cannot be set aside, the State must repeal the differentiated system.

Thus, a Member State may not invoke practical difficulties to extend tax relief to imported goods; this has frequently been confirmed in cases relating to environmental protection.

- In a judgment on the taxation of second-hand vehicles imported into Greece, the Court refused the argument of the Greek authorities according to which applying reduced rates for a special consumer tax on such vehicles would require individual control of each vehicle on import. Rather, the Court held that such difficulties 'cannot justify the application of internal taxation which discriminates against products from other Member States'.[124]

- In *Outokumpu Oy*, the Court condemned a system of differentiated taxation on the ground that it taxed imported electricity at a flat rate. Although this flat rate was lower than the highest rate applicable to electricity of domestic origin, it could lead, 'if only in certain cases, to higher taxation being imposed on imported electricity'.[125] The technical difficulty of applying differentiated rates to imported electricity was not taken into account.[126]

- In the same vein, the Court held in *Stadtgemeinde Frohnleiten* that: 'While it may indeed be extremely difficult for the Austrian authorities to ensure that [contaminated] sites located in other Member States...satisfy the requirements laid down in the Austrian legislation', this cannot justify the application of 'the exemption applicable to waste from disused hazardous sites...in Austria' when importers of foreign waste cannot benefit from this exemption.[127]

The Court's refusal to take into consideration practical difficulties arising from the extension of tax relief to imported products could jeopardize environmental taxation schemes.[128] The case law has obvious practical consequences: if a Member State cannot, for practical reasons, provide tax relief aimed at domestic anti-pollution products to similar imported products, it will have to repeal its differentiated tax system.

3.5 Concluding remarks

The increasing need to employ fiscal means to encourage undertakings as well as consumers to improve their environmental performance can lead to the creation of charges likely to hinder the free movement of goods. One must evaluate the validity of such charges with regard to Articles 28, 30, and 110 TFEU, provisions that have been held to be directly applicable before domestic courts.[129]

---

[122] Opinion AG Mayras in Case 21/79 *Commission v Italy* (n 109), para. 21.
[123] Case 21/79 *Commission v Italy* (n 109), para. 15.
[124] Case C-375/95 *Commission v Greece* (n 117), para. 47.   [125] *Outokumpu Oy* (n 104), para. 41.
[126] *Outokumpu Oy* (n 104), para. 39.   [127] *Stadtgemeinde Frohnleiten* (n 88), paras 70 and 71.
[128] See Opinion AG Mayras in Case 21/79 *Commission v Italy* (n 109), para. 1.
[129] Case C-57/65 *Lütticke* [1966] ECR 205, paras 210–11.

The lessons that can be drawn from this section are twofold.

First, given that an array of technical, scientific, economic, and political considerations are likely to tailor the scope of environmental tax regimes, constant distinctions are drawn between different categories of product. Sometimes these disctinctions are drawn from the intrinsic features of the products; they can also been drawn from the processes from which they were produced.[130] As a result, these distinctions are likely to discriminate *de facto* foreign products, as was highlighted in *Outokumpu Oy*. Therefore, the question is not whether that particular discrimination is arbitrary or unjustified, but whether there is discrimination. In that respect, the prohibitory regime embodied in Article 110 TFEU appears to be much stricter than those flowing from Articles 34, 35, and 36 TFEU.

That said, Member States still have some leeway if they can prove that foreign products are not likely to be taxed more heavily than home-produced products, that their tax system is based on objective criteria, and that it has a legitimate object. As such means also correspond to a prevention policy encouraged by the EU lawmaker, these tax regimes should be perceived favourably. Indeed, differential taxation based on objective environmental criteria is possible if it does not lead to any form of discrimination. Moreover, the national legislator is competent to fix tax rates according to the aims it wishes to pursue.

Finally, to conduct a differentiated tax policy properly, a Member State may require the importer to produce evidence of the criteria for environmental production, as long as such requirements are not harsher than those applying to similar domestic products or disproportionate in respect of the pursued aim—the elimination of fraud.[131]

4. Prohibition of Quantitative Restrictions and of Measures Having Equivalent Effect to Quantitative Restrictions to Trade

4.1 Introductory remarks

Certain aspects of national legislation on product standards are likely to fall under the concept of 'measures having equivalent effect' to 'quantitative restrictions' on imports—Article 34 TFEU—and on exports—Article 35 TFEU.

Because of the preference given to free movement of goods within the framework of the internal market, pursuant to Article 3(3) TEU and Article 26 TFEU,[132] these two provisions are of considerable importance in the EU legal order.

It should be noted that Articles 34 and 35 TFEU only apply to barriers not covered by other Treaty provisions. As seen previously, barriers resulting from customs duties, taxation, or State aid are covered by, respectively, Articles 28 and 30 TFEU, Article 110 TFEU, and Article 107 TFEU, which constitute *lex specialis* for those fields. As far as environmental measures are concerned, they are likely to fall within the scope of Treaty

---

[130] A good case in point is the Finnish energy tax scheme the validity of which was questioned in *Outokumpu Oy* (n 104).

[131] Case 21/79 *Commission v Italy* (n 109), para. 15.   [132] See ex Arts 3(c) and 14 EC.

provisions on goods as well as on services.[133] The TFEU provisions on free movement of goods and services are mutually exclusive. In this respect, *Commission v Ireland* is a good case in point.[134] The fact that an invitation to tender for the construction of a water main in an Irish municipality related to a service did not preclude the application of Article 34 TFEU on the ground that the clause at issue required the asbestos pressure pipes to conform to Irish standards. Indeed, the clause related to the intrinsic qualities of the pipes, irrespective of the purpose of the invitation to tender.

As there has been much discussion on the issue of conflict between national environmental policy and these provisions of the TFEU,[135] we shall briefly examine the characteristics of this regime before underlining the practical difficulties shown by the case law of the Court of Justice.

If the wording of Articles 34 and 35 TFEU is concise, the meaning and therefore the scope of these provisions have given rise to questions of interpretation. Contrary to the case law on food additives where the Court of Justice defined clear limits, the Court's case law concerning the environment oscillates between the aim of preserving the internal market and the desire to recognize environmental protection as being of public interest. Moreover, the variety of situations concerned—promotion of renewable energy, conservation of biodiversity, waste management, regulation of harmful substances, etc—does not make the life of the commentator any easier. There are many questions, for instance regarding the validity of extra-territorial measures, as well as the lessening of the distinction between measures applying equally and without distinction and measures applicable with distinction, that have not yet been fully resolved by the Court of Justice, as though it is not at ease with the subject.

4.2 Personal scope

Besides Member States, EU institutions and, to some extent, individuals are bound by Article 34 TFEU.

---

[133] See the discussion in Chapter 6.

[134] Case 45/87 *Commission v Ireland* [1988] ECR 4929.

[135] N. de Sadeleer: *Le droit communautaire and les déchets* (Brussels/Paris: Bruylant/LGDJ, 1995) 73–162; 'Les limites posées à la libre circulation des déchets par les exigences de protection de l'environnement' (1993) 5:6 *CDE* 672–96; *Environmental Principles* (Oxford: OUP, 2002) 341–54; *Commentaire Mégret. Environnement et marché intérieur* (Brussels: ULB, 2010) 363–412; D. Geradin, *Trade and the Environment. A Comparative Study of EC and US Law* (Cambridge: CUP, 1997); L. Krämer, 'L'environnement et le Marché unique' (1993) 1 *RMC* 48 and 'Environmental Protection and Article 30 TFEU' (1993) *CML Rev* 111–43; D. Misonne and N. de Sadeleer, 'Is There Space in the EU for National Product-Related Measures?' in M. Pallemarets (ed.), *EU and WTO Law: How Tight is the Legal Straitjacket for Environmental Product Regulation* (Brussels: VUB Press, 2006) 45–82; A. Notaro, *Judicial Approaches to Trade and Environment. The EC and the WTO* (London: Cameron & May, 2003); J. Scott, 'On Kith and Kine: Trade and Environment in the EU and WTO' in J. H. H. Veiler (ed.), *The EU, the WTO, and the NAFTA* (Oxford: OUP, 2000) 126–33; H. Temmink, 'From Danish Bottles to Danish Bees: The Dynamics of Free Movement of Goods and Environmental Protection—A Case Law Analysis' (2001) I *YbEEL* 61–102; G. Van Calster, *International & EU Trade Law. The Environmental Challenge* (London: Cameron & May, 2000); C. Vial, *Protection de l'environnement et libre circulation des marchandises* (Brussels: Bruylant, 2006); J. Wiers, *Trade and Environment in the EC and the WTO. A Legal Analysis* (Groeningen: Europa Law, 2002); and A. R. Ziegler, *Trade and Environmental Law in the European Community* (Oxford: Clarendon Press, 1996).

4.2.1 *Member States*

Articles 34 and 35 TFEU essentially target measures taken by a public authority. They apply *ratione personae* to Member States and thus to persons exercising State authority, as they apply to legal persons governed by public law.[136] Given that in most Member States environmental competences have been allocated to regional—Belgium, Germany, Italy, and Spain—or local entities,[137] the personal scope of these provisions is extremely broad. As far as environmental issues are concerned, they are likely to encompass a myriad of different types of public undertakings responsible for a variety of functions ranging from water treatment to land planning. By way of illustration, in *Fra.bo* the Court ruled that Articles 34 and 35 are applicable to a private law association with *de facto* rule-making competence for the standardization and certification of products used in drinking water.[138]

4.2.2 *EU institutions*

Even if the principle of free movement of goods applies less strictly to EU institutions than to Member States,[139] the former are also required to comply with these provisions in framing their legislation.[140]

Therefore, the EU institutions may not, through secondary law, enable Member States to behave in a manner that violates TFEU provisions on the free movement of goods. The Court of Justice made clear that conflicts should be avoided by interpreting secondary law so as not to infringe Treaty law.[141] In this connection, the following examples are illustrative of the ways in which the Court has assessed the compatibility of EU environmental regimes with the principle of free movement of goods.

- A number of French waste oil exporters raised doubts as to the validity of the former waste oil directive, particularly with regard to its provisions which envisage the possibility of exclusive zones being assigned to waste oil undertakings. The Court held that given that the waste oil directive must be seen 'in the

---

[136] Case 434/85 *Allen* [1988] ECR I-1245, para. 19; Case C-292/92 *Hünermund* [1993] ECR I-6787.

[137] A good example of a regional MEE may be found in Case C-2/90 *Commission v Belgium* ('*Walloon Waste*') [1992] ECR I-4431, and of a local MEE in Case 380/87 *Balsamo* [1989] ECR 2491.

[138] Case C-171/11 *Fra.bo* [2012] OJ C287/12, paras 31–2.

[139] Opinion AG Poiares Maduro of 14 September 2004 in Case C-41/02 *Commission v Netherlands* [2004] ECR I-11375, paras 30–3. See also F. G. Jacobs, 'Recent Developments in the Principle of Proportionality in EC Law' in E. Ellis (ed.), *The Principle of Proportionality in the Laws of Europe* (Oxford: Hart Publishing, 1999) 21 and T. Tridimas, 'Proportionality in European Community Law: Searching for the Appropriate Standards of Scrutiny' also in Ellis, 66; Kapteyn and Verloren Van Themaat (n 91), 640; H. Unperath and A. Johnston, 'The Double-Headed Approach to the ECJ concerning Consumer Protection' (2007) 44 *CML Rev* 1237–84.

[140] Joined Cases 80 & 81/77 *Commissaires réunis* [1978] ECR I-1978, para. 297; Case 15/83 *Denkavit Nederland* [1984] ECR I-2171, para. 15; Case C-51/93 *Meyhui* [1994] ECR I-3879, para. 11; Case C-114/96 *Kieffer and Thill* [1997] ECR I-3629, para. 27; Case C-469/00 *Ravil v Bellon* [2003] ECR I-5053, para. 86; Case C-108/01 *Consorzio del Prosciutto* [2003] ECR I-5121, para. 53; Case C-434/02 *Arnold André v Herford* [2004] ECR I-11825, para. 57; Case C-210/03 R *Swedish Match* [2004] ECR I-11893, para. 59; and Joined Cases C-154 & 155/04 R *Alliance for Natural Health* [2005] ECR I-6451, para. 47.

[141] K. Engsig Sørensen, 'Reconciling Secondary Legislation and the Treaty Rights of Free Movement' (2011) 36 *EL Rev* 339–61.

perspective of environmental protection, which is one of the Community's essential objectives', 'any legislation dealing with the disposal of waste oils must be designed to protect the environment'. In addition, as far as the free movement of goods is concerned, the directive 'must be construed...in light of the obligation not to create barriers to intra-Community trade'.[142] It follows that the right to create zones for the collection of waste oils does not automatically authorize national authorities to establish barriers to exports. In other words, the directive may not be applied in a manner contrary to Article 35 TFEU.

- As regards a regulation on substances that deplete the ozone layer, which prohibited the use and placing on the market of CFCs for firefighting, the Court held that these prohibitions had to be classified as MEEs.[143] However, environmental imperative requirement may limit the application of Article 34 TFEU, provided the principle of proportionality has been observed.[144]

- Limiting the placing on the market of vitamins to substances solely indicated in a 'positive' list—a regulatory technique often used in the environmental field—was also found to be a restriction under Article 34 TFEU.[145]

A further question arises as to the appropriate intensity of any review of the compatibility of EU legislation with Articles 34–36. EU institutions enjoy greater leeway than the Member States.[146] In *Alliance for Natural Health*, a case in which the Court was called upon to rule on the validity of a foodstuff directive, the Court held:

> The [EU] legislature must be allowed a broad discretion in an area such as that involved in the present case, which entails political, economic and social choices on its part, and in which it is called upon to undertake complex assessments. Consequently, the legality of a measure adopted in that area can be affected only if the measure is manifestly inappropriate having regard to the objective which the competent institution is seeking to pursue.[147]

4.2.3 *Individuals*

As a matter of principle, provisions on the free movement of goods do not apply to individuals,[148] as opposed to provisions in competition law. The Court clearly put an end to this controversy in its *Sapod Audic* judgment. There is therefore no horizontal effect. Typical in this respect is the example of 'buy local' campaigns that stress that long-distance transport of goods, such as food, entails significant environmental impact. Arguably, consumption of local products should be encouraged but, provided that such campaigns are promoted by private entities and cannot be attributed to the

---

[142] Case 240/83 *ADBHU* [1985] ECR 555, para. 13.
[143] Case C-284/95 *Safety Hi-Tech* [1998] ECR I-4301, para. 63; and Case C-341/95 *Safety Hi-Tech SRL* [1998] ECR I-4355, para. 61.
[144] *Safety Hi-Tech SRL* (n 143), paras 62–3.   [145] *Alliance for Natural Health* (n 140), para. 49.
[146] Oliver (n 76), 63–4; Temmink (n 135), 71.   [147] *Alliance for Natural Health* (n 140), para. 52.
[148] Case C-311/85 *Vereniging van Vlaamse Reisbureaus* [1987] ECR I-3801, para. 30. See also the implicit reasoning in Case C-325/00 *Commission v Germany* [2002] ECR I-9977.

State and are not financed by the government,[149] they escape the grasp of Article 34.[150] By the same token, the general obligation to identify packaging and thus affix the Green Dot logo, an obligation for which French law provided, results from a contract between two companies. If two legal persons entered into such a contract, the contractual provision could not be classified as a barrier under Article 34 TFEU.[151]

This statement must nevertheless be qualified, inasmuch as an individual's behaviour may affect free movement of goods if it was enabled by a Member State's failure to take action.[152] As regard environmental issues, the Court held in *Schmidberger* that when national authorities allow a protest of victims of noise pollution caused by traffic on a motorway the resulting MEE is proportionate to the constitutional values of the Member State.[153]

Could other types of action, such as a boycott of foreign products supported by consumers and environmental NGOs, be caught by Article 34 TFEU?[154] How exactly the Court will appy the principles developed in such cases as *Spanish Strawberries* remains to be seen.[155] Kapteyn and Verloren van Themaat clearly express the view that individual invitations to boycott foreign products fall outside the scope of Article 34 TFEU.[156] At least, to fall within the ambit of that provision, such actions should be buttressed by the State authorities.

4.3 Material scope of application of Articles 34 and 35 TFEU

4.3.1 *General considerations*

Two criteria are used to define the scope of Articles 34 and 35 TFEU, namely the nature of the 'goods' meant to move freely within the internal market and the nature of the barriers affecting those goods. In the absence of Treaty definitions of 'goods', 'quantitative restrictions', and 'measure having equivalent effect', one must refer to the Court of Justice's case law to determine the scope of these provisions.

4.3.1.1 The goods concerned

Nowhere in the Treaty is the concept of 'goods' defined. Both Articles 34 and 35 TFEU use the terms 'imports' and 'exports' rather than 'goods' or 'products'. In relation to all 'goods taken across a frontier for the purposes of commercial transactions . . . , whatever the nature of those transactions',[157] the concept of 'goods' is interpreted broadly and

---

[149] Case C-227/06 *Commission v Belgium* [2008] ECR I-46.
[150] J. Hojnik, 'Free Movement of Goods in a Labyrinth: Can *Buy Irish* Survive the Crises' (2012) 49 *CML Rev* 303.
[151] Case C-159/00 *Sapod Audic* [2002] ECR I-5031, para. 74.
[152] Case C-265/95 *Commission v France* [1997] ECR I-6959.
[153] Case C-112/02 *Schmidberger* [2003] ECR I-5659, noted by M. Humphreys (2004) *Env LR* 190–203. The Court took care to underline differences with regard to *Commission v France* the judgment for which was delivered on 9 December 1997.
[154] See the impact on inter-State trade of the boycott of French products supported by different NGOs as a result of the Mururora nuclear test that took place in 1995. Eg Temmink (n 135), 79.
[155] Case C-265/95 *Commission v France* (n 152).
[156] Kapteyn and Verloren Van Themaat (n 91), 640.
[157] Case C-324/93 *Evans Medical* [1995] ECR I-563, para. 20.

can thus cover goods such as petroleum products,[158] works of art,[159] and electricity.[160] This definition may not depend on national classifications. As a result, specimens of wild animals caught and marketed are treated in the same way as any other good.[161] As regards waste, in *Walloon Waste*, the Court underlined the practical difficulty of applying a distinction between recyclable and non-recyclable waste insofar as this distinction 'is based on factors which are uncertain and liable to change in the course of time according to technical progress'.[162] Moreover, the value of waste must not be taken into account as all objects subject to ownership or obligations must benefit from the principle of free movement regardless of their positive or negative commercial value. Accordingly, non-recyclable or non-reusable waste has to be regarded as 'goods' the movement of which must in principle not be prevented.[163]

4.3.1.2 The measures concerned

Articles 34 and 35 TFEU only apply if the existence of a quantitative restriction or an MEE can be established. Given that it is unlikely to face quantitative restrictions, the definition of an MEE is therefore essential in the Court of Justice case law which, through a broad interpretation of free movement of goods, puts more store by the effect of the measure than by its legal nature. That said, whereas the Court opted for a discrimination criterion in determining the scope of Article 35, the Court made clear in *Cassis de Dijon* that all measures with an impact on intra-Community trade, discriminatory as well as non-discriminatory, were caught by Article 34 TFEU. As a consequence, one should differentiate between the scope of MEEs on imports (Subsection 4.3.2) and exports (Subsection 4.3.3).

4.3.2 *MEEs on imports*

4.3.2.1 The *Dassonville* formula

Since its *Dassonville* judgment of 11 July 1974, the Court of Justice has interpreted the concept of MEE broadly. According to the wording of the judgment, 'all trading rules enacted by Member States which are capable of hindering, directly or indirectly,

---

[158] Case 72/83 *Campus Oil* [1984] ECR 2727, para. 17.

[159] Case 7/68 *Commission v Italy* [1968] ECR 423.

[160] Case 6/64 *Costa v Enel* [1964] ECR 585; Case C-393/92 *Commune d'Almelo* [1994] ECR I-1477, para. 28; and Case C-158/94 *Commission v Italy* [1997] ECR I-5789, paras 14–20. In *Jägerskiöld v Gustafsson*, AG Fennelly acknowledged that it might 'appear somewhat surprising that the Court has treated electricity, despite its intangible character, as goods'. In his view, 'electricity must be regarded as a specific case, perhaps justifiable by virtue of its function as an energy source and, therefore, in competition with gas and oil'. See Opinion in Case C-97/98 *Jägerskiöld v Gustafsson* [1999] ECR I-7319, 7328–29.

[161] This is the case of different taxonomic groups: British grouse (*Lagopus lagopus scotius*) in Case C-169/89 *Gourmetterie Van den Burg* [1990] ECR I-2143; Canadian goose (*Branta canadensis*) in Case C-149/94 *Vergy* [1996] ECR I-299; bees (*Apis mellifera*) in Case C-67/97 *Bluhme* [1998] ECR I-8033; goldfinch (*Carduelis carduelis*) in Case C-202/94 *Godefredius van der Steen* [1996] ECR I-355; macaw (*Ara macao*) in Case C-510/99 *Tridon* [2001] ECR I-7777; and wild mammals in Case C-219/07 *Andibel* [2008] ECR I-4475.

[162] *Walloon Waste* (n 137), para. 27. Case law of the US Supreme Court agrees with this interpretation: 'all objects of interstate trade merit commerce clause protection; none is excluded at the outset....Solid waste even if it has no value is an article of commerce'. All waste may thus move freely between states pursuant to the commerce clause of the US Constitution (*Philadelphia v New Jersey* 437 US 617, 622–3 (1978)).

[163] *Walloon Waste* (n 137), paras 27–8.

actually or potentially, intra-Community trade are to be considered as measures having an effect equivalent to quantitative restrictions'.[164] Repeated on countless occasions, this formula is still regularly cited in judgments. Its striking feature is its sheer breadth.[165] For an MEE to be prohibited, it need not necessarily apply to imports or exports; it is sufficient that it is applicable to them. Nor is it necessary that it has a direct and appreciable effect on inter-State trade.[166] Furthermore, the measure need not intervene at the time of crossing a border; its effects may be felt later, once inside the importing country.[167] Finally, to be prohibited the measure need not render import or export impossible; it is sufficient for these operations to be rendered more difficult for there to be an MEE.[168]

In *Cassis de Dijon*, the Court clarified that MEEs, not limited to measures directly affecting imports, encompassed measures that are 'applicable without distinction' to foreign and domestic goods, as a foreign producer may find it more difficult to respect these rules than a national producer. According to settled case law, 'in the absence of harmonization of legislation, obstacles to free movement of goods which are the consequence of applying, to goods coming from other Member States where they are lawfully manufactured and marketed, rules that lay down requirements to be met by such goods' constitute MEEs prohibited by Article 34 TFEU.[169] The condition that the goods were 'lawfully manufactured and marketed in another Member State' reflects 'the obligation to comply with the principle of mutual recognition of products'.[170] Mutual recognition can be defined as 'a principle whereby the sale of goods lawfully produced and marketed in one Member State may not be restricted in another Member State without good cause'.[171] It follows that the importer can work on the basis of a single regulation by the home State instead of having to overcome the hurdle of dealing with both the home State and the domestic regulation.[172] However, as discussed later, the principle of mutual recognition has to some extent been neutralized by the mandatory requirement doctrine.[173]

The incorporation under ex Article 28 EC (Art. 34 TFEU) of national measures which are indistinctly applicable has in any event permitted a considerable extension of the control of obstacles to trade between the Member States, which in turn gave rise to difficulties regarding the justification of national environmental measures. We shall

---

[164] Case 8/74 *Dassonville* [1974] ECR 837.

[165] P. Oliver, 'Of Trailers and Jet-Skis: Is the Case Law on Article 34 TFEU Hurtling in a New Direction?' (2011) 33 *Fordham Intl LJ* 1423; Barnard (n 47), 92.

[166] Case 16/83 *Prantl* [1984] ECR 1299, para. 20.

[167] Case 222/82 *The Apple and Pear Development Council* [1983] ECR 4083.

[168] *Dassonville* (n 164); and Case C-128/89 *Commission v Italy* [1990] ECR I-3239.

[169] Case 120/78 *Cassis de Dijon* [1979] ECR 649.

[170] Case C-110/05 *Commission v Italy* [2009] ECR I-519, para. 34 and the case law cited therein; Case C-108/09 *Ker-Optika* [2010] ECR I-12213, para. 48, noted by N. de Sadeleer (2011) 2 *EJCL* 435–44.

[171] *Cassis de Dijon* (n 169), para. 14.

[172] A. Rosas, 'Life after *Dassonville* and *Cassis*: Evolution but not Revolution' in M. Poiares Maduro and L. Azoulai (eds), *The Past and Future of EU Law: The Classics of EU Law Revisited on the 50th Anniversery of the Treaty of Rome* (Oxford: Hart Publishing, 2010) 440.

[173] N. Bernard, 'On the Art of Not Mixing One's Drinks: *Dassonville* and *Cassis de Dijon* Revisited' in M. Poiares Maduro and L. Azoulai (eds), *The Past and Future of EU Law: The Classics of EU Law Revisited on the 50th Anniversary of the Treaty of Rome* (Oxford: Hart Publishing, 2010) 460.

later examine the importance of the *summa divisio* between distinctly and indistinctly applicable measures as regards the possibility of justification by Member States.[174]

4.3.2.2 Examples of MEEs on imports aiming at environmental protection

MEEs aiming at environmental protection can have highly variable legal and factual characteristics. They can be based on agreements,[175] a legislative framework, or incentives.[176] In matters relating to the environment, the Court has faced a flurry of domestic measures of varying legal nature. In a growing body of case law, the Court has considered the compatibility of national environmental measures with Article 34 TFEU, as illustrated by the following examples. Much of this case law has been in the form of Article 267 TFEU preliminary references.

- Legislation prohibiting traffic of heavy goods vehicles over 7.5 tonnes on a highway of paramount importance for inter-Community trade is an MEE, despite the existence of alternative routes or of other means of transport capable of allowing the goods to be transported.[177]

- The statutory obligation for private electricity supply undertakings to purchase, at a minimum price higher than its value, electricity produced in their supply area from renewable energy sources, falls within the scope of Article 34 TFEU inasmuch as it prevents them from importing electricity from other Member States.[178]

- A 'positive list' of wild mammals 'is liable—since it is applied to specimens from another Member State—to restrict inter-State trade for the purposes of [Article 34 TFEU]'.[179]

- The requirement that aircraft be registred provided that they comply with noise emission thresholds is caught by Article 34 TFEU.[180]

It should be noted that most of these environmental measures were 'applicable without distinction' to foreign and domestic goods. However, as discussed later, the distinction to be drawn between measures 'applicable without distinction' and those indistinctly applicable is a fine one.[181]

Moreover, one need not establish that the challenged measure has actually significantly impeded the import or export of goods;[182] it suffices to demonstrate that the measure as it exists on paper is likely to hinder trade for the measure to be deemed to have equivalent effect.[183] Litigants are spared the task of 'adducing potentially complex and costly economic evidence' as to the extent to which national measures impede

---

[174] See the discussion below in Section 5.2.4.   [175] Case C-3/91 *Exportur* [1992] ECR I-5529.
[176] Case 249/81 *Commission v Ireland* [1982] ECR 4005, paras 27–9; and Case C-325/00 *Commission v Germany* [2002] ECR I-9977, para. 24.
[177] Case C-320/03 P *Commission v Austria* [2005] ECR I-3593, paras 66 and 67, noted by M. Humphreys (2007) 9 *Env L Rev* 137–47.
[178] Case C-379/98 *PreussenElektra* [2001] ECR I-2099.
[179] Case C-219/07 *Andibel* [2008] ECR I-4475, para. 26.
[180] Case C-389/96 *Aher-Waggon* [1998] ECR I-4473.
[181] See Sections 5.2.4 and 5.4.2.   [182] Case 16/83 *Prantl* [1984] ECR 1299, para. 20.
[183] Case 12/74 *Commission v Germany* [1975] ECR 181, para. 14.

access to the national market.[184] In fact, most environmental measures do not render the import or export of goods impossible; they merely render them more difficult, as illustrated by the following examples.

- The 'fact that ... there are alternative routes or other means of transport capable of allowing the goods in question to be transported' by heavy goods vehicles contributing to the limit values of air quality to be exceeded 'does not negate the existence of an obstacle'.[185]

- In dissuading trade in mammals and oysters as a result of systems of a 'positive' list and of licences granted by administrative authorities, a Member State hinders inter-State trade.[186]

- In a similar vein, the possibility for producers of dangerous substances, prohibited in principle, to obtain an exemption to continue to place their product on the market does not negate its classification as an MEE.[187]

- By entailing additional expense for traders, the marking requirement for batteries containing dangerous substances discourages the import of such goods.[188]

Moreover, Article 34 TFEU cannot be excluded on the basis of the absence of competing production on the territory of other Member States.[189] Even an increase in imports of the goods subject to an MEE to a quantitative restriction—*in casu* non-reusable packaging—will not prove 'that there is no discrimination against producers of natural mineral water' from other Member States.[190] It is therefore not necessary to consider statistical evidence as to the volume of imports or exports affected by the measure at issue in order to prove a true reduction of imports or exports.[191]

A potential barrier to trade requires a hypothetical comparison, based on general economic experience, between the situation that arose and the situation as it would have been in the absence of the contested measures. However, the Court may apply a strict and circumstanciated interpretation to the national barrier. For instance, in the German reusable water bottles case, the Court held that there was discrimination in the light of *in concreto* statistical data, showing the more frequent use of non-reusable—but

---

[184] A. L. Sibony, 'Can Market Access be Taken Seriously?' (2012) 2 *EJCL-REDC* 325. See Opinion AG Bot in Case C-110/05 *Commission v Italy* [2009] ECR I-519, para. 31.

[185] Case C-320/03 *Commission v Austria* [2005] ECR I-3593, paras 66 and 67. Indeed, by forcing transport undertakings 'to seek viable alternative solutions for the transport of goods' the Member State in question was capable of limiting trading opportunities between northern Europe and the north of Italy (paras 67 and 68).

[186] Case C-219/07 *Andibel* [2008] ECR I-4475, paras 21–2.

[187] In fact, the obligation for an economic operator to obtain an exemption from a national measure may in itself be a quantitative restriction or a measure having equivalent effect (see notably Case 82/77 *Van Tiggele* [1978] ECR 25, para. 19; and Case 251/78 *Denkavit Futtermittel* [1979] ECR 3369, para. 11; regarding exemptions for the prolonged use of dangerous substances, see Case C-473/98 *Toolex Alpha* [2000] ECR I-5681, para. 37).

[188] Case C-143/03 *Commission v Italy* [2004] not reported, para. 30 (only available in French and Italian).

[189] Case C-184/96 *Commission v France* [1998] ECR I-6197, paras 15–18.

[190] Case C-463/01 *Commission v Germany* [2004] ECR I-11705, para. 65.

[191] Case 12/74 *Commission v Germany* (n 183), para. 14; Case 261/85 *Commission v UK* [1988] ECR 547. See Oliver (n 76), 94.

recyclable—packaging by foreign mineral-water producers than by German producers, who tended to use reusable packaging as required by national legislation.[192]

Last, there is a general view, reflected in the Court's consistent case law, that there is not even a *de minimis* exception to Article 34 TFEU.[193] In this vein, the Court applied that provision in several environmental cases irrespective of the market effects of the measures at issue.

- As is clearly illustrated in *Bluhme*, an MEE may constitute a restriction on a very small fraction of imports of beehives. One of the arguments put forward by the Danish authorities was that the prohibition fell outside Article 34 TFEU as being *de minimis*, since it covered only 0.3 per cent of Danish territory. Advocate General Fennelly dismissed that argument on the ground that 'the slight effect of the decision, in volume terms, cannot, in itself, prevent the application of Article [34] of the Treaty'.[194] The conclusions of the Court were completely in line with that reasoning.

- In cases on the reuse of bottles for sale in Germany, the Court of Justice reminded parties that the extent of the barrier should not be taken into consideration, as a restrictive measure must be classified as an MEE 'even though the hindrance is slight and even though it is possible for the products to be marketed in other ways'.[195]

To conclude, the result of the *Dassonville* and *Cassis* case law is that the Court has been casting the Article 34 TFEU net so broadly that the provision captures not only protectionist measures but also bona fide environmental regulations. However, the most contentious questions surrounding the scope of this 'all-encompassing principle'[196] arose in the course of subsequent cases.

4.3.2.3 Selling arrangements

Although the judgment in *Keck* and subsequent case law did not reverse *Dassonville* and *Cassis de Dijon* case law,[197] it narrowed down the scope of Article 34 TFEU by removing 'certain selling arrangements'—sales at a loss, rules on advertising, opening of stores on Sundays, etc—from the scope of that provision as long as those arrangements are equal

---

[192] Case C-463/01 *Commission v Germany* (n 190), para. 60.

[193] Joined Cases 177/82 & 178/82 *Van de Haar* [1984] ECR 1797, para. 13; Case 16/83 *Prantl* [1984] ECR 1299, para. 20; Case 269/83 *Commission v France* [1985] ECR 837, para. 10; and Case 103/84 *Commission v Italy* [1986] ECR 1759, para. 18. Recent case law by the ECJ does not always clearly indicate whether there is a *de minimis* rule regarding Art. 34 TFEU. See, on the one hand, eg Case C-16/83 *Prantl* [1984] ECR 1299, para. 20; Joined Cases 177 & 178/82 *Van de Haar*, previously in this fn, para. 13; Case C-269/83 *Commission v France* [1985] ECR 837, para. 10; and Case C-158/94 *Commission v Italy* [1997] ECR I-5789, para. 18; and, on the other hand, eg Case C-266/96 *Corsica Ferries* [1998] ECR I-3949, para. 31; Case C-44/98 *BASF* [1999] ECR I-6269 and the implicit reasoning in Case C-254/98 *TK-Heimdienst* [2000] ECR I-151, para. 30.

[194] Opinion AG Fennelly in *Bluhme* (n 161), para. 16.

[195] Case C-463/01 *Commission v Germany* (n 190); and Case C-309/02 *Radlberger and Spitz* [2004] ECR I-11763, paras 63 and 68.

[196] Rosas (n 172), 437.

[197] Kapteyn and Verloren Van Themaat (n 91), 632; M. Poiares Maduro, *We, the Court. The European Court of Justice and the European Economic Constitution* (Oxford: Hart Publishing, 1998) 79.

in impact on both domestic and imported goods.[198] In so doing, the Court drew a distinction between selling arrangements and product requirements. On the one hand, selling arrangements fulfilling the *Keck* conditions are not subject to any type of justification. On the other, measures concerning the dimensions, weight, form, size, composition, designation, labelling, and presentation of goods do fall within the scope of Article 34.

That said, *Keck* has come in for considerable criticism precisely because the Court placed too much emphasis on factual and legal equality to the detriment of market access.[199] In addition, most of the selling arrangements reviewed recently by the Court have not been found to fall outwith the scope of Article 34 TFEU.[200]

Insofar as legal rules aiming to protect the environment primarily concern the characteristics of goods (eg the toxicity of a chemical product, the origin or rarity of a plant or animal species, the danger of waste, labelling, the concentration of hazardous substances) rather than selling arrangements, it is unlikely that the Court of Justice or the national courts will be faced with national regulation on the selling arrangements for said goods. Hence, as far as environmental issues are concerned, product bans, product standards, registration requirements, and emissions thresholds have to be considered as MEEs. To date, as illustrated by the following examples, few environmental measures have been classified as concerning selling arrangements under the *Keck* case law.

- The prohibition on importing bees to an island was found not to fall within the scope of the selling arrangement exemption.[201]

- Moreover, the Court found that legislation requiring the marking of heavy metal concentrations in batteries and accumulators before their sale in the Member State of origin, and thus before their marketing in the Member State of that legislation, did not concern selling arrangements.[202] Indeed, such legislation entails the adaptation and new packaging of the goods.

- Neither the deposit system encouraging the reuse of mineral water bottles, through the use of reusable glass bottles, nor the mandatory identification of packaging with a green dot can be considered selling arrangements.[203] In this respect, the Court distinguished the obligation for packaging producers to comply with certain technical requirements under Article 34 TFEU from the 'general obligation to

---

[198] Joined Cases C-267 & C-268/91 *Keck* [1993] ECR I-6097.

[199] F. Picod, 'La nouvelle approche de la Cour de justice en matière d'entraves aux échanges' (1998) 2 *RTDE* 169; A. Mattera, 'De l'arrêt *"Dassonville"* à l'arrêt *"Keck"*: l'obscure clarté d'une jurisprudence riche en principes novateurs et en contradictions' (1994) 1 *RMUE* 117; S. Weatherill, 'After *Keck*: Some Thoughts on How to Clarify the Clarification' (1996) 33 *CML Rev* 885; R. Kovar, '*Dassonville, Keck* et les autres: de la mesure avant toute chose' (2006) 2 *RTDE* 213; M. Poiares Maduro, '*Keck*: The End? The Beginning of the End? Or just the End of the Beginning?' (1994) *Irish Journal of European Law* 36; L. Gormley 'Two Years after *Keck*' (1996) 19 *Fordham Intl LJ* 866; C. Barnard, 'Fitting the Remaining Pieces into the Goods and Persons Jigsaw?' (2001) 26 *EL Rev* 35.

[200] E. Spaventa, 'Leaving *Keck* Behind? The Free Movement of Goods after the Rulings in *Commission v Italy* and *Mickelsson and Roos*' (2009) 34 *EL Rev* 920 and 922.

[201] *Bluhme* (n 161), para. 21.   [202] Case C-143/03 *Commission v Italy* (n 188), para. 29.

[203] Case C-159/00 *Sapod Audic* [2002] ECR I-5031, para. 73; and Case C-463/01 *Commission v Germany* (n 190), para. 68

identify the packaging collected for disposal by an approved undertaking', an obligation that is likely to be regarded as a selling arrangement.[204]

- Given that the provisions of the German waste packaging legislation (VerpackV) do not affect the marketing of drinks produced in Germany and that of drinks from other Member States in the same manner, these measures cannot fall outside the scope of Article 34 TFEU.[205]

Furthermore, Article 34 TFEU does not apply either to the advertising prohibition for goods that are hazardous to the environment or to the obligation to limit the marketing of dangerous substances to approved undertakings, provided that these measures 'apply to all relevant traders operating within the national territory' and do not distinguish goods, legally or factually, according to their origin. For instance, in *De Agostini* the Court applied the *Keck* formula in a case concering the prohibition in a TV broadcast on using the words 'environmentally friendly' and similar phrases implying that a detergent was beneficial for the environment.[206] In particular, State authorities may regulate however they like where and whom can sell hazardous goods or under which conditions such goods can be sold provided their measures do not have discriminatory effect.[207] However, total bans on advertising can be discriminating per se.[208] It follows that a measure restricting to specific operators the sale of hazardous substances falls outside the scope of Article 34 TFEU.

As will be discussed in the next subsection, Advocate General Kokott suggested in *Swedish Watercraft* the extension of the *Keck* formula to arrangements for product use since the 'characteristics of arrangements for use and selling arrangements . . . are comparable in terms of the nature and intensity of their effects on trade in goods'.[209] However, the Court departed from her Opinion.

4.3.2.4 A three-pronged approach to the concept of MEEs falling within the ambit of Article 34 TFEU

Since *Keck*, MEEs have been divided into two categories: product rules and selling arrangements. The rationale for this distinction is that both categories have a different impact on intra-Union trade. The functioning of the internal market would be hindered if goods which comply with the legislation of the Member State of origin, also needed to comply with product rules elsewhere in the Union; whereas the impact of selling arrangements is much more limited. Arguably, the latter measures do not impose extra costs on importers; their purpose is not to regulate trade.[210]

However, two judgments handed down by the Grand Chamber on 10 February 2009 (the *Italian Trailers* case) and by the Second Chamber of the Court on 4 June 2009

---

[204] *Sapod Audic* (n 203), para. 73; and Case C-463/01 *Commission v Germany* (n 190), paras 70–3.
[205] See *Radlberger and Spitz* (n 195), para. 73.
[206] Joined Cases C-34, 35, & 36/95 *De Agostini and TV-Shop* [1997] ECR I-3843, paras 21 and 31.
[207] Temmink (n 135), 75.   [208] Oliver (n 76), 133.
[209] Opinion AG Kokott in Case C-142/05 *Mickelsson and Roos* ('*Swedish Watercraft*') [2009] ECR I-4273, para. 52.
[210] P. Craig and G. de Búrca, *EU Law: Text, Cases, and Materials*, 3rd edn (Oxford: OUP, 2003) 648.

(*Swedish Watercraft*) made far-reaching changes to this two-pronged approach to the concept of an MEE.[211] These judgments are of specific interest both from the point of view of the scope of Article 34 TFEU as well as review of the necessity of the measures concerned. Of particular salience is the extent to which that provision restricts the hard core of environmental policy: the ability of national authorities to regulate the use of hazardous products.[212] The fact that three Advocates General delivered specific Opinions on these two cases and also that the Court handed down its *Swedish Watercraft* judgment on 4 June 2009 after the Swedish criminal court had referred its questions on 22 February 2005 mirror the difficulties the highest European court has faced in tracing the borders of national regulatory autonomy escaping the free movement of goods provisions.

In the two cases at hand, as well as in subsequent cases,[213] the Court identified three categories of measure that will now be covered by Article 34 TFEU. Accordingly, the two-pronged approach—on the one hand, national measures prescribing the characteristics of goods and, on the other, the selling arrangements—has been sidelined.

The first category involves measures which have the object or effect of treating products originating from other Member States less favourably.[214] In other words, it covers all national measures which are directly or indirectly discriminatory. It follows that whenever they have the object or the effect of discriminating against foreign producers, all measures governing the characteristics of a product, its use, as well as selling arrangements fall into this first category.

The second category concerns measures which, where national laws have not been harmonized, regulate the requirements which these products must satisfy, even if these rules are indistinctly applicable to all products (ie double-burden rules). This corresponds to the category of measures relating to the intrinsic characteristics of the products as defined under *Cassis de Dijon*.[215] In contrast to the first category, measures falling within the scope of the second category do not aim to discriminate against foreign products. By way of illustration, such would be the case where national regulations lay down technical standards on the placing on the market of pesticides or chemical substances.

In fact, this second category is difficult to distinguish from the first, particularly so where the 'actual characteristics of the products' are concerned. Indeed, it is difficult to draw a line between measures tantamount to indirect discrimination and indistinctly applicable measures. What is more, the second category establishes an exception to

---

[211] Case C-110/05 *Commission v Italy* ('*Trailers*') [2009] ECR I-519; *Swedish Watercraft* (n 209). As regards the first judgment, eg A. Rigaux, 'Définition des mesures d'effet équivalent' (2009) 4 *Europe* 158; C. Barnard, 'Trailing a New Approach to Free Movement of Goods?' (2009) 68 *CLJ* 288–90; and Barnard (n 47), 104–8. As regard the second judgment, eg A. Rigaux, 'Restrictions à l'usage des produits' (2009) 4 *Europe* 19–22. See also Oliver (n 76), 125–31. As regards the two judgments, see N. de Sadeleer, 'L'examen, au regard de l'article 28 CE, des règles nationales régissant les modalités d'utilisation de certains produits' (2009) 162 *JDE* 247–50; T. Horsley, (2009) 46 *CML Rev* 2001–19.

[212] N. de Sadeleer, *Commentaire Mégret. Environnement et marché intérieur* (Brussels: ULB, 2010).

[213] Case C-108/09 *Ker-Optika* [2010] ECR I-12213, paras 48–51, noted by N. de Sadeleer (2011) 2 *EJCL* 435–44.

[214] *Trailers* (n 211), para. 36; and *Ker-Optika* (n 213), para. 49.

[215] Case 120/78 *Rewe-Zentral* [1979] ECR 649. See Section 4.3.2.1.

'selling arrangements' within the meaning of the *Keck* jurisprudence,[216] which led certain commentators to speculate whether that case law had been superseded.[217]

Finally, the final category of this trilogy consists of 'any other measure which hinders access of products originating in other Member States to the market of a Member State'.[218] Vigorous debate ensued as to how to interpret these terms.[219] It is submitted that this category covers non-discriminatory measures, which do not fall within the scope of the first two categories, but which do prevent or impede access to the market for imported products. As we shall see later, this third category embraces authorization requirements, restrictions on transport, as well as the way in which the use of products is regulated.[220] For instance, a measure falls into this residual category where it has the effect of preventing consumers from using products according to 'the specific and inherent purposes for which they were intended or of greatly restricting their use'.[221]

Table 5.2 shows how the three categories of measure now covered by Article 34 TFEU unfold.

There are three points to be made about this new arrangement.

First, selling arrangements have not disappeared as such. They may be caught by the first category inasmuch as they are discriminatory,[222] or by the third category if they prevent access to the market for the importing Member State. Table 5.3 identifies three types of environmental measure likely to be classed as MEEs—product requirements, selling arrangements, and restrictions on use—and their respective regimes.

Second, the inclusion of the third category—access to market—is a novel feature of the case law.[223] In effect, the Court of Justice is placing emphasis on a market access criterion, independent of any discrimination test, thereby complying with its earlier case law in *Dassonville*. It follows that measures merely restricting and not just prohibiting the use of a product fall within the scope of Article 34 TFEU.[224] Whether market access will become the new yardstick against which national measures have to be assessed remains to be seen.[225] Indeed, it is still unclear what the term 'access' means.[226] In particular, the question arises as to what degree of access to the national

---

[216] *Trailers* (n 211), para. 36.

[217] Rosas (n 172), 445; Oliver (n 76), 129–30; Barnard (n 47), 104–8; and Barnard (n 211). See also the ten articles in (2012) 2 *EJCL-REDC*.

[218] *Trailers* (n 211), para. 37; *Swedish Watercraft* (n 209), para. 24.

[219] Spaventa (n 200), 921–2; Horsley (n 211), 2016. See also A. Fromont and C. Verdure, 'La consécration du critère de l'acccès au marché en matière de libre circulation des marchandises: mythe ou réalité?' 47 *RTDE* (2011) 716–48.

[220] Spaventa (n 200), 920.   [221] *Swedish Watercraft* (n 209), para. 58.

[222] As far as selling arrangements are concerned, the Court appears to consider that they operate as an exception to the *Dassonville* formula, provided that the two requirements established in *Keck* are met. *Ker-Optika* confirms that certain selling arrangements fall outwith the scope of Art. 34 TFEU. See *Ker-Optika* (n 213), para. 51.

[223] Rosas (n 172), 445; Oliver (n 76), 129–30; Barnard (n 47), 105.   [224] Horsley (n 211), 2007.

[225] G. Stratemans, 'Market Access, The Outer Limits of Free Movement of Goods and . . . the Law?' in M. Bulterman et al. (eds), *Views of European Law from the Mountain. Liber Amicorum P. J. Slot* (Alphen: Wolters Kluwer, 2009) 93.

[226] Oliver (n 76), 129–30; Horsley (n 211), 2014; J. Snell, 'The Notion of Market Access: A Concept or Slogan' (2010) *CML Rev* 470.

Table 5.2 Categories of MEE

Categories of MEE	Principles	Test	Features of environmental MEEs
1st category	Principle of non-discrimination	Measures discriminating directly or indirectly against foreign producers. As a result, all measures governing the characteristics of a product, its use, as well as selling arrangements that require higher level requirements than those for domestic ones are caught by this category	Eg an outright ban on advertising
2nd category	Principle of mutual recognition (*Dassonville*)	Product requirements to be met by goods that have been 'lawfully manufactured and marketed' in other Member States, even if those rules are indistinctly applicable. In effect, these indistinctly applicable standards bar access to the domestic market to substitutable goods in the way they are marketed in another Member State	Eg product standards related to form, size, dimension, weight, trade description, composition, packaging, labelling and presentation of goods, safety requirements, thresholds of hazardous substances, dangerous properties
2nd category	Access of products to national markets (*Trailers*)	'Any other measure which hinders access of products originating in other Member States'	Eg prohibitions or restrictions on the use of the goods, authorization requirements, and restrictions on transport

Table 5.3 Types of environmental measure caught by Article 34 TFEU

Object	Differentiated product requirements	Selling arrangements	Restrictions on use
Illustrations regarding environmental policy	Eg product standards	*De jure* or *de facto* restrictions on where, when, and by whom hazardous substances may be sold. Eg restrictions on selling hazardous goods to qualified undertakings, advertising restrictions	Eg restriction on transport, use, etc
Point at which the measure is adopted	Upstream	Downstream	Downstream
Case law	*Cassis de Dijon*	*Keck*	*Trailers*
Test	2nd category	1st or 3rd category	3rd category
Regime	Presumption of illegality	Presumption of legality provided that the arrangements apply to all traders operating within the national territory and affect in the same manner in law and in fact the selling of domestic products and of those from other Member States	Assessment of the impact of the measure on consumers' behaviour

market must be hindered.[227] Some authors take the view that such a test is a pointless addition to the already very broad scope of Article 34.[228]

Third, it is still premature to determine the real impact of this trilogy. In several recent judgments the Court has referred to these three categories of measure[229] whereas it has ignored the new arrangement in other judgments such as the *Brenner II* case.[230] No doubt, there will continue to be wrangling over the approach adopted by the Court. On the one hand, measures relating to sales on the internet only fall within the scope of Article 34 TFEU if their effect is discriminatory, even if they have a significant effect on access to the national market; on the other hand, a measure that has no impact on the market will not fall foul of the discrimination test on the ground that it applies to the product's characteristics.

As far as environmental issues are concerned, a broad interpretation of the market access test is likely greatly to enlarge the scope of Article 34 TFEU. As a result, Member States may be deprived of their right to conduct policies that are not aimed at protecting their national market. Since the 1970s, a number of hazardous products and substances have been subject to authorization before being placed on the market, as well as to numerous restrictions regarding their use.[231] Recently, with the aim of promoting sustainable patterns of production and consumption, some Member States have developed an integrated product policy (IPP). As opposed to specific product policies, IPP addresses the whole life cycle of products, from extraction of natural resources, through design, manufacture, assembly, marketing, distribution, sale, and use, to their eventual disposal as waste.[232] In addressing the product's life cycle, public authorities aim to reduce their cumulative environmental impacts—from 'cradle to grave'. In effect, although a product can be designed to cause as little environmental impact as possible, inappropriate use and disposal are likely to cause significant environmental damage. Indeed, consumers may still use them in an environmentally unfriendly way. By way of illustration, the use of energy-saving lightbulbs brings considerable environmental benefits, but these advantages can be offset if lights are not switched off when not in use.[233] Consequently, the life-cycle approach takes into consideration the whole product system.[234] In improving the environmental performance of products throughout their life cycle, Member States are more likely to reduce access to their market to other products. As a result, they will be obliged to justify the

---

[227] See Case C-456/10 *ANETT* [2012] nyr, para. 30.   [228] Sibony (n 184), 333.
[229] *Ker-Optika* (n 213), noted by A. Rigaux (2011) 2 *Europe* 19–22; Case C-385/10 *Elenca* [2012] OJ C379/3, para. 23. See also N. de Sadeleer, 'Restrictions of the Sale of Pharmaceuticals and Medical Devices such as Contact Lenses over the Internet and the Free Movement of Goods' (2011) 19 *Eur J Health L* 1–27.
[230] Case C-28/09 *Commission v Austria* [2011] nyr. See also *Fra.bo* (n 138).
[231] With respect to restrictions on the use of chemicals already placed on the market, see REACH Regulation, Arts 67–73. See also de Sadeleer (n 212), 207–47.
[232] At a Member State level, few States, notably the Nordic countries, the Netherlands, and Austria articulated at the beginning of the new millennium comprehensive policies on products and the environment. In addition, EU institutions have begun to heed to a more comprehensive product-oriented environmental policy with a view to enhancing sustainable production and consumption.
[233] Preamble to the Communication from the Commission to the Council and the European Parliament—Integrated Product Policy—Building on Environmental Life-Cycle Thinking, COM/2003/302 final.
[234] See, eg, Commission Recommendation 2011/696/EU on the definition of nanomaterial [2011] OJ L275/38, fifth recital.

proportionality of each of these measures in accordance with Article 36 or the rule of reason.

4.3.2.5 Measures governing the use of products falling within the scope of Article 34 TFEU

In both the *Trailers* and *Swedish Watercraft* cases, the Court did not consider that national measures governing the use of products fall outside the scope of Article 34 TFEU on the ground that they can be treated on a par with selling arrangements.

The first case, involving an infringement action against Italy, concerned a general prohibition on mopeds registered in Italy from pulling a trailer, irrespective of the condition of the road surface. In sharp contrast to the second case, the prohibition was absolute. In the second case, a reference was made to the Court in the course of criminal proceedings brought by the Swedish Prosecutor's Office against two boatmen for failure to comply with a prohibition on use of personal watercraft. The challenged measure concerned a general prohibition, mitigated by a regime of exceptions, on using watercraft in Sweden outwith specially designated waterways.

In these two cases, the national measures at stake were neither product requirements to which the *Cassis de Dijon* case law would apply nor selling arrangements in line with the *Keck* jurisprudence. In addition, the regulations concerned had the effect of discouraging consumers from purchasing the vehicles, either because their use was prohibited or because it was heavily regulated. The cases had one further aspect in common: in the absence of any harmonization rules at an EU level, the Member States were entitled to set the level of protection which they considered appropriate, provided that they respected the proportionality principle.

These two cases gave the Court the opportunity to specify, for the first time, the extent to which national measures which have the effect of limiting the use of certain products should be reviewed in accordance with Article 34 TFEU. Indeed, the Court has seldom had to deal with measures regulating the use of products.[235] In her Opinion delivered on 14 December 2006 in the *Swedish Watercraft* case, Advocate General Kokott proposed, based on the need for consistency, that the *Keck* case law should be applied by analogy and, therefore, that arrangements for the use of products should not be brought within the scope of Article 34 TFEU.[236] As stated in her Opinion, the regulations governing arrangements for use and selling arrangements for products were comparable 'in terms of the nature and the intensity of their effects on trade in goods'.[237] In fact, in contrast to technical prohibitions relating to products, selling arrangements and arrangements for use in principle only produce their effects after the importation of the product. The regulation of these arrangements therefore only has an

---

[235] Case 119/78 *SA des Grandes distilleries Peureux* [1975] ECR 975; and *Toolex* (n 187).

[236] Opinion AG Kokott in *Swedish Watercraft* (n 209), paras 55 and 56. This interpretation was supported by P. Wenneraas, 'Towards an Ever Greener Union? Competences in the Field of the Environment and Beyond' (2008) 45 *CML Rev* 1654. Other legal scholars discarded that view: P. Oliver and S. Enchelmaier, 'Free Movement of Goods: Recent Developments in the Case Law' (2007) 44 *CML Rev* 678 and 679.

[237] Opinion AG Kokott in *Swedish Watercraft* (n 209), para. 52.

indirect impact on the sale of goods, insofar as consumers may be discouraged from purchasing them.[238]

In sharp contrast, in their Opinions delivered in *Commission v Italy* in 2006 and 2008, Advocates General Léger and Bot defended the opposing argument according to which arrangements for use cannot be removed from the scope of Article 34 TFEU.[239] Moreover, according to Advocate General Bot, national rules were contrary to the Treaty if they impede a product's access to the market regardless of the aim pursued by the measure in question.[240] Having been invited by the Court in the first case to present their opinions on the question of whether Article 34 TFEU could apply to selling arrangements, the positions adopted by the Member States were, at the very least, contrasting.[241]

On two occasions the Court has held that a national measure regulating the use of a product fell within the scope of Article 34 TFEU.[242] It therefore follows that the concept of an MEE within the meaning of Article 34 TFEU covers all other generally applicable measures which impede access to the market of a Member State for products originating in other Member States, where these totally ban the use of a product or have 'a considerable effect on the behaviour of the consumers'.[243] As a result, such measures cannot be reviewed in the light of the criteria laid down in *Keck*. In so doing, the Court placed greater emphasis on the effect that the measure has on access to the market than on the nature of the rules in question, which did not contain requirements relating to the characteristics of the product.[244] Whereas the case law has traditionally focused on the effects of the measure on suppliers, the impact of the measure on consumers' behaviour must henceforth be taken into consideration.[245]

We will now examine the three categories resulting from these two cases: (1) measures completely prohibiting the use of a product; (2) measures preventing users from using products for the specific and inherent purposes for which they were intended; and (3) measures greatly restricting their use (see Table 5.4).

The first category does not leave any room for discussion. In fact, where the authorities prohibit all use of a product, they indirectly prevent its commercialization. Knowing that they are not permitted to use a given product, consumers have practically

---

[238] Opinion AG Kokott in *Swedish Watercraft* (n 209), para. 53.

[239] Opinion AG Léger and AG Bot in *Trailers* (n 211), para. 136.

[240] Opinion AG Bot in *Trailers* (n 211), para. 136.

[241] Pursuant to Art. 44(4) of the Rules of Procedure, on 9 November 2006 the Third Chamber decided to refer the case back to the Court in order that it might be reassigned to a formation composed of a greater number of judges. At a later stage, the Court ordered the re-opening of the oral procedure and the holding of a hearing. In addition, the Member States other than Italy were invited to answer the question of the extent to which and the conditions under which national provisions which govern not the characteristics of goods but their use, and which apply without distinction to domestic and imported goods, are to be regarded as MEEs within the meaning of Art. 34 TFEU.

[242] *Trailers* (n 211), para. 58.

[243] *Trailers* (n 211), para. 56; *Swedish Watercraft* (n 209), paras 26 and 27.

[244] Opinion AG Bot in *Trailers* (n 211), paras 109–111. See Barnard (n 211), 290.

[245] I. Lianos, 'Shifting Narratives in the European Internal Market' (2010) *Eur Business L Rev* 733; Sibony (n 184), 733.

Table 5.4 Categories of measure governing the use of products caught by Article 34 TFEU

1st category	Prohibition of all use of a product
2nd category	Inability of users to use a product for the 'specific and inherent purposes' for which it was intended
3rd category	Measures greatly restricting the use of a product on account that they have a considerable influence on the behaviour of consumers

no interest in buying it.[246] Whether some environmental restrictions on the use of products are so restrictive as to be tantamount to a ban remains to be seen. As discussed previously, most of the bans are subject to derogations.[247] Moreover, *Swedish Watercraft* and *Sandström* involved limitations on the use of watercraft in Sweden rather than an absolute prohibition.

As regards the second category, the inability of users to use a product for the 'specific and inherent purposes' for which it was intended also amounts to an MEE on imports. Such measures are closely related to the definition of the product itself. With regard to the *Swedish Watercraft* case, the possibilities for use of the watercraft were extremely marginal at the time the questions were referred to the Court.[248] Another case in point is the prohibition by a Member State of the practice of motocross at all places and at all times. Such a measure would have had the effect of discouraging followers of the sport from purchasing that type of motorcycle. Riding on tarmacked roads on a motorcycle with the intention of riding over obstacles hardly amounts to an 'interest' and in this case, since the interest in riding a motocross bike is rather limited, the measure in question by definition prevented bikers from using their vehicles for the specific and inherent purposes for which they were intended. Accordingly, such a measure constitutes an MEE.

The third category—measures having 'a considerable influence on the behaviour of consumers'—gives rise to conflicting opinions. Indeed, if the influence is not deemed to be 'considerable', the measure at issue falls outside the ambit of Article 34 TFEU.[249] In other words, a mere impact on sales of imports is insufficient to engage the provision. Given that mere restrictions are likely to apply across the whole product market— chemicals, pesticides, genetically modified organisms (GMOs), etc—they would be a 'rather ineffective attempt at protectionism'.[250] Some authors have voiced concerns over the subjective appraisal entailed by such an approach.[251] Indeed, the nature of the criteria of 'considerable influence' on the behaviour of consumers and 'great restriction' of the use of the products are eminently fuzzy. In particular, Barnard takes the view that this threshold requirement does appear to contradict the well-established no *de*

---

[246] See, by analogy, Case C-265/06 *Commission v Portugal* [2008] ECR I-2245, para. 33, concerning the affixing of tinted film to the windows of motor vehicles.

[247] See the discussion in Chapter 4, Section 5.4.

[248] *Swedish Watercraft* (n 209), paras 25 and 28; Case C-433/05 *Sandström* [2010] ECR I-2885, para. 32.

[249] G. Davies, 'The Court's Jurisprudence on Free Movement of Goods' (2012) 2 *EJCL-REDC* 364.

[250] S. Weatherill, 'The Road to Ruin: "Restrictions on Use" and the Circular Lifecycle of Article 34 TFEU' (2012) 2 *EJCL-REDC* 227.

[251] Sibony (n 184), 338; P. Oliver, 'The Scope of Article 34 TFEU after *Trailers*' (2012) *EJCL-REDC* 313, 316.

minimis rule.[252] In any event, the *Perlata* test must apply:[253] mere or minor restrictions on use the effects of which would be 'too uncertain or too indirect' should in no event fall under the scope of Article 34 TFEU.[254] More fundamentally, one could object that sensitive regulatory choices regarding the mere use of products should be subject to judicial review on the ground that the Court of Justice would be forced to assess the necessity of these choices.[255]

Arguably, one is left in the dark as to how to interpret these criteria. Heavy restriction on use is not the same as total restriction on use. What thresholds should apply? Does a 25 per cent reduction in sales amount to a 'great restriction' on use of the product? Clearly, a case-by-case analysis is called for. That said, when faced with these measures, will national courts elevate themselves to the status of experts or will they show modesty in requiring the submission of market studies, investigations, or even opinion surveys in order to determine the impact of the disputed regulation on consumer choice? Are such investigations a viable option?

It is submitted that this appraisal is capable of calling into question a broad range of measures which seek to guarantee public safety or health or to protect workers, consumers, or the environment. In contrast to the second category, a product falling into the third category can still be used according to its specific and inherent purpose. However, given the restrictions placed on its use, consumers are likely to be discouraged from purchasing it. Indeed, several regulations concerning not the composition of products but rather their use are likely to fall into this latter category. Examples are prohibitions on SUVs from driving on roads not specifically equipped for their use, sports vehicles from exceeding speed limits of 120–30 km/h on motorways, smoking in public places, or sowing GMOs outwith a limited area. Similarly, measures preventing adolescents from using sunbeds due to the risk of skin cancer would also be likely to fall foul of the principle of the free movement of goods where those rules would have 'a considerable influence on the behaviour' of this category of consumer. Surely all these regulations are likely to 'heavily restrict the use' of these products. Admittedly, it is open to question whether the development of such case law is consistent with the numerous Treaty amendments that have modified the hierarchy of values.[256]

4.3.2.6 Limits to the material scope of Article 34 TFEU

The material scope of Article 34 TFEU does have certain limits. Legal commentators have long debated whether MEEs the effects of which are both 'too indirect and too uncertain' should be deemed to impede inter-State trade and whether they should fall within the scope of Article 34 TFEU. In a handful of cases, the Court has accepted that some restrictions may be so 'uncertain and indirect' or 'too random and indirect' in

---

[252] C. Barnard, 'What the *Keck*? Balancing the Needs of the Single Market with State Regulatory Autonomy in the EU and the US' (2012) 2 *EJCL-REDC* 214. Regarding the no *de minimis* rule, see Section 4.3.2.2.

[253] Case C-379/92 *Peralta* [1994] ECR I-3453, para. 24.

[254] Oliver (n 76), 127–8 and 131. See the discussion in Subsection 4.3.2.4.

[255] M. Fallon and D. Gerard, 'Trailing the Trailers in Search of a Typology of Barriers' (2012) 2 *EJCL-REDC* 258.

[256] See Chapters 1 and 2 and Conclusions of Part I.

their effects as not to be regarded as capable of hindering trade.[257] Related to the intensity of obstacles to inter-State trade and not to the quantity of goods, this rule of remoteness entails a subjective element.[258] As Advocate General Kokott has pointed out in *Swedish Watercraft*, the criteria of 'uncertainty and indirectness' are 'difficult to clarify and thus do not contribute to legal certainty'.[259]

For the convenience of representation, five cases have been chosen with respect to environmental issues where the Court implicitly applied a rule of remoteness.

- In *Kramer*[260] the Court was asked to rule on the compatibility of fishing conservation quotas with Articles 34 and 35 TFEU and the common market organization for fish. The Court held that the compatibility of such measures limiting fish production depended on the global system established by the basic Community rules in the sector concerned and the objective of those rules. The Court took into consideration the nature of the product in question, fish. Whilst the conservation measures restricted production in the short term, by fixing catch quotas they were precisely aimed to avoid a long-term reduction in the quantities of fish brought to market.[261] Therefore, these measures were consistent with the Treaty provisions guaranteeing the free movement of goods.

- The Court seems to have implicitly affirmed the existence of such a remoteness rule in its *Peralta* judgment on the discharge of dangerous substances at sea.[262] In this case, the captain of a ship accused of dumping harmful chemical substances at sea contrary to Italian environmental legislation had argued that the legislation was in breach of Article 34 TFEU, since it created an obstacle to the import of those substances into Italy. The Court pointed out that the purpose of the Italian legislation was not to regulate trade in goods with other Member States and that the restrictive effects such environmental measure might have on the free movement of goods were 'too uncertain and indirect' for the obligation which it laid down to be regarded as being an MEE.[263]

- By the same token, in *DIP v Bassano di Grappa* the Court took the view that urban-planning laws restricting the opening of new shops in town centres were not aiming at regulating trade in goods with other Member States and had 'too uncertain and indirect' restrictive effects to constitute MEEs.[264]

- However, in *Bluhme*, a case concerning the prohibition on importing bees into part of the Danish territory, the Court held that the Danish measure had a 'direct and immediate impact on trade' even though the number of bees was fairly limited.[265]

---

[257] Case C-96/94 *Centro Servizi Spediporto v Spedizioni Maittima del Golfo* [1995] ECR I-2883; Case C-379/92 *Peralta* [1994] ECR I-3453; Case C-134/94 *Esso Española v Comunidad Autónoma de Canarias* [1995] ECR I-4223; Case C-266/96 *Corsica Ferries v Ministero dei Trasporti* [1998] ECR I-3949, para. 31; Case C-44/98 *BASF* [1999] ECR I-6269, para. 16; and Case C-254/98 *TK-Heimdienst* [2000] ECR I-151, para. 30. See Oliver (n 76), 95–6.
[258] Oliver (n 76), 96.   [259] Opinion AG Kokott in *Swedish Watercraft* (n 209), para. 46.
[260] Cases 3, 4, & 6/76 *Kramer* [1976] ECR 1279, paras 55–9.   [261] *Kramer* (n 260), paras 56–9.
[262] *Peralta* (n 253), para. 24.   [263] *Peralta* (n 253), para. 25.
[264] Case C-140/94 *DIP v Bassano di Grappa* [1995] ECR I-3257, para. 29. However, such measures may fall under the Treaty provisions on establishment. See Joined Cases C-570/07 & C-571/07 *Blanco Pérez and Chao Gómez* [2010] ECR I-4629.
[265] *Bluhme* (n 161), para. 22.

- Last, according to Advocate General Jacobs, a brief delay to traffic on a road occasionally used for intra-Community trade would appear not to fall within the scope of Article 34 TFEU, even though 'longer interruption on a major transit route' because of an environmental demonstration 'may none the less call for a different assessment'.[266] If that reasoning were to be followed, the test of remoteness would cover the same ground as a *de minimis* rule.[267]

4.3.3 *MEEs on exports*

In contrast to Article 34 TFEU on which there is a considerable body of case law, it is only in exceptional circumstances that the Court has had the opportunity to consider the scope of Article 35 TFEU—50 cases in total. The *Groenveld* judgment is the starting point for appreciating the difference between Articles 34 and 35 TFEU.[268] The Court has held that Article 34 concerns only 'national measures which have as their specific object or effect the restriction of patterns of exports and thereby the establishment of a difference in treatment between the domestic trade of a Member State and its export trade, in such a way as to provide a particular advantage for national production or for the domestic market of the State in question'.[269] In ruling in this manner, the Court refused to extend the *Cassis* case law to restrictions on exports. Accordingly, non-discriminatory environmental measures fall beyond the scope of Article 35 and as a result do not need any specific justification when, according to the *Cassis* judgment, they are qualified as MEEs within the meaning of Article 34 TFEU. In short, Article 35's scope is more limited than that of Article 34 TFEU.

Hence, this is a striking dichotomy, the consequences of which have been discussed in detail by Mattera.[270] The following arguments have been proposed with the intention of justifying that distinction.

First, the rationales underlying Articles 34 and 35 TFEU are different. On the one hand, the Member State is inclined to protect its own domestic market and to limit imports into its territory on economic protectionist grounds. By contrast, the State seeks to favour exports. It follows that the Court must examine restrictions on exports in a less detailed manner compared to restrictions on imports.

Second, in requiring a demonstration of different treatment between national goods and those which are exported, the Court is seeking to guard itself against the risk of being submerged in litigation relating to national measures with no direct relationship to the free movement of goods.[271] If the MEE on exports were extended to all discriminatory measures, such measures would be prohibited by virtue of Article 35 TFEU, unless the Member State was able to justify their legitimacy and proportionality. Moreover, were Article 35 TFEU to apply to all measures applied without distinction,

---

[266] Opinion AG Jacobs in Case C-112/00 *Schmidberger* [2003] ECR I-5659, para. 65.
[267] Oliver (n 76), 96.
[268] Case C-15/79 *Groenveld* [1979] ECR 3409; Case 155/80 *Oebel* [1981] ECR 1993.
[269] *Oebel* (n 268), para. 15; Case 172/82 *Inter-Huiles* [1983] ECR 555, para. 12; and Case 203/96 *Dusseldorp* [1998] ECR I-4075, para. 40.
[270] M. A. Mattera, *Marché unique*, 2nd edn (Paris: Jupiter, 1992) 510–22.
[271] Oliver (n 76), 135.

various classes of goods would not be subject to either the legislation of the country of origin or that of destination.[272] This would set in motion a deregulatory trend, which would be detrimental to levels of social and environmental protection. In this respect, *Oebel* is a good case in point: although the challenged measure restricted night work, it was held to comply with Article 35 TFEU.[273]

Consider also environmental measures relating to the production of goods. Imagine the case of a permit that prohibits the use of a particular manufacturing technique because it is harmful to the environment. Although it would prevent the manufacturer from producing goods intended for export to other Member States, if the *Groenveld* doctrine were not to be followed, it would fall within the reach of Article 35 TFEU. Needless to say, such an interpretation would jeopardize pollution control of listed installations.

The waste management judgments handed down by the Court are completely in line with *Groenveld*.

- In *Inter-Huiles*, the Court reached the conclusion that the partitioning of the market for the recovery of waste oil was inconsistent with the directive on the disposal of that type of waste.[274] In addition, the Court emphasized that given the discriminatory effect of the French measures, its conclusion was reinforced by Article 35 TFEU.[275] Given that the French undertakings authorized to collect waste oil were able to purchase these residues at a low, regulated price, they benefited from an advantage as against foreign competitors. That said, the reference to the discrimination criterion appears to be ancillary.[276]

- In *Dusseldorp*, a case concerning the prohibition on exporting oil filters unless their treatment abroad is of a superior quality to that in the Netherlands, the object and effect of the Dutch export ban was to restrict exports and to confer an advantage on domestic waste installations.[277]

On the other hand, some commentators have complained that the *Groenveld* case law entailed the risk of a 'dual charge' on exporters.[278] Indeed, since it concerns rules governing manufacturing, whilst at first sight the exporter is only subject to one set of regulations, namely those of the country of origin, nothing prevents it from being subsequently subject to other provisions in the country of destination. This would result in the imposition of a dual charge.

Nonetheless, the *Groenveld* case law has been subject to some variation, at least in formal terms. It should also be added that the *Groenveld* case law has been limited to

---

[272] J. Snell and M. Andenas, 'How Far? The Internal Market and Restrictions on the Free Movement of Goods and Services' (2000) *Intl & Comp LJ* 376; A. Dawes, 'Importing and Exporting Poor Reasoning: Worrying Trends in Relation to the Case Law on the Free Movement of Goods' (2007) 8:8 *German LJ* 769.

[273] Case C-155/80 *Oebel* [1981] ECR 1993.

[274] Case 172/82 *Inter-Huiles* [1983] ECR 555, para. 11.   [275] *Inter-Huiles* (n 274), para. 12.

[276] L. Gormley, 'Free Movement of Goods and the Environment' in J. Holder (ed.), *The Impact of EC Environmental Law in the UK* (Chichester: Wiley & Sons, 1997) 291.

[277] Case 203/96 *Dusseldorp* [1998] ECR I-4075, para. 42.

[278] W.-H. Roth, 'Exports of Goods and Services within the Single Market: Reflections on the Scope of Articles 29 and 49 EC' in T. Tridimas and P. Nebbia (eds), *European Union Law for the Twenty-First Century: Rethinking the New Legal Order* (Oxford: Hart Publishing, 2006) 36–42.

goods only and has never been extended to other major freedoms such as the free movement of services.[279]

Given the specialist nature of our subject, this section will only comment on the variations in cases concerning the transit of goods with reference to environmental protection.[280] The judgment related to the prohibition imposed by Austria on the transit by trucks heavier than 7.5 tonnes along a motorway crossing an Alpine valley. According to the national authorities, the measure was justified by the obligation to comply with EU air pollution standards. Moreover, the Austrian measure concerned sought to promote combined road and rail transport across the Alps. It transpired that the measure mainly affected the transport of goods between northern Italy and southern Germany, which thus transited through Austria, at the heart of the EU. In its judgment the Court of Justice did not appear to draw any distinction between the arrangements applicable to Article 34 TFEU and those applicable to Article 35.[281] However, as noted previously, in the *Groenveld* judgment the Court expressly rejected the *Dassonville* holding with regard to limits on exports. It will also be noted that a shift in meaning occurs between the *Schmidberger* case and the Inn motorway case, since in the latter judgment the Court returns to the *Schmidberger* formula.[282] That said, the Court did not clearly state whether it would consider the prohibition on the use of the Inn motorway as discriminatory. It is therefore a matter of regret that the Court did not rule more clearly on this point.[283] Subsequently, the Court limited itself to holding that the Austrian regulation was justified by a mandatory requirement.

Following these variations, some commentators have regretted the lack of coherence in the case law on the internal market.[284] In fact, to simplify matters, the traditional restrictive definition of restrictions on exports did not stand up well to the logic of the internal market for the free movement of goods which seeks to remove barriers to free exchanges from a global perspective, regardless of their direction. Criticisms have specifically pointed to the fact that it would be more advisable to apply a uniform test for access to the market both for Article 34 as well as Article 35 TFEU. Nonetheless, we take the view that the respective function of these two Treaty provisions is quite distinct, as explained previously.

Thirty years after the *Groenveld* judgment, in *Gysbrechts*, a case concerning Belgian consumer protection law, Advocate General Trstenjak proposed a complete rethink of the approach adopted by the Court in 1979. For various reasons, which cannot be analysed here due to lack of space, the Advocate General proposed to the Court that it extend the reach of Article 35 to all measures applied without distinction.[285] The Court did not consider it necessary to discuss in detail all the arguments put forward by the

---

[279] Case C-384/93 *Alpine Investments* [1995] ECR I-1141.

[280] This issue is discussed in A. Defossez, 'L'histoire d'une divergence et d'une possible réconciliation: l'article 29 TCE' (2009) 1 *CDE* 18.

[281] Case C-320/03 *Commission v Austria* [2005] ECR I-9871.

[282] Case C-112/00 *Schmidberger* [2003] ECR I-5659, para. 56.

[283] A. Rigaux casenote under Case C-205/07 *Gysbrechts* (2009) *Europe* 29.

[284] A. Dawes, 'A Freedom Reborn? The New Yet Unclear Scope of Art. 29 EC' (2009) 34 *EL Rev* 639; M. Szydlo, 'Export Restrictions within the Structure of Free Movement of Goods. Reconsideration of an Old Paradigm' (2010) 47 *CML Rev* 735–89.

[285] Opinion AG Trstenjak in Case C-205/07 *Gysbrechts* [2008] ECR I-9947.

Table 5.5 Tests for export restrictions caught by Article 35 TFEU

Groenveld	Discrimination resulting from a formal distinction between the domestic measure and the export
Gysbrechts	*De facto* discriminatory effect of the measure on export

Advocate General who, in her long and particularly detailed Opinion, had weighed up the relevance of the various arguments involved. In any event, the Court did not wish to be as ambitious as its Advocate General. The Court made some minor changes to the imbalance between the criteria applicable to Article 34 and those applicable to Article 35 TFEU.[286] It essentially grounded its view on the *Groenveld* case law, in order to establish whether the measure concerned was indeed an MEE pursuant to Article 35 TFEU. In purely formal terms, continuity in case law is assured, and the overly audacious approach endorsed by Advocate General Trstenjak was rejected. However, the Court noted that although it was applicable without distinction to all operators, the Belgian measure as a matter of fact had a greater effect on exports, and for this reason amounted to an MEE. A reading of this paragraph may give rise to different and partially divergent interpretations.[287] We shall follow the interpretation adopted by Oliver, according to which the definition of a restriction on exports was extended beyond a test of strict discrimination.[288]

This means that there is no longer a requirement for *de jure* different treatment for exported goods in order to amount to a restriction on free movement. A *de facto* difference in treatment is sufficient in order for the restriction on exports to be prohibited under Article 35 TFEU. Table 5.5 differentiates the nature of the two tests.

Finally, the Court referred to 'mandatory requirements', since the disputed national measure related to consumer protection, and for this reason was not covered by Article 36 TFEU.[289] Therefore, nothing leads to the conclusion that the Court has now abandoned its traditional approach in order to adopt a test based on access to the market.

4.4 Territorial scope

In principle, provisions on free movement of goods apply only if the contested national measure impedes inter-State trade, with the exception of purely national situations— that is, situations that do not have a foreign element likely to link them to trade between Member States.[290] Hence, Articles 34 and 35 TFEU apply only to goods passing between Member States; those moving within a Member State are not caught by the provisions. In this connection, it should not be lost from view that some EU

---

[286] *Gysbrechts* (n 285), para. 43. See A. Defossez, 'Arrêt *Gysbrechts*: le droit de rétractation du consommateur face au droit de l'UE' (2009) *REDC* 549–59 and n 280; Oliver (n 76), 139–40; A. Rigaux, case note (2009) *Europe* 28; Dawes (n 284), 639; W.-H. Roth, case note (2010) 47 *CML Rev* 509.

[287] Defossez (n 280), 18.   [288] Oliver (n 76), 140.

[289] *Gysbrechts* (n 286), paras 45 and 47. See Section 6.2.3.

[290] Case 152/78 *Commission v France* [1980] ECR I-2299; Joined Cases 314–16/81 & 83/82 *Waterkeyn* [1982] ECR I-4337; Case 98/86 *Mathot* [1987] ECR I-809; Case 168/86 *Rousseau* [1987] ECR I-1000.

directives and regulations entailing complete harmonization restrict themselves exclusively to harmonizing transfrontier issues. By way of illustration, Regulation (EC) No. 1013/2006 on shipments of waste[291] regulates the transfrontier movement of waste between Member States but not within each Member State. This may be illustrated by another example. When fish caught by a British ship are landed in the United Kingdom, Article 34 does not apply, as the ship is assimilated to British territory for these purposes.[292]

However, the application of Article 34 TFEU cannot be excluded on the sole basis of the fact that all elements of the case are limited to the borders of one Member State.[293] As regards environmental protection, the Court certainly seems to have conceded that Articles 34 and 35 TFEU may apply to local situations, as the following cases show.

- Danish legislation prohibiting the import of bees from other Member States onto part of the Danish territory, to preserve an endemic taxon of wild bees, was found to be compatible with Article 36 TFEU, despite being classified as an MEE.[294]

- The Court also held that a Copenhagen municipal regulation for collecting and retreating building waste destined for recovery, on the basis of which certain undertakings were conferred with an exclusive right to manage waste produced in the municipality, was contrary to Article 35 TFEU inasmuch as this municipal measure constituted, in law or in fact, an obstacle to exports of waste to other Member States.[295]

- In *Sapod Audic*, the Court did not hesitate to answer a preliminary question on compatibility with Article 34 TFEU of a French measure requiring the marking of recyclable packaging, although the facts of the case were solely limited to the French territory.[296]

- Conversely, the Dutch Council of State refused to apply ex Article 28 EC to interprovincial trade on the ground that all the facts were confined within the Netherlands.[297]

5. Exceptions to Free Movement of Goods

5.1 Introductory remarks

While Articles 28, 30, and 110 TFEU prohibit CEEs to customs duties and discriminatory internal taxation, MEEs may be allowed for 'reasons' or 'justifications' of three

---

[291] Regulation (EC) No. 1013/2006 on shipments of waste [2006] OJ L190/1.

[292] Oliver (n 76), 53.

[293] Joined Cases C-1 & 176/90 *Aragonessa de Publicitat Exterior* [1991] ECR I-4151; Case C-47/90 *Delhaize* [1992] ECR I-3669; Case C-184/96 *Commission v France* [1998] ECR I-6197; and Joined Cases C-321–4/94 *Pistre* [1997] ECR I-2343, paras 44 and 45.

[294] *Bluhme* (n 161), para. 20.

[295] Case C-209/98 *Entreprenorforeningens Affalds* [2000] ECR I-3743, para. 42.

[296] Case C-159/00 *Sapod Audic* [2002] ECR I-5031, paras 72–5. See in a similar vein, Opinion AG Jacobs delivered on 17 January 2002, paras 71 and 72.

[297] Raad van State 24 December 1998 [1998] AB 153. See Temmink (n 135), 85–7.

kinds of exception. It follows that given the existence of these exceptions, the free movement of goods, even though it constitutes 'one of the fundamental principles of the Treaty', is not absolute.[298] Hence, Articles 34 and 35 TFEU do not enshrine a general freedom to trade or the right to unhindered pursuit of commercial activities.[299] Given that these provisions aim to remove restrictions on imports and exports of goods rather than to deregulate the national economy,[300] they must not be confused with Article 16 EUCFR which recognizes 'the freedom to conduct a business in accordance with Community law and national laws and practices'. This section addresses the exceptions to MEEs on imports and the following section addresses the more complex issue of the justifications of MEEs having an extra-territorial dimension.

The first of these groups of exceptions can be found in Article 36 TFEU. As will be seen, the ageing character of this provision and its ever strict interpretation do not make the work of national authorities any easier.

Created through case law following the *Cassis de Dijon* judgment, a specific ground of justification concerns environmental policy as such. Accordingly, environmental protection in its own right is deemed to be an 'overriding requirement relating to the public interest' (ie a 'mandatory requirement').

Finally, since the *Schmidberger* judgment, fundamental rights, some of which reinforce environmental protection,[301] create a new exemption in the EU system.

The first two derogations must nevertheless be interpreted narrowly.[302] As for the third, case law is still evolving and has not yet settled the matter. Moreover, in all cases the burden of proof of their relevance is borne by the Member State, not by the Commission.[303]

Last, it should be noted that nothing precludes an MEE being justified on different grounds. For instance, some of the Article 36 TFEU justifications are complementary to the environmental protection mandatory requirement. Therefore, a measure on waste management hindering trade may be justified on the basis of Article 36 TFEU with respect to health protection, as it may be justified on the basis of environmental protection as a mandatory requirement. Along the same lines, in *Swedish Watercraft* the Court held that the Swedish regulation restricting the use of such craft was justified on grounds of protection of animals, plants, and humans, as well as on environmental protection grounds.[304] With respect to measures on GMOs and animal husbandry, public morality has been regularly invoked as an aspect of the justification relating to protection of human health and the environment.[305] By the same token, MEEs may be justified by considerations relating to different mandatory requirements. By way of

---

[298] Case C-112/00 *Schmidberger* [2003] ECR I-5659, para. 78.

[299] Case C-292/92 *Hünermund* [1993] ECR I-6787.

[300] Opinion AG Poiares Maduro in Cases C-158/04 & C-159/04 *Alfa Vita* [2006] ECR I-8135, paras 37 and 41.

[301] See the discussion in Chapter 2, Section 1.   [302] Case 46/76 *Bauhuis* [1977] ECR I-5.

[303] Case 45/87 *Commission v Ireland* [1988] ECR I-4929; Case C-128/89 *Commission v Italy* [1990] ECR I-3239; Case C-13/91 *Debus* [1992] ECR I-3617; and Case C-17/93 *Van der Veldt* [1994] ECR I-3537. See also Communication from the Commission on the Single Market and the Environment, COM(99) 263.

[304] *Swedish Watercraft* (n 209), paras 31–3.

[305] Case C-1/96 *Compassion* [1998] ECR I-1251, para. 66; and Case C-165/08 *Commission v Poland* [2009] ECR I-6843, para. 55.

illustration, motor vehicle registration requirements hindering the free movement of goods may be justified by mandatory requirements such as road safety and protection of the environment.[306]

After an overview in Subsection 5.2 of the characteristics shared by these exceptions, the ways in which they apply to environmental measures are examined in more concrete detail in subsequent sections.

5.2 Convergence and difference between Article 36 TFEU justifications and mandatory requirements

5.2.1 *Convergence: pre-eminence of non-economic values over free trade*

The first two derogations share common features: MEEs will be deemed to be in conformity with Articles 34 and following of the TFEU provided that they pursue non-economic aims.[307]

Be they admitted on the basis of a mandatory requirement or on the basis of Article 36 TFEU, reasons of general interest are of a non-economic nature. Expressing general interest, they indicate a supremacy of non-commercial values over the free movement of goods. It follows that one may invoke neither Article 36 TFEU nor a mandatory requirement for economic reasons. This is confirmed by Article 114(10) TFEU, which allows Member States to adopt more stringent protection measures within the framework of derogations only for 'non-economic reasons referred to in Article 36'.

The Court has proved itself to be uncompromising with regard to national measures aiming at profitability of waste-treatment plants, refusing to apply the rule of reason to them on the ground that these measures aim to protect an economic sector.[308] By way of illustration, the Court took the view that aims of a purely economic nature underpinned Dutch restrictions on the exports of oil filters with a view to ensuring a sufficient supply of the filters for use as a fuel in Dutch waste-treatment installations.[309] However, a measure's concomitant contribution to economic objectives does not by itself exclude the application of Article 36 TFEU. For instance, in *Nertsvoedersfabriek* the Court expressed the idea that the profitability of undertakings collecting animal waste might be necessary for protecting public health.[310] Accordingly, the obligation to ensure a sufficient supply of material to domestic undertakings might ensure a public interest rather than purely economic benefits.

---

[306] Case C-314/98 *Sneller* [2000] ECR I-8633, para. 55. The competent national authorities are required to demonstrate in a concrete manner how a roadworthiness test is appropriate or how it is necessary in order to safeguard consumer protection and protection of the environment. An abstract reference to such objectives is not in itself sufficient to justify such a test. See Case C-150/11 *Commission v Belgium* [2012] OJ C355/5, para. 57.

[307] Case 7/61 *Commission v Italy* [1961] ECR 317; Case 288/83 *Commission v Ireland* [1985] ECR 1761; and Case C-324/93 *Evans Medicals* [1995] ECR I-563.

[308] Case 172/82 *Inter-Huiles* [1983] ECR I-555; Case 203/96 *Dusseldorp* [1998] ECR I-4075.

[309] *Dusseldorp* (n 308), para. 44.

[310] On the obligation to deliver poultry offal only to licensed rendering plants, see Case 118/86 *Nertsvoederfabriek* [1987] ECR 3883, para. 15. See also J. Snell, 'Economic Aims as Justification for Restrictions on Free Movement' in A. Schrauwen (ed.), *Rule of Reason* (Groeningen: Europa Law, 2005) 43.

5.2.2 *Convergence: use of exceptions is only allowed in the case of negative harmonization*

Neither Article 36 TFEU justifications nor the rule of reason can be eternally invoked. These justifications remain applicable 'as long as full harmonization of national rules has not been achieved'.[311] In other words, as long as the EU lawmaker has not pre-empted the field (exhaustive, full, or complete harmonization), that is, as long as harmonization remains incomplete, Member States may invoke either one of the reasons written in Article 36 TFEU or a mandatory requirement.[312] Thus, these exceptions should be viewed only as temporary acceptance, pending EU action, of national measures ensuring that they reveal the pre-eminence of certain other values over free trade.[313]

As far as pesticides are concerned, until the entry into force of former Directive 91/414/EEC, there were no common harmonized rules relating to the production and marketing of plant protection products. In the absence of harmonization, it was therefore 'for the Member States to decide what degree of protection of the health and life of humans they intended to assure...having regard to the fact that their freedom of action is itself restricted by the Treaty'.[314] By the same token, until the entry into force of the REACH Regulation, EC legislation did not preclude a Member State from regulating the industrial use of trichloroethylene, a chemical substance classified as a category 3 carcinogen.[315]

Furthermore, minimum harmonization may be exhaustive in nature and as a result preclude stricter national measures. A case in point is *World Farming*: although the veal calves directive laid down minimum standards, the Court held that it was exhaustive in nature and excluded the application of stricter national standards outside the national territory.[316]

Conversely, Member States may no longer rely on Article 36 TFEU or a mandatory requirement if secondary law has fully harmonized a particular field.[317] In other words, as soon as obligations contained in directives and regulations fully replace national standards, national law must be interpreted pursuant to those obligations and no

---

[311] See Case 215/87 *Schumacher* [1989] ECR 617, para. 15; Case C-369/88 *Delattre* [1991] ECR I-1487, para. 48; Case C-347/89 *Eurim-Pharm* [1991] ECR I-1747, para. 26; Case C-62/90 *Commission v Germany* [1992] ECR I-2575, para. 10; and Case C-320/93 *Ortscheit* [1994] ECR I-5243, para. 14.

[312] Total harmonization pre-empts national regulators from enacting more stringent measures whereas minimum harmonization permits Member States to maintain or to introduce more stringent standards than those prescribed by the EU lawmaker. See M. Dougan, 'Minimum Harmonization and the Internal Market' (2000) 37 *CML Rev* 855.

[313] Gormley (n 276), 289 and 'The Genesis of the Rule of Reason in the Free Movement of Goods' in A. Schrauwen (ed.), *Rule of Reason* (Groeningen: Europa Law, 2005) 24.

[314] Case 104/75 *De Peijper* [1981] ECR 613; Case 272/80 *Biologische Produkten* [1981] ECR 3277, para. 12.

[315] *Toolex* (n 187), paras 27–33.

[316] Case C-1/96 *World Farming* [1998] ECR I-1251. See Scott (n 135), 128–33; Dougan (n 312), 873.

[317] See, among others, Case 5/77 *Tedeschi* [1977] ECR 1555, para. 35; Case 148/78 *Ratti* [1979] ECR 1629, para. 36; Case 251/78 *Denkavit Futtermittel* [1979] ECR 3369, para. 14; Case 190/87 *Moormann* [1988] ECR 4689, para. 10; Case 215/87 *Schumacher* [1989] ECR 617, para. 15; Case C-369/88 *Delattre* [1991] ECR I-1487, para. 48; Case C-62/90 *Commission v Germany* [1992] ECR I-2575, para. 10; Case C-323/93 *Centre d'insémination de la Crespelle* [1994] ECR I-5077, para. 30; and Case C-320/93 *Ortscheit* [1994] ECR I-5243, para. 14. Regarding the non-exhaustive character of food additives, see Case C-121/00 *Walter Hahn* [2002] ECR I-9193.

longer with reference to Article 36 TFEU or the mandatory requirement. As a result, Member States lose the possibility of adopting standards that are more restrictive than those contained in secondary law, either by reference to a mandatory requirement or by invoking one of the justifications provided in Article 36 TFEU.[318] By way of illustration, in *Nordiska Dental* the Court stated that the Swedish prohibition on exporting dental amalgams containing mercury was incompatible with Directive 93/42 concerning medical devices—a 'new approach' directive—on the ground that that directive covered environmental considerations.[319]

However, State authorities still have room for manoeuvre when harmonization measures require more detailed rules before becoming applicable.[320]

Given that the EU lawmaker has adopted a vast body of legislation harmonizing the conditions under which goods are entitled to be placed on the market and to circulate within the EU,[321] Member States' room for manoeuvre appears to be rather limited as regards the adoption of product standards. Thus, in order to know whether the proposed national measure falls within the scope of EU secondary law, it is necessary to assess the extent to which the instruments of EU law which appear, a priori, to be relevant to the issue are harmonized. This is not an easy task. Indeed, harmonization may never be equated with uniformity.[322] For instance, it is possible that an EU directive or regulation governs only some aspects of an issue, or only certain products, or only some stages in the life cycle of those products. By way of illustration, the EU regulation which sets eco-labelling rules for products does not necessarily harmonize the rules relating to the composition of those products or requirements relating to their energy efficiency.[323]

Finally, Member States are only allowed to depart from harmonized secondary law related to the functioning of the internal market insofar as EU law expressly provides for exemptions under Article 114(4)–(10) TFEU.[324] Yet, even if the rule of secondary

---

[318] Case C-102/98 *Commission v Germany* [1998] ECR I-6871.

[319] Case C-288/08 *Nordiska Dental* [2009] ECR I-11031, para. 30, noted by L. Krämer (2010) 7:1 *JEEPL* 124–8; and Case C-26/11 *Belgische Petroleum Unie* [2013] nyr, para. 27.

[320] As regards the completeness of the annexes of the REACH Regulation, see N. de Sadeleer, 'Room for Manoeuvre of the EC and EFTA Member States in the Face of Harmonization of Chemicals' in N. de Sadeleer (ed.), *Implementing Precaution. Approaches from the Nordic Countries, the EU and USA* (London: Earthscan, 2007) 330–51. With respect to the entry into force of a directive laying down zootechnical and pedigree requirements for the marketing of pure-bred animals, see *Bluhme* (n 161), paras 10–13.

[321] The Commission takes the view that half of the trade in goods within the EU is regulated by harmonized legislation. Eg Commission, 'A single market for goods'.

[322] The nature of the EU instrument in question has a major influence on the powers devolved to the Member States. In the case of a directive, Member States must adopt proper implementation rules; they have some latitude in choosing the way they consider the most appropriate in order to reach the objectives set by the directive. Regulations and decisions, on the contrary, are directly applicable and do not require, in principle, a formal transposition at Member State level. Nevertheless, the nature of the instrument does not reveal what leeway is afforded to the Member States as regards the result to be achieved. In order to assess whether the Member State may strengthen the objective set at EU level by maintaining or adopting stricter national measures, it is necessary to look at the legal basis of the EU measure. See Chapter 4, Section 4.2. See also Temmink (n 135), 66.

[323] European Parliament and Council Regulation (EC) No. 66/2010 on the EU Ecolabel [2010] OJ L27/1.

[324] Case 5/77 *TTJ* [1977] ECR 1555; and Case 138/78 *Ratti* [1979] ECR 1609.

law enables a Member State to adopt stricter standards,[325] the national measure must still conform with Articles 34 and 35 TFEU.[326]

As illustrated by the following examples, negative and positive harmonization complement each other in that secondary law—*lex specialis*—regardless of whether it allows more protective measures, must be interpreted in conformity with TFEU provisions—*lex generalis*.[327]

- In *Walloon Waste*, the Court held that the regional ban on imports of hazardous waste was incompatible with Directive 84/361/EEC on hazardous waste that permitted solely case-by-case restrictions on imports. Turning to the movements of waste not covered by that directive, the Court held that the Walloon prohibition could be justified by a mandatory requirement.[328] The paradoxical result of that judgment was that the Belgian authorities could uphold their ban on non-hazardous waste whereas their ban on hazardous waste was found to be unjustified.

- In only providing for minimal emission standards, Directive 80/51/EEC on aircraft noise enables Member States to provide for more restrictive noise limits.[329] However, by refusing to register a Danish aeroplane in Germany on the ground that it did not respect German noise limits, more restrictive than those for which the directive provides, the German authorities had not taken into account other provisions of the TFEU, notably Article 34.[330]

- A similar problem arises regarding secondary law on waste management, which may not be interpreted in such a way that would allow Member States to restrict the principle of free movement of goods.[331] One difficulty lies in the fact that secondary EU law often provides for different rules according to the method of waste management. As a result, a Member State may implement a directive on waste management in such a way that national law is then contrary to the principle of free movement of goods.[332] In later judgments, the Court took stock of the distinction to be drawn between waste bound for disposal and waste recovered. Pursuant to the principle of recovery affirmed in *Dusseldorp*, the principle of free movement applies unconditionally to waste intended to be recovered in another Member State, whereas waste bound for disposal is goods to which restrictions apply.[333]

---

[325] Such is the case for Art. 192 TFEU regarding the environment or Art. 169 para. 5 TFEU for consumer protection; see also the exemption systems in consumer protection for which directives based on Art. 114 TFEU provide, such as Directive 94/62/EC on packaging [1994] OJ L365/10.
[326] Regarding waste management, see Case 203/96 *Dusseldorp* [1998] ECR I-4075. On nature conservation, see Case C-510/99 *Tridon* [2001] ECR I-7777, para. 53.
[327] Case C-352/93 *Phytheron International* [1997] ECR I-1729; and Case C-105/94 *Celestini* [1997] ECR I-2971 noted by E. Gippini-Fournier (1998) 35 *CML Rev* 962.
[328] *Walloon Waste* (n 137).
[329] Case C-389/96 *Aher-Waggon* [1998] ECR I-4473, para. 15.
[330] *Aher-Waggon* (n 329), para. 16.   [331] *Dusseldorp* (n 326).
[332] Case 172/82 *Inter-Huiles* [1983] ECR 555; Case 295/82 *Rhône-Alpes Huiles* [1984] ECR 575; and Case 240/83 *ADBHU* [1985] ECR 531.
[333] N. de Sadeleer and M. Wemaëre, 'Valorisation et élimination des déchets: une distinction à clarifier' (2007) 2 *RDUE* 329–66.

5.2.3 *The incomplete character of EU environmental harmonization*

The formal existence of secondary law does not preclude the application of Article 36 TFEU or of mandatory requirements. Indeed, for such a purpose, full harmonization is required. As long as this is not the case, Member States may invoke grounds contained in Article 36 TFEU or a mandatory requirement with a view to impeding the free movement of goods.[334]

In the technical fields such as those examined, ruled by directives and regulations that never fully harmonize the relevant sectors, as the following examples show, a lawyer is faced with difficult situations.

- Waste may be classified as hazardous by a Member State despite not appearing in the list contained in Directive 91/689/EEC on hazardous waste, as the latter does not create full harmonization.[335]

- Before the entry into force of the REACH Regulation, there was not full harmonization of EC legislation on chemical substances, which enabled Member States to prohibit hazardous substances on their territory.[336]

- Similarly, there is not full harmonization of national systems for the encouragement of packaging reuse, as Article 5 of Directive 94/62/EC on packaging and packaging waste allows Member States to encourage, in conformity with the TFEU, reuse systems of packaging that can be reused in an environmentally sound manner.[337]

- Given that Directive 91/414 concerning the placing of plant protection products on the market does not contain any provision which specifically governs the conditions for the granting of marketing authorization for plant protection products in the context of parallel imports,[338] a Member State is entitled, pursuant to Article 36 TFEU, to subject a farmer who imports a plant protection product as a parallel import solely for the needs of his farm to a simplified authorization procedure.[339]

- In providing for measures aimed at protecting native species of fish against invasive species, the Netherlands does not aim to protect endangered species under the scope of the Habitats Directive and may therefore invoke Article 36 TFEU.[340]

- As they do not apply to older vehicles, directives providing for anti-pollution emission standards to be respected upon registration of motor vehicles do not prohibit Member States from cancelling licence plates of foreign vehicles that do not respect emission standards, through the use of one of the derogations.[341]

---

[334] Case C-323/93 *Centre d'insémination de La Crespelle* [1994] ECR I-5077; Case C-249/92 *Commission v Italy* [1994] ECR I-4311; and Case C-3/99 *Cidrerie Ruwet* [2000] ECR I-8749.

[335] Case C-318/98 *Fornasar* [2000] ECR I-4785, para. 46.

[336] *Toolex* (n 187), paras 27–33.

[337] Case C-463/01 *Commission v Germany* (n 190), paras 37–45.

[338] Opinion AG Trstenjak in Joined Cases C-260/06 & C-261/06 *Escalier and Bonnarel* [2007] ECR I-9717, para. 8.

[339] *Escalier and Bonnarel* (n 338), paras 34 and 36.

[340] Case C-249/07 *Commission v Netherlands* [2008] ECR I-174, paras 42 and 43.

[341] Case C-524/07 *Commission v Austria* [2008] ECR I-187, paras 46 and 47.

- Given that former Directive 80/57 on the limitation of noise emissions from subsonic aircraft merely laid down minimum standards, Germany was permitted to impose stricter noise standards as regard the registration of aircraft.[342]

- Since the Wild Birds Directive aims to protect bird populations present in their natural habitat, the protective regime is not extended to wild birds bred and reared in captivity.[343] Indeed, such an extension would serve 'neither the need for the conservation of the natural environment,..., nor the objective of long-term protection and management of natural resources as an integral part of the heritage of the peoples of Europe'.[344] As a result, Member States remain competent to regulate trade in species of wild birds which have been bred and reared in captivity, provided that their measures are justified in accordance with Article 36 TFEU.

On the other hand, many provisions of the former Waste Shipment Regulation (EEC) No. 259/93, now replaced by Regulation 1013/2006, have a 'full' character,[345] even though this remains a complex issue.[346]

It may be that a national measure is only partially covered by a rule of full harmonization. In such an event, the Court of Justice will simultaneously have to examine conformity of the national measure with Article 36 TFEU or mandatory requirements, pursuant to the rule of reason, and with secondary law.

- In *Walloon Waste*, for example, Belgium was condemned for having prohibited imports of hazardous waste, which was a harmonized sector, but not those of household and building waste, which was not harmonized.[347]

- Similarly, in *Jean Harpegnies* it was unclear whether the goods in question were covered by full harmonization, which would have precluded Belgium from invoking Article 36 TFEU. The Court held that as long as they were not fully harmonized, imported pesticides could be controlled by national authorities.[348]

5.2.4 *Divergence: indistinctly applicable measures and measures applicable without distinction*

There is still a major difference between these two types of derogation from the basic rule that all obstacles to the free movement of goods shall be eliminated. Given that the

---

[342] *Aher-Waggon* (n 329), paras 15 and 16.

[343] Case C-149/94 *Didier Vergy* [1996] ECR I-299, para. 15.

[344] *Didier Vergy* (n 343), para. 13; Case 100/08 *Commission v Belgium* [2009] ECR I-140, para. 106.

[345] Case 324/99 *DaimlerChrysler* [2001] ECR I-9897, para. 33. See also references made by the ECJ in that judgment. If, despite the explicit possibility in the Regulation on transboundary movements of waste for Member States to adopt general or partial prohibitions of shipments of waste bound for disposal national authorities, the Member States choose not to adopt such measures, the principles of proximity and self-sufficiency require that such a State be prohibited from imposing barriers to free movement of waste within its territory. The ECJ has thus stressed the fact that the regulation creates full harmonization in this field (Case C-221/06 *Stadtgeneinde Frohnleiten* [2007] ECR I-9643, para. 67).

[346] Originally the stance of the ECJ regarding the full character of harmonization was unclear as regards both the Framework Directive on waste and Regulation (EEC) No. 259/93. See *Dusseldorp* (n 326), paras 35 and 36.

[347] *Walloon Waste* (n 137), para. 20.   [348] Case C-400/96 *Jean Harpegnies* [1998] ECR I-5121.

exception to the fundamental principle of the free movement of goods must be construed narrowly, mandatory requirements can only justify measures that apply without distinction to imports as well as to domestic products.[349] As long as there is no arbitrary discrimination or disguised restriction to trade, differentiated national measures may be justified on grounds contained in Article 36 TFEU, but not by mandatory requirements.[350] As a result, while the rule of reason requires that measures be applicable without distinction, Article 36 TFEU has the advantage, for national authorities, of covering environmental protection measures that are not applicable without distinction to domestic and imported goods. As a result, national authorities could be inclined to the view that their environmental measures should be justified on the basis of a jusitification listed under Article 36 TFEU rather than on the basis of a mandatory requirement. However, as will be examined later, this distinction has been called into question since the *Walloon Waste* case.[351]

5.3 Grounds of justification for environmental measures embodied in Article 36 TFEU

5.3.1 *Scope*

Article 36 TFEU allows Member States to adopt or to maintain quantitative restrictions or MEEs, inasmuch as the latter are justified by the need to preserve certain interests, exhaustively listed.[352] However, Article 36 TFEU is not necessarily the best solution for Member States.

First, while it concerns the general values Member States have traditionally protected (eg 'public morality', 'public policy', 'public security', and the protection of 'health and life of humans, animals or plants'), Article 36 TFEU does not mention a specific ground of justification as regards environmental protection.[353]

Moreover, even if environmental concerns can permeate the grounds of justification contained in Article 36 TFEU, the latter is interpreted strictly, as it allows exceptions to the principle of free movement of goods.[354] Article 36 TFEU does not allow the justification of measures not covered by Articles 34 and 35 TFEU.[355] For instance, Article 36 TFEU does not constitute an exception to the prohibition of customs duties and CEEs enshrined in Article 28 TFEU.[356]

Furthermore, the protection of such interests may certainly never lead to 'arbitrary discrimination' or to 'disguised restrictions' to trade between Member States.

---

[349] Joined Cases C-1 & 176/90 *Aragonesa* [1991] ECR I-4151, para. 13; *Walloon Waste* (n 137), para. 34. See also Toth (n 57), 393–4; Oliver (n 76), 219–20; Barnard (n 47), 115.

[350] Case 7/61 *Commission v Italy* [1961] ECR 317; Case 113/80 *Irish Souvenirs* [1981] ECR I-1625, para. 11; Case 288/83 *Commission v Ireland* [1985] ECR 1761; Case 229/83 *Leclerq* [1985] ECR 135, para. 22; and *Aragonesa* (n 349), para. 13.

[351] See Section 5.4.2.   [352] Case 46/76 *Bauhuis* [1977] ECR 5.

[353] Nor does Art. XX of the GATT.

[354] *Bauhuis* (n 352); *Leclerq* (n 350); Case 95/81 *Commission v Italy* [1982] ECR 2204; Case 113/81 *Commission v Ireland* [1981] ECR 1625; and Case 13/78 *Eggers* [1978] ECR 1935.

[355] Case 13/68 *Salgoil* [1968] ECR 661 and esp. 676; Case 153/78 *Commission v Germany* [1979] ECR 2555 and esp. 2564; and Case 34/79 *Henn and Darby* [1979] ECR 3795.

[356] See the discussion in Section 2.

Finally, as will be examined later, to prevent the abuse of rights given by Article 36 TFEU, the Court does not give Member States invoking one of these exceptions absolute discretionary power as to the level of protection of these interests. To be justified under Article 36 TFEU, a restrictive measure must be proportional to the pursued aim.[357]

5.3.2 *Grounds of justification likely to encompass environmental concerns*

5.3.2.1 Protection of health and life of humans

Many environmental protection measures aim to protect 'public health'[358] and can be justified on the basis of that objective, which is reinforced by the fact that EU environmental policy has the aim, pursuant to Articles 191(1) and 169(1) TFEU, to 'contribute to...protecting human health'. As a result, it is perfectly feasible for a measure contributing to environmental protection in general, and more specifically to the protection of human health, to fall within the scope of Article 36 TFEU. For example, at the end of their useful life tyres become waste, the accumulation of which is associated with risk to humans. In tropical areas, specific risks to human life and health include the transmission of dengue fever, yellow fever, and malaria through mosquitoes which use tyres as breeding grounds. Therefore, taking regulatory actions to minimize the adverse effects of waste tyres aims at improving public health.[359]

Given that the health and life of humans 'rank foremost among the assets and interests protected by the Treaty'[360] and that public health protection 'must take precedence over economic considerations',[361] the Court has proved to be in favour of Member State discretion whenever public health is at stake. Indeed, it is settled case law that each Member State is free to choose its own level of protection within the limits set by Article 36 TFEU. Accordingly, in the absence of EU harmonization, given that the subject matter has not been harmonized, it is for the Member States to determine the level of protection which they wish to afford to public health and the means to be employed in order to achieve it, while taking free movement of goods into account.[362]

---

[357] See Section 7.

[358] Given that the Treaties have not conferred full and absolute competence on the EU as regards health policy, such competence remains largely shared between the Union and its Member States, as attested to by Arts 6(a) and 168 TFEU.

[359] See Report of the Appellate Body in *Brazil—Measures Affecting Imports of Retreaded Tyres*, 12 June 2007, AB-2007-4.

[360] Case 215/87 *Schumacher* [1989] ECR 617, para. 17; Case C-347/89 *Eurim-Pharm* [1991] ECR I-1747, para. 26; Case C-62/90 *Commission v Germany* [1992] ECR I-2575, para. 10; Case C-320/93 *Ortscheit* [1994] ECR I-5243, para. 16; Case C-322/01 *Deutscher Apothekerverband* [2003] ECR I-14887, para. 103; *Toolex* (n 187), para. 38; Case C-141/07 *Commission v Germany* [2008] ECR I-6935, para. 46; Joined Cases C-570/07 & C-571/07 *Blanco Pérez* [2010] ECR I-4629; Joined Cases C-171/07 & C-172/07 *Apotheker-kammer* [2009] ECR I-4171, para. 19; and Case C-108/09 *Ker-Optika* [2010] ECR I-12213, para. 58.

[361] Case C-183/95 *Affish* [1997] ECR I-4315, paras 43 and 57. This judgment confirms the case law of *UK v Commission* concerning export prohibitions on beef and veal due to contamination by bovine spongiform encephalopathy (BSE). See Case C-180/96 *UK v Commission* [1996] ECR I-2265; Case T-76/96 *Pfizer* [1996] ECR II-815.

[362] Case 104/75 *De Peijper* [1976] ECR 613, para. 15; Case 272/80 *Biologische Produkten* [1981] ECR 3277; Case 174/82 *Sandoz* [1983] ECR 2445; Case C-293/94 *Brandsma* [1996] ECR I-3159; Case C-375/90

In particular, since the level may vary from one Member State to another, Member States should be allowed a measure of discretion in determining that level, 'according to particular social circumstances and to the importance attached by those States to a legitimate objective under [EU] law'.[363] Besides, the precautionary principle may play a key role in justifying health measures adopted in the face of uncertainty.[364]

Health protection, mentioned in Article 36 TFEU, has often been used to validate sanitary measures partially concerning environmental policy, such as:

- measures restricting the marketing and use of phytopharmaceutical products[365] and substances harmful to workers and to the environment;[366]

- animal waste management,[367] registration of aircraft to limit noise pollution,[368] and measures encouraging renewable energy,[369] which concern both health protection policy and environmental policy.

However, Article 36 TFEU does not permit measures on the management of natural resources, such as the creation of a deposit and recycling system for empty packaging, eco-labelling, remediation of contaminated soils when there is no health risk, or quantitative water management.[370]

5.3.2.2 Protection of health and life of animals or plants

As nature conservation is an integral part of environmental policy pursuant to Article 192 TFEU, the legal basis for EU acts for the protection of wild fauna and flora,[371] the ground of justification linked to the 'protection of health and life animals or plants' is the cornerstone of national legislation on the protection of species of wild fauna and flora. Furthermore, recognizing that animals are sentient beings, Article 31 TFEU thus requires that full regard must be paid to their welfare. These two grounds are not limited to domestic animals or crops,[372] and can thus serve to validate national

---

Commission v Greece [1993] ECR I-2055; *Blanco Pérez* (n 360); and *Apothekerkammer* (n 360), paras 18 and 19.

[363] Case C-443/02 *Schreiber* [2004] ECR I-7275, para. 48; Case C-110/05 *Commission v Italy* [2009] ECR I-519, para. 65; Case C-141/07 *Commission v Germany* [2008] ECR I-6935; Case C-219/07 *Andibel* [2008] ECR I-4475, para. 31; and *Blanco Pérez* (n 360), para. 44 and the cases cited therein.

[364] N. de Sadeleer, 'The Precautionary Principle in European Community Health and Environmental Law' in N. de Sadeleer (ed.), *Implementing Precaution. Approaches from the Nordic Countries, the EU and USA* (London: Earthscan, 2007) 18–35.

[365] Case 272/80 *Biologische produkten* [1981] ECR 3277, para. 87; Case 125/88 *Nijman* [1989] ECR 3533; Case 94/83 *Heijn* [1984] ECR 3263; Case 54/85 *Mirepoix* [1986] ECR 1067; *Schreiber* (n 363).

[366] *Toolex* (n 187).

[367] Case 118/86 *Nertsvoederfabriek Nederland* [1987] ECR 3883, para. 15.

[368] *Aher-Waggon* (n 329), paras 19–25.

[369] Case C-379/98 *PreussenElektra* [2001] ECR I-2099, para. 75.

[370] Case 302/83 *Commission v Denmark* [1988] ECR 4607, para. 9.

[371] See in particular, Council Directive 79/409/EEC on the conservation of wild birds [1979] OJ L103/1; Habitats Directive 92/43/EC. See N. de Sadeleer and C.-H. Born, *Droit international et communautaire de la biodiversité* (Paris: Dalloz, 2004) 481–568.

[372] The WTO DSB also accepts a broad interpretation of these concepts in the light of international law for nature conservation (Report of the Appellate Body in *United States—Import Prohibition of Certain Shrimp and Shrimp Products* 12 October 1998 WT/DS58/AB/R and in *United States—Import Prohibition of Certain Shrimp and Shrimp Products—Recourse to Article 21.5 of the DSU by Malaysia* 22 October 2001 WT/DS58/AB/RW).

measures for nature conservation, as illustrated by numerous judgments of the Court of Justice.

- In the *Biological Resources of the Sea* case, the Court held that measures on the conservation of fish stocks adopted by the Netherlands in effect guaranteed optimum exploitation and thus the prosperity of the fishing sector.[373] Should such measures have the effect of reducing the quantity of fish on the market, they will not necessarily be prohibited by Treaty law.

- Regarding wild birds, the Court held that Article 36 TFEU covered the conservation not only of wild bird species in Europe[374] but also parrots born and bred in captivity, even though the species occurs in the wild in a French overseas department, French Guiana in this case.[375]

- The threat of extinction of indigenous species of crayfish or of subspecies of wild bees by the introduction of invasive species was found to be justified pursuant to Article 36 TFEU.[376]

- National measures may provide for broad protection, encompassing not only species but also subspecies as well as distinct populations. In the *Bluhme* case, the Court considered that 'measures to preserve an indigenous animal population with distinct characteristics contribute to the maintenance of biodiversity by ensuring the survival of the population'.[377] The Court used this reasoning to consider that 'the establishment … of a protection area within which the keeping of bees other than Laesø brown bees is prohibited', by reason of the recessive character of the latter's genes, 'therefore constitutes an appropriate measure in relation to the aim' of biodiversity conservation. In addition, the population of bees at risk must not face an immediate danger of extinction for the exception to be justified.

- Article 36 TFEU applies also to the protection of biodiversity and fish stocks that could be endangered by imports of harmful exotic organisms.[378]

- A national regulation under which it is prohibited to trade in mammals belonging to species other than those expressly referred to in that legislation can be justified on grounds, inter alia, of the protection of the health and life of humans or animals.[379] However, the Member States must abide by the conditions laid down by the Court's jurisprudence on food additives.

- In order to justify an MEE, the Member State has to demonstrate which 'indigenous animal population whose features are distinctive' falls within the scope of the protective measure.[380]

If these grounds of justification are evidently important for nature conservation, they do not however justify measures on natural resource management or IPP measures.

---

[373] Joined Cases 3, 4, & 6/76 *Kramer* [1976] ECR 1279, para. 59.
[374] Case 169/89 *Gourmetterie Van den Burg* [1990] ECR I-2143.
[375] Case C-510/99 *Tridon* [2001] ECR I-7777.
[376] Case C-131/93 *German Crayfish* [1994] ECR I-3303; and *Bluhme* (n 161).
[377] *Bluhme* (n 161), para. 33.
[378] Case C-249/07 *Commission v Netherlands* (n 340), para. 43.   [379] *Andibel* (n 363), para. 28.
[380] Case 100/08 *Commission v Belgium* [2009] ECR I-140, para. 96.

The concept of 'the environment' is both broader and more complex than that for wildlife protection.[381]

5.4 Environmental protection as a mandatory requirement

5.4.1 *Including the environment in the* Cassis de Dijon *case law*

Taken to extremes, a broad interpretation of both the *Dassonville* and *Cassis* formulae place at risk any type of environmental measure restricting market access to products originating from other Member States. Six years after delivering its *Cassis de Dijon* judgment,[382] the Court of Justice was compelled to state, in a case on waste exports, that environmental protection was a mandatory requirement justifying restrictions to the economic freedoms of the Treaty by EU instutions.[383] The Court held in this case that environmental protection was 'one of the Community's essential objectives', and later in the *Danish Bottles* case as well as in a number of subsequent cases approved environmental measures on the basis of such a mandatory requirement.[384]

The mandatory requirement is a powerful tool to justify environmental measures that cannot be justified in the light of the grounds listed in Article 36 TFEU. However, since Article 35's scope does not cover non-discriminatory measures, the mandatory requirement enunciated in *Cassis de Dijon* was deemed to be useless in the context of restrictions on the exports of goods. Given that this case law is likely to evolve, we shall address this issue in depth in the next section.

Nothing prevents the combination of the mandatory requirement relating to environmental protection with other mandatory requirements. For instance, national legislation on the delivery of certificates of registration for new vehicles can thus be justified both by mandatory requirements on road safety and by such requirements on environmental protection.[385] By the same token, although it hinders the free movement of goods, a positive list that prohibits the keeping of animals which do not belong to the species or categories referred to in that list is deemed to pursue several legitimate objectives, namely the welfare of animals kept in captivity, the 'protection of the health and life of humans or animals', as well as 'the protection of the environment'.[386]

However, it is difficult to define the line separating Article 36 TFEU from a mandatory requirement regarding environmental protection. While national legislation on pesticides was assessed by reference to Article 36 TFEU,[387] the mandatory requirement was invoked for cases on waste management.

As many environmental measures nowadays concern resource conservation and management (recycling to produce secondary raw material, re-use of products, renewable energy, eco-labelling, . . .), in the framework of sustainable development and

---

[381] See the discussion in Chapter 1, Section 2.
[382] Case 120/78 *Rewe-Zentral* [1979] ECR 649, para. 8.
[383] Case 240/83 *ADBHU* [1985] ECR 531.
[384] See notably Case 302/86 *Commission v Denmark* [1988] ECR 4604, para. 9; *Aher-Waggon* (n 329); Case C-213/96 *Outokumpu* [1998] ECR I-1777, para. 32; Case C-176/03 *Commission v Council* [2005] ECR I-7879, para. 41; and Case C-320/03 *Commission v Austria* [2005] ECR I-9871, para. 72.
[385] Case C-314/98 *Snellers Auto's* [2000] ECR I-8633, para. 55.   [386] *Andibel* (n 363), paras 27–9.
[387] Case 272/80 *Biologishe Produkten* [1981] ECR 3277, para. 13.

without reference to health or to the protection of wild fauna and flora, the mandatory requirement continues to play an important role.

5.4.2 *The relevance of excluding environmental measures applicable with distinction from the rule of reason*

As discussed in the introduction to this section, an MEE can be justified by a mandatory requirement provided that the measure is applicable without distinction. However, as underlined by case law, environmental measures have a tendency *de facto* to discriminate products according to their origin, their nature, their environmental impact, or their disposal.[388] In this connection, a few examples will suffice.

Even if it seems to be applicable without distinction, the German deposit system for mineral-water bottles, aiming to encourage the reuse of packaging, creates additional costs for foreign producers of natural mineral water. In the German mineral-water bottles cases, the Court of Justice underlined the obligation for mineral-water producers established in another Member State to bottle the water at source, under Directive 80/777/EEC. If the bottles are manufactured from glass, their weight exceeds that of plastic bottles in non-reusable packaging, and this difference in weight then entails higher fuel consumption and increased tonnage for transport. Non-reusable packaging, on the other hand, avoids the cost of transport back to the spring, thereby significantly reducing costs incurred by foreign producers.[389]

To cite another example, imagine a prohibition by the British authorities to market a taxon of bees from the continent on their territory with the aim of protecting indigenous taxa. It would be allowed under Article 36 TFEU, as it is not an arbitrary discrimination. The opposite can be said for a prohibition on discharging non-hazardous waste coming from abroad, which could be justified merely by reference to a mandatory requirement and not to Article 36 TFEU. Indeed, although this measure aims at preserving the capacity of national landfill sites, to avoid the dumping of waste anywhere, it is clearly discriminatory. It will therefore, in principle, not be allowed on the basis of the rule of reason. By the same token, in regulating motorway traffic by banning some categories of lorries, municipalities are likely to affect more considerably road hauliers from other Member States than domestic road hauliers on account of the exemptions granted for transports of goods having their origin and destination in the regulated area.

Maintaining such a distinction is controversial at best. Since the *Walloon Waste* case, the line between measures applicable without distinction, falling within the scope of the rule of reason, and discriminatory measures, to which Article 36 TFEU may apply, is not entirely clear, in particular regarding the eight cases we shall briefly examine.

---

[388] Opinion AG Jacobs in *PreussenElektra* (n 369), para. 233.

[389] *Radlberger and Spitz* (n 195); Case C-463/01 *Commission v Germany* [2004] ECR I-11705, para. 61, noted by N. Bringmann (2003–04) 4 *RAE-LEA* 694–704. See also Opinion AG Ruiz-Jarabo Colomer in Case C-463/01 *Commission v Germany*, para. 50. See C. True, 'The German Drinks Can Deposit: Complete Harmonization or a Trade Barrier Justified by Environmental Protection?' (2005) 2 *JEEPL* 142–50.

- In *Danish Bottles*, in spite of Advocate General Sir Gordon Slynn's underlining of the *de facto* applicability of the distinction of the contested legislation, the ECJ only mentioned such a discriminatory character to prove that the national approval system in question was a barrier to EU trade that was disproportionate in the light of its environmental aim.[390]

- In *Walloon Waste*, although the Court reaffirmed that the mandatory requirement was applicable only to equally applicable measures,[391] it proceeded to eschew the application of the test. The Court emphasized that in assessing whether the barrier in question was discriminatory, account had to be taken of 'the particular nature of waste',[392] in the light of the principle that environmental damage should be remedied at source and of the principles of self-sufficiency and proximity. Pursuant to these principles, it was for each region, commune, or local authority 'to take appropriate steps to ensure that its own waste [is] collected, treated and disposed of'. Accordingly, such waste had to be disposed of as close as possible to its source.[393] Against this background, the Court concluded that in view of the differences between waste produced locally and waste produced elsewhere, the ban on all waste imports into Wallonia was non-discriminatory in nature.[394]

- In *Dusseldorp*, the Court did not resolve the question of whether a discriminatory restriction on exports could be justified by mandatory requirements relating to protection of the environment.[395]

- In *Aher-Waggon*, which concerned German legislation requiring compliance with noise limitation standards for aircraft registration on German territory, the contested legislation directly discriminated against imported aircraft, in that aircraft previously registered in other Member States could not be registered in Germany, while similar aircraft previously registered in Germany retained their registration. Nevertheless, the Court held that such a barrier could be justified by requirements of public health and environmental protection, without examining whether the challenged measure was distinctly or indistinctly applicable.[396]

- In *PreussenElektra*, despite calls by Advocate General Jacobs for greater legal certainty, the ECJ did not clearly state whether Member States could justify discriminatory measures by environmental protection. The Court held that the obligation to purchase electricity from renewable energy sources was 'useful for protecting the environment in so far as it contributes to the reduction in emissions of greenhouse gases', noting that this measure 'is also designed to protect the health and life of humans, animals and plants'.[397] This was said to justify the

---

[390] Case 302/88 *Commission v Denmark* [1988] ECR 46. See the contrary Opinion AG Slynn [1988] ECR I-4622 and 4623.

[391] *Walloon Waste* (n 137), para. 34.   [392] *Walloon Waste* (n 137), para. 34.

[393] *Walloon Waste* (n 137), para. 34.   [394] This reasoning has been criticized by a number of authors. See L. Hancher and H. Sevenster, case note (1993) 30 *CML Rev* 351; Geradin (n 135), 19–20.

[395] Case 203/96 *Düsseldorp* [1998] ECR I-4075, paras 44 and 49.

[396] *Aher-Waggon* (n 329), para. 19.

[397] *PreussenElektra* (n 369), paras 73 and 75. Does it mirror a shifting of the place of environmental protection from a mandatory requirement to an EU policy in its own right? Eg L. Gormley, 'The Genesis of the Rule of Reason in the Free Movement of Goods' in A. Schrauwen (ed.), *Rule of Reason* (Groeningen: Europa Law, 2005) 32.

discriminatory rule obliging electricity suppliers to purchase all electricity produced from renewable energy sources from producers of renewable energy within
the respective supply area.

- A judgment of 14 December 2004 on the compatibility of a mineral-water deposit
  system in Germany is also unclear on this issue. While the German legislation
  seemed to be *de facto* applicable with distinction, inasmuch as its application
  created additional costs for foreign producers, the ECJ held that this system was
  suitable for the purpose of attaining the desired objective, reducing the amount of
  waste to be disposed of.[398]

- If, according to the Commission, a measure prohibiting traffic of heavy goods vehicles
  on a section of a motorway in Austria primarily threatened foreign transport
  companies and was therefore not applicable without distinction, the Court did
  not see fit to examine the question, considering that the measure could be justified
  by mandatory requirements insofar as it was sufficiently proportionate having
  regard to the legitimate aim pursued, namely protection of the environment.[399]

- On the validity of a system prohibiting the registration of second-hand motor
  vehicles previously registered in other Member States, the Court considered that
  there was no need to examine arguments on health protection separately from
  those on environmental protection even if domestic and foreign cars were treated
  differently.[400] The Court considered such a system suitable for the purpose of
  attaining the aim of pollution reduction.

- Finally, as regards the justification of regulations on the use of watercraft in
  Sweden, the Court reached the conclusion that the measure under review was
  justified by the objective of environmental protection as well as the protection of
  health and life of humans, animals, and plants. Although the Court considered
  that the two justifications were closely related, it focused its attention on the
  environmental justification.[401] The restrictions on use at issue were justified
  irrespective of the fact that they were likely to be distinctly applicable.

Despite their lack of shared characteristics, these judgments indicate that the Court
refuses to resolve the duality between mandatory requirements and the grounds of
justification mentioned in Article 36 TFEU. Many authors[402] and some Advocates

---

[398] The ECJ held that contested provisions of German legislation 'do not affect the marketing of drinks
produced in Germany and that of drinks from other Member States in the same manner' (Case C-463/01
Commission v Germany [2004] ECR I-11705, para. 69; and *Radlberger and Spitz* (n 195), para. 63).
[399] Case C-320/03 *Commission v Austria* [2005] ECR I-9871, paras 84 and 85.
[400] Case C-524/07 *Commission v Austria* [2008] ECR I-187, para. 56.
[401] *Swedish Watercraft* (n 209).
[402] P. Oliver, 'Some Further Reflections on the Scope of Articles 28–30 (ex-Articles 30–36 CE)' (1999)
CML Rev 783, 804–6; Oliver (n 76), 220; Temmink (n 135), 90–2; Jans and Vedder (n 80), 249; S. de Vries,
Tensions within the Internal Market (Groeningen: Europa Law, 2006) 62; Rosas (n 172), 445; de Sadeleer
(n 212), 391; C. Timmermans, 'Creative Homogeneity' in *Liber Amicorum in Honour of Sven Borberg*
(Brussels: Bruylant, 2006) 475. Moreover, the Court of Justice invoked mandatory requirements in cases
relating to the protection of consumers where one could, at the very least, say that there was uncertainty
regarding the 'applicable without distinction' character of a national measure (see, eg, Cases C-34–6/95 *De
Agostini* [1997] ECR I-3843, paras 44 and 45; Case C-120/95 *Decker* [1998] ECR I-1831, paras 36 and 39).

General[403] consider that measures applicable without distinction for environmental protection should be justifiable on the basis of a mandatory requirement. Such a development would be welcome, as it is difficult to understand why similar grounds such as 'plant protection' should be treated any more favourably than environmental protection.

5.5 Fundamental rights and national constitutional values

The importance of Articles 2, 6, 8, and 10 ECHR, and of Article 37 EUCHR, on environmental protection was underlined in Part I. As they apply both to the EU and to Member States, fundamental rights are a legitimate interest justifying, in principle, restrictions to economic rights for which primary EU law provides. A court must therefore balance the interests in question and establish, with regard to all circumstances of the case, whether such a balance between economic rights and fundamental rights has been respected.

It was in a case concerning noise pollution that the Court of Justice first unveiled a new derogation, in a judgment on the freedom of environment campaigners to mount a 30-hour blockade of trans-alpine transport through a tunnel in a protest that the authorities had tacitly permitted to go ahead. The Court held that although the protest was an MEE and was thus prohibited by Article 34 TFEU, it could be justified by a fundamental right stemming from both Article 10 ECHR and the Austrian constitution.[404] The fact that the national authorities had not prohibited such a protest, which hindered free movement of trade, was thus found not to be contrary to Articles 34 and 35 TFEU when combined with Article 4(3) TEU (ex Art. 10 EC). Given that the fundamental right at issue was to demonstrate against nuisance caused by the transit of trucks, the demonstrators' actions were not protectionist in intent.[405] Taking into account the fact that the protest in *Schmidberger* was authorized, it was perhaps deemed to be more acceptable that the French farmers' riots. Whether demonstrators' motives have to be taken into account in order to assess the justification remains to be seen.

Inasmuch as trade restrictions usually stem more from regulations than from the desire of citizen groups or NGOs to oppose the marketing of a product deemed hazardous in the name of free speech and the freedom to demonstrate, it is likely that this third derogation will not often be invoked. That said, one might expect in the future an increase in citizens' actions—boycotts, destruction of GM crops, destruction of goods, etc—hindering trade.[406] As a result, the *Schmidberger* case law could be further refined.

---

[403] Opinion AG Jacobs in *PreussenElektra* (n 369), paras 232 and 233; Opinion AG Geelhoed in Case C-320/03 *Commission v Austria* (n 399), para. 107; Opinion AG Trstenjak in Case C-28/09 *Commission v Austria* (n 230), para. 89.

[404] Case C-112/02 *Schmidberger* [2003] ECR I-5659, para. 74, noted by C. Brown (2003) 40 *CML Rev* 1499 and R. Agerbeek (2003) *EL Rev* 255. While Austria argued that the protest was justified by a mandatory requirement in the general interest concerning the environment, the ECJ rectified the claim stating that the pursued aim was the protection of free speech.

[405] Opinion AG Jacobs in *Schmidberger* (n 404), para. 96. Compare with Case C-265/95 *Commission v France* [2008] ECR I-6959. See also Oliver (n 76), 245.

[406] As regards animal welfare, during the 1990s animal groups opposed the export of calves from the UK on the ground that Directive 91/629/EEC laying down minimal standards for the protection of the calves

Table 5.6 Conditions to be fulfilled to admit measures hindering inter-State trade

No complete harmonization at EU level	Secondary legislation entailing complete harmonization precludes Member States from justifying their measures under Article 36 TFEU or a mandatory requirement
Legitimate objective of public interest	The measure must pursue a legitimate objective of public interest. Given that the environment has been recognized as 'a major objective in EU law' by the Court of Justice, Member States can invoke a mandatory requirement
Non-economic nature of the measures	Expressing general interest, Member States can invoke neither Article 36 TFEU nor a mandatory requirement for economic reasons
Respect for the principle of non-discrimination	In order to be justified by a mandatory requirement, the measure must not draw distinctions on the basis of the nationality of products or producers. On the other hand, nature protection and health-related measures can apply with distinction to domestic and foreign products
Necessity and proportionality	The measure must have a causal link to the objective pursued and be appropriate for achieving it

It should also be mentioned that the Court went further in its *Omega* judgment.[407] The case did not concern a right requiring Member States not to act—freedom of expression, even if this impedes economic freedom—but the obligation for States to intervene to ensure human dignity, which could be compromised by the actions of third parties. Similar reasoning could be used for fundamental rights for environmental protection, enshrined in many national constitutions, which set the framework for State intervention. In applying the rationale of the *Omega* judgment, one finds that the protection of such rights is 'a legitimate interest which, in principle, justifies a restriction of the obligations imposed by Community law'.[408] Moreover, one should assess the requirement of enforcing constitutional law in the light of the importance given to the right by that constitution. Member States whose constitution specifically values environmental protection could more easily follow such logic than others. It is not necessary for this conception to be 'shared by all Member States'.[409]

Table 5.6 summarizes the conditions to be fulfilled to admit MEEs.

6. Extra-Territorial Dimension of the Exceptions to the Free Movement of Goods

6.1 Extra-territorial dimension of environmental policy: current situation

As water, air, fauna, and flora are *res communes*, things shared by the entire world, environmental protection policy does not necessarily limit itself to the sole territory of

---

did not sufficiently regulate the transport of these animals over long distances. See S. Elworthy, 'Crated Calves and Crazy Cows: Live Animals and Free Movement of Goods' in Holder (n 276), 304–11.

[407] Case C-36/02 *Omega* [2004] ECR I-9609. It should be noted that the preliminary questions concerned infringements of free movement of both goods and services. Although the ECJ did not answer questions relating to the infringement of Art. 34 TFEU, the case is of great importance for free movement of goods. See, on the question of the constitutional right to dignity and its nature, T. Ackerman (2005) 42 *CML Rev* 110–15.

[408] *Omega* (n 407), para. 35.   [409] *Omega* (n 407), para. 37.

a Member State or to that of the EU. As a result, many environmental measures have an extra-territorial dimension. That said, care should be taken in distinguishing between different types of environmental measure having an extra-territorial dimension.

First, a Member State's measure may prevent the impact on its territory of pollution and nuisance created by an undertaking or an activity located in another Member State. Hence, the prohibition on importing goods from another Member State is justified by the environmental threat of means of production in the State of origin.

Second, other measures may be taken with the aim of protecting the environment at a global level: protection of the ozone layer, fight against climate change, restrictions on trade in endangered species, etc. The object of such measures is to protect the global commons. As stated earlier, the territorial scope of rules adopted on the basis of Article 192 TFEU is not limited to Member States' territories, as the objectives of environmental policy cover among others, pursuant to Article 191(1) TFEU, worldwide environmental problems.[410] Furthermore, the international duties of the EU can force it to adopt rules with an extra-territorial scope. To protect themselves from this 'green imperialism', several developing States consider these measures to be an unacceptable interference in their domestic affairs.

Third, nothing prohibits the EU from opposing exports of hazardous products to third States, notably third world States,[411] or imports of products—endangered species, scarce resources—on the ground that their consumption threatens their existence in the State of origin. For instance, the CITES regulation prohibits imports of species of wild fauna and flora that would be threatened with extinction if they continue to be traded. The import prohibition on ivory in Europe aims to ensure the survival of wild elephants on the African and Asian continents not to satisfy European consumers' needs.[412]

Fourth, the EU or a Member State could look at the ways in which the product has been manufactured, irrespective of its intrinsic qualities, which could make it harmful to the environment on consumption or use. Control by importing States of these non-product-related process and production methods refers to the conditions under which products are made. Control of these methods is likely to encompass working conditions, fair trade, environmental protection, ethical conduct, and natural resource consumption. By way of illustration, the prohibition on importing pelts unless the country of origin has itself established a regime meeting humane trapping standards, seeks to balance trade and animal welfare concerns.[413] Although they do not impinge on the final product, they are likely to alter the environment at an earlier stage or to affect workers' health.

---

[410] See Chapter 1, Section 6.2 and Chapter 4, Section 2.5.

[411] Regulation (EC) No. 1013/2006 on shipments of waste ([2006] OJ L190/1) prohibit waste exports to non-OECD countries to protect both the environment and human health in these countries. See also European Parliament and Council Regulation (EC) No. 689/2008 concerning the export and import of dangerous chemicals [2008] OJ L204/1.

[412] Council Regulation (EC) No. 338/97 on the protection of species of wild fauna and flora by regulating trade therein [1997] OJ L51/3.

[413] Council Decision 98/142/EC concerning the conclusion of an Agreement on international humane trapping standards between the European Community, Canada and the Russian Federation and of an Agreed Minute between Canada and the European Community concerning the signing of the said Agreement [1998] OJ L42/40. See further M. Bouwman, P. Davies, and C. Redgwell, *Lyster's International Wildlife Law*, 2nd edn (Cambridge: CUP, 2010) 687.

This can be illustrated by the following example. Imagine a regulation restricting the marketing of vegetables to organic products, the production of which precludes the use of pesticides and other chemicals. In so doing, the regulation focuses on the source of the pollution rather than the nutritional properties of the organic products. As a result, non-organic products would be restricted even though they do not contain any pesticides. In fact, the environmental benefits—or, seen through a different lens, the costs—of such a regulatory approach are not localized in the importing State but in the State of manufacture.[414]

Another example can be drawn from Directive 2009/28/EC on the promotion of the use of energy from renewable sources.[415] Biofuel production is likely to increase land encroachment causing rainforests and peatlands to be ploughed up to meet the increased demand for biofuels. With the aim of warding off these ecological threats, the directive sets out sustainability criteria in order to bear the impact of 'indirect land use change' (ILUC).[416] In so doing, the EU lawmaker has endorsed an ecosystemic conservation approach outside the EU.

Other examples relate to furniture manufactured from wood managed according to sustainable specifications[417] or fish harvested according to special harvesting methods, such as the type of equipment used or the health of the fish stock with a view to ensuring that 'stock is not overfished'.[418]

Where Member States limit, in their inter-State trade relations, imports and exports from other Member States on the basis of extra-territorial considerations, three hypotheses must be distinguished:

(1) The prohibition on importing goods from another Member State is justified by the environmental threat of means of production in the State of origin.

(2) A Member State prohibits exports of certain products insofar as it suspects their use in a manner which could damage the environment of third States.

(3) The field is covered by full harmonization.

6.2 Restrictions on imports justified by extra-territorial considerations

A Member State may wish to preserve certain natural resources by limiting its imports of goods from third States. These are measures having equivalent effect to import restrictions. Where their object is to protect interests that could be regarded, by their nature, as common to all Member States, can they nonetheless be justified? To date, this question has been examined in only a handful of cases.

---

[414] R. Bonsi, A. L. Hammett, and B. Smith, 'Eco-Labels and International Trade: Problems and Solutions' (2008) 42:3 *JWT* 416.

[415] Directive 2009/28/EC [2009] OJ L140/16.

[416] Biofuels and bioliquids taken into account for the purposes referred to in points (a), (b), and (c) of para. 1 must not be made from raw material obtained from land with a high biodiversity value.

[417] In 1992, the Austrian authorities considered enacting a regulation requiring the labelling of all timber and timber products originating from tropical rainforests. Amid controversy from the trade realm, the proposal was later shelved. See J. Heissenbuttel et al., 'Forest Certification' (1995) 4 *Journal of Forestry* 6–10.

[418] See UN Food and Agriculture Organization (FAO), *Guidelines for the Ecolabelling of Fish and Fishery Products from Marine Capture Fisheries* (Rome: FAO, 2009) 9.

The *Gourmetterie van den Burg* case concerned the validity of a prohibition on marketing a particular species of bird in the Netherlands (the Scottish red grouse: *Lagopus lagopus scotius*), legally hunted on the territory of another Member State (the United Kingdom). As the name conveys, the species is not found in the wild in the Netherlands. The Court had to assess whether the Dutch authorities could prohibit the sale of the species in the Netherlands. As far as Article 36 TFEU is concerned, the Court took the view that the Bird Protection Directive exhaustively regulates the Member States' powers as regards the marketing of game birds. However, Article 14 of the directive expressly authorized the Member States to enact more stringent measures than those provided under the directive. Consequently, the Court had to determine the scope of the room for manoeuvre conferred by Article 14 on the Member States. Although he was contending with the proportionality of the prohibition at issue, Advocate General van Gerven concluded that, in view of the transfrontier nature of the protection of birds expressly recognized both by international and EU law, a 'Member State can rely on the concern for animal life in another Member State to justify a restriction on the free movement of goods'.[419] Against this background, the Court stressed that the directive granted specific protection to migratory and endangered bird species. Accordingly, the Member States were authorized, pursuant to Article 14, to introduce stricter measures to protect that species 'even more effectively' whereas they were precluded from doing so with regard to other bird species.[420] It follows that extra-territorial conservation measures are confined either to migratory species of birds or to endangered birds. This reasoning sparked controversy on account that the Birds Directive provides for a general system of protection for all wild birds.[421]

Along the same lines, in *PreussenElektra* the Court admitted the justification put forward by the German authorities. Promoting renewable sources of electricity was consistent with a mandatory requirement on the grounds that the German MEE focusing on climate change could be regarded as a measure addressing not strictly the national interest but interests common to all Member States.[422]

One can deduce from these judgments that national measures on environmental protection may, under certain circumstances, have extra-territorial effects. To some extent, Article 36 TFEU could justify a national prohibitory measure, if it complies with the room for manoeuvre left by the EU lawmaker to the Member States.

6.3 Restrictions on exports justified by extra-territorial considerations

6.3.1 *States*

At the outset it should be stressed that Member States would appear to have no interest in restricting the exports of goods produced on their territory.[423] As a result, in a

---

[419] Opinion AG van Gerven in Case 169/89 *Gourmetterie Van den Burg* [1990] ECR I-2143.
[420] *Gourmetterie Van den Burg* (n 419), para. 12.
[421] See L. Krämer, *European Environmental Law. Casebook* (The Hague: Kluwer, 1993) 152–9; Scott (n 135), 132.
[422] *PreussenElektra* (n 369), paras 73–4.   [423] See the discussion in Section 4.3.3.

competitive market Article 35 TFEU has given rise to less case law than Article 34 TFEU, with the exception of waste management.

However, legislation based on environmental protection may in certain cases aim to protect a Member State's industry or to preserve rare natural resources,[424] through limiting the export of sensitive goods such as waste or hazardous chemicals. The reason is simple: pursuant to the principles of self-sufficiency and proximity, found both in international and EU law, Member States may wish to oppose the export of their waste, either because it would be discharged in appalling conditions elsewhere—Southern Italian cases caused quite a stir in this regard[425]—or to cover the costs of technologically advanced domestic waste-treatment installations. Indeed, it is tempting for domestic undertakings to avoid costs incurred by the disposal of waste in domestic waste-disposal facilities by exporting them to other Member States. In restricting waste exports, the national regulator aims at protecting the domestic market against foreign competitors. Also, the export of used goods (eg used cars, WEEE) and their subsequent unsuitable waste treatment (eg land-filling, dumping, etc) in the receiving countries can contribute to a considerable loss of resources.[426]

As discussed previously, such environmental measures can be considered to be an MEE within the meaning of Article 35 TFEU, as long as they create a difference of treatment based on the nationality of economic operators.[427]

6.3.2 *Justification of export restrictions caught by Article 35 TFEU*

When examining a French system for the collection and disposal of waste oils, seemingly valid with regard to secondary law, the Court held that it was not valid with reference to Article 35 TFEU.[428] The contested system, based on the approval of waste collectors and creating zones of exclusive collection and disposal, effectively forced waste oil holders and collectors to deliver them to approved French waste-disposal undertakings and thus prohibited waste oil exports to other Member States, where they could be incinerated at lower cost. To elude the prohibition contained in Article 35 TFEU, the approval system would have had to apply to all economic operators treating waste oils, regardless of the location of the installation.

One could initially ask whether such export restrictions can be justified by reference to Article 36 TFEU or to a mandatory requirement. According to the *Groenveld* doctrine,[429] as measures falling within the scope of Article 35 TFEU are discriminatory,

---

[424] China has set quotas to restrict its rare-earth exports that are essential for a range of sensitive technologies, including wind turbines and smartphones. China claims that the restrictions are designed to protect dwindling natural resources and the environment. Such export restraints have been challenged before the WTO. See *China—Measures Related to the Exportation of Various Raw Materials* 30 January 2012 WT/DS394/AB/R, WT/DS395/AB/R, and WT/DS398/AB/R.

[425] Case C-297/08 *Commission v Italy* [2010] ECR I-1749, paras 86, 99, and 103. See also *Di Sarno v Italy*, 10 January 2012.

[426] EEA, *The European Environment 2010. State and Outlook* (Copenhagen: EEA, 2010) 75.

[427] See the discussion in Section 4.3.3.

[428] Case 172/82 *Inter-Huiles* [1983] ECR 555, (1983) 3 CMLR 485; Case 295/82 *Rhône-Alpes Huiles* [1984] ECR 575; and Case 240/83 *ADBHU* [1985] ECR 531, paras 14 and 15. See also Case C-37/92 *Vanacker* [1993] ECR I-4947.

[429] Case 15/79 *Groenveld* [1979] ECR 3409; Case 155/80 *Oebel* [1981] ECR 1993.

the rule of reason, concerning only measures applicable without distinction, is of little help.[430] It follows that restrictions on non-hazardous waste can never be justified by a mandatory requirement since such measures are discriminatory in nature. Nor can they be justified by virtue of Article 36 TFEU on the ground that there is no health risk. However, 30 years later in *Gysbrechts*, the Court took the view that the Belgian measure could be justified by a mandatory requirement, since the disputed national measure related to consumer protection.[431]

Second, one could also ask whether Member States may justify their export restrictions not to protect environmental interests found in the State in question, but those of another Member State. To date, the Court has never clearly answered the question, perhaps for fear of opening Pandora's box.[432] Moreover, most authors have stated that the case law on this matter is all but clear.[433]

In different judgments on the environment, the ECJ was unwilling to give extraterritorial effect to Article 36 TFEU.

- *Inter-Huiles* is a case in point. In France, the obligation placed on oil producers to use exclusively the services of domestic licensed operators for the recycling of their waste oil implicitly prohibited the export of these products. The Court refuted environmental arguments by the French Government supporting the prohibition to export French waste oils abroad, on the ground that 'the environment is protected just as effectively when the oils are sold to an authorised disposal or regenerating undertaking of another Member State as when they are disposed of in the Member State of origin'.[434] In other words, as soon as the environment is protected in a similar manner in all Member States through the application of a directive, national authorities may no longer adopt protective measures that are more restrictive with the aim of protecting the environment of a third State. One might conversely deduce that in the absence of harmonization, a Member State may take into account the consequences of waste disposal abroad when adopting legislation on the movement of waste.

- In *Nertsvoerderfabriek*, on a Dutch implicit prohibition on exporting poultry offal, the Court allowed the possibility of invoking Article 36 TFEU, but only when necessary for health protection, at the moment of the collection and transport of

---

[430] Kapteyn and Verloren Van Themaat (n 91), 628.

[431] Case C-205/07 *Gysbrechts* [2008] ECR I-9947, paras 45 and 47.

[432] On the other hand, certain Advocates General have adopted a more definite stance. AG Trabucchi in his Opinion delivered in the *Dassonville* Case and AG Léger in his Opinions in Case C-5/94 *Lomas* [1996] ECR I-2553, paras 33–9 and in Case C-1/96 *Compassion in World Farming* [1998] ECR I-1251, para. 56 considered that Art. 36 TFEU may only be invoked for the protection of national interests.

[433] Kapteyn and Verloren Van Themaat (n 91), 658; Wiers (n 135), 65; Vial (n 135), 227–8; Jans and Vedder (n 80), 239, Oliver (n 76), 236–7.

[434] *Inter-Huiles* (n 428), para. 14. One might wonder whether the Court should have answered the French Government's arguments. In the present case, Art. 36 TFEU could not be invoked as the field was fully harmonized (Opinion AG Rozes, 571). The AG had foreseen the possibility of using exemptions stemming from the rule of reason but refuted the argument as the French legislation in question was not applicable without distinction to both French and foreign goods (Opinion of AG Rozes, 577).

waste on domestic territory.[435] The prohibition on exporting is therefore linked to national health concerns.

- In *Dusseldorp*, a case concerning the prohibition on exporting oil filters unless their treatment abroad is of superior quality to that in the Netherlands, the Court held that a Member State may only oppose transfer insofar as it respects the principle of proportionality.[436] In the case in question, processing techniques in Germany for the recovery of oil filters were similar to those of the Dutch undertaking responsible for the waste treatment.[437] One may wonder whether the ECJ would have adopted the same view if the treatment abroad had been of inferior quality to the national treatment.

In the light of this case law, the Court seems to open, to some extent, the possibility for an extra-territorial scope of Article 36 TFEU for human health protection in another Member State. As environmental problems gain every day a greater transnational dimension, it is submitted that extension of the case law to environmental concerns that could be regarded as common to all Member States is truly necessary, particularly where common interests—biodiversity, climate change, ozone, fisheries, etc—are at stake.[438]

6.4 Full harmonization

As soon as the EU lawmaker has provided for full harmonization, such export restrictions can be enacted exclusively within the framework of EU legislation.[439]

On the subject of waste exports, the difficulty lies in the fact that national legislation on waste treatment varies greatly between Member States. It is worth recalling that 'the fact that one Member State imposes less strict rules than another Member State does not necessarily mean that the latter's rules are disproportionate and hence incompatible with Community law'.[440] Since the entry into force of Waste Shipment Regulation (EEC) No. 259/93, replaced in 2006 by Regulation 1013/2006, Member States may no longer object to such shipments unless they do so on grounds for which the Regulation provides.

- In *DaimlerChrysler* the Court held that when a Member State authorizes exports of waste for disposal, it may only require that landfill sites and incinerators abroad meet the requirements of the State of dispatch.[441] In other words, whenever there is full harmonization, which was the case of the former Regulation (EEC)

---

[435] Case 118/86 *Nertsvoerderfabriek* [1987] ECR 3883, para. 16.
[436] Case C-203/96 *Dusseldorp* [1998] ECR I-4075, para. 33, noted by N. Notaro (1999) 6 *CML Rev* 1317, and N. de Sadeleer and P. Nihoul (1999) 1 *Amén-Env* 23–7. See G. Van Calster, 'Court Criticises Restrictions on Free Movement of Waste' (1999) 2 *EL Rev* 178.
[437] *Dusseldorp* (n 436), para. 47.   [438] Jans and Vedder (n 80), 294.
[439] *Compassion in World Farming* (n 432), paras 57–60. In this case, even though Directive 91/629/EEC empowered Member States to enact more stringent measures, the Court expressed the view that such measures were permitted only if they related to calves within the jurisdiction of the Member State and if they were in accordance with Treaty law.
[440] Case C-294/00 *Gräbner* [2002] ECR I-6515, para. 46.
[441] Case 324/99 *DaimlerChrysler* [2001] ECR I-9897, para. 64.

No. 259/93,[442] national authorities may not rely upon Article 36 TFEU with a view to adopting legislation protecting interests elsewhere as well as their own.

- On the other hand, on the matter of the grounds of objections to waste shipments, for which Article 7(4)(a) of Regulation (EEC) No. 259/93 provides, the Court found that the competent authority of dispatch could object to waste shipments, 'assessing the effects on health and the environment of the recovery envisaged at the destination'. If it does so in conformity with the principle of proportionality, the authority may rely on its own criteria, 'even where those criteria are stricter than those in force in the State of destination'.[443] The German authority of dispatch could therefore object to shipments on the basis not of concerns regarding waste transport but of its recovery in Italy.

7. Proportionality of Environmental Measures Contrary to Articles 34 and 35 TFEU

7.1 Functions of the principle of proportionality

Once an MEE has been justified under Article 36 TFEU or the rule of reason, the Member State is free to determine the level of protection it wishes to pursue. To prevent the principle of free movement of goods from becoming nugatory, the Court has put in place a series of criteria to assess the proportionality of the measures justified under the aforementioned exceptions. The principle of proportionality allows assessment of the means used—ban, prohibition, approval, authorization, restriction on use, etc—with reference to the objectives pursued—health or environment—to best take into account the legitimate interests of undertakings in freely trading their goods. As stakeholders necessarily adopt opposite stances regarding the adequacy of the level of protection in this field, one must stress that the proportionality principle is ideologically neutral and does not aim to favour environmental interests over economic interests or to create such a hierarchy of values out of thin air.

As these criteria are applied in a flexible and evolutionary manner, it is difficult to establish a fixed definition of the principle. Nevertheless, certain Advocates General, whose point of view has been echoed by several authors, managed to compile a list of conditions for the application of the principle, by dividing it into three successive tests. The *Fedesa* judgment also echoes this systematic approach. The three tests apply as follows: prohibitory measures are valid if they are 'appropriate and necessary in order to achieve the objectives legitimately pursued by the legislation in question; when there is a choice between several appropriate measures recourse must be had to the least onerous and the disadvantages caused must not be disproportionate to the aims pursued'.[444] As will be seen, the Court applies these tests in different ways and does not always distinguish them clearly.

---

[442] *DaimlerChrysler* (n 441), para. 42. In contrast, it is possible according to Article 12 c) of 1013/2006 Regulation, to oppose the transfer on the account of lower treatment standards in the importing country than those of the country of dispatch.

[443] Case C-277/02 *EU-Wood-Trading GmbH* [2004] ECR I-11957, para. 54.

[444] Case 331/88 *Fedesa* [1990] ECR 4023, para. 13. See, to the same effect, Opinion AG van Gerven in Cases C-312/89 *Sidef Conforama* and C-332/89 *Marchandise* [1991] ECR I-997, para. 14; and Opinion AG Poiares Maduro in Case C-434/04 *Jan-Erik Anders Ahokainen* [2006] ECR I-9171, paras 23–6.

7.2 First test: 'suitability' of the measure with regard to the objective pursued

As it is not necessary to kill a fly with a sledgehammer, the measure should not be excessive with regard to the problem. The principle of proportionality thus requires that the measure be adequate, suitable with a view to attaining its objective. This first stage is known as the 'suitability test' or 'adequacy test'.

The first question to answer is whether the facts noted by the national authorities justify a need for a measure to protect the environment. Does the current situation or risk of environmental degradation require Member State intervention? In order to be deemed suitable, the measure at issue must be linked to the objective pursued. It must constitute a reasonably intelligible means of ensuring the removal of the nuisance. It may therefore be useful for a national authority to underline the reasons behind the contested measure with a view to demonstrating that it reflects the best methodological approach to deal with the environmental risk. In that respect, the coherence of the approach endorsed is the essence of this first requirement.[445] Additionally, the more coherent and intelligible a measure is, the more suitable it will be deemed to be. Conversely, a measure that does not prevent harm to the environment, despite claiming to do so, will be unacceptable.

The following cases are illustrative of ways in which environmental measures fulfil this first condition.

- To assess whether the obligation for electricity supply undertakings to purchase electricity produced from renewable energy sources is compatible with Article 34 TFEU, 'account must be taken, first, of the aim of the provision in question, and, second, of the particular features of the electricity market'. Several factors, such as the integration principle and the international obligations of the EU to fight climate change, can plead for a favourable assessment of the contested measure.[446]

- Insofar as a national measure on a deposit-and-return system intended to ensure the reuse of packaging of bottles encourages producers and retailers to opt for reusable packaging and encourages consumers to return empty packaging to retail outlets, the Court held that such system is an 'indispensable element' to the reduction of waste to be disposed of as well as to increase the proportion of empty packaging returned.[447] Moreover, given that the reduction of waste to be discharged is one of the general objectives of waste-management policy, such a national measure is deemed to be adequate.

- It is necessary for the survival of a bee species threatened with extinction to create a protection area hindering the free movement of bees sold freely elsewhere.[448]

- Restricting the use of watercraft to a limited number of designated waters is adequate for the purpose of protecting the environment.[449]

---

[445] G. Mathisen, 'Consistency and Coherence as Conditions for Justification of Member State Measures Restricting Free Movement' (2010) 47 *CML Rev* 1036.

[446] *PreussenElektra* (n 369).

[447] Case C-302/86 *Commission v Denmark* [1988] ECR 46, para. 13; Case C-463/01 *Commission v Germany* [2004] ECR I-11705, paras 76 and 77; and *Radlberger and Spitz* (n 195), paras 77 and 78.

[448] *Bluhme* (n 161), para. 37. [449] *Swedish Watercraft* (n 209), para. 34.

- According to Advocate General Geelhoed's Opinion in the Inn motorway case,[450] the adequacy of the measure must be assessed with reference to such criteria as the following:
    - the effectiveness of the measure (is it likely that the measure will lead to the foreseen emission reduction within a reasonable time frame?);
    - the question whether the measure can be put into practice (is the measure an effective means of attaining the objective?);
    - its enforceable character (can economic operators be forced to adapt their behaviour in the desired way?).

7.3 Second test: control of the necessity of public authority intervention

7.3.1 *Ratio*

Second, the principle of proportionality implies a comparison of measures likely to attain the desired result and the selection of the one with the least disadvantages. If it appears that an alternative measure would meet the target while hindering inter-State trade to a lesser degree, the contested measure is no longer necessary and must be deemed disproportionate. The national measure must therefore be necessary in attaining the objective pursued. An alternative measure is not considered less restrictive on the ground that it better attains the desired result, but rather because it impinges the free movement of goods to a lesser degree.[451] The question arises then as to whether, by directing a similar amount of its resources into an alternative measure, the Member State could 'achieve the same result at a lower cost to intra-Community trade'.[452]

7.3.2 *Assessment of the availability of least burdensome measures: a gamut of environmental measures*

In the light of the variety of interests and factors to take into consideration,[453] a Member State often has a choice between numerous measures.[454] Caution is therefore necessary when a plaintiff claims that 'other' measures would be 'more effective', 'more proportionate', or 'less restrictive'. While this may be the case in considering one specific interest, it may not necessarily be the case when measures are assessed with reference to other, competing, interests.[455]

The Member State must be able to compare the advantages and disadvantages of each national measure that might attain the aim pursued. Nonetheless, a Member State

---

[450] Opinion AG Geelhoed in Case C-320/03 *Commission v Austria* (n 399), para. 65.
[451] Mathisen (n 445), 1043.
[452] Opinion AG Poiares Maduro in Case C-434/04 *Jan-Erik Anders Ahokainen* [2006] ECR I-9171, para. 25.
[453] See the discussion in Chapter 4, Section 2.
[454] The proportionality of the prohibition on imports of canned beer and carbonated drinks is still under discussion. Indeed, the question concerns the least restrictive system: prohibition of the deposit and collection of cans, the branding of products, eco-taxes, and the fixing of objectives for the reuse of certain types of containers. See Opinion delivered on 13 September 2001 by AG Ruiz-Jarabo Colomer in Case C-233/99 *Haugsted Hansen*, para. 41. No judgment was ever delivered.
[455] Opinion AG Geelhoed in Case C-320/03 *Commission v Austria* (n 399), para. 66.

only has the obligation of resorting to the measure least restrictive to free movement of goods if it 'has a choice between various measures to attain the same objective'.[456] Where the environmental or the health risk is so significant, the Member State might have no other choice but to ban or to regulate the product or the substance.

Therefore, when the planned measure gravely hinders free movement of goods, national authorities must carefully examine the possibility of adopting less restrictive measures, and they may only set them aside if they are clearly insufficient to attain the objective. This can be illustrated by the following cases.

- On the matter of a total traffic ban on a section of motorway constituting a vital route of communication between certain Member States, the Court held in *Bremer I* that 'given the declared objective of transferring transportation of the goods concerned from road to rail, those authorities were required to ensure that there was sufficient and appropriate rail capacity to allow such a transfer' before deciding to implement the contested measure.[457] Indeed, adopting such a radical measure forced national authorities to 'examine carefully the possibility of using measures less restrictive of freedom of movement, and discount them only if their inadequacy, in relation to the objective pursued, was clearly established'.[458]

- As regards the necessity of an MEE, the presentation of a certificate with a view to enabling the award of an ecological bonus under the terms of the Environmental Round Table for demonstration vehicles imported into France was excessive, and therefore disproportionate having regard to the environmental objective pursued.[459]

There are many illustrations of the necessity test regarding waste management.

- Dutch legislation provided for mandatory treatment of animal carcasses, and for the measure to be justified on the basis of Article 36 TFEU, such an obligation would have to be 'essential' to the functioning of the Dutch disposal system for that type of waste.[460]

- The *Danish Bottles* case takes on particular significance for the assessment of necessity of bottle-reuse measures. With the aim of diminishing the amount of waste, the Danish authorities wished to encourage reuse of bottles. In their view, this approach offered the highest level of environmental protection. On the one hand, manufacturers were required to market their drinks only in reusable containers. On the other, on the account that a limited amount of authorized containers would allow consumers to return their packaging to any beverage retailer, the Danish authorities required both domestic producers and importers

---

[456] Case 27/81 *Fietje* [1981] ECR 2481; Case 220/81 *Robertson* [1982] ECR 2349; Case 261/81 *Lebensmittelwerke v De Smedt* [1982] ECR 3961, para. 12; Case 124/81 *Commission v UK* [1983] ECR 203; Case 155/82 *Commission v Belgium* [1983] ECR 531; Case 247/81 *Commission v Germany* [1984] ECR I-1111; and Case 154/85 *Commission v Italy* [1987] ECR 2717.
[457] Case C-320/03 *Commission v Austria* (n 399), paras 87–8.
[458] Case C-320/03 *Commission v Austria* (n 399), para. 87.
[459] Case C-443/10 *Philippe Bonnarde* [2011] OJ C347/6, para. 38.
[460] Case 118/86 *Nertsvoederfabriek* [1987] ECR 3883, para. 14.

to use only approved containers.[461] This second measure was likely to oblige foreign producers to manufacture or purchase containers that were already approved, which would involve substantial additional costs. Both the general obligation and the container-approval regime were challenged by the Commission. The upshot of the judgment was that the broad requirement to market exclusively returnable containers was upheld on the ground that this was an 'essential element' of a system aimed at improving environmental protection, whereas the complementary requirement to restrict the use of non-approved containers was disproportionate to the environmental objective pursued.[462] Although this complementary measure ensured 'a very considerable degree of protection of the environment',[463] it was nonetheless disproportionate. It follows that environmental imperatives must not be taken into account at the highest level, particularly when they hinder trade disproportionately. Some have argued that the judgment was contradictory since the Court gave the Member States considerable leeway to carry out their environmental policy in the first part, yet took it back in the second part of the judgment.[464]

The same can be said for nature conservation. Secondary EU law does not prohibit Member States from adopting more restrictive measures than the EU legislator, as long as these measures are necessary for the aim pursued.

- The prohibition of trade in a species of macaw, a parrot found in the neotropic ecozone and the placing of which on the market is ruled by the CITES Convention, is compatible with the TFEU 'only to the extent that it is necessary for effectively achieving the objective of the protection of the health and life of animals', an objective mentioned in Article 36 TFEU.[465]

- The prohibition on importing exotic crayfish on German territory must be proportionate to the aim pursued, the protection of indigenous crayfish.[466]

- Inasmuch as the scope of Directive 79/409/EEC on the conservation of wild birds does not apply to specimens born and bred in captivity, Member States may adopt legislation on trade of the latter in conformity with the principle of proportionality.[467] To assess the possibility of attaining the objective with less restrictive rules, one must resort to a specific analysis, through the use of scientific studies.[468]

- In Belgium, the limiting of trade in wild birds to birds having a metallic ring impeded the import of birds with plastic rings or microchips, methods that are

---

[461] Non-approved containers had to be returned to the retailer who sold the beverage; they could be recycled instead of reused.

[462] Case 302/86 *Danish Bottles* [1998] ECR 4607, paras 13 and 21.

[463] *Danish Bottles* (n 462), para. 20.

[464] S. Walker, *Environmental Protection versus Trade Liberalization: Finding the Balance* (Brussels: Saint Louis, 1993) 83.

[465] Case C-510/99 *Tridon* [2001] ECR I-7777, para. 53.

[466] Case C-131/93 *Commission v Germany* [1994] ECR I-3303.

[467] Case C-149/94 *Didier Vergy* [1996] ECR I-299, para. 15; and Case C-480/03 *Hugo Clemens* [2004] not reported, para. 17.

[468] *Hugo Clemens* (n 467), para. 19.

authorized in other Member States. The Court held that such an obligation was disproportionate to the aim pursued, namely the fight against fraud.[469]

The Court has sometimes taken care not to examine such considerations.

- In its *Walloon Waste* and *PreussenElektra* cases[470] the Court did not fully examine the proportionality of the contested measures, limiting itself to an analysis and confirmation of the necessity of the measures.

- Regarding measures prohibiting trade in parrots born and bred in captivity, the Court stated that it could not assess the proportionality of the measure in the absence of a scientific study that the national judge had to commission.[471]

- Judgments can also seem brief and lacking when the proportionality of EU harmonization is questioned.[472]

7.3.3 *The neutrality of the necessity test*

The necessity test is not necessarily neutral, and may therefore hide subjective assessments of the interests present. Indeed, in many cases concerning the environment, the Court of Justice has compared measures that did not necessarily share the same degree of effectiveness, before choosing an alternative yet less effective measure, without taking into account technical and scientific reasons for adopting the contested measures.[473] The Court thus deemed the following to be comparable:

- the obligation to return waste oils to waste collectors for recycling within the national territory and the possibility of handing them over to foreign collectors permitted to incinerate them;[474]

- the prohibition on importing exotic animals to protect indigenous wild species and the possibility of importing these exotic species subject to the requirement of preliminary veterinary checks;[475]

- the obligation to obtain administrative approval to trade bottles and the obligation to reuse said bottles;[476]

- a system prohibiting registration of old vehicles previously registered in other Member States, on the ground that such vehicles do not comply with anti-pollution standards, and a taxation system dissuading use of such vehicles or encouraging their destruction.[477]

---

[469] Case C-100/08 *Commission v Belgium* [2009] ECR I-140, paras 103–5.
[470] *Walloon Waste* (n 137); and *PreussenElektra* (n 369).   [471] *Tridon* (n 465), para. 58.
[472] Case C-284/95 *Safety High-Tech* [1998] ECR I-4301, para. 64.
[473] It is true that Member States do not always succeed in convincing the Court of the necessary character of the measure both in terms of efficiency and economy. See Case C-524/07 *Commission v Austria* [2008] ECR I-187, para. 61.
[474] Case 172/82 *Inter-Huiles* [1983] ECR 555, para. 14.
[475] *German Crayfish* (n 376), para. 24. See, in particular, Opinion AG van Gerven at para. 14.
[476] *Danish Bottles* (n 462), para. 21.
[477] Case C-524/07 *Commission v Austria* (n 473), para. 61.

As a result, the Court must be extremely careful in reviewing the necessity of various measures the effectiveness of which is likely to vary significantly.

An examination of a more recent judgment reveals the Court's tendency to intensify yet further its proportionality review. The *Brenner II* case involved a measure restricting the circulation on a segment of motorway in Austria of certain types of heavily polluting trucks—lorries of over 7.5 tonnes carrying certain goods—which could have been replaced by a less restrictive measure, such as a general speed limit applicable to all vehicles. The motorway is one of the principal land transport routes between certain Member States. The more severe measure applied by the Austrian authorities was justified, on their account, by the obligation imposed by a directive laying down quality objectives for certain atmospheric pollutants which had been regularly exceeded due to high traffic levels. Contrary to the arguments submitted by the Commission, the Court held that the contested measure was adequate and consistent.[478] Since the case involved the necessity test, the Court paid considerable attention to the examination of alternative measures available to the national authorities. According to the judgment, the national authorities must furnish proof in support of the comparison, given that the Court will carry out a detailed examination of the studies on which their policing measure is based.[479] Although Austria had based its position on the 'actual' speed of trucks in order to justify the contested ban, which was applicable to these trucks only, while travelling on one particular section of the motorway—rather than setting a permanent speed limit applicable to all vehicles—the Court ruled that such reasoning was invalid. On the contrary, it held that only a maximum permitted speed (with which it was for the national authorities to ensure compliance) could act as the basis for the adoption of such a strict MEE as the one adopted in that case. In effect, had the imposition of a permanent speed limit[480] been considered, according to the studies reviewed, that permanent limitation would have been more effective from the point of view of emissions of certain pollutants than a sectoral restriction. However, since the pollution-reducing potential for each of the measures was relatively similar, there is a question whether such a finding of a failure to comply with Treaty law was sufficiently justified, taking account also of the reliability of the methods for assessing emissions based on 'projections', which were used in this case.

7.3.4 *Temporal scope of the measure at issue*

The Court occasionally holds as incompatible measures providing undertakings with too brief a time frame to adapt to a new regulatory system without necessarily refuting the validity of the system in question. In other words, the necessity for the ban is only accepted where it is mitigated by effective implementation of a temporary regime of exceptions that allows the undertakings to adjust their operations.

---

[478] Case C-320/03 *Commission v Austria* (n 399), para. 133.
[479] Case C-320/03 *Commission v Austria* (n 399), paras 144–8.
[480] One of the alternatives was to replace the variable speed limit with a permanent 100 km/h speed limit.

- Despite its contribution to the reduction of waste, the German deposit and recycling system for mineral-water packaging was found to be disproportionate. The Court held that the six-month period between announcement of the new system and its entry into force did not allow producers of natural mineral water 'to adapt their production and their management of non-reusable packaging waste to the new system'.[481] The proportionate character of the German system was therefore assessed in the light of the general principle of legitimate expectations of economic operators, which requires that economic operators have sufficient time to adapt to new legislative constraints.[482]

- A transition period limited to two months between adoption and entry into force of a prohibition on heavy goods vehicles on an Austrian trans-alpine motorway, the aim of which was to adhere to anti-pollution standards, was found to be 'clearly insufficient reasonably to allow the operators concerned to adapt to the new circumstances'.[483]

- In *Swedish Watercraft*, the need for the prohibition was only accepted because it was mitigated by effective implementation of a regime of exceptions which allowed for watersport activity.[484] In order to determine whether it was reasonable to take 11 months in order to designate the areas where the sport was allowed, the national court had to take into account the fact that these designations were adopted 'following consultations with the municipalities and other parties concerned'.[485]

7.3.5 *Assessment of the least burdensome measure in the light of the objective pursued*

The necessity of suitable measures is greatly influenced by the level of protection set by the Member State.[486] Given that the principle of subsidiarity enshrined in Article 5(3) TEU underlies EU environmental policy,[487] undertakings are likely to encounter important discrepancies as regards standards on the placing on the market of hazardous products. Indeed, standards applied in Germany are known to be more stringent than those applied in Portugal or Bulgaria.[488] However, this does not mean that the most stringent national standards should be replaced by measures found in other States. According to settled case law:

> The fact that one Member State imposes less stringent rules than another Member State does not mean that the latter's rules are disproportionate and hence

---

[481] Case C-463/01 *Commission v Germany* [2004] ECR I-11705, para. 80; and *Radlberger and Spitz* (n 195), para. 81.
[482] The Court did not answer the claim of the European Commission according to which the entire German system was disproportionate inasmuch as it ignored the specific situation of mineral water to be transported over long distances.
[483] Case C-320/03 *Commission v Austria* (n 399), paras 87–90; Opinion Geelhoed in Case C-320/03 *Commission v Austria* (n 399), para. 115.
[484] *Swedish Watercraft* (n 209), para. 39.   [485] *Sandström* (n 248), para. 39.
[486] Ziegler (n 135), 82.   [487] See the discussion Chapter 3, Section 2.2.
[488] C. Koutalakis, A. Buzogany, and T. Börzel, 'When Soft Regulation is Not Enough: The Integrated Pollution Prevention and Control Directive of the EU' (2010) 4 *Regulation & Governance* 329–44.

incompatible with [EU] law. The mere fact that a Member State has chosen a system of protection different from that adopted by another Member State cannot affect the appraisal as to the need for and proportionality of the provisions adopted.[489]

Given that the Member States are not required to apply the lowest level of protection within the EU,[490] they may dismiss less restrictive alternatives[491] on the ground that they would not secure the appropriate level of domestic protection. This raises the question whether less restrictive alternatives protect the Member State's interests as effectively as the challenged measure. Given the complexities of environmental policy, this appreciation is rather delicate. It is submitted that the Member States should enjoy a rather wide margin of appreciation in determining, according to the specificities of the environmental issues and the importance they attach to environmental values, the measures that are likely to achieve concrete results most efficiently.[492]

Indeed, one might initially consider whether the Court has sufficient technical proficiency for the comparison of different measures, notably as regards their projected results, in complex fields such as environmental protection and public health protection.

Second, in judgments on the non-essential character of national measures, the Court has often used simple statements without resorting to more reliable data. As it focuses on ascertaining the effect of the contested measure on access to the domestic market, it tends to favour weaker competing measures as soon as they are less restrictive to trade.

Finally, in comparing the disadvantages of the contested measure and of alternative measures, there is a risk that the Court will always prefer a more reasonable measure to a more rigorous one; a choice that may take place at the expense of the aim pursued. Such a method clearly goes against the principle requiring a high level of environmental protection found in Treaty law by virtue of Article 3(3) TEU and Article 191(2) TFEU as well as in national laws.[493]

7.3.6 Assessment of the least burdensome measure in the light of the effectiveness of the available measures

The Court has occasionally excluded the use of other measures on the ground that the latter are less effective. The following three cases are illustrative of the manner in which the Court has dismissed the effectiveness of alternative measures.

In *Aher-Waggon*, the Court took the view that 'limiting noise emissions from aircraft is the most effective and convenient means of combating the noise pollution which they

---

[489] See, inter alia, Case C-108/96 *Mac Quen and Others* [2001] ECR I-837, paras 33 and 34; Case 219/07 *Andibel* [2008] ECR I-4475, para. 31; Case C-100/08 *Commission v Belgium* [2009] ECR I-140, para. 95; *Trailers* (n 211), para. 65.

[490] Case C-384/93 *Alpine Investment* [1995] ECR I-1141; and Case C-124/97 *Läärä* [1999] ECR I-6067, para. 36.

[491] The consideration of alternative solutions could be seen as a prerequisite before taking draconian measures such as 'a total traffic ban on a section of motorway constituting a vital route of communication between certain Member States'. See Case C-320/03 *Commission v Austria* (n 399), para. 87.

[492] *Trailers* (n 211), para. 65; *Swedish Watercraft* (n 209), para. 39. See by analogy Case C-394/97 *Heinonen* [1999] ECR I-3599, para. 43.

[493] See Chapter 1, Section 7.2.

generate. It prevails thus over alternative measures'.[494] The Court observed that alternative measures to carry out noise reduction in the vicinity of airports would be extremely costly. In addition, the restriction was applied to all aircraft irrespective of their origin and did not prevent aircraft registered in another Member State from being used in Germany.

In this connection, *Toolex* is a case in point. The prohibition of trichloroethylene, a carcinogenic chemical substance, was held to be more effective than an alternative suggested by the European Commission (ie thresholds of exposure) in reducing the risk of cancer. Indeed, many difficulties due to scientific uncertainty arise with the implementation of such exposure thresholds which limits the effectiveness of the exposure standards proposed by the Commission.[495] The prohibitory measure, which was more restrictive, was found to be necessary inasmuch as it both reduced the number of users and encouraged the use of substitutable products.[496] Moreover, the Court held that the Swedish system of individual exemptions to the prohibition on trichloroethylene was adequate and proportionate, as it improved protection of workers while taking into account the requirements necessary to allow the undertaking to remain in operation. The proportionality of this system was reinforced by the fact that exemptions were granted subject to the condition that there was no less harmful substitutable product and that the applicant undertook an obligation to seek an alternative solution which would be less harmful to the environment and public health.[497]

In *Swedish Watercraft*, involving the Swedish ban on the use of watercraft, the parties argued that the Swedish authorities could have chosen a less severe regime which would in principle permit the use of such craft, provided that they were not used in areas considered to be sensitive, such as a limited number of nature sanctuaries and bathing areas. However, the Court held that this alternative was not as effective as the prohibition ultimately put in place. By analogy with the *Italian Trailers* case, the Court took the view that 'Member States cannot be denied the possibility of attaining' the objective of protecting the environment 'by the introduction of general rules which are necessary on account of the particular geographical circumstances of the Member State concerned and easily managed and supervised by the national authorities'.[498] In other words, the Court acknowledged that a Member State may maintain more stringent trade-restricting measures if compliance with less restrictive alternative measures would entail a heavier administrative burden. Put simply, the costs incurred by national administrations may mean that this aspect gathers momentum.

In support of the latter view, attention should be drawn again to the fact that it is easier for public authorities to control the restricted use of vehicles in specifically designated areas than it is elsewhere. In addition, such measures appear to be far more effective. In *Swedish Watercraft* it was obvious that wild birds such as loons and shorebirds would be better protected by a general prohibition covering the whole

---

[494] *Aher-Waggon* (n 329).

[495] *Toolex* (n 187), para. 45. On the impossibility of defining an intake threshold due to scientific shortfalls, see also Case 53/80 *Eyssen* [1981] ECR 409.

[496] Opinion of AG Mischo presented on 21 March 2000, para. 65.

[497] *Toolex* (n 187), paras 46 and 47.   [498] *Swedish Watercraft* (n 209), para. 36.

country on the use of watercraft rather than by a tedious designation of a patchwork of small nature sanctuaries.[499] Since they are found on every stretch of water, shorebirds are certainly not restricted to a handful of protected areas. Returning to our motocross example in which the sport is regulated in heavily populated Member States such as the Netherlands and Belgium, here too the practice is only authorized in specially designated locations, in order to reduce noise pollution and guarantee road safety. In this case, the addressees of the rule know the locations where they are able to practise their sport. Outside those areas, they are likely to be subject to administrative fines. In line with the previous judgment, the Court accepted in *Swedish Watercraft* the need for the more severe alternative on efficiency grounds. That said, the authorities are called on to flesh out this general proportionality assessment into concrete measures, such as the obligation to identify the waters in which noisy or dangerous sport activities can be carried out.[500]

The Court has also required that less caution be taken 'when new elements change the perception of a risk or show that that risk can be contained by less restrictive measures'.[501] In such cases, one must adapt legislation falling within the scope of Article 34 TFEU.

7.3.7 *Assessment of the least burdensome measure in the light of international obligations*

EU law cannot be insulated from international law. As secondary law may reinforce the necessity of national measures hindering trade, so provisions of international law may act as grounds for necessity as shown by the following examples.

- The prohibition on waste imports in Wallonia is justified by the principles of proximity and self-sufficiency, enshrined in an international convention on transboundary movements of waste.[502]

- Similarly, the conservation of an indigenous animal species through protective measures hindering trade is recognized both in international law and in secondary law, and its validity must be deemed to stem from Article 36 TFEU.[503]

- The obligation for German economic operators to purchase wind energy from national producers must be examined in the context of the UN Framework Convention on Climate Change.[504]

- A national regulation under which it is prohibited to trade in mammals belonging to species other than those expressly referred to in that legislation can be justified because animal welfare pursues a legitimate objective, namely the welfare of animals, the importance of which was reflected, in particular, in the adoption by

---

[499] *Swedish Watercraft* (n 209), para. 30.
[500] *Swedish Watercraft* (n 209), para. 39. See Spaventa (n 200), 926.
[501] Case C-504/04 *Agrarproduktion Staebelow* [2006] ECR I-679, para. 40.
[502] *Walloon Waste* (n 137), para. 35.   [503] *Bluhme* (n 161), paras 36 and 38.
[504] *PreussenElektra* (n 369), para. 74.

the Member States of the protocol on the protection and welfare of animals, annexed to the EC Treaty.[505]

7.3.8 *A gamut of environmental measures: bans, restrictions, and positive and negative lists*

The intensity of the review of proportionality is likely to vary significantly from one measure to another. As alluded to earlier, in some cases neither the EU nor Member States have any choice on the matter. Some products are thus totally prohibited because of their harmful nature[506] and the dangers are so significant that any alternative to prohibition would be deemed unreasonable. It should be noted that the Court considers that 'a decision to prohibit marketing' constitutes 'the most restrictive obstacle to trade in products lawfully manufactured and marketed in other Member States'.[507] Therefore, it is not certain whether bans would easily pass the test of proportionality.[508] At the other end of the spectrum, more lenient measures that merely restrict the use of hazardous products are less likely to be subject to a strict necessity test.[509]

Let us turn to the more fundamental questions that arise with respect to positive and negative listing. On the one hand, negative lists expressly prohibit the products or the substances that can either be placed on the market or used. It therefore follows that traders can freely trade in products that are not listed.[510] This regulatory technique is particularly favourable to traders.

On the other hand, for the marketing of certain goods a number of international, EU, and national regulations require prior inclusion of those goods on an 'authorized list' or 'positive list'. This regulatory approach makes marketing of those goods more difficult and more expensive, and consequently hinders trade between the Member States.[511] The Court has consistently held that legislation which makes the holding of animals or the use of hazardous substances subject to prior inclusion of the species/ category to which they belong in a 'positive list'—and which also applies to specimens of species or substances which are legally held or produced in other Member States—is in compliance with EU law only if three conditions are satisfied.[512]

First, the drawing up of such a list and any subsequent amendment 'must be based on objective and non-discriminatory criteria'.[513] By way of illustration, physiological, ethological, and ecological needs, the level of threat to human or animal health or to an

---

[505] Case 219/07 *Andibel* [2008] ECR I-4475, para. 27; Case 100/08 *Commission v Belgium* [2009] ECR I-140, para. 91.

[506] See, eg, Council Directive 79/117/EEC prohibiting the placing on the market and use of plant protection products containing certain active substances [1979] OJ L33/36; Commission Directive 1999/77 on asbestos [1999] OJ L207/18.

[507] Case C-333/08 *Commission v France* [2010] ECR I-757, para. 89.

[508] Jans and Vedder (n 80), 285.

[509] Fallon and Gerard (n 255), 262–3. See, eg, Case 110/05 *Commission v Italy* [2009] ECR I-519, para. 67.

[510] Regarding restrictions on the placing on the market and use of certain dangerous substances, preparations, and articles, see Reach Regulation, Title VIII.

[511] Case C-24/00 *Commission v France* [2004] ECR I-1277, para. 23; and *Andibel* (n 505), para. 23.

[512] *Andibel* (n 505), paras 32–6; and Case 100/08 *Commission v Belgium* (n 505), paras 97–101.

[513] *Andibel* (n 505), para. 34; and Case 100/08 *Commission v Belgium* (n 505), para. 98.

Table 5.7 Positive and negative listings of wildlife

Convention on International Trade in Endangered Species of Wild Fauna and Flora (CITES)	Council Regulation (EC) No. 338/97 of 9 December 1996 on the protection of species of wild fauna and flora by regulating trade therein	1986 Belgian Law on Animal Welfare
Negative list	Negative list	Positive list
Annex I of the Convention prohibits, eg, trade in orang-outang, chimpanzee, bonobos. As a result, all the animals not listed can be traded and held	The purchase, offer to purchase, acquisition for commercial purposes, display to the public for commercial purposes, use for commercial gain and sale, keeping for sale, offering for sale or transporting for sale of specimens of the species listed in Annexes A and B shall be prohibited (Art 8(1) and (5)). As a result, all the animals not listed can be traded	Only animals belonging to the species included in the list may be held, imported, or traded in Belgium. Conversely, animals which do not belong to the species or categories referred to in the national list shall not be held, imported, or traded

ecosystem, and the risk of escape are deemed to be 'objective and non-discriminatory criteria' justifying a postive list of wild mammals that can be traded.[514]

Secondly, that legislation 'must make provision for a procedure enabling interested parties to have new species or a new substance included in the national list. The procedure must be one which is readily accessible, which presupposes that it is expressly provided for in a measure of general application, and can be completed within a reasonable time, and, if it leads to a refusal to include the product at issue—it being obligatory to state the reasons for that refusal—the refusal decision must be open to challenge before the courts'.[515]

Last, an application to obtain the inclusion of a product or substance in that national list may be refused by the competent administrative authorities only if the holding of specimens of that species poses 'a genuine risk to the protection of or compliance with the interests' justifying the MEE.[516]

Table 5.7 illustrates the extent to which decision-makers can frame positive and negative lists with the aim of protecting wildlife.

7.4 Third test: proportionality *stricto sensu* of the measure

In assessing the proportionality of an MEE, the courts have to examine both its relevance and its essential character. Should these two requirements be fulfilled, some consider that a third test is necessary: an analysis of the measure itself, not through comparison with other measure, to determine whether the advantage provided is disproportionate with regard to the damage caused to inter-State trade.[517] Thus, the Member State must

[514] *Andibel* (n 505), para. 26.
[515] *Andibel* (n 505), para. 35; and Case 100/08 *Commission v Belgium* (n 505), para. 99.
[516] *Andibel* (n 505), above, para. 36; and Case 100/08 *Commission v Belgium* (n 505), para. 100.
[517] W. van Gerven, 'Principe de proportionnalité abus de droit et droits fondamentaux' (1992) *JT* 306 and 'The Effect of Proportionality on the Actions of Member States of the European Community: National Viewpoints from Continental Europe' in Ellis (n 139), 38; G. de Búrca, 'The Principle of Proportionality and its Application in EC Law' (1993) 13 *YbEL* 105–50.

demonstrate that 'the level of protection it decides to afford to its legitimate interests is commensurate with the degree of interference this causes in intra-Community trade'.[518] This should be the case with a draconian measure that has barely any environmental benefit.

As a result, a national measure protecting the environment and restricting trade should therefore be deemed disproportionate if it can be substituted by a less restrictive measure (violation of the second test) or if it causes excessive prejudice to commercial interests (violation of the third test). This should lead case law only to validate measures that are both essential (second test) and reasonable (third test). Therefore, the *stricto sensu* proportionality test may oblige a Member State to reduce its level of protection, in spite of the effectiveness of the measure.

At the request of several Advocates General, the Court of Justice has occasionally mentioned this third test, without, however, applying it as such, insofar as it always invalidated the contested measures on the basis of their non-essential character. For instance, in the *Danish Bottles* case Advocate General Slynn expressed the view that 'There has to be a balancing test between the free movement of goods and environmental protection, even if in achieving the balance the high standard of protection sought has to be reduced. The level of protection must be a reasonable level'. In adjudicating that the Danish measure requiring approved containers was disproportionate, the Court implicitly supported Advocate General Slynn's views.[519] Indeed, the Court weighed the level of environmental protection with the free movement of goods and reduced it on account that it was not reasonable. Thus far, this is the only case where a measure has been held unlawful because of its excessive character in regard to environmental protection.

With the exception of the *Danish Bottles* case, the other Court judgments on proportionality of environmental MEEs concentrate exclusively on the first and second tests. For instance, 16 years after adjudicating the *Danish Bottles* case, the Court did not review the level of environmental protection pursued by the German authorities as regards the requirement to reuse water bottles.[520] Moreover, there has been much criticism of the application of the proportionality criterion in the assessment of measures protecting the environment.[521] Such criticism relates to the practical difficulty of comparing advantages and disadvantages of environmental protection, and it echoes the theoretical impossibility of balancing environmental protection and the proper functioning of the internal market. Moreover, given that the Court is ill-equipped to define appropriate regulatory policy in the context of weighing conflicting interests, this gives rise to issues of legitimacy.[522]

---

[518] Opinion AG Poiares Maduro in Case C-434/04 *Jan-Erik Anders Ahokainen* [2006] ECR I-9171, para. 26. See Case C-112/00 *Schmidberger* [2003] ECR I-5659, para. 81.

[519] *Danish Bottles* (n 462), para. 21.

[520] Case C-463/01 *Commission v Germany* (n 481); *Radlberger and Spitz* (n 195).

[521] L. Krämer: 'L'environnement et le marché unique européen' (1993) 1 *RMUE* 48; 'Environmental Protection and Article 30 EEC Treaty' (n 135), 123 and 124; *EC Environmental Law*, 6th edn (London: Sweet & Maxwell, 2007), 113–19; N. de Sadeleer, *Les principes du pollueur-payeur de prévention et de précaution* (Brussels: Bruylant-AUF, 1999) 352–89; *Environmental Principles* (n 135), 296–301; Jans and Vedder (n 80), 287–8; J. H. Jans, 'Proportionality Revisited' (2000) 27:3 *LIEI* 239–65; Scott (n 135), 163.

[522] M. Poiares Maduro, *We, The Court: The European Court of Justice and the European Economic Constitution* (Oxford: Hart Publishing, 1997).

In the *Schmidberger* judgment, the question was not confronted in terms of the hierarchy of general principles or fundamental duties but of coexistence. The Court of Justice thus established the conditions for compatibility between the right to freedom of expression, on the one hand, and the fundamental freedom to the movement of goods, on the other, without ruling on their respective places in the hierarchy of norms. The resolution of the conflict between these two freedoms involves weighing up the interests in play, a balancing operation which must take account of the margin of appreciation of the Member States.

8. Internal Market Preventive Control Procedures of National Technical Rules

8.1 Introductory remarks

Review of the compatibility of national measures hindering the free movement of goods in the light of Treaty law is governed by a reactive approach. In addition, judicial intervention mainly has a corrective effect: it can only remove particular obstacles to free trade.[523] With a view to overcoming these shortcomings, the EU lawmaker has adopted different acts, among which is Directive 98/34/EC, requiring the Member States to notify to the Commission their draft regulations setting technical standards before their enactment. Also, in 2008 the EU lawmaker adopted additional regulations furthering the original preventive approach.

As a result, a wide variety of regulatory measures—taxes, subsidies, bans, restrictions on use—deployed at the national level to limit the environmental impact of products whether upstream in their conception ('specification' of their characteristics) or downstream in their production ('other requirements imposed on the product for the purpose of environmental protection') are subject to these preventive arrangements.

In sharp contrast to the directives and regulations regulating the placing on the market of several hazardous products, the acts commented on in this section are procedural and not substantive in nature. Insofar as the efficacy of the notification procedure established by this directive has been reinforced by the principles inferred by the Court of Justice, this case law will be taken into account.

8.2 Notification Directive 98/34, an instrument of transparency at the service of the internal market

8.2.1 Objective

The goal of Directive 98/34/EC[524] (the Notification Directive) consists in preventing the re-emergence of technical obstacles to trade between Member States.[525] With the objective of ensuring as full a protection as possible to the free movement of goods,

---

[523] Barnard (n 47), 127.

[524] [1998] OJ L24/37. Repealing Directive 83/189/EEC, Directive 98/34/CE was amended shortly after its adoption by European Parliament and Council Directive 98/48/EC ([1998] OJ L207/18).

[525] Case C-194/94 *CIA Security International* [1996] ECR I-2201, para. 40.

which is one of the foundations of the EU,[526] this procedural directive completes the prohibition on MEEs within the meaning of Articles 34 and 35 TFEU, as well as the harmonization of national regulations through secondary law.[527] It can be described as an instrument of cooperation between the Commission and the Member States to ensure the smooth functioning of the internal market.

Thirty years after its entry into force, the Notification Directive has proved to be a fundamental internal market instrument. Unparalleled in other fields, this procedure for creating *ex ante* control over drafts of national technical regulations today exercises considerable influence on the product standard policies implemented by certain Member States. Its impact on the adoption of product standards by the national authorities is undeniable: so far, more than 12,300 drafts have been notified.[528] Thanks to the standstill period, both the Commission as well as the other Member States may request that the proposed legislation be adapted in order to reduce the risk of restrictions on the free movement of goods.

8.2.2 *Territorial scope*

The geographical scope of the directive has been gradually extended. It applies to all Member States, members of the EEA (Norway, Iceland, and Liechtenstein), EFTA States (Switzerland), as well as Turkey.

8.2.3 *Material scope*

8.2.3.1 **Introductory note**

The scope of the Directive has been gradually broadened to cover all measures relating to industrially manufactured products, agricultural products, including fish products, and information society services. The directive's scope is thus particularly broad. Having regard to the specialist nature of this book, the directive's obligations on information society services will not be discussed.

Constituting the linchpin of the directive, the notification (Art. 8) and standstill (Art. 9) procedures apply to the adoption of any 'draft technical regulation', that is defined as a function of its effects and not of its objective. In spite of the fact that the measures apply indiscriminately to domestic products and to imported products and that they pursue the objective of environmental protection, they are liable to be subject to the obligation to notify the Commission.[529] Similarly, the procedure also applies to rules falling in the area of criminal law.[530]

Given that it can include legislation as well as any form of secondary legislation, the concept of 'draft technical regulation' is extremely broad. It can also include measures such as administrative circulars, departmental guidelines, codes of practice, voluntary

---

[526] *CIA Security International* (n 525), para. 40; Case C-13/96 *Bic Benelux* [1997] ECR I-1753, para. 19; and Case C-226/97 *Lemmens* [1998] ECR I-3711, para. 32.

[527] *CIA Security International* (n 525), para. 40; *Bic Benelux* (n 526), para. 19.

[528] F. Herlitz, 'La politique de prévention des obstacles aux échanges de marchandises et de services de la société de l'information' (2008) 3 *RDUE* 405.

[529] *Bic Benelux* (n 526), para. 20.   [530] *Lemmens* (n 526), para. 20.

agreements, etc, if such documents recommend the use of given specifications or standards.[531]

In addition, in contrast to the Technical Barrier to Trade (TBT) Agreement, the Notification Directive does not contain any *de minimis* rule and does not operate any differentiation based on the value of the goods at issue or the importance of the market concerned. Accordingly, even draft technical rules with negligible economic impact are subject to the requirements for notification and standstill.

However, given that the directive's scope is distinct from the provisions of the TFEU on free movement of goods, the concept of 'draft technical regulation' is narrower than general case law on the concept of MEEs; for instance, the directive does not cover measures restricting certain selling arrangements. In effect, the directive applies as a function of the concept of a technical rule and does not depend on the criteria governing the applicability of the Treaty provisions examined earlier. It follows that compliance with the preventive control procedure does not have the effect of precluding the further application of Treaty provisions.

8.2.3.2 Prerequisites

According to a highly complex definition, the concept of 'draft technical regulation' must satisfy three prerequisites.

First, the drafts must be imputable to State authorities. Even though the directive may embrace draft regulations adopted only in part of a Member State, such as a region or a Land, drafts adopted by local authorities fall outside its scope.

Second, observance of the national draft must be 'compulsory, *de jure* or *de facto*'.

Third, the national draft must fall within the scope of one of the various categories of measure that are defined in Article 1(11): 'technical specifications', 'other requirements', 'national regulations prohibiting specific uses of a product', and 'rules on services'. Since the first three categories are likely to encompass a great number of environmental rules, we will endeavour to specify their scope.

8.2.3.3 Technical specification

Defining 'the characteristics required of a product', the 'technical specification' is thus referring, pursuant to Article 1(3), to 'levels of quality, performance, safety or dimensions, including the requirements applicable to the product as regards the name under which the product is sold, terminology, symbols, testing and test methods, packaging, marking or labelling and conformity assessment procedures'. The specification must therefore apply to the characteristics of the product or its packaging. Since a product cannot be placed on the market unless it complies with the 'technical specification', such specifications will directly affect the marketing of the product. The specification can serve a multitude of goals, such as consumer protection or protection of the environment.

Clearly, technical specifications abound within environmental law: maximum permitted thresholds of toxic substances in products with a risk profile, obligation to use

---

[531] Department of Trade and Industry (DTI), *Avoiding New Barriers to Trade. Directive 98/34/EC. Guidance for Officials* (2002) 1.

specific substances in the production of goods, composition, dimensions, tonnages, resistance, etc. A national draft requiring that bottles intended to contain mineral water comply with certain specifications regarding the characteristics of their packaging will accordingly fall within the ambit of the concept of technical specifications.

Underscoring the importance of the preventive control introduced by the notification regime in the area of technical standards and regulations, the Court of Justice has interpreted the different categories of 'technical specifications' broadly.[532] As far as environmental measures are concerned, it subjects several types of regulation to the preventive regime among which one encounters regulations concerning the quality of water and the production and marketing of some molluscs,[533] the composition, classification, packaging, and labelling of pesticides,[534] the prohibition on the marketing of cottonbuds not made from biodegradable materials,[535] and the prohibition on the extraction, importation, processing, use, marketing, treatment, and disposal in the national territory, as well as exportation, of asbestos, asbestos products, and products containing asbestos.[536]

Accordingly, a variety of draft environmental measures covering lead in petrol, marine anti-fouling paints, anglers' lead fishing weights, pesticides, hazardous substances, organic solvents, labelling to be placed on furs, asbestos, waste disposal, refrigerants in non-refillable containers, pesticides, animal by-products, hook-size restrictions, oil storage, water quality, catering waste, sludge, packaging waste, and end-of-waste criteria for the production and use of tyre-derived rubber materials, have been notified by State authorities to the Commission.[537]

Moreover, the Court has held that national measures requiring that special signs, markings, or labels be placed on goods must be classified as technical regulations.[538] The following environmental measures have been classified as technical specifications:

- distinctive signs affixed to products which are subject to a tax levied on them due to the environmental damage which they are deemed to cause;[539]

- the obligation of 'marking or labelling' imposed on producers and importers of products marketed in packaging in order to determine which packaging will be handled by an organization responsible for their recycling.[540]

That said, a distinction must be drawn between, on the one hand, enabling measures which are not subject to the requirement of notification on the ground that they do not

---

[532] The case law is mainly related to the definitions in Directive 83/189/EEC now replaced by Directive 98/34/EC.

[533] Case C-61/93 *Commission v Netherlands* [1994] ECR I-3607.

[534] Case C-289/94 *Commission v Italy* [1996] ECR I-4405.

[535] Case C-303/04 *Lidl Italia* [2005] ECR I-7865.

[536] Case C-279/94 *Commission v Italy* [1997] ECR I-4743, para. 30.

[537] N. de Sadeleer, 'Internal Market Preventive Controls of National Technical Standards and their Impact on Environmental Measures' (2011) 8:3 *JEELP* 258.

[538] Case C-317/92 *Commission v Germany* [1994] ECR I-2039, para. 25; Case C-443/98 *Unilever* [2000] ECR I-7535; Case C-145/97 *Commission v Belgium* [1998] ECR I-2643; Case C-65/05 *Commission v Greece* [2006] ECR I-10341, para. 61.

[539] *Bic Benelux* (n 526), paras 25 and 26.

[540] Case C-159/00 *Sapod Audic* [2002] ECR I-5031, para. 46.

constitute a new specification and, on the other, implementation measures which are taken on the basis of these enabling provisions. Such measures must be notified.[541]

It follows that a provision which obliges the producer or importer of packaging to 'identify', without however requiring it to place a marking or label on this packaging, does not specify the characteristics required of a product and, accordingly, will not be classified as a technical specification.[542] Nonetheless, the national court may reach the conclusion, having regard to all the factual and legal evidence, that the enabling provision to identify the packaging must be interpreted as amounting to a technical specification. This is not precluded by the fact that the detailed rules regarding the marking or labelling are yet to be defined.[543]

8.2.3.4 Other requirements

Considered as 'technical regulation', pursuant to Article 1(4) the 'other requirements' cover 'all requirements, other than a technical specification, imposed on a product for the purpose of protecting... the environment and which affect [a product's] life cycle after it has been placed on the market, such as conditions of use, recycling, reuse or disposal.'[544]

However, in order to qualify as 'other requirements', these conditions must be likely to have 'a significant influence on the composition or nature of the product or its marketing'.

The essential difference with the concept of 'technical specification' lies in the fact that the 'other requirement' does not necessarily apply to the product as such or its packaging; rather, it amounts to a measure regulating its use after it is placed on the market.

As far as environmental measures are concerned, drafts of measures which impose specific obligations regarding the conditions for using a product—labels on packaging, obligation to reuse the discarded product, obligation seeking to impose a return or reuse system for packaging, or even the separate collection of certain products,[545] consumer notices, etc—must be notified to the European Commission.[546]

8.2.3.5 National regulations prohibiting specific uses of a product

By virtue of Article 1(11), national authorities responsible for environmental protection must take particular account of a third category of technical regulations that encompass: 'laws, regulations or administrative provisions... prohibiting the manufacture, importation, marketing or use of a product...', which are particularly numerous in the areas of waste management and chemical substances. These regulatory measures are supposed to 'leave no room for any use which can reasonably be made

---

[541] Case C-317/92 *Commission v Germany* (n 538), para. 26.

[542] Case C-278/99 *Vandenburg* [2001] ECR I-2015, para. 20; *Sapod Audic* (n 540), para. 30.

[543] *Sapod Audic* (n 540), paras 33 and 34.

[544] This concept was included in Directive 94/10/EC, at the time of the second amendment of the text. Regarding the scope of the different waste management techniques encapsulated in the Waste Framework Directive, see N. de Sadeleer, 'Déchets' (2013) 1934 *Jurisclasseurs Europe* 1–20.

[545] European Commission, *A guide to the procedure of information in the field of technical Standards and regulations and the rules on the Information Society services* (2005) 21.

[546] For further illustrations, see de Sadeleer (n 537), 260.

of the product concerned other than a purely marginal one'.[547] It follows that draft regulations prohibiting the manufacture of a substance such as DTT or asbestos would appear in any event to be subject to the obligation to notify, even though the planned measures would not hinder the free movement of goods.

Insofar as Directive 98/34/EC does not apply to national measures aiming at 'the protection of persons, in particular workers, when products are used, provided that such measures do not affect the products' (Art. 1(12) *in fine*), a national draft regulation restricting the use of devices considered to be dangerous to some categories of qualified workers is exempt from the notification procedure.

8.2.3.6 *De facto* technical regulations

In addition to the three categories mentioned earlier, the directive provides examples of various '*de facto* technical regulations'.

(i) Voluntary agreements

By virtue of Article 1(11) 'voluntary agreements to which a public authority is a contracting party and which provide, in the general interest, for compliance with technical specifications or other requirements or rules on services...' are subject to the procedural requirements.

Generally speaking, whereas a technical specification is mandatory, compliance with a voluntary agreement is optional. For instance, imported goods which do not comply with technical requirements cannot be placed on the market, whilst a good that does not comply with the requirements of a voluntary eco-label is not prevented from entering the domestic market. That said, voluntary agreements could hinder access to the domestic market. Indeed, domestic undertakings that are able to bear the extra costs incurred by voluntary certification of their environmentally friendly products might overpower foreign undertakings not endowed with such resources.

Under Article 1(11), the voluntary agreements must provide 'for compliance' with technical specifications or other requirements. Contrary to technical product standards which focus on the intrinsic qualities of a product, voluntary agreements promoting the labelling of environmentally friendly products may require compliance with a number of 'other requirements' such as a life-cycle analysis of the environmental impacts of the product, and in particular assessment of the environmental impact of process and production methods.[548]

Since the obligations to collect and recover waste provided for under secondary law are increasingly often contained in voluntary agreements concluded between public authorities and certain branches of industry,[549] where they have not been notified to the Commission, such agreements may be deemed inapplicable. Moreover, failure to notify or non-compliance with the standstill period are liable—in accordance with the

---

[547] Case C-267/03 [2005] *Lindberg* ECR I-3247, para. 77.
[548] See, in particular, European Parliament and Council Regulation (EC) No. 1980/2000 on a revised Community eco-label award scheme [2000] OJ L37/1, Art. 2(2)(b).
[549] See Chapter 4, Section 4.4 and Chapter 9.

Unilever case law, confirmed in the area of waste management by the *Sapod Audic* judgment—to affect contractual relations between private individuals.

(ii) Fiscal measures

Attention should also be drawn to the fact that, by virtue of Article 1(11), 'technical specifications or other requirements or rules on services which are linked to fiscal... measures affecting the consumption of products... by encouraging compliance with such technical specifications or other requirements or rules on services' are also considered *de facto* technical regulations. In other words, where they promote respect for technical standards, fiscal measures also amount to *de facto* technical regulation.

For instance, a draft regulation providing for an environmental fee on plastic bags is likely to be considered a '*de facto* technical regulation'. Confronted with the issue of mandatory marking of products subject to environmental tax, in order to ensure that the collection of environmental tax is monitored, the Court of Justice held in *Bic Benelux* that this obligation could in no way be regarded as exclusively a fiscal accompanying measure, which was at that time subject to a derogatory notification regime. Accordingly, an obligation 'to affix specific distinctive signs to products which are subject to a tax levied on them on account of the environmental damage which they are deemed to cause', constitutes a 'technical regulation'.[550]

However, pursuant to Article 8(1)(vi), observations and detailed opinions regarding technical specifications or other requirements relating to fiscal or financial measures which may be issued by the Commission and by the other Member States may concern 'only the aspect which may hinder trade and not the fiscal or financial aspect of the measure'. It follows that neither the Commission nor the Member States can challenge the tax basis or the tax rates. Only the aspects of the draft fiscal regulation which might hinder trade in goods are subject to the assessment.

(iii) Financial measures

Finally, 'financial measures affecting the consumption of products... by encouraging compliance with such technical specifications or other requirements' are also considered *de facto* technical regulations. Therefore, public subsidies encouraging the purchase of energy-saving devices—photovoltaic power generation, wind turbines to produce electricity, tax incentives granted to clean vehicles which met certain emission limits or equipped with catalytic converters—are subject to the notification and standstill procedure. However, the Notification Directive does not cover financial measures carried out in support of certain enterprises or products, pursuant to Articles 107 TFEU.[551]

8.2.4 Prior notification and suspension of draft technical rules

8.2.4.1 Obligation to inform

In order to prevent the adoption of technical regulations from giving rise to measures having an equivalent effect to a quantitative restriction on trade in goods, Directive

---

[550] *Bic Benelux* (n 526), paras 25 and 26.   [551] See Chapter 12.

98/34/EC establishes a procedure for prior notification to the Commission for any 'draft technical regulation' planned by the Member States. However, Member States are not required to communicate a modified draft provided that the modification is not 'significantly altering its scope'.[552] In this connection, the Court ruled that a relaxation of the conditions of use of a product reduced the possible impact of a technical regulation on trade.[553]

Since the objective of Article 8(1) of the directive is to permit the Commission as well as the other Member States that could be affected by the proposed regulation to obtain information that is as complete as possible in order to enable them to exercise their powers as effectively as possible, the Member States must provide the complete text containing the draft technical rule,[554] accompanied, depending on the circumstances, by a statement of the reasons for and the basic legislative or regulatory provisions. Thus, the Court judged that only a throughout communication of an Italian law on asbestos could allow the Commission to evaluate the exact scope of the technical rules it eventually contained.[555] However, by virtue of Article 8(5), compliance with these formalities releases the Member State from the requirement to notify the draft a second time within the context of other regulatory procedures.

Of particular importance regarding environmental protection, the communication of draft technical regulations which seek to limit the marketing or use of substances, preparations, or chemical products on the grounds of public health or the protection of consumers or the environment must also include the scientific evidence justifying their adoption, including by virtue of Article 8(1)(4) an analysis of the risks. This assessment must be carried out in accordance with the general principles for risk assessment enshrined in the REACH Regulation.

8.2.4.2 Obligations placed on the Commission and other Member States

The draft brought to the attention of the Commission is subsequently transmitted to the other Member States. The Member State which has notified the draft is then subject to a standstill obligation and thus required to suspend its adoption to allow sufficient time for it to be examined by the Commission and the other Member States.

If neither a Member State nor the Commission takes any action on the notification during the three-month standstill period, the Member State is free to adopt the draft technical regulation at the end of that period.

Member States may state their opinion that the planned measure may constitute an obstacle to the free movement of goods. If another Member State or the Commission comment on the draft, the originating Member State is required pursuant to Article 8(2) to take such comments into account as far as possible in the subsequent preparation of the regulation.

If the draft is considered to be a barrier to trade, a detailed opinion[556] may be submitted by the Commission or another Member State and this will extend the

---

[552] Art. 8(1).
[553] *Sandström* (n 248), paras 47 and 48. [554] Case C-289/94 *Commission v Italy* (n 534), para. 41.
[555] Case C-289/94 *Commission v Italy* (n 534), paras 39 and 40.
[556] It is not at all clear what is meant by 'detailed opinion' in Art. 9(2).

Table 5.8 Standstill obligations relating to the notification of draft regulation of products

Notification	Initial standstill period of 3 months
Comments from the Commission or other Member State	No further standstill
Detailed opinion from the Commission or other Member State	Further standstill period of 3 months
Intention of the Commission to propose a harmonized measure	Extension of the standstill period to 12 months
Adoption of a common position by the Council during the 12-month standstill period	Extension of the standstill period to 18 months

standstill period for a further three months.[557] During that period, the originating Member State must report to the Commission on the action it proposes to take.

If the Commission announces its intention to propose a directive on the matter, the Member State is then called upon to postpone the adoption of the draft for 12 months. The freezing of the national draft may facilitate the adoption at EU level of a harmonization measure that is likely to hinder the functioning of the internal market to a lesser degree.[558] See Table 5.8 for an overview of the standstill obligations in this regard.

That said, on conclusion of the procedure the Member State is still entitled to adopt its draft technical regulation even though it has been subject to a detailed opinion. A copy of the definitive text must be sent to the Commission without further justification.[559] Indeed, by virtue of Article 8(2), the Member State is merely required 'to take such comments into account in the subsequent preparation of the technical regulation'.

In that respect, the notification and suspension procedure provided for under the Notification Directive is quite distinctive from the authorization procedure provided for under Article 114(6) TFEU.[560] Moreover, the hurdles to overcome are not as high as those under Article 34 TFEU. In fact, the Member State notifying the draft is not required to justify the measure in the light of Article 36 TFEU or the rule of reason.

8.2.4.3 Limits to the notification requirements

In spite of the fact that they are scattered over various provisions and drafted without particular concern for consistency, limits have nevertheless been placed on the obligation to notify the draft immediately. Only the extent of the limits which affect national policies on environmental matters will be discussed here.

In accordance with Article 9(7), the notification of the draft regulation is not required in cases where there are 'urgent reasons, occasioned by serious and unforeseeable circumstances relating to the protection of public health or safety, the

---

[557] Art. 9(2).

[558] By way of illustration, the draft regulation on prohibition of imports of furs of animals caught by leghold traps, notified by the UK under former Directive 83/189/EEC, met much resistance. As a result, this submission led the Commission to submit its own proposal on the matter, that became Regulation (EEC) No. 3254/91 of 4 November 1991 prohibiting the use of leghold traps in the Community and the introduction into the Community of pelts and manufactured goods of certain wild animal species originating in countries which catch them by means of leghold traps or trapping methods which do not meet international humane trapping standards [1991] OJ L308/1. See Gormley (n 276), 301.

[559] Art. 8(3).

[560] N. de Sadeleer, 'Procedures for Derogations From the Principle of Approximation of Laws under Article 95 EC' (2003) 40:4 *CML Rev* 889–915. See the discussion in Chapter 7, Section 3.

protection of animals or the preservation of plants'.[561] Likewise, under Article 8(1) the notification does not take place if it 'merely transposes the full text of an international or European standard, in which case information regarding the relevant standard shall suffice'.

Besides, pursuant to Article 10(1), first indent, Articles 8 (notification requirement) and 9 (standstill requirement) are not applicable in cases of 'compliance with binding [EU] acts which result in the adoption of technical specifications or rules on services'. The wording of this provision clearly raises several interpretative difficulties. The term 'comply' must be interpreted as to 'act in accordance with'.[562] According to the case law, whenever the harmonization measure offers a sufficiently substantial margin of appreciation to the national authorities, the transposing legislation cannot copy it in full. Accordingly, the national measure could not benefit from this exemption.[563] In *Sapod Audic* the Court of Justice rejected the argument according to which the French obligation to identify by way of appropriate labelling packaging destined to be collected and processed by an approved waste-management undertaking did not fall within the ambit of former Directive 83/189/EEC on the ground that the national arrangements were intended to transpose Waste Framework Directive 75/442/EEC. According to the Court, inasmuch as this directive leaves Member States 'a significant degree of freedom', the disputed national measure did not have the purpose of conforming with the EU secondary law on waste.[564]

Finally, by virtue of Article 10(1), third indent, where Member States 'make use of safeguard clauses provided for in binding [EU] acts', Articles 8 and 9 are not applicable. The conditions in respect of the implementation of safeguard clauses, which imply EU control proceedings, will now be examined.[565]

8.2.5 *Private enforcement*

Given that Directive 98/43 promotes 'a regulated dialogue' between the Member State proposing the draft, the Commission, and the other Member States,[566] one may wonder whether failure to make the notification required under that directive is able to be invoked by an individual in order to render the technical regulation in question inapplicable. Indeed, according to the *Enichem Base* case law, individuals may not derive any right from the fact that the Member State has not respected the procedures laid down by the directives for communicating draft regulations prior to their adoption.[567]

---

[561] As far as the emergency proceeding is concerned, the Court of Justice implicitly indicated that the existence of motives allowing invocation of this proceeding did not exempt the Member States from their obligation to notify their technical rules. Case C-289/94 *Commission v Italy* (n 534), para. 26.

[562] *Shorter Oxford English Dictionary,* vol. 1 (Oxford: OUP, 2002).

[563] Case C-289/94 *Commission v Italy* (n 534), paras 36, 43, and 44.

[564] *Sapod Audic* (n 540), paras 43–6.

[565] See the discussion in Chapter 7, Section 3.4.1.   [566] Barnard (n 47), 129.

[567] Case C-380/87 *Enichem Base* [1989] ECR 2491. The Court recently confirmed that the obligation that Directive 75/442/EEC on waste imposes on the Member States to inform the Commission of planned implementation measures did not give individuals any right which they may enforce before national courts (*Sapod Audic* (n 540), paras 58–63).

The situation is, however, different under the notification procedure. Breach of the requirement to notify,[568] as well as the adoption of a national technical rule during the period of suspension,[569] constitute 'a substantial procedural defect'[570] of such a nature as to entail two consequences.

First, all State bodies are under an obligation not to apply not only technical rules which were not communicated during the drafting stage to the European Commission, but also any technical rule adopted without respecting the standstill period imposed by the directive.

Second, the defect will result in the non-applicability of the technical rules to individuals, and will therefore not be open to challenge on account of the prohibition on horizontal direct effect. However, according to *Lemmens* case law, this requirement of non-application only applies where the technical rules 'hinder the use or the marketing of a product which was not in conformity' with these rules.[571] It follows that the mere qualification of a measure as a technical specification is not sufficient to render it inapplicable to private individuals. Its inapplicability depends on the extent to which the measure restricts the free movement of goods.

The invalidity or unenforceability of a contract which was purportedly concluded in accordance with a technical rule affected by such a defect is governed by national law, subject to compliance with the principles of equivalence and effectiveness. In *Sapod Audic*, a dispute involving a packaging waste-management company and one of its affiliates, the Court of Justice followed its judgment in *CIA Security International*, holding that it was for the national court to refuse to apply a technical regulation, in accordance with Directive 83/189, concerning the identification of the packaging concerned.[572] Moreover, the severity of the action to be applied in such case, such as nullity or unenforceability of the contract, has to be governed by national law.[573]

8.3 Other notification procedures under internal market directives

It will be immediately clear that some secondary environmental legislation includes notification rules intended to guarantee respect for the internal market. This is the case in particular for Directive 94/62/EC of 20 December 1994 on packaging and packaging waste, that obliges the Member States to notify any more ambitious recycling targets than the rates required under the directive.[574] The *ratio legis* here is to prevent disruption to recycling markets.[575]

8.4 Information for economic operators

Although for more than half a century the EU institutions have committed themselves to guaranteeing the free movement of goods by dismantling all State tariff or non-tariff

---

[568] *CIA Security International* (n 525), para. 48; *Lemmens* (n 526), para. 33.
[569] Case C-443/98 *Unilever* [2000] ECR I-7535, para. 34.
[570] *CIA Security International* (n 525), para. 48; *Unilever* (n 569), para. 45; *Lemmens* (n 526), para. 33; *Sandström* (n 248), para. 23.
[571] *Lemmens* (n 526), para. 35.   [572] *Sapod Audic* (n 540), para. 51.
[573] *Sapod Audic* (n 540), para. 52.   [574] Packaging Directive 94/62/EC.
[575] De Sadeleer, *Le droit communautaire et les déchets* (n 135), 395–6.

measures, the balance of this action remains mixed, especially due to technical short-comings (harmonization of national regulations in different forms). In order to maintain the dynamics of the internal market, three legislative texts were adopted by the European Parliament and the Council on 9 July 2008. These three texts aim at setting out:

- a common framework for the marketing of products;[576]
- the requirements for accreditation and market surveillance relating to the mar-keting of products;[577]
- procedures relating to the application of certain national technical rules to prod-ucts lawfully marketed in another Member State.[578]

Despite their technical differences, these three regulations make up a coherent set of rules in the service of the same goal—the free movement of goods in the internal market. By facilitating the implementation of the principle of mutual recognition, this body of legislation reinforces the framework for the policing powers vested in the Member States in the absence of harmonization.[579] This means that the competences of the Member States in matters concerning the regulation of products which do not fall within the reach of a directive or a harmonization regulation will be significantly more controlled than they were in the past. Accordingly, this new legislative framework contributes to reinforcing a construction which originated from judge-made law.

Regulation (EC) No. 764/2008 relating to the application of certain national tech-nical rules to products lawfully marketed in another Member State is of special interest for the national administrations responsible for health and the environment. The regulation complements Directive 98/34/EC that lays down a preventive control for the adoption of any draft technical regulation concerning any product, in ensuring that, following the adoption of such a technical regulation, the principle of mutual recognition is correctly applied in individual cases to specific products. In contrast to the directive that applies to regulatory measures, the regulation applies in individual cases.

In enhancing the correct application of the principle of mutual recognition by the Member States, Regulation (EC) No. 764/2008 aims to minimize the possibility of technical rules 'creating unlawful obstacles to the free movement of goods between Member States'.[580] Its principal goal is to improve information for economic operators regarding the decisions taken by the national authorities relating to their products.

---

[576] European Parliament and Council Decision 768/2008/EC on a common framework for the market-ing of products, and repealing Council Decision 93/465/EEC [2008] OJ L218/82.

[577] European Parliament and Council Regulation (EC) No. 765/2008 setting out the requirements for accreditation and market surveillance relating to the marketing of products and repealing Regulation (EEC) No. 339/93 [2008] OJ L218/30.

[578] European Parliament and Council Regulation (EC) No. 764/2008 laying down procedures relating to the application of certain national technical rules to products lawfully marketed in another Member State and repealing Decision 3052/95/EC [2008] OJ L218/21.

[579] R. Kovar, 'Le législateur communautaire encadre le régime de la mise des produits dans le marché intérieur' (2008) 44:2 *RTDE* 289–311.

[580] Recital 4.

The administrative decision must be directed to an economic operator and must concern a product lawfully marketed in another Member State which is not subject to harmonized EU law. Pursuant to Article 2, the direct or indirect effect of that decision must be the prohibition of a product, the modification or additional testing of that product, and its withdrawal. Moreover, the decision must be based on a technical rule. In addition to the requirements regarding the intrinsic properties of the product, such as levels of quality, performance, or safety, the 'technical rule' includes 'any other requirement which is imposed on the product or type of product for the purposes of protecting consumers or the environment, and which affects the life-cycle of the product after it has been placed on the market, such as conditions of use, recycling, reuse or disposal, where such conditions can significantly influence the composition, nature or marketing of the product or type of product'.[581] As discussed previously, these 'other requirements' are likely to encompass a number of waste-management and environmental producer responsibility rules. However, a requirement that the placing of a product on the market be subject to prior authorization should, as such, not constitute a technical rule within the meaning of this regulation. Accordingly, a decision to exclude or remove a product from the market exclusively on the ground that it does not have valid prior authorization should not constitute a decision to which the regulation applies.[582]

Before regulating the product or its placing on the market, the national authority is required to issue to the economic operator concerned a written notice of its intention, specifying the technical rule which will act as a basis for its decision and providing the technical or scientific information which will justify its decision. In addition, the national authority is called upon to communicate to the operator the overriding reasons of public interest for imposing national technical rules on its product and why less restrictive measures cannot be as effective. Thus, as stressed by Barnard, the burden of proof has been shifted from the trader to the State of destination that must justify on which grounds the product cannot be marketed.[583] In the case of failure to notify within the period laid down in the regulation, the product is deemed to be lawfully marketed in the Member State. The economic operator concerned must be allowed to present its observations within a time limit of 20 days. The decision, which must contain reasons, specifies the procedure which the operator should follow in order to challenge the decision, should it decide to do so. Moreover, in order to improve the information provided to businesses, the Member States must establish 'Product Contact Points'.

8.5 Concluding remarks

Given the shortcomings of negative harmonization, the EU lawmaker has adopted different procedural acts aiming to improve the free movement of goods that fall outside the scope of EU harmonization. These notification and information procedures complement the rules of primary law that were analysed in the previous sections.

---

[581] Art. 2(2)(b)(ii).		[582] Recital 12.		[583] Barnard (n 47), 136.

In laying down a procedure for the provision of information in the field of technical standards and regulation, the Notification Directive is intended to help to avoid the creation of new regulatory barriers to trade within the EU. Given that draft technical regulation can cover a host of environmental measures including bans, quotas, import and export permits, prior informed consent procedure, mandatory labelling schemes, certification procedure, testing procedure, warning notices, labelling requirements, and emission thresholds that are likely to determine which product can be placed on the market, its scope covers a gamut of environmental measures.

In addition, the notification and standstill procedures increase transparency, since national draft regulations are brought to the attention of the authorities and interested parties before being enacted.

More recently, Regulation (EC) No. 764/2008 frames how national authorities monitor compliance with national technical rules on goods not covered by harmonized EU law. Member States which prohibit access for these goods to their markets are obliged to make contact with the enterprise and to produce detailed objective reasons for refusal.

Given that the objective of both Directive 98/43/EC and Regulation (EC) No. 764/2008 is to strengthen the internal market by improving the free movement of goods, these acts may be seen as additional deterrents to the development of a national environmental product policy.

6

Freedom of Establishment, Free Movement of Services, and the Environment

1. Introduction

Since services today make up more than two-thirds of EU GDP and are the main source of job creation, the manner of wealth creation may be regulated comprehensively for environmental purposes in the same way as goods. As a result, certain obstacles of an administrative nature may also affect economic operators which wish to establish themselves in other Member States by virtue of the right of establishment contained in Article 49 TFEU, as well as those which provide services in another Member State without, however, establishing themselves there pursuant to the free movement of services under the terms of Articles 56 and 57 TFEU.

Moreover, the increasing interpenetration between categories of goods and services, as well as the position occupied by environmental services in Directive 2006/123/EC on services in the internal market (hereinafter 'Services Directive'), underscore the risk of conflicts between national measures intended to protect the environment and the free movement of services.

That said, barriers to the freedom of establishment for service providers and barriers to the free movement of services between Member States cannot be removed solely by relying on direct application of Articles 49 and 56 TFEU, since addressing them on a case-by-case approach through infringement proceedings is deemed to be inefficient.

Against this background, in 2006 the EU lawmaker adopted the Services Directive—a 'legal framework' that aims at achieving 'a genuine internal market for services'.[1]

Having regard both to the specialist nature of this book as well as the fact that few conflicts between these fundamental freedoms and national environmental measures have been ruled on by the Court of Justice, this chapter will be limited, following a brief overview of the requirements contained in Treaty law, to a discussion of the various provisions contained in the Services Directive.

As confirmed by the dual aspect of the Services Directive, there are points of intersection between the freedom of establishment and the freedom to provide services which constitutes, pursuant to Article 26(2) TFEU, together with the free movement of goods, one of the four basic freedoms of movement underlying the internal market. Indeed, the freedom to provide services may be facilitated by the establishment of new logistical bases—waste-treatment plants—which make it possible to offer services to citizens of the host country as well as to those of other Member States. Accordingly, this chapter addresses these two freedoms simultaneously.[2]

2. Treaty Law

2.1 Freedom of establishment

In precluding any national measure which, even though it is applicable without discrimination on ground of nationality, is liable to hinder or to render less attractive the exercise by EU citizens of the freedom of establishment,[3] Article 49 TFEU guarantees to every citizen of a Member State the right to establish themselves stably within another Member State with a view to pursuing an independent economic activity there. In contrast to the freedom to provide services, the economic activity relevant for the freedom of establishment cannot be pursued on a temporary basis in the host country, only in a stable and continuous manner.

However, it is settled law that 'restrictions on freedom of establishment which are applicable without discrimination on grounds of nationality may be justified by overriding reasons relating to the general interest, provided that the restrictions are appropriate for securing attainment of the objective pursued and do not go beyond what is necessary for attaining that objective'.[4] Most importantly, from our perspective,

---

[1] European Parliament and Council Directive 2006/123/EC on services in the internal market [2006] OJ L376/36, recitals 6 and 12.

[2] There is a rather fine line between freedom of establishment and freedom of services, in particular when the service provider spends a substantial amount of time in the Member State where the service is provided. The difference may be one of degree rather than of substance, the decisive factor being the duration which is not the subject of a clear-cut definition. See Opinion AG Jacobs in Case C-76/90 *Säger* [1991] ECR I-4221, paras 25 and 26. See C. Barnard, *The Substantive Law of the EU*, 3rd edn (Oxford: OUP, 2007) 367–8, A. G. Toth, *The Oxford Encyclopaedia of European Community Law*, vol. II (Oxford: OUP, 2005) 316.

[3] See, inter alia, Case C-299/02 *Commission v Netherlands* [2004] ECR I-9761, para. 15; and Case C-140/03 *Commission v Greece* [2005] ECR I-3177, para. 27.

[4] Case C-169/07 *Hartlauer* [2009] ECR I-1721, para. 44; Joined Cases C-171/07 & C-172/07 *Apothekerkammer des Saarlandes and Others* [2009] ECR I-4171, para. 25; and Joined Cases C-570/07 & C-571/07 *Blanco Pérez and Chao Gómez* [2010] ECR I-4629, para. 61.

such overriding reasons recognized by the Court include, among others, environmental protection[5] as well as town and country planning.[6] To date, the Court of Justice has seldom had the opportunity to rule on the validity of restrictions to the right to freedom of establishment on environmental protection grounds. In this connection, three cases will suffice.

With respect to land planning, legislation which makes the establishment of any large retail establishment on the territory of the Autonomous Community of Catalonia conditional upon the issue of prior authorization, falls within the concept of 'restriction' for the purposes of Article 49 TFEU, since it is capable of hindering the exercise by that undertaking of freedom of establishment, by preventing it from freely pursuing its activities through a fixed place of business.[7]

Spain argued that the restrictions on the location and size of large retail establishments which follow from the prohibition on setting up such establishments outside the consolidated urban areas of a limited number of municipalities were appropriate for achieving objectives relating to town and country planning and environmental protection. Indeed, by confining the location of large retail establishments to population centres, where the demand is greatest, and by limiting the size of establishments in less populous areas, the contested legislation seeks to avoid polluting car journeys, to counter urban decay, to preserve an environmentally integrated urban model, to avoid new road building, and to ensure access by public transport. Contrary to the assertions made by the Commission, the Court held that restrictions relating to the location and size of large retail establishments appear to be 'methods suitable for achieving the objectives relating to town and country planning and environmental protection'.[8] However, the Court took the view that Spain had not produced sufficient evidence to explain the reasons for which the restrictions at issue were necessary to achieve the objectives pursued.[9]

Relatedly, the requirement to obtain a licence before opening a large retail establishment has been regarded as an appropriate means of achieving the objective of environmental protection and of town and country planning. Indeed, the adoption of measures a posteriori (if setting up a retail establishment already built should prove to have a negative impact on environmental protection), appears a less effective and more costly alternative to the system of prior authorization.[10] The judgment is thus based on the assumption that prevention is better than cure.[11] However, purely economic considerations, such as the application of ceilings for market share and the impact on existing retail trade, cannot constitute an overriding reason in the public interest.[12]

Moreover, the establishment of a committee, with responsibility for drawing up a report before any decision on the issuing or refusal of a licence is taken (account being

---

[5] Case C-384/08 *Attanasio Group* [2010] ECR I-2025, para. 50.
[6] Case C-400/08 *Commission v Spain* [2011] OJ C152/2, para. 74. See, by analogy, Case C-567/07 *Woningstichting Sint Servatius* [2009] ECR I-9021, para. 29 and the cases cited therein.
[7] Case C-400/08 *Commission v Spain* (n 6), para. 64. As regards drugstores, see *Blanco Pérez and Chao Gómez* (n 4), para. 54.
[8] Case C-400/08 *Commission v Spain* (n 6), para. 79.
[9] Case C-400/08 *Commission v Spain* (n 6), paras 83–5.
[10] Case C-400/08 *Commission v Spain* (n 6), para. 92.
[11] See Chapter 1, Section 7.4.   [12] Case C-400/08 *Commission v Spain* (n 6), para. 97.

taken in particular of aspects of town and country planning and environmental protection), is appropriate for ensuring achievement of the objectives pursued in that regard by that provision.[13] However, sectoral interest represented in that committee cannot be restricted to existing local trade.[14]

Finally, Spanish law provides for a 'negative silence system' by providing that failure to grant a licence within the period allowed constitutes an implied decision rejecting the application. Such a regime is aiming at ensuring legal certainty in the event that the authority responsible for ruling on the application does not take an express decision within the period allowed. Moreover, it enables the party which made the application to apply to the courts. Given that this system is easily managed and supervised by the competent authorities, the Court of Justice held that the measure at issue achieves the objectives, such as environmental protection, town and country planning, and consumer protection.[15]

Let us now turn to another case raising similar questions. The EFTA Court found against Norwegian legislation providing, on the one hand, for concessions for an unlimited period of time for public undertakings which had acquired dams with a view to producing hydroelectric energy whilst, on the other hand, applying different concession arrangements with time limits for foreign undertakings.[16] The difference in treatment amounted to indirect discrimination within the meaning of Article 31(1) of the Treaty on the European Economic Area (TEEA), a provision reproduced in identical form by Article 49 TFEU.[17] Nevertheless, the EFTA Court found that nothing prevented Norway from establishing the contested regime pursuant to Article 125 TEEA—a provision equivalent to Article 228 TFEU—which sought to guarantee a certain level of public control over that sector of the economy.[18] According to the Court, the exercise of control over the dams by the public authorities could be classified as an overriding reason relating to the public interest justifying discriminatory arrangements where such control furthers other legitimate public interests, such as protection of the environment and the security of energy supplies.[19] However, the Court did not see how the protection of the environment could be better guaranteed by Norwegian public undertakings benefiting from an unlimited concession than it could by private undertakings. According to the EFTA Court, it was incumbent upon Norway to demonstrate whether other measures, such as more exacting administrative requirements, could reach the goal of environmental protection in an equally effective manner.

However, internal restrictions will not be caught by Article 49 TFEU. In a case concerning the decision by a municipality to establish, without a prior call for tenders, a

---

[13] Case C-400/08 *Commission v Spain* (n 6), para. 108.
[14] Case C-400/08 *Commission v Spain* (n 6), para. 111.
[15] Case C-400/08 *Commission v Spain* (n 6), paras 124 and 125.
[16] Case E-2/06 *Surveillance Authority v Norway* [2007] EFTA Ct. Rep. 164, paras 64–7.
[17] Art. 31(1), first para. reads: 'Within the framework of the provisions of this Agreement, there shall be no restrictions on the freedom of establishment of nationals of an EC Member State or an EFTA State in the territory of any other of these States. This shall also apply to the setting up of agencies, branches or subsidiaries by nationals of any EC Member State or EFTA State established in the territory of any of these States'.
[18] *Surveillance Authority v Norway* (n 16), para. 73.
[19] *Surveillance Authority v Norway* (n 16), paras 78–81.

financial company to run the solid urban waste-collection service, the Court held that Article 49 TFEU did not apply on the ground that the case was confined in all respects to a single Member State.[20]

2.2 Freedom to provide services

By virtue of Article 56 TFEU, the freedom to provide services is ensured by the prohibition of restrictions capable of hindering its exercise. In brief, as regards the scope of that provision, the Court refrained from taking a bold approach comparable to *Dassonville*; rather, it endorsed a more subtle approach 'combining the discrimination standard with the restriction approach'.[21] Nonetheless, the freedom enshrined in Article 56 TFEU is subject to important limitations. Both the TFEU as well as the Court of Justice have put in place a range of grounds of justification, authorizing Member States to maintain restrictions where they are justified by virtue of Article 52 TFEU on grounds of 'public policy, public security or public health' or satisfy one of the 'overriding reasons relating to the public interest' recognized by the Court of Justice due to their non-economic nature.[22] Such overriding reasons may justify the application of authorizations or other administrative restrictions justified by environmental considerations. However, reasons of a purely economic nature are not accepted. In addition, the restrictions must be applied in a non-discriminatory manner and should be proportionate.

That said, in contrast to the case law on free movement of goods discussed previously, only in very exceptional cases has the Court of Justice had the opportunity to examine the compatibility of restrictions justified on environmental protection grounds with reference to Article 56 TFEU.[23] This may be explained by the fact that free movement of goods was long regarded as a *lex generalis*, a view which has now been abandoned.[24]

---

[20] Case C-108/98 *RI.SAN* [1999] ECR I-5219, para. 23.

[21] W.-H. Roth, 'The European Court of Justice's Case Law on Freedom to Provide Services: Is *Keck* Relevant?' in M. Andenas and W.-H. Roth (eds), *Services and Free Movement in EU Law* (Oxford: OUP, 2004) 14–15.

[22] The list of derogations set out in Art. 52 TFEU is clearly narrower than that set out in Art. 36 TFEU. Referring to three justifications (public policy, public security, or public health), Art. 52 TFEU does not mention the environment. However, the Court has made it possible to complete this list through the concept of 'overriding reasons relating to the public interest'. As with the *Cassis de Dijon* case law on free movement of goods (see Chapter 5, Section 4.3.2.1), the Court of Justice has permitted Member States to justify their restrictions on grounds of emerging society values, such as protection of consumers, the environment, workers, and the urban environment including town and country planning.

[23] Concerning the procurement contracts of services in the transport sector, see Case C-513/99 *Concordia Bus Finland* [2002] ECR I-7213, para. 57.

[24] Since Art. 57 TFEU holds that the provisions of services are only considered as such 'in so far as they are not governed by the provisions relating to freedom of movement for goods', the notion of service has traditionally taken on a residuary nature. By way of illustration, recital 76 of the Services Directive emphasizes where this line in drawn. At present, when a national measure affects both the freedom to provide services and the free movement of goods, the Court of Justice reviews it against one of those fundamental freedoms if it turns out that, under the circumstances of the case, one is ancillary compared to another and can be related to it. Eg Case C-275/92 *Schindler* [1994] ECR I-1039, para. 22; Case C-390/99 *Canal Satélite Digital* [2002] ECR I-607, para. 31; Case C-71/02 *Karner* [2004] ECR I-3025, para. 46; Case C-36/02 *Omega* [2004] ECR I-9609, para. 27; and Case C-108/09 *Ker-Optika* [2010] ECR I-12213, para. 43. In *Frohleiten*, the Court ruled that the Austrian waste taxation scheme was not imposed on a supply of services by the operator of the waste disposal site but was instead imposed on products. See Case C-221/06 *Stadtgemeinde Frohleiten* [2007] ECR I-9643, para. 39.

However, given the increasing importance of international trade in services, it might be expected that the Court of Justice would rule on a greater number of conflicts opposing environmental measures and the freedom to provide services.

Moreover, in contrast to goods, conflicts as regard the scope of that freedom cover a variety of situations: on the one hand, service providers might pursue their activity in the Member State where the service is provided whereas, on the other hand, service receivers might move between Member States in search of cheaper or better quality environmental services.[25] As stressed by Barnard, domestic regulation of services tends to be more complex than that on goods because 'it is not just the service itself but also the service provider, its staff, and equipment' that are subject to restrictions.[26] The following examples are illustrative of the ways in which the Court of Justice has balanced free movement of services against environmental protection concerns.

- The freedom to provide services was raised in relation to the validity of a certification procedure in France which applied to foreign undertakings in competition with national undertakings where the foreign undertakings had already been certified by the relevant foreign authorities.[27] Even though the Flemish company, the directors of which were subject to criminal proceedings, offered its French customers a removal service for waste oil, the Court limited itself to addressing the preliminary reference exclusively from the point of view of the free movement of goods, rather than the freedom to provide services as proposed by Advocate General Lenz. The involvement of goods—the waste collected—seems to have led the Court to preclude the regime of free movement of services.

- The application of legislation punishing the discarding of harmful chemical substances does not breach the principle of non-discrimination contained in Article 56 TFEU solely on the ground that other Member States apply less rigorous sanctions.[28]

- On environmental protection grounds, Article 56 TFEU prohibits Member States from preventing the operator of a harbour from renting more than a specific number of moorings to boat owners resident in another Member State.[29]

- Pursuant to this provision, private bodies which control biological agricultural produce are not required to maintain an establishment in the Member State concerned.[30]

- An activity which consists of making fishing waters available to third parties, for consideration and upon certain conditions, to allow them to fish constitutes a provision of services which, if it has a cross-frontier character, is covered by Articles 56 TFEU et seq. The fact that this right may be the subject of trade is not sufficient to bring it within the scope of Treaty provisions on the free movement of goods because the goods are intangible.[31]

---

[25] Barnard (n 2), 355.   [26] Barnard (n 2), 407.
[27] Case C-37/92 *Vanacker* [1993] ECR I-4947. See N. de Sadeleer, 'L'agrément des collecteurs de déchets au regard des règles de droit communautaire' (1993) 4 *Amén-Env* 237.
[28] Case C-379/92 *Peralta* [1994] ECR I-3453, para. 47.
[29] Case C-224/97 *Ciola* [1999] ECR I-2517, para. 19.
[30] Case C-404/05 *Commission v Germany* [2007] ECR I-10239, para. 52; and Case C-393/05 *Commission v Austria* [2007] ECR I-10195, para. 61.
[31] Case C-97/98 *Jägerskiöld* [1999] ECR I-7319, para. 36.

- A tax on waste disposal does not cover the provision of a service but of a good and therefore falls within the ambit of Article 110 TFEU.[32] By contrast, a tax on satellite dishes reflecting 'the desire to prevent the uncontrolled proliferation of satellite dishes in the municipality and thereby preserve the quality of the environment' is liable to hinder the freedom to provide services. Such a tax is not necessary where other less severe urban planning measures—for instance, the adoption of requirements concerning the size of the dishes, their position, and the way in which they are fixed to the building or its surroundings or the use of communal dishes—would contribute to safeguarding the 'quality of the urban environment'.[33] On the other hand, the imposition of a tax on mobile communications infrastructures which does not have the effect of rendering the provision of services between Member States more difficult than the provision of purely internal services is not incompatible with Article 56 TFEU.[34]

3. Services Directive

3.1 Introductory comments

3.1.1 *Impacts on environmental policy*

Starting from the assumption that barriers to the creation of a market in services 'cannot be removed solely by relying on direct application of Articles [49] and [56 TFEU]', the Services Directive has the goal of 'remov[ing] barriers to the freedom of establishment for providers in Member States and barriers to the free movement of services as between Member States and to guarantee recipients and providers the legal certainty necessary for the exercise in practice of those two fundamental freedoms of the Treaty'.[35]

Although it is less ambitious compared to the Commission's initial draft—particularly due to abandonment of the country of origin principle—the directive is nevertheless of great practical importance.

First, the replacement of *ex post* judicial review which had previously been preferred by positive harmonization represents a step forward. Moreover, a horizontal *ex ante* administrative approach has been provided for.

Second, in general terms the directive requires the reduction of administrative burdens on service providers. In providing for a simplification of procedures,[36] the mutual recognition of certificates and attestations,[37] the implementation of a 'point of single contact',[38] as well as rights to information,[39] Chapter II of the directive makes considerable efforts at administrative simplification, which may occur to the detriment of environmental requirements.

---

[32] Case C-108/98 *RI.SAN* [1999] ECR I-5219, paras 39–47.
[33] Case C-17/00 *De Coster* [2001] ECR I-9445, paras 36 and 38.
[34] Joined Cases C-544 & 545/03 *Mobistar SA v Commune de Fléron* and *Belgacom Mobile SA v Commune de Schaerbeek* [2005] ECR I-7723, para. 35.
[35] Services Directive, recitals 43, 45, 47, and 48.
[36] Services Directive, recitals 5 and 6.   [37] Services Directive, Art. 6 and recital 48.
[38] Services Directive, Art. 5(3).   [39] Services Directive, Art. 7.

Although the academic literature has stressed the fact that this harmonization ultimately made few significant changes to the general principles inferred by the Court of Justice from Articles 49 and 56 TFEU,[40] environmental protection neverthe-less features in several derogations contained in Chapter III concerning freedom of establishment for service providers as well as in Chapter IV concerning the free movement of services. Moreover, the provisions of Chapter IV which apply to services which do not require any movement of people or which are offered on a temporary basis are without doubt of less interest for undertakings wishing to invest in the field of water and waste management than the provisions of Chapter III, which covers services offered by persons established in another Member State. In addition, the directive introduces certain innovations associated with administrative assistance between the Member States. We shall not engage in further discussion of a text which has already been commented on in detail elsewhere,[41] except to highlight its implications for national environmental regulations.[42]

3.1.2 *Scope*

The importance of the Services Directive stems from the breadth of its field of applica-tion, which covers a significant number of consultancy activities in environmental matters, such as management consultancy services and certification and testing.[43] However, the broad area falling under the Commission's proposal was significantly reduced during the course of negotiations. Moreover, the text of the directive is littered with derogations which are not always completely consistent.[44] The scope of the directive is particularly varied given the introduction by several Articles of certain exceptions, some of which overlap. That said, it is possible to systematize certain levels of exception out of this legal melange. A number of them cover various services which may relate to the exploitation of natural resources or environmental protection.

3.1.2.1 Exclusions stemming from the definition of the concept of service

First and foremost, several services are excluded from the scope of the directive on the account that they fall outside the notion of 'service'. Non-economic services of general interest are formally precluded.[45] This first exclusion applies to activities in respect of which the general rules contained in Treaty law cannot apply because they do not constitute services within the meaning of Treaty law. Conversely, services of general

---

[40] *Mobistar SA v Commune de Fléron* and *Belgacom Mobile SA v Commune de Schaerbeek* (n 34), para. 37.

[41] C. Barnard, 'Unravelling the Services Directive' (2008) 45 *CML Rev* 323–94; M. Fallon and A. C. Simon, 'La directive «Services»: quelle contribution au marché intérieur?' (2007) *JTDE* 34; V. Hatzopoulos, 'Que reste-t-il de la directive sur les services?' (2007) 3–4 *CDE* 320; A.-L. Sibony and A. Defossez, 'Liberté d'établissement et libre prestation de services 2007–2008' (2009) 45:3 *RTDE* 514–30.

[42] For Spain, J. J. Pernas Garcia, 'La incidencia de la normativa de servicios en el derecho amiental. Técnicas preventivas de protección ambienal y normativa de servicios: particularizado de la evaluación de impacto ambiental y de la ordenación administrativa de la gestión de residuos' (2010) 2 *Revista de Dret Catalana* 1.

[43] Services Directive, recital 33.

[44] Fallon and Simon (n 41), 34; Hatzopoulos (n 41), 320.

[45] Services Directive, Art. 2(2)(a).

economic interest (SGEIs),[46] which are services performed for economic consideration, do fall within the scope of the directive:[47] for instance, the treatment of waste is deemed to be a service of general economic interest.[48] In order to determine whether a service of general interest constitutes an economic service, an assessment has to be carried out on a case-by-case basis in the light of all the characteristics of the service.[49] That said, as regards SGEIs, the Member States are not bound to liberalize those services.[50] In addition, the requirements applied to these services have to be evaluated insofar as they do not obstruct the performance of the task assigned to them.[51]

As far as the environment is concerned, it is important to note that services 'connected with the exercise of official authority',[52] including pollution oversight activities fall outside the directive's scope.[53] Furthermore, since the directive aims to control the 'requirements' which the Member States place on access to, or exercise of, a service activity, the latter 'applies only' to these requirements,[54] which has the effect of precluding the regulation of the use of land[55] and, by analogy, pollution control measures.

3.1.2.2 Exclusions of certain categories of service

A number of services, such as services in the field of transport and financial services, fall outside the scope of the directive.[56] In addition, it should be noted that the Services Directive does not apply to the field of taxation.[57] Similarly, Article 17—a provision which covers freedom of services—exempts additional categories of services harmonized by specific directives. Finally, as discussed later, several environmental services are excluded from the obligations relating to the freedom to provide services.

3.2 Freedom of establishment for service providers

It is important briefly to note that although initially the Court of Justice was relatively favourable to the wholesale application of the regulations to the recipient State, it has progressively limited the discretionary power of the Member States over persons who wish to establish themselves in that State. Chapter III of the Services Directive codifies these principles. In relation to the freedom of establishment of service providers, the directive distinguishes between two types of obstacle: those resulting from authorization schemes (Arts 9–13) and those resulting from other 'requirements' (Arts 14 and 15).

---

[46] See Chapter 1, Section 3.2.   [47] Services Directive, recital 17.
[48] Services Directive, Art. 17(1)(e).   [49] Services Directive, recital 34.
[50] Services Directive, Art. 1(2).   [51] Services Directive, Art. 15(4) and recital 17.
[52] Services Directive, Art. 2(2)(i). Regarding the definition of 'official authority', see Case 2/74 *Reyners* [1974] ECR 631.
[53] Regarding the exercise of powers relating to the protection of the environment which are typically those of a public authority and the non-application of competition law, see Case C-343/95 *Diego Cali e Figli* [1997] ECR I-1547. See the discussion in Chapter 8, Section 1 and Chapter 11, Section 2.
[54] Fallon and Simon (n 41), 34; Hatzopoulos (n 41), 320.
[55] Services Directive, recital 9.   [56] Services Directive, Art. 2(2).
[57] Services Directive, Art. 2(3).

3.2.1 *Authorization schemes*

As a matter of principle, Article 9 restricts the Member States' room for manoeuvre to subject access to a service activity to an authorization scheme. However, pursuant to Article 9(1)(a), (b), and (c), an authorization scheme applying to the establishment of an activity may be permitted, provided that it does not discriminate against the provider in question and it is not disproportionate compared to an 'overriding reason relating to the public interest'. Going beyond the provisions set out in Article 52 TFEU, these 'reasons' are those 'recognised as such in the case law of the Court of Justice'. In particular, they include, in accordance with Article 4(8), grounds of justifications concerning 'the protection of consumers,..., workers,..., the protection of the environment and the urban environment, the health of animals,...' This list, which is not exhaustive, includes a fundamental difference between arrangements governing establishments and the regime for services where the directive places draconian limits on permissible justifications. Be that as it may, it will be seen that the framers of the directive expressly specified the environment as a justification both under Chapter III and under Chapter IV.

Also the environment *lato sensu* must be regarded as an overriding reason relating to the public interest justifying the maintenance of a national authorization scheme to which the establishment of a foreign service provider may be subject. The same also applies to authorizations which are time-limited.[58] In this way, authorization schemes for listed installations,[59] which are limited in time, may be justified by 'overriding reasons relating to the public interest'.[60]

Importantly from an environmental perspective, although they might be justified, authorization procedures are subject to a number of restrictions. For instance, the directive favours a 'negative silence system', which provides that failure to grant the authorization within the time period set in accordance with the regulation constitutes an implied decision granting the application.[61] This provision contradicts the opposite 'negative silence system'—failure to grant the authorization within the time period amounts to a refusal—that was approved by the Court of Justice in the Catalan supermarket case commented on in Section 2.1.[62] Finally, by virtue of Article 12, 'a selection procedure from among several candidates' guaranteeing impartiality and transparency is permitted 'where the number of authorisations available for a given activity is limited because of the scarcity of available natural resources or technical capacity'. This selection procedure does not, however, prevent Member States from

---

[58] Services Directive, Art. 11(1)(c).

[59] Given that the authorization regime is broadly defined (Art. 4(6)), the derogation also covers operators' registration schemes which are very common for waste management and operation of listed installations. See, eg, European Parliament and Council Directive 2008/98/EC on waste [2008] OJ L308/3, Art. 26(c).

[60] P. Thieffry, *Droit de l'environnement de l'UE* (Brussels: Bruylant, 2007) 698.

[61] Services Directive, Art. 13(4). Nonetheless, environmental objectives or other overriding reasons relating to public interest allow Member States to maintain authorization schemes less favourable to applicants.

[62] Case C-400/08 *Commission v Spain* (n 6), paras 124 and 125. It should be noted that environmental objectives or other overriding reasons relating to public interest allow the Member States to maintain authorization schemes less favourable to the applicants.

giving consideration, in particular, to 'public health, health and safety,..., the protection of the environment...and other overriding reasons relating to the public interest'.[63]

3.2.2 *Requirements prohibited or subject to evaluation*

Pursuant to Articles 14 and 15, a range of 'requirements' which may be imposed on the establishment of an activity are either expressly prohibited or subject to an evaluation of their non-discriminatory nature, necessity, and proportionality.

Among the requirements prohibited per se under Articles 15, foreign operators cannot be obliged to provide a financial guarantee or to take insurance from a provider established in the host Member State. Such a prohibition impacts on national listed installations legislation which obliges operators to provide a financial guarantee from a national financial institution.

In addition, Member States were called on to examine whether their other environmental measures were consistent with the conditions listed in Article 15(2). It follows that for certain Member States, the collection and treatment of waste must comply with requirements to be evaluated by virtue of Article 15(1) and (2). These may, in particular, relate to requirements laid down by environmental agencies regarding the minimum number of qualified employees and establishments, compulsory tariffs for dumping or incinerating waste, and conditions which reserve access to the service activity in question to particular providers by virtue of the specific nature of the activity.[64] Again, 'overriding reasons relating to the public interest', which include protection of the environment *lato sensu*,[65] may justify the maintenance of these requirements.[66] However, since 2007 the adoption of new requirements has been subject to a control regime[67] which will have the effect of significantly limiting the discretionary power of the Member States.

3.3 Free movement of services

As far as the exercise of the free movement of services embodied in Chapter IV is concerned, Article 16(1), first sentence, stipulates a clear rule: service providers have the right to provide their services from their place of establishment in all other Member States, and Member States must respect that right, guaranteeing both 'free access to service' as well as their 'free exercise' within its territory.[68]

The access to, or exercise of, a service activity in a foreign country may not be subject to any conditions other than those mentioned previously unless they are first covered by one of the four grounds permitted in a closed list encompassing the grounds of justification of 'public policy, public security, public health and the protection of the environment' ('principle of necessity') and that they satisfy the additional 'principles' of

---

[63] Services Directive, Art. 12(3).
[64] See, in particular, Services Directive, Art. 15(2)(d), (e), (f), and (g).
[65] Services Directive, Art. 4(8).   [66] Services Directive, Art. 15(3)(b).
[67] Services Directive, Art. 15(6).   [68] Services Directive, Art. 16(1), second sentence.

non-discrimination, and proportionality.[69] According to the case law of the Court of Justice, the law of the country of destination applies on a non-discriminatory basis. Moreover, the principle that the law of the country of destination should apply operates to the detriment of the rule advocated by the Commission that the law of the country of origin should take precedence. On this point, the directive is not innovative.

As discussed previously, it is settled case law that authorization or licence may already be justified on various grounds involving environmental protection.

Whereas Chapter III of the Services Directive accepts that 'overriding reasons relating to the public interest' which embrace several factors relating to the environment *lato sensu*[70] may be invoked in order to regulate the establishment of service activities, Chapter IV is decidedly more restrictive as far as services are concerned.[71] The Member States may only justify—by virtue of Article 16(1), third sentence and Article 16(3)—restrictions where they are 'justified for reasons of public policy, public security, public health, or the protection of the environment'. On the other hand, they may not justify them on either consumer protection or animal health grounds; both issues which are related to the question of the environment.[72] Certain commentators regret this 'substantial reduction' of grounds of justification.[73]

Article 16(2) lists those restrictions which are prohibited. Most interestingly, from our perspective, the requirements affecting 'the use of equipment and material which are [an] integral part of the service provided' are prohibited under this second paragraph.[74] Accordingly, environmental agencies are not allowed to regulate the use of hazardous substances 'which are [an] integral part of the service provided'.

In any event, as far as the free movement of services is concerned, the Member States have the right by virtue of Article 17 to invoke certain 'additional derogations from the freedom to provide services'. It is important to distinguish between services of general economic interest (para. 1) and other areas that are mostly governed by EU law (paras 2 et seq.).

First, the freedom to provide services enshrined in Article 16, discussed previously, does not apply to certain SGEIs that are provided in another Member State, including in particular the services of 'water distribution and supply services and waste water services' and 'the treatment of waste' in accordance with Article 17(1)(d) and (e). In contrast to the postal, gas, and electricity sectors which are covered by sectoral directives, these two categories of service have not as yet been subject to a harmonization as extensive as in other sectors. This derogation from the requirement of the free provision of services does not, however, mean that the rules of the host country automatically

---

[69] Services Directive, Art. 16(1), third sentence.   [70] Services Directive, Art. 4(8).

[71] These four grounds of justification are set out in the framework of both the 'necessity principle' that applies when Member States control service activities (Art. 16 (1)(3)(c)), as well as the justification of the derogation (Art. 16(3)). It should also be noted that although the first three imperative requirements of public interest are expressly mentioned in Art. 52 TFEU, environment protection is not. S. D'Acunto, 'Directive service: radiographie juridique en dix points' (2007) 2 *RDUE* 303.

[72] If harmonization is of a minimal nature, this exclusion should not raise any problems.

[73] Fallon and Simon (n 41), 37 fn 18; K. Peglun, 'Libre prestation de services dans la directive 2006/123/CE' (2008) 44(1) *RTDE* 100; Barnard (n 41), 363; and Sibony and Defossez (n 41), 525.

[74] Services Directive, Art. 16(2)(f).

apply; the matter is left to rules specific to the relevant fields and remains in any event subject to the principles of non-discrimination, necessity, and proportionality.[75]

Second, pursuant to Article 17(1)(e) the freedom to provide services does not apply to transfers of waste.[76]

Last, Article 18 provides 'in exceptional circumstances' for a case-by-case derogation.

4. Conclusions

The rapid replacement of a manufacturing economy by an economy dominated by services will increase litigation in which national measures come up against the rules on freedom of establishment and freedom to provide services. Due to the feebleness of the obligations contained in it, the Services Directive has clearly disappointed many internal market enthusiasts. Given the significant number of exceptions relating to exploitation of natural resources and environmental protection, the national authorities will undoubtedly not be obliged to review fundamentally their regulatory approach.

However, whilst the directive is not as broad-sweeping as the initial draft, the fact remains that it marks a significant change in the perspective of the EU's approach, which will not fail to have an impact on control of polluting activities. On the one hand, the administrative simplification exercise brought about by this directive will prove to be a precious support for service providers. Hopefully, this exercise may have the effect of expanding competition in the anti-pollution technology industry. On the other hand, this exercise is also liable to result in a reduction in the rigour of administrative authorization regimes that are an indispensable instrument in controlling economic operators providing services which cause harm to the environment.

---

[75] S. D'Acunto, 'Directive service: radiographie juridique en dix points' (2007) 2 *RDUE* 303.

[76] It should be noted that the Directive refers to Regulation (EEC) No. 259/93 on shipments of waste ([1993] OJ L30/1) although this regulation has been replaced by Regulation (EC) No. 1013/2006 on the shipments of waste ([2006] OJ L190/1).

7

National Provisions Derogating from Secondary Law

1. Introduction

Distortions to competition caused by diverging national policies may be more easily combated through the adoption of rules harmonized for the whole Union. In fact, by reining in the power of the Member States to adopt autonomous policy measures, uniform rules would better guarantee the free movement of goods and services than provisions of Treaty law taken alone. Moreover, since secondary legislation has comprehensively harmonized this area of law, it has taken the place of national law.[1] This means that Member States are prevented from further relying on Article 36 TFEU or a rule of reason in order to circumvent their obligations under secondary law.[2] Nevertheless, various mechanisms provided for under Treaty law enable the Member States to retain a certain degree of autonomy.

As discussed in Part I, after the entry into force of the Single European Act (SEA), the rules of secondary law on environmental protection were principally developed along two tracks: they were adopted either on the basis of ex Article 130s EC (Art. 192 TFEU) or pursuant to ex Article 100a EC (Art. 114 TFEU) which is the legal base for harmonization measures having as their object the establishment and the functioning of the internal market.[3] However, the power to enact more stringent standards than those embodied in secondary law varies depending on the legal base chosen by the Union legislator. In effect, for each of these provisions the Treaty provides for fundamentally distinct exceptions. In contrast to Article 193 TFEU, which establishes the principle of minimum harmonization in areas relating to environmental protection, Article 114 restricts Member States' powers to enact derogating provisions.

This chapter is concerned with comparing the conditions for enacting more stringent environmental measures under the environmental policy (Art. 193 TFEU) and the internal market policy (Art. 114(4)–(10) TFEU).

2. Enactment of More Stringent Environmental Measures Pursuant to Article 193 TFEU

2.1 Introductory remarks

Departing from the *Titanium Dioxide* judgment, during the course of the 1990s the Court of Justice stressed the pivotal role which ex Article 130s EC (Art. 192 TFEU) was called upon to play as the legal basis for legislation with the object and purpose of protecting the environment.[4]

The ability for the lawmaker to rely on that provision amounted to a notable exception to the concept of maximum harmonization. The provision was in line with the previous practice of Community institutions which, by incorporating reservations into the directives adopted on the basis of ex Articles 100 and 235 EEC, granted broad

---

[1] Case C-350/97 *Monsees* [1999] ECR I-2921, para. 27.
[2] See the discussion in Chapter 5, Section 5.2.2.
[3] See the discussion in Chapter 3, Section 4.4 and Chapter 4, Section 5.5.
[4] Case C-155/91 *Commission v Council* [1993] ECR I-939. See the discussion Chapter 3, Section 4.4.

autonomy to the Member States. In contrast to acts previously adopted on the basis of these two provisions of the EEC Treaty, under which the right to enact more stringent rules than the Community standards was subject to the existence of a provision of secondary law that expressly recognized that right, Article 130t EC (Art. 193 TFEU) enshrined this right in general terms, which consisted of a specific application of the principle of subsidiarity.[5]

This provision, which has not been subject to major modifications during the course of various Treaty amendments, runs as follows:

> The protective measures adopted pursuant to Article 192 shall not prevent any Member State from maintaining or introducing more stringent protective measures. Such measures must be compatible with the Treaties. They shall be notified to the Commission.

Accordingly, any Member State may at any time freely decide to maintain or adopt more stringent standards than those provided for under an act adopted on the basis of Article 192 TFEU. The importance of Article 193 TFEU can be illustrated by the following examples.

- A regulation such as the CITES Regulation, which was adopted pursuant to Article 192 TFEU, does not prevent any Member State from maintaining or introducing more stringent protective measures, which must be compatible with the Treaty.[6] By the same token, a refusal to recognize 'CITES' certificates validly issued by foreign authorities in order to obtain an exception for the prohibition on the marketing of specimens of wild animals born and bred in captivity, amounts to a more stringent protective measure within the meaning of Article 193 TFEU.[7]

- The addition of a hazardous substance to a closed list amounts to a 'more stringent protective measure'.[8]

2.2 Material scope

The question whether a national measure falls within the ambit of Article 193 TFEU cannot be disregarded since the adoption of 'more stringent protective measures' must comply with relevant substantive and formal conditions.

Stricter national measures pursuant to Article 193 TFEU may only be adopted with reference to the EU harmonization rule enacted under Article 192 TFEU.[9] Member States are thus precluded from invoking Article 193 TFEU with a view to departing

---

[5] Opinion AG Cosmas in Case C-318/98 *Fornasar* [2000] ECR I-4785, para. 35.

[6] Case C-510/99 *Tridon* [2001] ECR I-7777, para. 45.

[7] Case C-100/08 *Commission v Belgium* [2009] ECR I-140, para. 60.

[8] *Fornasar* (n 5), paras 45–8. Even where the harmonization appears to be complete, EU directives expressly empower the Member States to depart from the EU regime in enacting more stringent measures. Eg pursuant to Art. 7(2) of Directive 2008/98/EC on waste ([2008] OJ L312/3), a Member State may consider waste as hazardous waste where, even though it does not appear as such on the list of waste, it displays some hazardous properties.

[9] The Belgian Constitutional Court held that the ETS set out in Directive 2003/87/EC may be extended to other categories of undertaking that do not fall within the scope of the directive in accordance with Art. 193 TFEU (Belgian CA, 92/2006, 7 June 2006). However, one could contest such an interpretation on the ground that such measures do not fall within the scope of Art. 193 TFEU.

from standards laid down by a directive dealing with the functioning of the internal market. However, nothing precludes the EU lawmaker from authorizing the national authorities to depart, under certain conditions, from their preventive obligations.[10]

In addition, the question must be raised whether all environmental measures likely to fall within the scope of an Article 192 TFEU-based directive or regulation must be enacted pursuant to Article 193 TFEU. The following distinction must be made: first, since Directive 2009/147/EC protects all bird populations of every species of wild bird found in Europe,[11] any stricter national measures governing the protection of game must fall within the ambit of Article 193 TFEU; secondly, since Directive 92/43/EC on habitats only protects a limited number of wild species, any measures taken in relation to species not falling under the scope of this directive will not be covered by Article 193 TFEU.[12]

2.3 Substantive conditions

The power of the Member States to adopt more stringent measures is not, however, absolute. The expression 'more stringent measures' implies that these measures may not be different from those decided at Union level, but they must consist in the extension of the harmonization rule by pursuing a greater level of protection.[13] In other words, the objectives of the national measure must coincide with those stated in the measure of secondary law. This means that the Member States may neither lower the level of protection nor change the arrangements for implementing secondary law.[14] Likewise, the adoption of more stringent arrangements under Article 193 TFEU cannot release the Member States from the obligation to transpose the whole directive.[15] In particular, the Member States cannot eschew their obligations regarding the control of discharge of pollutants into the aquatic environment on the ground that their quality objectives are more stringent than the measures provided for under the aquatic pollution directive.[16]

The definition of the extent of the protection to be achieved is left to the Member States.[17] Indeed, it is a matter for the latter to examine whether it is appropriate to extend the field of application of the Union standard, to increase its thresholds, to introduce more stringent procedural arrangements, to list additional substances or activities to be regulated, or to remove exceptions.[18]

---

[10] By virtue of Art. 15(4) of Directive 2010/75/EU on Industrial Emissions ([2010] OJ L334/17), the competent authority granting the operating licence for listed installations may, in specific cases, set less strict emission limit values 'where an assessment shows that the achievement of emission levels associated with the best available techniques...would lead to disproportionately higher costs' compared to the accruing environmental benefits.

[11] Case C-202/94 *Godefredius van der Steen* [1996] ECR I-355, paras 16 and 17.

[12] See, eg, Case C-294/07 *Commission v Netherlands* [2008], paras 31–7.

[13] L. Krämer, *EC Environmental Law*, 6th edn (London: Sweet & Maxwell, 2007) 127.

[14] Case C-194/01 *Commission v Austria* [2004] ECR I-4579, para. 39.

[15] Case C-322/00 *Commission v Netherlands* [2003] ECR I-11267.

[16] Case C-184/97 *Commission v Germany* [1999] ECR I-7837, para. 41.

[17] Case C-6/03 *Deponiezweckverband Eiterköpfe* [2005] ECR I-2753, para. 61.

[18] In its first judgment on pollution cases under the Environmental Liability Directive (ELD), which backed up the 'polluter pays' principle enshrined in this directive, the Court of Justice did not consider Art.

Moreover, reliance on Article 193 TFEU is subject to two further limits: first, that the relevant measures respect secondary law where there has been complete harmonization in the area and, second, that they are compatible with the Treaties. These two restrictions require more detailed discussion.

2.3.1 *Complete harmonization*

As far as secondary law is concerned, the exhaustive nature of the Union measure, even if it consists in a minimum standard, has the effect of preventing Member States from justifying more stringent protective measures by relying on Article 36 TFEU.[19] This mechanism is, however, open to criticism because it allows the institution drafting the measure of secondary law to conceptualize the harmonization in such a way that Member States will be prevented from adopting more stringent arrangements even where this is expressly permitted under Treaty law.

- As regards the protection of domestic animals, an issue closely related to environmental law, the Court of Justice has held that a Member State cannot object to the exportation of veal on the ground that the directive laying down minimum standards for the protection of calves 'regulated exhaustively the Member States' powers'.[20]

- By not transposing into regional law the exceptions provided for in the measure of secondary law for arrangements prohibiting the marketing of creosote, a Belgian regional authority violated Directive 76/769/EEC which, for the purposes of EU law,[21] amounted to complete harmonization.[22]

- One may wonder whether complete harmonization regimes adopted on the basis of Article 192 TFEU might violate Article 193 TFEU. In this regard, it is important to note that Advocate General Cosmas stated that Directive 91/689/EC concerning hazardous wastes was contrary to Article 193 TFEU as well as the precautionary principle. According to the Advocate General, by laying down an exhaustive list of hazardous waste, the directive limited the powers of the national authorities to subject other waste to the more stringent arrangements applicable to hazardous waste.[23]

However, most directives adopted on the basis of Article 192 TFEU do not result in complete harmonization. As shown in the following examples, the Member States enjoy fairly broad room for manoeuvre in this case. Introduced by Directive 2003/87/EC establishing a scheme for greenhouse gas emission allowance trading within the Community (the ETS Directive),[24] carbon emissions trading may be extended to other categories of undertaking which are not covered by that directive, in accordance with

---

193 TFEU in determining the room for manoeuvre left to the Member States as regards the link of causation. See Case C-378/08 *Agusta* [2010] ECR I-1919, para. 56.

[19] Chapter 5, Section 5.2.2.
[20] Case C-1/96 *Compassion in World Farming* [1998] ECR I-1251, paras 65–8.
[21] Joined Cases C-281 & 282/03 *Cindu Chemicals* [2005] ECR I-8069.
[22] Ceb no. 177.488 *nv VFT BELGIUM* [2007].
[23] Opinion AG Cosmas in *Fornasar* (n 5), paras 54 et seq.
[24] European Parliament and Council Directive 2003/87/EC establishing a scheme for greenhouse gas emission allowance trading within the Community and amending Council Directive 96/61/EC [2003] OJ L275/32.

Article 193 TFEU.[25] One could also argue by analogy that since Directive 94/62/EC on packaging and waste packaging does not amount to complete harmonization, a Member State may introduce environmental taxes on packaging.[26]

That said, the more stringent protective measure must not undermine the coherence of the harmonization rule.[27] For example, the emissions trading regime introduced by the ETS Directive provided for a fine of €100 per ton of carbon not returned. The directive also indicates that payment of the fine did not amount to a release from the obligation. Therefore, Article 193 TFEU does not permit Member States from providing for payments as an alternative to the obligation arising from Article 16(3) of the directive on the operator 'to surrender an amount of allowances equal to those excess emissions'. On the other hand, nothing prevents Member States from increasing the amount of the fine to €150, or even €200. However, if the amount were to become disproportionate, the Member State would jeopardize the proper functioning of the system, which would undoubtedly run contrary to Article 193 TFEU.

It is also necessary to address a further issue. The ETS Directive amended Integrated Pollution Prevention and Control (IPPC) Directive 2001/1/EC by inserting a new clause that sets out that IPPC authorizations cannot include emission limits for greenhouse gases (GHG) that fall within the ETS scheme. However, some Member States would like to impose caps on carbon emissions by requiring new power stations to include carbon-capture technology. The Commission has taken the view that such national initiatives are not now legally possible due to the amendments made to the IPPC Directive. The question therefore arises as to whether the ETS Directive does inhibit national initiatives.

2.3.2 *Compatibility with Treaty law*

We now turn to the second limit, consisting in the requirement for the more stringent protective measure to be compatible with Treaty law.[28] In addition, the expression 'in accordance with the Treaty' is often inserted into the texts of secondary law which is particularly the case for the regulation of the transfrontier movement of waste adopted on the basis of Article 192 TFEU. Having been called upon to specify the scope of these terms, the Court of Justice held that a stricter national measure adopted with regard to the exportation of waste could not 'be subject to a further and separate review of its compatibility with Articles [34, 35, and 36 TFEU]'.[29]

This interpretation of the expression 'in accordance with the Treaty' is complex because a distinction must be drawn between two situations: where the more stringent protective measure does not affect trade between the Member States and where it impinges upon the free movement of goods.

---

[25] Belgian CA, 92/2006, 7 June 2006; Case T-16/04 *Arcelor SA* [2010] OJ C100/35, para. 179.
[26] Belgian CC, 186/2005, 14 December 2005.
[27] Case C-2/97 *Borsana* [1998] ECR I-8597, para. 37.
[28] See J. Jans, 'Minimum Harmonization and the Role of the Principle of Proportionality' in M. Führ, R. Wahl, and P. von Wilmowsky (eds), *Umweltrecht und Uwmeltwissenschaft. Festschrift für E. Rehbinder* (Berlin: Erich Schmidt Verlag, 2007) 705–17.
[29] Case C-324/99 *DaimlerChrysler* [2001] ECR I-9897, para. 44.

This first situation concerns a measure which does not undermine the principle of the free movement of goods. In *Deponiezweckverband Eiterköpfe*, the Court of Justice provided the following clarifications regarding the conformity of this type of national measure taken pursuant to Article 193 TFEU. In particular, the Court took the view that:

> 62 In that context, in so far as it is a matter of ensuring that the minimum requirements laid down by the Directive are enforced, the Community principle of proportionality demands that measures of domestic law should be appropriate and necessary in relation to the objectives pursued.
>
> 63 In contrast, and inasmuch as other provisions of the Treaty are not involved, that principle is no longer applicable so far as concerns more stringent protective measures of domestic law adopted by virtue of Article [193 TFEU] and going beyond the minimum requirements laid down by the Directive.
>
> 64 As a result, the reply to the second question has to be that the Community-law principle of proportionality is not applicable so far as concerns more stringent protective measures of domestic law adopted by virtue of Article [193 TFEU] and going beyond the minimum requirements laid down by a Community directive in the sphere of the environment, inasmuch as other provisions of the Treaty are not involved.

Another case in point would be *Azienda Agro-Zootecnica Franchini*. Regarding the proportionality of nature protection measures, the Court ruled that, 'In view of its limited scope' an environmental-protection measure prohibiting the location of new wind turbines in Natura 2000 sites is not liable to jeopardize the European Union in developing new and renewable forms of energy, as established for EU policy by Article 194(1)(c) TFEU.[30]

Therefore, as long as other provisions of the Treaty are not undermined, the general principle of proportionality will not apply to a national measure providing for the expansion of an obligation contained in secondary law.[31] In other words, the intention expressed by the national authorities to go beyond the minimum requirements contained in the harmonization instrument cancels out the requirement to carry out a proportionality test. The justification for the restriction made to the application of a general principle of law lies without doubt in the fact that, as far as the application of Article 193 TFEU is concerned, 'it falls to the Member States to define the extent of protection to be achieved'.[32]

---

[30] Case C-2/10 *Azienda Agro-Zootecnica Franchini Sarl* [2010] ECR I-5031, para. 57.

[31] *Deponiezweckverband Eiterköpfe* (n 17), paras 63 and 64. By analogy, see *Borsana* (n 27), para. 40. In contrast, the principle of proportionality applies to more stringent national measures in the area of fisheries. In *Karanikolas* the Court ruled that the national prohibition of the use of certain types of fishing net that went beyond the minimum requirements of an EU fisheries regulation, and which was adopted before the entry into force of that regulation, was valid provided that 'that prohibition is in conformity with the common fisheries policy, that it does not go beyond what is necessary to achieve the objective pursued and that it is not contrary to the principle of equal treatment, those being matters which it is for the national court to determine.' Case C-453/08 *Karanikolas* [2010] ECR I-7895, para. 58.

[32] *Deponiezweckverband Eiterköpfe* (n 17), para. 61.

This reasoning is completely acceptable. For present purposes, the dispute concerned the increase in protection thresholds for landfills. Even if waste is deposited there, landfills are still listed installations which, contrary to waste, do not move from one Member State to another. Consequently, any increase in the protection thresholds will not have the goal of limiting the importation into Germany of waste produced in Austria or Italy. It flows from that reasoning that only the national courts are empowered to adjudicate on whether more protective standards applying to landfills are deemed to be compatible with the fundamental freedoms, such as freedom of enterprise.

On the other hand, it may be the case that other provisions of the Treaty are called into question through the exercise of national regulatory powers. Even where it is permitted both under Treaty law as well as under secondary law, a protective measure that goes beyond the EU harmonization standards must respect the principle of the free movement of goods or other EU general principles of law. Article 193 TFEU does not, therefore, give the Member States carte blanche to determine their protection thresholds where those thresholds are likely to give rise to conflicts with other Treaty provisions. By way of illustration, the Member States cannot rely on Article 193 TFEU in order to justify environmental levies contrary to Article 110 TFEU[33] or an authorization scheme at odds with Article 34 TFEU.

Accordingly, where they are likely to obstruct trade between the Member States, national measures which go beyond the minimal EU environmental standards must pass the necessity and proportionality tests.

The following cases illustrate the extent of the proportionality test as applied by the Court of Justice.

- The Netherlands was not able to justify arrangements preventing the exportation of hazardous recoverable waste, even though it complied with the requirements of secondary law.[34]

- Similarly, national measures restricting the transfer of waste cannot be systematically presumed to be compatible with secondary law solely because they are intended to implement one or more environmental principles, such as the principles of proximity and self-sufficiency.[35] In addition to respecting the Waste Shipment Regulation, a national scheme restricting the transfer of waste must also respect the general principles laid down in the Treaty. Nor was it possible for the Netherlands to oppose the export of dangerous waste for recovery on the ground that the percentage of recoverable waste in the State of destination was insufficient compared to the percentage of recovery achieved in the Netherlands.[36] By the same token, the classification of the shipment of waste deemed to be exported with the aim of being recovered cannot be changed by the competent authority ex officio.[37] The fact that the regulation was founded on the environmental legal base had no bearing on the interpretation. According to Pagh, the

---

[33] See the discussion in Chapter 5, Section 3.
[34] Case C-203/96 *Chemishe Afvalstoffen Dusseldorp* [1998] ECR I-4075, para. 49.
[35] Case C-324/99 *DaimlerChrysler* [2001] ECR I-9897.
[36] Case C-113/02 *Commission v Netherlands* [2004] ECR I-9707.
[37] Case C-6/00 *ASA* [2004] ECR I-1961.

opposite interpretation would jeopardize the whole procedural scheme regarding control of the transfrontier movement of waste.[38] In other words, given the extent of harmonization, there is no room for stricter national measures in that field.

- Although an environmental directive stipulating that certain minimum noise limits be respected authorized national authorities to adopt more stringent standards, this directive does not, however, permit them to oppose the first registration of aircraft previously registered in another Member State prior to the directive being implemented.[39]

- In its judgment on reusable packaging in Germany, the Court of Justice held that the interpretation of the expression 'in accordance with the Treaty' could not be transposed into the directive on packaging.[40]

- Even though it amounted to a more stringent protective measure, the Belgian regulation preventing the marketing of indigenous European birds born and bred in captivity, which were legally marketed on the territory of other Member States, amounted to a measure having equivalent effect to a quantitative restriction within the meaning of Article 34 TFEU.[41]

By the same token, Article 193 TFEU cannot be invoked with a view to circumventing the duty of loyal cooperation enshrined in Article 4(3) TEU. The proposal to list a chemical substance in the annex to a mixed agreement is not permitted by Article 193 TFEU.[42]

This analysis can be taken a little further. It would appear that when the national authorities pursue a level of protection greater than that imposed under Union law within the framework of acts adopted on the basis of Article 192 TFEU, the courts should view them in a favourable light. In effect, such measures generally aim to optimize environmental protection on the basis of circumstances specific to the Member State, such as the vulnerability of ecosystems, the difficulties encountered during inspection missions, etc. These measures often prove to be necessary in order to guarantee the effectiveness of secondary law. It follows that these measures should not be struck down unless they have a significantly disproportionate effect on the free movement of goods between Member States.

One may also wonder whether a more stringent measure is proportional pursuant to Article 193 TFEU. According to the Dutch Council of State, the sole fact of adopting stricter emissions standards than the emission standards laid down in a Community directive does not mean that they are unreasonable.[43]

---

[38] P. Pagh, 'The Battle on Environmental Policy Competences. Challenging the Stricter Approach: Stricter Might Lead to Weaker Protection' in R. Macrory (ed.), *Reflections on 30 Years of EU Environmental Law* (Groeningen: Europa Law, 2006) 10.

[39] Case C-389/96 *Aher-Waggon* [1998] ECR I-4473, paras 15 and 16.

[40] Case C-463/01 *Commission v Germany* [2004] ECR I-11705, para. 50.

[41] Case C-100/08 *Commission v Belgium* [2009] ECR I-140, paras 94 et seq. See the discussion in Chapter 5, Section 7.3.2.

[42] Case C-246/07 *Commission v Sweden* [2010] ECR I-3317, para. 102. See Chapter 3, Section 3.3.2.

[43] R.v.St., Case AB 1985 [1984], 44.

2.4 Formal conditions

As far as formal requirements are concerned, the exercise of this right is subject to a specific formality consisting in the notification of the measure to the Commission. Requested only for information purposes, this notification is not part of an authorization regime. Moreover, no time limit is specified for notification of the national regulation. Implementation of the system for notification, however, requires the Commission and the Member States to cooperate in good faith. It is necessary for the Member States to notify their provisions as soon as possible in order to enable the Commission to carry out its review effectively.[44] However, failure by the Member States to comply with their notification obligation under Article 193 TFEU does not in itself render unlawful the more stringent protective measures thereby adopted.[45]

3. Procedures for Derogations From the Principle of Approximation of Laws Under Article 114 TFEU

3.1 Introductory remarks

During the course of negotiations for the SEA, some Member States expressed their reservations over the proposed new Article 100a EEC (since the Treaty of Amsterdam revised and renumbered as Art. 95 EC and later as Art. 114 TFEU), a provision from which the original intention was that derogations could not be made. Such an imposed harmonization would not only have restricted these Member States' room for manoeuvre, but would also have forced them to reduce the level of protection which they had granted their workers and consumers, and also their environment. In order to allay their fears, the framers of the SEA moderated the effects of majority voting by inserting a derogation mechanism into paragraph 4 of Article 100a EEC.

Despite any misgivings which this derogation mechanism may have provoked at the time, few Member States exercised their rights.[46] Before 1 May 1999, the date of entry into force of the Treaty of Amsterdam, Article 100a(4) EEC had only been invoked a few times, generally with the intention of retaining national regulations on chemical substances. Due to the complexity of the scientific questions raised by such derogation requests, the European Commission made, from 1992 to 1999, no more than ten decisions on their validity, in general taking several years to examine the relevant issues.

Practice has thus shown this gap in the principle of the uniform application of EU law not to have been as alarming as was initially thought.[47] Besides being interpreted in

---

[44] Case C-319/97 *A. Kortas* [1999] ECR I-3143, para. 35.

[45] Case C-2/10 *Azienda Agro-Zootecnica* [2010] ECR I-5031, para. 53. See, by analogy, Case 380/87 *Enichem Base* [1989] ECR 2491, paras 20–3; Case C-209/98 *Sydhavnens Sten & Grus* [2000] ECR I-3743, para. 100; and Case C-159/00 *Sapod Audic* [2002] ECR I-5031, paras 60–3.

[46] Several commentators were of the opinion that para. 4 of ex Art. 100a EEC would provoke a major rupture in internal market policy. See P. Pescatore, 'Some Critical Remarks on the European Single Act' (1987) 24 *CML Rev* 9.

[47] Ph. Léger (ed.), *Commentaire article par article des Traités UE et CE* (Brussels: Hebing & Lichtenhahn, 2000) 931; P. Craig and G. de Búrca, *EU Law: Text, Cases, and Materials*, 3rd edn (Oxford: OUP, 2003), 1189.

a relatively strict manner by Advocates General and theorists alike, reliance on the derogation mechanism provided for in paragraph 4 of ex Article 100a EEC was discouraged due to the interpretative difficulties generated by the provision.

Owing to its ambiguity, Article 100a(4) had to be reformed. The growing influence of sustainable development and environmental concerns also gave rise to calls for a rebalancing of equilibrium between the internal market and non-commercial interests. The search for a new compromise was all the more justified by the fact that consumer law and a substantial part of environmental law were dealt with under the auspices of the internal market.

During the course of the negotiations for the Treaty of Amsterdam, an opportunity presented itself for giving greater consideration to non-commercial interests, including the concept of sustainable development that was at the time encapsulated in Article 2 EC (Art. 3 TEU), and affirming in Article 6 EC (Art. 11 TFEU) the principle of integrating environmental needs with other EC policies.[48] This increased environmental protection in the Treaty logically required the revision of Article 100a EEC—a provision guaranteeing the establishment of the internal market. The new provision would also be duly renumbered as Article 95 EC, and since the entry into force of the Treaty of Lisbon as Article 114 TFEU. Two lines of thought were selected by the framers of the Amsterdam Treaty in order to place non-commercial values on a firmer footing within the context of the construction of the internal market.

First, paragraph 3 of Article 114 TFEU obliges EU institutions, for the purposes of establishing of the internal market, to pursue a higher level of protection 'concerning health, safety, environmental protection and consumer protection'. This requirement was supposed to avoid the Commission being swamped by a plethora of demands for derogations by those Member States wishing to achieve a higher level of protection. While the level of protection guaranteed under EU law does not necessarily have to be the highest possible, this does not mean that it is non-existent, weak, feeble, or even intermediate. As discussed previously, this obligation is additionally subject to judicial review.[49]

Substantial modifications were subsequently made to the derogation procedure to the advantage of Member States wishing to guarantee a higher degree of protection than that accomplished by the EC harmonization measures.[50] Article 114 TFEU now

---

[48] See Chapter 1, Section 5.   [49] See Chapter 1, Section 7.2.4.1.

[50] For initial commentary on this new provision, see S. Albin and S. Bär, 'Nationale Alleingänge nach Amsterdam—Der neue Art. 95 EGV: Fortschritt oder Rückschritt für den Umweltschutz?' (1999) *Natur und Recht* 185; R. Verheyen, 'The Environmental Guarantee in European Law and the New Article 95 EC Treaty in Practice—A Critique' (2000) 1 *RECIEL* 180–7; H. Sevenster, 'The Environmental Guarantee after Amsterdam: Does the Emperor Have New Clothes?' (2000) 1 *YbEEL* 291–310; N. de Sadeleer: 'Les dérogations nationales à l'harmonisation du marché intérieur' (2013) 2 *RDUE* 233–66; 'Procedures for Derogations from the Principle of Approximation of Laws under Article 95 of the EC Treaty' (2003) 40 *CML Rev* 889–915; *Commentaire Mégret. Environnement et marché intérieur* (Brussels: ULB, 2010) 428–46; J. H. Jans and H. Vedder, *European Environmental Law*, 4th edn (Groeningen: Europa Law, 2008) 111–21; P. Wennerås, 'Fog and Acid Rain Drifting from Luxembourg over Art. 95(4)' (2003) *EELR* 169–78; M. Onida, 'The Practical Application of Article 95(4) and 95(5) EC Treaty' in M. Pallemaerts (ed.), *EU and WTO Law: How Tight is the Legal Straitjacket for Environmental Product Regulation?* (Brussels: VUB Press, 2006) 83–117; C. Vial, 'Une nouvelle intensité dans la prise en compte des exigences de la protection de l'environnement' (2003–04) 4 *RAE-LEA* 617–27; L. Defalque et al., *Commentaire J. Mégret. Libre circulation*

includes two derogation mechanisms. In keeping with past practice, one of the derogatory mechanisms authorizes—at EU level—Member States to depart from the harmonizing measure (para. 10), while the other mechanism allows them, in the absence of an express indication in EU secondary law, to maintain or adopt measures more stringent than EU harmonization measures (paras 4–7).

3.2 Maintenance or introduction of national provisions derogating from internal market harmonization measures in accordance with Article 114(4)–(7) TFEU

Paragraphs 4 and 5 of the new Article 114 authorize Member States to implement, on condition of respect for certain conditions, more stringent measures than those provided for by an EU harmonizing norm, even though the relevant directive, decision, or regulation does not expressly recognize that right. The two paragraphs run as follows:

> 4. If, after the adoption by the Council or by the Commission of a harmonization measure, a Member State deems it necessary to maintain national provisions on grounds of major needs referred to in Article 36, or relating to the protection of the environment or the working environment, it shall notify the Commission of these provisions as well as the grounds for maintaining them.
>
> 5. Moreover, without prejudice to paragraph 4, if, after the adoption by the Council or by the Commission of a harmonization measure, a Member State deems it necessary to introduce national provisions based on new scientific evidence relating to the protection of the environment or the working environment on grounds of a problem specific to that Member State arising after the adoption of the harmonization measure, it shall notify the Commission of the envisaged provisions as well as the grounds for introducing them.

In contrast to Article 193 TFEU,[51] which establishes the principle of minimum harmonization in areas relating to environmental protection,[52] the conditions for implementation of paragraphs 4 and 5 of Article 114 are strictly circumscribed *ratione materiae, personae et temporis*. Due to the significance of the disputes which these derogation mechanisms have given rise to in the recent past, a detailed examination of the manner in which such mechanisms are implemented should be made. The Court of Justice handed down several judgments which provide a number of important clarifications. Despite these judgments, however, various questions remain.

3.2.1 *Personal scope of application of the derogation*

Neither the text of paragraph 4 of ex Article 100a EEC nor that of the new Article 114 TFEU specifies which Member States can invoke the derogation mechanism. This begs

---

des personnes et des capitaux. Rapprochement des legislations (Brussels: IEE, 2006) 233–7; M. G. Doherty, 'The Application of Article 95(4)–95(6) of the EC Treaty: Is the Emperor Still Unclothed' (2008) 8 *YbEEL* 48–79.

[51] See the discussion in Section 2.

[52] M. Dougan, 'Minimum Harmonization and the Internal Market' (2000) 37 *CML Rev* 853–85.

the question whether only the minority Member States enjoy the right, or whether it should also extend to those Member States which voted in favour of the EU harmonization measure. The answer is quite straightforward. By suppressing the expression 'qualified majority' which was present in paragraph 4 of ex Article 100a, the Treaty of Amsterdam put an end to this unproductive debate. Every Member State can now petition for the adoption of more stringent national measures, irrespective of its position within the Council.[53] The ability of every Member State to adopt, under Article 114(5), stricter national norms after the coming into force of an EU harmonizing measure, confirms the validity of such an interpretation.

3.2.2 *Material scope of application of the derogation*

Paragraphs 4 and 5 of Article 114 apply only to harmonization measures adopted on the basis of paragraph 1 of that Article. It should also be noted that it is now possible for a Member State to derogate not only from a harmonization measure adopted by the Council, but also from an implementing measure adopted by the Commission by virtue of Article 291 TFEU. This is not without significance in the light of the considerable regulatory powers which have been accorded to the Commission, in particular to set the threshold for protection regarding health and environmental issues.

Given that paragraph 4 of ex Article 100a EEC could authorize derogations with the potential to restrict the free internal market, Advocate General Tesauro judged that its material scope should be subject to a strict interpretation.[54] Is this interpretation valid *mutatis mutandis* for the new version of Article 114? Given the recent evolution of the case law of the Court of Justice enshrining the principle of integrating environmental concerns within the framework of the internal market,[55] such a restrictive interpretation is no longer certain to be appropriate where invocation of the derogation clause is justified on environmental grounds. In fact, as the discussion in Part I of the book has evidenced, the modifications introduced into the Lisbon Treaty constrain the principle of the functioning of the internal market to accommodating other values which the Court similarly regards as essential.

3.2.3 *Temporal scope of application of the derogation*

Most authors have argued that the ex Article 100a(4) EC derogation mechanism precluded the adoption of new national legislation more stringent than the harmonization measures.[56] The Treaty of Amsterdam put an end to that controversy by

---

[53] Opinion AG Tizzano in Case C-3/00 *Denmark v Commission* [2003] ECR I-2643, para. 78.

[54] According to AG Tesauro, 'Since [Article 100a (4) EEC] creates an exception to the principles of uniform application of EC law and unity of the market, it must, like all provisions which allow derogations, be strictly interpreted, so as to ensure that it is not extended to cases other than those specifically provided for in it' (para. 4 of his Opinion in Case C-41/93 *Commission v France* [1994] ECR I-1829).

[55] Case C-379/98 *PreussenElektra AG* [2001] ECR I-2099, para. 76. See in particular the arguments set out by AG Jacobs in his Opinion (paras 230–1).

[56] The clear and precise formulation of the words, 'If, after the adoption . . ., a Member State deems it necessary to apply national provisions' seemed a priori to preclude the subsequent adoption of more stringent measures. In addition, the term 'apply' had in fact to be contrasted with the terms 'maintain' and

expressly allowing the introduction of new national measures. Regarding temporal scope, two situations can now be distinguished: on the one hand, the Member States can 'maintain' under paragraph 4 national measures following the adoption of an EU harmonization measure; on the other hand, they can at any time 'introduce' under paragraph 5 of Article 114 new measures subject to the Commission's approval. It is nonetheless evident that the conditions required for the adoption of new national regulations are much stricter than those applying to the maintenance of existing national norms.

3.2.4 *Justification of the request for derogation*

As explained later, the conditions applicable under paragraph 4 to the maintenance of national measures which predate an EU measure differ substantially from those which relate under paragraph 5 to the adoption a posteriori of a national measure.

3.2.4.1 Maintenance of existing national measures derogating from internal market harmonization measures

In order to gain Commission approval, a national measure imposing a higher level of protection than the EU harmonization measure must respect the following procedural requirements.

The Member State is obliged to notify the Commission of its desire to maintain national measures due to 'major needs referred to in Article 36 TFEU, or relating to the protection of the environment or the working environment'. On a narrow reading, these 'major needs'[57] justifying recourse to the derogatory mechanism are less numerous that mandatory requirements in the general interest laid down in *Cassis de Dijon*.[58] Given the restrictive interpretation to which Article 36 'reasons' are subject,[59] the framers of the Treaty of Amsterdam nevertheless deemed it necessary to include the phrase 'the protection of the environment or the working environment'. Whereas the concept of environment is interpreted broadly,[60] protection of the working environment applies to nothing more than non-economic considerations relating to the safety, health, and hygiene of workers, which are closely related to environmental issues.[61]

Having said that, Member States should encounter fewer difficulties in conserving protective measures than in adopting new ones, because the latter can relate only to 'the protection of the environment or the working environment'.

The wording of the fourth paragraph calls for several observations. First, the invocation of concerns of public health, the environment, or the working environment

---

'establish' in ex Art. 130t EEC (Art. 176 EC), a provision conferring on Member States a temporally unlimited right to take more stringent measures than those foreseen under the EC norm. See also the Opinion of AG Tizzano in Case C-3/00 *Denmark v Commission* (n 53), para. 71.

[57] Too great an importance should not be placed on the choice of the term 'major needs' as opposed to 'compelling reasons' found in *Cassis de Dijon*. See D. Simon, 'Commentaire de l'article 100A' in *Traité instituant la CEE. Commentaire article par article* (Paris: Economica, 1992) 569; Léger (n 47), 937.

[58] Opinion AG Tesauro in Case C-41/93 *France v Commission* (n 54), para. 5.

[59] See above the discussion in Chapter 5, Section 5.3.2.

[60] See above the discussion in Chapter 1, Section 1.

[61] For a case in point, see Case C-473/98 *Toolex Alpha* [2000] ECR I-5681.

seems to preclude the possibility of having regard to considerations extraneous to the supposed hazard. Accordingly, the Commission deemed that arguments based on technological need and risk of misleading consumers—in support of a national regime forbidding the use of sulphites in foods since these substances did not 'perform a technical function... [or] correspond to a technical need which... [could not] be satisfied by other economically and technically usable methods'—not pertinent for the purposes of public health. In this particular case, the national authorities bore the burden of demonstrating the sanitary risk and could not simply point to the possibility of replacing such food additives with other substances.[62] Nevertheless, the Court of Justice judged that the technological need to use food additives was 'closely related to the assessment of what is necessary in order to protect public health. In the absence of a technological need justifying the use of an additive, there is no reason to incur the potential health risk resulting from authorization of the use of that additive'.[63]

That said, nothing prevents Member States from citing non-scientific data with a view to confirming the admissibility of a national measure which has already been scientifically justified. Where the risk is shown to be plausible, such reasons can justify the maintenance of a stricter measure. It should be added that the substitution principle, recently acknowledged by the Court in *Toolex*,[64] will be a significant factor in reviewing the proportionality of national requests for derogations. Indeed, the principle of encouraging the replacement of harmful substances with less noxious substances, which as yet appears only sporadically throughout EU law,[65] should have a moderating effect on the need to prove the necessity of the protective measure under review.

As far as the wording of the new paragraph 4 is concerned, the condition of 'specificity' of risk—found in paragraph 5—need not be satisfied in order for national measures to be maintained. The Court of Justice recently confirmed this interpretation: 'It follows that neither the wording of Article 114(4) TFEU nor the broad logic of that article as a whole entails a requirement that the applicant Member State prove that maintaining the national provisions which it notifies to the Commission is justified by a problem specific to that Member State.'[66] Thus the Commission cannot, as it has in the past, demand that national authorities furnish proof of the specificity of the risks

---

[62] Decision 1999/830/EC relating to national provisions notified by Denmark relating to the use of sulphites, nitrites and nitrates in foodstuffs [1999] OJ L329/1, paras 20 and 21.

[63] Case C-3/00 *Denmark v Commission* (n 53), para. 82.

[64] *Toolex* (n 61), paras 46 and 47. The Court recognized in this judgment that the conditions imposed on the granting of a derogation are 'compatible with the substitution principle... which consists in the elimination or reduction of risks by means of replacing one dangerous substance with another, less dangerous substance' (para. 47).

[65] Council Directive 89/391/EC on the introduction of measures aiming to encourage improvements in the health and safety of workers at work [1989] OJ L183/1; European Parliament and Council Directive 2004/37/EC on the protection of workers from the risks related to exposure to carcinogens or mutagens at work [2004] OJ L158/0, Art. 4(1); Council Directive 98/24/EC on the protection of health and safety of workers relating to the risk of exposure to chemical agents at work [1998] OJ L131/11; European Parliament and Council Directive 98/8/EC concerning the placing of biocidal products on the market [1998] OJ L123/1, Art. 10(5)(i); Council Directive 1999/13/EC on the limitation of emissions of volatile organic compounds due to the use of organic solvents in certain activities and installations [1999] OJ L85/1, Art. 5(6).

[66] Case C-3/00 *Denmark v Commission* (n 53), para. 59.

cited.[67] The Advocate General's Opinion in that case went against this interpretation, on the ground that any derogation from the principle of uniform application of Community law and the unity of the internal market is subject to a strict interpretation.[68]

Finally the placing by the Treaty framers of 'the protection of the environment or the working environment' and 'major needs referred to in Article 36' on a similar footing in paragraph 4 of Article 114 seems implicitly to have abolished the supplementary *Cassis de Dijon* condition, according to which the national measure should be 'indistinctly applicable'. As discussed previously, this interpretation is not without practical significance for the Member States.[69] Thus, a distinctly applicable national measure could be maintained subject to approval by the Commission, even where it has already been subject to harmonization. By contrast, such a measure could not in the context of a negative harmonization be covered by *Cassis de Dijon* due to its 'distinctly applicable' character.

3.2.4.2 Introduction of a new national measure derogating from internal market harmonization measures

The fact that conditions relating to the maintenance of a more stringent rule have become less strict seems justified. In such cases, the national regime predates EU harmonization. The EU legislature was aware of this, even if it did not consider it opportune to take further consideration of the fact.[70] The introduction of a new measure could, on the other hand, constitute a more significant danger undermining the internal market.[71]

The term 'apply' used in the original version of Article 100a(4) was interpreted by the majority of commentators as preventing Member States from adopting more stringent measures after the adoption of an EU harmonization measure. Henceforth, Member States are empowered, under the terms of paragraph 5 of Article 114, to adopt more stringent measures after the entry into force of the harmonizing measure. Some Member States regard this as one of the principal benefits of the Treaty of Amsterdam. Nevertheless, the reasons which can justify invoking this second derogation mechanism appear less numerous than those which justify the maintenance of existing national norms. Only 'the protection of the environment' and the 'working environment'[72] can be invoked. This precludes the possibility of founding a derogation on a requirement

---

[67] Accordingly, the Commission, in its 1994 decisions on the maintenance of German and Danish regimes prohibiting pentachlorophenol, placed particular emphasis on the fact that those Member States were exposed to high levels of dioxin (Decision 94/783/EC [1994] OJ L316/43 (Germany), para. 7; Decision 96/211/EC [1996] OJ L68/32 (Denmark), para. 6). On the other hand, in its decision on the prohibition of pentachlorophenol (PCP) in the Netherlands, the Commission no longer applied the condition (Decision 1999/831/EC [1999] OJ L329/15 (Netherlands), para. 58). Academic literature confirms the point of view expressed here. See Verheyen (n 50), 80–187; Sevenster (n 50), 236.

[68] Opinion AG Tizzano in Case C-3/00 *Denmark v Commission* (n 53), paras 67–77.

[69] See the discussion in Chapter 5, Sections 5.2.4 and 5.4.2.

[70] Case C-512/99 *Germany v Commission* [2003] ECR I-845, para. 41; and Case C-3/00 *Denmark v Commission* (n 53), para. 58.

[71] Léger (n 47), 936.

[72] The reference to protection of the working environment is more problematic because Art. 114(2) TFEU expressly precludes the adoption of measures relating to 'the rights and interests of employed persons'. It should, however, be noted that the majority of chemical regulations based on Art. 114(1) TFEU only concern worker protection incidentally. See REACH Regulation, Annex I, 5.1.1.

such as the Article 36 protection of human health.[73] There is therefore a fine line between the justifications embodied in paragraph 5 of Article 114 and those contained in Article 36 TFEU. It should not be forgotten that under Article 191(2), the concept of 'environment' includes protection of public health which is itself expressly enshrined in Article 36. The Commission has justified the maintenance of national measures prohibiting pentachlorophenol on both sanitary and environmental grounds (which itself illustrates the indeterminacy of the distinction between the two grounds for justification); yet it has also blocked the adoption of new measures based on the principle of protection of human health. The Commission does not, therefore, seem to be endorsing a broad interpretation of the concept of 'environment'. All attempts to determine the precise scope of the public interest at stake appear destined to fail.[74]

That said, the second derogation mechanism is subject to stricter conditions because 'the adoption of new national legislation is more likely to jeopardize harmonization. The EU institutions could not, by definition, have taken account of the national text when drawing up the harmonization measure.'[75] Indeed, new unilateral measures are likely to jeopardize the functioning of the internal market.[76] Hence, national measures should satisfy three requirements: the risk that the measure is supposed to counter should be specific to the Member State requesting the derogation, it should manifest itself after the adoption of the harmonization measure, and should be supported by scientific proof. These conditions are clearly cumulative.[77] Each requires some clarification.

Specificity of the problem   First, the 'problem' or risk justifying the intervention of the Member State should be 'specific' to the applicant Member State. The intention of the framers of the Treaty of Amsterdam was clearly to avoid the adoption of all regulations of general character. In other words, particular demographic, geographic, or epidemiological circumstances should render the problem particular to the State requesting the derogation.[78] As under consumer law,[79] the geographic or social

---

[73] See Case C-3/00 *Denmark v Commission* (n 53), para. 58; Case C-512/99 *Germany v Commission* (n 70), para. 41. The Commission in particular relied on this argument in rejecting the German prohibition of the commercialization of organostanic compounds (Decision 2001/570/EC [2001] OJ L202/37, para. 76). See also Decision 2000/509/EC on Belgian provisions [2000] OJ L205. On the exclusion of human health, see Sevenster's critique (n 50), 301–2.

[74] See the discussion in Chapter 1, Section 1.

[75] Case C-512/99 *Germany v Commission* (n 70), para. 41; and Case C-3/00 *Denmark v Commission* (n 53), para. 58.

[76] Case C-3/00 *Denmark v Commission* (n 53), para. 58.

[77] See Case C-512/99 *Germany v Commission* (n 70), para. 81; Joined Cases C-439/05 P & C-454/05 P *Land Oberösterreich and Republic of Austria v Commission of the European Communities* [2007] ECR I-7441, para. 57.

[78] On this question, see the decisions on the prohibition of PCP taken in respect of Germany and Denmark (above). In its Decision 1999/830/EC (n 67), the Commission considered whether the Danish population had a greater risk of allergy than other populations, due to genetic disposition, diet, and natural environment (para. 32). In its Decisions 2001/570/EC ([2001] OJ L202/37) and 2000/509/EC ([2000] OJ L205/7) on organostanic compounds, the Commission refused to give consideration to the accumulation of TBT in the ecosystems surrounding German and Belgian naval ports (para. 74 of Decision 2001/570/EC).

[79] In different judgments handed down in the area of food additives, the Court of Justice has considered consumer habits when conducting its proportionality test of national measures prohibiting particular substances. See Case 174/82 *Sandoz* [1983] ECR 2445; Case 227/82 *Van Bennekom* [1983] ECR 3883; Case 97/83 *Melkunie* [1983] ECR 2367; and Case C-247/84 *Motte* [1985] ECR 3887. This case law is not, however, pertinent to monitoring of the implementation of para. 5 of Art. 95, to the extent that consumer protection is not covered by this derogation mechanism.

conditions of the interested State—for example, population density, degree of indus-
trialization, the extent of cross-frontier pollution, vulnerability of the groundwater,
historic record of pollution, etc—exacerbate the impact of particular problems.[80] *A
contrario*, the condition of risk specificity prohibits the adoption of national measures
designed to solve a problem common to the whole of the EU.

Having said that, the term 'specific' should not be given too strict an interpretation; it
is not absolutely necessary that the problem be present exclusively within the Member
State requesting the derogation, since it is potentially possible for it to occur on the
territory of other Member States. As emerged during the course of the BSE epidemic, a
risk discovered at a given moment on the territory of one Member State can rapidly
spread to other countries. This interpretation of the term 'specific' seems justified in the
light of the wording of paragraph 7 of Article 114, which obliges the Commission
immediately to examine the feasibility of adapting the EU harmonizing norm following
a decision in favour of a national measure. The possibility of such an adaptation is only
meaningful if the problem arises or is susceptible to arising in other Member States.

It is no longer necessary to conclude that the appearance of an identical problem in
two Member States would be likely to prevent them from jointly requesting more
stringent national measures. This argument already seems to have been confirmed by
Commission practice, with the prohibition of the use of pentachlorophenol (PCP)
being authorized at the request of Germany and Denmark.[81]

However, several cases have given rise to debate.

- With respect to the prohibition of the cultivation of seed and planting material
  composed of or containing GMOs in the Land Oberösterreich, the Republic of
  Austria claimed that the territory of the Land Oberösterreich contained unusual or
  unique ecosystems that required separate risk assessments from those conducted
  for Austria as a whole or in other similar areas of Europe. The Commission
  dismissed the Austrian request taking into consideration the findings of the
  European Food Safety Agency (EFSA) concerning the absence of scientific evidence demonstrating the existence of a specific problem. Both the General Court
  and the Court of Justice held that Austria had failed to establish sufficient evidence
  capable of invalidating the concrete findings set out by the Commission in its
  contested decision.[82] In particular, Austria had not adduced any scientific evidence
  proving the existence of 'unusual' ecosystems.[83]

- In its request in favour of more stringent limits on the emissions of particulate
  matter by diesel-powered vehicles, the Dutch Government claimed that for a
  problem to be specific to a Member State within the meaning of paragraph 5, it

---

[80] This interpretation is supported by AG Kokott. See Opinion in Case C-405/07 P *Netherlands v
Commission* [2008] ECR I-8301, para. 88.
[81] See the four decisions of the Commission on the prohibition of PCP imposed by different Member
States: for Germany, see the Commission Communication 92/C 334/04 [1992] OJ C334/8 and Decision
94/783/EC [1994] OJ L316/43; for Denmark, see Decision 96/211/EC [1996] OJ L68/32; for the Netherlands, Decision 1999/831/EC [1999] OJ L329/15.
[82] Cases T-366/03 & T-235/04 *Land Oberösterreich* [2005] ECR II-4005, para. 67; and Cases C-439/05
P & C-454/05 P *Land Oberösterreich* (n 77), paras 65 and 66.
[83] Cases C-439/05 & C-454/05 P *Land Oberösterreich* (n 77), para. 66.

was not necessary that it was the result of an environmental danger within that State alone. Although the General Court acknowledged that for a problem to be specific 'it is not necessary that it [is] the result of an environmental danger within that State alone', the Court rejected the Government's argument relating to the interpretation of the criterion of specificity as lacking any factual basis.[84] That judgment was set aside by the Court of Justice on the ground that the Commission was obliged to demonstrate that there were no specific problems. Such an obligation flows from the Commission's obligation 'both to examine all the relevant elements of the individual case and to give an adequate statement of the reasons for its decision'.[85]

To conclude, the Member State requesting the Commission's approval does not have to demonstrate a difference from all other Member States.

Date of emergence of the problem As is well known, in particular with respect to climate change, 'environmental problems are notorious for only revealing themselves gradually'.[86] Nonetheless, Article 114(5) TFEU, requires that the problem must arise after the 'adoption'—and not at the end of the implementation period—of the harmonization measure.[87] Any strict interpretation of that condition could render the whole procedure nugatory. It is submitted that this condition does not preclude the possibility of the risk already being present at the moment of drafting, or even adoption, of the EU harmonization measure, and only later manifesting itself.

Scientific evidence Finally, the right to introduce a national measure more stringent than the EU standard must be justified in the light of 'new scientific evidence'. To the extent that the draft of the EU harmonization measure proposed by the Commission must already take into consideration in accordance with Article 114(3) 'any new development based on scientific facts', the novel character of the scientific evidence has to be assessed in the light of those scientific discoveries which occurred after the adoption of the norm. In assessing the national request for a derogation, the Commission is likely to consult external experts[88] with a view to obtaining their opinion on the soundness of the scientific evidence put forward by the Member State.[89]

There is a noticeable lack of congruence in the Article between the terms 'scientific facts' in paragraph 3 and the 'scientific evidence' of paragraph 5. In the German version, the terms correspond to 'Wissenschaftliche Ergebnisse' and 'Wissenschaftliche Erkenntnisse'. In the French version, the 'faits scientifiques' of paragraph 3 are placed in opposition to the paragraph 5 'preuves scientifiques nouvelles'. By the same token, in the Spanish version, the 'hechos científicos' are distinct from the terms 'novedades científica'. On a semantic analysis, the English word 'evidence'—as opposed to

---

[84] Case T-182/06 *Netherlands v Commission* [2007] ECR I-1983, paras 63–72.

[85] Case C-405/07 P *Netherlands v Commission* [2008] ECR I-8301, para. 66.

[86] Doherty (n 50), 62.

[87] Case C-512/99 *Germany v Commission* (n 70), para. 80; and Cases C-439/05 & C-454/05 P *Land Oberösterreich* (n 77), para. 57.

[88] By way of illustration, for national measures regulating the placing on the market and use of GMOs, the Commission seeks the opinion of EFSA. See Cases T-366/03 & T-235/04 *Land Oberösterreich* (n 82), para. 12.

[89] Cases C-439/05 & C-454/05 P *Land Oberösterreich* (n 77), para. 32.

'proof'—does not necessarily imply that the cause of damage to the environment or workers' health must be proved; 'evidence' can consist of an indication of a possible link between the factor in question and the damage which occurs.[90] Also, the Member States requesting the derogation should only have to provide a minimum of data on the relation of cause and effect between the regulated activity and the suspected damage, rather than having to furnish irrefutable proof.

However, this requirement must not be subject to a literal interpretation, as it is possible for scientific evidence already existing at the time of the adoption of the EU harmonization measure, but not entirely validated at that point in time, to justify the pursuit of a higher level of protection.[91] In addition, nothing prevents new scientific evidence from being advanced by a minority of researchers or solely by national research institutes.[92] In fact, the Court of Justice takes the view that, 'A Member State may base an application to maintain its already existing national provisions on an assessment of the risk to public health different from that accepted by the Community legislature when it adopted the harmonisation measure from which the national provisions derogate'.[93] Accordingly, the serious nature of the scientific evidence gathered by the Member State matters more than scientific consensus. As a matter of course, this interpretation should be endorsed in the light of the precautionary principle.

Furthermore, the possibility for national authorities to refer to uncertain risks seems in any event justified, given the Commission's obligation to take into account the precautionary principle when examining the serious nature of the scientific proof advanced by a Member State.[94]

Having said that, decisions made by the Commission in respect of measures proposed by Belgium and Germany intending to restrict the commercialization of organostanic products due to the endocrinal disturbances which these substances cause—notably on the sex of marine mussels—show that it is intent on giving a particularly strict interpretation to the aforementioned conditions.[95] Nevertheless, the Court of Justice is keen to adopt a more lenient view regarding the nature of the risk assessment. The Court, for instance, has recently accepted that 'the applicant

---

[90] S. Bär and R. A. Krämer, 'European Environmental Policy after Amsterdam' (1998) 10:2 *JEL* 22.

[91] The rate of adoption of regulatory measures designed to protect stratospheric ozone demonstrates the point at which political decisions become dependent on the result of scientific research resulting from work over many years. There is thus always a time-lag between the scientific discovery and the political decision.

[92] *European Communities—Measures Concerning Meat and Meat Products* 16 January 1998 WT/DS26&48/AB/R, § 194.

[93] Case C-3/00 *Denmark v Commission* (n 53), para. 64.

[94] The Commission already applies this principle when it addresses requests for derogation. It has accordingly, in four decisions handed down on 26 October 1999 relating to the prohibition of the use of a chemical agent (creosote), found that measures aimed at reducing the probability of prolonged exposure of the skin to this substance were justified in the light of the principle. See Decision 1999/835/EC on notified UK provisions on the restriction of the marketing of creosote [1999] OJ L329/82, para. 110; Decision 1999/833/EC relating to national provisions notified by Germany relating to restrictions on the marketing of creosote [1999] OJ L329/43, para. 99; Decision 1999/834/EC relating to national provisions notified by Sweden relating to restrictions on the marketing of creosote [1999] OJ L329/63, para. 108; Decision 1999/832/EC relative to national provisions notified by the Netherlands relating to restrictions on the marketing of creosote [1999] OJ L329/25, para. 104. See also the criticisms of Verheyen (n 50), 180–7.

[95] Decisions 2001/570/EC ([2001] OJ L202/37) and 2000/509/EC ([2000] OJ L205/7) on organostanic compounds. Regarding the Commission's practice, see Doherty (n 50), 55–8.

Member State may, in order to justify maintaining such derogating national provisions, put forward the fact that its assessment of the risk to public health is different from that made by the Community legislature in the harmonization measure. In the light of the uncertainty inherent in assessing the public health risks posed by, inter alia, the use of food additives, divergent assessments of those risks can legitimately be made, without necessarily being based on new or different scientific evidence.'[96] This case law is consistent with the precautionary principle which allows public authorities to base their assessment either on qualitative or on quantitative methods.[97]

3.3 Control of requests for derogations provided for in Article 114(4) and (5) TFEU

3.3.1 *Control procedure*

Paragraph 6 of the new Article 114 sets out both the formal and substantive conditions which must be fulfilled in order to secure a derogation.

> The Commission shall, within six months of the notifications as referred to in paragraphs 4 and 5, approve or reject the national provisions involved after having verified whether or not they are a means of arbitrary discrimination or a disguised restriction on trade between Member States and whether or not they shall constitute an obstacle to the functioning of the internal market.

In the absence of a decision by the Commission within this period, the national provisions referred to in paragraphs 4 and 5 shall be deemed to have been approved. When justified by the complexity of the matter and in the absence of danger to human health, the Commission may notify the Member State concerned that the period referred to in this paragraph may be extended for a further period of up to six months.

3.3.1.1 Formal conditions

The Court of Justice declared in a judgment in 1999 that the possibility provided for in paragraph 4 of ex Article 100a EEC presupposed respect for the procedure laid down for this purpose. It accordingly concluded that Italy was not entitled to invoke this derogation mechanism in order to derogate from a directive harmonizing gas appliances, since it had not adhered to the appropriate procedures.[98] Member States requesting the granting of derogations must therefore respect the formal requirements of Article 114(6) TFEU.

The request for derogation must be registered with the Commission; however, a deadline for notification is not specified. Justification of the request is a prerequisite for effective control by the Commission, with Article 114(4) and (5) requiring that the Member State reveal 'the grounds' for maintaining or adopting national measures. This can be founded on any scientific argument—toxicological, epidemiological, ecological,

---

[96] Case C-3/00 *Denmark v Commission* (n 53), para 63.
[97] Commission Communication on the precautionary principle, COM(2000) 1, para. 5.1.3. See the discussion in Chapter 1, Section 7.6.
[98] Case C-112/97 *Commission v Italy* [1999] ECR I-1821.

etc—capable of providing a sound basis for the level of protection.[99] The implementation of the notification system inevitably requires close cooperation between the Commission and the Member States. As far as the latter are concerned, they are bound by Article 4(3) TEU to notify as early as possible such national measures which they intend to continue applying are incompatible with a harmonization measure.[100] Notification of the maintenance of existing measures should thus follow as quickly as possible, allowing the Commission to rule before the expiry of the implementation period of the harmonization measure, thus avoiding the situation where measures having direct effect conflict with the application of the national measures. The Member State should therefore ensure that a period of at most six months separates the notification of its provisions from the end of the implementation period of the EU measure. As far as the Commission is concerned, it must display corresponding diligence in examining the national provisions submitted to it as quickly as possible.

Although not mandatory under Article 114, the Commission has adopted the practice of informing the other Member States when it receives a request under Article 114(4)–(5), with a view to giving them the chance to express an opinion on the request for derogation. Because the procedure is initiated at the request of a Member State seeking the approval of national provisions derogating from a harmonization measure adopted at EU level, the Commission in turn must be able, within the prescribed period, to obtain the information which proves to be necessary without being required once more to hear the applicant Member State.[101] This informal procedure is in fact similar to that provided for in Directive 98/34/EC of 22 June 1998,[102] which laid down a procedure for the provision of information in the field of technical standards and regulations by which the Commission immediately brought any notifications of proposed technical rulings to the attention of other Member States in order to allow them to make observations.

It should be pointed out that no provision allows for the application in favour of the applicant Member State of the principle of the right to be heard in the decision-making procedure laid down in Article 114(4) and (6) EC, which relates to the approval of national provisions derogating from a harmonization measure adopted at EU level. Due to the specificity of the procedure, the Court of Justice has held that 'the principle of the right to be heard does not apply to the procedure provided under Article 114(4) and (6) EC.'[103] Where a Member State's request is considered to be incomplete, one may wonder when the clock should start running for the Commission's decision. The central issue is whether the Commission must in such cases reject the request or

---

[99] Regarding the absence of scientific argument, see Decision 2006/255/EC of 14 March 2006 concerning national provisions imposing on supermarkets an obligation to place genetically modified foods on separate shelves from non-genetically modified foods, notified by Cyprus pursuant to Article 95(5) of the EC Treaty ([2006] OJ L92/12).

[100] *Kortas* (n 44), para. 35.

[101] Case C-3/00 *Denmark v Commission* (n 53), para. 48.

[102] European Parliament and Council Directive 98/34/EC laying down a procedure for the provision of information in the field of technical standards and regulations and of rules on Information Society services [1998] OJ L204/37. See the discussion in Chapter 5, Section 8.

[103] Case C-3/00 *Denmark v Commission* (n 53), para. 50.

whether it can demand additional information, which would then have the effect of delaying the start of the time period.

3.3.1.2 Substantive conditions

(i) Introductory remarks

Once it receives the notification the Commission is obliged, as Guardian of the Treaties, to verify whether the maintenance or adoption of the national provisions responds to the requirements contained in paragraph 6. In particular, the provisions proposed must not constitute either 'a means of arbitrary discrimination or a disguised restriction on trade between Member States or an obstacle to the functioning of the internal market'. The two first criteria—'a means of arbitrary discrimination or a disguised restriction on trade between Member States'—have been taken from Article 36 TFEU; this once again shows how close the links are between this provision and Article 114 TFEU. The third criterion—no 'obstacle to the functioning of the internal market'—is particularly ambiguous and, incidentally, is not found in so many words elsewhere in the Treaty, although similar terms can be found.[104] At first sight, any national provision derogating from the EU harmonizing measure is capable of hindering the free movement of goods and should as such be precluded. Since this interpretation is problematic: the third requirement is taken to constitute just one element to be considered by the Commission when testing the validity of the national measure. In other words, the Commission can only apply a proportionality test and is thus only able to reject those national measures which constitute major obstacles 'to the functioning of the internal market'.[105]

If it finds that all three conditions are satisfied, the Commission approves the relevant national provisions; in the contrary case, it rejects the request.

Account must also be taken of the fact that the Commission's assessment differs significantly from the case law regarding both Article 36 TFEU and *Cassis de Dijon*. Under Article 114 TFEU, the Member State bears the burden of proof for demonstrating that the EU standards are inappropriate for addressing the risks it is facing. In contrast, when invoking either Article 36 TFEU or *Cassis de Dijon*, the Member States are endowed with the right to choose their level of protection on account that there is no previous EU standard.[106]

---

[104] Art. 107(3)(c) TFEU.

[105] The Commission considers thus that 'the concept of obstacle to the functioning of the internal market as referred to in Article 114(6) has to be understood as a disproportionate effect in relation to the pursued objective, in order to preserve the useful character of the procedure'. See Decision 2012/160/EU concerning the national provisions notified by the German Federal Government maintaining the limit values for lead, barium, arsenic, antimony, mercury, and nitrosamines and nitrosatable substances in toys [2012] OJ L80/19, para. 89.

[106] Accordingly, in the absence of EU harmonization, given that the subject matter has not been harmonized, it is for the Member States to determine the level of protection which they wish to afford to public health and the means to be employed in order to achieve it, whilst also taking free movement of goods into account. See Case 104/75 *De Peijper* [1976] ECR 613, para. 15; Case 272/80 *Biologische Produkten* [1981] ECR 3277; Case 174/82 *Sandoz* [1983] ECR 2445; Case C-293/94 *Brandsma* [1996] ECR I-3159; Case C-375/90 *Commission v Greece* [1993] ECR I-2055; Joined Cases C-570/07 & C-571/07 *Blanco Pérez and Chao Gómez* [2010] ECR I-4629; and Joined Cases C-171/07 & C-172/07 *Apothekerkammer des Saarlandes* [2009] ECR I-4171, paras 18 and 19. See also Case T-198/12 R *Germany v Commission* [2013] nyr.

Article 114 expressly places the burden of proof of showing that the conditions are satisfied on the Member State requesting the derogation.[107] At this stage, the Commission can be confronted with three possibilities:

- the information provided by the Member State is incomplete; the Commission must then reject the request on the ground that it does not have a sufficiently sound basis in science;

- whilst the information provided by the national authorities is complete, it does not demonstrate the necessity of deviating from the harmonization measure; the Commission rejects the request unless it can be justified by recourse to the precautionary principle;

- the request is so complex that the Commission has neither the time nor the expertise to verify the data submitted. In this case, the Commission must make a prima facie ruling.

(ii) Principle of proportionality

The structure of Article 114 allows the Commission a certain degree of discretion when exercising its control.[108] One may wonder whether the Commission must at this stage be as strict as the Court of Justice when it examines the proportionality of a national measure under Article 36 TFEU or in the light of a mandatory requirement.[109] In other words, can the Commission restrict itself to verifying whether a national measure satisfies the requirements of paragraph 6 of Article 114, or should it also assess the measure's proportionality? In his Opinion in *France v Commission*, Advocate General Tesauro stressed that 'the principle of proportionality, a general principle of EU law, must also be applied in appraising the grounds relied on by a Member State as a basis for continuing to apply its own rules by way of derogation from the harmonization measures'. He went on to say that this control should even 'be inspired by more stringent criteria' than those adopted by the Court for the purposes of the application of Article 36 TFEU 'in that there is no possibility of not taking account of the standards of protection already laid down by the harmonization rules'.[110] Against this background, the Commission, did not accept a Danish measure concerning the use of sulphites, nitrites, and nitrates in food products on the ground that they went beyond

---

[107] The Court of Justice stressed in Case C-3/00 *Denmark v Commission* (n 53) that 'it falls to the applicant Member State to prove that those national provisions ensure a level of health protection which is higher than the Community harmonization measure and that they do not go beyond what is necessary to attain that objective'. See para. 64. See also, eg, Decision 1999/830/EC [1999] OJ L329/1, para. 18; and Decision 2001/570/EC [2001] OJ L202/37, para. 65. See Opinion AG Tizzano in Case C-3/00 *Denmark v Commission* (n 53), para. 101.

[108] Léger (n 47), 943, para. 81.   [109] See the discussion in Chapter 5, Section 7.

[110] Various authors considered that derogations requested under para. 4 of ex Art. 100a EEC could not avoid a proportionality test. See B. Langeheine, 'Le rapprochement des législations nationales selon l'article 100 A du traité C.E.E.: l'harmonisation communautaire face aux exigences de protection nationale' (1989) 328 *RMC* 357; H.-J. Glaesner, 'L'article 100A: un nouvel instrument pour la réalisation du marché commun' (1989) *CDE* 622, 624.

that which was necessary in order to achieve the objective of the protection of health.[111] Advocate General Tizzano supported this strict interpretation in his Opinion on the validity of the Commission decision prohibiting Danish food safety measures.[112] However, in this case the Court found that, in its decision on the application of the Danish authorities, the Commission had failed to take into account the 'highly critical' opinion of the Scientific Committee for Food regarding the scientific basis of the EC harmonization measure's thresholds of the permissible residual amounts of nitrites and nitrates in foodstuffs.[113]

(iii) Right to be heard

According to the General Court, 'the authors of the Treaty intended that that procedure should be speedily concluded in order to safeguard the applicant Member State's interest in being certain of the applicable rules, and in the interest of the proper functioning of the internal market'.[114] As a consequence, the right for the Member State lodging the request to be heard does not apply either to paragraph 4 or to paragraph 5 procedure.[115]

(iv) Statement of reasons

Nonetheless, the Commission cannot dismiss the request on the sole ground that it is not sufficiently justified. Its decision must fully satisfy the obligation to provide a statement of reasons provided for in Article 296(2) TFEU, as interpreted by the Court of Justice. Accordingly, the Commission is bound to explain in such a way that, on the one hand, the Court can exercise its control and, on the other hand, that both Member States and interested nationals can understand the circumstances in which the Commission has correctly applied EU law.[116] It cannot therefore restrict itself to merely observing that the national regulation is compatible with paragraphs 4 and 5 'without explaining the reasons of fact and law on account of which the Commission considered that all the conditions contained in Article 100a(4) were to be regarded as fulfilled in the case in point'.[117]

---

[111] Decision 1999/830/EC on national provisions notified by Denmark concerning the use of sulphites, nitrites, and nitrates in foodstuffs [1999] OJ L329/1. In its statement on the single market and the environment (COM(99) 263), the European Commission nonetheless indicated that the principles contained in Art. 175 EC (Art. 192 TFEU) would be rigorously applied when assessing national provisions invoked under paras 4 and 5 of Art. 95 (Art. 114 TFEU). According to the Commission, the justifications advanced by the Member States must be substantiated, not only legally but also from a scientific, technical, and economic perspective.

[112] See Opinion AG Tesauro in Case C-41/93 *France v Commission* (n 53), paras 99–105.

[113] Case C-3/00 *Denmark v Commission* (n 53), paras 109–15.

[114] Case C-3/00 *Denmark v Commission* (n 53), para. 49; and Cases C-439/05 & C-454/05 P *Land Oberösterreich and Austria* (n 77), paras 40 and 41; Joined Cases T-366/03 & T-235/04 *Land Oberösterreich* (n 82), para. 43; and Case T-69/08 *Poland v Commission* [2010] ECR II-5629, para. 62.

[115] Case C-3/00 *Denmark v Commission* (n 53), paras 49 and 50; and Cases T-366/03 & T-235/04 *Land Oberösterreich* (n 82), paras 41 and 43.

[116] Case C-41/93 *France v Commission* (n 54), para. 34. In this particular case, France contested the validity of a Commission decision confirming German regulations concerning the prohibition of PCP, which were more stringent than the EC harmonizing norm. Following the judgment in this case, the Commission reconfirmed the derogation, adopting Decision 94/783/EC [1994] OJ L316/43.

[117] Case C-41/93 *France v Commission* (n 54), para. 36.

(v) Tacit consent to the adoption of national derogating measures

The Treaty of Amsterdam introduced a major modification to the control procedure. Whilst the procedure provided for in ex Article 100a(4) precluded Member States from applying a national regulation which departed from the harmonizing rules without having first obtained Commission approval,[118] paragraph 6 of Article 114 now allows for an extension of the period within which the Commission has to make a ruling. The authors of the Treaty intended, in the interests of both the applicant Member State and the proper functioning of the internal market, that the approval procedure 'should be speedily concluded'.[119] Thus, the Commission has six months in which either to approve or reject the national request. In the absence of a Commission decision, the national measure is deemed to have been approved.[120]

This implicit authorization mechanism puts the Member States in a stronger position since the silence of the Commission is now equivalent to tacit approval of the national measure, whereas this would previously have prevented the measure's maintenance.

The six-month period is set in motion on the first working day following receipt of the request from the national authorities. The need to perform extra testing cannot have the effect of interrupting the time limit. By the same token, a decision adopted by the Commission before the six-month deadline but not notified to the Member State concerned during that period does not interrupt the six-month time limit set out in paragraph 6.[121] Such a decision is accordingly vitiated by an error of law and is likely to be annulled.[122]

The complexity of the risk assessment procedures[123] can, however, lead the Commission to postpone the inquiry's six-month deadline for up to six more months—that is, up to a total of 12 months—unless prolonging the time limit would constitute a danger to human health.[124] Oddly enough, whilst the six-month deadline cannot be extended where there is a danger to human health, it can be extended in the case of irreversible damage to the environment.

3.3.2 *Impact of the control procedure on national law*

In *Kortas*, the Court of Justice confirmed the primacy of the provisions of a directive adopted on the basis of ex Article 100a EEC—to the extent that it satisfied general requirements as to clarity, precision, and unconditional character and that the period for implementing the directive into national law had passed—over a more stringent

---

[118] *Kortas* (n 44), para. 27.
[119] Case C-3/00 *Denmark v Commission* (n 53), para. 49; Case T-69/08 *Poland v Commission* (n 114), para. 62.
[120] This condition is valid both for requests to maintain national provisions predating the act of harmonization and for requests to adopt new national provisions.
[121] Case T-69/08 *Poland v Commission* (n 114), para. 62.
[122] Case C-398/00 *Spain v Commission* [2010] ECR I-5643, para. 34; and Cases C-439/05 & C-454/05 P *Land Oberösterreich* (n 77), para. 37.
[123] See the discussion on the precautionary principle in Chapter 1, Section 7.6.
[124] Cases C-439/05 & C-454/05 P *Land Oberösterreich* (n 77), para. 40; and Case T-69/08 *Poland v Commission* (n 114), para. 60.

national regime (prohibition of a colorant in food products) justified by major needs based on Article 36 TFEU regarding public health.[125] The fact that the Commission delayed assessing a Swedish request for derogation did not prejudice the primacy of EU law over national law. This case law indicated that Member States intending to invoke paragraph 4 of Article 100a EEC could not apply their own regulatory regimes after the end of the EU norm's implementation period until the Commission confirmed the request. The provisions of the harmonized measure which have direct effect could no longer apply after such approval was given.[126]

The Court justified its position on the ground that the EU harmonization measures would have been deprived of their effect if Member States could retain the right unilaterally to apply national provisions departing from them. The ambiguity occasioned by any other conclusion as to the regime applicable in a particular Member State would not only have gone against the principle of legal certainty, but also would have undermined the primacy of EU law.[127]

Viewed from a more practical perspective, the solution accepted by the Court of Justice obliged the Member States to suspend the effects of their regulations until the Commission could rule on their request, running the risk of having to wait several years for the Commission's decision. This gave rise to significant difficulties for Member States wishing to maintain coherent normative policies at national level. As has already been shown, these difficulties led the framers of the Treaty to impose on the Commission a strict deadline for assessing derogation requests (either six months, or at most one year).

Under the new Article 114, Member States have the right to maintain national measures during the implementation period, to the extent that this does not compromise the realization of the objectives of the EU harmonization measure.[128] They should nevertheless give the Commission the necessary time to process their application, six or 12 months. If the Commission rejects the application, the provisions of the harmonized measure which have direct effect will immediately apply. This will preclude the Member State from maintaining its national measures.

Given the exceptional nature of the Member States' recognized powers, Commission approval constitutes 'in every sense an authorization ... to derogate from the harmonizing measure, with the result that a refusal would place the State in question under an obligation to bring its own legislation into line with the requirements decided on by the Commission'.[129] The words 'approve or reject' in paragraph 6 must accordingly be understood as authorizing Member States to apply more stringent national measures on the sole condition that they have first been approved by the Commission. The result of this is that it is entirely in the interests of national authorities wishing to maintain a more stringent measure to lodge their request as quickly as possible after the publication of the harmonization measure in the Official Journal, so that the Commission can rule before the expiry of the implementation period.

---

[125] *Kortas* (n 44).   [126] Opinion AG Saggio of 28 January 1999 in *Kortas* (n 44).
[127] On this point, see Opinion AG Tesauro in Case C-41/93 *France v Commission* (n 54), para. 9.
[128] Case C-129/96 *Inter-Environnement Wallonie* [1997] ECR I-441.
[129] Opinion AG Tesauro in Case C-41/93 *France v Commission* (n 54), para. 8.

A remaining doubt concerns the suspension mechanism where paragraph 9 of Article 114 permits both the Member States and the Commission to contest before the Court of Justice the validity of national measures which would, in the light of paragraph 6 of Article 114, have their effects suspended. One may wonder at the utility of court proceedings where the contested national measure would not have been applied in any event. The modifications incorporated by the Treaty of Amsterdam do not, therefore, remove all doubts relating to suspensions resulting from the assessment procedure.

3.3.3 *Impact of the Commission's decision on harmonized EU law*

Where the Commission rejects an application, the Member State must, in conformity with Article 4(3) TEU, refrain from adopting any measure liable to jeopardize the realization of the Treaty's aims. The national authority must therefore bring its regulation into line with the standard set by the harmonization measure.

On the other hand, if the Commission approves the application, the Member State can, depending on the case, maintain its national regulation or adopt a rule more stringent than the EU harmonization measure. Article 114 TFEU does not specify whether there is any temporal limitation to the maintenance of an existing standard or the adoption of a new national standard. Where the derogation has been approved, it should in principle subsist as long as the conditions set out in paragraph 6 are satisfied.

Moreover, under paragraph 7 a favourable decision entails an obligation for the Commission to 'immediately examine whether to propose an adaption' to EU law.[130] Although it is not bound to reach any particular conclusion, this requirement nevertheless enhances the dynamic forces driving the realization of the internal market. The EU standards which shape this market would therefore be adapted in conformity with the regulatory progress achieved by particular Member States. In addition, according to the Court of Justice, 'such an adaptation could be appropriate when the national provisions approved by the Commission offer a level of protection which is higher than the harmonization measure as a result of a divergent assessment of the risk to public health.'[131] That said, it would be difficult for the Commission, which is endowed with wide discretion, to be censured for any delay in proposing an amendment to the EU act at issue.[132]

In addition, in order to reinforce this dynamic Article 114(8) provides that 'when a Member State raises a specific problem on public health in a field which has been the subject of prior harmonization measures, it shall bring it to the attention of the Commission which shall immediately examine whether to propose appropriate measures to the Council'. If the Commission refuses to set in motion this levelling-up procedure, it has a duty to show that it is not possible to extend the protection regime to the internal market as a whole. Be that as it may, this obligation should allow space for national initiatives to contribute to the constant adaptation of EU law in the light of scientific progress, as required by Article 114(3) TFEU.

---

[130] Art. 114(7) TFEU.   [131] *Kortas* (n 44), para. 65.   [132] Léger (n 47), 946, para. 88.

Finally, any modifications made to EU harmonizing norms following the granting of a derogation by the Commission should at the very minimum guarantee, in accordance with both Article 3(3) TEU and Article 114(3) TFEU, a higher level of environmental protection.[133]

3.3.4 *Objections by other Member States*

Since the approval—or absence thereof—of the request for derogations constitutes a decision of the Commission for the purposes of Article 288 TFEU, the Member State making the request can contest it under Article 263 TFEU.[134]

Article 114(9) establishes a simplified breach procedure before the Court of Justice, under which the Commission or Member State can bring the matter directly before the Court if they consider 'that another Member State is making improper use of the powers provided for in this Article'. Avoiding pre-trial procedures, this action can be brought even before the Commission has ruled on the request, as well as after the request's refusal by the Commission. It can thus lead to a rapid judicial condemnation of every abuse of the derogatory regime. This specific remedy does not prejudice the Member State from lodging an action for annulment by virtue of Article 263. In fact, this procedure has not as yet been applied.

3.4 Safeguard clauses in harmonization measures

3.4.1 *Clauses provided for in paragraph 10 of Article 114*

The existence of a safeguard clause in a directive based on Article 114 is often necessary to allow the Court of Justice to treat EU legislation as being exhaustive; this has the effect of preventing Member States from invoking Article 36 TFEU.[135]

Moderating the effects of majority voting, paragraph 10 of Article 114 provides that directives, decisions, and regulations which have as their object the establishment and functioning of the internal market can:

> in appropriate clauses include a safeguard clause authorizing Member States to take, for one or more of the non-economic reasons referred to in Article 36, provisional measures subject to a EC control procedure.

The purpose of paragraph 10—replicating paragraph 5 of ex Article 100a EEC—is to allow a Member State, subject to an EU control procedure, to adopt temporary measures

---

[133] See the discussion in Chapter 5, Section 7.2.   [134] Glaesner (n 110), 625.

[135] It is settled case law that where directives provide for the harmonization of measures designed to safeguard the protection of the health of animals and people and setting down Community procedures to ensure adherence, recourse to Art. 30 EC is no longer justified; appropriate controls must be made and protective measures undertaken within the framework laid down by the harmonization directive. See inter alia: Case 5/77 *Tedeschi* [1977] ECR 1555, para. 35; Case 148/78 *Ratti* [1979] ECR 1629, para. 36; Case 251/78 *Futtermittel* [1979] ECR 3369, para. 14; Case 190/87 *Moormann* [1988] ECR 4689, para. 10; Case C-323/93 *Centre d'insémination de la Crespelle* [1994] ECR I-5077, para. 30; Case C-99/01 *Linhart* [2002] ECR I-9375, para. 18.

in the event of a sudden and unforeseen danger to health, life, etc.[136] This paragraph does nothing beyond giving formal recognition to a practice followed for a long time by the Council when adopting harmonization measures under Article 94 (ex Art. 100) EC.[137] To the extent that this possibility is addressed directly to the EU legislature and not to the Member States, the safeguard clause provided for in paragraph 10 is different from the derogation procedures under paragraphs 4 and 5 of Article 114.

The majority of regulations and directives founded on Article 114 contain safeguard clauses encompassing environmental risks.[138]

The insertion of such a safeguard clause into an instrument of EU legislation must satisfy several conditions.

First, the clause must allow Member States to deal with exceptional situations of limited duration. Given that the circumstances must be exceptional, a national measure which unilaterally imposes a general prohibition on the marketing of GMO seed, clearly infringes the provisions regarding safeguard clauses set out under secondary law.[139] As regards the duration of the measure, in *Greenpeace v France* the Court of Justice held that the precautionary principle was in particular expressed in the safeguard clause of Directive 90/220/EC, which provided for provisional limitations or bans on the use and sale of GMOs. When relying on the wording of this safeguard clause, the measures of prohibition or limitation taken by national authorities are only authorized for as long as is necessary for a new decision to be taken by the EU authorities.[140]

Second, it must be justified in the light of the non-economic reasons mentioned in Article 36 TFEU, such as public morality and the protection of health and life of humans, animals, or plants. No reference is made to protection of the environment. The absence of an 'environmental' safeguard clause is all the more incomprehensible given the specific emphasis placed on environmental protection in paragraphs 3–5 of Article 114 and that several environmental directives are based on Article 114. It would nevertheless be possible to fill the substantive gap in paragraph 10 by reference to the second subsection of Article 174(2)(2), which provides that 'in this context, harmonization measures answering environmental protection requirements shall include, where appropriate, a safeguard clause allowing Member States to take provisional measures, for non-economic environmental reasons, subject to a Community inspection procedure'.

---

[136] Craig and de Búrca (n 47), 1186.

[137] C. D. Ehlermann, 'The Internal Market Following the SEA' (1987) 24 *CML Rev* 398.

[138] Directive 98/34/EC on information society services [1998] OJ L204/37, Art. 7; Directive 2001/18/EC on the deliberate release into the environment of genetically modified organisms [2001] OJ L106/1, Art. 23; Regulation (EC) No. 1829/2003 on genetically modified food and feed [2003] OJ L268/1, Art. 34; REACH Regulation, Art. 129; and Regulation (EC) No. 1107/2009 concerning the placing of plant protection products on the market [2009] OJ L 309/1, Art. 71. Moreover, Art. 6 of Packaging Directive 94/62/EC provides for a derogation from the rate of recycling and recovery in favour of 'Member States which have, or will, set programmes going beyond the targets of para. 1(a) and (b) and which provide to this effect appropriate capacities for recycling and recovery'.

[139] Case C-165/08 *Commission v Poland* [2009] ECR I-6843, para. 61.

[140] Case C-6/99 *Greenpeace France* [2000] ECR I-1676, para. 44. Comments by Legal and Romi in (2000) *AJDA* 452; G. Vaqué, 'El principio de precaución en la jurisprudencia del TJCE: la sentecia "Greenpeace France"' (2001) 2 *Comunidad Europea Aranzadi* 33–43.

Third, in line with the case law on free movement of goods, the safeguard clauses can authorize the Member States to depart from harmonization for 'non-economic reasons referred to in Article 36'.[141]

In invoking safeguard clauses, Member States have to overcome additional hurdles in particular with respect to measures limiting the placing on the market of GMOs. Regarding burden of proof, the Court ruled in *Monsanto Agricultura Italia* that 'protective measures, notwithstanding their temporary character and even if they are preventive in nature, can be adopted only if they are based on a risk assessment which is as complete as possible in the particular circumstances of an individual case'.[142] Moreover, in Joined Cases C-58–68/10 *Monsanto and Others*, regarding the substantive conditions for emergency measures adopted pursuant to Novel Food Regulation (EC) No. 1829/2003, the Court of Justice ruled that Member States are required to establish, in addition to urgency, the existence of a situation which is likely to constitute a clear and serious risk to human health, animal health, or the environment.[143] In contrast to *Greenpeace v France*,[144] the Court did not invoke the precautionary principle in that judgment.

Finally, in accordance with principles traditionally applicable to safeguard clauses, the application of a derogation clause under paragraph 10 should also be subject to a 'control procedure' normally undertaken by the Commission. In practice, the safeguard clause entails an obligation for the Member State to notify the Commission of the derogating measures taken, in order to enable the latter to ascertain whether they are consistent with the relevant legislation. Generally speaking, the Commission will either authorize the provisional measure for a defined time period or require the Member State to revoke the provisional measure. As a result, the interim national measure is temporary. It can also be concluded that such a clause could be subject to a proportionality test identical to that used by the Court in respect of measures having equivalent effect contrary to Articles 34 and 35 TFEU.

Is the effect of Article 114(10) TFEU to preclude the possibility of the EU legislature enacting, in line with procedure under the ex Article 100 regime, provisions expressly authorizing Member States to preserve more stringent rules on environmental protection in the long term? In the light of the general context within which this paragraph is situated, the adoption of a long-term derogation mechanism would at first sight appear to be precluded: the safeguard clause should be temporary insofar as it is required to cover 'provisional measures'. The Commission's capacity to grant derogations definitively by applying paragraphs 4 and 5 of Article 114 confirms, moreover, a restrictive interpretation of the scope *ratione materiae et temporis* of paragraph 10. Nevertheless, this practice shows that the insertion of safeguard clauses which permit the granting of long-term derogations remains generally admissible.[145]

---

[141] The requirement only to consider arguments of a non-economic nature is redundant since Art. 36 TFEU precludes arguments of a purely economic nature. See the discussion in Chapter 5, Section 5.2.1.

[142] Case C-236/01 *Monsanto Agricoltura Italia* [2003] ECR I-8105, para. 107.

[143] Cases C-58–68/10 *Monsanto and Others* [2011] OJ C311/8, para. 76. See M. Weimer, 'The Right to Adopt Post-Market Restrictions of GM Crops in the EU' (2012) 3 *EJRR* 447.

[144] Case C-6/99 *Greenpeace France* [2000] ECR I-1676.

[145] See Art. 6(6) of Packaging Directive 94/62/EC which permits Member States, in certain circumstances, to set recycling targets higher than provided for in the Directive.

Finally, the insertion of a safeguard clause into a directive does not preclude the possibility of a Member State invoking paragraphs 4 and 5 of Article 114. However, the existence of such a clause could be beneficial to the Member State.

3.4.2 Safeguard procedures under the 'new approach'

Harmonization on a product-by-product basis has been criticized for being time-consuming as well as costly.[146] According to the new approach for technical normalization,[147] whereas technical harmonization was restricted to 'essential requirements' dealing mainly with health and environmental protection, standard-setting became the province of non-EU standardization bodies, such as CEN and CENELEC. These bodies can find themselves entrusted with the task of developing technical specifications 'needed for the production and placing on the market of products conforming to the essential requirements established by the Directives' adopted on the basis of Article 114 TFEU. In so doing, the EU lawmaker has left significant room for manoeuvre to these bodies as to how to satisfy these 'essential requirements'.

While these technical specifications maintain their status as voluntary norms,[148] they effectively oblige the Member States to recognize a presumption of conformity with the essential requirements established by the directives for those products manufactured in accordance with those technical specifications. The resolution of 7 May 1985 on the 'new approach' provides that safeguard procedures be inserted into directives with a view to allowing either the Commission or a Member State to challenge norms emanating from the standardization bodies. For example, Directive 94/62/EC of 20 December 1994 on packaging and packaging waste authorizes both the Member States and the Commission to appeal to the committee established by Directive 98/34/EC if they consider that the norms elaborated by the CEN 'do not entirely meet the essential requirements' in respect of production, composition, reusability, and value of the packaging. On the basis of advice given by the committee, the Commission can 'withdraw' such norms adopted by the standardizing bodies from the Official Journal. In this way (answering the Danish and Belgian challenge to the validity of several norms proposed by the CEN concerning packaging on the ground that the priority given to incineration and energy conservation compromised the prevention principle, and as such was contrary to the compelling reasons provided for in Annex II to the Directive), the Commission decided not to publish certain norms harmonized by the CEN.[149]

---

[146] S. Farr, *Harmonisation of Technical Standards in the EC* (Chichester: Wiley, 1992) 5.

[147] Council Resolution 85/C 136/01 on a new approach to technical harmonization and normalization [1985] OJ C136/1. Council Resolution 2000/C 141/01 on the role of normalization in Europe [2000] OJ C141/1.

[148] Annex II to Resolution 85/C 136/01 states that 'these technical specifications are not mandatory and maintain their status of voluntary standards'. See also Art. 4 of European Parliament and Council Directive 2001/95/EC on general product safety ([2002] OJ L11/4) which requires that the Commission shall call on the European standardization bodies to draw up standards which satisfy general safety requirements.

[149] Commission Decision 2001/524/EC on the publication of references to the norms EN 13428:2000, EN 13429:2000, EN 13430:2000, EN 13431:2000 and EN 13432:2000 in the Official Journal of the European Communities within the context of the implementation of the Directive 94/62/EC on packaging and packaging waste [2001] OJ L190/21.

4. Conclusions

One may assume that minimum harmonization is appropriate in the environmental field because the thrust of EU environmental policy is to pursue the broad objectives enshrined in Article 192 TFEU and not to integrate markets.[150] However, neither the TEU nor the TEU require the Member States to pursue a higher level of environmental protection than that achieved at EU level. The possibility of enacting more stringent measures is simply an option left to the Member States. Moreover, such an option is likely to be interpreted strictly when the national measures hamper free trade. Account must also be taken of the fact that Article 193 TFEU has a symbolic function since Member States use their powers rather sparingly and incidentally.[151] Indeed, copy-and-paste transposition of environmental directives is strongly entrenched.

With respect to the functioning of the internal market, in order not to favour trade disproportionately to the detriment of other values recognized by the Treaties, Article 114 TFEU provides a certain number of guarantees. It states that measures proposed at the EU level concerning health, safety, environmental, and consumer protection are to take as a base a high level of protection, taking account in particular of any new development based on scientific facts. Such requirements must be approved. High standards foster innovation and, as a result, improve the competitiveness of European undertakings. In addition, environmental measures can be much more effective at an EU than at a national, let alone a local level. Obviously, uniform standards enhance a common playing field. In sharp contrast, the fact that each Member State would decide for itself its own standards is likely to result in significant differences in environmental quality and may hamper economic integration.

So why does it matter whether there is room for more stringent national product-related measures? It matters for the following reason. National authorities may contend with the level of environmental protection afforded under harmonized legislation, in particular where they are intent upon pursuing more ambitious objectives than the EU standards. Under Article 114(3), the Commission is called upon to base its proposal on a high level of protection. However, this level has never been optimal. Moreover, whether the European Parliament and the Council are ready to endorse the level proposed by the Commission remains to be seen.[152] Furthermore, Article 114 offers the Commission much latitude for approving such national measures and, as a result, the consent procedure has been applied in a very strict manner to the detriment of the environmental goals pursued by several Member States.[153]

Finally, this latitude is contained within limits which are not always very clear. Indeed, in spite of the clarifications brought about by the Treaty of Amsterdam in

---

[150] S. Weatherill, 'Pre-Emption, Harmonization and the Distribution of Competence' in C. Barnard and J. Scott (eds), *The Law of the Single European Market* (Oxford: Hart Publishing, 2002) 59.

[151] Pagh (n 38), 8; J. H. Jans, 'Gold Plating of European Environmental Measures?' (2009) 6:4 *JEEPL* 417–35.

[152] D. Misonne, *Droit européen de l'environnement et de la santé: l'ambition d'un niveau élevé de protection* (Louvain: Anthémis, 2010) 277–9.

[153] Doherty (n 50), 52.

relation to the safeguard clause mechanisms, the new Article 114 in turn generates its own share of questions. Where certain modifications appear at first sight to be favourable to Member States, others, notably those which regulate the process of scrutiny for new measures, strongly limit their room for manoeuvre. The Court of Justice has inevitably been called upon to settle disputes. Whether the judgments commented on in this chapter attempt to strike a balance between the efficacy of the internal market and the defence of a range of interests held dear by a 'risk society' remains to be seen. Once again, the importance which is accorded by the EU Courts to certain meta-principles—the requirement for a high degree of protection, precaution, substitution, free movement of goods—is a determining factor in the resolution of these disputes.

PART II

CONCLUSIONS

At the outset, interactions between environmental protection measures and the free movement of goods and services, enshrined in the TFEU, are at odds with one another. As the previous discussion has evidenced, numerous measures covering all aspects of environmental policy restrict in one way or another inter-State trade even though that may not be their objective. Moreover, both negative and positive harmonization is likely to restrict the Member States' regulatory powers to protect the environment. Given that conflicts do not oppose primary law against national law, secondary law may also be relied on by economic operators objecting to environmentally restrictive measures. Thus, under the terms of the directive on packaging and packaging waste, Germany favoured the reuse of bottles which, however, brought it into conflict with a directive obliging the producers of mineral water to fill their bottles at source.[1] Similarly, as noted in Part I, the Netherlands requested the Commission that it be allowed to adopt more stringent measures pursuant to Article 114(5) TFEU than those provided for under a directive harmonizing the rules applicable to the marketing of motor vehicles. The Dutch authorities relied on the need to respect a directive on air quality where the thresholds had been exceeded due to atmospheric pollution caused by cars.[2]

Attempts to reconcile the conflicts between these fundamental freedoms and environmental protection have not always been characterized by coherence. The overall impression generated by this heterogeneity of cases is thus one of confusion. To make matters worse, the boundaries between the Treaty provisions commented on are constantly under strain. Nonetheless, it is clear from that a change of emphasis within the case law, which had for too long favoured commercial interests, is underway.

This development has come about, on the one hand, due to a deterioration in environmental circumstances and, on the other hand, due to the fact that, as noted in Part I, the Treaties have struck a better balance between the internal market and sustainable development; two objectives that have been placed on an equal footing. It follows that when the Member States have to take action against environmental risks,

---

[1] Case C-309/02 *Radlberger and Spitz* [2004] ECR I-11763; and Case C-463/01 *Commission v Germany* [2004] ECR I-11705.

[2] Cases C-439/05 & C-454/05 R *Land Oberösterreich* [2007] ECR I-7441.

they must have sufficient room for manoeuvre and must not become reliant on the sluggishness of the Union's decision-making procedures.

The case law analysed in Part II has thrown up more questions than it resolves on issues such as the validity of eco-taxes, measures having an extra-territorial dimension, measures restricting the use of products, and the scope of mandatory requirements.

In further pursuit of these developments, the following propositions will be made for the courts.

As far as the determination of the similar nature of categories of products liable to fall within the ambit of Article 110 TFEU is concerned, in accordance with the integration clause—Article 11 TFEU—the Court should draw finer distinctions, having regard to environmental considerations which underscore the specific character of certain systems of taxation. Tax arrangements should not violate Article 110 TFEU where insurmountable or significant practical difficulties prevent a Member State from extending tax breaks to imported goods and the national authorities have taken all possible steps in order to overcome those obstacles.

The criterion of 'considerable influence on the behaviour of consumers' which a national measure regulating the use of a product must have in order to be considered tantamount to a measure having equivalent effect must be interpreted narrowly. Such an interpretation is required in order to avoid entire areas of policing regulations being rendered nugatory.

Due to a growing interpenetration between health and the environment and the difficulty in tracing a dividing line between matters falling under Article 36 TFEU and an imperative requirement, it would be advisable either to include environmental protection grounds under Article 36 TFEU, or to accept that environmental measures may be justified on the grounds of an imperative requirement even if they are distinctly applicable. Moreover, granting privileged status to environmental protection by virtue of Article 37 EUCFR should lead the courts to recognize that this interest has a more substantial legal value than that currently attributed to the category of 'imperative requirements in the general interest'.

The Court would have to recognize an extra-territorial scope to Article 36 TFEU when this provision is relied on in order to protect components of the EU common heritage located within the territory of another Member State or to protect the global commons. In particular, where there is consensus at EU level to protect the environment at the continental or the global level, such extra-territorial measures should be permitted under Treaty law.

Given the marked differences between domestic environmental policies within the EU, in the absence of harmonized rules there should be no review of the Member State's chosen level of protection. Accordingly, ambitious environmental objectives justify the tailoring of restrictive measures the necessity of which should be reviewed only by reference to the level of protection being pursued.

The necessity test cannot conceal an axiological review of proportionality *stricto sensu*. Moreover, when applying this test, the EU Courts should show greater regard for the efficacy of the measures concerned by taking account of the specific circumstances of the fight against environmental degradation and the obligations resulting from international law; the costs and the technical difficulties of implementing the various facets of the alternative should be carefully weighed up. It is also advisable to take into consideration the limited capacities of the national administrations charged with the implementation of increasingly broad and complex regulations. Finally, it would appear that when the EU lawmaker is incapable of setting a common protection threshold for the 28 Member States, the Court of Justice should not substitute its own balancing of interests for that of the national authorities.

The specific features of environmental policy should also be taken into account when applying Articles 49 and 56 TFEU as well as the Services Directive.

The obligation on the authorities to provide evidence of risk through scientific proof must be relaxed in accordance with the precautionary principle enshrined in Article 191 TFEU. When confronted with uncertainty, the precautionary principle authorizes the national authorities to take action even where they have not attained complete certainty. Since the uncertainty may continue, this principle does not apply only within the ambit of safeguard clauses. If recourse to rigorous scientific analyses appears to be justified, it will again be necessary to grant the national authorities the possibility of basing their decision on minority views that nonetheless respect rigorous scientific methodology.

Finally, the Court need not review the proportionality of enhanced protection measures adopted on the basis of Article 193 TFEU when they do not limit the economic freedoms enshrined by the Treaty. Where this is not the case, the need for these national measures must be considered in a favourable light because they are consistent with the expansion of a minimal level of harmonization which is, by its very essence, unsatisfactory. The requirements laid down in paragraphs 4 and 5 of Article 114 TFEU must be interpreted in such a way that a high level of environmental protection is not diminished.

PART III

COMPETITION LAW AND THE ENVIRONMENT

Part III Introduction

The principle encroachments on free competition are caused by the behaviour of the Member States and private undertakings and fall within the scope, respectively, of Treaty law provisions regulating the freedom of movement of goods and competition, both of which have the objective of establishing the internal market.[1] As competition law seeks to prevent economic operators from re-establishing barriers to trade which have been dismantled in accordance with the law on the internal market, this area of EU law therefore complements the freedom of movement[2] discussed in Part II.

On the other hand, the maintenance of a system of free and undistorted competition appears to be inextricably linked to the implementation of environmental policy for the following reasons. First, competition and environmental policies go hand in hand: the placing of artificial restrictions on competition between undertakings has the effect of isolating them from forces which might encourage them to innovate, either through introducing new less polluting products or by using more effective energy-saving or resource-saving manufacturing processes. Second, the polluter-pays principle calls for the incorporation of hidden costs into the price of goods and services with a view to clarifying the true economic choices. Proclaimed in Article 192(2) TFEU, this environmental principle should foster competition between undertakings and encourage them to reduce emissions by using more innovative production and disposal techniques.[3]

However, relations between these two policies are far from idyllic. Four issues emerge as of particular importance.

First, by definition, the goals of competition policy do not necessarily overlap with those assigned to environmental policy. Whilst competition seeks to increase the

---

[1] P. Linth, 'The Influence of Competition Law on Free Movements Rules' in H. Kanninen, N. Korjuse, and A. Rosas (eds), *EU Competition Law in Context. Essays in Honour of Virpi Tiili* (Oxford: Hart Publishing, 2009) 20.

[2] Cases 56/64 & 58/64 *Grundig* [1996] ECR 429.

[3] See the discussion in Chapter 1, Section 7.6.

productivity of undertakings for the benefit in particular of consumers, initiatives followed in order to protect the environment aim to regulate the environmental impacts of industrial productivity. Accordingly, economic liberalism and the ensuing rules of free competition have never been favourably welcomed by environmentalists, who regard them more as factors which aggravate the environmental crisis.

Second, environmental policy pursued at the level of undertakings is not necessarily well adapted to comply with competition law. Since the external costs of pollution are not necessarily incorporated into the price of goods and services, the most enterprising undertakings in environmental terms that are able to produce and place on the market more environmentally friendly products, albeit that they may be more expensive, will experience difficulties in competing with rivals. In order to lower the cost of invest-ments to innovate, undertakings may be tempted to reach agreements between them-selves. This is also the case when they harmonize their practices with a view to attaining more efficiently the objectives set by lawmakers. In addition, public authorities also interfere with the market by favouring undertakings which sell electricity pro-duced from renewable energy or products manufactured from secondary raw materials. Competition may also be skewed where the national authorities conclude agreements with undertakings or where they put pressure on them to conclude agreements between themselves. Such agreements may allow undertakings to erect barriers against the entry of new economic operators on the market. In one way or another, all these courses of action are liable to restrict competition and, where these restrictions affect the conditions for trade within the EU, to breach Articles 101 and 102 TFEU.

Third, by permitting undertakings specializing in waste management or wastewater purification to offset their losses from less profitable operations taking place in less populated areas, public authorities grant them specific or exclusive rights, the com-patibility of which with the rules contained in the Treaty governing competition law should not be taken for granted. Similarly, arrangements regulating the collection and recycling of waste established by industry with the support of public authorities may create a real bottleneck for competing undertakings envisioning similar waste-management schemes. In fact, due to the limited number of sites available in urban areas for facilities for the collection of specific household waste—cardboard, paper, glass, metals, etc—it is hardly possible to increase the number of waste-collection facilities; such facilities will therefore have to be shared. Accordingly, some undertak-ings carrying out these tasks face either little or no competition. Whilst holding exclusive rights under the terms of Article 106 TFEU, they are therefore in a position to abuse their dominant position, thus violating Article 102 TFEU.

Finally, a further source of tension stems from the granting by public authorities of State aid in order to permit the recipient undertakings to comply with their legal obligations under environmental law or to encourage them to invest in less polluting technologies, but at the risk of distorting competition. These State aids must be authorized by the Commission pursuant to Article 107(3) TFEU.

The objective of Part III is to review the various conflicts between national envir-onmental measures as well as the conduct of undertakings in this field and EU competition law. In so doing, we will analyse the extent to which environmental protection considerations have been hitherto integrated into EU competition law and assess whether a traditional economic posture may frustrate further integration. Given the specialist nature of our analysis, only cases which have a direct relationship with the protection or management of the environment will be discussed.[4] As far as the extent of the various provisions that deal with competition in the TFEU is concerned, readers will be referred to studies dedicated to EU competition law.[5] The discussion will be structured as follows. Chapter 8 discusses the basic concepts of undertakings and relevant markets in the light of environmental considerations. Chapters 9 and 10 review the manner in which the key provision of the TFEU implementing competition policy, Articles 101 and 102, regulate the conduct of private undertakings restricting competition through restrictive agreements or abuse of dominant position. In Chapter 11 we consider the application of EU competition law to environmental regulation and Chapter 12 reviews the State aid arrangements for environmental protection.

Despite this targeted approach, the exercise in systematization to which Part III is dedicated remains delicate. Indeed, it must be remembered that the dividing line between these Treaty provisions is not easy to trace. For instance, the border between contractually-based and unilateral actions of undertakings is never completely water-tight. Moreover, the question as to whether Article 106 TFEU has been violated is premised on an examination of the applicability of Articles 101 and 102 TFEU, since Article 106 TFEU provides public undertakings or those entrusted with the operation of public services with the possibility of exemptions in particular from competition law. In addition, the upheavals to which the application of Articles 101 and 102 TFEU were subject in 2004 have not been without impact on the practices of undertakings in the environmental sector. Although ex Article 81 EC (Art. 101 TFEU) has been subject to a centralized control regime since 1962, the difficulties and costs entailed by this pro-cedure[6] spurred the Council to replace it with a regime of decentralized controls.[7]

---

[4] See, in particular, F. O. W. Vogelaar, 'Towards an Improved Integration of EC Environmental Policy and EC Competition Policy: An Interim Report' (1995) *Fordham Yearbook*, ch. 21, 529; D. Geradin, 'Droit européen de la concurrence et protection de l'environnement' (1999) spec. ed. *Amén.-Env* 50; M. Gremminger, M. Laurila, and G. Miersch, 'The Commission Defines Principles of Competition for the Packaging Waste Recovery Markets' (2001) 3 *Competion Policy Newsletter* 29; L. Idot, 'Environnement et droit communautaire de la concurrence' in J.-V. Masclet (ed.), *La Communauté européenne et l'envir-onnement* (Paris: La Documentation française, 1997) 383; D. Geradin, 'EC Competition Law and Envir-onmental Protection: Conflict or Compatibility?' (2002) 2 *YbEEL* 117–54; C. London, 'Competition and Environment: An Ecologically Rational Agreement' in R. Macrory (ed.), *Reflections on 30 Years of EU Environmental Law* (Groeningen: Europa Law, 2006) 150; N. de Sadeleer, *Commentaire Mégret. Envir-onnement et marché intérieur* (Brussels: ULB, 2010) 460–526; P. Thieffry: 'Protection de l'environnement et droit communautaire de la concurrence' (2009) *JurisClasseur environnement*, vol. 2140; *Droit de l'envir-onnement de l'UE*, 2nd edn (Brussels: Bruylant, 2011) 914–1046; H. Vedder, *Competition Law & Environ-mental Protection in Europe* (Groeningen: Europa Law, 2003) 478; J. H. Jans and H. Vedder, *European Environmental Law*, 4th edn (Groeningen: Europa Law, 2012) 297–335; and S. Kingston, *Greening EU Competition Law and Policy* (Cambridge: CUP, 2011).

[5] See J. Faull and A. Nickpay, *The EC Law of Competition*, 2nd edn (Oxford: OUP, 2007) 1844; P. Roth and V. Rose, *Bellamy & Child: European Community Law of Competition*, 6th edn (Oxford: OUP, 2010) 1679.

[6] Regulation (EC) No. 1/2003 on the implementation of the rules on competition laid down in Articles 81 and 82 of the Treaty [2003] OJ L1/1, recital 3.

[7] See L. Idot, *Droit communautaire de la concurrence. Le nouveau système de mise en œuvre des articles 81 et 82 CE* (Brussels: Bruylant, 2004) 368; P. Nihoul (ed.), *La décentralisation dans l'application du droit de la concurrence. Un rôle accru pour le praticien?* (Brussels: Bruylant, 2004) 262.

Thereafter, the agreements, decisions, and concerted practices covered by Article 101(1) TFEU could be authorized without any requirement for a prior decision by the Commission, as was the case under the terms of Regulation No. 17 implementing Articles 85 and 86 EC.[8] Where such agreements, decisions, and practices do not respect the conditions stipulated under Article 101(3) TFEU they are prohibited, irrespective of any prior administrative control.[9] Similarly, abuse of a dominant position covered by Article 102 TFEU is outlawed under the same circumstances.[10]

Insofar as all aspects of Articles 101 and 102 TFEU are directly applicable,[11] the national competition authorities (NCAs) along with the national courts now carry out new functions, in particular upholding individual rights flowing from these two provisions.[12] The NCAs are now competent to enforce these rights in individual cases. Moreover, undertakings may require enforcement of these provisions in national courts. Acting both on their own initiative or following a complaint, the NCAs and the national courts may order either the cessation of an infringement or the taking of interim measures. They may also impose fines or penalties.[13] There is no doubt that this decentralization of competition law will result in the gradual disengagement of the European Commission from environmental protection matters and, conversely, in a more marked involvement of the NCAs. The national authorities now have competence to apply Article 101 TFEU as a whole, whilst prior to the reform of competition law only the Commission could apply the third paragraph of this provision. In any event, the Commission, the NCAs, and the national courts are required to cooperate closely.[14] As the decentralized system of EU competition enforcement is still in its infancy, it is difficult to assess the extent to which NCAs and national courts are keen on integrating environmental considerations into the framework of Articles 101 and 102 TFEU.

Before examining the various areas of tension, it is important to consider to what extent the integration clause enshrined in Article 11 TFEU may clarify the arrangements governing exceptions from a new perspective. Although it cannot have the result of automatically legitimizing environmental agreements restricting competition or abuse of a dominant position, this provision may nonetheless encourage both the Commission as well as the NCAs to display greater sensitivity to specific issues relating to environmental policy when examining the compatibility of the conduct of an undertaking with the relevant Treaty provisions. In effect, as emphasized later, Article 101(3) TFEU is couched in open-textured terms leaving a great deal of leeway to

---

[8] EEC Council, Regulation No. 17, First Regulation implementing Articles 85 and 86 of the Treaty [1962] OJ L13/204.

[9] Regulation (EC) No. 1/2003 [2003] OJ L1/1, Art. 1(1).

[10] Regulation (EC) No. 1/2003, Art. 1(1)–(3).

[11] Given the room for manoeuvre left by the third paragraph of Art. 101 TFEU, one may wonder whether the Council's declaration is lawful. Eg W. Moschel, 'Change of Policy in European Competition Law' (2009) 37 *CML Rev* 495.

[12] Regulation (EC) No. 1/2003, sixth and seventh recitals.

[13] Regulation (EC) No. 1/2003, Arts 5 and 6.

[14] Regulation (EC) No. 1/2003, Art. 11. See, in this respect, the Commission Notice on the cooperation between the Commission and the courts of the EU Member States in the application of Articles 81 and 82 EC [2004] OJ C101/54.

integrate non-competition interests into the assessment of restrictive agreements. In this regard, although this issue is still controversial, it is submitted that the oversight authorities are bound by an obligation to refrain from exempting restrictive agreements where the content or consequences would be manifestly harmful for environmental protection or would breach secondary environmental law.[15]

Since competition is simply an instrument in the service of the internal market, the compatibility of an agreement should not be examined exclusively with reference to the need to maintain undistorted competition.[16] The integration clause encapsulated in Article 11 TFEU might allow the competent authorities to relax their standards of review relating to undertakings' conduct where they make a significant contribution to environmental objectives set by public authorities. In other words, it would thus encourage NCAs or the Commission to view environmentally friendly types of agreement or arrangement in a favourable light. However, where there is no scope at all for interpreting Treaty provisions in a way that is likely to enhance environmental integration, Article 11 is not relevant.[17] For instance, if an agreement impairing the environment does not restrict competition, it cannot be prohibited.

---

[15] Vedder (n 4), 185; Jans and Vedder (n 4), 304.

[16] Therefore, the stabilization of employment, an objective which is linked to economic and social policy, may come within the framework of the objectives to which reference may be had pursuant to Art. 85(3) EC. See Case C-26/76 *Metro* [1977] ECR 1877, para. 43. The same applies to taking into account the environment when examining the compatibility of State aid. See the discussion in Chapter 12.

[17] Kingston (n 4), 790.

8

The Concepts of Undertakings and the Relevant Market in the Light of Environmental Considerations

Articles 101–102 TFEU apply only to undertakings defined as entities engaged in economic activity operating in a relevant market. It is the aim of this introductory chapter to examine the extent to which environmental factors are likely to be decisive in defining the concepts of undertakings and the relevant market in which they operate.

1. Undertakings

The existence of a voluntary agreement between undertakings or a dominant position held by an undertaking conditions the application of Articles 101 and 102 TFEU, although its form and object are of little importance.[1] In other words, the fact that an agreement is justified on environmental protection grounds does not stand in the way of the application of the first paragraph of Article 101.[2] So far, EU and national courts have not applied a rule of reason with a view to excluding environmental agreements from the scope of the first paragraph of Article 101 or dominant position from the scope of Article 102 TFEU.[3]

---

[1] Case C-41/90 *Höfner and Elser* [1991] ECR I-1979, para. 21.

[2] The same reasoning applies to an advantage granted through State resources to an undertaking. Insofar as such an advantage fulfils the conditions laid down in Art. 107(1) TFEU, it is deemed to be State aid no matter its positive impact on the environment.

[3] The Court of Justice held that a regulation prohibiting lawyers from entering into an association with accountants fell outside the scope of the first paragraph. See Case C-309/09 *Wouters* [2002] ECR I-1577.

Given the pre-eminence of the State in controlling hazardous activities, it comes as no surprise that authorities play a key role in the conclusion of environmental agreements or in the conferral of special and exclusive rights upon services of general economic interest (SGIE). Whenever the State acts directly through a body which forms part of the public administration or indirectly through a legal entity which it endows with specific or exclusive rights, it is necessary to determine, on a case-by-case basis, whether it is carrying on an economic activity (action *de jure gestionis*) or whether it is acting as a public authority (action *de jure imperii*).[4] To put it differently, a distinction must be drawn 'between a situation where the State acts in the exercise of official authority and that where it carries on economic activities of an industrial or commercial nature by offering goods or services on the market'.[5]

Action *de jure gestionis* Brief mention should be made that only economic activities carried on by undertakings offering goods or services on a given market are covered by the EU rules governing competition.[6] When carrying on an economic activity, the State may be regarded as an undertaking for the purposes of competition law. The status and financing of a body does not change its status as an undertaking. It follows that if the municipalities are responsible for the collection of household waste and its subsequent processing, they are still nonetheless not exempt from the rules of competition law when concluding agreements with third party undertakings to carry out further processing. Indeed, when contracting with third party undertakings, the municipalities effectively enter into the economic cycle of waste management.[7] Accordingly, whenever local authorities conclude agreements with a company charged with responsibility for the management and recycling of household waste, this amounts to an economic activity of an industrial and commercial nature falling within the ambit of Article 101 TFEU. The same applies for agreements concluded between associations of undertakings,[8] as well as agreements concluded between local authorities carrying on economic activities of an industrial and commercial nature.[9] The fact that these agreements are concluded pursuant to a statutory obligation does not mean that they amount to an exercise of regulatory powers.[10]

Action *de jure imperii* By guaranteeing free competition between undertakings, Articles 101 and 102 TFEU do not seek to limit the Member States' prerogatives over public policies which, depending on the circumstances, may fall within the ambit of

[4] The Court of Justice addresses this issue in a flexible and practical way. See *Höfner and Elser* (n 1); Case 118/85 *Commission v Italy* [1987] ECR 2599, para. 10; and Cases C-159 & 160/91 *Poucet and Pistre* [1993] ECR I-637.

[5] Case 118/85 *Commission v Italy* (n 4), para. 7; and Case C-343/95 *Diego Cali e Figli* [1997] ECR I-1547, para. 16.

[6] The qualification of an entity as an undertaking subject to competition law will not be commented upon here. See, eg, A. Autenne, 'La notion d'entreprise en droit européen de la concurrence: retour sur un concept clé pour déterminer la sphère d'application de l'ordre concurrentiel' in A. Puttemans (ed.), *Actualité du droit de la concurrence* (Brussels: Bruylant, 2006) 147; W. Wils, 'The Undertaking as Subject to EC Competition Law and the Imputation of Infringements to Natural or Legal Persons' (2000) *Eur LR* 99.

[7] Commission Decision 2001/663/EC *Eco-Emballages* [2001] OJ L233/37, para. 37.

[8] Commission Decision 91/301/EEC *ANSAC* [1991] OJ L152/54.

[9] Commission Decision 2001/663/EC *Eco-Emballages* (n 7), para. 70.

[10] Commission Decision 2001/663/EC *Eco-Emballages* (n 7), para. 70.

other Treaty provisions.[11] Therefore, the pursuit of an activity that involves the exercise of public authority is not subject to the Treaty rules on competition.[12] Where, due to their nature, their object, and the rules to which they are subject, the activities concerned are associated with the exercise of the prerogatives of public authorities, they do not fall under EU competition law.[13]

In this connection, the case *Diego Cali* highlights the extent to which companies performing anti-pollution services on behalf of public authorities do not fall within the ambit of EU competition law. The Court of Justice found that an undertaking entrusted by a public authority to carry out preventive environmental surveillance tasks was not an undertaking 'since it carried out services relating to the protection of the environment which were not of an economic nature.... The anti-pollution surveillance ... is a task in the public interest which forms part of the essential functions of the State as regards protection of the environment. Such surveillance is connected by its nature, its aim and the rules to which it is subject with the exercise of powers relating to the protection of the environment which are typically those of a public authority.'[14] It should be noted that the Court drew a distinction between preventive control and curative environmental services, the latter likely to be qualified as an economic activity.[15]

Nonetheless, given that in accordance with the polluter-pays principle environmental costs must be internalized in the price of goods and services, it is likely that environmental services may increasingly become economic activities falling within the ambit of Article 101(1) TFEU.[16]

2. Assessment of the Relevant Market

2.1 Introductory remarks

The relevant market to which environmental agreements relate must be assessed, first, in terms of the products or services concerned and, second, in terms of geographic area.[17] The relevant market is determined according to criteria similar to those applicable in order to ascertain the existence of a dominant position.[18] Moreover, an

---

[11] Opinion AG Tesauro in Case C-2/91 *Meng* [1992] ECR I-5751.

[12] In *Reyners*, AG Mayras defined official authority as that which arises 'from the sovereignty and majesty of the State; for him who exercises it, it implies the power of enjoying the prerogatives outside the general law, privileges of official power and powers of coercion over citizens'. See Opinion AG Mayras in Case 2/74 *Reyners* [1994] ECR 631.

[13] Thus social security organizations, such as those for sickness and old-age insurance (*Poucet and Pistre* (n 4)), as well as Eurocontrol (Case 118/85 *Commission v Italy* (n 4), para. 30) have not been considered to be undertakings.

[14] *Diego Cali e Figli* (n 5), paras 20 and 22; noted in (1997) 5 *CMLR* 484.

[15] J. H. Jans and H. Vedder, *European Environmental Law*, 4th edn (Groeningen: Europa Law, 2008) 299.

[16] Jans and Vedder (n 15), 299.

[17] Commission Notice on the definition of relevant market for the purposes of Community competition law [1997] OJ C372/5, para. 7. On the fundamental significance that should be given to the determination of the relevant market in which the undertaking might be able to engage in abuses which hinder effective competition, see Case C-242/95 *GT-Link* [1997] ECR I-4449, para. 36.

[18] Case T-62/98 *Volkswagen* [2000] ECR II-2707.

examination of the market cannot be limited solely to the objective characteristics of the relevant products and services, but must also encompass 'the competitive conditions and the structure of supply and demand on the market'.[19]

2.2 Relevant markets in products and services

The relevant market covers 'all those products and/or services which are regarded as interchangeable or substitutable by the consumer by reason of their characteristics, their prices, and their intended use'.[20] The decisive factor in determining the market is therefore whether the products or services are interchangeable, as they must have a sufficient degree of substitutability in order for them to belong to a single market.[21] The possibility for competition must be judged within the context of the market comprising the products or services which, with respect to their characteristics, are particularly suitable for satisfying constant needs and are only to a limited extent interchangeable.[22]

When determining substitutability one should take into account 'not only from the supply side but also . . . the demand side, which remains, in principle, the most effective assessment criterion.'[23] It should be noted that markets are often interlinked on the demand side (joint tenders by several municipalities or undertakings) as well as the supply side (companies tendering for contracts outside their regions of origin).

2.2.1 *Demand side*

On the demand side, consumers must be able to consider the products or services as interchangeable or substitutable. If, for example, consumers consider that an environmentally friendly product—a hybrid motor vehicle—does not compete with a more polluting product—a traditional motor vehicle—this product constitutes a free-standing market. As a result, where there is no uniform market encompassing both hybrid motor vehicles and traditional motor vehicles, the producer of hybrid vehicles is more likely to be in a position to abuse any dominant position.

---

[19] Case 322/81 *Michelin v Commission* [1983] ECR 3461, para. 37; Case T-65/96 *Kish Glass v Commission* [2000] ECR II-1885, para. 62; Case T-219/99 *British Airways v Commission* [2003] ECR II-5917, para. 91; and Case T-301/04 *Clearstream v Commission* [2003] ECR II-5917, para. 48.

[20] Commission Notice on the definition of relevant market for the purposes of Community competition law [1997] OJ C372/5, para. 7. See, eg, Commission Decision 2001/837/EC *DSD* [2001] OJ L319/1, para. 83. The approach to relevant market definition is the same in the context of Arts 101 and 102 TFEU as in the Merger Regulation. See Commission Regulation (EC) No. 802/2004 implementing Council Regulation (EC) No. 139/2004 on the control of concentrations between undertakings [2004] OJ L133/1, Annex I, s. 6. In looking at the relevant market, careful consideration is given to a number of cases decided by the Commission pursuant to Art. 4 of Council Regulation 139/2004 on the control of concentrations between undertakings [2004] OJ L24/1.

[21] Case C-53/92 P *Hilti* [1994] ECR I-667. See H. Vedder, *Competition Law and Environmental Protection. Towards Sustainability* (Groeningen: Europa Law, 2003) 203.

[22] Case T-65/96 *Kish Glass v Commission* [2000] ECR II-1885, para. 62; confirmed by Case C-241/00 P *Kish Glass v Commission* [2001] ECR I-7759; Cases T-191/98 & T-212–14/98 *Atlantic Container Line v Commission* [2003] ECR II-3275; Case T-219/99 *British Airways v Commission* [2003] ECR II-5917, para. 91.

[23] Case T-177/04 *Easy Jet v Commission* [1994] ECR I-1931, para. 99.

It will also be possible to establish, on the basis of customer attitude, that ecological products are not interchangeable with products which, whilst having the same intended use, do not have the same environmental qualities.[24]

After a brief look at the relevant services market, the focus will shift to the relevant products market.

Regarding delineation of the relevant service markets, waste management operations, ranging from collection to disposal, are still a major issue. In effect, environmental services performed by private waste-management undertakings are particularly diverse.[25] Since they enable only one type of waste to be processed adequately due to its specific technical features, waste-processing methods are not interchangeable. Therefore, the technical nature of waste-processing operations entails a limitation on the number of economic operators capable of gaining a foothold within the market concerned. This position has been confirmed by the General Court.[26] Accordingly, this market fragmentation entails risks for the undertakings providing such specialized services of being viewed as holding a dominant position.

It comes as no surprise, as may be seen in the light of the following cases, that the identification of the relevant market is a touchy subject. The majority of Commission decisions authorizing mergers in the waste-management sector distinguish a variety of separate markets. In this connection, a few examples will suffice.

- Separate markets exist for the collection of non-hazardous waste and the treatment and disposal of non-hazardous waste.[27]

- By the same token, collection and sorting markets of non-hazardous waste may even constitute separate markets.[28]

- Similarly, a permit issued to a company charged with the collection and recycling of waste is liable to limit substitutability with other services offered in the sector.[29]

- In the Netherlands, incineration of non-hazardous waste is a market separate from the market for landfill of non-hazardous waste on account that waste may only be land-filled if it is proven that there is no incineration capacity available.[30]

- The market for the collection of waste can be further delineated in the ordinary household waste-collection services and ordinary industrial and commercial waste-collection services on the account that, on the demand side, these services are not substitutable.[31]

---

[24] S. Kingston, *Greening EU Competition Law and Policy* (Cambridge: CUP, 2011) 208–9, 211.

[25] Case C-480/06 *Commission v Germany* [2009] ECR I-4747. See the list of operations defined in Waste Framework Directive 2008/98/EC, Art. 3.

[26] Case T-419/03 *Alstoff Recycling Austria v Commission* [2011] ECR II-975, para. 71.

[27] Cases COMP/M.295—*SITA–RPC/SCORI*; COMP/M.283—*Waste management International/SAE*; COMP/M.448—*GKN/Brambles/Leto Recycling*; and COMP/M.4576—*AVR/Van Gansewinkel*, para. 10.

[28] European Commission, DG Competition Paper Concerning Issues of Competition in Waste Management Systems, 22 September 2005, para. 37; Case COMP/M.295—*SITA—RPC/SCORI*; Case COMP/M.283 *Waste Management International/SAE*.

[29] CA Paris, 11 September 2009, *DKT International v Eco-Emballages*, RG no. 2009/16626.

[30] Case COMP/M.4576 *AVR/Van Gansewinkel*, decision of 3 April 2007, para. 12.

[31] Case COMP/M.5464—*Veolia Eau/Societe des Eaux de Marseille/Société des Eaux d'Arles/Société Stephanoise des Eaux*, decision of 30 July 2009, para. 27; Case COMP/M.4576—*AVR/Van Gansewinkel*, decision of 3 April 2007, para. 10.

- A distinction between different categories of waste is appropriate where a limited number of municipalities tender large contracts for long duration for household waste while for industrial and commercial waste, numerous customers only contract services for the short to medium term.[32]

- In the *Waste Management International* case, the Commission concluded, taking account of various factors such as regulation and high transport costs, that the market for the disposal of non-hazardous waste constituted an autonomous market.[33]

- When there are factual and legal differences between an individual scheme for taking back packaging and participation in a collective scheme for taking back the same packaging by an approved company similar to DSD,[34] these schemes may only substitute for one another on a limited basis; they therefore amount to distinct markets.

On the other hand, nothing precludes different waste activities being encompassed within a single relevant market. In sharp contrast with the previous cases, in France the Cour de cassation reversed a judgment of the Court of Appeal which had accepted the argument of the Conseil de la Concurrence (Competition Council) that the elimination of domestic waste in controlled landfills related to a market distinct from that for incineration and composting. The fact that disposal in a controlled landfill made it possible to avoid the production of final waste did not mean, according to the Cour de cassation that this method of waste processing was not interchangeable with incineration and composting.[35] This means that the landfilling of waste in authorized landfills is not a market different from that for incineration.

2.2.2 *Supply side*

The substitutability of the goods or services concerned must also be analysed from the supply side. Environmental considerations may also operate at this stage. Recourse to environmentally friendly techniques—for example, the replacement of a hazardous substance by a less toxic substance—is likely to make the substitution of one product by another more difficult.[36]

- In its decision issued regarding the compatibility of the French Eco-Emballages and the German DSD arrangements, the Commission identified three relevant markets: that in services offered to producers in taking over their obligation to take back and recover their packaging waste, that in the selective collection and sorting of household packaging waste, and finally that for recovery services.[37]

---

[32] Case COMP/M.4576—*AVR/Van Gansewinkel*, decision of 3 April 2007, para. 10.
[33] Case IV/M.283 *Waste Management International/SAE*.
[34] Commission Decision 2001/837/EC *DSD* (n 20), para. 98.
[35] Fr. Cass., 22 May 2001, *Société routière de l'Est parisien*, BOCC [2001], 529. See P. Thieffry, 'Protection de l'environnement et droit communautaire de la concurrence' (2002) 123 *Juris-Classeur* 3.
[36] Vedder (n 21), 203.
[37] Commission Decision 2001/663/EC *Eco-Emballages* (n 7), paras 48–50; European Commission, DG Competition Paper on Waste Management (n 28), para. 7. See P. Kienapfel and G. Miersch, 'Competition Issues in Waste Management Systems' (2006)1 *Antitrust* 52–6.

- By the same token, the supply of waste-management services for non-hazardous waste is distinct from the supply of hazardous waste.[38]

- Similarly, the regulation by local authorities of the collection and processing of building waste produced within a municipality may have the effect of conditioning, on the supply side, the characteristics of the relevant market.[39]

- Water supply services, including all services ranging from production to distribution to the consumers are distinct from collection and wastewater treatment services.[40]

The issue of administrative approval to a company responsible for collecting, sorting, and recycling household packaging waste may also contribute to delineating the market concerned. On the supply side, a regime of administrative approval is not comparable to a regime authorizing producers of packaging to collect their waste individually. In this connection, the DSD scheme is a good case in point. The conditions placed on waste collecting and recycling undertakings such as DSD to comply with a number of requirements on behalf of their members—such as to achieve a coverage rate for certain geographic areas, to achieve certain recovery rates, etc—have the effect, on the supply side, of conditioning the relevant market. This means that a collective scheme for taking back packaging waste, under the terms of which a single company—DSD—processes all the waste produced by its participants, is distinct, on the supply side, from arrangements authorizing producers of packaging to collect their waste on an individual basis.[41] In effect, since DSD was the only undertaking which had established a collective service for collecting and recovering packaging waste in Germany, there was no short-term substitutability of supply which would have allowed other service providers to propose a competing household waste-collection scheme without having to make significant investment. As a result, the Commission concluded that the Germany company DSD held a dominant position in the collection and recovery of packaging waste.[42]

The relevant *products market* also deserves attention. In contrast to the 2011 guidelines on horizontal agreements, the former 2001 guidelines provided clarification on the types of market liable to be affected by environmental agreements which could be prohibited pursuant to Article 101(1) TFEU. When the agreements concern a pollutant that is not itself a product, the relevant market encompasses that of the

---

[38] Case M.295 *SITA—RPC/SCORI*; and Case M.283 *Waste Management International/SAE*.

[39] Case C-209/98 *Sydhavnens* [2000] ECR I-3743, paras 57–61. In this particular case, the Court of Justice considered that it was for the national court to define the relevant market in comparison with the facts it had at its disposal.

[40] Case IV/M.1365—*FCC/Vivendi*, decision of 4 March 1999; Case COMP/M.1633—RWE *Umwelt/ Vivendi/Berliner Wasserbetriebe*, decision of 13 September 1999; Case COMP/M.5464—*Veolia Eau/Société des Eaux de Marseille/Société des Eaux d'Arles/Société Stephanoise des Eaux*, decision of 30 July 2009, para. 16. See also Decision of the French Competition Council no. 02-D-44 of 11 July 2002 relative à la situation de la concurrence dans les secteurs de l'eau potable et de l'assainissement, notamment en ce qui concerne la mise en commun des moyens pour répondre à des appels d'offres.

[41] Commission Decision 2001/834/EC *DSD* (n 20), paras 75–9.

[42] Commission Decision 2001/834/EC *DSD* (n 20), paras 95–7.

Table 8.1 Waste flow recovery targets

Waste stream	Directive	Year	Min. recovery	Min. recycling
Household waste	2008/98/EC	2020		50% overall of household waste (glass, metal, paper, and plastic) 70% construction and demolition waste (excl. soil and stone)
Packaging total	94/62/EC	2008	60%	55%
Packaging glass	94/62/EC	2008	60%	60%
Packaging paper and plastics	94/62/EC	2008	60%	60%
Packaging metals	94/62/EC	2008	60%	50%
Packaging plastics	94/62/EC	2008	60%	22,5%
Packaging wood	94/62/EC	2008	60%	15% incl. reuse
WEEE, large household appliances		2006	80%	75% incl. reuse
WEEE, IT, telecoms, and consumer equipment		2006	75%	65% incl. reuse
WEEE, small household appliances; lighting equipment; tools; toys; leisure and sports equipment		2006	70%	60% incl. reuse
WEEE, gas discharge lamps		2006		80%
Accumulators and batteries	2006/66/EC	2012	25%	50%
ELD	2002/96/EC	2012		85% incl. reuse
Biodegradable waste diverted from landfills	2008/98/EC	2016		reduction to 35% of the 1995 level

product into which the pollutant is incorporated.[43] As a result, if fly ash is incorporated into a concrete mix, the latter is the one considered as the product market.

In this connection, waste issues deserve further attention. When waste has characteristics which are so specific that it must be processed in accordance with a highly specialized process, it becomes sub-categorized. Distinctions may therefore be drawn between waste—which may be cardboard, iron, or aluminium—since each of these materials thus constitutes a distinct market.[44] This fragmentation of the markets for waste processing is a result of EU legislation on waste that sets a number of targets for reuse, recycling, and recovery for different waste streams including household waste, accumulators and batteries, end-of-life vehicles (ELV), packaging and waste electrical and electronic equipment (WEEE). As shown in Table 8.1, these targets require separate collection and subsequent treatment operations of different categories of waste in order to achieve a high level of recycling.[45]

---

[43] Guidelines on horizontal agreements, para. 182.

[44] C. Verdure, *La conciliation des enjeux économiques et environnementaux dans le secteur des déchets* (Brussels: Faculté de droit de l'Université Saint-Louis, 2013) 271.

[45] Packaging Directive 92/46/EC, Art. 7; Directive 2006/66/EC on batteries and accumulators and waste batteries and accumulators [2006] OJ L266/1, Art. 7.

Furthermore, distinct markets may even coexist in relation to one single material such as glass. In effect, since clear glass and coloured glass are processed in different recycling centres, there are two specific markets depending on the colour of the glass.[46] Consequently, the fact that undertakings use different recycling procedures for different categories of glass means that the relevant markets are different.[47] Due to the fragmentation of the market for waste resulting from the presence of numerous distinct categories, the markets for the products concerned will never be of significant size. The following cases are testament to the ongoing fragmentation process occurring in the field of waste management.

- In practice, the Commission distinguishes between different types of market as a function of the type of waste, namely between non-hazardous and hazardous waste. Distinct markets for goods are identified for these two categories.[48]

- Landfilling is part of a different market from recycling, composting, or incineration.[49]

- Incineration of specific hazardous waste in special installations represents a separate product market where there is no substitution.[50]

- Given that different technologies and facilities are required to recover platinum metals, on the one hand, and gold and silver, on the other, there are separate relevant product markets for the recovery of these categories of precious metals.[51]

- Finally, in a case involving building waste in the municipality of Copenhagen, the Court of Justice held that the national court would have to determine whether the processing of environmentally non-hazardous building waste could amount to a different market from the processing of other types of waste.[52]

2.3 Relevant geographic market

The relevant geographic market can be defined 'as the territory in which all traders operate in similar conditions of competition with regard specifically to the relevant products'.[53]

---

[46] Case COMP/M.4576, *AVR v Van Gansewinkel*, decision of 3 April 2007, para. 13.

[47] Case COMP/M.4576 (n 46), para. 13.

[48] Case IV/M. 916—*Lyonnaise des eaux v Suez*, decision of 5 June 1997, para. 22; European Commission, DG Competition Paper on Waste Management (n 28), para. 5.

[49] Conseil de la concurrence français, décision 98-D-61, 6 octobre 1998, relative à la situation de la concurrence dans le secteur du traitement des ordures ménagères en Ile de France; Case COMP/M.5464—*Veolia Eau/Société des Eaux de Marseille/Société des Eaux d'Arles*, para. 28.

[50] COMP/M.4318-*Veolia/Cleanaway*, decision of 21 September 2006, para. 31.

[51] Case COMP/M.3213 *Umicore/OMG Precious Metals Group*, decision of 29 July 2003, para. 15.

[52] *Sydhavnens* (n 39), para. 61.

[53] Case T-83/91 *Tetra Pak v Commission* [1994] ECR II-755, para. 91; Case T-128/98 *Aéroports de Paris* [2000] ECR II-3929, para. 40. In particular, it 'comprises the area in which the undertakings concerned are involved in the supply of products or services, in which the conditions of competition are sufficiently homogeneous and which can be distinguished from neighbouring areas because the conditions of competition are appreciably different in those areas'. See Commission Regulation (EC) No. 802/2004 implementing Council Regulation (EC) No. 139/2004 on the control of concentrations between undertakings, Annex I, s. 6. See, eg, Commission Decision 2001/837/EC *DSD* (n 20), para. 100.

As may be seen in the light of the following cases, the geographic market may be local, national, or cover the whole EU.

2.3.1 *EU-wide market*

Several geographic markets are EU-wide. This is indeed the case of the EU emissions trading scheme (ETS) which set up an EU cap-and-trade system for greenhouse gas (GHG) emission allowances.

In relation to waste management, the following examples are also illustrative of factors leading to EU-wide markets.

- The market in services for recycling household waste and marketing secondary raw material generated from the recycling of waste is likely to be EU-wide.[54]

- Where there is insufficient treatment capacity at national level, the market for treatment of hazardous waste may be EU-wide.[55]

2.3.2 *National market*

Despite certain tendencies towards internationalization,[56] especially under the influence of secondary legislation, to date most markets for the collection and recycling of waste remain essentially organized on either a regional or a national level.[57] Against this background, it should be noted that the Court of Justice considers that 'an agreement extending over the whole of the territory of a Member State by its very nature has the effect of reinforcing the compartmentalization of markets on a national basis, thereby holding up the economic interpenetration which the treaty is designed to bring about and protecting domestic production'.[58]

Moreover, the characteristics of environmental policy may also be used to delineate the relevant geographic market, in particular when national regulations governing the collection and recycling of waste draw distinctions between different national markets, in accordance with the principles of proximity and self-sufficiency.[59] This calls for a few words of explanation.

In seeking to attain full autonomy over waste disposal, State or substate polities are pursuing the goal of self-sufficiency.[60] For this reason, such political units constitute relevant reference markets in geographic terms. Furthermore, with a view to reducing the transport of waste, the principle of proximity leads undertakings to have their waste

---

[54] European Commission, DG Competition Paper on Waste Management (n 28), para. 46.
[55] Case IV/M.295 *SITA—RPC/Scori*, decision of 19 March 1993; Case COMP/M.4576 *AVR v Van Gansewinkel*, para. 18.
[56] European Environment Agency (EEA), *Waste Without Borders in the EU? Transboundary Shipments of Waste*, EEA Report 2009/1 (Copenhagen: EEA, 2009) 8–11.
[57] Commission Decision 2001/834/EC *DSD* (n 20), paras 88 and 89.
[58] Case 8/72 *Cementhandelaren* [1972] ECR 992, para. 29.
[59] European Parliament and Council Regulation (EC) No. 1013/2006 on shipments of waste [2006] OJ L190/1, Art. 11(1)(a); Waste Framework Directive, Art. 16.
[60] Case C-2/90 *Commission v Belgium* ('*Walloon Waste*') [1992] ECR I-4431; Case C-17/09 *Commission v Germany* [2010] ECR I-4, para. 16.

processed close to the place where it is produced. The application of this principle amounts to an additional factor in the delineation of the geographic area where the undertaking holds a dominant position.[61] Accordingly, the factor of the distance covered between production and disposal of the waste has an impact on the definition of the geographic market.[62]

In addition, markets may also have a national dimension particularly where environmental rules are predominantly national in character. Furthermore, markets are national, primarily due to different competitive conditions in different countries resulting from the fact that environmental law is harmonized by directives rather than unified by regulations.[63] In particular, the waste management sector is highly fragmented. Admittedly, taxes, subsidies, prices, means of collection and treatment—disposal, recycling, reuse, recovery, disposal, etc—may vary significantly from Member State to Member State. This can be illustrated by the following cases.

- The Commission found that as far as the services provided by DSD were concerned, the geographic market for collection and recycling arrangements for household packaging waste and the application of the 'Green Dot' covered the whole of Germany[64] and that, consequently, the company was in a position to abuse its dominant position.

- This prerequisite was also satisfied where the dominant position is held over the territory of a Member State as a whole following the granting of a specific right to a Dutch undertaking for the incineration of all hazardous waste produced in the Netherlands.[65]

- The relevant geographic market for the treatment of hazardous waste is considered to be national, since only a few treatment facilities exist in Sweden, all of which receive and treat waste from all Swedish regions.[66]

- The geographic market for the collection of non-hazardous waste in the Netherlands is national in scope.[67] Although demand must be regarded as local, where local or regional markets for the collection of waste are interlinked to a wider, national market, the relevant geographic market is also national in scope.[68]

- Where export impediments and capacity shortages in neighbouring Member States lead to a situation where Dutch non-hazardous waste can only be incinerated in the country where it is produced, that country constitutes a separate geographic market.[69]

---

[61] Conseil de la Concurrence (France), décision no. 03-D-61 du 17 décembre 2003 relative à des pratiques mises en œuvre sur le marché de la fourniture et de la location de chariots à déchets au CHU de Nantes.

[62] Kingston (n 24), 219.

[63] See the discussion in Chapter 4, Section 4.2.

[64] Commission Decision 2001/834/EC *DSD* (n 20), paras 91, 100–3. See also Case T-151/01 *DSD v Commission* [2007] ECR II-1607, para. 47. As regard the French waste packaging scheme, see Commission Decision 2001/663/EC *Eco-Emballages* (n 7), para. 52.

[65] Case C-203/96 *Chemische Afvalstoffen Dusseldorp* [1998] ECR I-4075, para. 60.

[66] Case COMP/M.2897 *Sita Sverige AB/Sydkraft Ecoplus*, para. 14.

[67] Case COMP/M.4576—*AVR v Van Gansewinkel*, paras 15 and 19.

[68] Case COMP/M.4576 (n 67), para. 16.   [69] Case COMP/M.4576 (n 67), para. 17.

- The relevant geographic market of water distribution and wastewater treatment in France covers the national territory on the ground that the contracts awarding public service are either national or EU and apply equally to all contractors (principle of equal treatment between service providers).[70] Similarly, the geographic market for municipal waste collection and related services is national in scope due to countrywide public tender procedures.[71]

2.3.3 *Local market*

In appropriate circumstances, nothing prevents part of the territory of a Member State from also constituting a substantial part of the common market for the purposes of Article 102 TFEU. Markets may thus have regional or even local dimensions. The Court of Justice has found Articles 101 and 102 TFEU to apply to regional markets on two occasions.

- In relation to an exclusive electricity concession on part of the territory of a Member State, the Court of Justice held that if there were sufficiently important links between the regional electricity distributors in the Netherlands in order for the latter to adopt a uniform stance on the market, these undertakings collectively held a dominant position.[72]
- As far as the assessment of a local market is concerned, it should be noted that in *Sydhavnens* the Court of Justice invited the referring national court to consider whether the geographic area covered by the building waste recycling agreement constituted a substantial part of the common market having specific regard to the significance of the volume of waste produced and processed in the municipality of Copenhagen in relation to building waste processing operations as a whole in Denmark.[73]

As is clear from the following Commission decisions, where the collection of waste is organized by municipalities and the demand for the service is local, the market will thus have a local dimension.

- The market for household waste disposal and the recovery of sewage sludge in France has been found to be local on account that waste-management plans are adopted at the level of the department.[74]
- By the same token, the geographic market for landfill operations in Sweden consists of a catchment area within a 200 km radius of the installation.[75]

---

[70] Case COMP/M.5464—*Veolia Eau/Société des Eaux de Marseille/Société des Eaux d'Arles/Société Stephanoise des Eaux*, decision of 30 July 2009, para. 17.

[71] Case M.916—*Lyonnaise des Eaux/Suez* and Case M.2897—*SITA Sverige AB/Sydkraft Ecoplus*.

[72] Case C-393/92 *Commune d'Almelo* [1994] ECR I-1477, paras 42 and 43. See also Case C-18/93 *Corsica Ferries Italia* [1994] ECR I-1812, para. 41.

[73] *Sydhavnens* (n 39), para. 64.

[74] Case COMP/M.5464—*Veolia Eau/Société des Eaux de Marseille/Société des Eaux d'Arles/Société Stephanoise des Eaux*, decision of 30 July 2009, para. 31.

[75] Case COMP/M.2897 *Sita Sverige AB/Sydkraft Ecoplus*, para. 12. However, the Commission has left the exact geographic market definition open.

Finally, when public authorities purchase more environmentally friendly goods and services according to public procurement procedures, their calls for tender could delineate the market.[76] In that regard, the market covered by calls for tender would in itself constitute the relevant market for the purposes of competition law.[77] As a result, the relevant geographic market for collection of ordinary waste would be national, in view of the mainly countrywide public tender procedures.[78]

3. Conclusions

As has been seen, environmental considerations have an influence on both the delineation of the market for products and services as well as their geographic size.[79] Although it may prove to be a relatively fine distinction,[80] a trend has emerged in favour of differentiating between relevant markets, notably in the waste-management sector, on the basis of criteria such as the characteristics of the residues, the nature of the facilities and waste-treatment methods, or the specificity of the environmental legislation.

Additionally, the parcelling out of markets for products and services on the basis of environmental criteria such as the flow of waste, environmental regulations, impediments to waste transfer, etc leads to the delineation of extremely narrow markets within which only a limited number of economic operators are present. If the segmentation of waste management is taken to extremes, one would encounter only one or two operators processing specific waste within a very limited geographic market. Thus, for the Ile de France there would only be one economic operator processing clear glass, one operator processing batteries for the Province of Western Flanders, and one operator processing used bottles for the Land of Schleswig-Holstein.

Admittedly, it will be easier for an undertaking operating over a very specialist market to hold a dominant position than an undertaking operating in a vast market. This results in the risk of an increase in dominant positions.[81] On the other hand, considering the very limited geographic scope of these markets, it is not certain that a 'substantial part' of the internal market would be affected within the meaning of Article 102 TFEU.[82]

---

[76] In spite of the specificity of waste law, the disposal of biowaste is subject to Council Directive 92/50/EEC relating to the coordination of procedures for the award of public service contracts ([1992] OJ L209/1). See Case C-17/09 *Commission v Germany* (n 60), para. 18. See also Case C-26/03 *Stadt Halle* [2005] ECR I-1.

[77] Verdure (n 44), 282.

[78] Case IV/M.916 *Lyonnaise des Eaux/Suez* and Case IV/M.1059 *Suez Lyonnaise des Eaux/BFI*.

[79] Jans and Vedder (n 15), 298; Thieffry (n 35), 922.

[80] European Commission, DG Competition Paper on Competition in Waste Management (n 28), paras 33–47.

[81] Kingston (n 24), 210, 212.   [82] Verdure (n 44), 283.

9

Article 101 TFEU

1. Introduction

Environmental agreements have multiplied over the course of recent years, notably in the waste management sector. These may come in extremely varied form by virtue of the authorities involved (local, regional, national, or EU), the obligations (mandatory or voluntary), the objectives (general, qualitative, or quantified), or the parties (eg horizontal agreements concluded between all producers of a specific category of waste or vertical agreements concluded between the producers of packaging, distributors, collectors, and disposers of packaging waste).

Vertical relationship may exists between waste-to-energy facilities and the presence on the upstream market of an ordinary waste-collection scheme. In relation to waste, a vertical relationship may occur between collection/transport activities, intermediate storage facilities, and recovery or disposal treatment facilities.

As regards personal scope, it is sometimes the undertakings or federations of undertakings which take concerted action, with or without the encouragement of public authorities, regarding the action to be taken. On other occasions, it is public authorities themselves which conclude agreements with the undertakings of a specific sector—energy, services, manufacturing, etc—in order to require them to adopt a more environmentally friendly approach.[1]

As regards material scope, the agreements or arrangements may entail the simultaneous abandonment by a whole industrial sector of an obsolete mode of operation, the development of new technologies, the promotion with consumers of a brand image highlighting the environmentally friendly efforts of a group of undertakings, or the anticipation or replacement of a binding regulation with self-regulatory procedures.

---

[1] See the discussion in Chapter 4, Section 4.4.

Moreover, both goods and services as well as industrial property rights—for example, a trade mark certifying that the packaging is subject to a waste-management procedure— may be subject to such arrangements. Clearly, 'newer, more environmentally-friendly agreements are more technically advanced'.[2] In enhancing product quality, these agreements are likely to increase consumer choice,[3] pool know-how, and improve innovation.[4] The cases that will be commented upon in the coming chapters illustrate the diversity which characterizes the world of arrangements concerning the environment.

Given that the Commission and national authorities strongly advocate the use of voluntary agreements, the mushrooming of these agreements raises the potential of conflicts with competition law. In effect, the rationale behind these agreements is to enable undertakings to achieve environmental protection objectives by restricting competition.[5]

Despite their diversity, these agreements raise difficulties that are often identical for the purposes of competition law, and irrespective of whether they are justified by environmental considerations.

Although the Commission gave a certain number of indications regarding the validity of arrangements concerning the environment in its 2001 guidelines on horizontal cooperation agreements,[6] the new 2011 guidelines on horizontal cooperation agreements,[7] as well as the 2000 guidelines on vertical restraints,[8] do not by contrast mention or barely mention this type of arrangement. As a result, the following sections will mainly discuss the 2001 guidelines applying to horizontal cooperation agreements.[9]

2. Prohibition

As discussed previously, paragraph 1 of Article 101 TFEU outlaws all anti-competitive behaviour resulting from an independent agreement between two or more undertakings which is liable to affect trade between Member States and which has as its object or effect the prevention, restriction, or distortion of competition within the common market. This provision therefore covers contractual agreements. Under the terms of paragraph 2, such arrangements are automatically void. Even before the entry into force of Regulation (EC) No. 1/2003,[10] this provision was recognized as having direct

---

[2] Commission Guidelines on the applicability of Article 101 of the Treaty on the Functioning of the European Union to horizontal co-operation agreements (hereafter '2011 Guidelines on horizontal cooperation agreements') [2011] OJ C11/01, para. 329.

[3] 2011 Guidelines on horizontal cooperation agreements, para. 308.

[4] 2011 Guidelines on horizontal cooperation agreements, para. 2.

[5] A. Boute, 'Environmental Protection and EC Anti-Trust Law: The Commission's Approach for Packaging Waste Management Systems' (2006) 15 *RECIEL* 147.

[6] Communication 2001/C3/02 Guidelines on the applicability of Article 81 of the EC Treaty to horizontal cooperation agreements ([2001] OJ C3/1). Hereafter '2001 Guidelines on horizontal agreements'.

[7] According to para. 18 fn 1, 'These guidelines do not contain a separate chapter on "environmental agreements" as was the case in the previous guidelines. Standard-setting in the environment sector, which was the main focus of the former chapter on environmental agreements, is more appropriately dealt with in the standardisation chapter of these guidelines. In general, depending on the competition issues "environmental agreements" give rise to, they are to be assessed under the relevant chapter of these guidelines, be it the chapter on R&D, production, commercialisation or standardisation agreements.'

[8] Communication of the Commission, Guidelines on vertical restraints [2000] OJ C291/1.

[9] 2011 Guidelines on horizontal cooperation agreements.

[10] Council Regulation (EC) No. 1/2003 on the implementation of the rules on competition laid down in Articles 81 and 82 of the Treaty [2003] OJ L1/25.

effect and, accordingly, as conferring a right on individuals which the national courts must protect.[11]

Article 101(1) TFEU only applies if the various prerequisites specified therein have been satisfied. Arrangements are not in actual fact prohibited per se. Moreover, the effects of an agreement on competition must be marked and not insignificant.[12]

As regards the vague nature of the obligations contained in the numerous environmental agreements, especially those concluded with public authorities, one may wonder whether they are liable to fall within the reach of Article 101 TFEU. In its 2001 communication on horizontal cooperation agreements, which still provides an adequate framework to assess the validity of anti-competitive environmental agreements, the Commission provided a number of indications in order to distinguish between environmental agreements falling within the ambit of paragraph 1 and those which do not. Consequently, agreements which do not impose any precise individual obligation on the parties or in which the obligations are drawn up in a loosely binding manner are not subject to the first paragraph prohibition. The same applies to agreements which specify the environmental performance of products that do not appreciably affect product and production diversity in the relevant market.[13]

By contrast, when the environmental targets of the agreement mask a disguised cartel aimed at excluding competitors from the market or at discouraging potential competitors from entering it, the agreement falls under Article 101(1) TFEU.[14]

Finally, the Commission indicates a third category of arrangements which cover a major share of a sector at national or EU level, as well as those which appreciably restrict the parties' ability to devise the characteristics of their products or the way in which they produce them. These agreements are liable to fall under paragraph 1 due to their potential impact on competition.[15]

It follows that when environmental agreements offer the parties significant freedom of action in the choice of technical and economic methods, they do not significantly affect product diversity or only weakly influence decisions to purchase. In this case, they do not fall within the ambit of Article 101 TFEU. By way of illustration, the Commission ruled that the commitment made by the Association of European Automobile Manufacturers significantly to reduce CO_2 emissions from new cars set out loosely defined targets leaving much leeway to the undertakings which were members of the association. Accordingly, each car producer was free to set its own emission standards. Therefore, the agreement at issue was not appreciably restricting competition. On the other hand, when

---

[11] Case C-242/95 *GT-Link* [1997] ECR I-4449, para. 57. See Arts 5 and 6 of Regulation (EC) No. 1/2003, provisions acknowledging that the third paragraph of Art. 101 TFEU has direct effect.

[12] From this point of view, the Commission precluded the first paragraph of Art. 81 EC from applying to agreements considered of minor importance. See Commission Notice on agreements of minor importance which do not appreciably restrict competition under Article 81(1) EC (Art. 101(1) TFEU) [2001] OJ C368/07.

[13] 2001 Guidelines on horizontal agreements, paras 184 and 185; Commission Notice—Guidelines on the application of Article 81(3) of the Treaty [2004] OJ C101/08, paras 20 and 21 ([2004] OJ C101/97). Thus, a cooperation agreement concluded between Europe's leading motor manufacturers with the aim of improving research on environmental impact did not infringe Art. 101 TFEU provided that the research was not directly used for a specific vehicle. See 28th Annual Report on Competition Policy (1998), para. 130.

[14] 2001 Guidelines on horizontal agreements, para. 188.

[15] 2001 Guidelines on horizontal agreements, para. 189.

undertakings holding a significant share of the market notably restrict their technical or technological ability to manufacture their goods or the way in which they produce them, their agreement is liable to fall foul of the prohibition.

3. Exceptions to the Prohibition

The prohibition introduced under paragraph 1 of Article 101 TFEU is subject to exceptions, set out in paragraph 3, which provide for the possibility of exempting arrangements which would normally be prohibited, provided that their benefits for the establishment of the internal market outweigh the resulting disadvantages for competition. In contrast to the former procedure under which agreements were to be notified to the Commission which was competent to grant exemptions, this paragraph may now be relied upon by undertakings as a defence with a view to maintaining their restrictive agreements.[16] Hence, parties must assess for themselves whether their agreements fulfil the conditions laid down in the third paragraph. Neither the Commission, nor national competition authorities (NCAs), nor courts are empowered to issue *ex ante* exemptions.

Such exemptions may come in two forms.

First, under the former procedural agreements, certain category exemption regulations have been adopted with a view to relaxing administrative controls.[17] These exemption regulations represented a net advantage for the parties to the agreement, which benefit from an exemption *ex ante* from the requirement to notify their agreements. The Commission is now redesigning block exemptions to make them more business friendly.[18] Although no group exemption regulations at present refer to environmental protection, there is no doubt that a certain number of them are eligible to benefit from this type of exemption.[19] This gives a better guarantee of legal certainty than under Regulation (EC) No. 1/2003.

Second, as the Commission no longer grants individual exemptions, the parties to an agreement which does not fall under an exemption regulation may consider that it satisfies the prerequisites specified under Article 101(3) TFEU. It is a matter for them to assess themselves the compatibility of their practices with competition law. When proceeding in this manner, they have every interest in taking into account the decision-making practice of the Commission prior to the entry into force of Regulation (EC) No. 1/2003. For this reason, it is considered appropriate here to review the decisions taken by the Commission prior to 2004.

---

[16] 2011 Guidelines on horizontal cooperation agreements, para. 48.
[17] Commission Regulation (EC) No. 772/2004 on the application of Article 81(3) of the Treaty to categories of technology transfer agreements [2004] OJ L123/11.
[18] D. Chalmers, G. Davies, and G. Monti, *European Union Law* (Cambridge: CUP, 2010) 995.
[19] Some agreements might fall within the scope of Commission Regulation (EC) No. 2659/2000 on the application of Article 81(3) of the Treaty to categories of research and development agreements [2000] OJ L304/7. In the Decision *KSB/Goulds/Lowara/ITT*, environmental considerations were taken into account in order to assess whether a research agreement could fall within the scope of Commission Regulation (EU) No. 1217/2010 on the application of Article 101(3) TFEU to certain categories of research and development agreements [2010] OJ L335/36. See Commission Decision 91/38/EEC *KSB/Goulds/Lowara/ITT* [1991] OJ L19/25.

When the agreement does not fall under any of the categories for which the exemption is automatic, the parties which assert in their defence that their agreement satisfies the conditions specified under paragraph 3 are required to establish that the benefits secured by their agreement outweigh the disadvantages. This analysis constitutes an integral part of the self-assessment exercise. The benefits must be considered objectively and not from the subjective point of view of the parties to the agreement.[20]

Paragraph 3 requires that four cumulative conditions be respected,[21] which do not however contain the word environment. Thus, the agreement must (1) contribute to improving the production or distribution of goods or to promoting technical or economic progress; (2) while allowing consumers a fair share of the resulting benefits; (3) without imposing restrictions on the undertakings which are not indispensable to the attainment of these objectives; and (4) without eliminating competition in respect of a substantial part of the production. In accordance with Article 11 TFEU, these conditions should be interpreted in line with environmental requirements.

We shall examine the scope of these conditions in the light of Commission practice prior to the entry into force of Regulation (EC) No. 1/2003. Whether NCAs and national courts would be keen to depart from the Commission's practice remains to be seen.

3.1 First condition: contribution to the promotion of technical and economic progress

For restrictive agreements to be exempted under paragraph 3, they must first contribute to improving the production or distribution of goods or to promoting technical or economic progress. Under the terms of Regulation (EC) No. 1/2003, the parties to the agreement must ascertain the benefits which the agreement creates. Therefore, environmental protection may only be taken into consideration where it contributes to the achievement of these objectives. As far as the practice prior to the entry into force of Regulation (EC) No. 1/2003 is concerned, this condition did not appear to raise any great difficulties.[22] Before 1 May 2004, that is under Regulation No. 17 implementing Articles 85 and 86 EC, the majority of environmental agreements which had the goal of reducing the polluting activities of industries or of promoting the placing on the market of more ecological products, were authorized by the Commission on the ground that they contributed to the promotion of technical and economic progress. Since 2003, account must be taken of the fact that EU environmental product policy has gradually placed much more emphasis on a life-cycle approach.[23] Accordingly, the agreements focusing on a life-cycle approach should contribute to technical progress. On the other

---

[20] Cases C-56 & 58/64 *Consten* [1966] ECR 42.

[21] Case T-34/92 *Fiatagri* [1994] ECR II-905.

[22] In its 25th Annual Report on Competition Policy (1995), the Commission considered that the protection of the environment had to be 'regarded as a factor which contributes to improving production or distribution or to promoting economic or technical progress' (para. 85).

[23] Regulation (EE) No. 66/2010 on the EU Ecolabel [2010] OJ L27/1, recitals 1 and 5. See also the Commission Green Paper on Integrated Product Policy (COM(2001) 68 final).

hand, a countrywide collection and recycling system for household waste fulfils that condition in view of its considerable economies of scale and scope.[24]

3.2 Second condition: allowing consumers a fair share of the benefits

Once the beneficial nature of an agreement has been established on a technical or economic level, the parties should ensure that the benefits resulting from it do not favour exclusively the parties to the agreement rather than consumers as a whole.

The concept of 'consumers' has always been interpreted broadly by the Commission. As regards the compatibility of a reinsurance pool with Article 101 TFEU, this concept may cover insurers, the insured, the victims, as well as the environment.[25] By the same token, in addition to being environmentally friendly, the gasification of coal as well as the sale of new water pumps allowing for energy savings offer undeniable benefits for consumers.[26]

The deal reserved for users is supposed to be fair. This implies that the disadvantages caused by the limitation on competition must be offset by the benefits which users may draw from the agreement or concerted practice. For a long time, according to the Commission's interpretation, 'fair share of the benefit' referred primarily to the existence of more favourable prices for consumers.[27] In other words, environmental benefits were subordinate to cost savings. By way of illustration, the participation of manufacturers and distributors subject to a take-back and recycling obligation in a countrywide system dispensing them of that obligation, is likely to result in cost savings compared to the option of fulfilling their obligations individually. As a result, the cost savings attained over the term of the agreement will be passed on to the consumer.[28]

As far as environmental agreements are concerned, the Commission's interpretation was far from satisfactory. Indeed, since the majority of these environmental agreements involved an increase in production costs, and accordingly in the sale price of the goods, consumers did not receive any immediate economic benefit in terms of lower prices. Moreover, agreements to limit the pollution emitted by industrial installations do not necessarily improve the quality of the goods produced, and hence result in cost saving.[29] More fundamentally, genuine 'environmental benefits cannot be linked to

---

[24] Cases COMP/D3/35470—*ARA and COMP D3/35473—ARGEV, ARO*, decision of 16 October 2003, [2004] OJ L75/59, para. 270.

[25] Commission Decision 92/96/EEC *Assurpol* [1992] OJ L37/16, para. 39.

[26] Commission Decision 83/669/EEC *Carbon Gas Technologie* [1983] OJ L376/17; Commission Decision 91/38/EEC *KSB/Goulds/Lowara/ITT* (n 19).

[27] Where the agreement had not led to lowering of consumer prices, the Commission was keen to take into account other advantages that were provided to consumers. However, the Commission would make sure that these other advantages would significantly compensate the price increase. See Decision 91/38/EEC *KSB/Goulds/Lowara/ITT*.

[28] Cases COMP D3/35470—*ARA and COMP D3/35473—ARGEV, ARO*, decision of 16 October 2003, [2004] OJ L75/59, para. 272.

[29] However, insufficient attention has been paid to the fact that the agreements at issue were likely to have positive long-term repercussions on the price of the commercialized goods. Indeed, restrictive agreements anticipating the entry into force of binding environmental standards are likely to improve in the long-run the competitive position of the signatory undertakings.

any individual or specific consumer due to their diffuse nature'.[30] It has also been argued that economic valuation does not easily allow the translation into economic value of every environmental improvement.

In 2000, in its *CECED* decision,[31] the Commission began to ascribe greater weight to the genuine environmental benefits accruing from an agreement falling within the ambit of Article 101 TFEU. The Commission took the view that the environmental benefits incurred by an agreement concluded by washing machine producers with a view to phasing out inefficient machines 'appear to be more than seven times greater than the increased purchase costs of more energy-efficient washing machines'.[32] Such environmental benefits for society would adequately allow consumers a fair share of benefits even if no benefits accrued to individual purchasers. In other words, collective benefits to society as a whole were akin to 'consumer benefits'. It follows that non-competition public policy considerations could progressively be taken into account by the Commission.[33]

This initial approach was endorsed in the 2001 guidelines on the applicability of Article 101 TFEU to horizontal cooperation agreements, in which the Commission clearly asserted that improvement in technical quality from the point of view of environmental protection had become an essential element in the eyes of consumers. Therefore, it envisaged an assessment of the second condition from a broader perspective than that which it had traditionally adopted. By virtue of the 2001 guidelines, alongside advantages to individual consumers, benefits may also be created for society as a whole. However, these benefits must have the effect of offsetting the agreement's negative effects on competition.[34] As a consequence, assessment of the benefits granted by the agreement must be carried out in two stages. Where consumers benefit individually from the positive effects of an agreement, within a reasonable time-scale,[35] it is not necessary to establish the environmental or global benefits. It should, moreover, be noted that the benefit drawn by consumers may consist in an improvement in product quality, a criterion which may clearly offset the increase in price which would result from the implementation of the agreement.[36] Against this background, the Commission held in its DSD and ARA decisions that due to economies of scale stemming from collective waste-management schemes, the benefits gained could be passed on to consumers. Accordingly, these restrictive agreements could be seen as

---

[30] D. Casey, 'Disintegration: Environmental Protection and Article 81 EC' (2009) 15:3 *ELJ* 370.

[31] Commission Decision 2000/475/EC *CECED* [2000] OJ L187/47. The Commission approved for the first time an agreement aiming at stopping production of ineffective machines on the ground that there was 'a positive contribution to the EU's environmental objectives, for the benefit of present and future generations'.

[32] Commission Decision 2000/475/EC *CECED* (n 31), para. 56.

[33] Casey (n 30), 362–72. Prior to that, the Commission had already considered that cooperation between different undertakings marketing less energy-consuming pumps was not only beneficial to the environment but also useful for consumers due to their quality. See Commission Decision 91/38/EEC *KSB/Goulds/Lowara/ITT* (n 19), para. 25.

[34] 2001 Guidelines on horizontal agreements, para. 193.

[35] The fact that the benefit is not immediate must not lead to dismissing the exemption. See Guidelines on the application of Article 81(3) of the Treaty, para. 87.

[36] Guidelines on the application of Article 81(3) of the Treaty, paras 86 and 102–4.

'very consumer-friendly'.[37] That said, non-competition purposes cannot subjugate the economic efficiency methodology underpinning Article 101 TFEU.[38]

Oddly enough, during the course of the same decade the Commission decided to endorse a more restrictive approach. In this respect, the White Paper on Modernisation[39] and the subsequent guidelines[40] represent a turning point in the Commission's interpretation of the role of the environmental integration clause. In particular, the Commission espoused in the White Paper on Modernisation the view that the objective of paragraph 3 was 'to provide a legal framework for the economic assessments of restrictive practices and not to allow application of competition rules to be set aside because of political considerations'.[41]

In its 2011 guidelines on horizontal cooperation agreements, the Commission failed to flesh out Article 11 TFEU into an assessment of the compatibility of restrictive horizontal agreements. However, the Commission's move to discard public interest considerations from the scope of paragraph 3 may be the result of the decentralization of the enforcement of Article 101 TFEU.[42]

To conclude, although the 2011 guidelines belittle the issue of environmental integration, the denial cannot in itself revoke the application of Article 11 TFEU. It is submitted that Article 101(3) TFEU must be interpreted in such a way as to embrace the genuine environmental benefits accruing from agreements falling within the scope of the first paragraph of that provision.[43] On the other hand, as regards the self-assessment exercise under Regulation (EC) No. 1/2003, it is doubtful whether the concept of consumers will one day be extended to persons who only indirectly benefit from the conclusion of environmental agreements consisting in the adoption of more stringent anti-pollution rules, such as residents living near industrial installations who are not, however, the consumers of the products manufactured by those installations.[44]

It should be noted that the General Court acknowledges that environmental benefits are likely to justify anti-restrictive agreements. In *Alstoff Recycling* the Court expressed the view that the benefits for the organization of collection and recycling of household waste in Austria offset the anti-competitive effects.[45]

---

[37] Commission Decision 2001/834/EC *DSD*, para. 147; Commission Decision 2004/208/EC *ARA/ARGEU/ARO* [2004] OJ L75/59, para. 272.

[38] A. Komminos, 'Non-Competition Concerns: Resolution of Conflicts in the Integrated Article 81 EC', Working Paper 08/05, University of Oxford Centre for Competition Law and Policy 10; L. Idot, 'L'intérêt général: limite ou pierre angulaire du droit de la concurrence' (2007) *JTDE* 225.

[39] Commission White Paper on Modernisation of the Rules Implementing Articles 85 and 86 of the Treaty [1999] OJ C123/1.

[40] Guidelines on the application of Article 81(3) of the Treaty, para. 33.

[41] White Paper on Modernisation, para. 57.

[42] Casey (n 30), 374.

[43] S. Kingston, 'Integrating Environmental Protection and EU Competition Law: Why Competition Isn't Special' (2010) 6 *ELJ* 780–805.

[44] Regarding an agreement on the use of technologies aiming at reducing atmospheric pollution, the Commission did not take into account the advantage for the whole undertaking, considering that 'the cost advantages resulting from the improvements mentioned above will be passed on to consumers in the form of downward pressure on lamp prices'. See Commission Decision 94/986/EC *Philips-Osram* [1994] OJ L378/37, para. 27. The Commission did not contemplate whether the measures would benefit third parties.

[45] Commission Decision 94/986/EC *Philips-Osram* (n 44), para. 80.

3.3 Third condition: indispensable restrictions

The parties must also verify whether the restrictions contained in their agreement are 'indispensable' in order to contribute to the promotion of 'technical or economic progress'. In cases where they are presented with less anti-competitive solutions, they must refrain from concluding the agreement. As the Commission has regularly pointed out in the past, this third condition retains its full force in the area of environmental agreements.[46]

Certain agreements examined by the Commission have been manifestly disproportionate. Accordingly, it was not necessary to reserve the award of a conformity label *de facto* to the exclusive importers of washing machines in order to guarantee water quality in Belgium.[47] Similarly, in relation to an agreement concluded by German water bottle producers which was likely to foreclose market entry to outsiders, the Commission stressed that the restrictions of competition had to be indispensable to achieve the environmental objectives.[48] Generally speaking, the Commission takes a negative view of multilateral tariffs or price fixing as a result of the implementation of an environmental agreement. Hence, agreements entailing uniform and fixed fees do not fulfil this condition. In this connection, the Dutch VOTOB agreement is a good case in point. Six Dutch undertakings hammered out an agreement with a view to increasing uniformly their fees for use of their tank-storage facilities. Given that the charges were both uniform and fixed, the efforts carried out by each undertaking in implementing the new environmental standards were not deemed to be relevant. Hence, there was less incentive to invest as efficiently as possible. As a result, the Commission considered that the agreement was restrictive of competition.[49]

Due to the concentration of economic operators, the waste-processing sector has raised, and will continue to raise, particular difficulties.[50] For example, the flexibility offered under Directive 94/62/EC on packaging and packaging waste[51] has permitted the emergence, on a national level, of different packaging collection and recycling schemes which are implemented by economic operators under the oversight of the relevant Member State authorities. When taking on the obligations of the packaging producers, the companies charged with the collection and recovery of waste generally require their members to transfer to them all obligations for the material as a whole. The indispensable nature of these exclusivity clauses has been examined on several occasions by the Commission, in particular in its decisions concerning the British, French,[52] German,[53] Dutch,[54] and Austrian[55] arrangements.

---

[46] 22nd Annual Report on Competition Policy (1992), para. 77; 25th Annual Report on Competition Policy (1995), para. 85.

[47] Commission Decision 82/371/EEC *Naewe-Anseau* [1982] OJ L167/39.

[48] *Spa Monopole/GDB* mentioned in 23rd Annual Report on Competition Policy (1993), para. 240.

[49] 22nd Annual Report on Competition Policy (1992), paras 177–86.

[50] Boute (n 5), 146–59; European Commission, DG Competition Paper Concerning Issues of Competition in Waste Management Systems, 22 September 2005.

[51] Packaging Directive 94/62/EC.

[52] Commission Decision 2001/663/EC *Eco-Emballages* [2001] OJ L233/37, para. 37.

[53] Commission Decision 2001/834/EC *DSD* [2001] OJ L319/1.

[54] Commission Decision 2004/208/EC *ARA/ARGEU/ARO* (n 37).

[55] Cases COMP D3/35470—*ARA* and COMP D3/35473—*ARGEV, ARO*, decision of 16 October 2003, [2004] OJ L75/59, paras 281–7; Case T-419/03 *Alstoff Recycling* [2011] ECR II-975, paras 274–7.

- With regard to the take-back arrangements for packaging waste in the United Kingdom, Valpack, the Commission accepted that the 'all or nothing' approach was necessary in order to finance investment, especially due to the innovative nature of the system.[56]

- As far as the French Eco-Emballages arrangements were concerned, the Commission concluded that due to the right granted to producers and local authorities to rescind their contracts with the company authorized to process household waste, these arrangements did not have the effect of unduly limiting their freedom of choice and action.[57]

- Similarly, the setting of a minimum take-back price payable by the waste-collection firm to the local authorities did not violate Article 101(1) TFEU where setting the price enabled local authorities to avoid having to deal with market fluctuations. Accordingly, the contract which granted the company Eco-Emballages the principle licence to use the 'Green Dot' did not create an unjustifiable exclusive right.[58]

- With a view to redeeming the investments made by DSD in order to establish facilities for the collection of household waste that were appropriate given the recycling targets imposed by German legislation, exclusive contracts with a duration of 13 or 15 years were concluded between the operator of a collective system, DSD, and household waste-collection companies. According to the plaintiffs, this exclusivity clause had the effect of hindering third party collection companies from gaining access to the market. The Commission found that an exclusivity clause with a shorter duration, such as eight years, would allow the collection companies to redeem their investments.[59]

- The Commission also toned down an exclusivity clause prohibiting DSD from requiring its prior authorization for the shared use of facilities by competitor collection companies. In the eyes of the Commission, the fact that these facilities could be used by competitors was not only necessary in order to maintain competition over this type of market but also, consequently, over the markets for the recovery of the waste collected. The General Court held that the obligation imposed by the Commission to guarantee the shared use of the collection facilities was proportionate.[60]

- The obligation for a waste-management undertaking to contract with only one partner per disposal region for the entire contract period was to ensure lasting and reliable collection services, which were indispensable for the success of the system as a whole. The Commission took into consideration that it would be almost impossible in practice and in economic terms to duplicate the collection infrastructure in the household waste sector across the whole of Austria.[61]

[56] 28th Annual Report on Competition Policy (1998), para. 132.
[57] Commission Decision 2001/663/EC *Eco-Emballages* (n 52), paras 73–8.
[58] Commission Decision 2001/663/EC *Eco-Emballages* (n 52), para. 82.
[59] Commission Decision 2001/834/EC *DSD* (n 53), para. 155.
[60] Case T-289/01 *Der Grüne Punkt* [2007] ECR II-1691, paras 170, 177, and 192.
[61] Cases COMP D3/35470—*ARA* and COMP D3/35473—*ARGEV, ARO*, decision of 16 October 2003, [2004] OJ L75/59, paras 281–7; *Alstoff Recycling* (n 55), para. 79.

In order to ensure that their agreement is indispensable, the parties have every interest in verifying its economic efficiency.[62] In this regard, a cost–benefit analysis ascribing environmental measures with economic value is likely to establish the indispensable nature of an agreement which will bring exclusively environmental benefits.[63]

In this connection, the CECED decision is a good case in point. The agreement that was concluded by the vast majority of washing machine manufacturers in the EU aimed at phasing out the production as well as the importation of inefficient machines. In addition to reducing consumer choice, the agreement prevented 'manufacturers and importers from competing through a full range of energy categories'.[64] The energy efficiency standard for washing machines adopted by the sector illustrates the need to weigh up the advantages and benefits of the various options. It was possible for undertakings to adopt measures which had less effect on competition than a common product standard likely significantly to reduce consumer choice, such as campaigns seeking to inform consumers of the energy efficiency of washing machines following the award of an EU Eco-label. This would be less restrictive of competition than a phase-out of inefficient machines. However, it is necessary for these alternative measures to bring identical benefits to those resulting from the agreement, which involves the setting of a common efficiency standard for washing machines. Where this is not the case, the indispensable nature of the restrictions to competition provided for under the agreement is confirmed.[65]

3.4 Fourth condition: elimination of competition

The agreement or concerted practice may not have the effect of eliminating competition for a substantial part of the goods or services concerned. However, certain arrangements may result in the elimination of all forms of competition within the sector.

- This was the case for a pool of Danish oil companies which divided up the total contributions from its members when cleaning up service station sites that had been polluted by accidentally discarded hydrocarbons. The pool associated the reopening of a decontaminated service station with the payment of a significant penalty, rather than reimbursement of the clean-up costs, which violated Article 101 TFEU.[66]

- Similarly, several agreements concluded in Germany by the company DSD with various waste-management undertakings did not respect this fourth condition. It may be recalled that the company operates on behalf of the packaging industry by collecting and recycling the packaging that it has placed on the market. DSD does not itself collect the used packaging and instead contracts out the service to

---

[62] 2001 Guidelines on horizontal agreements, para. 195.
[63] 2001 Guidelines on horizontal agreements, para. 196.
[64] Commission Decision 2000/475/EC *CECED* (n 31), paras 31–2. Although the 2011 Guidelines on horizontal cooperation agreements do not expressly refer to the *CECED* decision, the Commission provides an example of an agreement similar to the *CECED* case. See para. 329.
[65] Commission Decision 2000/475/EC *CECED* (n 31), paras 58–63.
[66] 24th Annual Report on Competition Policy (1994), para. 421.

local waste-processing undertakings (both local authority and private) which are guaranteed collection areas on an exclusive basis. Initially, the service contracts stipulated that the operators of the waste collected could not sell the materials recovered themselves. They were required to hand it over free of charge to the recycling companies designated by DSD according to the 'zero price' principle. The Commission challenged this principle on the ground that it infringed Article 101(1)(a) TFEU. The Commission took the view that the restriction of competition stemmed from the fact that the collecting undertakings operating for DSD could not themselves sell the materials owned by them.[67]

That said, the requirement of maintaining effective competition is satisfied where the parties still enjoy a marginal degree of room for manoeuvre.[68]

4. Conclusions

The lessons learned both from the practice of the Commission and the EU case law therefore retain their significance insofar as they best permit undertakings, within the ambit of the self-assessment of their agreements, to assess the compatibility of the agreements with competition law.

To conclude, it is rare for agreements to have the principal objective of protecting the environment. The *Assurpol* decision must be regarded as an exception. On the other hand, for other agreements the environment is often little more than an ancillary consideration and the agreement's merits on this score only offer a complementary argument which does not call into question the traditional approach.[69]

Regarding the conditions under paragraph 3, the benefit to consumers is still a stumbling block. It is submitted that the concept of 'consumers' must be interpreted broadly and not exclusively in the light of more favourable pricing policies. In effect, a narrow reading of paragraph 3 curtails the discretion of the NCAs whilst not enhancing consistency between environmental and competition policy.

---

[67] Paras 40 and 48 of the Communication pursuant to Art. 19, para. 3, of Regulation No. 17 of the Council [1997] OJ C100/4.

[68] Although the CECED agreement was concluded by undertakings representing 90 per cent of the industry, the Commission took the view that competition was not completely eliminated. In effect, the parties were still able to compete on features such as price, quality, technical performance, and service. Commission Decision 2000/475/EC *CECED* (n 31), para. 64.

[69] P. Thieffry, *Droit de l'environnement de l'UE*, 2nd edn (Brussels: Bruylant, 2011) 936.

10

Article 102 TFEU

1. Introduction

Up until the mid-1980s, abuses of dominant position were rarely objected to in the environmental sector. However, following the granting of whole swathes of exclusive and special rights by the national authorities to a number of undertakings intervening on behalf of their members—Fost plus, Valipack, DSD, Eco-Emballages etc—competitor companies started to challenge their dominant positions.[1]

2. Abuse of Dominant Position

Article 102 TFEU does not in itself prevent an undertaking from occupying a dominant position in the market. Nonetheless, the Court of Justice has constantly stated that 'whilst the finding of a dominant position does not in itself imply any criticism of the undertaking concerned, that undertaking has a special responsibility, irrespective of the causes of that position, not to allow its conduct to impair genuine undistorted competition on the common market'.[2]

The holding of a particularly significant market share is in itself evidence of the existence of a dominant position.[3]

---

[1] H. Vedder, *Competition Law and Environmental Protection in Europe. Towards Sustainability* (Groeningen: Europa Law, 2003) 201–2.

[2] Case T-201/04 *Microsoft Corp v Commission* [2007] ECR II-3601, para. 229. See, eg, Case 322/81 *Michelin v Commission* [1983] ECR 3461, para. 57; Case T-228/97 *Irish Sugar v Commission* [1999] ECR II-2969, para. 112; Case C-202/07 P *France Télécom v Commission* [2009] ECR I-2369, para. 105; and Case C-457/10 P *AstraZeneca v Commission* [2012] OJ C301/18, para. 134.

[3] This is the case for a market share of 50 per cent (Case C-62/86 *Akzo* [1991] ECR I-3439, para. 60; Case T-83/91 *Tetra-Pak* [1994] ECR II-755, para. 109), or even of a market share adding up to 70–80 per cent (Case T-30/89 *Hilti* [1991] ECR II-1439, para. 92, confirmed by Case C-53/92 P *Hilti* [1994] ECR I-667; Cases T-191 & T-212–14/98 *Atlantic Container Line* [2003] ECR II-3275, para. 907).

- Given that DSD was the only undertaking to offer a household recycling system in Germany, the Commission took the view that DSD would thus have a market share of 100 per cent.[4]

- As the position in Europe of a group producing automatic recovery machines for empty beverage containers had continuously exceeded 95 per cent of the market since 1997 and that, on all the relevant markets, the group's market shares were many times larger than those of its competitors, the group was deemed to be a dominant undertaking for the purposes of Article 102 TFEU.[5]

- In the same vein, the granting of exclusive rights to process hazardous waste on the territory of a Member State as a whole confers on the undertaking concerned a dominant position in a substantial part of the common market.[6]

- On the other hand, where the market share of an inter-municipal waste-processing company does not exceed 10 per cent of the regional market and 5 per cent of the national market, there is no dominant position.[7]

However, only abuses are prohibited. Whilst it does not define the concept of abuse, Article 102(2) TFEU nonetheless provides various examples of abusive practices which largely overlap with the examples of illegal agreements mentioned in Article 101(1) TFEU.

Abuse is an objective concept, the assessment of which implies an examination of the effects of the behaviour of an undertaking in a dominant position on the structure of competition in the relevant market rather than the goals pursued by that undertaking.[8]

Although as an objective concept abuse 'does not require the existence of intent, intent is nevertheless not irrelevant.'[9]

Moreover, even though the concept of abuse of dominant position is not always crystal-clear, the view taken by the Court of Justice in *Hoffmann-La Roche* should be borne in mind:

> The concept of abuse is an objective concept relating to the behaviour of an undertaking in a dominant position which is such as to influence the structure of a market where, as a result of the very presence of the undertaking in question, the degree of competition is weakened and which, through recourse to methods different from those which condition normal competition in products or services on the basis of the transactions of commercial operators, has the effect of hindering the maintenance of the degree of competition still existing in the market or the growth of that competition.[10]

---

[4] Commission Decision 2001/463/EC *DSD* [2001] OJ L166/1, para. 95.

[5] Case T-155/06 *Tomra* [1995] ECR I-865, para. 10; Case C-549/10 P *Tomra* [2012] OJ C165/6.

[6] Case C-203/96 *Chemische Afvalstoffen Dusseldorp* [1998] ECR I-4075, para. 60. See also Commission Decision of 2001/463/EC *DSD* (n 4), para. 95.

[7] Conseil de la concurrence, 21 mars 2008, decision 2008-P/K-10-AUD, *FEGE v Idelux*.

[8] Case C-310/93 P *BPB Industrie et British Gypsum* [1995] ECR I-865; and Case C-333/94 P *Tetra-Pak International* [1996] ECR I-5951.

[9] Case T-321/05 *AstraZeneca v Commission* [2010] ECR II-02805, para. 334.

[10] Case 85/76 *Hoffmanm-La Roche v Commission* [1979] ECR 461, para. 91.

Irrespective of whether it results from a category exemption regulation or a self-assessment exercise under Regulation (EC) No. 1/2003, the fact that a practice respects Article 101(3) TFEU does not exempt it from the prohibition contained in Article 102 TFEU.[11] Leaving aside the case of an undertaking holding a dominant position by virtue of exclusive rights conferred upon it by public authorities where they satisfy the prerequisites specified in Article 106(2) TFEU, abuse of a dominant position is not subject to any exception.

Where dominant positions held by undertakings specializing in the environmental sector fall under Article 102 TFEU, the integration clause enshrined in Article 11 TFEU cannot call into question the scope of the application of the provision.

Article 102 TFEU is now regularly applied in the environmental protection sector, at times in conjunction with Article 101 TFEU.[12]

As will be seen, the effects of an abuse of a dominant position may, amongst other things, consist in the unlawful fixing of prices that do not reflect the cost of the product or service, the restriction of production, markets, and technological developments, the imposition of discriminatory conditions as well as the lack of access to essential facilities.

2.1 Unfair pricing

The sale at disproportionately high prices or billing of services which will not be provided, as well as the granting of price reductions to certain operators, violate Article 102 TFEU.

Since it holds a dominant position, an undertaking which sells products of a higher ecological quality, which are therefore more expensive, could abuse its position. However, this interpretation should be nuanced. In effect, extra costs in producing environmentally friendlier products should be taken into account in assessing whether price levels are excessive. By way of illustration, in *Albion Water* the UK Competition Appeal Tribunal took the view that 'a central element in determining whether a price was excessive was to determine the cost actually incurred by an analysis of the relevant cost structure. To determine the direct costs and appropriate cost allocation was therefore fundamental. It was necessary to allocate relevant cost to the activity in question, together with an appropriate contribution towards common costs.'[13] In a nutshell, the UK Competition Appeal Tribunal concluded that the prices charged by the owner of a water system were justified in order to ensure compliance with environmental standards and regulations.

Article 102 also applies to undertakings which due to their dominant position demand from their suppliers products that are more environmentally friendly. In effect, each of these undertakings either directly or indirectly imposes on its clients

---

[11] Case T-51/89 *Tetra-Pak* [1990] ECR II-358; and Case C-333/94 *Tetra-Pak* [1996] ECR I-5951.

[12] DSD's contract practices were thus examined under Arts 101 and 102 (ex Arts 81 and 82 EC). See Commission Decisions 2001/837/EC and 2001/463/EC.

[13] *Albion Water Ltd v Water Services Regulation Authority (formerly Director General of Water Services) (Aquavitae (UK) Ltd and others intervening)* [2006] All ER (D) 222 (Oct.).

purchase or sale prices that can be too high or too low, or even discriminatory, in order to freeze out competitors.

By providing its customers with a service exempting them from the obligation to collect and recycle their packaging waste, the fee regime operated by the German collection and recycling company DSD threw new light on this question. In this instance, the payment of a fee for use of the 'Green Dot' mark was linked to the quantity of packaging marked rather than the quantity of packaging actually collected by DSD. As a result, undertakings could be charged even for products that would never be collected through the DSD scheme. Accordingly, this fee did not reflect the real cost of the service provided by DSD for its members (collecting and recycling discarded packaging). In other words, use of the Green Dot mark did not coincide with the actual use of services provided by DSD, which provided its customers with an exemption service for recycling their packaging waste. This resulted in a violation of the principle of proportionality.[14] The Commission required DSD to grant licences for use of its Green Dot mark, even though the packaging bearing the mark could be disposed of using competitors' systems. Moreover, DSD's argument that the Commission's decision had the effect of negating the distinctive character of the mark was rejected.

The General Court and the Court of Justice upheld the Commission's argument that the payment of the fee for all packaging sold, irrespective of its collection by DSD, was to be regarded as abuse of a dominant position.[15] DSD's arguments that this obligation would undermine the goals of the German statute governing recycling, trade mark law, and the requirements of the proper functioning of the system were rejected by the General Court.[16]

As far as trade mark law was concerned, the General Court and the Court of Justice emphasized that the producer or distributor of packaging did not transfer to DSD a specific amount of packaging intended for branding with the mark but rather a quantity of material—plastic, cardboard, etc—which DSD was to take back and recover.[17] The argument put forward by DSD that the obligation that had been imposed on it would have the effect of depriving the mark of its distinctive character was dismissed on the ground that the Green Dot mark did not make it possible to determine with any degree of certainty *ex ante* whether a type of packaging would actually be processed by the collection scheme which covered it. The essential function of the mark was to signal to the consumer that the company selling the packaged product participated in a collection scheme capable of processing the packaging. This also meant that the exclusivity of the mark was not essential for the final consumer (eg such-and-such a packaging branded with such-and-such a mark must be brought within the ambit of that scheme). Indeed, the consumer cannot know whether his

---

[14] Commission Decision 2001/837/EC, [2001] OJ L319/, paras 111 and 112 confirmed by Case T-151/01 *DSD v Commission* [2007] ECR II-1607, para. 164.

[15] Case T-151/01 *DSD v Commission* (n 14), paras 107–17 and 126–33; Case C-385/07 P *Der Grüne Punkt-DSD* [2009] ECR I-06155, para. 143.

[16] Case T-151/01 *DSD v Commission* (n 14), para. 164.

[17] Case T-151/01 *DSD v Commission* (n 14); Case C-385/07 P *Der Grüne Punkt-DSD* (n 15), paras 110–18.

packaging will actually be disposed of by DSD or under a competitor exemption system.[18]

Last, the Commission ruled that an Italian consortium for the collection and recycling of used lead batteries, Cobat, sold its waste at discriminatory prices since the Italian undertakings benefited from more favourable pricing than foreign undertakings.[19]

2.2 Restrictions on production and markets

An obvious case involving a market restriction should be mentioned here. Having received a complaint from a Belgian producer of mineral water, in 1989 the Commission commenced proceedings against GDB, an association of German undertakings placing on the national market mineral water packaging.[20] It claimed that the German market in mineral water was inaccessible, first due to the packaging order which prohibited the sale of exported water in any packaging other than reusable glass and, second, due to the fact that it was impossible for foreign undertakings to join the GDB pool which managed a system for taking back reusable glass bottles. Such access for foreign retailers was deemed to be essential in order to compete on the German mineral water market. In this case, although the Commission did not question the German regulation on waste packaging, it did find that, in view of its nature, the GDB agreement constituted an abuse of dominant position within the meaning of Article 102 TFEU.

Moreover, in *Dusseldorp* the Court of Justice held that the obligation introduced by the Dutch authorities to assign the processing of certain categories of hazardous waste to an undertaking which processed it on an exclusive basis in the Netherlands resulted 'in the restriction of outlets in a manner contrary to Article [106(1) TFEU] in conjunction of Article [102 TFEU] of the Treaty'.[21]

2.3 Discriminatory conditions

With the intention of encouraging the production of environmentally friendly products, an undertaking could abuse its dominant position by requiring its suppliers or customers to respect very specific standards of conduct even though such standards are not required for similar products. In this event, the suppliers or customers could claim that the conditions of purchase or sale were discriminatory. However, the actions of an undertaking with a dominant position may always be justified by the fact that the products concerned constitute their own market, which is distinct from that in less

---

[18] Case T-151/01 *DSD v Commission* (n 14), paras 142–5.

[19] V. Baccaro, 'Collecte et recyclage des batteries usagées en Italie: droits exclusifs, exigences environnementales et droit de la concurrence' (2011) 1 *CPN* 40.

[20] This case, which did not lead to the adoption of a decision by the Commission, is related in the 14th Annual Report on Competition Policy (1993) 170.

[21] Case C-203/96 *Dusseldorp* (n 6), para. 63.

environmentally friendly products. In this case, the distinction would override the complaint of discriminatory behaviour.[22]

By the same token, pricing policy might be used as a discriminatory device. In *COBAT*,[23] the Commission suspected that a consortium (COBAT) had coordinated the collection and recycling of used batteries in Italy thus abusing a dominant position on the Italian market for recyclable lead waste. COBAT organized tender procedures for collectors and assigned the winners exclusive territories. Thus, undertakings that were not selected could only operate as subcontractors of the other firms. These exclusive collection zones gave rise to unnecessary discrimination between collectors. In addition, as regards the sale of waste, COBAT seemed to pay Italian recycling firms much lower prices than those in force on the European market for similar products. After COBAT amended its rules, the Commission decided to end the proceedings: any undertaking possessing the necessary authorization would now be able to collect and recycle waste without being subject to any territorial restrictions or exclusivity conditions. Furthermore, sales by COBAT to the recycling firms both in Italy and abroad would be effected according to the criterion of best market price.

2.4 Access to essential facilities

Refusal to allow access for the use of essential facilities entails the violation of Article 102 TFEU where there are no objective justifications for such refusal and where such refusal would ultimately eliminate all competition on that market.

In other words, 'it is clear from that case-law that, in order for the refusal by an undertaking which owns a copyright to give access to a product or service indispensable for carrying on a particular business to be treated as abusive, it is sufficient that three cumulative conditions be satisfied, namely, that that refusal is preventing the emergence of a new product for which there is a potential consumer demand, that it is unjustified and such as to exclude any competition on a secondary market.'[24] Even though this last requirement has been the subject of controversy, the Court of Justice's view should be borne in mind, according to which, 'it is determinative that two different stages of production may be identified and that they are interconnected, inasmuch as the upstream product is indispensable for the supply of the downstream product'.[25]

In *SPA Monopole v GDB*, the Belgian mineral water producer Spa was refused access to the pool of reusable glass bottles and crates set up by the association of German

---

[22] Vedder (n 1), 211–12.

[23] Europa Press Release IP/00/1351, 23 November 2000, available at <http://europa.eu/rapid/press-release_IP-00-1351_en.htm>.

[24] Case C-418/01 *IMS Health* [2004] ECR I-5039, para. 38. For further developments see Joined Cases 6 & 7/73 *Commercial Solvents Corporation v Commission* [1974] ECR 223; Case 238/87 *Volvo* [1988] ECR 6211; Cases C-241/91 P & C-242/91 P *Radio Telefis Eireann v Commission* [1995] ECR I-743; Case C-7/97 *Bronner* [1998] ECR I-7791; Case T-201/04 *Microsoft Corp v Commission* (n 2); and Case T-321/05 *AstraZeneca v Commission* (n 9).

[25] Case C-418/01 *IMS Health* (n 24), para. 45.

mineral water producers (GDB). The Commission took the view that access to the GDB pool was essential in order to compete effectively in the mineral water market.[26]

2.5 Tying

An undertaking which occupies a dominant position may want to consolidate its market share by ensuring that its customers are tied.[27] Thus, the dominant undertaking may unlawfully prevent the entry of competitors into the market by binding, either *de facto* or *de iure*, companies which purchase its goods or services, and thereby prevent them from dealing with competitor suppliers. In this event, it is necessary to guarantee equal opportunities between competitors, particularly for less powerful competitors.[28]

In the DSD case, producers were forced to set up separate distribution channels in order to circumvent the DSD collection system. As the Commission pointed out, unfair commercial terms exist where an undertaking in a dominant position fails to comply with the principle of proportionality. By giving undertakings a choice between paying an unreasonable licence fee or introducing separate packaging and distribution channels, DSD was imposing unfair commercial terms.[29] The extra costs resulting from the need to introduce separate packaging and distribute channels was a *de facto* tie to the DSD system.

3. Conclusions

Dominant positions held by undertakings carrying out environmental services do not fall beyond the reach of Article 102 TFEU. Moreover, where a discriminatory price remains a discriminatory price or a discount remains a discount, the question of environmental integration does not arise. Indeed, competition law applies in a manner detached from other social issues.

Given that environmental management schemes are constantly evolving and that the limits of the scope of Article 102 is not clear-cut, it could be that new categories of abuse are likely to be challenged under the provision.

---

[26] 23rd Annual Report on Competition Policy (1993), para. 240.
[27] See Communication from the Commission, Guidance on the Commission's enforcement priorities in applying Article 82 of the EC Treaty to abusive exclusionary conduct by dominant undertakings, paras 47–62.
[28] Case 202/88 *France v Commission* [1991] ECR 1271, para. 51.
[29] Commission Decision 2001/463/EC *DSD* (n 4), para. 112.

11

Environmental Regulation and EU Competition Law

1. Introduction

Although activities which do not display any economic feature fall beyond the reach of competition law,[1] public undertakings as well as undertakings to which the State grants special and exclusive rights are subject to the principle of equal treatment. They are therefore placed on an equal footing with private undertakings. However, this requirement is not absolute, as exceptions have been provided for in favour of services of general economic interest (SGEIs).

The question before us now is whether and to what extent these exceptions may be invoked by undertakings charged by public authorities with cleaning up pollution or managing environmental services (wastewater treatment, disposal of hazardous waste, inspection of hazardous products, renewable energy, etc). Without doubt, the search for a balance between the contradicting requirements of SGEIs and compliance with competition law is no easier in the environmental sector than in other areas such as social services.

By restricting this discussion to the limited number of environmental cases which have dealt with this problem, we shall not attempt to take stock more generally here of the case law on the compatibility of SGEIs with competition law which is, to say the least, varied.

---

[1] As a result, services of general interest (SGI) will not need to be assessed in relation to Art. 106(2) TFEU. Regarding the distinction between SGI and SGEI, see M. Donny, 'Les notions de services d'intérêt général et de services d'intérêt économique général' in J.-V. Louis and S. Rodrigues (eds), *Les services d'intérêt économique général et l'Union européenne* (Brussels: Bruylant, 2006) 4–38.

2. Anti-Competitive State Regulation

Does the TFEU allow national regulations governing the exercise of economic activities by undertakings to produce, even indirectly, anti-competitive effects? At first sight, there can be no confusion between the behaviour of undertakings, the goal of which is to earn profits, and the regulatory activity of the State which pursues the general interest.[2] Insofar as it applies exclusively to the actions of undertakings, competition law does not impinge upon governmental regulations aiming at protecting the environment. Accordingly, national legislation regulating the exercise of the economic activity of undertakings falls beyond the material scope of competition law.[3] As is clear from the following examples, the traditional criterion for exercising regulatory powers makes it possible to trace a dividing line between the two.

- By way of illustration, the establishment of monopolies by a Member State in areas where waste is collected cannot itself be placed on an equal footing with the behaviour of an undertaking.[4]

- Similarly, the fact that national authorities approve identical price scales for take-back agreements for packaging 'is the result of a measure taken by the State and does not constitute a restrictive practice'.[5]

- Moreover, sectoral agreements with quasi-regulatory effects concluded between public authorities and the private sector concerning environmental matters do not in principle fall under the ambit of Article 101 TFEU for the simple reason that the public authority is not acting as an economic operator. Only subordinate agreements adopted in accordance with these sectoral agreements are capable of falling within the reach of Article 101(1) TFEU.

That said, as far as cleaning up pollution is concerned, the activities of the State and those of private undertakings are increasingly closely intertwined. This is particularly the case where national regulation favours or consents to the adoption of an agreement with anti-competitive effects, or replaces one with a view to consolidating the agreement. Therefore, in accordance with the Court of Justice's case law, regulations adopted in the public interest cannot undermine the effectiveness of competition law.[6] Such agreements are considered contrary to Article 101 TFEU, read in conjunction with Article 4(3) TEU, and the 27th additional protocol.

Three situations in which actions by a Member State are likely to breach competition law have thus been identified within the case law of the Court of Justice, where:[7]

---

[2] See the discussion in Chapter 8, Section 1.

[3] Case 30/87 *Bodson* [1988] ECR 2479, para. 18.

[4] According to the Opinion of AG Lenz in Case C-37/92 *Vanacker* [1993] ECR I-4947, para. 40, the application of Art. 86(2) EC presupposes conduct by an undertaking. See also Opinion AG Tesauro in Case C-320/91 *Corbeau* [1993] ECR I-2533, para. 14.

[5] Commission Decision 2001/663/EC *Eco-Emballages* [2001] OJ L233/37, para. 37.

[6] Case C-332/89 *Marchandise ea* [1991] ECR I-1027, para. 22.

[7] G. Marenco, 'Le Traité CEE interdit-il aux Etats membres de restreindre la concurrence' (1986) 3–4 *CDE* 285 et seq.

- a Member State requires or favours the conclusion of agreements, decisions, or concerted practices with anti-competitive effects;
- it reinforces the effects of agreements, decisions, or concerted practices in existence prior to the anti-competitive effects;
- it deprives its regulations of their status as State rules by delegating to private operators responsibility for taking decisions to intervene in economic matters.[8]

The Court requires that contested national measures be directly linked with anti-competitive behaviour by private undertakings, even if the measure taken alone would objectively have an effect equivalent to that of an agreement prohibited under Article 101 TFEU.[9] In the absence of such a causal link, the compatibility of the State measure cannot be assessed with reference to Articles 4(3) TEU and 101(1) TFEU, as well as Article 27 of the additional protocol.

As far as the first scenario is concerned (State regulation requires or favours the adoption of restrictive agreements), it could be the case that, rather than requiring the establishment of a system for the collection of household waste, the national measure recommends or even requires the producers of packaging to cooperate amongst themselves in order to place standardized packaging on the market. Consequently, State regulation compelling private waste-management undertakings to conclude a restrictive agreement would be in breach of Article 4(1) TEU read together with Article 101 TFEU provided there is a causal link between the contested regulation and the conduct by private undertakings infringing competition law. In contrast, EU competition law is not infringed where a State regulation imposes very strict environmental standards on its own undertakings and, as a result, penalizes them vis-à-vis their foreign competitors. In *Peralta*, the Court of Justice had to judge whether Italian legislation imposing an absolute prohibition on the discharge of tank-flushing liquids into the high seas only on vessels registered in the State in question, even though those vessels were equipped with decontamination equipment prescribed by international agreements ratified by the EU, was distorting competition. The Court held that the legislation at issue did not require or foster anti-competitive conduct nor did it reinforce the effects of a pre-existing agreement.[10]

As regards the second and third scenarios, it will be far from easy to demonstrate the existence of a direct link between the role of the State and the anti-competitive behaviour of undertakings. Unless 'they simply reproduce the elements of an agreement, decision or concerted practice between economic agents in that sector'[11] (second

---

[8] Case 267/86 *Van Eycke* [1988] ECR 4769, para. 18. In relation to this hypothesis, the Court of Justice judged that 'les entreprises doivent fonctionner sous la surveillance des pouvoirs publics ou être soumises à la discipline du marché mais qu'elles ne doivent pas se voir conférer des attributs de puissance publique, alors qu'elles ne représentent que des intérêts particuliers' (R. Joliet, 'Réglementations étatiques anticoncurrentielles et droit communautaire?' (1988) 4 *CDE* 370).

[9] Case C-2/91 *Meng* [1993] ECR I-5791; Case C-185/91 *Reiff* [1993] ECR I-5801; Case C-245/91 *Ohra* [1993] ECR I-5851; and Case C-35/99 *Arduino* [2002] ECR I-1529, para. 34. See on that point, B. Van der Esch, 'La loyauté fédérale et subsidiarité à propos des arrêts du 17 novembre 1993 dans les affaires C-2/91 (*Meng*), C-245/91 (*Ohra*) et C-185/91 (*Reiff*)' (1994) 5–6 *CDE* 524; N. Reich, 'The "November Revolution" of the European Court of Justice: *Keck*, *Meng* and *Audi* Revisited' (1994) *CML Rev* 459. See also Case C-153/93 *Delta Schiffart* [1994] ECR I-2517.

[10] Case C-379/92 *Peralta* [1994] ECR I-3453, para. 22.

[11] *Meng* (n 9), para. 19.

scenario), the Member State measure would not appear to run contrary to Article 101(1) TFEU, especially where there are differences, which may be minor, between the latter agreement and the preceding one.[12]

Similarly, when the Member State deprives its regulations of 'their official character by delegating to private traders responsibility for taking decisions affecting the economic sphere' (third scenario), the authorities should authorize the sector concerned to establish product or emissions standards in order that this technique of encouraging self-regulation may be examined with reference to Articles 101 and 102 TFEU. In the light of the case law, Geradin considers that Member States are not prevented 'from entrusting committees composed of experts from industry with the duty to implement environmental objectives fixed in legislation'.[13]

To sum up, the Court of Justice clearly wishes to avoid excessive interference of Union law with the competences of the Member States, which would result in two tiers of review of the legality of national regulations: the first in relation to the free movement of goods and services and the second in the light of the rules on undistorted competition.

Although this case law has not yet been applied in the area of environmental law, certain Member State measures, in particular regarding the recycling of waste, may encourage undertakings to conclude agreements which are liable to fall within the ambit of the prohibition resulting from the joint application of these two Treaty provisions.

3. Special, Exclusive Rights, and SGEIs

3.1 Article 106(1) TFEU: principle of equal treatment

As previously discussed, given that the Court of Justice has restricted the application of Article 4(1) TEU to cases where there is a causal link between the State measure and the conduct of private undertakings in breach of Articles 101 and 102 TFEU, environmental regulations are not likely to fall foul of EU competition law.

The Treaty does not call into question the freedom of Member States to conduct their own economic policy by creating public undertakings or by granting special and exclusive rights to private undertakings. These legal privileges granted to economic operators cover two distinct legal categories. Certain rights grant the beneficiary a monopoly over a market as a whole (exclusive rights), whilst others have the effect of regulating conditions for accessing a specific market (special rights).[14] Although the

---

[12] D. Geradin, 'Droit européen de la concurrence et protection de l'environnement' (1999) *Amén-Env* 50.

[13] D. Geradin, 'EC Competition Law and Environmental Protection: Conflict or Compatibility?' (2002) 2 *YEEL* 117, 134.

[14] As for the distinction between the two categories of right, see Case 202/88 *Commission v France* [1991] ECR 1223. See S. Rodrigues, *La nouvelle régulation des services publics en Europe* (Paris: Tec & Doc, 2000) 498.

TFEU gives no definition of either 'exclusive rights'[15] or 'special rights', these concepts have been defined by the Commission.[16]

By virtue of Article 106(1) TFEU, this freedom does not, however, permit the States from departing from the principles of the free movement of goods and freedom of competition. The principle of equal treatment is to be interpreted broadly as it implies a requirement to respect all the provisions of the Treaty, and not simply those relating to competition, since the latter are only mentioned by way of example.

In the field of competition, under the terms of Article 106(1) TFEU, the provisions which seek to guarantee competition, and more specifically Articles 101 and 102 TFEU, are fully applicable to the Member States where they manage public undertakings or grant undertakings exclusive or special rights. As a matter of practice, Member State liability usually arises under Article 106(1) TFEU in conjunction with Article 102 TFEU.

In an age in which undertakings are increasingly charged, in the name of the principle of economic efficiency, with carrying on activities which were traditionally reserved to the public sector, in particular with regard to waste management and the treatment of wastewater, the question of the validity of the concession of exclusive and special rights is ever more keenly felt. In effect, most tasks to prevent pollution or to manage environmental services conferred upon specialized undertakings could not be carried out unless certain economic and technical prerequisites are satisfied, which call for the granting of 'special or exclusive rights' within the meaning of Article 106(1) TFEU. The pursuit of a genuine environmental objective may render the service provided by the undertaking endowed with special or exclusive rights less competitive than comparable services rendered by competitors.[17]

- For example, on the basis of the criteria of appropriateness, public authorities may grant special rights to a limited number of undertakings to exploit limited natural resources.

- Similarly, exclusive rights may be granted in return for an obligation incumbent upon the beneficiary to serve an entire geographical area on a continuous basis, including those areas which are not profitable.[18]

On the one hand, the concession of these rights may be justified in the interests of efficiency. Indeed, the presence of one single economic operator to process dangerous waste may prove less onerous for public authorities if it is necessary for them to subsidize the activity. On the other hand, granting those rights may also be justified by the fact that the undertakings which benefit commit themselves to fulfilling public service obligations.[19] Clearly, these rights may have the effect of limiting competition.

---

[15] It is clear from the Court's case law that exclusive rights are to be understood as rights granted 'in an exclusive manner by a measure adopted by a State to a limited number of undertakings in all or part of the national territory'. Opinion AG Léger in Case C-209/98 *Sydhavnens* [2000] ECR I-3743, para. 53.

[16] Commission Directive 2006/111/EC on the transparency of financial relations between Member States and public undertakings as well as on financial transparency within certain undertakings [2006] OJ L318/17, Art. 2(f) and (g).

[17] M. Reese and H.-J. Koch, 'Public Waste Management Services in the Internal Market and the Interpretation of Article 106 TFEU' (2011) 8:1 *JEELP* 28–9.

[18] See, in that respect, the French system of collection of used oils the validity of which was disputed in Case 172/82 *Interhuiles* [1983] ECR 555.

[19] Geradin (n 13).

Therefore, the question arises as to whether, when exercising their special or exclusive rights, the undertakings approved by public authorities violate the obligations resulting from Articles 101 and 102 TFEU. It should be noted that that merely creating a dominant position by granting exclusive rights within the meaning of Article 106(1) TFEU is not in itself incompatible with Article 102 TFEU. It is settled case law that 'a Member State is in breach of the prohibitions contained in those two provisions only if the undertaking in question, merely by exercising the exclusive rights granted to it, is led to abuse its dominant position or when such rights are liable to create a situation in which that undertaking is led to commit such abuses'.[20]

However, as discussed in the next section, the framers of the Treaty sought to prevent too severe an application of competition rules from jeopardizing a public monopoly responsible for essential services from the point of view of the general interest.

3.2 Article 106(2) TFEU: SGEIs

3.2.1 *The State*

Article 106(2) TFEU offers Member States the possibility of freeing themselves from the requirement to comply with competition law, subject to specific conditions. SGEIs[21] are subject to competition law 'in so far as the application of such rules does not obstruct the performance, in law or in fact, of the particular tasks assigned to them'.

The existence of SGEIs will thus enable a Member State to carry out a practice in principle prohibited under Articles 101 and 102 TFEU. Accordingly, Article 106(2) provides a significant exception to the principle of equal treatment. Hence, the fact that an undertaking is charged with the management of an environmental protection service may justify a derogation from the rules of competition law. In addition, tasks 'of general economic interest' were symbolically recognized after the entry into force of the Treaty of Amsterdam under Article 14 TFEU and Article 36 EUCFR.

Nevertheless, the lawfulness of exclusive and special rights has been subject to numerous reservations, since Article 106(2) TFEU must be interpreted narrowly.[22] However, the case law has followed different tracks: in some of its judgments, the Court of Justice has held that the use made of exclusive rights may under certain

---

[20] Case C-260/89 *Elleniki Radiofonia Tileorassi* [1991] ECR I-2925, para. 37; Case C-179/90 *Merci Convenzionali Porto di Genova* [1991] ECR I-5889, paras 16 and 17; Case C-323/93 *Centre d'Insémination de la Crespelle* [1994] ECR I-5077, para. 18; Case C-163/96 *Raso and Others* [1998] ECR I-533, para. 27; and Joined Cases C-115/97, C-116/97 & C-117/97 *Brentjens* [1999] ECR I-6025, para. 93.

[21] SGEI must abide by minimum requirements such as the presence of an act of a public authority entrusting the operators with an SGEI activity, the universal and compulsory nature of that activity, the reasons why the Member State considers that the service in question, because of its specific nature, merits being characterized as an SGEI and being distinguished from other economic activities. See Case T-289/03 *BUPA ea v Commission* [2008] ECR II-81, para. 172.

[22] Case 127/73 *BRTE v Sabam et Fonior* [1974] ECR 51, para. 19; Case C-41/90 *Höfner* [1991] ECR I-979; Case C-179/90 *Merci* [1991] ECR I-5889; and Case C-260/89 *Elleniki Radiofonia Tileorassi* [1991] ECR I-2925. See also European Commission, DG Competition Paper Concerning Issues of Competition in Waste Management Systems, 22 September 2005, para. 54. In addition, the development of trade must not be affected to an extent that would be 'contrary to the interests of the EU'.

circumstances prove to be unlawful, whilst in other cases it had suggested that the simple exercise of an exclusive right or a special right almost automatically entails abuse of a dominant position.

In short, in order to be permitted, special or exclusive rights conferred upon an SGEI must, according to this complex jurisprudence, be 'necessary' in order to permit the undertaking to carry out its task.[23] Competition law cannot therefore be set aside unless its application obstructs the performance of the task given to a public undertaking or one charged with providing a public service.[24] If the special or exclusive right can be replaced by another measure leading to an identical result, the measure which restricts competition must accordingly be considered unlawful. Measures which are least detrimental to competition are therefore preferred. In brief, this amounts to a proportionality test.

The economic feasibility of the task is crucial in this regard. It is not, though, necessary to establish that the survival of the undertaking is under threat. By way of illustration, in *Almelo* the Court of Justice paid heed to 'the economic conditions in which the undertaking operates, in particular the costs it has to bear and the legislation, particularly concerning the environment, to which it is subject'.[25] The obligation on the holder of the right to carry out its task in conditions of economic equilibrium presupposes that it will be possible to offset profitable sectors against those which are not.[26] With respect to household and commercial waste, it is generally necessary to cross-subsidize unprofitable service segments in order to ensure full coverage of the territory. If that were not the case, private undertakings would restrict themselves to covering only the most lucrative segments of the waste-recovery markets to the detriment of other areas.[27]

Finally, as discussed in Chapter 12, as an exception to the body of rules contained in the Treaty, the second paragraph of Article 106 TFEU may also be relied on in order to authorize State aid which may violate Article 107 TFEU.

3.2.2 *SGEIs in an environmental context*

The paragraph 2 regime is a priori applicable to the numerous undertakings charged with a public services relating to environmental protection. However, it is necessary for public authorities to be in a position to establish that granting these rights is essential from the point of view of the general interest. The following undertakings have been charged with the management of SGEIs.

- Water utility companies established by public authorities in order to ensure the regular supply and distribution of water under conditions which fully guarantee the protection of public health.[28]

---

[23] Case C-320/91 *Corbeau* [1993] ECRI-2533, para. 14; and Case C-159/94 *Commission v France* [1997] ECR I-5815, para. 49. Regarding the necessity test in the environmental field, see eg Case C-203/96 *Dusseldorp* [1998] ECR I-4075, para. 65; and *Sydhavnens* (n 15), para. 74.

[24] On the criteria of appreciation of the failing, see Rodrigues (n 14), 521–31.

[25] Case C-393/92 *Commune d'Almelo* [1994] ECR I-1508, para. 77.

[26] *Corbeau* (n 23), para. 17.   [27] Reese and Koch (n 17), 35.

[28] Commission Decision 82/371/EEC *Navewa-Anseau* [1982] OJ L167/65.

- A company given the task, through a non-exclusive concession governed by public law, of ensuring the supply of electricity in part of the national territory with a particularly rigorous specification ('cahier des charges');[29] this judgment is, however, an illustration of the joint application of Articles 101, 102, and 106 TFEU; undertakings authorized to recycle building waste produced in the territory of the municipality of Copenhagen.[30]
- A compulsory consortium for processing used batteries in Italy.[31]
- Advocate Genral Rozès argued in the *Interhuiles* case that waste-collection undertakings authorized by the French authorities could be considered as having been charged with the operation of an SGEI by virtue of the obligation incumbent upon them to collect and recycle waste oils.[32]
- Finally, in *Dusseldorp* Advocate General Jacobs took the view that the 'waste management function might well be said to constitute a SGEI'.[33]

On the other hand, the European Commission does not consider the following State aids to be SGEIs within the meaning of Article 106(2) TFEU.

- State aid intended to promote the production of newsprint from recycled paper, since the market already provided that type of service. By contrast, a service consisting in the collection of waste paper amounts more to a service which should be provided by the public authorities.[34]
- State aid granted to an undertaking operating a landfill site for hazardous waste, since it was not certain whether, as the beneficiary of exclusive rights granted by the Dutch authorities, it was the only company able to provide that type of service.[35]
- Conversely, aid granted to undertakings treating hazardous waste and amounting to 100 per cent of their operating deficit consists of an SGEI.[36] The Commission took into consideration that there was a market failure in this case.

3.2.3 *Case law on the necessity of environmental measures*

As far as the environment is concerned, the Court of Justice has accepted that particularly heavy environmental burdens may have an impact on the assessment of the necessary character of the restrictions applied to competition for the performance

---

[29] Case C-393/92 *Almelo* [1994] ECR I-1477, para. 46.
[30] *Sydhavnens* (n 15), paras 75 and 76.
[31] V. Baccaro, 'Collecte et recyclage des batteries usagées en Italie: droits exclusifs, exigences environnementales et droit de la concurrence' (2011) 1 *CPN* 40, 39–41.
[32] Opinion AG Rozès in *Interhuiles* (n 18).
[33] Opinion AG Jacobs in *Dusseldorp* (n 23), para. 103.
[34] Commission Decision 2003/814/EC on the State aid which the United Kingdom is planning to implement for a newsprint reprocessing capacity support under the WRAP programme [2003] OJ L314/26.
[35] Commission Decision 2003/C 196/03 State aid—Netherlands, Operating aid in favour of AVR for dealing with hazardous waste [2003] OJ C196/6.
[36] Commission Decision 2006/237/EC on the aid measures implemented by the Netherlands for AVR for dealing with hazardous waste [2006] OJ C84/37, para. 78.

of a task of general interest. *Almelo* is a good case in point.[37] The case concerned a clause granting an exclusive concession according to which the local distributors were bound to the beneficiary undertaking. Here, the need to respect environmental obligations made it necessary to rein in competition law. By considering the regulatory constraints which the undertaking had to deal with, the Court departed from a strictly economic analysis. Taking into account policing measures, in particular with reference to environmental protection, is therefore an integral part of the analysis of whether the restrictions imposed on competition law are necessary. Three waste management cases raise some of the same issues, but in the context of an entirely different set of facts.

3.2.3.1 *Dusseldorp*

In *Dusseldorp* the Court of Justice reversed its narrow understanding of the notion of restricting competition. It effectively broadened the extent of control over the need to confer an exclusive right.[38] The case concerned Dutch undertakings which were confronted with the refusal by a minister to export certain categories of hazardous waste to Germany. This refusal was justified by the Dutch authorities on the grounds, first, that there were no processing methods of a higher quality in Germany compared to the technique used in the Netherlands and, second, that the treatment capacity in the Netherlands was sufficient. Moreover, the waste was to be turned over to a Dutch undertaking which had been granted the exclusive right to process it; its permit was in particular subject to conditions that were intended to prevent undesirable price increases. Its profitability depended on a regular supply of waste intended for use as fuel. Moreover, a break in the supply would oblige it to use a less environmentally friendly fuel.

The Court found that, in practice, the national measures preventing exports entailed granting an exclusive right to the undertaking charged with incinerating hazardous waste in the Netherlands. This right was not, however, necessary for the general interest. Account should have been taken of the fact that the process in the German installation was not of a lower environmental standard than that in the Dutch installation.[39] Thus, it was not essential from an environmental perspective to require a measure amounting to a prohibition to export waste. This reasoning therefore draws heavily on the proportionality principle which predominates the argument of financial equilibrium developed in the *Corbeau* judgment.[40]

Finally, it was not so much the conferral of the exclusive right to incinerate waste in the Netherlands which was called into question here as the combination of this exclusive right with the ministerial prohibition on the exportation of the waste.[41] The ministerial prohibition had the effect of reinforcing the monopoly granted to the Dutch undertaking and, accordingly, permitting it to restrict access to the German market in breach of Article 102 TFEU.

---

[37] Case C-393/92 *Almelo* [1994] ECR I-1477.   [38] *Dusseldorp* (n 23).
[39] *Dusseldorp* (n 23), para. 20.   [40] Rodrigues (n 14), 526.   [41] Geradin (n 13), 52.

3.2.3.2 *Sydhavnens*

In view of the more nuanced position adopted by the Court of Justice in the *Sydhavnens* judgment concerning the granting of an exclusive right to process a specific category of waste,[42] the scope of the *Dusseldorp* judgment needs to be put into perspective. With regard to the application of the necessity test to the measure taken by the municipality of Copenhagen to grant exclusive rights for processing building waste to three undertakings, the Court of Justice placed particular emphasis on the fact that an alternative measure involving less restrictive effects on competition (eg a regulation requiring undertakings exclusively to recycle their building waste) would not have been as effective as the arrangements put in place by the municipal authorities.[43] The Court paid particular attention to the fact that the contested arrangements envisaged the creation of a recycling centre with high capacity to ensure its profitability in order to confront an environmental problem which was considered to be serious.[44] Moreover, the exclusive right was limited both temporally and geographically.[45] Consequently, conferring an exclusive right proved to be necessary in order to accomplish the task of an SGEI.[46] This case, which was favourable to the SGEI, stands in contrast to other more stringent case law. It is only in exceptional cases that the Court permits derogations in a limited number of areas, which include social and environmental protection.[47]

3.2.3.3 *DSD*

Finally, the General Court held that the obligation imposed on DSD, a company charged with a take-back and recovery service for packaging waste in Germany, not to prevent waste collection undertakings from concluding contracts with competitors in order to share the use of collection facilities, did not 'threaten the attainment on economically acceptable conditions' of the SGEI.[48] Similarly, the fact that DSD would no longer be paid, following a decision taken by the Commission, for use of the mark applied on the packaging covered by competitor systems was not of such a nature as to call into question the SGEI which had, under the circumstances, been granted to that company.[49]

4. Conclusions

The Treaty strikes a balance between competition and the public provision of SGEIs. Member States are endowed with much discretion in deciding which environmental schemes qualify as SGEIs[50] and can confer upon them the appropriate special and exclusive rights inasmuch as those rights are necessary to permit the undertakings to carry out their tasks. Moreover, according to the case law, where the possibilities for an economically sustainable service are limited, cross-subsidies between the profitable and the unprofitable segments may be permitted.

---

[42] *Sydhavnens* (n 15).   [43] *Sydhavnens* (n 15), para. 80.   [44] *Sydhavnens* (n 15), paras 78–81.
[45] *Sydhavnens* (n 15), para. 79.   [46] *Sydhavnens* (n 15), para. 81.
[47] L. Idot, 'Concurrence et services d'intérêt général. Bref bilan des évolutions postérieures au traité d'Amsterdam' in Louis and Rodrigues (n 1), 56.
[48] Case T-289/01 *Der Grüne Punkt* [2007] ECR II-1691, para. 208.
[49] *Der Grüne Punkt* (n 48), para. 101.   [50] Reese and Koch (n 17), 45.

12

State Aids and Environmental Protection

1. Introduction

Although they still occupy a marginal place, State aids in the environmental domain nonetheless constitute one of the spearheads of national environmental protection policies and the fight against global warming, as shown by the diverse nature of the initiatives taken in this area. First, given the costs of investments borne by the private sector in order to comply with environmental regulations, public authorities are inclined to give financial assistance to their undertakings. The EU lawmaker may even authorize the granting of such aids in order to compensate for costs incurred by the implementation of harmonized standards.[1] Second, State aids can also be granted with a view to encouraging undertakings at the forefront of technological innovation in pollution abatement. Since there is no let-up in the expansion of environmental policy into new areas, such as renewable energy and eco-products,[2] State aids have become more widespread. Containing both 'positive' (subsidies, loans, direct investments, etc) and 'negative' (tax relief, preferential tariffs, tax remission, exemption from the obligation to pay fines, or other pecuniary penalties, guarantees, etc) measures,[3] they may come in extremely varied forms. This complex and evolving situation inevitably calls for a nuanced approach.

Whilst State aids appear to be a not insignificant asset for ensuring the success of a public environmental protection policy, a number of subsidies are also likely to hamper environmental policy. Typical in this respect is the Common Fisheries Policy (CFP): the basic condition for the success of its reform is the reduction in overcapacity in fishing fleets which is still supported by subsidies. Clearly, this overcapacity creates economic pressure to set fishing quotas at levels which are too high from an ecological point of view and lead to illegal fishing activity.[4] Another case in point is the over-allocation of GHG emissions allowances. In 2006, Member States over-allocated the carbon allowances free of charge to a number of major polluters. On the one hand, this led to a collapse of the price of the allowances and endangered the whole trading scheme; on the other hand, the windfall profits caused significant distortion of competition.[5]

That aside, some State aids may benefit national undertakings to the detriment of competitors and, for this reason, undermine the system of free and non-distorted competition required in particular under Article 107 TFEU. They may also sit awkwardly alongside the polluter-pays principle, enshrined in Article 192(2) TFEU, which requires polluting undertakings to bear the costs of their pollution-reduction investments.[6]

In order for an environmental measure to be considered to breach Article 107 TFEU, it is necessary to provide evidence, first, that it amounts to a State aid as defined by this

---

[1] The EU lawmaker may authorize Member States to grant State aid with the aim of compensating costs incurred from environmental obligations. Eg by virtue of Art. 10a(6) of ETS Directive 2003/87/EC, Member States may adopt financial measures in favour of sectors determined to be exposed to a significant risk of carbon leakage due to costs relating to greenhouse gas (GHG) emissions passed on in electricity prices, in order to compensate for those costs. Such financial measures have to be granted in accordance with State aid rules.

[2] See the discussion in Chapter 4, Section 6.2.

[3] Case C-126/01 *GEMO* [2003] ECR I-4397, para. 28.

[4] SRU [German Advisory Council on the Environment], *Fischbestände nachhaltig bewirtschaften. Zur Reform der Gemeinsamen Fischereipolitik*, no. 16 (Berlin, 2011).

[5] Due to this over-allocation, the price of allowances fell in one month from almost €30 to €12. Eg J. de Sépibus, 'Scarcity and Allocation of Allowances in the EU Emissions Trading Scheme—A Legal Analysis', *NCCR Trade Working Paper 2007/32*, 36.

[6] See the discussion in Chapter 1, Section 7.6.

provision, and which does not fall under any of the exceptions listed in paragraphs 2 and 3. One is struck by the great legal uncertainty which still reigns regarding both the concept of State aids as well as the issue of their compatibility with the provisions of the Treaty.

The first section of this chapter is dedicated to substantives rules whilst the second deals briefly with procedural rules. Since this study will be limited to commentary on the different arrangements for environmentally friendly aids,[7] the general rules will not be analysed. For these issues, readers should consult the more general studies dedicated to controls over State aids.

Finally, where it is necessary to control the conduct of States and not those of undertakings, the decentralization of powers from the Commission to the national authorities is more difficult to assure than it is when implementing Articles 101 and 102 TFEU.[8]

2. Substantive Conditions

2.1 Introductory remarks

Before deciding on the compatibility of aid with Treaty State aid provisions, the Commission has to clarify if State aid is involved. Given that the definition of State aid is by no means straightforward, this is a rather challenging task. In fact, Article 107 TFEU does not provide any definition of the concept of State aid. Moreover, measures falling under this provision are not identified with reference to their form, their objectives, or the activities to which they apply. According to settled case law, in

---

[7] G. van Calster, 'Greening the EC's State Aid and Tax Regimes' (2000) 21 *ECLR* 294; H. Vedder, *Competition Law & Environmental Protection in Europe. Towards Sustainability* (Groeningen: Europa Law, 2003) 478; A. Alexis, 'Protection de l'environnement: la mise en application du principe du pollueur-payeur' (2003–04) 4 *RAE-LEA* 629–40; J. de Sépibus, *Die Umweltschutzsubvention im Gemeinschaftsrecht* (Bern: Peter Lang, 2003); G. Facenna, 'State Aid and Environmental Protection' in A. Biondi, P. Eeckhout, and J. Flynn (eds), *The Law of State Aid in the European Union* (Oxford: OUP, 2004) 245–64; A. Kliemann, 'Aid for Environmental Protection' in M. S. Rydelsky (ed.), *The EC State Aid Regime. Distortive Effects of State Aid on Competition and Trade* (London: Cameron & May, 2006) 315–46; A. Winterstein and B. Tranholm Schwarz, 'Helping to Combat Climate Change: New State Aid Guidelines for Environmental Protection' (2008) 2 *Competition Policy Newsletter* 12–20; E. Kutenicova and A. Seinen, 'Environmental Aid' in W. Mederer, N. Pesaresi and, M. Van Hoof (eds), *EU Competition Law*, vol. 4, State aids (Leuven: Claeys & Casteels, 2008); U. Soltesz and F. Schaltz, 'State Aid for Environmental Protection. The Commission's New Guidelines and the New General Block Exemption Regulation' (2009) 6:2 *JEEPL* 141–70; N. de Sadeleer, *Commentaire Mégret. Environnement et marché intérieur* (Brussels: ULB, 2009) 503–26; and 'State Aids and Environmental Protection: Time for Promoting the Polluter-Pays Principle' (2012) 2 *NJEL* 3–31; P. Thieffry, *Droit de l'environnement de l'UE*, 2nd edn (Brussels: Bruylant, 2011) 963–1047; and S. Kingston, *Greening Competition Law and Policy* (Cambridge: CUP, 2011) 379–433.

[8] Although ex Art. 81 EC (Art. 101 TFEU) has been subject to a centralized control regime since 1962, the difficulties and costs entailed by these procedural arrangements spurred the Council to replace that regime with one of decentralized controls. See Council Regulation (EC) No. 1/2003 on the implementation of the rules on competition laid down in Articles 81 and 82 of the Treaty [2003] OJ L1/1. Thereafter, the agreements, decisions, and concerted practices covered by Art. 101(1) TFEU could be authorized without any requirement for prior decision by the Commission, as was the case under the terms of Regulation No. 17 implementing Articles 85 and 86 of the EC Treaty. Regarding the possibility of decentralizing State aid control, see J. Hettne, 'Public Services and State Aid—Is a Decentralisation of State Aid Policy Necessary?' (2011)14 *SIEPS* 1–7.

order to be classified as State aid, a measure must satisfy four conditions.[9] For the sake of clarity, the prerequisites set out by the Court of Justice are examined in a slightly different order:

- an advantage must be conferred on the recipient of the aid;
- the advantage must be of State origin;
- the aid must have a selective nature;
- and the aid must be liable to affect trade between the Member States.

These conditions often end up becoming entangled, which highlights the evolutionary and pragmatic nature of the concept of State aid. On the one hand, the EU Courts are careful to ensure that the concept of State aid is sufficiently broad whilst, on the other hand, they also seek to constrain it out of concern for legal certainty.

2.2 First condition: advantage conferred on the recipient

2.2.1 *Introductory comments*

First, the recipients of State aid must be undertakings and not private persons.[10] Accordingly, tax relief granted to private individuals purchasing cars equipped with catalytic converters would not fall within the scope of Article 107 TFEU.[11]

Second, in order to amount to State aid, the measure must create an advantage for its beneficiary. It is thus necessary to establish 'whether the recipient undertaking receives an economic advantage which it would not have obtained under normal market conditions'.[12] Against this background, the notion of advantage has been very broadly interpreted and is wider than that of subsidy.[13] Accordingly, any measure which, in different forms, reduces the financial burdens that normally apply to a company amounts to an advantage for the purposes of Article 107(1) TFEU.

On the other hand, granting relief from abnormal burdens relating to the provision of an SGEI pursuant to Article 106(2) TFEU does not create an advantage for the

---

[9] Case C-142/87 *Belgium v Commission* ('*Tubemeuse*') [1990] ECR I-959, para. 25; Joined Cases C-278–280/92 *Spain v Commission* [1994] ECR I-4103, para. 20; Case C-482/99 *Stardust* [2002] ECR I-4397, para. 68; Case C-280/00 *Altmark* [2002] ECR I-7747, para. 74; and Case C-345/02 *Pearle and Others* [2004] ECR I-7139, para. 32.

[10] For the definition of an undertaking, see Case C-41/90 *Höfner* [1991] ECR I-1979, para. 21.

[11] E. Garbitz and V. Zacker, 'Scope for Action by the EC Member States for the Improvement of Environmental Protection under EEC Law: The Example of Environmental Taxes and Subsidies' (1989) *CML Rev* 429. The Commission, for its part, intervening in accordance with ex Art. 88 EC (Art. 108 TFEU), carried out a thorough analysis of the German and Dutch fiscal exemptions for 'clean' cars. It finally raised no objection against the implementation of those measures. See 15th Annual Report on Competition Policy, 224 and 225. The question arose as to whether an environmental tax exemption on international flights granted to transit passengers at Schiphol Airport and not to other passengers using Dutch airports was deemed to be a State aid granted to that specific airport. The Dutch Supreme Court doubted whether the advantage granted to transit passengers could lead to a factual advantage for the airlines or Schiphol Airport. See HR, 4 October 2009, LJN BI3451.

[12] Case C-301/87 *SFEI* [1996] ECR I-3547, para. 60.

[13] Joined Cases C-328/99 & C-399/00 *Italy and SIM 2 Multimedia v Commission* [2003] ECR I-4035, para. 35; Joined Cases C-393/04 & C-41/05 *Air Liquide Industries Belgium* [2006] ECR I-5293, para. 29; and Joined Cases T-425/04, T-444/04 & T-456/04 *France Télécom v Commission* [2010] ECR II-2099, para. 232.

recipient undertaking, since the compensation does not exceed the real cost of the service including a reasonable profit.[14] By way of illustration, 'the consideration for the services performed by the collection of disposal undertakings' does not constitute State aid, which means that a levy on the sale of certain goods, the revenue from which is used to indemnify undertakings collecting and/or recycling waste oils, cannot be regarded as financing State aid.[15]

The following measures have been qualified as State aid within the meaning of Article 107 TFEU:

- Selling a plot of land to a private undertaking by a public undertaking, when the purchase price would not have been obtained by the buyer under normal market conditions.[16]

- Tendering for a contract aiming to increase the capacity of a newspaper waste recycling plant that had the effect of conferring an advantage on the bidder, on account that the authorities were not intervening as private investors.[17]

2.2.2 Undertakings' liability to bear the environmental costs

As far as environmental measures are concerned, in order to ascertain whether a recipient undertaking receives an advantage, the Commission takes into consideration the polluter-pays principle, which makes it possible to assess liability for the costs generated by the pollution concerned. Following the Commission's reasoning in *Gemo*, a case regarding the financing by slaughterhouses of operators collecting and disposing of animal carcasses and slaughterhouse waste, Advocate General Jacobs took the view that 'a given measure will constitute State aid where it relieves those liable under the polluter-pays principle from their primary responsibility to bear the costs'.[18] Without referring to this environmental principle, the Court of Justice ruled that the disposal of such waste had to be 'considered to be an inherent cost of the economic activities of farmers and slaughterhouses'.[19] As a result, an advantage was granted to those undertakings.

Furthermore, granting exemptions from certain regulatory obligations or their financing may for that reason fall within the ambit of Article 107 TFEU. Accordingly,

---

[14] Compensation granted to undertakings entrusted with the operation of SGEIs falls outside the scope of Art. 107 TFEU on the ground that such compensation does not represent an advantage. However, four conditions must be fulfilled. See Case C-280/00 *Altmark* [2002] ECR I-7747, paras 89–93.

[15] Case 240/83 *ADBHU* [1985] ECR I-531, para. 18. In relation to the compensation approach, see Opinion AG Jacobs in *GEMO* (n 3), paras 97 et seq.

[16] See Joined Cases T-127, 129 & 148/99 *Diputación Foral de Álava ea v Commission* [2002] ECR II-1275, para. 73; and Case T-274/01 *Valmont Nederland v Commission* [2004] ECR II-3145, para. 45.

[17] Commission Decision 2003/814/EC on the State aid C61/2002 which the United Kingdom is planning to implement for a newsprint reprocessing capacity support under the WRAP programme [2003] OJ L314/26.

[18] Opinion AG Jacobs in *GEMO* (n 3), para. 69.

[19] *GEMO* (n 3), para. 31. AG Jacobs had considered that 'the provision free of charge of a collection and disposal service for dangerous animal waste [was relieving the]...farmers and slaughterhouses of an economic burden which would normally, in accordance with the polluter-pays principle, have to be borne by those undertakings'. See Opinion AG Jacobs in *GEMO* (n 3), para. 64.

the Commission has concluded in various cases that by financing costs which would normally fall on the recipient undertaking, the public authorities have granted State aid. For example, where the authorities decide to finance the elimination of industrial dust emitted by an undertaking, they are granting aid because the decision has the effect of exempting the undertaking from the costs relating to the elimination of its waste.[20] In fact, under the terms of the polluter-pays principle, the producer of the waste is responsible for its disposal and recycling. Intervention by a public authority in favour of an undertaking will in that case be tantamount to an economic advantage for the latter and, accordingly, must be classified as State aid within the meaning of Article 107 TFEU. Similarly, a steel producer cannot be released from its obligation to manage its waste and to recycle industrial dust.[21]

2.2.3 *Granting of tradable emission rights*

Finally, the question arises as to whether the granting of tradable emission rights entails an advantage. Account must be taken of the fact that some emission rights are granted free of charge (grandfathering) whereas others are sold or auctioned. An example would be the emissions trading scheme (ETS). During the two first phases (2005–07 and 2008–12), ETS Directive 2003/87/EC[22] allowed Member States to auction off a limited number of allowances (5–10 per cent). As a result, 90–95 per cent of the allowances were granted free of charge.[23] Although allowances to emit GHG will be auctioned from 2013,[24] ETS Directive 2003/87/EC still provides for derogations.[25] Where these commodities are granted for free, sold, or auctioned, the undertakings can trade in intangible assets representing market value for a specific period. It thus follows that the undertakings enjoy the advantage of being able to monetize the economic value of the allowance.

Admittedly, there is increasing support for the view that where the distribution of the allowances involves grandfathering or where they are sold by State authorities below market price, there is an advantage for the recipient undertaking: 'the advantage

---

[20] Commission Decision 1999/227/ECSC on aid granted by the Land of Lower Saxony (Germany) to *Georgsmarienhütte GmbH* [1997] OJ C323/4.

[21] Commission Decision 1999/227/ECSC (n 20).

[22] Directive 2003/87/EC establishing a scheme for greenhouse gas emission allowance trading within the Community [2003] OJ L275/32.

[23] However, the Commission did not request formal notification of the National Allocation Plans (NAP) as State aids under Art. 108(3) TFEU. In assessing the validity of the plans under Directive 2003/87/EC, the Commission reminded the applicant Member States that it was not excluded that their NAPs implied State aid. See letter of the Commission of 17 March 2004 quoted in Case T-387/04 *EnBW Energie Baden-Württemberg AG* [2007] ECR II-1201. See also Commission Decision on the first French NAP C(2004) 3982/7 final; and Commission Decision on the first Polish NAP C(2005) 549 final. It should be noted that the Commission has never opened a formal State aid investigation.

[24] See ETS Directive 2003/87/EC, Art. 10(1); and preamble to European Parliament and Council Directive 2009/29/EC amending Directive 2003/87/EC so as to improve and extend the greenhouse gas emission allowance trading scheme of the Community [2003] OJ L140/63, recital 19.

[25] Pursuant to Art. 10c(1) of the ETS Directive, until 2020 certain Member States are allowed to grant allowances free of charge to installations for electricity production. See Communication from the Commission, Guidance document on the optional application of Article 10c of Directive 2003/87/EC [2011] OJ C99/9.

flows essentially from the fact that the state has handed out for free something that is tradable'.[26] In its 2008 guidelines discussed later, the Commission took the view that 'tradable permit schemes may involve State aid in various ways, for example, when Member States grant permits and allowances below their market value and this is imputable to Member States'.[27] The 2012 guidelines endorse the same interpretation.[28]

In this respect, the Dutch NO_x trading scheme is a good case in point.[29] Within the framework of the NO_x national emission ceiling established by Directive 2011/81, the Netherlands set a cap-and-trade scheme for 250 of its largest and most polluting facilities. According to this scheme, the undertakings had to comply with a specific emission abatement standard either by reducing their own emissions or by purchasing emission allowances from other undertakings. If an undertaking exceeded the national emission standard, it was required to compensate for the surplus during the following year. Consequently, the Dutch undertakings were authorized to trade emission allowances between them. In contrast with other cap-and-trade schemes, the quantity of tradable allowances was not laid out in advance on the ground that they were awarded according to the additional reduction the undertakings could achieve in relation to the national standard. In infringement proceedings brought by the Commission against the Netherlands, the question arose as to whether the tradability of the emission allowances constituted an advantage for the undertakings subject to the scheme.

Taking the view that the national authorities were conferring a market value on these tradable allowances, both the General Court and the Court of Justice held that the measure had to be regarded as 'an economic advantage which the recipient undertaking could not have obtained under normal market conditions'.[30] The argument that the allowances were mitigating efforts taken by the undertakings to attain the national emission standard was rejected on the ground that 'the costs of reducing those emissions fall within the charges to which the budget of the undertaking is normally subject'.[31]

In fact, the mere existence of windfall profits militates against the negation of any economic advantage conferred on the recipient undertaking.[32]

2.3 Second condition: State resources

2.3.1 *Introductory comments*

To be classified as State aid within the meaning of Article 107 TFEU, the advantage must, first, be granted 'directly or indirectly through State resources and, second, be

---

[26] J. H. Jans and H. Vedder, *European Environmental Law*, 4th edn (Groeningen: Europa Law, 2008), 321.

[27] Paras 55 and 139.

[28] Commission, Guidelines on Certain State Aid Measures in the context of the greenhouse gas emission allowance trading scheme post-2012 [2012] OJ C158/4. See M. Stoczkiewicz, 'Free Allocation of EU ETS Emission Allowances to Installations for Electricity Production from a State Aid Law Perspective' (2012) 3:3 *Envt Economics* 99–107.

[29] Case C-279/08 P *Commission v Netherlands* [2011] OJ C311/6.

[30] Case T-233/04 *Netherlands v Commission* [2008] ECR II-591, para. 63; and Case C-279/08 P *Commission v Netherlands* (n 29), para. 91.

[31] Case C-279/08 P *Commission v Netherlands* (n 29), para. 89.

[32] J. de Sépibus, 'The EU Emissions Trading Scheme Put to the Test of State Aid Rules', NCCR Trade Working Paper 2007/34, 12.

imputable to the State'.[33] These conditions are cumulative. Accordingly, the concept of 'aid' is defined in particularly broad terms in that it applies to all forms of assistance granted by a Member State or through State resources in any form whatsoever. By way of illustration, the following measures have been considered to involve the transfer of public resources and, therefore, to fall within the scope of Article 107 TFEU:

- a levy applied in order to finance the operations of a national manure bank on Dutch pig breeders which produced more manure than they could use;[34]
- the management of animal waste provided free of charge by private undertakings for farmers and slaughterhouses, as 'the organisation of that service originates with the public authorities'.[35]

Moreover, the distinction made between 'aid granted by a Member State' and aid granted 'through State resources' signifies that State aids may be granted by all levels of government, as well as public and private bodies over which the Member State exercises decisive influence.[36] As far as environmental policy is concerned, measures taken by local authorities as well as environmental agencies are caught by Article 107 TFEU if they concern public resources.

This condition is not always fulfilled. For instance, subsidies awarded to an under-taking with a view to covering the costs incurred by the clean-up of contaminated soil does not involve a transfer of State resource, inasmuch as the undertaking is bound to reimburse the sum to the State.[37] By the same token, the obligation to pay a charge for each car registered for the first time in the Netherlands in order to finance a private undertaking in charge of collecting and recycling car wrecks and founded by a voluntary agreement between undertakings that was rendered compulsory by Dutch public authorities, did not involve a transfer of public resources. First, it is a legal obligation and, second, payment of the charge was voluntary because manufacturers and importers could obtain exemption if they themselves ensured the recycling of the car wrecks.[38] Given that only private undertakings were involved in the scheme, the benefits were not granted out of State resources. Conversely, when they favour some recycling undertakings, charges paid by commercial undertakings relating to their vehicles may be considered State resources and, thus, State aid.

2.3.2 *Emission trading scheme and transfer of State resources*

Much ink has been spilled over the question whether the gratuitous allocation of allowances is tantamount to a transfer of State resources.

---

[33] Case C-482/99 *Stardust* [2002] ECR I-4397, para. 24; and *GEMO* (n 3), para. 24.
[34] Commission Decision 92/316/EEC concerning aid envisaged by the Netherlands Government in favour of an environmentally-sound disposal of manure [1992] OJ L170/34.
[35] *GEMO* (n 3), para. 26.
[36] Case C-379/98 *PreussenElektra* [2001] ECR I-2099, para. 58; and Case C-222/07 *UTECA* [2009] ECR I-1407, para. 34.
[37] Commission Decision 1999/272/EC on the measure planned by Austria for the clean-up of the Kiener Deponie Bachmanning landfill [1999] OJ L109/51.
[38] Commission Decision 2002/204/EC on the waste disposal system for car wrecks implemented by the Netherlands [2002] OJ L68/18.

As a starting point for analysis of this challenging question it should be stressed that the measure must be imputable to the Member State. The fact that an EU act, such as the ETS Directive, obliged Member States to allocate GHG emission allowances free of charge did not prevent the allocation from being qualified a State aid inasmuch as the national authority was endowed with sufficient room for manoeuvre when implementing the directive. Given that the ETS Directive offered the national authorities much discretion during the two first phases of the scheme (2005–08, 2008–12), the condition was easily fulfilled.[39]

Second, the advantage must be granted 'directly or indirectly through state resources'. Since the proceeds resulting from the sale of allowances did not constitute the Member States foregoing revenue, several commentators have argued that this was not the case.[40] However, the view taken by these authors can no longer be sustained. Indeed, it is settled case law that the advantages granted to certain undertakings entailing 'an additional burden for the public authorities in the form of an exemption from the obligation to pay fines or other pecuniary penalties' fall within the ambit of Article 107 TFEU.[41] It therefore follows that a national cap-and-trade scheme offering free of charge the possibility for undertakings covered by it to trade in emission allowances in order to avoid the payment of fines and conferring on these allowances the character of tradable intangible assets confers an advantage granted through State resources.[42] In effect, the State could have sold such allowances or put them up for auction.[43] Thus, there is a transfer of State resources in the form of loss of State resources.

Similarly, the fact that a Member State does not take advantage of the possibility granted to it under secondary legislation to auction off GHG emissions allowances is attributable to the State and financed from the public purse.[44] As is clear from the following example, by deciding not to sell allowances to installations for electricity production, the State is depriving itself of revenue that it could earn, were it to auction them instead.[45] On the other hand, where allowances are sold at market price, there is no transfer of State resources.

However, the issue free of charge of green certificates does not entail the transfer of State resources insofar as these certificates merely acknowledge that green electricity has been produced by the recipient undertaking.[46]

---

[39] De Sépibus (n 32), 7–8.

[40] C.-S. Schweer and L. Bernhard, 'Emissionshandel und EG-Beihilfenrechts' (2004) 7 *RdE* 153–80.

[41] Case C-295/97 *Piaggio* [1999] ECR I-3735, para. 42.

[42] Case C-279/08 P *Commission v Netherlands* (n 29), para. 106.

[43] Opinion AG Mengozzi in Case C-279/08 P *Commission v Netherlands* (n 29), para. 87.

[44] The Commission acts along the same line: see J. de Sépibus, 'The European Emission Trading Scheme Put to the Test of State Aid Rules' (2009) 17:4 *Environmental Liability* 126; Thieffry (n 7), 769.

[45] Pursuant to Art. 10c(1) of the ETS Directive, until 2020 certain Member States are allowed to grant allowances free of charge to installations for electricity production. Thus, these Member States are not required to use the option of transitional allocation. Accordingly, the Commission takes the view that these allowances fall within the ambit of Art. 107 TFEU. See Communication from the Commission, Guidance document on the optional application of Article 10c of Directive 2003/87/EC [2011] OJ C99/9.

[46] Commission Decision of 25 July 2001 on green certificate in the Belgian electricity sector, No. 550/2000.

2.3.3 *Foregoing State resources is inherent in environmental regulation*

As will become clear from the following examples, it is not always easy to distinguish between State aid and a classical regulatory measure. Indeed, measures which do not entail direct or indirect financial burdens for the State do not normally fall within the concept of State aid, even where they represent an advantage for the undertakings concerned. Typical in this respect is the *Preussen Elektra* case.[47] The Court of Justice found that, even though it gave some economic advantage to producers of this type of electricity, and entailed a diminution in tax receipts for the State, that latter consequence was an inherent feature of such a legislative provision. Accordingly, the obligation to purchase electricity produced from renewable sources at minimum prices did not involve any direct or indirect transfer of State resources to the electricity production companies.[48] Hence, there was no direct connection between the German measure at issue and the possible loss of revenue. Consequently, the German arrangements did not involve a transfer of State resources.

The opposite solution prevails where there is a sufficiently direct connection between the measure and the foregoing of State revenue. For instance, where the State has, with respect to a cap-and-trade scheme, the choice between grandfathering or selling or auctioning them, the foregoing of resources cannot be considered inherent 'to the instrument designed to regulate the emissions of pollutants'.[49]

2.3.4 *Failure to implement environmental law*

Insufficient attention has hitherto been paid to the fact that environmental law suffers from the reticence of the authorities charged with applying it. All too often their indifference, negligence, incompetence, or even resignation, prevail over their obligations to apply the mandatory rules contained both in international law as well as secondary EU law. These shortcomings give national undertakings advantages that are sometimes considerable, as the latter may not incorporate environmental externalities into the price of their goods and services in accordance with the polluter-pays principle. However, in the absence of a transfer of State resources, these shortcomings fall beyond the definition of State aid.[50]

2.4 Third condition: selectivity

2.4.1 *Environmental measures and selectivity*

Although they may comply with the previous two conditions, State measures will not amount to State aid within the meaning of the Treaty if they are not selective. In fact, in

[47] *PreussenElektra* (n 36), para 85.   [48] *PreussenElektra* (n 36), paras 54 and 59.
[49] Case C-279/08 P *Commission v Netherlands* (n 29), para. 111; and Opinion AG Mengozzi in Case C-279/08 P *Commission v Netherlands* (n 29), para. 92.
[50] Thus, in a case where the Spanish authorities had not required a producer of synthetic fibres to implement waste-management standards, the Commission dismissed a complaint according to which the shortcomings were tantamount to State aid. Given that there was not a transfer of State resources, the Commission ruled that Art. 107 TFEU was inapplicable (Commission Notice C-66/97 on certain measure undertaken in favour of Sniace [1998] OJ C49/2).

order for a State measure to be considered equivalent to State aid, it is further necessary for it to favour 'certain undertakings or the production of certain goods', rather than indiscriminately benefiting all undertakings situated within the Member State.[51] This criterion reflects the thinking that the more an aid measure is selective, the more likely it is that it will distort competition.

The following arrangements fulfil the prerequisites for selectivity:

- Granting a rebate on a tax on the consumption of energy solely to undertakings manufacturing goods constitutes a selective advantage likely to lead to the qualification of State aid.[52] In fact, a tax scheme establishing distinctions between manufacturing undertakings and undertakings furnishing services is not justified inasmuch as the consumption of energy by those sectors is harmful to the environment.[53]

- A measure aiming at facilitating the replacement of industrial vehicles by new vehicles was deemed to be selective when it targeted certain undertakings particularly small and medium-sized enterprises (SMEs), 'albeit that they are not limited in number'.[54] 'The exclusion of undertakings that are not SMEs from the benefit of the Spanish Plan cannot be justified on the basis of the nature and scheme of the system of which it forms part'.[55]

- The fact that the free collection of animal waste essentially benefited farmers and slaughterhouses underlined the fact that it did not constitute an arrangement of a general nature.[56]

2.4.2 *General measures of economic policy and selective measures*

Selective State aids stand in opposition to so-called general measures of economic policy which are not aimed at favouring specific products or sectors, but at all undertakings in the national territory, without distinction. These general measures cannot constitute State aid[57] provided they are justified by the nature of the general structure of the system under which they fall. In effect, an economic benefit granted to an undertaking constitutes State aid only if, by displaying a degree of selectivity, it favours certain undertakings or the production of certain goods.

However, the criterion of selectivity is fulfilled where the administration called upon to apply arrangements of a general nature uses its discretionary power with regard to

---

[51] The reference geographical framework is not necessarily the national geographical framework when a measure is taken by a substate entity enjoying both an institutional, procedural, economic, and financial autonomy as far as its autonomous powers are concerned. See Case C-88/03 *Portugal v Commission* [2006] ECR I-7115; Joined Cases C-428–434/06 *Unión General de Trabajadores de La Rioja* [2008] ECR I-6747; and Joined Cases T-211 & 215/04 *Government of Gibraltar v Commission* [2008] ECR II-3745.

[52] Case C-143/99 *Adria-Wien Pipeline* [2001] ECR I-8365, paras 43–53.

[53] *Adria-Wien Pipeline* (n 52), para. 52.

[54] Case C-351/98 *Spain v Commission* [2002] ECR I-8031, para. 40.

[55] Case C-351/98 *Spain v Commission* (n 54), para. 41.   [56] *GEMO* (n 3), para. 38.

[57] *Adria-Wien Pipeline* (n 52), para. 35; and Case T-55/99 *CETM v Commission* [2000] ECR II-3207, para. 40.

the application of the regulatory measure, and where this discretionary power has the effect of favouring certain undertakings or the production of certain goods.[58]

That said, the dividing line between measures which may constitute public subsidies, on the one hand, and measures forming part of a State's general system, on the other, may sometimes be difficult to ascertain.[59] As far as environmental policy is concerned, the distinction between general and selective measures proves to be particularly delicate. For example, the financing of a waste incinerator or a landfill by the public authorities will not benefit any particular undertaking. However, if it appears that an undertaking would be favoured by such infrastructure due to the fact that it would be the principal beneficiary, the prerequisite of selectivity would be met. This example shows how difficult it is to trace the dividing line between investments in public infrastructure and State aid.

In this regard the following question arises: must arrangements applicable to all industrial sectors, which are not *de iure* selective, but which *de facto* apply to a limited number of sectors, be considered to fall within Article 107(1) TFEU? The Netherlands NO_x trading scheme case offers valuable insights into this issue.[60] The question arose as to whether the national cap-and-trade scheme granting free allowances to 250 large polluting facilities favoured a certain group of undertakings within the meaning of Article 107 TFEU. The 250 recipient undertakings were subject to the cap-and-trade scheme since their thermal capacity was more than 20 MWth whereas the smaller undertakings were bound to comply with emission ceilings without the possibility of taking part in the scheme.

The General Court held that the measure was not selective for the following reasons: 'the beneficiary undertakings are determined in accordance with the nature and general scheme of the system, on the basis of their significant emissions of NO_x and of the specific reduction standard to which they are subject' and that 'ecological considerations justify distinguishing undertakings which emit large quantities of NO_x from other undertakings'.[61] The General Court further held that 'that objective criterion is furthermore in conformity with the goal of the measure, that is, the protection of the environment and with the internal logic of the system'.[62] Therefore, it was possible to draw a distinction between the two categories of plant.

However, the Court of Justice objected to this reasoning. In line with its previous case law, it held that: 'Article [107(1) TFEU] does not distinguish between measures of State intervention by reference to their causes or their aims but defines them in relation to their effects'. Regarding the objective of the measure at issue, the Court endorsed the same reasoning as in its previous *British Aggregates* judgment: 'even if environmental protection constitutes one of the essential objectives of the [EU], the need to take that objective into account does not justify the exclusion of selective measures from the scope of Article [107(1) TFEU], as account may, in any event, usefully be taken of the

---

[58] Joined Cases T-92/00 & T-103/00 *Diputación Foral de Álava ea v Commission* [2002] ECR II-1385, paras 23, 31, and 35.

[59] Opinion AG Ruiz-Jarabo Colomer in Case C-6/97 *Italy v Commission* [1999] ECR I-2981, para. 27.

[60] Case C-279/08 P *Commission v Netherlands* (n 29).

[61] Case T-233/04 *Netherlands v Commission* (n 30), para. 99.

[62] Case T-233/04 *Netherlands v Commission* (n 30).

environmental objectives when the compatibility of the State aid measure with the common market is being assessed pursuant to Article [107(3) TFEU]'.[63] In particular, the Court stressed that the fact that all national facilities were subject to emission reduction obligations was not sufficient to obliterate the differentiation introduced by the national authorities between the 250 largest polluting plants and the other plants.[64] The Court also considered that the quantitative criterion to select the 250 major plants could not be regarded as inherent to the general scheme to reduce industrial atmospheric pollution.[65]

2.4.3 *Environmental taxes and selectivity*

By definition, the arrangements governing State aids (Arts 107 and 108 TFEU) and those governing distortions resulting from different treatment under tax law (Arts 28, 30, and 110 TFEU) do not cover identical ground.[66] Despite the existence of these two regimes, tax regulation is nonetheless liable to fall under the scope of the arrangements governing State aid. In other words, the fact that a tax measure complies with the requirements of provisions governing the free movement of goods does not therefore imply that it will be lawful under the terms of Article 107 TFEU.

Clearly, the application of this provision to environmental taxation[67] is a particularly delicate issue when the revenue from the taxation is allocated to public bodies which have the task of assisting undertakings to comply with their obligations under environmental law, or even to comply with more stringent environmental standards. Moreover, with a view to promoting more environmentally friendly economic innovation, eco-taxation provides for distinctions to be made between different categories of goods or services in accordance with environmental considerations, which generally manifest themselves in the form of exemptions which may benefit certain categories of undertakings or the production of certain goods. In addition, the adoption of new tax arrangements, especially with reference to the fight against climate change, may disadvantage certain categories of undertaking such as steelworks that are confronted with strong international competition. As a result, exemptions from environmental taxes may on occasion be granted to polluting undertakings in order to permit them to absorb the impact of new tax arrangements and, on other occasions in order to remain competitive compared to foreign undertakings not subject to the same fiscal constraints.[68] Finally, exemptions may also be granted with a view to enticing undertakings to develop less polluting technologies.

---

[63] Case C-279/08 P *Commission v Netherlands* (n 29), para. 75.
[64] Case C-279/08 P *Commission v Netherlands* (n 29), para. 76.
[65] Case C-279/08 P *Commission v Netherlands* (n 29), para. 76; Opinion AG Mengozzi, para. 55.
[66] Opinion AG Geelhoed in Case C-174/02 *Streekgewest* [2005] ECR I-85, para. 28.
[67] An environmental tax has been defined by the Commission as a tax the base of which has a negative effect on the environment or which seeks to tax certain activities, goods, or services so that environmental costs may be included in the price. See General Block Exemption Regulation (EC) No. 800/2008, Art. 17 (10); and the 2008 guidelines on environmental aids, para. 40.
[68] In this connection, the Austrian energy tax at issue in *Adria-Wien Pipeline* (n 52) is a good case in point.

The question whether tax exemption arrangements have the effect of favouring 'certain undertakings or the production of certain goods' arose repeatedly when the first national regimes to fight global warming were adopted. The climate change tax in the United Kingdom provided an exemption in favour of a certain number of operators which used certain technology, which created an advantage for them over other users which were forced to buy electricity taxed on the basis of environmental considerations. The UK authorities stipulated that the exceptional arrangements applied to all undertakings which used the said technology, regardless of the extent of their exploitation. Having concluded that these criteria were objective, the Commission found that the exemption was justified with regard to the general structure of the system into which it was incorporated.[69]

It follows that whenever environmental tax reductions or exemptions are inherent in the logic of a national tax system, they fall outside the scope of Article 107(1) TFEU, provided that the conditions examined previously are not satisfied. This may be illustrated by the following example. The Danish lawmaker exempted undertakings covered by the EU ETS from a carbon tax on fuel consumption for production purposes.[70] Whereas the Danish authorities argued that the exemption was inherent in the logic of the ETS, the Commission took the view that the proposed exemption deviated from the logic of the system used as a reference which was the energy tax system and not the Danish ETS. The logic of that system was to tax each energy product consumed. As a result, the selectivity of the proposed exemption could not be justified by the nature and logic of the tax system.

The national authorities must in any event take particular care to ensure that tax exemptions or reductions do not have the effect of benefiting certain companies to the detriment of their competitors and, therefore, satisfy the criterion of specificity which is one of the prerequisites for the application of Article 107(1) TFEU. The position of the Court of Justice on this question in *Adria-Wien Pipeline*, the Norwegian electricity tax, and *British Aggregates* is instructive.

In *Adria-Wien Pipeline*, the Court of Justice was called upon to examine a partial exemption from payment of an environmental tax on the consumption of natural gas and electricity by undertakings, an exemption which had not been granted only to undertakings producing tangible goods. This case is undoubtedly of great interest. The Court held that granting benefits to undertakings the principal activity of which consisted in the manufacture of tangible goods was not justified by the nature or the general structure of the contested tax system. Since the consumption of energy by undertakings producing tangible goods was as damaging to the environment as that of undertakings providing services, the environmental considerations underlying the tax arrangements did not justify different treatment of these two sectors.[71] The Court did

---

[69] Commission Decision to open the proceeding concerning aid C 18/2001—Climate change [2001] OJ C185/03/22.

[70] Commission Decision 2009/972/EC on aid scheme 41/06 which Denmark is planning to implement for refunding the CO_2 tax on quota-regulated fuel consumption in industry (C(2009) 4517), para. 44. See S. Hoe, 'Regulering af CO_2 med afgifter og kvoter—en dobbeltregulering?' (2011)2 *NELJ* 87.

[71] *Adria-Wien Pipeline* (n 52), para. 52. See V. Golfinopoulos, 'Concept of Selectivity Criterion in State Aid Definition Following the *Adria-Wien* Judgment—Measures Justified by the Nature or General Scheme of a System' (2003) 10 *ECLR* 543.

not accept the argument by the Austrian Government, which was inspired by the idea of maintaining the competitiveness of undertakings producing tangible goods, according to which partial reimbursement of the environmental taxes was justified by the fact that those undertakings had been proportionally more affected by the tax than the other undertakings.[72] Moreover, it was irrelevant whether the situation of the recipient of the measure had improved or worsened compared to the previous state of the law or, by contrast, had not changed over time.[73] It was only necessary to verify whether the State measure had the effect of favouring 'certain undertakings or the production of certain goods' within the meaning of Article 107(1) TFEU.[74] Only a measure which is justified by the nature or general structure of the system into which it is incorporated will not satisfy the requirement of selectivity.[75]

In a similar environmental tax case, the EFTA Court endorsed the Court of Justice's reasoning. The EFTA authority claimed that under the Norwegian electricity tax system several tax exemptions were selective in nature on the ground that they favoured, within the meaning of Article 61(1) of the Agreement on the European Economic Area, manufacturing and mining industries compared to the service and building sectors. The aid in question could not be justified on the basis of the nature or general scheme of the tax system since the exemption of sectors that consume the most electricity ran counter to the aim of the electricity tax, namely to ensure a more efficient use of electric power. The EFTA Court dismissed the applicants' arguments that the tax exemption was non-selective.[76]

In *British Aggregates*, the General Court departed from the classical case law of the Court of Justice. The question arose as to whether an environmental tax on aggregates providing for an exemption in favour of aggregates produced from waste from the extraction of minerals created a selective advantage. The General Court held that the tax break was not selective. In particular, it took care to underscore the margin of appreciation of the State: the Member States were free, when weighing up the different interests in play, to define their priorities in the area of environmental protection and accordingly to determine the goods and services which they decided to subject to this eco-tax.[77] Moreover, the General Court justified this reasoning in view of the integration clause contained in ex Article 6 EC (Art. 11 TFEU).[78] As a result, the fact that such a levy did not apply to all similar activities which had a comparable environmental

---

[72] *Adria-Wien Pipeline* (n 52), para. 44.   [73] *Adria-Wien Pipeline* (n 52), para. 41.

[74] In his Opinion, AG Misho took the view that reimbursement rules favouring the manufacturing sector but discriminating against the services sector did not constitute State aid on the ground that the scheme was part of 'a new general system of ecology taxes which from the moment of its conception was based on the principle that the primary and secondary sectors of the national economy could not reasonably be taxed proportionately to the whole of their electricity and gas consumption'. See Opinion AG Misho in *Adria Wien Pipeline* (n 52), para. 42. The objectivity of the criteria of the tax perception and the reimbursement's subordination to criteria established by the legislature and not by the administrative authorities attested, in his view, to the existence of an overall system of energy taxation (para. 43).

[75] *Adria-Wien Pipeline* (n 52), para. 42.

[76] Joined Cases E-5/04, E-6/04 & E-7/04 *Fesil ASA and Finnfjord Smelteverk AS* (Case E-5/04), *Prosessindustriens Landsforening and others* (Case E-6/04), *The Kingdom of Norway* (Case E-7/04) v *EFTA Surveillance Authority* [2005], EFTA Ct. Rep. 2005, p. 117, paras 76–87.

[77] Case T-210/02 *British Aggregates v Commission* [2006] ECR II-2789, para. 86.

[78] Case T-210/02 *British Aggregates* (n 77), para. 117.

impact does not mean that similar activities, which were not subject to the levy, benefit from a selective advantage.[79]

This 'highly innovative' reasoning[80] has, however, been objected to by the Court of Justice which found that the General Court had misconstrued Article 107(1) TFEU.[81] According to the Court of Justice, this approach ended up cancelling out the effects of the aid measure having regard to the goal pursued by the tax arrangements, namely 'the environmental objective'. This went against the traditional interpretation given to this provision of the Treaty, which did not distinguish between measures of State intervention by reference to their causes or aims but defined them in relation to their effects.[82]

As a result, the selectivity of the non-imposition of an environmental tax on operators in comparable situations could not be assessed in the light of the objective being pursued by the tax authority, independently of the effects of the fiscal measure in question.[83] Moreover, 'the need to take account of requirements relating to environmental protection, however legitimate, cannot justify the exclusion of selective measures, even specific ones such as environmental levies, from the scope of Article [107(1) TFEU]'.[84] In addition, as Advocate General Mengozzi underlined, 'neither the competence enjoyed by the Member States in matters relating to taxation or the environment, nor the principle laid down by Article [11 TFEU] of the integration of environmental protection requirements into the definition and implementation of Community policies, justifies the wholesale removal of public measures that could distort competition from the ambit of the supervisory power conferred on the Commission by the Treaty rules on State aid'.[85]

The Court of Justice decided to refer the case on British tax aggregates back to the General Court on account of the error of law discussed previously. The Commission contended that an exceptional burden on a narrow economic sector does not involve State aid to all other sectors not subject to the levy. Contrary to the Commission's contention, in its second judgment the General Court held that in order to classify a domestic tax measure as 'selective':

- first, it is necessary to begin by identifying and examining the common taxation regime applicable (in this case the specific tax system applicable to aggregates);

- second, it is in relation to this 'normal' tax regime that it is necessary 'to assess and determine whether any advantage granted by the tax measure at issue may be selective by demonstrating that the measure derogates from that common regime inasmuch as it differentiates between economic operators who, in the light of the

---

[79] Case T-210/02 *British Aggregates* (n 77), para. 115.

[80] Opinion AG Mengozzi in Case C-487/06 P *British Aggregates v Commission* [2008] ECR I-10505, para. 96.

[81] Case C-487/06 P *British Aggregates* (n 80), para. 86.

[82] Case C-241/94 *France v Commission* [1996] ECR I-4551, para. 21; Case C-342/96 *Spain v Commission* [1999] ECR I-2459, para. 23; and Case C-75/97 *Belgium v Commission* [1999] ECR I-3671, para. 46. See also Case C-279/08 P *Commission v Netherlands* (n 29), para. 75.

[83] Case C-487/06 P *British Aggregates* (n 80), para. 87.

[84] Case C-487/06 P *British Aggregates* (n 80), para. 92.

[85] Opinion AG Mengozzi in Case C-487/06 P *British Aggregates* (n 80), para. 102; Opinion AG Mengozzi in Case C-279/08 P *Netherlands v Commission* (n 29), para. 63.

objective assigned to the tax system of the Member State concerned, are in a comparable factual and legal situation'.[86]

On the ground that the aggregates levy entailed distinctions the effects of which were to favour 'the production of certain goods' within the relevant economic sector, the General Court went on to assess whether these distinctions were justified by the tax scheme's logic and its environmental objective (shift from raw materials to by-products).[87] Given that the differentiations clearly derogated from the rationale of the normal tax framework, the General Court annulled the Commission's decision that found the British levy at issue did not amount to State aid.

To conclude, even if the eco-tax can be described as an exceptional fiscal burden on a narrowly defined sector, that in itself does not mean that the tax falls outside the scope of the prohibition laid down in Article 107 TFEU. Moreover, its environmental objective is not sufficient to exclude it from the scope of that provision. However, neither the Commission nor the General Court can disregard the environmental objective underpinning a tax scheme in assessing whether the differentiations between economic operators are consistent with the general tax framework. Finally, the environmental integration clause enshrined in Article 11 TFEU should lead the Commission to take into account environmental goals pursued by the national lawmaker not when classifying the measure but exclusively when assessing its compatibility with paragraph 3 of Article 107 TFEU.[88]

By contrast, both the Commission and the General Court held that the criterion of selectivity was not fulfilled in the following situations:

- where a Member State grants tax breaks on all products which are less polluting and takes care to avoid discriminating against foreign products;[89]

- when Germany applied the general regime of tax exemption to the arrangements put in place by German nuclear power stations for the purpose of the disposal of their radioactive waste and the permanent closure of their plants, and did not benefit the operators of these nuclear power stations compared to other subjects liable to pay the tax, which meant that the arrangements applied did not satisfy this condition;[90]

- finally, when the Netherlands planned tax measures in favour of non-polluting cars which complied with EU standards in advance, since these measures were granted independently of the origin of the vehicles.[91]

However, even if the regime of exemptions is considered to amount to State aid, nothing prevents the Commission from approving it. Indeed, both the 2008 guidelines on State aid for environmental protection[92] as well as the Commission General Block

---

[86] Case T-210/02 RENV *British Aggregates v Commission* [2012] OJ C118/21, para. 49.
[87] Case T-210/02 RENV *British Aggregates* (n 86), para. 68.
[88] Case C-487/06 P *British Aggregates* (n 80), para. 92; and Opinion AG Mengozzi, para. 102.
[89] Commission Communication of 26 March 1997 on environmental taxes and charges in the Single Market [1997] OJ C224/6.
[90] Case T-92/02 *Stadtwerke Schwäbisch Hall v Commission* [2006] ECR II-11, paras 43–53.
[91] 20th Annual Report on Competition Policy, nos 199 et seq.
[92] 2008 guidelines, paras 151–60.

Exemption Regulation (EC) No. 800/2008 (hereafter 'GBER')[93] accept that environ-mental tax reductions or exemptions may be compatible with Article 107(3)(c) TFEU. Such exceptions, which must be of a temporary nature, must however be necessary and proportionate.[94]

2.4.4 *Hypothecation of the tax for State aid*

It is also important to consider the hypothecation of the tax for the State aid.

In the *SWNB* and *Pape* cases,[95] the plaintiffs challenged the legality of environmental taxes to which they had been subject, claiming that they were intended to finance State aid. In these two cases, the Court of Justice found that only the taxes which 'constitute the method of financing an aid measure, so that they form an integral part of that measure' suffer the same fate as the aid measure itself. Indeed, for a tax, or part of a tax, to be regarded as forming an integral part of an aid measure, it must be hypothecated to the aid measure under the relevant national rules.[96] It follows that these criteria are not satisfied where the revenue from the environmental tax is not allocated to a group of taxpayers.

In *Pape*, the Court of Justice held that since the national legislation at issue left to the authorities the decision on how to distribute the revenue from the tax on waste, there was no 'hypothecation' between the ecological tax and the aid considered.[97] Similarly, in *SWNB* the fact that the revenue from a tax on waste did not have any impact on the level of aid granted in a sector in the form of tax exemption should lead the national courts to conclude that there was no 'hypothecation'.[98] In sum, the fact that the fiscal advantage resulting from the exemption is balanced out by an increase in the tax is not sufficient to establish the existence of hypothecation.

2.5 Fourth condition: negative impact on trade between Member States

Finally, for the State measure at issue to be considered State aid, it must be liable to affect trade between Member States. In particular, it is still necessary to establish that the benefit has a negative impact on competition as well as on the free movement of goods. Clearly, these two conditions are inextricably linked.

---

[93] Commission Regulation (EC) No. 800/2008 declaring certain categories of aid compatible with the common market in application of Articles 87 and 88 of the Treaty [2008] OJ L214/3.

[94] 2008 guidelines, paras 155 and 157–9.

[95] Case C-174/02 *Streekgewest* [2005] ECR I-85, para. 25; and Case C-175/02 *Pape* [2005] ECR I-127, para. 15. See M. Dony, *Commentaire Mégret. Contrôle des aides d'Etat* (Brussels: ULB Press, 2008) 395–6, nos 726 and 727. See also Commission Decision 98/384/EC on aid granted by the Netherlands to a hydrogen peroxide works in Delfzijl [1998] OJ L171/36.

[96] *Streekgewest* (n 95), para. 26. According to AG Geelhoed, 'indicative of the existence of such a link are the following criteria: the extent to which the aid measure concerned is financed from the revenue of the levy and is thus dependent; the extent to which the revenue from the levy is intended solely for the specific aid measure; the extent, apparent from the legislation concerned, of the binding nature of the link between the revenue from the levy and its specific earmarking as an aid measure; the extent to which and the manner in which the combination of the levy and aid measure influences competition in the (sub)sector or business sphere concerned'. See Opinion in *Streekgewest* (n 95), para. 35.

[97] Case C-175/02 *Pape* [2004] ECR I-127, para. 16.

[98] *Streekgewest* (n 95), paras 28 and 29.

The Commission tends to regard the first condition as having been fulfilled automatically.[99] Indeed, when aid granted by the State strengthens the position of an undertaking vis-à-vis other undertakings competing in intra-Community trade, the latter must be regarded as affected by that aid.[100] By way of illustration, due to the fact that it reduces the cost of products, a waste-management measure 'appears to be an economic advantage liable to distort competition'.[101]

The second condition regarding the impact on intra-Community trade is also easily fulfilled. It is settled case law that 'when aid granted by a Member State strengthens the position of an undertaking compared with other undertakings competing in intra-Community trade, the latter must be regarded as affected by that aid'.[102] For instance, the Court of Justice held that a French measure exempting the costs of carcass disposal for farmers and slaughterhouses constituted an advantage for national exports and affected intra-Community trade.[103]

Two exceptions should, however, be mentioned. The Commission found that trade between Member States is not affected where the beneficiaries are public or private bodies providing local or regional public services which have not been opened up to competition from commercial vehicle operators established in other Member States. In effect, given the absence of liberalization of a specific type of transport, beneficiaries do not compete with commercial vehicle operators in other Member States.[104] Accordingly, the State aid in question could not affect trade between Member States unless the beneficiary transport undertakings were in competition with foreign undertakings. Additionally, under the terms of Regulation (EC) No. 1998/2006,[105] so-called *de minimis* aids, which do not exceed €200,000 over a period of three years and are granted to the same undertaking, do not fulfil the prerequisite affecting competition or trade.

3. Exemptions

3.1 Introductory remarks

In principle, the prohibition of State aid is neither absolute nor unconditional and is subject to numerous exceptions. In this regard, the absence from Treaty law of express exceptions for environmental protection measures has not prevented the emergence of

---

[99] Commission Decision 2006/63/EC on the aid scheme which Italy (Region of Piedmont) is planning to implement for the reduction of airborne pollution in its territory [2006] OJ L32/82.

[100] Case 730/79 *Philip Morris v Commission* [1980] ECR 2671, para. 11; and Case C-310/99 *Italy v Commission* [2002] ECR I-2289, para. 84.

[101] *GEMO* (n 3), para. 33.

[102] Case 730/79 *Philip Morris Holland v Commission* [1980] ECR 2671, para. 11; Case C-53/00 *Ferring* [2001] ECR I-9067, para. 21; and Case C-372/97 *Italy v Commission* [2004] ECR I-3679, para. 52; Opinion AG Jacobs in Cases C-278–280/92 *Spain v Commission* [1994] ECR I-4103, para. 33. See also Commission Decision on the second German NAP of 29 November 2006, para. 2.2. Where Member States decide to grandfather allowances to installations for electricity production, Art. 10c(3), (5)(e), and (6) of the ETS Directive sets out a number of requirements to avoid distortion of competition.

[103] *GEMO* (n 3), paras 42 and 43.

[104] Commission Decision 98/693/EC concerning the Spanish Plan Renove Industrial system of aid for the purchase of commercial vehicles Plan Renove Industrial [1998] OJ L329/23.

[105] Commission Regulation (EC) No. 1998/2006 on the application of Articles 87 and 88 of the Treaty to de minimis aid [2006] OJ L379/5.

an administrative praxis favourable to granting these types of aid on the basis of Article 87(2) and (3) EC, which has now become Article 107 TFEU.[106]

Whereas paragraph 2 lists certain categories of aid which are deemed compatible with the internal market, paragraph 3 lists other categories which may be considered compatible with Article 107 TFEU.

Article 107(2)(b) TFEU sets out the aids 'to make good the damage caused by natural disasters or exceptional occurrence'. Given that these aids are characterized by a solidarity approach, they are for that reason fully admissible. In principle, aids relating to environmental matters do not fall under this paragraph. However, the granting of an aid under the terms of this provision should be possible in cases where public authorities have to deal with far-reaching changes to ecosystems caused by natural disasters or exceptional occurrences (drought, fire, wide-scale pollution, reduction of fishing resources, etc).[107] For instance, floods occurring in the Netherlands—likely to increase with climate change—gave rise to aid falling within the ambit of that paragraph.[108] Countries where the standard of living is abnormally low have also been authorized to grant State aid in accordance with Article 107(3)(a) TFEU.[109]

By contrast, paragraphs (b) and (c) of Article 107(3) TFEU contain two grounds for exemption that are likely to be much more relevant for environmental aid. These paragraphs run as follows:

(b) aid to promote the execution of an important project of common European interest or to remedy a serious disturbance in the economy of a Member State;

(c) aid to facilitate the development of certain economic activities or of certain economic areas, where such aid does not adversely affect trading conditions to an extent contrary to the common interest.

Under the terms of paragraph (b), concerted action by different Member States as part of the fight against a common threat, such as environmental pollution were, until 2001, accepted by the Commission. Since 2001, State aid can always be admitted on the basis of paragraph 3(b), in exceptional circumstances, provided that it respects conditions such as the 'exemplary' and 'substantive' contribution of an 'important project of common European interest'.[110] However, that exemption must be interpreted narrowly[111] and, consequently, the mere fact that investments may have been able to establish the use of a new technology does not necessarily mean that the project is in the general interest.[112]

---

[106] *Adria-Wien Pipeline* (n 52), para. 31.

[107] As yet, the Commission has not accepted that State aid granted in response to sensitive modifications to the natural environment will be allowed in accordance with Art. 107(2)(b) TFEU. See Commission Decision 108/C 291/05 [1998] OJ C291/4, p. 11.

[108] XXIVth Competition Report, para. 354.   [109] State aid N 495/2009-Latvia.

[110] The 2008 guidelines, paras 147–50 state that this exemption applies as a secondary ground.

[111] Case C-21/06 *Germany v Commission* [2009] Removed from the register on 27 April 2006, para. 70.

[112] Joined Cases 62 & 72/87 *Glaverbel v Commission* [1988] ECR I-1595, paras 22 and 25.

When applying paragraph (c) which grants a broad margin of appreciation,[113] the Commission has adopted various guidelines setting out the criteria for compatibility of certain environmental aids and which have accordingly been used as a basis for its practice. Thus, since 1994 this paragraph has operated as the legal basis for the adoption of a range of Commission guidelines.[114] By accordingly specifying the categories of State aid that are compatible with Article 107 TFEU, the Commission has established a quasi-regulatory competence.

It is also important to point out that the incorrect application of obligations stemming from secondary environmental legislation does not prevent the Commission from assessing the compatibility of the contested aid with Article 107 TFEU. Thus, the General Court did not uphold the argument by four operators of hotels which challenged the granting of State aid to a competitor on the ground that the hotel project had not been subject to an impact assessment as required by the Environmental Impact Assessment Directive on the assessment of the effects of certain public and private projects on the environment. Indeed, where an infringement of that directive 'is liable, in an appropriate case, to proceedings for a declaration that the Member State has failed to fulfil its obligations under [Article 258 TFEU]', it cannot constitute a serious difficulty as regards the Commission's assessment of the compatibility of the disputed aid with the common market.[115] That said, it is submitted that where State authorities do not comply with EU environmental law, the Commission is called on by virtue of Article 11 TFEU to assess the compatibility of the aid at issue with the environmental requirements, even if the aid complies with State aid requirements.

In accordance with its 2005 action plan on State aid,[116] the Commission has concluded that State aid should not be granted other than with a view to achieving an objective of common interest, correcting market failures, or favouring social and regional cohesion, or even sustainable development. These aids must accordingly create adequate incentives proportionate to their objectives and distort competition as little as possible.[117] This 2005 action plan resulted in a remodelling of the control exercised by the Commission: first, it led to the adoption in 2008 of new guidelines on environmental aids decidedly more complete than the previous ones; second, it resulted in the inclusion by the Commission of numerous criteria relating to environmental protection aids in the GBER.[118] As a result, national authorities have to assess whether their aid measures aiming to improve the environment are likely to be justified

---

[113] It is settled case law that the Commission, in the application of Art. 107(3)(c) TFEU, has wide discretion, 'the exercise of which involves complex economic and social assessments which must be made in a Community context'. See, inter alia, Case 310/85 *Deufil v Commission* [1987] ECR 901, para. 18; Case C-91/01 *Italy v Commission* [2004] ECR I-4355, para. 43; Case C-351/98 *Spain v Commission* [2002] ECR I-8031, para. 74; Case C-409/00 *Spain v Commission* [2003] ECR I-1487, para. 93; Case C-91/01 *Italy v Commission* [2004] ECR I-4355, para. 43; and Case C-21/06 *Germany v Commission* (n 111), para. 50.

[114] 2008 guidelines, para. 12.

[115] Case T-158/99 *Thermenhotel* [2004] ECR II-1, para. 159.

[116] 'State Aid Action Plan—Less and better targeted state aid: a roadmap for state aid reform 2005–2009', COM(2005) 107 final, paras 45 and 46.

[117] 2005 Action Plan, paras 10 and 11.

[118] Commission Regulation (EC) No. 800/2008 declaring certain categories of aid compatible with the common market in application of Articles 87 and 88 of the Treaty [2008] OJ L214/3.

under one of the heads of the 2008 guidelines or be exempted from notification in accordance with the provisions of the GBER.[119] Hierarchically superior, the GBER will be examined before the guidelines. In addition, special emphasis will be placed on the legal nature of these two instruments.

3.2 General Block Exemption Regulation

In order to guarantee effective oversight of granting State aid and to simplify administrative management, without however weakening the Commission's control, in 1998 the Council[120] granted the Commission the power to issue regulations declaring certain categories of horizontal aid compatible with the internal market and to exempt them from the notification requirement provided for in Article 108(3) TFEU.

On the basis of the experience which it obtained due to the previous environmental guidelines,[121] the Commission has incorporated several categories of environmental protection aid into the GBER.[122] Consolidating the previous systems of block exemptions into one instrument, the GBER, for the first time, contains a cluster of exemptions in the environmental field. Accordingly, it exempts from the notification requirement investment aid for environmental protection of €7.5 million per undertaking per investment project.[123] There is a clear advantage: not being subject to the standstill obligation,[124] the aid measures can be implemented immediately. In contrast to the 2008 guidelines, discussed later, operating aid does not fall within the scope of the regulation.

The essential utility of these new arrangements consists in the reduction of the administrative burden of the Commission, which is no longer required to exercise prior control pursuant to Article 108(3) TFEU over aid regimes that are compatible with the criteria specified in the GBER.[125] By contrast, State aids which are not covered by this regulation remain subject to the notification requirement provided for under Article 108(3) TFEU,[126] irrespective of whether they comply with the conditions specified under the 2008 guidelines.

Finally, the GBER varies the distribution of competences between the Commission and the national courts, as the latter may now verify directly whether State aid satisfies

---

[119] GBER, Arts 17–25. On that subject, see Kutenicova and Seinen (n 7), para. 4.394; Soltesz and Schaltz (n 7), 141–70; Thieffry (n 7), 781–833.

[120] Council Regulation (EC) No. 994/98 on the application of Articles 92 and 93 of the Treaty establishing the European Community to certain categories of horizontal State aid [1998] OJ L142/1. The Commission, when it adopts regulations exempting categories of aid, must specify the purpose of the aid, the categories of beneficiaries and thresholds limiting the exempted aid, the conditions governing the accumulation of aid, and the conditions of monitoring. See recital 6.

[121] GBER, recital 3.

[122] GBER, Arts 17–25. On that subject, see Kutenicova and Seinen (n 7), para. 4.394; Soltesz and Schaltz (n 7), 141–70; Thieffry (n 7), 988.

[123] GBER, Arts 3 and 6(1)(b).

[124] TFEU, Art. 108(3); and Council Regulation (EC) No. 659/1999 laying down detailed rules for the application of Article 93 of the EC Treaty [1989] OJ L83/1, Art. 3.

[125] GBER, Art. 3.

[126] TFEU, Art. 108(1); and Council Regulation (EC) No. 659/1999, Art. 2(1).

the criteria of compatibility laid down by the Commission and whether it may in consequence be granted without prior notification to the Commission.[127]

3.3 2008 environmental guidelines

3.3.1 *General considerations for State aid guidelines*

Given the vagueness of the Treaty provisions on State aid and the initial unwillingness of the Council to enact secondary legislation with the aim of fleshing out the exemption criteria, the Commission has made a virtue out of a necessity and developed exemption criteria through a host of soft law instruments.[128] Since the beginning of the 1970s, the Commission has become aware that it will not be able to eliminate State aid completely. Resolutely pragmatic, it has delineated the scope of the exceptions through a succession of guidelines the object of which is to simplify the task of Member States wishing to provide assistance to their undertakings. Where it uses the technique of guidelines, the Commission must respect the following obligations: first the guidelines may not in any way derogate from Treaty provisions;[129] second, the Commission is bound by the general rules which it has adopted, and may not set them aside in individual cases. Reference to the guidelines amounts to a proper statement of reasons.[130]

Since 1974, various guidelines have been issued in the field of environmental law which both increases legal certainty and the transparency of decision-making.[131] Whereas the first guidelines[132] authorized the granting of 'aid to promote the execution of an important project of common European interest', pursuant to ex Article 92(3)(b) EEC, they were replaced by a series of guidelines (respectively in 1994,[133] 2001,[134] and 2008[135]) which based the new exemption regimes on Article 87(3)(c) EC ('aids to facilitate the development of certain economic activities or of certain economic areas') which has now become Article 107 TFEU. Moreover, since the 1974 guidelines were merely transitional, it quickly became apparent that the elimination of State aid was nothing more than pie in the sky. In addition, the Commission has progressively expanded the scope of the exceptions.

In contrast to the GBER, the guidelines do not exempt national authorities from the requirement to notify aids to the Commission, even where they are compatible with their requirements. That said, the Member States will find useful indications in the

---

[127] J.-P. Kepenne, 'Révolution dans le système communautaire de contrôle des aides d'Etat' (1998) 2 *RMUE* 136.

[128] M. Blauberger, 'From Negative to Positive Integration? European State Aid Control Through Soft and Hard Law', Discussion Paper 08/4, Max Planck Institute for the Study of Societies, 2008, 6.

[129] Case C-382/99 *Netherlands v Commission* [2002] ECR I-5163, para. 24; Case C-310/85 *Deufil v Commission* [1987] ECR I-901, para. 22; and Case T-214/95 *Het Vlaams Gewest v Commission* [1998] ECR II-717, para. 79.

[130] Case T-288/97 *Frituli Venezia Giulia v Commission* [2001] ECR II-1169, para. 72.

[131] 2008 guidelines, para. 12.   [132] Doc. SEC(74) 4264.

[133] Community guidelines on State aid for environmental protection [1994] OJ C72/1.

[134] Community guidelines on State aid for environmental protection [2001] OJ C37. See Dony (n 95), 249–58.

[135] Community guidelines on State aid for environmental protection [2008] OJ C82/1.

guidelines regarding the criteria which the EU executive will apply when examining an aid. Accordingly, when the criteria established by the guidelines are respected, the prospective aid will be viewed favourably by the Commission.

Finally, nothing prevents the Commission from examining and, where appropriate, approving aid which exceeds the thresholds provided for under the guidelines on the basis of Article 107(3)(c) TFEU, 'unless it has explicitly adopted a position on the question concerned in its guidelines'.[136] The Commission must therefore take into account the fact that environmental protection constitutes an essential objective of the EU and that environmental concerns must be incorporated into other policies in accordance with Article 11 TFEU.[137]

3.3.2 *Content of the 2008 guidelines*

In force since 1 April 2008, the new 2008 guidelines replace the 2001 guidelines and will be in force until 31 December 2014. As discussed previously, they are complemented by the GBER. Thus, they are one of the spearheads of the policy to combat pollution and global warming. They stipulate that aids will 'primarily be justified' on the basis of Article 107(3)(c) TFEU.[138]

Until the end of 2014, the granting of State aids which do not fall within the scope of the GBER have to be assessed by the Commission with reference to the criteria laid down in the guidelines. Since it applies to all State aids intended to assure environmental protection in all sectors governed by the Treaty,[139] including those which are subject to specific EU rules on state aid (SMEs), the field of application of these guidelines is particularly broad. Accordingly, the Commission may examine an aid with reference to several provisions of EU law, even if it means applying to it the more favourable arrangements.

A 'standard' examination is required for State aid measures for amounts below a certain threshold (2008 guidelines, ch. 3) whilst a more detailed examination is required for aids above that threshold (2008 guidelines, ch. 5). Indeed, as regards aid measures likely to entail a higher risk of distortion of competition, further scrutiny appears to be necessary.

The following aids are subjected to a close examination:

- investment aid: where the aid amount exceeds €7.5 million for one undertaking;
- operating aid for energy saving: where the aid amount exceeds €5 million per undertaking for five years;
- operating aid for the production of renewable electricity and/or combined production of renewable heat: the aid is granted to renewable electricity installations at sites where the resulting renewable electricity-generation capacity exceeds 125 MW;

---

[136] Case T-375/03 *Fachvereinigung Mineralfaserindustrie v Commission* [2007] ECR II-121, para. 143.
[137] *Fachvereinigung Mineralfaserindustrie* (n 136), para. 142.
[138] *Fachvereinigung Mineralfaserindustrie* (n 136), para. 12.
[139] *Fachvereinigung Mineralfaserindustrie* (n 136), para. 59.

- operating aid for the production of biofuel: when the aid is granted to a biofuel-production installation at sites where the resulting production exceeds 150,000 tonnes per year;
- operating aid for cogeneration: where aid is granted to a cogeneration installation with the resulting cogeneration electricity capacity exceeding 200 MW. Aid for the production of heath from cogeneration will be assessed in the context of notification based on electricity capacity.

The 2008 guidelines build on the results of the previous guidelines.[140] As hinted at previously, an undertaking does not have an incentive to go beyond mandatory standards if the cost of doing so exceeds the benefit for the undertaking; although State aid may be an incentive for improving environmental protection. Conversely, aid to assist undertakings to comply with EU standards already in force should not be authorized on the ground that such aid would not lead to a higher level of environmental protection.[141] Since 1994, the Commission has only accepted aids to investment which comply with new mandatory standards or other new legal obligations.[142] Aids for investment in existing installations are in principle prohibited on the ground that they run contrary to the polluter-pays principle.[143] Similarly, according to the provisions of the GBER, operating aid is not in principle authorized.[144]

Even though the 2008 guidelines essentially concern investment aid, they provide several exemption regimes in favour of operating aid on energy efficiency grounds,[145] renewable energy,[146] and cogeneration.[147] These aids, which do not fall under the GBER, must therefore be assessed in accordance with the criteria laid down in the 2008 guidelines.

Investment aid may be granted up to a gross amount equal to 50 per cent of eligible costs,[148] which may be increased depending on the size of the undertaking.[149] The

---

[140] The previous guidelines allowed State aid aiming at adapting listed installations to new environmental standards. The General Court set out criteria distinguishing the adaptation of old installations from their replacement by new ones. See Case T-150/95 *UK Steel Association v Commission* [1997] ECR II-1433. The General Court also held that aid awarded to an Italian steel mill was not compatible with the 1992 guidelines, which laid down as a condition of eligibility for aid that the investment must bring the plant into conformity with new standards. In this case, the plant was operated according to existing standards and the investment had no connection with the entry into force of new standards. Inasmuch as those standards were neither new nor binding, the undertaking was not entitled to rely on the 1992 guidelines. See Case T-176/01 *Ferriere Nord v Commission* [2004] ECR II-3931, paras 123–5.

[141] 2008 guidelines, para. 45.

[142] The absence of clarity in the judicial qualification of the aid as an operating aid or an aid for investment may lead the Court of Justice to annul the Commission decision for lack of statement of reasons. See Case C-351/98 *Commission v Spain* [2002] ECR I-8031, paras 81 and 82; and Case C-409/00 *Commission v Spain* [2003] ECR I-1487, paras 96–9.

[143] According to the 2008 Environmental Guidelines 'it is essential that aid be classified as aid for investment or operating aid in order to determine whether it may be authorized under those Guidelines'. See Case C-351/98 *Commission v Spain* (n 142), para. 77.

[144] 2008 guidelines, para. 73.

[145] 2008 guidelines, paras 99 et seq. See also the investment aid to highly efficient power plants authorized under the Guidelines on certain State aid measures in the context of the greenhouse gas emission allowance trading scheme post-2012 [2012] OJ C158/11.

[146] 2008 guidelines, para. 107.   [147] 2008 guidelines, para. 119.

[148] 2008 guidelines, para. 76.   [149] 2008 guidelines, paras 77–9.

calculation of the amount of aid is based on supplementary environmental investment costs rather than on the total cost of the investments.

In addition, by virtue of both the GBER and the 2008 guidelines, SMEs are entitled to an increased level of aid.[150]

3.3.3 *Categories of environmental State aid covered by the GBER and the 2008 guidelines*

The 2008 guidelines list 12 categories of aid measures, some of which are not covered by the GBER. Moreover, the maximum aid is higher for aid covered by the 2008 guidelines than for that referred to in the GBER.[151] Table 12.1 lists the categories of aid as well as their regulatory bases.

Table 12.1 Classification of environmental aids

Categories of aid	Provisions
Investment aid enabling undertakings to go beyond EU standards for environmental protection or increase the level of environmental protection in the absence of Community standards	Paras 73–84 of the guidelines; Art. 18 GBER
Aid for the acquisition of new transport vehicles	Paras 85 and 86 of the guidelines; Art. 19 GBER
Aid for early adaptation to future EU standards for SMEs	Paras 73–84 of the guidelines; Art. 20 GBER
	The GBER is only applying to SMEs.
Aid for environmental studies	Paras 91–3 of the guidelines; Art. 24 GBER
Environmental aid for energy-saving measures	Paras 94–100 of the guidelines; Art. 21 GBER The GBER only covers investment aid and not operating aid
Environmental aid for the promotion of energy from renewable sources	Paras 101–11 of the guidelines; Art. 23 GBER
	The GBER only covers investment aid and not operating aid
Environmental investment aid for high-efficiency cogeneration	Paras 112–25 of the guidelines; Art. 22 GBER
Aid for waste management	Paras 126–31 of the guidelines
Aid for the remediation of contaminated sites	Paras 132–4 of the guidelines
Aid for the relocation of undertakings	Paras 135–8 of the guidelines
Aid involved in tradable permit schemes	Paras 139–41 of the guidelines
Aid in the form of reductions or exemptions from environmental taxes	Paras 151–9 of the guidelines; Art. 25 GBER
	The GBER only applies to tax reductions harmonized at the European level

---

[150] 2008 guidelines, para. 79; and GBER, Art. 18(4)(2).   [151] GBER, recital 49.

3.3.4 *Consistency of environmental State aid with the polluter-pays principle*

At first sight, State aid runs counter not only to competition law but also to a principle at the heart of environmental policy, the polluter-pays principle. In fact, due to the granting of aid to cover investments to combat pollution, the recipient undertaking will not incorporate into its costs any externalities relating to environmental degradation and will instead transfer responsibility to society. As a result, the polluter will be relieved of bearing the burden of the costs of its pollution. The TFEU provides no guidance for resolving this conflict. However, the following are some of the reasons for considering that granting Sate aid is likely to be compatible with the polluter-pays principle.

First, an overzealous application of the environmental principle is not acceptable; indeed, since 1975 the Commission has recognized the difficulties inherent in an immediate and wholesale application of the principle.[152] Recognizing the limits to which the principle is subject, the Commission accepts that it does not prevent the granting of State aid.[153]

Second, certain categories of aid make it possible to rectify market failures[154] where the market does not allow for the incorporation of negative externalities into the price of goods and services. Such affirmative action will prevent the best players from being penalized. For example, given the competitive advantage which producers of energy from fuel or coal gain over the producers of energy from renewable sources, there will be a case for public authorities to correct that advantage. In this regard, tax regimes favourable to undertakings which develop more environmentally friendly production methods are compatible with the polluter-pays principle.[155] Similarly, State aid which satisfies the criteria contained in the 2008 guidelines or the GBER is considered to be compatible with the polluter-pays principle.[156]

Third, the ability to grant State aid may also permit Member States to adopt standards that are more stringent than EU standards by lowering unsustainable burdens incumbent upon certain undertakings.[157]

This does not, however, mean that any form of aid may be admitted, in fact quite the opposite. Since under the terms of the polluter-pays principle internalization of the costs of pollution must be given priority, State aid may only be granted sparingly, and especially for incentives for the undertaking to make additional investments which permit it to go beyond mandatory standards, or to invest in renewable energy.[158] The granting of aid is nothing but a 'last resort', an 'alternative',[159] or a 'second-best

---

[152] In its Council Recommendation 75/436/Euratom, ECSC, EEC regarding cost allocation and action by public authorities on environmental matters ([1975] OJ L194/1), the Council had already recognized that the granting of State aid was deemed to be transitory.

[153] 2008 guidelines, paras 6–9.   [154] 2008 guidelines, para. 24.

[155] This is the position adopted by the Commission. See Stoczkiewicz (n 28), 185–6.

[156] S. V. Budlong, 'Article 130r(2) and the Permissibility of State aids for Environmental Compliance in the EC' (1992) *Columbia J Transntl Law* 465; M. Stoczkiewicz, 'The Polluter Pays Principle and State Aid for Environmental Protection' (2009) 6:2 *JEELP* 171–96.

[157] 2008 guidelines, para. 26.   [158] 2008 guidelines, para. 43.

[159] See the 23th Annual Report on Competition Policy, para. 166 and the 1994 guidelines, para 1.4.

option'[160] since the polluter-pays principle remains the rule.[161] Some aid is certainly incompatible with this principle. This is the case for aid intended to offer breathing space for undertakings in order to facilitate their adaptation to new standards, or to remain competitive internationally. They serve no purpose in the fight against pollution.[162] By the same token, where allowances are granted free of charge with a view to helping undertakings to meet environmental standards, they are deprived of any incentivizing effect.

In addition, where the Commission seeks to reconcile competition policy with environmental policy in the light of the polluter-pays principle, the 2008 guidelines and the GBER will only accept State aid that is capable of being justified by the need to apply more stringent environmental protection standards than those provided under EU law or, where no standards have been adopted by the Union, that are likely to increase the level of protection resulting from the activities of the undertaking.[163] The aid must therefore have an incentivizing effect.[164] Accordingly, it cannot guarantee activities the economic viability of which offers cause for concern. This means that the aid cannot cover investments designed to permit undertakings to bear the costs resulting from bringing their operations into line with existing EU environmental provisions.[165]

The role played by the polluter-pays principle was underlined in *GEMO* by Advocate General Jacobs:

> In its State aid practice the Commission uses the polluter-pays principle for two distinct purposes, namely (a) to determine whether a measure constitutes State aid within the meaning of [Article 107(1) TFEU] and (b) to decide whether a given aid may be declared compatible with the Treaty under [Article 107(3) TFEU].
>
> In the first context, that of [Article 107(1) TFEU], the principle is used as an analytical tool to allocate responsibility according to economic criteria for the costs entailed by the pollution in question. A given measure will constitute State aid where it relieves those liable under the polluter-pays principle from their primary responsibility to bear the costs.
>
> In the second context, that of [Article 107(3) TFEU], the polluter-pays principle is used by contrast in a prescriptive way as a policy criterion. It is relied on to argue that the costs of environmental protection should as a matter of sound environmental and State aid policy ultimately be borne by the polluters themselves rather than by States.[166]

---

[160] 2008 guidelines, para. 24.   [161] 2008 guidelines.

[162] See, eg, the illustrations given by the Commission in 2008 guidelines, para. 36.

[163] 2008 guidelines, paras 43 and 74; and GBER, Arts 18 and 19. For an example of aid allowed to go beyond the level of protection set out in the national legislation, see Commission Decision 98/251/EC on the proposal of Austria to award aid to the Hoffmann-La Roche company [1998] OJ L103/28.

[164] 2008 guidelines, paras 27–9.

[165] 2008 guidelines, para. 75. Thus, when the aid granted to an undertaking has the effect of allowing the authorities to confirm with environmental obligations stemming from EU secondary law, notably regarding the recycling of packaging waste, it is not granted with a view to exceeding the standards applying to the recipient undertaking. In that event, the incentive criterion set out in the 2001 guidelines has not been respected. See Commission Decision 2003/814/EC on the State aid C 61/2002 which the United Kingdom is planning to implement for a newsprint reprocessing capacity support under the WRAP programme [2003] OJ L314/26, para. 119.

[166] Opinion AG Jacobs in *GEMO* (n 3), paras 68–70.

To conclude, the polluter-pays principle therefore provides a standard for analysis which makes it possible to determine on whom the costs fall in order to establish whether a given measure constitutes State aid pursuant to Article 107(1) TFEU. A State measure which relieves those actors of those costs is thus to be regarded as an economic advantage capable of constituting State aid.[167]

3.3.5 *Consistency of environmental State aid with the proportionality principle*

It is not sufficient that an aid has positive environmental effects in order to be justified or exempted pursuant to either the 2008 guidelines or the GBER. The proportionality principle requires that a subsidy cannot be higher than the level necessary in order to achieve the environmental protection goals pursued. When national authorities invoke environmental protection considerations, they must therefore establish the necessary link between the restriction placed on competition and the goal of protecting the environment. This means that aid will be struck down where a measure of a different nature, which would have had less of an impact on trade or competition, could have been adopted. The 2008 guidelines place particular emphasis on the proportionality of the aid, since it must 'be limited to the minimum needed to achieve the protection sought'.[168] As a result, all economic benefits which the investment entails must in principle be extracted from the extra net costs.[169]

As shown by the following cases, proportionality has always played a decisive role in leading the Commission to limit the anti-competitive effects of these aids to a bare minimum.

- In order to encourage the disposal of surplus manure in an ecological manner, the Dutch government sought to establish a regime of aid,[170] consisting in financing the construction and exploitation of treatment facilities for the organic waste by a 'national manure bank'.[171] These arrangements, which were intended to encourage producers of manure to deliver their excess waste to the national bank rather than to dispose of it in the environment, were to be totally financed by revenue from a levy paid by pig breeders which produce an excess of manure. The Commission observed that the intervention of the national bank would permit manure-processing facilities to be built more quickly and, for this reason, could reinforce the competitive position of intensive breeding in the Netherlands. Moreover, since the processing of excess manure would lead to the production

---

[167] Opinion AG Jacobs in *GEMO* (n 3), paras 71 and 72.

[168] 2008 guidelines, paras 30 et seq. See also the 2005 State Aid Action Plan, para. 20, according to which the positive impact of aid depends on whether it is proportionate in the sense that the expected change in behaviour could not be achieved with less aid.

[169] 2008 guidelines, para. 31.

[170] Commission Decision 92/316/EEC concerning aid envisaged by the Netherlands Government in favour of an environmentally-sound disposal of manure [1992] OJ L170/34.

[171] The Commission had initially exempted, by virtue of Art. 92(3)(c) EC, the aid necessary for the construction of the first installations for the disposal of manure. See Commission Communication on the basis of Article 93(2) EC, addressed to other Member States and interested third parties, concerning aid envisaged by the Netherlands Government in favour of attempts projects of the disposal of manure [1991] OJ C82/3.

of solid organic fertilizer, the aid concerned was also likely to favour the competitive position of manure-processing undertakings compared to the producers of organic and chemical fertilizers. The Commission concluded that the aid concerned could only be regarded as compatible with the common market pursuant to ex Article 92(3)(c) EEC (Art. 107(3)(c) TFEU), provided that it did not exceed the fixed costs (consisting in the administrative and construction costs and the costs for maintenance of the storage infrastructure) and provided that it did not last longer than an initial period of two years. All operating aid for installations was therefore considered to be prohibited.

• Similarly, the Commission concluded that an initiative taken in order to assist a paper manufacturer to transfer its production site with a view to reducing its impact on the local environment could not benefit from an exemption from the prohibition on granting State aid due in particular to the absence of any requirement for such an aid in order to achieve the objective pursued.[172]

• By the same token, it found that a Walloon regional regulation which provided for the granting of aid not only to undertakings which installed new less polluting equipment—the recycling and recovery of waste were eligible—but also to producers of the equipment was manifestly disproportionate to the objectives which it was supposed to pursue.[173]

• In 1989 it opposed the granting of a measure of aid by the French Air Quality Agency to industries which carried out investment into desulphurization on the ground that, due to its importance, it could have anti-competitive effects.[174]

• For the chemical industry, the Commission found that investments intended not to combat ecological damage but to prevent catastrophic occurrences and to guarantee the safety of adjacent homes could not be subsidized since they amounted to an essential element of the activity of the undertakings concerned.[175]

• The Commission finally found that an aid seeking to subsidize the production of newspaper which could have been exempted under the terms of Article 107(3)(c) TFEU did not satisfy the prerequisites of necessity and proportionality, since the investments appeared to be disproportionate compared to the objective of recycling waste.[176] In this case, the financing of a paper recycling plant did not appear to be proportionate on the ground that it did not result in a reduction in the quantity of waste deposited in landfill, but that it encouraged the use of recycled paper for the production of newspapers.

---

[172] Commission Decision 93/564/EEC concerning aid the Italian Government intends to grant to Cartiere del Garda [1993] OJ L273/51.

[173] Commission Communication on the basis of Article 93, para. 2, EC, addressed to other Member States and interested third parties, concerning the environmental investment aids [1994] OJ C100/5. The proceedings were closed after a modification of the regulation by the Walloon Region.

[174] 21st Annual Report on Competition Policy (1990), no. 198.

[175] Commission Decision 98/251/EC on the proposal of Austria to award aid to the Hoffmann-La Roche company [1998] OJ L103/28, para. II, C, b); and Commission Decision 98/384/EC on aid granted by the Netherlands to a hydrogen peroxide works in Delfzijl [1998] OJ L171/36, para. VI, C.

[176] Commission Decision 2003/814/EC *WRAP programme* (n 165), paras 188 and 189.

On the other hand, the Commission has shown greater flexibility when the anti-competitive effects of aid do not prove to be disproportionate.

- In February 1990 the Commission approved the granting of tax relief to Danish undertakings which used at least 50 per cent of recycled material as raw materials for production. This relief was justified by the fact that undertakings using recycled material produce quantities of waste decidedly greater than undertakings which use non-recycled material with the result that they end up being penalized by the tax on waste disposal.[177]

- The Commission also adopted a more pragmatic approach when approving temporary relief from environmental taxation arrangements necessary in order to prevent national undertakings from being disadvantaged on the international market.[178]

4. Procedural Standards

4.1 Introductory remarks

Article 108 TFEU, as well as Council Regulation (EC) No. 659/1999 of 22 March 1999 laying down detailed rules for the application of Article 93 EC,[179] regulate the control procedure for State aid which is operated by the Commission. In contrast to the new arrangements for applying Article 101 TFEU, the Commission continues to be notified of all plans to grant aid,[180] the application of which must moreover be suspended pending the Commission's ruling. As discussed previously, the existence of guidelines specifically dedicated to aid does not relieve the States of their obligation to notify all their aid arrangements. By contrast, aid falling within the scope of application of the GBER is not subject to the notification requirement.

Member States are subject to precise obligations in order to facilitate the task of the Commission and to prevent it from being confronted with a fait accompli. After the notification stage, the Member State has every interest in informing the Commission of the environmental justifications capable of rendering its aid compatible with the internal market.[181] If the Commission considers the prospective aid to be incompatible with the internal market, it initiates a control procedure which may lead to the adoption of a decision ordering the suspension or modification of the contested aid. If the Member State does not comply with this decision within the term limit set, the Commission or any other Member State may refer the matter to the Court of Justice.[182]

Competitor undertakings of the beneficiaries of aid may formulate observations when the Commission initiates the Article 107(2) TFEU procedure. With regard to

[177] 23rd Annual Report on Competition Policy (1993), p. 283, no. 420.
[178] Commission Decision 92/411/ECSC on the granting of aid to steel undertakings by the Danish and Dutch Governments [1992] OJ L223/28.
[179] Council Regulation (EC) No. 659/1999 [1999] OJ L83/1. Since the adoption of this regulation, Art. 93 EC became Art. 88 EC then Art. 108 TFEU.
[180] See GBER, Art. 9.
[181] Case C-382/99 *Netherlands v Commission* [2002] ECR I-5163, para. 81.
[182] Council Regulation (EC) No. 659/1999, Art. 23(1).

such actions, the Court of Justice has consolidated the status of competitors by granting
them the right to challenge a refusal by the Commission to initiate the Article 107(2)
TFEU procedure against new aids.[183] Moreover, the Court has recognized the direct
effect of the last sentence of Article 108(3) TFEU. This means that applicants may
rely on the provision before the national courts and that the latter may, where
applicable, apply it. Even though national courts may punish violations of the
obligation of prior notification to the Commission, they cannot declare the aid as
such to be incompatible with the internal market—a decision which falls exclusively
to the Commission.

4.2 'Parties concerned' within the meaning of Article 108(2) TFEU

The following question has also been subject to debate. In order to qualify as 'parties
concerned' within the meaning of Article 108(2) TFEU, must the competitive position
on the market of third parties be affected by the granting of the aid concerned?

In a judgment of 16 September 1998, the General Court did not recognize this status
as being applicable to an undertaking which complained that the aid concerned
entailed an increase in taxes on waste which it was obliged to pay. The Court found
that the undertaking had to pay the tax in its objective capacity as the producer of waste
on the same ground as any other operator in the same situation, which meant that it
could not argue that the aid concerned affected its competitive position on the market.
The Court added that to follow the applicant's reasoning would amount to recognizing
that any taxpayer would be a concerned party within the meaning of Article 108(2)
TFEU.[184] On the other hand, tax relief granted to undertakings which are current or
potential customers of the applicant directly affects its competitive position on the
market, with the result that it has the status of a concerned party.[185]

As regards a levy on waste accompanied by some exclusions which assumed the
character of State aid, the Court of Justice considered that Article 108(3) TFEU had to
be interpreted 'as meaning that it may be relied on by a person liable to a tax forming
an integral part of an aid measure levied in breach of the prohibition on implementation referred to in that provision, whether or not the person is affected by the distortion
of competition resulting from that aid measure'.[186] In that way, the Court adopted an
extensive conception of the interest on which persons liable to a tax may rely. Even
though they are not affected by the distortion of competition, individuals liable to
environmental tax can invoke the direct effect of Article 108(3) TFEU. They will not
have to demonstrate that they were affected by the aid.

---

[183] It should be noted that undertakings may face an uphill battle when challenging Commission
decisions taken within the framework of the EU ETS and not pursuant to Art. 4(3) of Regulation 659/
1999. See Case T-387/04 *EnBW Energie Baden-Württemberg AG* (n 23), para. 41.
[184] Case T-188/95 *Waterleiding Maatschappij Noord-West Brabant* [1998] ECR II-3713, paras 67
and 68.
[185] *Waterleiding Maatschappij Noord-West Brabant* (n 184), para. 80.
[186] Case C-174/02 *Streekgewest* [2005] ECR I-85, para. 21.

5. Conclusions

Given the broad scope of the notion of State aid, a number of environmental measures are likely to fall within the ambit of the prohibition laid down in Article 107 TFEU. That did not prevent the Commission from developing its own vision of a well-tailored State aid policy for protection of the environment. The broad criteria laid down in paragraph 3 have been fleshed out into a complex cluster of soft law instruments (guidelines) and hard law (GBER). The guidelines criteria do not deprive the Commission from playing a key role in weighing up the positive environmental impacts of the national measure against the potential negative effects for competition and trade. Through this balancing test, the Commission is called upon to assess whether the aid is appropriate and necessary in order to attain the objective of common interest. The incentive effect of the aid is taken into consideration. Clearly, the thresholds laid down by the Commission significantly influence national environmental policies.

It should be kept in mind that the criteria laid down by the Commission must be consistent with both the polluter-pays principle and the environmental integration clause. Admittedly, State aid which represents a threat to the protection of the environment must be prohibited by the Commission, even if it complies with competition law requirements. By contrast, State aid which is manifestly beneficial for the environment should be more easily accepted where its anti-competitive effects are not disproportionate.

Be that as it may, competition law will not on its own resolve the problems of pollution, as it is nothing more than an instrument in the service of environmental policy.

PART III

CONCLUSIONS

Although environmental and competition policy have hitherto been able to evolve with perfect independence—the former due to an intense regulatory approach and the latter through the case law of the Commission and the Court of Justice concerning the application of Articles 101, 102, 106, and 107 TFEU—the interactions between the two have recently become intense and may be the cause of legal problems.

On the one hand, environmental law is by nature likely to increase competition between undertakings, which must express in monetary terms the environmental costs resulting from their activities. A strict application of the regulations should lead first to the disappearance of economic operators which are not able to respect the new environmental requirements and, second, should encourage other undertakings to equip themselves with less polluting methods of production. Only the most competitive operators, and hence the least polluting, will therefore remain on the market, with the risk of creating oligopolies.

On the other hand, however, the interaction between the two policies may also be detrimental to the conservation of natural resources. In fact, competition law may act as a brake to investments made by undertakings seeking to pursue an environmental policy since, in accordance with Articles 101 and 107 TFEU, they may not in principle conclude agreements between themselves in order to fulfil environmental targets more effectively, nor may they benefit from State aid.

The application of Articles 101 and 102 presupposes that various prerequisites have been met, although it is not easy to comply with them in relation to environmental matters. Indeed, as has been shown, it is difficult to trace the dividing line between the involvement of private undertakings and the prerogatives of public authorities. Similarly, the determination of the market for products and services as well as the geographic market often proves to be a delicate matter, taking account of the specific features of the environmentally friendly products or waste.

Environmental protection appears to be ancillary to a somewhat traditional economic approach. The analysis of the practice of the Commission, in particular with respect to waste management schemes, highlights the extent to which that institution takes into account environmental considerations as long as they are intertwined with genuine economic benefits. As a result, environmental improvements that cannot be translated into economic values may not justify restrictive agreements. So far, the

Commission appears to be unwilling to allow NCAs and national courts to balance competing policy objectives. This a priori exclusion of public considerations can be explained by the Commission's attempt to reinforce the direct effect of Articles 101 and 102. Whether NCAs and national courts will be ready to depart from the Commission's narrow approach remains to be seen.

Through its influence, both negative and positive, on the development of competition law, the Article 11 TFEU integration clause may, to a certain extent, alleviate these tensions. It is submitted that the practices, agreements, and State aids which represent a threat to the protection of the environment must be prohibited by the Commission, even if they comply with competition law requirements. By contrast, the practices and agreements which are manifestly beneficial for the environment should be more easily accepted where their anti-competitive effects are not disproportionate. However, the continued granting of State aids is more controversial since they are not entirely compatible with the polluter-pays principle, which the principle of integration rightly has the effect of extending to competition law. Be that as it may, competition law will not resolve the problems of pollution on its own, as it is nothing more than an instrument in the service of environmental policy.

Final Conclusions

Both primary law and secondary law have recently undergone important changes.

As regards primary law, it is now necessary to take seriously the place occupied by environmental questions since its development over the past three decades has undoubtedly been significant. Environmental protection was originally asserted as an essential value by the Court of Justice, and not the framers of the EEC Treaty, with the purpose of expanding the list of justifications for national measures hindering the free movement of goods. Initially, enshrining this value was more reactive than proactive but thereafter, having been affirmed as 'action' under the SEA, the environment subsequently transformed into a 'policy' with the adoption of the Maastricht Treaty. With the Treaty of Amsterdam, the requirement of a 'high level of protection and improvement of the environment' was imposed in relation to all Community policies. With the entry into force of the Lisbon Treaty, the simultaneous recognition of the three pillars of sustainable development and the principle of a high level of environmental protection within the EUCFR has made it possible to take stock of the path followed since the adoption of the Treaty of Rome. The Union's goals are no longer solely economic, but also environmental. Furthermore, the proper functioning of the internal market must be accommodated with a non-market value, the legal protection of which is nonetheless also essential.

It could certainly be argued that in comprising one of the numerous facets of the general interest, environmental protection does not raise any more specific issues than other values such as public health, consumer protection, education, or the promotion of cultural diversity. However, such reasoning disregards the requirement of sustainable development enshrined in Article 3(3) TEU. In effect, sustainable economic growth goes hand in hand with the conservation of national resources for the benefit of future generations, the improvement of living standards, the protection of workers against industrial nuisances, consumer awareness of their ecological impact, as well as the conservation of biodiversity. From this perspective, environmental protection ends up providing an incentive for more responsible economic growth, thereby averting the risk of an apocalypse as proclaimed by a significant number of scientists. There is, indeed, an implicit hierarchy of values under primary law.

In laying down qualitative requirements, the requirements of integration, a high level of protection, and the principles of environmental law are more than just simple policy guidelines. Although some of these provisions do not give absolute priority to environmental protection, the fact remains that they have, on the one hand, been called for by the courts according to a teleological interpretation whilst, on the other hand, providing for a balancing of interests. In other words, by obliging institutions to display particular sensitivity to environmental protection, they limit their room for manoeuvre. Therefore, neither the institutions nor the Member States may content themselves with pursuing their policies without ambition. It follows that judicial control of compliance with these provisions should be stringent, since the institutions cannot disregard requirements imposed by primary law. Moreover, the extent of this power of review should not be limited to objecting to any levelling-down of standards, but should also guarantee that secondary law is ambitious, since policies must be proactive.

Nevertheless, primary law still contains imperfections in that it authorizes the institutions to improve the level of environmental protection but, in contrast, does not establish a right *to* the environment. Neither the Charter of Fundamental Rights nor the ECHR are of any particular assistance.

At this stage, one may certainly rejoice in the fact that the framers of the Treaties weighed up interests, set out objectives, proclaimed principles, called for the de-compartmentalization of policies, and framed in broad terms the scope for intervention in order to protect the environment. Furthermore, the role played by the EU Courts is also to be welcomed. The Court of Justice has shown particular sensitivity towards the Member States' obligation to comply with the objectives set out in the directives and regulations. In addition, Member States are frequently sanctioned, with reference to the theory of *effet utile* which is so dear to the Court, on the ground that they have exceeded their margin of appreciation. Basing its reasoning on environmental principles, the Court also adopts a predominately proactive approach when interpreting certain directives and regulations.

However, there is a question whether secondary law lives up to the ambitions asserted in the Treaties. There is no doubt that the devil lies in the regulatory detail or, rather, the regulatory mess. The structure put in place by the institutions is so elaborate and incomplete that it is easy to become lost in the confusion. Levels of protection are constantly changing, because the objective is certainly not to eliminate all risks, but instead to ensure that damage remains within limits which are deemed acceptable, having regard to the capacity for absorption and dilution and resilience of ecosystems. Moreover, subsidiarity, proportionality, regional differentiation, lack of resources, and the weakness of enforcement also act as brakes on any endeavours to implement an ambitious policy.

The protection regimes will continue to be ineffective for as long as they remain within the confines of specific environmental protection sectors. In accordance with the integration clause, de-compartmentalization is required. Indeed, policies which have focused on production targets for more than five decades will gradually have to pay heed to environmental concerns. Nevertheless, the path ahead which must be followed in order to reconcile economic development with the conservation of natural resources, under the aegis of the concept of sustainable development, remains littered with pitfalls.

Environmental law and economic law often appear to clash. As was seen in Parts II and III, whether they are adopted by the Union or by the Member States, environmental measures must ensure that the economic freedoms enshrined in primary law are not breached. Nevertheless, the EU has become much more than an integrated economic area: due to the rebalancing of the objectives pursued by the Treaties, it must be acknowledged that economic law does not override environmental law.

Reconciliation is therefore the order of the day. For instance, environmental measures may benefit from requirements relating to the internal market, without thereby being exclusively subject to market imperatives. In effect, the preference is to harmonize 28 different legal systems with a view to guaranteeing the free movement of goods and services. If the mandatory requirements of primary law are correctly applied by the EU lawmaker, the global level of environmental protection should be reinforced as a result. To name another example, competition law, which is more heavily focused on consumer protection, should favour the opening up of new markets and technological innovations which are less of a drain on energy and natural resources. The law on State aids should be used to abolish financial aid to economic activities which are harmful to the environment and, conversely, to encourage companies to innovate in this area.

Considering the severity of the ecological crisis, the economic model implemented by the European Union will certainly have to evolve, not so much in terms of unlimited growth, but rather in qualitative terms. Technological innovation will play an essential role in this regard. There is no doubt—and scientists are in full agreement on this point—that our model of consumption cannot be generalized at the end of this century to eleven million people, unless the regenerative capacity of our ecosystems can be increased tenfold, which is of course impossible. Lawyers cannot ignore this fact.

Selective Bibliography

1. EU LAW: GENERAL WORKS

Berlin, D., *Commentaire J. Mégret. Politique fiscale* (Brussels: ULB, 2012).

Blumann, C. (ed.), *Commentaire J. Mégret. Politique agricole commune et politique de la pêche* (Brussels: ULB, 2011).

Chalmers, D., Davies, G., and Monti, G., *European Union Law* (Cambridge: CUP, 2010).

Craig, P. and de Búrca, G., *EU Law: Text, Cases, and Materials*, 3rd edn (Oxford: OUP, 2003).

Hilson, C., 'Rights and Principles in EU Law: A Distinction without Foundation' (2008) 15 *MJ* 193.

Kapteyn, P. and Verloren Van Themaat, P., *Introduction to the Law of the European Communities*, 3rd edn (The Hague: Kluwer, 1998).

Léger, Ph. (ed.), *Commentaire article par article des Traités UE et CE* (Geneva: Helbing & Lictenhahn, 2000).

Louis, J.-V. and Ronse, T., *L'ordre juridique de l'UE* (Brussels: Helbing/Bruylant/LGDJ, 2005).

Macleod, I., Hendry, D., and Hyett, St., *The External Relations of the European Communities* (Oxford: OUP, 1996).

Mögele, R. and Erlbacher, F. (eds), *Single Common Market Organisation—Article-by-Article Commentary of the Legal Framework for Agricultural Markets in the EU* (Munich/Oxford/Baden-Baden: C. H. Beck/Hart Publishing/Nomos, 2011).

Nicolaides, P. and Geilmann, M., 'What is Effective Implementation of EU Law?' (2012) 19:3 *MJ* 383.

Pescatore, P., *The Law of Integration* (Leiden: Stijhol, 1974).ˈ

Poiares Maduro, M., *We, the Court: The European Court of Justice and the European Economic Constitution* (Oxford: Hart Publishing, 1997).

2. EU INSTITUTIONAL LAW (PART I)

2.1 General works

Andenas, M. and Türk, A. (eds), *Delegated Legislation and the Role of Committees in the European EU* (The Hague: Kluwer Law, 2000).

Barents, R., 'The Internal Market Unlimited: Some Observations on the Legal Basis of EU Legislation' (1993) 30 *CML Rev* 85.

Bast, J., 'New Categories of Acts after the Lisbon Reform: Dynamics of Parliamentarization in EU Law' (2012) 19 *CML Rev* 913.

Bergström, C. F., *Comitology* (Oxford: OUP, 2005).

Blumann, C., 'Un nouveau départ pour la Comitologie' (2011) 1 *CDE* 38.

Bradley, K. St C., 'The European Court and the Legal Basis of Community Legislation' (1998) 13:6 *EL Rev* 379.

Chalmers, D. and Tomkins, A., *EU Public Law* (Cambridge: CUP, 2007).

Chamon, M., 'EU Agencies between *Meroni* and *Romano* or the Devil and the Deep Blue Sea' (2011) 48:4 *CML Rev* 1055.

Christiansen, T. and Kirchner, E. (eds), *Committee Governance in the EU* (Manchester: Manchester University Press, 2000).

Close, E., 'Harmonization of Laws. Use or Abuse of Power under the EEC Treaty' (1978) 6 *EL Rev* 461.

Craig, P., *The Lisbon Treaty* (Oxford: OUP, 2010).

Craig, P., 'Delegated Acts, Implementing Acts and the New Comitology Regulation' (2011) 5 *EL Rev* 671.

Cremona, M., 'Balancing Union and Member State Interests: Opinion 1/2008, Choice of Legal Base and the Common Commercial Policy under the Treaty of Lisbon' (2010) 35 *EL Rev* 686.

Cullen, H. and Charlesworth, H., 'Diplomacy by Other Means: The Use of Legal Basis Litigation as a Political Strategy by the European Parliament and Member States' (1999) 36 *CML Rev* 1243.

De Búrca, G., 'The Principle of Proportionality and its Application in EC Law' (1993) 13 *YbEL* 105.

de Sadeleer, N. and Hachez, I., 'Hiérarchie et typologie des actes juridiques de l'UE' in N. de Sadeleer et al. (eds), *Les innovations du traité de Lisbonne* (Brussels: Bruylant, 2011) 45.

Dougan, M., 'The Treaty of Lisbon 2007: Winning Minds, Not Hearts' (2008) 45 *CML Rev* 659.

Emiliou, N., 'Opening Pandora's Box: The Legal Basis of Community Measures Before the Court of Justice' (1994) 19 *EL Rev* 488.

Estrella, A., *The EU Principle of Subsidiarity and Its Critique* (Oxford: OUP, 2002).

Franklin, C., 'The Burgeoning Principle of Consistency in EU Law' (2011) 30:1 *YEL* 66.

Frassoni, P., 'Is the Commission Still the Guardian of the Treaties?' (2009–10) 1 *RAE-LEA* 45.

Héritier, A. et al., *Ringing the Changes in Europe: Regulatory Competition and Transformation of the State* (Berlin/New York: de Gruyter, 1996).

Jacobs, F. G., 'Recent Developments in the Principle of Proportionality in EC Law' in E. Ellis (ed.), *The Principle of Proportionality in the Laws of Europe* (Oxford: Hart Publishing, 1999).

Joerges, C. and Vos, E., *EU Committees* (Oxford: Hart Publishing, 1999).

Kohler, C. and Engel, J.-C., 'Le choix approprié de la base juridique pour la législation communautaire: enjeux constitutionnels et principes directeurs' (2007) 1 *Europe* 4.

Labayle, H., 'L'ouverture de la boîte de Pandore. Réflexions sur la compétence de la Communauté en matière pénale' (2006) 3–4 *CDE* 379.

Maubernard, C., 'L'intensité modulable des compétences externes de la CE et de ses Etats membres' (2003) 39:2 *RTDE* 230.

Peers, S., 'The European Community's Criminal Competence: The Plot Thickens' (2008) 33 *EL Rev* 399.

Pescatore, P., 'Some Critical Remarks on the European Single Act' (1987) 24 *CML Rev* 9.

Peter, B., 'La base juridique des actes en droit CEE' (1994) 378 *RMC* 324.

Pichoustre, D., 'La compétence pénale de la Communauté' (2006) 12 *JTDE* 15.

Roller, G., 'Komitologie und Demokratieprinzip', *Kritische Viertelhahresschrift für Gesetzgebung und Rechtswissenschaft* 3 (2003) 249.

Rosas, A., 'The European Court of Justice and Public International Law' in J. Wouters, A. Nollkaemper, and E. de Wet (eds), *The Europeanisation of International Law* (The Hague: Asser Press, 2008) 71.

Senden, L., *Soft Law in EC Law* (Oxford: Hart Publishing, 2004).

Van Gerven, W., 'Principe de proportionnalité, abus de droit et droits fondamentaux' (1992) *JT* 306.

Van Gerven, W., 'The Effect of Proportionality on the Actions of Member States of the European Community: National Viewpoints from Continental Europe' in E. Ellis (ed.), *The Principle of Proportionality in the Laws of Europe* (Oxford: Hart Publishing, 1999) 38.

van Ooik, R., 'The European Court of Justice and the Division of Competence in the EU' in D. Obradovic and N. Lavranos (eds), *Interface Between EU Law and National Law* (Groeningen: Europa Law, 2007) 13.

2.2 Institutional dimension of EU environmental policy

Alemano, A. and Mahieu, S., 'The EFSA before the European Courts' (2008) 5 *EFFLR* 325.

Bouckaert, J., 'Artikel 130 S EEG als juridische basis voor afvalrichtlijn' (1993) 4 *TMR* 226.

Brinkhorst, L., 'Subsidiarity and European Community Environmental Policy. A Pandora's Box' (1991) 2 *EL Rev* 20.

de Sadeleer, N., 'Legal Basis of EC Environmental Legislation' (1993) 2 *JEL* 291.

de Sadeleer, N., 'Environmental Governance and the Legal Bases Conundrum' (2012) 31:1 *YEL* 1.

de Sadeleer, N., 'Particularités de la subsidiarité dans le domaine de l'environnement' (2012) 80 *D & S* 73.

de Sadeleer, N., 'Principle of Subsidiarity and the EU Environmental Policy' (2012) 9:1 *JEEPL* 63.

Demmke, C., 'Comitology in the Envrionmental Sector' in M. Andenas and A. Türk (eds), *Delegated Legislation and the Role of the Committees in the EC* (London: Kluwer, 2000).

Fajardo del Castillo, T., *La politica exterior de la Union Europea en materia de medio ambiente* (Madrid: Tecnos, 2005).

Fajardo del Castillo, T., 'Revisiting the External Dimension of the Environmental Policy of the EU: Some Challenges Ahead' (2010) 4:4 *JEEPL* 365.

Fisher, E., *Risk Regulation and Administrative Constitutionalism* (Oxford: Hart Publishing, 2007).

Geradin, D., 'The Legal Basis of the Waste Directive' (1993) 5 *EL Rev* 418.

Granvik, L., 'Incomplete Mixed Environmental Agreements of the EU and the Principle of Bindingness' in M. Koskenniemi (ed.), *International Law Aspects of the EU* (The Hague: Kluwer Law, 1998) 255.

Grimmeaud, D., 'The Integration of Environmental Concerns into EC Policies: A Genuine Policy Development?' (2000) *EELR* 207.

Haagsma, A., 'De milieuheffing in Europees-rechtelijk perspectief' (1980) *SEW* 512.

Haumont, F., *Droit européen de l'aménagement du territoire et de l'urbanisme* (Brussels: Bruylant, 2007).

Jans, J. H., 'Minimum Harmonization and the Role of the Principle of Proportionality' in M. Führ, R. Wahl, and P. von Wilmowsky (eds), *Umweltrecht und Uwmeltwissenschaft. Festschrift für E. Rehbinder* (Berlin: Erich Schmidt Verlag, 2007).

Krämer, L., 'Article 100A or 130S as a Legal Basis for Community Measures: Case C-300/89— *Titanium Dioxide*', *European Environmental Law Casebook* (London: Sweet & Maxwell, 1993) 21.

Krämer, L., 'The Environmental Complaint in EU Law' (2009) 6:1 *JEELP* 13.

Kulovesi, K., Morgera, E., and Munoz, M., 'Environmental Integration and Multi-Faceted International Dimensions of EU Law: Unpacking the EU's Climate and Energy Package' (2011) 48 *CML Rev* 829.

Lafferty, W. and Hovden, E., 'Environmental Policy Integration: Towards an Analytical Framework' (2003) 3 *Environmental Politics* 1.

Lee, M., 'The Environmental Implications of the Lisbon Treaty' (2008) 22:2 *Env L Rev* 131.

Lohse, E. J., 'Surprise? Surprise!—Case C-115/09 (*Kohlekraftwerk Lünen*)—A Victory for the Environment and a Loss for Procedural Autonomy of the Member States' (2012) 18:2 *EPL* 249–68.

Pagh, P., 'The Battle on Environmental Policy Competences. Challenging the Stricter Approach: Stricter Might Lead to Weaker Protection' in R. Macrory (ed.), *Reflections on 30 Years of EU Environmental Law* (Groeningen: Europa Law, 2006) 10.

Robinson, J., 'The Legal Basis of EC Environmental Law' (1992) 4:1 *JEL* 109.

Vedder, H., 'The Treaty of Lisbon and European Environmental Law and Policy' (2010) 22:2 *JEL* 285.

Wennerås, P., *The Enforcement of EC Environmental Law* (Oxford: OUP, 2007).

Wennerås, P., 'Towards an Ever Greener Union? Competence in the Field of the Environment and Beyond' (2008) 45 *CML Rev* 1674.

Wessmaier, M., 'The Integration of Environmental Protection as General Rule for Interpretating Law' (2001) 38 *CML Rev* 159.

Williams, R., 'The European Commission and the Enforcement of Environmental Law: An Invidious Position' (1994) 14 *YEL* 351.

2.3 External dimension of EU environmental policy

Bail, C., Falkner, R., and Marquard, H. (eds), *The Cartagena Protocol on Biosafety* (London: Royal Institute of International Affairs, 2002).

Birnie, P., Boyle, A., and Redgwell, C., *International Law and the Environment*, 3rd edn (Oxford: OUP, 2009).

Bonsi, R., Hammett, A. L., and Smith, B., 'Eco-Labels and International Trade: Problems and Solutions' (2008) 42: 3 *JWT* 407.

Bouwman, M., Davies, P., and Redgwell, C., *Lyster's International Wildlife Law*, 2nd edn (Cambridge: CUP, 2010).

Cardwell, P. J. and French, D., 'Who Decides? The European Court of Justice's Judgment on Jurisdiction in the MOX Plant Dispute' (2007) 19:1 *JEL* 125.

d'Agent, P., 'De la fragmentation à la cohésion systémique: la sentence arbitrale du 24 mai 2005 relative au "Rhin de fer"' in *Droit du pouvoir, Pouvoir du droit. Mélanges J. Salmon* (Brussels: Bruylant, 2007) 113.

de Sadeleer, N. and Born, C.-H., *Droit international et communautaire de la biodiversité* (Paris: Dalloz, 2004).

Dopagne, F., 'Arrêt "Intertanko": l'appréciation de la validité d'un acte communautaire au regard de conventions internationales' (2008) 152 *JDE* 241.

Gonzalez Gimenez, J., 'Régimen Comunitario de la contaminación por descargas procedentes de buques: la relación con las normas internacionales y la sentencia del TJCE sobre el asunto Interkanko' (2009) 34:13 *RDCE* 915.

Loibl, G., 'The Role of the European Union in the Formation of International Environmental Law' (2002) 2 *YbEEL* 223.

Marin-Duran, G. and Morgera, E., *Environmental Integration in the EU's External Relations* (Oxford: Hart Publishing, 2012).

Okowa, P., 'The EC and International Environmental Agreements' (1995) 15 *YEL* 169.

Pallemaerts, M., *Toxics and Transnational Law* (Oxford: Hart Publishing, 2003).

3. EU ENVIRONMENTAL LAW (PART I)

3.1 General works

Bandi, G. (ed.), *The Environmental Jurisprudence of the European Court of Justice* (Budapest: Szent Istvan Tarsulat, 2008).

Biondi, A. et al. (eds), *Scientific Evidence in the European Environmental Rule-Making* (The Hague: Kluwer Law, 2003).

Bogdan, M., 'The Treatment of Environmental Damage in Rome II' in J. Ahern and W. Binchy (eds), *The Rome II Regulation on the Law Applicable to Non-Contractual Obligations* (Leiden/Boston: Martinus Nijhoff, 2009) 219.

Bradley, K. St C. and Moore, M., 'Case Law of the European Court of Justice' (2003) 3 *YbEEL* 527.

Chalmers, D., 'Inhabitants in the Field of EC Environmental Law' in P. Craig and G. de Búrca (eds), *The Evolution of EU Law* (Oxford: OUP, 1999).

Davies, P., *EU Environmental Law* (Farnham: Ashgate, 2006).

de Sadeleer, N. and Poncelet, C., 'Protection Against Acts Harmful to Human Health and the Environment Adopted by the EU Institutions' (2012) 14 *CYELS* 177.

de Sadeleer, N., Roller, G., and Dross, M., *Access to Justice in Environmental Matters and the Role of NGOs* (Groeningen: Europa Law, 2005).

Douma, W. (ed.), *European Environmental Case Law* (The Hague: Asser Instituut, 2002).

Epiney, A., *Umweltrecht in der Europäischen Union* (Cologne: Heymanns, 1997).

García Ureta, A., *Derecho Europeo de la Biodiversidad* (Madrid: Gomez-Acebo & Pombo, 2010).

Grabitz, E. and Sasse, C., *Umweltkompetenz der Europäischen Gemeinschaften* (Berlin: E. Schmidt, 1977).

Guinchard, E. and Lamont-Black, S., 'Environmental Law—The Black Sheep in Rome II's Drive for Legal Certainty?' (2009) 11 *Env L Rev* 161.

Hedemann-Robinson, M., *Enforcement of EU Environmental Law* (London: Routledge-Cavendish, 2007).

Hedemann-Robinson, M., 'The EU and Environmental Crime' (2008) 20 *JEL* 279.

Hilson, C., *Regulating Pollution: A UK and EC Perspective* (Oxford: Hart Publishing, 2000).

Holder, J. and Lee, M., *Environmental Protection Law and Policy*, 2nd edn (Cambridge: CUP, 2009).

Jack, B., *Agriculture and EU Environmental Law* (Farnham: Ashgate, 2009).

Jacobs, F., 'The Role of the European Court of Justice' (2006) 18:2 *JEL* 185.

Jans J. H., 'Gold Plating of European Environmental Measures?' (2009) 6:4 *JEEPL* 417.

Jans, J. H. and Vedder, H., *European Environmental Law*, 4th edn (Groeningen: Europa Law, 2012).

Krämer, L., *European Environmental Law. Casebook* (The Hague: Kluwer, 1993).

Krämer, L., *Casebook on EU Environmental Law* (Oxford: Hart Publishing, 2002).

Krämer, L., '30 Years of EC Environmental Law: Perspectives and Prospectives' (2002) 2 *YBEEL* 163.

Krämer, L., 'Statistics on Environmental Judgments by the EC Court of Justice' (2006) 18:3 *JEL* 407.

Krämer, L., *EC Environmental Law*, 6th edn (London: Sweet & Maxwell, 2007).

Krämer, L., 'Sustainable Development in EC Law' in H.-C. Bugge and C. Voigt (eds), *Sustainable Development in International and National Law* (Groeningen: Europa Law, 2008).

Lee, M., *EU Environmental Law. Challenges, Change and Decision Making* (Oxford: Hart Publishing, 2005).

Lister, C., *EU Environmental Law* (Chichester: Wiley, 1997).

Louka, E., *Conflicting Integration. The Environmental Law of the EU* (Antwerp: Intersentia, 2004).

MacLeod, M. et al. (eds), *Understanding the Costs of Environmental Regulation in Europe* (Cheltenham: Edward Elgar, 2009).

Macrory, R., *Regulation, Enforcement and Governance in Environmental Law* (Oxford: Hart Publishing, 2010).

Markus, T., *European Fisheries Law. From Promotion to Management* (Groeningen: Europa Law, 2009).

Misonne, D., *Droit européen de l'environnement et de la santé: l'ambition d'un niveau élevé de protection* (Louvain: Anthémis, 2010).

Moreno Molina, A. M., *Derecho comunitario del medio ambiente* (Madrid/Barcelona: Marcial Pons, 2006).

Noiville, C. and de Sadeleer, N., 'La gestion des risques écologiques et sanitaires à l'épreuve des chiffres. Le droit entre enjeux scientifiques et politiques' (2001) 2 *RDUE* 389.

Pagh, P., *EU Miljøret* (Copenhagen: C. Ejler, 1996).

Pallemaerts, M. et al., *Drowning in Process? The Implementation of the EU 6th Environmental Action Programme* (London: Institute for European Environmental Policy, 2006).

Plaza Martin, V., *Derecho ambiental de la Unión europea* (Valencia: Tirant Lo Blanch, 2006).

Scott, J., *EU Environmental Law* (London: Longman, 2001).

Scott, J. (ed.), *Environmental Protection. European Law and Governance* (Oxford: OUP, 2009).

Sevenster, H., 'The Environmental Guarantee after Amsterdam: Does the Emperor Have New Clothes?' (2000) I *YEEL* 291.

Thieffry, P., *Droit de l'environnement de l'UE*, 2nd edn (Brussels: Bruylant, 2011).

Van Calster, G., *Handbook of EU Waste Law* (Richmond: Richmond Law & Tax, 2006).

Vedder, H., 'The Treaty of Lisbon and European Environmental Law and Policy' (2010) 22:2 *JEL* 289.

Verheyen, R., 'The Environmental Guarantee in European Law and the New Article 95 EC Treaty in Practice—A Critique' (2000) 1 *RECIEL* 180.

Vial, C., 'Une nouvelle intensité dans la prise en compte des exigences de la protection de l'environnement' (2003–04) 4 *RAE-LEA* 617.

von Homeyer, I., 'The Evolution of EU Environmental Governance' in J. Scott (ed.), *Environmental Protection: European Law and Governance* (Oxford: OUP, 2009).

Wakefield, J., 'Fisheries: A Failure of Values' (2009) 46 *CML Rev* 439.

Weale, A. et al., *Environmental Governance in Europe* (Oxford: OUP, 2000).

Wenerås, P., 'A New Dawn for Commission Enforcement under Articles 226 and 228 EC' (2006) 43 *CML Rev* 31.

Winter, G. (ed.), *European Environmental Law* (Aldershot: Dartmouth, 1995).

Winter, G., 'Constitutionalizing Environmental Protection in the EU' (2002) 2 *YBEEL* 76.

3.2 Environmental principles

Alemanno, A., 'Le principe de précaution en droit communautaire' (2001) 4 *RDUE* 917.

Alexis, A., 'Protection de l'environnement: la mise en application du principe du pollueur-payeur' (2003–04) 4 *RAE-LEA* 629.

Bugge, H. C., *Forurensnings-Ansvaret* (Oslo: Aschehoug, 1999).

Cheyne, I., 'Taming the Precautionary Principle in EC Law: Lessons from Waste and GMO Regulation' (2007) 4:6 *JEEPL* 468.

Christoforou, T., 'Science, Law and Precaution in Dispute Resolution on Health and Environmental Protection: What Role for Scientific Experts?' in *Le commerce international des OGM* (Paris: Documentation française, 2002) 213.

Cooney, R. and Dickson, B. (eds), *Biodiversity & the Precautionary Principle* (London: Earthscan, 2005).

Corcelle, G., 'La perspective communautaire du principe de précaution' (2001) 450 *RMC* 447.

D'Hondt, N., 'Environmental Law Principles and the Case Law of the Court of Justice' in M. Sheridan and L. Lavrysen (eds), *Environmental Law Principles* (Brussels: Bruylant, 2000) 141.

D'Hondt, N., *Integration of Environmental Protection into other European EU Policies. Legal Theory and Practice* (Groeningen: Europa Law, 2003).

de Sadeleer, N., 'Le statut juridique du principe de précaution en droit communautaire: du slogan à la règle' (2001) 1 *CDE* 79.

de Sadeleer, N., *Environmental Principles* (Oxford: OUP, 2002).

de Sadeleer, N., 'Polluter Pays, Precautionary Principles and Liability' in G. Betlem and E. Brans (eds), *Environmental Liability in the EU* (Cambridge: Cameron & May, 2006) 89.

de Sadeleer, N., 'The Precautionary Principle in EC Health and Environmental Law' (2006) 12 *ELJ* 139.

de Sadeleer, N., *Implementing the Precautionary Principle: Approaches from the Nordic Countries, the EU and USA* (London: Earthscan, 2007).

de Sadeleer, N., 'The Precautionary Principle as a Device for Greater Environmental Protection: Lessons from EC Courts' (2008) 18:1 *RECIEL* 3.

de Sadeleer, N., 'The Precautionary Principle Applied to Food Safety' (2009) 1 *EJCL* 147.

de Sadeleer, N., 'The Precautionary Principle in EU Law' (2010) 5 *Aansprakelijkheid Verzekering en Schade* 173.

de Sadeleer, N., 'The Polluter-Pays Principle in EU Law. Bold Case Law and Poor Harmonisation' in *Pro Natura. Festskrift til H.-C. Bugge* (Oslo: Universitetsforlaget, 2012) 405.

de Sadeleer, N., 'The Principle of a High Level of Environmental Protection in EU Law' in C. Zetterberg and L. Gipperth (eds), *Festskrift G. Michanek and J. Darpö* (Uppsala: Iustus, 2013).

Doherty, M., 'Hard Cases and Environmental Principles: An Aid to Interpretation?' (2002) 3 *YBEEL* 157.

Doherty, M., 'The Judicial Use of the Principles of EC Environmental Policy' (2002) 2 *Env L Rev* 251.

Douma, W. T., 'The Precautionary Principle. Its Application in International, European and Dutch Law', PhD, Groeningen, 2002.

Doyle, A. and Carney, T., 'Precaution and Prevention: Giving Effect to Article 130r Without Direct Effect' (1999) 8 *EEELR* 44.

Epiney, A., 'Environmental Principles' in R. Macrory (ed.), *Reflections on 30 Years of EU Environmental Law* (Groeningen: Europa Law, 2006) 21.

Hervé-Fournereau, N., 'Le principe d'intégration des exigences de la protection de l'environnement: essai de clarification juridique' in *Liber amicorum Jean RAUX, Le droit de l'Union européenne en principes* (Rennes: Apogée, 2006) 661.

Jans, J., 'Stop the Integration Principle' (2010) 33:5 *Fordham Intl LJ* 1547.

Macrory, R. (ed.), *Principles of European Environmental Law* (Groeningen: Europa Law, 2004).

Scotford, E., 'Mapping the Article 174(2) EC Case Law: A First Step to Analysing Community Environmental Law Principles' (2008) 8 *YBEEL* 20.

Szajkowska, A., 'The Impact of the Definition of the Precautionary Principle in EU Food Law' (2010) 47 *CML Rev* 173.

Vaqué, G., 'El principio de precaución en la jurisprudencia del TJCE: la sentecia "Greenpeace France"' (2001) 2 *Comunidad Europea Aranzadi* 33.

Weimer, M., 'Applying Precaution in EU Authorisation of Genetically Modified Products- Challenges and Suggestions for Reform' (2010) 16:5 *ELJ* 624.

Winter, G., 'The Legal Nature of Environmental Principles in International, EC and German Law' in R. Macrory (ed.), *Principles of European Environmental Law* (Groeningen: Europa Law, 2004) 399.

Winter, G., 'A Fundament and Two Pillars' in H.-C. Bugge and C. Voigt (eds), *Sustainable Development in International and National Law* (Groeningen: Europa Law, 2008) 25.

Zander, J., *Different Kinds of Precaution* (Cambridge: CUP, 2010).

3.3 Environmental secondary law

Beijen, B., 'The Implementation of European Environmental Directives: Are Problems Caused by the Quality of the Directives?' (2011) 20 *EEELR* 150.

Casotta, S. and Verdure, C., 'Recent Developments Regarding the EU Environmental Liability for Enterprises: Lessons Learned from Italy's Implementation of the "Raffinerie Mediterranée" Cases' (2012) 21 *EEELR* 156.

Christoforou, T., 'The Regulation of GMOs in the EU: The Interplay of Science, Law and Politics' (2004) 41 *CML Rev* 703.

de Sadeleer, N., *Le droit communautaire et les déchets* (Brussels/Paris: Bruylant/LGDJ, 1995).

de Sadeleer, N., 'EC Waste Law or How to Juggle with Legal Concepts. Drawing the Line between Waste, Residues, Secondary Materials, By-Products, Disposal and Recovery Operations' (2005) 2:6 *JEEPL* 46.

de Sadeleer, N., 'Habitats Conservation in EC Law: From Nature Sanctuaries to Ecological Networks' (2005) 5 *YbEEL* 215.

de Sadeleer, N., 'La directive 2004/35/CE relative à la responsabilité environnementale: avancée ou recul pour le droit de l'environnement des Etats membres?' in B. Dubuisson and G. Viney (eds), *Les responsabilités environnementales* (Brussels/Paris: Bruylant/LGDJ, 2005) 732.

de Sadeleer, N., 'Waste, Products and By-Products' (2005) 1:4 *JEEPL* 46.

de Sadeleer, N. and Poncelet, C., 'Protection Against Acts Harmful to Human Health and the Environment Adopted by the EU Institutions' (2012) 14 *CYELS* 177.

de Sépibus, J., 'Scarcity and Allocation of Allowances in the EU Emissions Trading Scheme—A Legal Analysis', NCCR Trade Working Paper 2007/32, 36.

Garcia Ureta, G., 'Habitats and Environmental Assessment of Plans and Projects' (2007) 2 *JEEPL* 84.

Holder, J., 'A Dead End for Direct Effect? Prospects for Enforcement of EC Environmental Law by Individuals' (1996) 8:2 *JEL* 313.

Howarth, W., 'Aspirations and Realities under the Water Framework Directive: Proceduralisation, Participation, and Practicalities' (2009) 21:3 *JEL* 391.

Koutalakis, C., Buzogany, A., and Börzel, T., 'When Soft Regulation is Not Enough: The Integrated Pollution Prevention and Control Directive of the EU' (2010) 4 *Regulation & Governance* 329.

Krämer, L., 'The Implementation of EC Environmental Directives within Member States: Some Implications of the Direct Effect Doctrine' (1991) 3:1 *JEL* 39.

Krämer, L., 'The European Commission's Opinions under Article 6(4) of the Habitats Directive' (2009) 21:1 *JEL* 70.

Lee, M., *EU Regulation of GMOs* (Cheltenham: Edward Elgar, 2008).

Macrory, R., 'Integrated Prevention and Pollution Control: The UK Experience' in C. Backes and G. Betlem (eds), *Integrated Prevention and Pollution Control—The EC Directive from a Comparative Legal and Economic Perspective* (The Hague: Kluwer Law, 1998).

Poncelet, C., 'The Emission Trading Scheme Directive: Analysis of Some Contentious Points' (2011) 20 *EEELR* 245.

Rhebinder, E., 'Environmental Agreements. A New Instrument of Environmental Policy', European University Institute, Jean Monnet Chair Paper RSC No 97/45, 1997.

Schnabl, G., 'The Evolution of Environmental Agreements at the Level of the EU' in E. Croci (ed.), *The Handbook of Environmental Voluntary Agreements* (Vienna: Springer, 2005) 104.

Thieffry, P., 'Les politiques européennes de l'énergie et de l'environnement: rivales ou alliées?' (2009–10) 4 *RAE-LEA* 783.

Toshkov, D., 'Embracing European Law: Compliance with EU Directives in Central and Eastern Europe' (2008) 9:3 *European Union Politics* 372.

Weimer, M., 'The Right to Adopt Post-Market Restrictions of GM Crops in the EU' (2012) 3 *EJRR* 447.

4. FREE MOVEMENT OF GOODS AND SERVICES (PART II)

4.1 General works

Albin, S. and Bär, S., 'Nationale Alleingänge nach Amsterdam—Der neue Art. 95 EGV: Fortschritt oder Rückschritt für den Umweltschutz?' (1999) 21:4 *Natur und Recht* 185.

Barnard, C., 'Fitting the Remaining Pieces into the Goods and Persons Jigsaw?' (2001) 26 *EL Rev* 35.

Barnard, C., 'Unraveling the Services Directive' (2008) 45 *CML Rev* 323.

Barnard, C., 'Trailing a New Approach to Free Movement of Goods?' (2009) 68 *CLJ* 288.

Barnard, C., *The Substantive Law of the EU*, 3rd edn (Oxford: OUP, 2010).

Barnard, C., 'What the Keck? Balancing the Needs of the Single Market with State Regulatory Autonomy in the EU and the US' (2012) 2 *EJCL-REDC* 201.

Bernard, N., 'On the Art of Not Mixing One's Drinks: *Dassonville* and *Cassis de Dijon* Revisited' in M. Poiares Maduro and L. Azoulai (eds), *The Past and Future of EU Law: The Classics of EU Law Revisited on the 50th Anniversary of the Treaty of Rome* (Oxford: Hart Publishing, 2010) 460.

Craig, P., 'The Evolution of the Single Market' in C. Barnard and J. Scott (eds), *The Law of the Single European Market* (Oxford: Hart Publishing, 2002).

D'Acunto, S., 'Directive service: radiographie juridique en dix points' (2007) 2 *RDUE* 303.

Davies, G., 'The Court's Jurisprudence on Free Movement of Goods' (2012) 2 *EJCL-REDC* 364.

Dawes, A., 'Importing and Exporting Poor Reasoning: Worrying Trends in Relation to the Case Law on the Free Movement of Goods' (2007) 8:8 *German LJ* 769.

Dawes, A., 'A Freedom Reborn? The New Yet Unclear Scope of Article 29 EC' (2009) 34 *EL Rev* 639.

de Sadeleer, N., 'Les dérogations nationales à l'harmonisation du marché intérieur' (2013) 2 *RDUE* 233–66.

de Sadeleer, N., 'Procedures for Derogations from the Principle of Approximation of Laws under Article 95 of the EC Treaty' (2003) 40 *CML Rev* 889.

de Sadeleer, N., 'L'examen, au regard de l'article 28 CE, des règles nationales régissant les modalités d'utilisation de certains produits' (2009) 162 *JDE* 247.

de Sadeleer, N., 'Restrictions of the Sale of Pharmaceuticals and Medical Devices such as Contact Lenses over the Internet and the Free Movement of Goods' (2011) 19 *Eur J Health L* 1.

de Sadeleer, N., 'Restrictions on the Use of Products' (2012) 2 *EJCL-REDC* 231.

Defalque, L. et al., *Commentaire J. Mégret. Libre circulation des personnes et des capitaux. Rapprochement des législations* (Brussels: ULB, 2007).

Defossez, A., 'Arrêt *Gysbrechts*: le droit de rétractation du consommateur face au droit de l'UE' (2009) 2 *REDC* 549.

Defossez, A., 'L'histoire d'une divergence et d'une possible réconciliation: l'article 29 TCE' (2009) 1 *CDE* 409.

Doherty, M. G., 'The Application of Article 95(4)–95(6) of the EC Treaty: Is the Emperor Still Unclothed' (2008) 8 *YbEEL* 48.

Dougan, M., 'Minimum Harmonization and the Internal Market' (2000) 37 *CML Rev* 855.

Egan, M., *Constructing a European Market* (Oxford: OUP, 2001).

Ehlermann, C. D., 'The Internal Market following the SEA' (1987) 24 *CML Rev* 398.

Engsig Sørensen, K., 'Reconciling Secondary Legislation and the Treaty Rights of Free Movement' (2011) 36 *EL Rev* 339.

Fallon, M. and Gerard, D., 'Trailing the Trailers in Search of a Typology of Barriers' (2012) 2 *EJCL-REDC* 249.

Fallon, M. and Simon, A. C., 'La directive "Services": quelle contribution au marché intérieur?' (2007) 136 *JTDE* 34.

Fromont, A. and Verdure, C., 'La consécration du critère de l'acccès au marché en matière de libre circulation des marchandises: mythe ou réalité?' (2011) 47 *RTDE* 716.

Glaesner, E., 'L'article 100A: un nouvel instrument pour la réalisation du marché commun' (1989) 25 *CDE* 622.

Gormley, L., 'Two Years after *Keck*' (1996) 19 *Fordham Intl LJ* 866.

Gormley, L., 'The Genesis of the Rule of Reason in the Free Movement of Goods' in A. Schrauwen (ed.), *Rule of Reason* (Groeningen: Europa Law, 2005).

Gormley, L., *EU Law of Free Movement of Goods and Customs Union* (Oxford: OUP, 2009).

Hatzopoulos, V., 'Que reste-t-il de la directive sur les services?' (2007) 3–4 *CDE* 320.

Hojnik, J., 'Free Movement of Goods in a Labyrinth: Can *Buy Irish* Survive the Crises' (2012) 49 *CML Rev* 303.

Kovar, R., '*Dassonville, Keck* et les autres: de la mesure avant toute chose' (2006) 2 *RTDE* 213.

Kovar, R., 'Le législateur communautaire encadre le régime de la mise des produits dans le marché intérieur' (2009) 44:2 *RTDE* 289.

Langeheine, B., 'Le rapprochement des législations nationales selon l'article 100A du traité C.E.E.: l'harmonisation communautaire face aux exigences de protection nationale' (1989) 328 *RMC* 357.

Lianos, I., 'Shifting Narratives in the European Internal Market' (2010) 21 *European Business L Rev* 733.

Mathisen, G., 'Consistency and Coherence as Conditions for Justification of Member State Measures Restricting Free Movement' (2010) 47 *CML Rev* 1036.

Mattera, A., *Marché unique*, 2nd edn (Paris: Jupiter, 1992).

Mattera, A., 'De l'arrêt "Dassonville" à l'arrêt "Keck": l'obscure clarté d'une jurisprudence riche en principes novateurs et en contradictions' (1994) 1 *RMUE* 117.

Oliver, P. 'Goods and Services: Two Freedoms Compared' in *Mélanges en l'honneur de M. Waelbroeck* (Brussels: Bruylant, 1999).

Oliver, P., 'Some Further Reflections on the Scope of Articles 28–30 (ex-articles 30–36 CE)' (1999) 36 *CML Rev* 783.

Oliver, P., *Oliver on Free Movement of Goods in the European Union*, 5th edn (Oxford: Hart Publishing, 2010).

Oliver, P., 'Of Trailers and Jet-Skis: Is the Case Law on Article 34 TFEU Hurtling in a New Direction?' (2011) 33 *Fordham Intl LJ* 1423.

Oliver, P. and Enchelmaier, S., 'Free Movement of Goods: Recent Developments in the Case Law' (2007) 44 *CML Rev* 649.

Peglun, K., 'Libre prestation de services dans la directive 2006/123/CE' (2008) 44:1 *RTDE* 100.

Picod, F., 'La nouvelle approche de la Cour de justice en matière d'entraves aux échanges' (1998) 2 *RTDE* 169.

Poiares Maduro, M., '*Keck*: The End? The Beginning of the End? Or Just the End of the Beginning?' (1994) 1 *Irish Journal of European Law* 36.

Poiares Maduro, M., *We, the Court: The European Court of Justice and the European Economic Constitution* (Oxford: Hart Publishing, 1998).

Rigaux, A., 'Définition des mesures d'effet équivalent' (2009) 4 *Europe* 158.

Rigaux, A., 'Restrictions à l'usage des produits' (2009) 4 *Europe* 19.

Rosas, A., 'Life after *Dassonville* and *Cassis*: Evolution but not Revolution' in M. Poiares Maduro and L. Azoulai (eds), *The Past and Future of EU Law: The Classics of EU Law Revisited on the 50th Anniversary of the Treaty of Rome* (Oxford: Hart Publishing, 2010).

Roth, W.-H., 'The European Court of Justice's Case Law on Freedom to Provide Services: Is *Keck* Relevant?' in M. Andenas and W.-H. Roth (eds), *Services and Free Movement in EU Law* (Oxford: OUP, 2004) 14.

Roth, W.-H., 'Exports of Goods and Services within the Single Market: Reflections on the Scope of Articles 29 and 49 EC' in T. Tridimas and P. Nebbia (eds), *European Union Law for the Twenty-First Century: Rethinking the New Legal Order* (Oxford: Hart Publishing, 2006) 1.

Sibony, A.-L., 'Can Market Access be Taken Seriously?' (2012) 2 *EJCL-REDC* 323.

Sibony, A.-L. and Defossez, A., 'Liberté d'établissement et libre prestation de services 2007–2008' (2009) 45:3 *RTDE* 514.

Simon, D., 'Commentaire de l'article 100A' in *Traité instituant la CEE. Commentaire article par article* (Paris: Economica, 1992) 569.

Snell, J., 'Economic Aims as Justification for Restrictions on Free Movement' in A. Schrauwen (ed.), *Rule of Reason* (Groeningen: Europa Law, 2005).

Snell, J., 'The Notion of Market Access: A Concept or Slogan' (2010) 47 *CML Rev* 470.

Snell, J. and Andenas, M., 'How Far? The Internal Market and Restrictions on the Free Movement of Goods and Services' (2000) 3 *Intl & Comp LJ* 376.

Spaventa, E., 'Leaving *Keck* Behind? The Free Movement of Goods After the Ruling in *Commission v. Italy* and *Michelsson and Roos*' (2009) 34 *EL Rev* 914.

Stratemans, G., 'Market Access, The Outer Limits of Free Movement of Goods and . . . the Law?' in M. Bulterman et al. (eds), *Views of European Law from the Mountain. Liber Amicorum P. J. Slot* (Alphen: Wolters Kluwer, 2009) 93.

Szydlo, M., 'Export Restrictions within the Structure of Free Movement of Goods. Reconsideration of an Old Paradigm' (2010) 47 *CML Rev* 735.

Toth, A. G., *The Oxford Encyclopaedia of European Community Law*, vol. II (Oxford: OUP, 2005).

Unperath, H. and Johnston, A., 'The Double-Headed Approach to the ECJ concerning Consumer Protection' (2007) 44 *CML Rev* 1237.

Weatherill, S., 'After *Keck*: Some Thoughts on How to Clarify the Clarification' (1996) 33 *CML Rev* 885.

Weatherill, S., 'Pre-Emption, Harmonization and the Distribution of Competence' in C. Barnard and J. Scott (eds), *The Law of the Single European Market* (Oxford: Hart Publishing, 2002).

Weatherill, S., 'The Road to Ruin: "Restrictions on Use" and the Circular Lifecycle of Article 34 TFEU' (2012) 2 *EJCL-REDC* 359.

4.2 The environmental dimension of the internal market

Arrowsmith, S. and Kunzlik, P. (eds), *Social and Environmental Policies in EC Procurement Law* (Cambridge: CUP, 2009).

de Sadeleer, N., 'Le droit communautaire de l'environnement, un droit sous-tendu par les seuls motifs économiques?' (1991) 4 *Amén-Envt* 217.

de Sadeleer, N., 'L'agrément des collecteurs de déchets au regard des règles de droit communautaire' (1993) 4 *Amén-Envt* 237.

de Sadeleer, N., 'Les limites posées à la libre circulation des déchets par les exigences de protection de l'environnement' (1993) 5:6 *CDE* 672.

de Sadeleer, N., *Commentaire J. Mégret. Environnement et marché intérieur* (Brussels: ULB, 2010).

de Sadeleer, N. and Wemaëre, M., 'Valorisation et élimination des déchets: une distinction à clarifier' (2007) 2 *RDUE* 329.

Farr, S., *Harmonisation of Technical Standards in the EC* (Chichester: Wiley & Sons, 1992).

Gormley, L., 'Free Movement of Goods and the Environment' in J. Holder (ed.), *The Impact of EC Environmental Law in the UK* (Chichester: Wiley & Sons, 1997) 289.

Krämer, L., 'L'environnement et le marché unique européen' (1993) 1 *RMUE* 48.

Misonne, D. and de Sadeleer, N., 'Is There Space in the EU for National Product-Related Measures?' in M. Pallemarets (ed.), *EU and WTO Law: How Tight is the Legal Straitjacket for Environmental Product Regulation?* (Brussels: VUB Press, 2006).

Pernas García, J. J., *Contratación pública verde* (Madrid: La Ley, 2009).

Pernas García, J. J., 'La incidencia de la normative de servicios en el derecho amiental. Técnicas preventivas de protección ambienal y normativa de servicios: particularizado de la evaluación de impacto ambiental y de la ordenación administrativa de la gestión de residuos' (2010) 2 *Revista de Dret Catalana* 1.

Temmink, H., 'From Danish Bottles to Danish Bees: The Dynamics of Free Movement of Goods and Environmental Protection—A Case Law Analysis' (2000) 1 *YEEEL* 61.

True, C., 'The German Drinks Can Deposit: Complete Harmonization or a Trade Barrier Justified by Environmental Protection?' (2005) 2 *JEEPL* 142.

Van Calster, G., 'Court Criticises Restrictions on Free Movement of Waste' (1999) 2 *EL Rev* 178.

Vial, C., *Protection de l'environnement et libre circulation des marchandises* (Brussels: Bruylant, 2006).

Wennerås, P., 'Fog and Acid Rain Drifting from Luxembourg over Art. 95(4)' (2003) 12:6 *EELR* 169.

Ziegler, A. R., *Trade and Environmental Law in the European Community* (Oxford: Clarendon Press, 1996).

4.3 The environmental dimension of EU trade law and international trade law

Geradin, D., *Trade and the Environment. A Comparative Study of EC and US Law* (Cambridge: CUP, 1997).

Notaro, A., *Judicial Approaches to Trade and Environment. The EC and the WTO* (London: Cameron & May, 2003).

Pallemaerts, M. (ed.), *EU and WTO Law: How Tight is the Legal Straitjacket for Environmental Product Regulation?* (Brussels: VUB Press, 2006).

Scott, J., 'On Kith and Kine: Trade and Environment in the EU and WTO' in J. H. H. Weiler (ed.), *The EU the WTO and the NAFTA* (Oxford: OUP, 2000).

Scott, J., 'International Trade and Environmental Governance: Relating Rules and Standards in the EU and the WTO' (2004) 15:2 *EJIL* 307.

Scott, J. and Vos, E., 'The Juridification of Uncertainty: Observations on the Ambivalence of the Precautionary Principle in the EU and the WTO' in Ch. Joerges and R. Dehousse (eds), *Good Governance in Europe's Integrated Market* (Oxford: OUP, 2002) 253.

Stockes, E., 'The Role of Risk Assessment in Precautionary Intervention: A Comparison of Judicial Trends in the EC and WTO' (2007) 4:6 *JEEPL* 461.

Van Calster, G., *International & EU Trade Law. The Environmental Challenge* (London: Cameron & May, 2000).

Vecchione, E., 'Is It Possible to Provide Evidence of Insufficient Evidence? The Precautionary Principle at the WTO' (2012) 13 *Chicago J Intl L* 153.

Walker, S., *Environmental Protection versus Trade Liberalization: Finding the Balance* (Brussels: Saint Louis, 1993).

Wiers, J., *Trade and Environment in the EC and the WTO. A Legal Analysis* (Groeningen: Europa Law, 2002).

5. COMPETITION LAW (PART III)

5.1 General works

Blauberger, M., 'From Negative to Positive Integration? European State Aid Control Through Soft and Hard Law', Discussion Paper 08/4, Max Planck Institute for the Study of Societies, 2008, 6.

Donny, M., 'Les notions de services d'intérêt général et de services d'intérêt économique général' in J.-V. Louis and S. Rodrigues (eds), *Les services d'intérêt économique général et l'Union européenne* (Brussels: Bruylant, 2006) 4.

Donny, M., *Commentaire J. Mégret. Contrôle des aides d'Etat* (Brussels: ULB, 2008).

Faull, J. and Nickpay, A., *The EC Law of Competition*, 2nd edn (Oxford: OUP, 2007).

Idot, L., *Droit communautaire de la concurrence. Le nouveau système de mise en œuvre des articles 81 et 82 CE* (Brussels: Bruylant, 2004).

Idot, L., 'Concurrence et services d'intérêt général. Bref bilan des évolutions postérieures au traité d'Amsterdam' in J.-V. Louis and S. Rodrigues (eds), *Les services d'intérêt économique général et l'Union européenne* (Brussels: Bruylant, 2006) 56.

Idot, L., 'L'intérêt général: limite ou pierre angulaire du droit de la concurrence' (2007) 142 *JTDE* 225.

Joliet, R., 'Réglementations étatiques anticoncurrentielles et droit communautaire?' (1988) 4 *CDE* 370.

Kepenne, J.-P., 'Révolution dans le système communautaire de contrôle des aides d'Etat' (1998) 2 *RMUE* 136.

Linth, P., 'The Influence of Competition law on Free Movements Rules' in H. Kanninen, N. Korjuse, and A. Rosas (eds), *EU Competition Law in Context. Essays in Honour of Virpi Tiili* (Oxford: Hart Publishing, 2009).

Marenco, G., 'Le Traité CEE interdit-il aux Etats membres de restreindre la concurrence?' (1986) 3–4 *CDE* 285.

Moschel, W., 'Change of Policy in European Competition Law' (2009) 37 *CML Rev* 495.

Nihoul, P. (ed.), *La décentralisation dans l'application du droit de la concurrence. Un rôle accru pour le praticien?* (Brussels: Bruylant, 2004).

Reich, N., 'The "November Revolution" of the European Court of Justice: *Keck*, *Meng* and *Audi* Revisited' (1994) 31 *CML Rev* 459.

Rodrigues, S., *La nouvelle régulation des services publics en Europe* (Paris: Tec & Doc, 2000).

Roth, P. and Rose, V., *Bellamy & Child: European Community Law of Competition*, 6th edn (Oxford: OUP, 2010).

Van der Esch, B., 'La loyauté fédérale et subsidiarité à propos des arrêts du 17 novembre 1993 dans les affaires C-2/91 (*Meng*), C-245/91 (*Ohra*) et C-185/91 (*Reiff*)' (1994) 5–6 *CDE* 524.

Wils, W., 'The Undertaking as Subject to EC Competition Law and the Imputation of Infringements to Natural or Legal Persons' (2000) 25:2 *Eur LR* 99.

5.2 The environmental dimension of competition law

Baccaro, V., 'Collecte et recyclage des batteries usagées en Italie: droits exclusifs, exigences environnementales et droit de la concurrence' (2011) 1 *CPN* 40.

Boute, A., 'Environmental Protection and EC Anti-Trust Law: The Commission's Approach for Packaging Waste Management Systems' (2006) 15 *RECIEL* 147.

Casey, D., 'Disintegration: Environmental Protection and Article 81 EC' (2009) 15:3 *ELJ* 370.

Geradin, D., 'Droit européen de la concurrence et protection de l'environnement' (1999) *Amén-Env* 50.

Geradin, D., 'EC Competition Law and Environmental Protection: Conflict or Compatibility?' (2002) 2 *YEEL* 117.

Gremminger, M., Laurila, M., and Miersch, G., 'The Commission Defines Principles of Competition for the Packaging Waste Recovery Markets' (2001) 3 *Competition Policy Newsletter* 29.

Idot, L., 'Environnement et droit communautaire de la concurrence' in J.-V. Masclet (ed.), *La Communauté européenne et l'environnement* (Paris: La Documentation française, 1997) 383.

Kingston, S., 'Integrating Environmental Protection and EU Competition Law: Why Competition Isn't Special' (2010) 6 *ELJ* 781.

Kingston, S., *Greening EU Competition Law and Policy* (Cambridge: CUP, 2011).

Komminos, A., 'Non-Competition Concerns: Resolution of Conflicts in the Integrated Article 81 EC', Working Paper 08/05, University of Oxford Centre for Competition Law and Policy, 10.

London, C., 'Competition and Environment: an Ecologically Rational Agreement' in R. Macrory (ed.), *Reflections on 30 years of EU Environmental Law* (Groeningen: Europa Law, 2006) 143.

Reese, M. and Koch, H.-J., 'Public Waste Management Services in the Internal Market and the Interpretation of Article 106 TFEU' (2011) 8:1 *JEELP* 28.

Thieffry, P., 'Protection de l'environnement et droit communautaire de la concurrence' (2002) 123 *Juris-Classeur* 3.

Vedder, H., *Competition Law and Environmental Protection in Europe. Towards Sustainability* (Groeningen: Europa Law, 2003).

Verdure, C., La conciliation des enjeux économiques et environnementaux dans le secteur des déchets (Brussels: Faculté de droit de l'Université Saint-Louis, 2013).

Vogelaar, F. O. W., 'Towards an Improved Integration of EC Environmental Policy and EC Competition Policy: An Interim Report' (1995) *Fordham Yearbook* 529.

5.3 State aids and environmental measures

Budlong, S. V., 'Article 130r(2) and the Permissibility of State Aids for Environmental Compliance in the EC' (1992) 30:1 *Columbia J Transntl L* 465.

de Sadeleer, N., 'State Aids and Environmental Protection: Time for Promoting the Polluter-Pays Principle' (2012) 2 *NJEL* 3.

de Sépibus, J., *Die Umweltschutzsubvention im Gemeinschaftsrecht* (Bern: Peter Lang, 2003).

de Sépibus, J., 'The EU Emissions Trading Scheme put to the Test of State Aid Rules', NCCR Trade Working Paper 2007/34, 12.

de Sépibus, J., 'The European Emission Trading Scheme Put to the Test of State Aid Rules' (2009) 17:4 *Environmental Liability* 126.

Facenna, G., 'State Aid and Environmental Protection' in A. Biondi, P. Eeckhout, and J. Flynn (eds), *The Law of State Aid in the European Union* (Oxford: OUP, 2004) 245.

Garbitz, E. and Zacker, V., 'Scope for Action by the EC Member States for the Improvement of Environmental Protection under EEC Law: The Example of Environmental Taxes and Subsidies' (1989) 26 *CML Rev* 429.

Golfinopoulos, V., 'Concept of Selectivity Criterion in State Aid Definition Following the Adria-Wien Judgment—Measures Justified by the Nature or General Scheme of a System' (2003) 10 *ECLR* 543.

Hoe, S., 'Regulering af CO_2 med afgifter og kvoter—en dobbeltregulering?' (2011) 2 *NELJ* 87.

Kliemann, A., 'Aid for Environmental Protection' in M. S. Rydelsky (ed.), *The EC State Aid Regime. Distortive Effects of State Aid on Competition and Trade* (London: Cameron & May, 2006) 315.

Soltesz, U. and Schaltz, F., 'State Aid for Environmental Protection. The Commission's New Guidelines and the New General Block Exemption Regulation' (2009) 6:2 *JEEPL* 141.

Stoczkiewicz, M., 'The Polluter Pays Principle and State Aid for Environmental Protection' (2009) 6:2 *JEELP* 171.

Stoczkiewicz, M., 'Free Allocation of EU ETS Emission Allowances to Installations for Electricity Production from a State Aid Law Perspective' (2012) 3:3 *Envt Economics* 99.

van Calster, G., 'Greening the EC's State Aid and Tax Regimes' (2000) 21 *ECLR* 294.

Winterstein, A. and Tranholm Schwarz, B., 'Helping to Combat Climate Change: New State Aid Guidelines for Environmental Protection' (2008) 2 *Competition Policy Newsletter* 12.

6. OFFICIAL DOCUMENTS

EUGLOREH, *The Report on the Status of Health in the European Union. Towards a Healthier Europe* (2009).

European Commission, A mid-term assessment of implementing the EC Biodiversity Action Plan, COM (2008) 864 final.

European Commission, Environment Policy Review 2008, COM (2009) 304.

European Environment Agency, *Europe's Environment. The Dobris Assessment* (Copenhagen: EEA, 1995).

European Environment Agency, *Environmental Taxes: Recent Developments in Tools for Integration* (Copenhagen: EEA, 2000).

European Environment Agency, *Late Lessons from Early Warnings: The Precautionary Principle 1896–2000* (Copenhagen: EEA, 2001).

European Environment Agency, *The European Environment. State and Outlook* (Copenhagen: EEA, 2005).

European Environment Agency, *Europe's Environment. The Fourth Assessment* (Copenhagen: EEA, 2007).

European Environment Agency, *Progress towards the European 2010 Biodiversity Target* (Copenhagen: EEA 2009).

European Environment Agency, *Waste Without Borders in the EU? Transboundary Shipments of Waste*, EEA Report 2009/1 (Copenhagen: EEA, 2009).

European Environment Agency, *The European Environment 2010. State and Outlook* (Copenhagen: EEA, 2010).

European Institute of Public Administration, *Delegated & Implementing Acts. The New Comitology* (Maastricht: EIPA, 2011) 15.

OECD, *Environmental Outlook to 2050* (Paris: OECD, 2012).

World Commission on Environment and Development (WCED), *Our Common Future* (Oxford: OUP, 1987).

World Bank, *Beyond Economic Growth. Meeting the Challenges of Global Development* (Washington DC: World Bank, 2000).

Index

University of Plymouth
Charles Seale Hayne Library
Subject to status this item may be renewed
via your Primo account

http:/primo.plymouth.ac.uk
Tel: (01752) 588588